INVESTMENTS
Analysis and Management

NINTH EDITION

INVESTMENTS
Analysis and Management

Charles P. Jones

North Carolina State University

 John Wiley & Sons, Inc.

ACQUISITIONS EDITOR Leslie Kraham
PROJECT EDITOR Cindy Rhoads
EDITORIAL ASSISTANT Jessica Bartelt
SENIOR PRODUCTION EDITOR Petrina Kulek
SENIOR MARKETING MANAGER David Woodbury
SENIOR DESIGN MANAGER Dawn Stanley
ILLUSTRATION EDITOR Anna Melhorn
PHOTO EDITOR Lisa Gee
COVER PHOTO Digital Vision/Getty Images
INTEXT CHAPTER OPENER PHOTO(S) Tim Barnett/PhotoDisc, Inc./Getty Images

This book was set in 10/12 Berkley by UG / GGS Information Services, Inc. and printed and bound by Donnelley/Willard. The cover was printed by Lehigh Press.

This book is printed on acid free paper.   ∞

To order books or for customer service, please call 1-800-CALL WILEY (225-5945).

Library of Congress Cataloging in Publication Data
Jones, Charles Parker,
    Investments : analysis and management / Charles P. Jones—9th ed.
        p. cm.
    Includes index.
    ISBN 0-471-45666-7 (alk. paper)
    1. Investments. 2. Investment analysis. I. Title.

  HG4521.J663 2004
  332.6–dc22

                                                          2003055577

ISBN 0-471-45666-7 (Domestic) 0-471-45184-3 (WIE)

Printed in the United States of America

10 9 8 7 6 5 4 3 2 1

To Kay and Kathryn
For making every year special
and to
Georgie,
Who continues with her active participation

Preface

THIS book is designed to provide a good understanding of the field of Investments while stimulating interest in the subject. This understanding can be quite valuable, because each of us must make various investment decisions during our lifetimes—definitely as individuals and possibly in our chosen careers.

My goal in this text is to help readers gain an appreciation of what is involved in (1) understanding what the investment opportunities are, (2) making good investment decisions, and (3) recognizing where investment problems and controversies arise and knowing how to deal with them.

Since this book is designed as an introduction to investments, descriptive material must be—and is—thoroughly covered. Equally important, however, the analytics of investments are presented throughout the discussion to help students reason out investment issues for themselves, and thus be better prepared when making real-world investment decisions. Terminology and trading mechanisms may change, but learning to analyze and evaluate investment opportunities carefully will pay off under any circumstances.

The book is written for the first course in investments, generally taught at the sophomore, junior, senior, or MBA level. Standard prerequisites include basic accounting, economics, and financial management. A course in statistics is very useful but not absolutely essential. I have sought to minimize formulas and to simplify difficult material, consistent with a presentation of the subject that takes into account current ideas and practices. Relevant, state of the art material has been simplified and structured specifically for the benefit of the beginning student. The emphasis in this text is on readability—making investments material readily accessible, as well as interesting and thoughtful, to the beginner who has modest prerequisites.

Organization of the Text

The text is divided into seven parts for organizational purposes. Part One provides the needed background for students before encountering the specifics of security analysis and portfolio management. The goal of this introductory set of chapters is to acquaint beginners with an overview of what investing is all about. After a general discussion of the subject in Chapter 1, the next four chapters describe the variety of securities available when investing directly, investing indirectly (investment companies and exchange-traded funds), the markets in which they are traded, and the mechanics of securities trading.

Part Two is concerned with an analysis of returns and risk, along with the basics of portfolio theory and capital market theory. Chapter 6 contains a careful and complete analysis of the critical concepts of risk and return that dominate any discussion of investments, including important calculations. Chapter 7 contains a complete discussion of expected return and risk for both individual securities and portfolios. The primary emphasis is on the essentials of Markowitz portfolio theory. This structure illustrates one of the primary characteristics of this text—introducing material only at the point it is needed, and only in the detail needed by beginning students. I believe this improves the flow of the material greatly, and keeps students from becoming mired in needless, and often tedious, details. Chapter 8 elaborates further on portfolio theory by considering the Markowitz principles applied to asset classes. Chapter 9 covers capital market theory and the capital-asset pricing market and arbitrage pricing theory.

Part Three discusses the analysis, valuation, and management of common stocks. Chapter 10 describes the most important valuation principles, including the dividend discount model and the P/E ratio model as well as other techniques. Chapter 11 discusses the passive and active approaches to selecting and managing stocks, and contains an up-to-date discussion of security analysts. Chapter 12 explains the efficient market hypothesis and provides some insights into the controversy surrounding this topic. As explained in Chapter 1, investors should be aware of and carefully consider this hypothesis, although it need not dominate their thinking and does not dominate the text. For example, Chapter 12 also discusses market "anomalies" or exceptions to the efficient market hypothesis, and these deserve careful consideration by investors.

Part Four covers fundamental analysis, the heart of security analysis. Because of its scope and complexity, three chapters are required to cover adequately the fundamental approach. The sequencing of these chapters—market, industry, and company—reflects the author's belief that the top-down approach to fundamental analysis is the preferable one for students to learn, although the bottom-up approach is also discussed. This section also discusses the other approach to common stock selection, technical analysis. Technical analysis is a well-known technique for analyzing stocks which goes back many years, and investors quite often have heard of one or more technical analysis tools.

In this ninth edition, Part Five covers the bond chapters. This allows users to cover stocks earlier in the course, and have more time to work with concepts involving stocks during the semester. Some parts of these chapters have been rewritten to make them more comprehensible and more in line with the Chartered Financial Analyst (CFA) study materials. Chapter 17 covers the major issues, yields and prices, and it also covers the important calculations that bond investors may need to use. Chapter 18 considers key issues such as yield curves, and analyzes the passive and active approaches to bond investing.

Part Six discusses the other major securities available to investors, derivative securities. Chapter 19 analyzes options (puts and calls), a popular investment alternative in recent years. Stock index options also are covered. Chapter 20 is devoted to financial futures, an important topic in investments. Investors can use these securities to hedge their positions and reduce the risk of investing.

Finally, Part Seven concludes the text with a discussion of portfolio management and the issue of evaluating portfolio performance. Chapter 21, a chapter first introduced in the sixth edition, is structured around the Association for Investment Management and Research's approach to portfolio management as a process. Chapter 22 is a logical conclusion to the entire book, because all investors are keenly interested in how well their investments have performed. Mutual funds are used as examples of how to apply these portfolio performance measures and how to interpret the results.

Special Features

This text offers several important features, some of which are unique.

   1. *The sequence of chapters has been carefully restructured and streamlined* from edition to edition, reflecting considerable experimentation over the years and a continuing search for the most effective organizational structure. The bond chapters have been repo-

sitioned in the ninth edition so that they follow all of the common stock material. This allows instructors to get to the material on stocks earlier in the semester, which I believe to be very desirable in terms of teaching the course.

2. I have diligently sought to ensure that *the text length is reasonably manageable* in the standard undergraduate investments course. Although it requires a very tight schedule, the entire text could be covered in a typical three-hour course, including limited use of supplementary material. However, many instructors choose to omit chapters, depending on preferences and constraints; doing so will cause no problems in terms of teaching a satisfactory investments course. For example, the chapters on fundamental analysis and technical analysis (Part Four) could be omitted, because the valuation and management of common stocks is fully covered in Part Three. Alternatively, the chapters on options and futures could be omitted if necessary. Another alternative is assigning some chapters, or parts of chapters, to be read by students with little or no class discussion.

3. *The pedagogy is specifically designed for the student's benefit.*

- Each chapter begins with a set of realistic *learning objectives*, which will aid the reader in determining what is to be accomplished with a particular chapter.
- Each chapter contains *key words* in boldface type. Key words are carefully defined as marginal definitions, and they also are included in the glossary. Other important words are italicized.
- Each chapter contains a *detailed summary* of "bulleted" points for quick and precise review.
- Each chapter contains an *extensive set of numbered examples*, designed to illustrate clearly important concepts.
- Each chapter contains an *extensive set of questions* keyed specifically to the chapter material and designed to review thoroughly the concepts in each chapter.
- Many chapters have a *separate set of problems* designed to illustrate the quantitative material in the chapters. Some of these problems can be solved in the normal manner, while others are best solved with available software. Included as part of some problem sets are demonstration problems that show the reader how to solve the most important types of problems.
- Many chapters contain *multiple and extensive questions and problems* taken from the Chartered Financial Analysts (CFA®) examinations. This allows students to see that the concepts and problem-solving processes they are studying in class are exactly the same as those asked on professional examinations for people in the money-management business.
- A distinctive feature of the first edition of this text was the use of *boxed inserts*, and the ninth edition continues this tradition. These inserts provide timely and interesting material from the popular press, enabling the student to see the real-world side of issues and concepts discussed in the text. These boxed inserts have been very carefully selected from the potentially large number available on the basis of their likely interest to the reader, their relevance in illustrating important concepts, their timeliness, and their overall appeal to students interested in learning about the world of Investments.
- Throughout the text, as appropriate, *Investments Intuition* sections are set off from the regular text for easy identification. These discussions are designed to help the reader quickly grasp the intuitive logic of, and therefore better understand, particular investing issues. Some *Practical Advice* sections are also available.
- Throughout the text, as appropriate, *Using the Internet* sections are set off from the regular text. These contain Web addresses dealing with a particular topic being discussed.

Changes in the Ninth Edition

The ninth edition has been thoroughly updated using the latest information and numbers available. At the time of publication, the data reflect the latest information available. Most of the data are through year-end 2002.

Important features in the ninth edition include:

- Part One contains the latest information available on newer concepts such as ETFs (exchange-traded funds) and ECNs (electronic communications networks) and the most current information on important trends such as discount/Internet brokers.
- Portfolio theory and capital market theory have been reorganized into three chapters within Part Two—Chapters 7 through 9.
- Chapter 10, on the valuation of common stocks, has been substantially revised to place less emphasis on the dividend discount model and more on alternative valuation techniques. Other discounted cash-flow approaches are also discussed.
- Chapters 13 through 16 provide an improved discussion of security analysis, making this section much more comprehensive and effective than in previous editions.
- The bond chapters have been moved to follow all of the common stock material. In the ninth edition, they become Chapters 17 and 18. Key parts of these chapters have been rewritten to make them more comprehensible and more in line with the CFA study materials.
- Some appendices have been removed from the text itself and are available on the Web site to students and users of the text. The appendices that remain in the text are deemed essential in terms of being readily available for reference.
- Relevant Internet sites are much more extensive and up-to-date, and occur at the point of discussion of the specific issue.
- Relevant questions from previous CFA examinations are included as part of the end-of-chapter questions and problems.

Supplements

The ninth edition includes a complete set of supplements:

- **Instructor's Manual.** For each chapter, chapter objectives, lecture notes, notes on the use of PowerPoint presentations, and additional material relevant to the particular chapters are included. Answers to all questions and problems in the text are provided. The Instructor's Manual has been carefully prepared by the author.
- **Test Bank.** The Test Bank includes numerous multiple-choice and true/false questions for each chapter as well as short discussion questions and problems. The majority of these questions have been extensively tested in class and are carefully checked. The Test Bank is also available in a computerized format which allows for customization of the material.
- **PowerPoints.** PowerPoint presentations which contain lecture outline material for each chapter are available.
- **Internet Exercises.** This interactive resource is part of the text Web site and provides exercises to accompany each chapter of the text. These exercises present practical investing situations with the use of Internet resources.
- **Software.** *The Investment Portfolio*, version 2.0, a Windows-based software package published by John Wiley & Sons, Inc., can be packaged with the text. It contains modules on portfolio management, equilibrium, statistics, valuation models, bonds,

options, futures, and evaluation, and includes data for use with all modules. Users may also enter their own data in spreadsheet or ASCII format. This software is now available with extensive documentation as well as a workbook.

❏ **Web Site.** John Wiley & Sons, Inc., makes available a Web site which allows adopters of the text to obtain additional materials located at *www.wiley.com/college/jones*.

❏ **Data File.** This file is available to adopters on the Web site to accompany this edition. It contains returns on financial assets from 1871. These definitive data have been developed over many years by Charles Jones and Jack Wilson at North Carolina State University. Adopters will have to register on-line within the text Web site in order to gain access to these particular data.

❏ **Videos.** NBR videos are available complimentary to adopters. These videos include footage on contemporary issues related to investments.

Acknowledgments

A number of individuals have contributed to this project. I particularly thank Jack W. Wilson, North Carolina State University, a highly valued friend and colleague who has offered many useful comments, provided material for some of the tables, figures, and appendices, and worked out many of the problems (including the extended problems) for the text. He has continued his valuable assistance by supplying data, graphs, suggestions, and insights. Some of the material used in this book and the accompanying supplements is based on Jack's pathbreaking work in the area of asset returns and has generously been made available by him, for which I am very grateful.

A text does not reach its ninth edition unless it has met the needs of a large number of instructors who find it to be a useful tool in assisting their teaching. The earlier editions of this text benefited substantially from the reviews of many instructors whose suggestions for improvements are found on many pages of this text. I owe a debt of gratitude to these teachers and colleagues, who helped on the first and second editions: Randall Billingsley, Virginia Polytechnic Institute and State University; Pat Hess, Ohio State University; Richard DeMong, University of Virginia; Keith Broman, University of Nebraska; Ron Braswell, Florida State University; Donald Puglisi, University of Delaware; Howard Van Auken, Iowa State University; James Buck, East Carolina University; Malcolm Torgerson, Western Illinois University; Eugene Furtado, Kansas State University; William B. Gillespie, St. Louis University; Edward Sanders, Northeastern University; P. R. Chandy, North Texas State University; D. Monath, University of Louisville; Larry J. Johnson, University of Tulsa; Stan Atkinson, University of Central Florida; Howard W. Bohnen, St. Cloud State University; James M. Tipton, Baylor University; William P. Dukes, Texas Tech University; A. Bhattacharya, University of Cincinnati; and Christopher Ma, University of Toledo.

I wish particularly to thank two users, John Groth of Texas A&M University and Seth Anderson of Auburn University, who supplied me with detailed comments, suggestions, and corrections in the course of using earlier editions.

In developing the third edition, I benefited greatly from still more instructors teaching this course, including Paul Bolstar, Northeastern University; John Lindvall, California Polytechnic State University; Robert McElreath, Clemson University; Roger Palmer, College of St. Thomas; John Williams, California State University—Northridge; Philip Swensen, Utah State University; Clark Holloway, University of South Carolina; James F. Feller, Middle Tennessee State University; Michael McBain, Marquette University; George S. Swales, Jr., Southwest

Missouri State University; Lalatendu Misra, University of Texas—San Antonio; Richard E. White, University of North Florida; Donald Monath, University of Louisville; Thomas R. Anderson, Babson College; Randall Billingsley, Virginia Polytechnic Institute and State University; John W. Ellis, Colorado State University; Thomas E. Eyssell, University of Missouri—St. Louis; James P. D'Mello, Western Michigan University; and Herbert Weinraub, University of Toledo. Their criticisms and suggestions have substantially affected the evolution of this text and made it a better book. In the development of the fourth edition, I had the benefit of additional input from instructors teaching this course, including Joel Barber, Florida International University; Gary Dokes, University of San Diego; Richard D. Gritta and R. Karanjia, Fordham University; Clotilde Perez, Universidad de Puerto Rico; Hadi Salavitabar, State University of New York—New Paltz; David Smith, State University of New York—Albany; Mo Vaziri, California State University—San Bernardino; Tony Wingler, University of North Carolina—Greensboro; and Dennis Zocco, University of San Diego. A number of chapters benefited from these additional comments and resulted in a yet better text.

The fifth edition was improved as the result of additional reviewers. I would like to thank John J. Dran, Jr., Northern Illinois University; Ron Silante, Pace University; Ravi Shulka, Syracuse University; Richard D. Gritta, University of Portland.

In developing the sixth edition, I benefited greatly from instructors teaching this course, including Bala Arshanapalli, Indiana State University; Christopher Blake, Fordham University; Vincent Deni, Oakland Community College; Clark Hawkins, New Mexico State University; Cheryl McGaughey, Angelo State University; Frederick Puritz, State University of New York—Oneonta; David L. Scott, Valdosta State University; Howard Van Auken, Iowa State University; Richard Voth, Pacific Union College; Stephen Avard, Texas A&M University; Richard B. Carter, Iowa State University; James F. Gatti, The University of Vermont; Carl Hubbard, Trinity University; Bruce McManis, Nicholls State University; Maury Randall, Rider University; Milan P. Sigetich, Southern Oregon State College; Glenn Wood, California State University—Bakersfield; and Dennis Zocco, University of San Diego.

The seventh edition benefited from reviews by: Joseph Volk, University of California Berkeley Extension; Howard Van Auken, Iowa State University; Dean Kiefer, Northern Kentucky University; Dennis Mahoney, University of Pennsylvania; Suresh Srivastava, University of Alaska—Anchorage; Mustafa Gultekin, University of North Carolina—Chapel Hill; James Gatti, University of Vermont; Halina Orlowski, Sacred Heart University; Bong-Soo Lee, University of Houston; and Philip Young, Southern Missouri State University.

I also received several valuable and insightful comments from the reviewers of the eighth edition throughout its phases of development. These reviewers include Jasmine Yur-Austin, California State University—Long Beach; Paul Bolster, Northeastern University; Richard Kish, Lehigh University; Richard B. Carter, Iowa State University; Kip Sigetich, Southern Oregon University; and William P. Dukes, Texas Technical University. In addition, Dr. Mazin Aljanabi was extremely helpful in making suggestions for corrections and for improvements. Dr Aljanabi has significantly helped me improve this text, and I am very grateful.

Finally, I owe a debt of gratitude to those instructors who reviewed my revised material for this ninth edition. These reviewers include:

Murad Antia, University of South Florida
Felix Ayadi, Texas Southern University
G. Glenn Baigent, St. John's University
Peter M. Basciano, Augusta State University

Richard J. Bauer, Jr., St. Mary's University
James Carden, University of Mississippi
Kurt Carrasquilla, Golden Gate University
Robert L. Chapman, Oral Roberts University
James J. Cordeiro, State University of New York—Brockport
Natalya Delcoure, University of Southern Alabama
Frederick Duncan, Winthrop University
Farzad Farsio, Montana State Univerity—Billings
James Feller, Middle Tennessee State University
TeWhan Hahn, University of Idaho
John Hammen, University of South Dakota
Ibrahim Helou, University of La Verne
Eric Higgins, Kansas State University
Brian Holland, Bethel College
David Hua, Notre Dame de Namur University
Stanley Jacobs, Central Washington University
Rajiv Kalra, Minnesota State University—Moorhead
Ashok K. Kapoor, Augsburg College
Dongcheol Kim, Rutgers University
Doseong Kim, University of Akron
Richard Kish, Lehigh University
Robert Kiss, Eastern Michigan University
Nick Laopodis, Fairfield University
Malek Lashgari, University of Hartford
Karyl Leggio, University of Missouri—Kansas City
William Lepley, University of Wisconsin—Green Bay
Bing Liang, Case Western Reserve University
Thomas Lloyd, Westmoreland County Community College
Charmen Loh, Rider University
Ann Macy, West Texas A&M University
Leslie Mathis, University of Memphis
James Milanese, University of North Carolina—Greensboro
Mbodja Mougoue, Wayne State University
Brigitte Muehlmann, Bentley College
Jim Murtagh, Rensselaer Polytechnic Institute
Michael Nugent, Dowling College, State University of New York—Stonybrook
Janet D. Payne, Southwest Texas State University
Trib Puri, University of Massachusetts—Dartmouth
Denis Raihll, West Chester University
Catherine Shenoy, University of Kansas
R. Bruce Swensen, Adelphi University
Amir Tavakkol, Kansas State University
J.M. Ventura, UABC
Richard Voth, Pacific Union College
Richard Warr, North Carolina State University
Tzjy-Jeng Wu, Pace University
Allan Zebedee, South Dakota State University

I would also like to thank my former editors at John Wiley & Sons, Inc., Rich Esposito, Joe Dougherty, and John Woods. John Woods worked hard to enhance the supplementary material to the third edition of the text and to provide the overall support necessary substantially to revise the material and improve the book in numerous ways. Whitney

Blake was most helpful in developing a top-of-the-line fourth and fifth edition, always displaying a "can-do" attitude. Marissa Ryan significantly aided in developing the seventh edition. Cindy Rhoads has been a large part of the eighth and ninth editions along with several others at Wiley, including Leslie Kraham, Jessica Bartelt, Petrina Kulek, David Woodbury, Dawn Stanley, and Anna Melhorn.

Finally, I would like to thank my family, who continue to put up with the interruptions caused by writing a book. Without their support, a project such as this is difficult at best. I thank in particular my wife, Kay, who has helped me tremendously in the preparation of various editions of this text. Kay and Kathryn make a difficult job bearable, and worth doing.

Charles P. Jones
North Carolina State University

Brief Contents

Contents

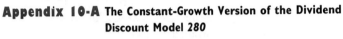

INVESTMENTS
Analysis and Management

chapter *1*

Understanding Investments

Chapter 1 provides the foundation for the study of Investments by analyzing what investing is all about. The critically important trade-off between expected return and risk is explained and important considerations that every investor must deal with in making investment decisions are analyzed. An organizational structure for the entire text is provided.

AFTER READING THIS CHAPTER YOU WILL BE ABLE TO:

▶ Understand why return and risk are the two critical components of all investing decisions.

▶ Appreciate the scope of investment decisions and the operating environment in which they are made.

▶ Follow the organization of the investment decision process as we progress through the text.

From the spring of 2000 through 2001, investors lost $5 trillion, or 30 percent of their wealth in stocks. During one week in July 2002, the major stock indexes declined about 7 percent. From the peak in March 2000, the S&P 500 Index, a measure of large stocks, lost about 50 percent of its value, whereas the Nasdaq Stock Market lost about 75 percent of its value. With volatility like this, should most investors avoid common stocks, particularly for their retirement plans?

In one recent year, the Asia Pacific Fund gained 109 percent, and the Turkish Investment Fund gained 152 percent. Should U.S. investors be participating in "emerging" stock markets? If so, how? Should most investors invest some part of their funds in international assets?

In the early 1990s, 75 percent of all company employees with self-directed retirement plans had none of their funds invested in stocks, although over the years stocks have significantly outperformed the alternative assets they did hold. Is this smart?

About two-thirds of all affluent Americans use financial advisers, a percentage that has been increasing. Will you need one?

For a recent 10-year period, only one-third of professionally managed stock portfolios were able to outperform the overall stock market. Why?

One stock returned 57,000 percent in less than eight years during the period 1990 to 1998. What is the chance an individual investor could have recognized this company's potential and gotten in on the ride?

Is it possible to have earned 40 percent or more investing in default-free Treasury bonds in a single year?

How can futures contracts, with a reputation for being extremely risky, be used to reduce an investor's risk?

What is the historical average annual rate of return on common stocks? What can an investor reasonably expect to earn from stocks in the future?

The objective of this text is to help you understand the investments field as it is currently understood, discussed, and practiced so that you can intelligently answer questions such as the preceding ones and make sound investment decisions that will enhance your economic welfare. To accomplish this objective, key concepts are presented to provide an appreciation of the theory and practice of investments.

Both descriptive and quantitative materials on investing are readily available. Some of this material is very enlightening; much of it is entertaining but debatable because of the many controversies in investments; and some of it is worthless. This text seeks to cover what is particularly useful and relevant for today's investment climate. It offers some ideas about what you can reasonably expect to accomplish by using what you learn, and therefore what you can realistically expect to achieve as an investor in today's investment world. Many investors have unrealistic expectations, and this will ultimately lead to disappointments in results achieved, or worse.

Learning to avoid the many pitfalls awaiting you as an investor by clearly understanding what you can reasonably expect from investing your money may be the single most important benefit to be derived from this text. For example, would you entrust your money to someone offering 36 percent annual return on riskless Treasury securities? Some 600 investors did and lost some $10 million to a former Sunday school teacher. Religious-based scams alone cost investors an estimated $1 billion in 2001. Or consider one of the largest Ponzi schemes in California history, which cost investors some $330 million. This scheme involved a fund promising 17 percent annual returns by investing in subprime mortgages. Victims included corporate executives, lawyers, and partners of accounting firms. Intelligent investors learn to say no and to avoid many of the mistakes that can be prevented by simply knowing when to say no.

The Nature of Investments

SOME DEFINITIONS

The term *investing* can cover a wide range of activities. It often refers to investing money in certificates of deposit, bonds, common stocks, or mutual funds. More knowledgeable investors would include other "paper" assets, such as warrants, puts and calls, futures contracts, and convertible securities, as well as tangible assets, such as gold, real estate, and collectibles. Investing encompasses very conservative positions as well as aggressive speculation. Whether your perspective is that of a college graduate starting out in the workplace or that of a senior citizen concerned with how to live after retirement, investing decisions can be very important to you.

Investment The commitment of funds to one or more assets that will be held over some future time period

Investments The study of the investment process

Financial Assets Pieces of paper evidencing a claim on some issuer

Real Assets Physical assets, such as gold or real estate

Marketable Securities Financial assets that are easily and cheaply traded in organized markets

An **investment** can be defined as the commitment of funds to one or more assets that will be held over some future time period. The field of **investments**, therefore, involves the study of the investment process. Investments is concerned with the management of an investor's wealth, which is the sum of current income and the present value of all future income. (This is why present value and compound interest concepts have an important role in the investment process.) Although the field of investments encompasses many aspects, as the title of this text suggests, it can be thought of in terms of two primary functions: analysis and management.

In this text, the term *investments* refers in general to financial assets and in particular to marketable securities. **Financial assets** are paper (or electronic) claims on some issuer, such as the federal government or a corporation; on the other hand, **real assets** are tangible assets such as gold, silver, diamonds, art, and real estate. **Marketable securities** are financial assets that are easily and cheaply tradable in organized markets. Technically, investments include both financial and real assets and both marketable and nonmarketable assets. Because of the vast scope of investment opportunities available to investors, our primary emphasis is on marketable securities; however, the basic principles and techniques discussed in this text are applicable to real assets.

Even when we limit our discussion primarily to financial assets, it is difficult to keep up with the proliferation of new products. Two such assets that did not exist a few years ago are SPDRs (Standard & Poor's Depository Receipts) and Direct Access Notes (corporate bonds designed for the average investor), both of which are discussed in a later chapter.

A PERSPECTIVE ON INVESTING IN FINANCIAL ASSETS

The investment of funds in various assets is only part of the overall financial decision making and planning that most individuals must do. Before investing, each individual should develop an overall financial plan. Such a plan should include the decision on whether to purchase a house, which for most individuals represents a major investment. In addition, decisions must be made about insurance of various types—life, health, disability, and protection of business and property. Finally, the plan should provide for emergency reserve funds.[1]

Portfolio The securities held by an investor taken as a unit

This text assumes that investors have established their overall financial plan and are now interested in managing and enhancing their wealth by investing in an optimal combination of financial assets. The idea of an "optimal combination" is important because our wealth, which we hold in the form of various assets, should be evaluated and managed as a unified whole. Wealth should be evaluated and managed within the context of a **portfolio**, which consists of the asset holdings of an investor. For example, if you own four stocks

---

[1] Personal finance decisions of this type are discussed in personal finance texts.

and three mutual funds, that is your portfolio. If your parents own 23 stocks, some municipal bonds, and some certificates of deposit (CDs), that is their portfolio of financial assets.

WHY DO WE INVEST?

We invest to make money! Although everyone would agree with this statement, we need to be more precise. (After all, this is a college textbook and those paying for your education expect more.) We invest to improve our welfare, which for our purposes can be defined as monetary wealth, both current and future. We assume that investors are interested only in the monetary benefits to be obtained from investing, as opposed to such factors as the psychic income to be derived from impressing one's friends with one's financial prowess.

Funds to be invested come from assets already owned, borrowed money, and savings or foregone consumption. By foregoing consumption today and investing the savings, investors expect to enhance their future consumption possibilities by increasing their wealth. Don't underestimate the amount of money many individuals can accumulate. By the mid-1990s, there were approximately 3 million households that qualified as "millionaires," and the number of individuals with $1 million portfolios had tripled over the past 12 years.

Investors also seek to manage their wealth effectively, obtaining the most from it while protecting it from inflation, taxes, and other factors. To accomplish both objectives, people invest.

The Importance of Studying Investments

THE PERSONAL ASPECTS

It is important to remember that all individuals have wealth of some kind; if nothing else, this wealth may consist of the value of their services in the marketplace. Most individuals must make investment decisions sometime in their lives. Some people may wish to improve the return from their "savings account" funds by investing in alternatives to insured savings accounts. Many employees can decide whether their retirement funds are to be invested in stocks or bonds.

Example 1-1

A good example of the investing decisions facing a typical individual, and the critical importance of making good investment decisions, is the Individual Retirement Account (IRA). IRAs are a primary method that Americans use to provide for their retirement. An estimated 42 percent of U.S. households, some 44 million, owned IRAs in mid-2001.

Under new legislation enacted in 2001, the annual contribution for 2002 for both traditional and Roth IRAs is $3,000. The limit increases to $4,000 in 2005 and $5,000 in 2008. IRA funds can be invested in a wide range of assets from the very safe to the quite speculative. IRA owners are allowed to have self-directed brokerage accounts, which offer a wide array of investment opportunities.

Since these funds may be invested for as long as 40 or more years, good investment decisions are critical, as shown by the examples in Table 1-1 for one individual contribut-

Table 1-1 Possible Payoffs from Long-Term Investing

Amount Invested per Year ($)	Number of Years	Final Wealth If Funds Are Invested at		
		5%	10%	15%
3000	20	99,198	171,825	307,320
3000	30	199,317	493,470	1,304,220
3000	40	362,400	1,327,770	5,337,000

ing $3,000 annually. Over many years of investing, the differences in results that investors realize, owing solely to the investment returns earned, can be staggering. Note that in the case of a $3,000 annual contribution for 40 years, the payoff at an earnings rate of 15 percent is over $5,000,000, whereas at an earnings rate of 10 percent, the payoff is $1.3 million, a great retirement fund but significantly less than $5+ million. Clearly, good investment decisions leading to higher returns can make a tremendous difference in the wealth that you can accumulate.

Some Practical Advice

▶ It's Your Money, and Your Decisions

A major revolution in personal finance is to provide employees with self-directed retirement plans (defined contribution plans rather than defined benefit plans) for which they must make investment decisions. The best example of this is a 401(k) plan offered by many employers, whereby employees contribute a percentage of salary to a tax-deferred plan, and the employer often matches part of the contribution. By mid-2002, these plans had over $1.5 trillion in assets, and 400,000 companies offered them. As of July 2002, some 42 million American workers were contributing part of their paychecks to 401(k) plans, with $12 billion flowing in each month. 401(k)'s today are the dominant form of retirement savings. Therefore, you need fully to understand your investing alternatives with 401(k) plans, and what you can reasonably expect to accomplish with them over your working lifetime.

Whereas traditional defined-benefit retirement plans guarantee retirees an amount of money each month, the new emphasis on self-directed retirement plans means that you will have to choose among stock funds, bond funds, guaranteed investment contracts, and other alternatives. By the beginning of 2000, about three-fourths of participant assets were invested in stocks. Your choices are many—many 401(k) participants can choose from thousands of mutual funds. Your success, or lack thereof, will directly affect your retirement benefits. Therefore, whereas employees in the past typically did not have to concern themselves much with investing decisions relative to their company's retirement plan, future employees will have to do so. This is a very important personal reason for studying the subject of investments!

Using the Internet

Investors can find many Web sites with so-called retirement calculators. For example, www.quicken.com offers a popular format. You input your age, salary, and current savings, make some assumptions about the rate of return you will earn and the inflation rate, indicate likely pension income and Social Security payments, and Quicken's Retirement Planner produces an estimate of terminal wealth at retirement, shortfalls, and amounts needed to be saved. Vanguard, the giant mutual fund company, offers extensive information on retirement planning at www.vanguard.com. Vanguard's Pre-Retirement Savings Modeler allows the user to enter personal and financial information and determine how long savings will last during retirement. At www.bloomberg.com, users can find (in the "Tools" section) a simplified retirement calculator that allows the user to calculate the annual contribution required to reach a goal, or the final amount that occurs from an annual contribution, given the number of years and an earnings rate.

Everyone needs to understand the importance of investing decisions as they affect your future retirement. It is estimated that the middle class in this country suffered a 13 percent decline in their total wealth from 1983 to 1998 despite this being one of the strongest stock markets in history. Further estimates suggest that more than 40 percent of households headed by someone between the ages of 47 and 62 years will be unable to replace half their preretirement income when they cease working. Even more worrisome, many people will have retirement income below the poverty line. Most workers today are unlikely to accumulate enough in their 401 (k) plans adequately to fund their retirement. Therefore, they need to make the very best investing decisions they can in order to enhance their retirement wealth.

The study of investments is more important than ever in the twenty-first century. After being net sellers of stocks from 1968 through 1990, individual investors have swarmed into the financial markets either by force (becoming part of a self-directed retirement plan) or by choice (seeking higher returns than those available from financial institutions). In the late 1990s, individuals increased their direct ownership of stocks, reversing the trend of the 1980s and early 1990s. By 1998, some 84 million individuals in the United States owned stocks.

Individual investor interest in the stock market is best expressed by the power of mutual funds (explained in Chapter 3), a favorite investment vehicle of small investors. Mutual funds are now the driving force in the marketplace. With so much individual investor money flowing into mutual funds, and with individual investors owning a large percentage of all stocks outstanding, the study of investments is as important as ever, or more so.

In the final analysis, we study investments in the hope of earning better returns in relation to the risk we assume when we invest. A careful study of investment analysis and portfolio management principles can provide a sound framework for both managing and increasing wealth. Furthermore, a sound study of this subject matter will allow you to obtain maximum value from the many articles on investing that appear daily in newspapers and magazines, which in turn will increase your chances of reaching your financial goals. Popular press articles will cover many important topics, such as the following nonexhaustive list. All of these issues are covered in the text, and learning about them will make you a much smarter investor:

1. Financial assets available to investors
2. Total rate of return vs. yield
3. Compounding effects and terminal wealth
4. Realized returns vs. expected returns
5. How to compare taxable bonds to municipal (tax-exempt) bonds
6. Index funds and mutual fund expenses
7. How diversification works to reduce risk
8. The asset allocation decision
9. The significance of market efficiency to investors

INVESTMENTS AS A PROFESSION

In addition to the above reasons for the importance of studying investments, the world of investments offers several rewarding careers, both professionally and financially. A study of investments is an essential part of becoming a professional in this field.

Investment bankers, who arrange the sale of new securities as well as assist in mergers and acquisitions, enjoyed phenomenal financial rewards in the booming 1980s and 1990s. Pay and bonuses for many of these people were huge—in the millions of dollars. Given the turmoil of 2000 to 2002, investment banking business dropped off sharply, and by mid-2002 was the slowest part of Wall Street's business. Of course, the need for investment bankers may increase in the future as the economy and stock market recover.

Top traders and salespeople seem to do best on Wall Street. In a typical good year, a junior bond trader on Wall Street can earn $300,000 to $400,000 or more, whereas an experienced bond trader can earn in the neighborhood of $750,000. A bond salesperson who sells to institutional investors can earn $200,000 or more if relatively inexperienced and $600,000 to $700,000 if experienced. Once again, however, conditions can change, and the severely depressed markets in the early years of the new millennium caused a significant change in the Wall Street landscape.

For those interested in doing research, which is less glamorous and less profitable for the firms involved, the good jobs on Wall Street still pay well. A security analyst on Wall Street with a few years of experience can earn $200,000 or more, whereas one with 10 years of experience can earn up to $500,000. In the past, top analysts, because of their effect on companies using a firm's investment banking services, were paid millions of dollars. Whether this will continue to be the case remains to be seen, but it is clear that security analysts have been under heavy criticism lately, and that firms who employ so called sell-side analysts are instituting new reforms.

A range of financial institutions—including brokerage firms and investment bankers as well as banks and insurance companies—need the services of investment analysts (also called security analysts, or simply analysts). Brokerage houses need them to support their registered representatives who in turn serve the public; for example, preparing the research reports provided to customers. Investment bankers need analysts to assist in the sale of new securities and in the valuation of firms as possible merger or acquisition candidates. Banks and insurance companies own portfolios of securities that must be evaluated in order to be managed. Mutual funds need analysts to evaluate securities for possible purchase or sale.

All the financial firms mentioned above need portfolio managers to manage the portfolios of securities handled by these organizations. Portfolio managers are responsible for making the actual portfolio buy and sell decisions—what to buy and sell, when to buy and sell, and so forth. Portfolio performance is calculated for these managers, and their jobs may depend on their performance relative to other managed portfolios and to market averages.

What about the 80,000 registered representatives (stockbrokers) employed in cities across the country? A few superbrokers earn $1 million or more per year. The average broker in the early 1990s earned almost $100,000 per year, although the median compensation (half above, half below) was $63,000. (More will be said about brokers as an occupation in Chapter 5).

Of course, the employment and pay for the various job types associated with Wall Street tends to be cyclical. Whereas the late 1990s were the great years for investors and investment firms and employees, the market declines of 2000 to 2002 brought a new reality. From the end of 2000 through mid-2002, Wall Street firms had cut employment by 7 percent, almost 30,000 people, and more cuts were expected. The securities industry's pretax profits in 2001 were half of what they were in 2000.

Finally, the number of financial planners continues to grow. This area has employment opportunities for people interested in the Investments field. As noted at the chapter outset, about two-thirds of all affluent Americans now use a financial planner. For a typical $1,000,000 portfolio, a financial adviser will charge $10,000 a year. Some planners charge by the hour, with the hourly rate in the $115 to $150 range.

No standard credentials exist for financial planners. Although most planners must register with the Securities and Exchange Commission as a Registered Investment Advisor (RIA), this involves only the filling out of a form providing information on education and background and the payment of a $150 registration fee. Otherwise, financial planners are bound only by the job requirements of professional organizations to which they belong, and individuals seeking a financial planner may wish to contact these organizations.[2]

[2] These include the National Association of Personal Financial Advisors (800-366-2732); the International Association for Financial Planning (800-945-4237); and the Institute of Certified Financial Planners (800-282-7526).

Designations that do connote training in the financial planning field include:

❑ Certified Financial Planner (CFP), awarded by the Certified Financial Planning Board of Standards, an industry group, requires course work and a five-part examination over two days
❑ Chartered Financial Consultant (ChFC) requires a comprehensive examination and often involves those with an insurance background
❑ Personal Financial Specialist, awarded by the American Institute of Certified Public Accountants to CPAs only, requires experience in personal financial planning and a comprehensive examination

Financial planners are compensated by three methods: fee based, commission based, or fee-and-commission based, which is the most common form of compensation. Planners indicate that they average about $100 an hour regardless of method of compensation. According to one survey, planners gross a little over $100,000 per year, primarily from selling products for commissions and from managing clients' assets for a percentage of the assets under management.

Chartered Financial Analyst (CFA) A professional designation for people in the investments field

Individuals interested in careers in the investments field, as opposed to financial planning, should consider studying to become a **Chartered Financial Analyst (CFA®)**. This is a professional designation for people in the investments area, not unlike the CPA designation for accountants. The CFA designation is widely recognized in the investments industry today. It serves as an indication that areas of knowledge relevant to investing have been studied and that high ethical and professional standards have been recognized and accepted. Details of the CFA program are included in Appendix 1-A. Throughout this text we will use relevant parts of the CFA curriculum, procedures, and philosophy, because it directly relates to a study of investments.

Understanding the Investment Decision Process

An organized view of the investment process involves analyzing the basic nature of investment decisions and organizing the activities in the decision process.

Common stocks have produced, on average, significantly larger returns over the years than savings accounts or bonds. Should not all investors invest in common stocks and realize these larger returns? The answer to this question is—to pursue higher returns investors must assume larger risks. Underlying all investment decisions is the trade-off between expected return and risk. Therefore, we first consider these two basic parameters that are of critical importance to all investors and the trade-off that exists between expected return and risk.

Given the foundation for making investment decisions—the trade-off between expected return and risk—we next consider the decision process in investments as it is typically practiced today. Although numerous separate decisions must be made, for organizational purposes, this decision process has traditionally been divided into a two-step process: security analysis and portfolio management. Security analysis involves the valuation of securities, whereas portfolio management involves the management of an investor's investment selections as a portfolio (package of assets), with its own unique characteristics.

THE BASIS OF INVESTMENT DECISIONS

Return Why invest? Stated in simplest terms, investors wish to earn a return on their money. Cash has an opportunity cost: By holding cash, you forego the opportunity to earn a return on that cash. Furthermore, in an inflationary environment, the purchasing power of cash diminishes, with high rates of inflation (such as that in the early 1980s) bringing a relatively rapid decline in purchasing power.

Investments Intuition

Investors buy, hold, and sell financial assets to earn returns on them. Within the spectrum of financial assets, why do some people buy common stocks instead of safely depositing their money in an insured savings account or a U.S. savings bond with a guaranteed minimum return? The answer is that they are trying to earn returns larger than those available from such safer (and lower yielding) assets. They know they are taking a greater risk of losing some of their money by buying common stocks, but they expect to earn a greater return.

Expected Return The *ex ante* return expected by investors over some future holding period

Realized Return Actual return on an investment for some previous period of time

In investments it is critical to distinguish between an **expected return** (the anticipated return for some future period) and a **realized return** (the actual return over some past period). Investors invest for the future—for the returns they expect to earn—but when the investing period is over, they are left with their realized returns. What investors actually earn from their holdings may turn out to be more or less than what they expected to earn when they initiated the investment. This point is the essence of the investments process: Investors must always consider the risk involved in investing.

Risk Investors would like their returns to be as large as possible; however, this objective is subject to constraints, primarily risk.[3] The stock market enjoyed the five greatest consecutive years of returns in its history during 1995 to 1999, with total returns each year in excess of 21 percent on a broad cross section of common stocks. Nevertheless, several professionally managed funds performed poorly relative to the market, and some managed to lose money in one or more of those years. As this example shows, marketable securities offering variable returns across time are risky. The investment decision, therefore, must always be considered in terms of both risk and return. The two are inseparable.

Risk The chance that the actual return on an investment will be different from the expected return

There are different types, and therefore different definitions, of risk. Risk is defined here as the uncertainty about the actual return that will be earned on an investment.[4] When we invest, we often expect some particular return, but there is a risk that what we in fact end up with when we terminate the investment—the actual return—will be different. Using the term *risk* in this manner, we find that the nominal (current dollar) return on a Treasury bill has no practical risk, because there is no reasonable chance that the U.S. government will fail to redeem these obligations as they mature in 13 or 26 weeks. On the other hand, there is some risk, however small, that Exxon or General Electric will be unable to redeem an issue of 30-year bonds when they mature. And there is a very substantial risk of not realizing the expected return on any particular common stock over some future holding period, such as a year, six months, one month, or even one day.

As we shall see in Chapter 7, Markowitz changed the study of Investments in a significant manner by quantifying risk as a statistical measure, the variance or standard deviation. This allows us to measure the risk of various assets and compare them.

---

[3] Although risk is the most important constraint on investors, other constraints clearly exist. Taxes and transaction costs are often viewed as constraints. Some investors may face legal constraints on the types of securities they can purchase or the amount they can hold.

[4] As we shall see in Chapter 7, expected return is a precise statistical term, not simply the return the investor expects. As indicated in our definition, risk involves chances, or probabilities, which will also be discussed in Chapter 7 along with measures of the dispersion in the expected return.

Risk-Averse Investor
An investor who will not assume a given level of risk unless there is an expectation of adequate compensation for having done so

It is easy to say that investors dislike risk, but more precisely, we should say that investors are risk averse.[5] A **risk-averse investor** is one who will not assume risk simply for its own sake and will not incur any given level of risk unless there is an expectation of adequate compensation for having done so. Note carefully that it is not irrational to assume risk, even very large risk, as long as we expect to be compensated for it. In fact, investors cannot reasonably expect to earn larger returns without assuming larger risks.

Investors deal with risk by choosing (implicitly or explicitly) the amount of risk they are willing to incur. Some investors choose to incur high levels of risk with the expectation of high levels of return. Other investors are unwilling to assume much risk, and they should not expect to earn large returns.

We have said that investors would like to maximize their returns. Can we also say that investors, in general, will choose to minimize their risks? No! The reason is that there are costs to minimizing the risk, specifically a lower expected return. Taken to its logical conclusion, the minimization of risk would result in everyone holding risk-free assets such as savings accounts and Treasury bills. Thus, we need to think in terms of the expected return-risk trade-off that results from the direct relationship between the risk and the expected return of an investment.

The Expected Risk-Return Trade-off Within the realm of financial assets, investors can achieve virtually any position on an expected return-risk spectrum such as that depicted in Figure 1-1. The line RF to B is the assumed trade-off between expected return and risk that exists for all investors interested in financial assets. This trade-off always slopes upward, because the vertical axis is expected return, and rational investors will not assume more risk unless they expect to be compensated for doing so. The expected return should be large enough to compensate for taking the additional risk; however, there is no guarantee that the additional returns will be realized.

Risk-Free Rate of Return   A return on a riskless asset, often proxied by the rate of return on Treasury securities

RF in Figure 1-1 is the return on a risk-free asset such as Treasury bills. This position has zero risk (on a practical basis, in the sense of default) and an expected return equal to the current rate of return available on risk-free assets such as Treasury bills. This **risk-free rate of return**, which is available to all investors, will be designated as RF throughout the text.

Figure 1-1 shows approximate relative positions for some of the financial assets that will be discussed in Chapter 2. As we move from risk-free Treasury securities to more risky corporate bonds, equities, and so forth, we assume more risk in the expectation of

Figure 1-1

The expected return-risk trade-off available to investors.

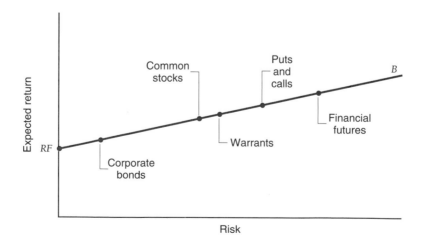

<hr />

[5] Do investors dislike risk? In economics in general, and investments in particular, the standard assumption is that investors are rational. Rational investors prefer certainty to uncertainty.

earning a larger return. Common stocks are quite risky, in relation to bonds, but they are not as risky as a speculative purchase of options (puts and calls) or futures contracts. (All of these terms are defined in Chapter 2.)

Obviously, Figure 1-1 depicts broad categories. Within a particular category, such as common stocks, a wide range of expected return and risk opportunities exists at any time.

The important point in Figure 1-1 is the trade-off between expected return and risk that should prevail in a rational environment. Investors unwilling to assume risk must be satisfied with the risk-free rate of return, RF. If they wish to try to earn a larger rate of return, they must be willing to assume a larger risk as represented by moving up the expected return-risk trade-off into the wide range of financial assets available to investors. In effect, investors have different limits on the amount of risk they are willing to assume and, therefore, the amount of return that can realistically be expected.[6]

Always remember that the risk-return trade-off depicted in Figure 1-1 is *ex ante*, meaning "before the fact." That is, before the investment is actually made, the investor expects higher returns from assets that have a higher risk. This is the only sensible expectation for risk-averse investors, who are assumed to constitute the majority of all investors. *Ex post* (meaning "after the fact" or when it is known what has occurred), for a given period of time, such as a month or a year or even longer, the trade-off may turn out to be flat or even negative. Such is the nature of risky investments!

STRUCTURING THE DECISION PROCESS

Investors can choose from a wide range of securities in their attempt to maximize the expected returns from these opportunities. They face constraints, however, the most pervasive of which is risk. Traditionally, investors have analyzed and managed securities using a broad two-step process: security analysis and portfolio management.

Security Analysis   The first part of the investment decision process involves the valuation and analysis of individual securities, which is referred to as **security analysis**. Professional security analysts are usually employed by institutional investors. Of course, there are also millions of amateur security analysts in the form of individual investors.

Security Analysis The first part of the investment decision process, involving the valuation and analysis of individual securities

The valuation of securities is a time-consuming and difficult job. First of all, it is necessary to understand the characteristics of the various securities and the factors that affect them. Second, a valuation model is applied to these securities to estimate their price, or value. Value is a function of the expected future returns on a security and the risk attached. Both of these parameters must be estimated and then brought together in a model.

The valuation process is difficult for common stocks. The investor must deal with the overall economy, the industry, and the individual company. Both the expected return and the risk of common stocks must be estimated. In addition, investors must consider the possibility that securities markets, particularly the equity markets, are efficient. In an efficient market, the prices of securities do not depart for any length of time from the justified economic values that investors calculate for them. Economic values for securities are determined by investor expectations about earnings, risks, and so on, as investors grapple with the uncertain future. If the market price of a security does depart from its estimated economic value, investors act to bring the two values together. Thus, as new in-

---

[6] In economic terms, the explanation for these differences in preferences is that rational investors strive to maximize their utility, the perception of which varies among investors. Utility theory is a complex subject; however, for our purposes, we can equate maximization of utility with maximization of welfare. Because welfare is a function of present and future wealth, and wealth in turn is a function of current and future income discounted (reduced) for the amount of risk involved, in effect, investors maximize their welfare by optimizing the expected return-risk trade-off. In the final analysis, expected return and risk constitute the foundation of all investment decisions.

formation arrives in an efficient marketplace, causing a revision in the estimated economic value of a security, its price adjusts to this information quickly and, on balance, correctly. In other words, securities are efficiently priced on a continuous basis. We discuss the full implications of this statement in Chapter 12.

Despite the difficulties, some type of analysis is performed by most investors serious about their portfolios. Unless this is done, one has to rely on personal hunches, suggestions from friends, and recommendations from brokers—all dangerous to one's financial health—or one chooses to follow a passive approach as explained below.

Portfolio Management The second major component of the decision process is **portfolio management**. After securities have been evaluated, a portfolio should be selected. Concepts on why and how to build a portfolio are well known. Much of the work in this area is in the form of mathematical and statistical models, which have had a profound effect on the study of investments in the last 30 years.

> **Portfolio Management**
> The second step in the investment decision process, involving the management of a group of assets (i.e., a portfolio) as a unit

Having built a portfolio, the astute investor must consider how and when to revise it. This raises a number of important questions. Portfolios must be managed regardless of whether an investor is active or passive:

A **passive investment strategy** involves determining the desired investment proportions and assets in a portfolio and maintaining these proportions and assets, making few changes. Even if investors follow a passive strategy, questions to be considered include taxes, transaction costs, maintenance of the desired risk level, and so on.

> **Passive Investment Strategy** A strategy that determines initial investment proportions and assets and makes few changes over time

An **active investment strategy** involves specific decisions to change the investment proportions chosen, or the assets in a particular category, based on the belief that an investor can profit by doing so. If the investor pursues an active strategy, the issue of market efficiency must be considered. If prices reflect information quickly and fully, investors should consider how this will affect their buy and sell decisions.

> **Active Investment Strategy** A strategy that seeks to change investment proportions and/or assets in the belief that profits can be made

The possibility that the stock market is efficient, as discussed above, has significant implications for investors. In fact, one's knowledge of and belief in this idea, known as the **Efficient Market Hypothesis (EMH)**, will directly affect how one views the investment process and makes investment decisions. Strong believers in the EMH may adopt, to varying degrees, a passive investment strategy because of the likelihood that they will not be able to find underpriced securities. These investors will seek to minimize transaction costs and taxes, as well as the time and resources devoted to analyzing securities, which, if the EMH is correct, should be correctly priced to begin with.

> **Efficient Market Hypothesis (EMH)**
> The proposition that security markets are efficient, with the price of securities reflecting their economic value

Investors who do not accept the EMH, or have serious doubts, pursue active investment strategies, believing that they can identify undervalued securities and that lags exist in the market's adjustment of these securities' prices to new (better) information. These investors generate more search costs (both in time and money) and more transaction costs, but they believe that the marginal benefit outweighs the marginal costs incurred.

Finally, all investors are interested in how well their portfolio performs. This is the bottom line of the investment process. Measuring portfolio performance is an inexact procedure, even today, and needs to be carefully considered.

Important Considerations in the Investment Decision Process for Today's Investors

Intelligent investors should be aware of the fact that the investment decision process as just described can be lengthy and involved. Regardless of individual actions, however, certain factors in the investment environment affect all investors. These factors should constantly be kept in mind as investors work through the investment decision process.

THE GREAT UNKNOWN

The first, and paramount, factor that all investors must come to grips with is uncertainty. Investors buy various financial assets expecting to earn various returns over some future holding period. These returns, with few exceptions, may never be realized. The simple fact that dominates investing, although many investors never seem to appreciate it fully, is that the realized return on an asset with any risk attached to it may be different from what was expected—sometimes, quite different.

At best, estimates are imprecise; at worst, they are completely wrong. Some investors try to handle uncertainty by building elaborate quantitative models, and others simply keep it in the back of their mind. All investors, however, are affected by it, and the best they can do is make the most informed return and risk estimates they can, act on them, and be prepared for shifting circumstances. Regardless of how careful and informed investors are, the future is uncertain and mistakes will be made.

As an illustration of how commonplace are the mistakes in judgments and estimates concerning the investments arena—indeed, they are inevitable—consider Box 1-1. *Smart Money*, an excellent monthly magazine designed for individual investors, publishes a "Reality Check" in each issue. These comments, which are representative of the total stream of comments on financial markets that appear regularly, illustrate how easily one's predictions and estimates can turn out to be incorrect. It is important to understand that the people making these comments are no more prone to error than anyone else. It is simply a fact that investing involves decisions about the future, and predictions and statements about the future will often be in error. All market participants, individual investors as well as the professionals, make errors.

BOX 1-1

Reality Checks

"I hate the word bubble because it means that imminently this thing is going to blow up in your face. Sure, every bull market has a speculative binge. I just don't think this is it."
—RALPH ACAMPORA, PRUDENTIAL SECURITIES' DIRECTOR OF TECHNICAL ANALYSIS, ON FORBES.COM, DEC. 16, 1999.

Though he's gotten many things right, this call blew up in Acampora's face. The speculative binge would end just three months later, and the Nasdaq is now 73 percent off its peak.

"I say he's doing a fine job, and when the market goes up, I hope they give him credit. If they're going to hold him accountable for a market going down, they ought to give him credit when the market goes up. I have all the confidence in the world in the secretary of the Treasury."
—PRESIDENT GEORGE W. BUSH, DEFENDING TREASURY SECRETARY PAUL O'NEILL AGAINST CALLS FOR HIS RESIGNATION, ON JULY 22, 2002.

Less than five months later, the S&P 500 was up 11 percent, but instead of giving O'Neill credit, President Bush gave him the boot. The market rallied on the news.

"There is no question in my mind that Michael (Capellas) intends to stay for an extended period of time. I think you will see him stick with it to bring the promises of the merger to fruition."
—MICHAEL WINKLER, CHIEF MARKETING OFFICER AND EXECUTIVE VICE PRESIDENT OF HEWLETT-PACKARD, IN A MAY 2002 INTERVIEW ON ITWORLD.COM.

There may have been questions in Capellas's mind, however. He jumped ship in November with a cash payout estimated at $14.4 million, less than six months after the merger, to become CEO of WorldCom. As for the promises of the merger, the stock has not returned to, much less surpassed, its May high. William Berry

SOURCE: *SmartMoney*, February 2003, p. 24. Reprinted by permission of *SmartMoney*. Copyright © 2003 *SmartMoney*. *SmartMoney* is a joint publishing venture of Dow Jones & Company, Inc. and Hearst Communications, Inc. All rights reserved worldwide.

Investors may, and very often do, use past data to make their estimates. They frequently modify these data to incorporate what they believe is most likely to happen. What is important to remember is that basing investment decisions solely on the past is going to lead to errors. A 10-percent average return on all stocks for the last 10 years in no way guarantees a 10-percent return for the next year, or even an average 10 percent return for the next 10 years.

Someone can always tell you what you should have bought or sold in the past. No one, however, can guarantee you a successful portfolio for next year or any other specified period of time, because no one can consistently forecast what will happen in the financial markets, including the professionals who are paid to make recommendations. Unanticipated events will affect the financial markets.

Investment decisions are both an art and a science. To succeed in investing, we must think in terms of what is expected to happen. We know what has happened, but the past may or may not repeat itself. Although the future is uncertain, it is manageable, and a thorough understanding of the basic principles of investing will allow investors to cope intelligently.[7]

THE GLOBAL INVESTMENTS ARENA

Now more than ever, investors must think of investments in a global context. Although foreign investments have been possible for a number of years, and some investors bought and sold on an international basis, most investors did not, particularly U.S. investors. However, as Figure 1-2 shows, the world has changed, and the United States no longer accounts for a majority of stock market capitalization in the world as it did in 1970. And the expectation is that the 47 percent shown for 2001 will shrink even more over time.

Consider this: Although roughly half of the world's market capitalization comes from foreign securities, Americans have invested only about 6 percent of their stock mutual fund money in foreign portfolios. Furthermore, less than 20 percent of the world's companies are listed in the United States. Today, more than ever, an international perspective is very important to all investors, and this particularly includes U.S. investors.

A global marketplace of round-the-clock investing opportunities is emerging, and the astute investor no longer thinks only of domestic investment alternatives. Why re-

Figure 1-2

U.S. and World Market Capitalizations, 1970 and 2001

Source: S&P data, Morgan Stanley, Federal Reserve.

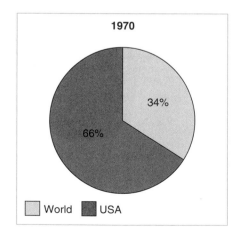

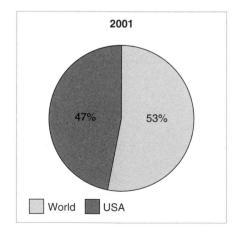

---

[7] In addition, some new tools and techniques are now being used that may help investors to make better decisions. These new techniques include neural networks, genetic algorithms, chaos theory, and expert systems.

strict yourself only to local investment opportunities if you can increase your returns or reduce your risk, or both, by investing on an international basis?

Business Week annually compiles the "Global 1000," which comprises the world's most valuable companies based on market value (price × number of shares). In 2002, U.S. corporations still accounted for more than half of the capitalization of the entire 1000 and dominated the top 25 positions. Nevertheless, some foreign companies clearly stand out. BP Oil, for example, was fourth in sales and eighth in market value. Nestle of Switzerland was thirtieth in market value, and Royal Dutch/Shell and BP Oil were fourth and fifth, respectively, in terms of profits. Clearly, U.S. investors should consider companies such as these when they invest.

From the standpoint of U.S. investors, an easy way to organize the global environment is to think of a global triad of opportunities. This triad can be summarized as Europe, Asia, and emerging markets.

Western European markets are well developed and offer investors numerous alternatives in what some observers feel will be the premier economic power of the future. A significant event occurred on January 1, 1999, with the launch of the European economic and monetary union, or EMU, along with the euro, Europe's common currency. The euro is the official currency of 11 countries. This marks a significant change for Europe and European financial markets.

The Japanese market is well known, having reached very high levels in the 1980s but followed by very low levels since. Some of the smaller Asian countries have enjoyed strong growth. China, of course, is a possible emerging economic power.

Emerging Markets
Markets of less developed countries, characterized by high risks and potentially large returns

Emerging markets continue to generate investor interest.[8] Several Asian markets are rapidly emerging. Despite many problems, some Latin American countries are beginning to emerge into stronger economies. Investors in emerging markets earned an average return of almost 70 percent in one recent year. Nevertheless, consistent with our discussion of the uncertainty involved in financial markets as well as the return-risk trade-off that underlies all investment decision, emerging markets peaked in 1994 and suffered a disastrous collapse in the mid-1990s. Consider the following limited examples—others could be chosen:

- Thailand devalued its currency in 1997, setting off a meltdown of Asian markets.
- Russian bonds collapsed in 1998.
- Brazil devalued its currency in 1999.
- Argentina suffered severe problems in 2001.

Despite these problems, emerging markets outperformed the S&P 500 in 2001 to 2002 when U.S. markets were doing so poorly. Investors should look ahead to future opportunities. For example, Mexico is regarded by many as having strong potential, and it is clearly tied to the U.S. economy. Coming out of the 2000 to 2001 recession, countries such as Mexico and Brazil should benefit from a worldwide recovery, because they are commodity exporters, and commodity prices typically recover early.

Why should investors be so concerned with international investing? First, many U.S. companies now derive a very large percentage of their revenues from abroad; Coca-Cola and Merck Pharmaceuticals are examples. The average company in the S&P 500 Composite Stock Index (an important measure of large U.S. companies) now derives in excess of 25 percent of its sales from abroad. This trend can be expected to continue.

---

[8] The World Bank classifies a stock market as "emerging" if its country's economy had less than $7,910 in U.S. dollars in per capita gross domestic product (GDP) in 1991.

Thus, U.S. investors investing in what traditionally are thought of as classic American companies are vitally affected by what happens abroad. A downturn in some key foreign companies, or an adverse movement in exchange rates, can have unhappy consequences for U.S. investors holding what they believe are solid U.S. companies. For example, when the dollar is strong, multinational producers are affected, because foreign currency revenues and operating profits are translated into fewer U.S. dollars when results are reported on the U.S. parent company's financial statements.

Second, U.S. investors should be aware of capital flows from abroad into domestic financial markets. By mid-2000, foreign governments and investors owned almost 40 percent of all Treasury bonds outstanding at the time. They also owned about 20 percent of U.S. corporate bonds and about 8 percent of U.S. equities. Of course, this dependence on foreign capital inflows can become a problem if these buyers sell their U.S. bonds, depressing bond prices and driving up yields. In mid-2002, the euro currency reached parity with the U.S. dollar, and even exceeded it, changing a relationship that had existed for years.

Third, the rates of return available in foreign securities have often been larger than those available from U.S. markets. For example, for several years in a row, the average compound rate of return for eight major Asian markets was approximately double that of the primary measure of U.S. stocks. In one year alone, the typical international investor enjoyed returns of roughly 40 percent, and the downside was plus 20 percent. Thus, by ignoring foreign investment opportunities, U.S. investors forego potentially larger returns relative to domestic returns only.

Ironically, the more globally integrated the world's economies become, the more U.S. investors need to consider foreign companies. Consider this: In many major industries today, the top 10 companies include relatively few U.S. companies. Many of the world's major players, and potentially valuable opportunities for investors, are foreign companies.

Fourth, adding foreign securities allows the investor to achieve beneficial risk reduction inasmuch as some foreign markets move differently than do U.S. markets. For example, when U.S. stocks are doing poorly, some foreign stocks may be doing well, which would help offset the poor U.S. stock performance. This risk reduction in a portfolio is a result of diversification. The simple point is that if domestic diversification in a portfolio reduces an investor's risk, which it clearly does, foreign diversification should provide even more risk reduction—and it does!

Given that international investing has now been going on for a number of years, it is not surprising that a recent analysis of international equity investing for the last 20 years concludes that "global portfolio diversification is no longer a new route to higher returns and lower risks, as it was two decades ago." Nevertheless, evidence for the past 20 years "indicates that thoughtful international equity diversification can improve the risk/return characteristics of investors' portfolios."[9]

Thus, we should consider foreign markets as well as the U.S. financial environment. We will do so throughout this text as an integral part of the discussion rather than as a separate chapter. Although the technical details may vary, the principles of investing are applicable to financial assets and financial markets wherever they exist.

Does a consideration of foreign investing ensure our success as investors? No, because of the first issue we discussed—the great unknown. As in any other area of investing, the experts are often wrong. Consider the following quote from an article in *The Wall Street Journal*: "As we entered the 1990s, many investment advisers, market pundits and

---

[9] Both quotes are from Richard O. Michaud, Gary L. Bergstrom, Ronald D. Frashure, and Brian K. Wolahan. "Twenty Years of International Equity Investing," *The Journal of Portfolio Management*, Fall 1996, p. 20.

well-meaning journalists were betting that the U.S. stock market was in for lackluster returns, but that foreign stocks might take up the slack. We couldn't have been more wrong."[10]

THE NEW ECONOMY VS. THE OLD ECONOMY

Traditionally, there was one large market of securities, ranging from the tiny company to the giant company, from very shaky companies to the very successful companies, from the purely domestic company to the multinational firms. In the late 1990s, investors got swept up in a new terminology, Old Economy stocks and New Economy stocks.

Old Economy stocks refer to the traditional "smokestack" companies and the traditional service, consumer, and financial companies. Examples include Ford, Eastman Kodak, Procter & Gamble, and Bank of America. They produce goods and services, sell them, show a profit, and reward their stockholders fairly consistently. These companies are typically successful, and have a lengthy history, but many of these companies are not considered to be exciting, because they are not directly involved in new technologies.

The New Economy stocks, such as Cisco, Oracle, and America On Line (AOL), have a heavy focus on technology. The New Economy also included the e-commerce stocks that had meteoric rises, and often very dramatic declines, such as eToys, The Street.com and DrKoop.com. Unlike the Old Economy stocks, many of these companies reported losses since they began, regardless of potential, and many subsequently failed.

What does this mean to investors? It illustrates that the world in general, and the investing world in particular, sometimes changes very quickly and investors may need to adjust to a changing environment. Many of the new e-commerce companies had no earnings, and therefore no P/E ratio, and no rational way to be valued. At one point, investors paid $500 per share for Amazon, a company with no profits. EBay has sold for a P/E ratio in the thousands. This was a brave new world, but if investors simply ignored the new technologies and trends, they missed stocks like Cisco, Dell, Microsoft, and Intel, all of which rewarded their shareholders tremendously for multiple year periods.

By early 2001, the technology stocks in general had suffered a dramatic decline, and this decline continued in 2002. Technology stocks simply collapsed—one of the greatest collapses in market history. This illustrates the importance of learning about rational investment principles that hold up over long periods of time. Ultimately, investors return to basic valuation principles, such as those we will learn about in this text.

THE RISE OF THE INTERNET

Any discussion of the investment decision process today must focus on the role of the Internet, which in a short time has significantly changed the investments environment. Now, all investors can access a wealth of information about investing, trade cheaply and quickly in their brokerage accounts, obtain real-time quotes throughout the day, and track their portfolios.

This is a true revolution—the Internet has democratized the flow of investment information. Any investor, at home, at work, or on vacation, can download an incredible array of information, trade comments with other investors, do security analysis, manage portfolios, check company filings with government agencies, and carry out numerous other activities not thought possible for a small investor only a few years ago. Although some of these information sources and/or services carry a fee, most of them are free.

---

[10] See Jonathan Clements, "Foreign Funk: Our '90s Advice Is Wrong So Far," *The Wall Street Journal*, October 1, 1996, p. C1.

In the new millennium, numerous on-line discount brokers are competing intensely for investor business. One large discount brokerage firm, Charles Schwab, has several million on-line accounts.

INSTITUTIONAL INVESTORS

Institutional Investors
Pension funds, investment companies, bank trust departments, life insurance companies, and so forth, all of whom manage large portfolios of securities

There are two broad categories of investors: individual investors and **institutional investors**. The latter group, consisting of bank trust departments, pension funds, mutual funds, insurance companies, and so forth, includes the professional money managers, who are often publicized in the popular press. The amount of money managed by these institutions is staggering. For example, in one recent year, Goldman, Sachs & Company managed some $16 billion in money market and bond funds. Two months after deciding to again manage stock portfolios (Goldman had abandoned this function some years earlier), wealthy individuals offered the company some $200 million to manage before it actually began accepting funds.

Given the figures for one financial company, it is not hard to see why, by the beginning of the 1990s, institutional investors in the United States held almost $6 trillion in assets. However, these institutional investors do not constitute a monolithic bloc of investors. Instead, they are made up of thousands of different organizations, most of which have multiple money managers.

The first issue to note about institutional investors is that their relative importance has changed. For 30 or more years up to the 1990s, it was the pension funds and corporate raiders who had the big impact on Wall Street. Although pension funds remain the primary institutional owner of common stocks, with about one-quarter of all stock, their importance has declined, because many plans have either been terminated or converted into self-directed plans. The private pension plans bought all of the net equities available in the 1960s and 1970s, whereas in the 1980s, corporate restructurings—mergers, acquisitions, and stock buybacks—took one-half trillion dollars of equity out of the market. In the 1990s, however, it was the mutual funds that were the primary buying force in the stock market. We will analyze mutual funds in detail in Chapter 3.

The second issue to note about institutional investors is their dual relationship to individual investors. On the one hand, individuals are the indirect beneficiaries of institutional investor actions, because they own or benefit from these institutions' portfolios. On a daily basis, however, they are "competing" with these institutions in the sense that both are managing portfolios of securities and attempting to do well financially by buying and selling securities.

Institutional investors are indeed the "professional" investors, with vast resources at their command. In the past, they were often treated differently from individual investors, because companies often disclosed important information selectively to some institutional investors. However, this situation changed significantly in October 2000 when Regulation Full Disclosure (FD) took place.

Regulation FD
Regulates communications between public companies and investment professionals by requiring that material information be disclosed to everyone at the same time

Regulation FD, which applies to almost all public companies, attempts to regulate communications between public companies and investment professionals. Companies are now prohibited from disclosing (intentionally) material, nonpublic information to specific types of investment professionals unless the company simultaneously publicly discloses the information. If a nonintentional disclosure is made of such information, the company must publicly disclose the information promptly.

Does the average investor have a reasonable chance in the market given the advantages of the institutional investors in terms of knowledge and resources? Yes—in the sense that he or she can generally expect to earn a fair return for the risk taken. On average, the individual investor will probably do just as well as the big institutional investors, because markets are usually quite efficient and securities fairly priced (as discussed in Chapter 12).

Some individual investors do even better either by superior skill and insight or luck. Furthermore, some opportunities can more easily be exploited by individual investors than by institutional investors.

Example 1-2 Individual investors can exploit a spin-off (defined as a division of a company that is turned into a separate publicly held company) better than institutional investors in some cases.[11] Some institutional investors will not purchase the new companies, because they often pay no dividends immediately after spin-off, and they may be too small to be held by some institutions. Furthermore, unless the spin-off is unusually large, it is often ignored by security analysts.

These companies often look unattractive at the time of spin-off, because they had problems as a division. However, these problems tend to be solved by a new, proactive management, and these companies become attractive as take-over candidates.

A study of 150 spin-offs found that the average three-year total return was about 75 percent, 30 percentage points higher than a comparable group of companies. In fact, several studies have found that over a period of one to three years, these stocks generally do well. In contrast, initial public offerings, which may enjoy great success on their first day of trading, generally track the overall market.

Investors are advised to defer purchases of spin-offs until they have been trading for a few weeks, because some institutions may sell the shares they received in the spin-off, and prices are often lower weeks later than at the time trading begins in the new companies. With a newly energized management team who have stock options, these companies often take off and do very well.

Relative to our discussion above about the Internet, individual investors are now on a more competitive basis with institutional investors given the information they can access. Furthermore, we would expect the market to become more efficient, because information is even more quickly and freely available.

The question of how well individual investors do relative to institutional investors raises the issue of market efficiency, which we consider in Chapter 12. All intelligent investors who seek to do well when investing must ultimately come to grips with the issue of market efficiency.

Organizing the Text

The following chapters are organized around the two major components of the investment decision process: asset valuation (security analysis) and portfolio management. The Investments business has traditionally been divided into these two broad areas, each of which encompasses a wide spectrum of activities.

Four chapters of background material follow this introductory chapter to form Part I, which covers background. The financial assets available to investors—both from direct investing and indirect investing—are examined in separate chapters, followed by a discussion of the securities markets in which they trade. This, in turn, is followed by an analysis of how securities are actually traded.

[11] See "Personal Investing," *Fortune*, April 18, 1994, pp. 31–32.

Part II deals with the important issues of return and risk, which underlie all investment decisions. Chapter 6 covers returns that investors have earned in the financial markets in the past, along with the risk involved, because investors must have an understanding of the results of investing in major assets such as stocks and bonds if they are to make intelligent estimates of the future. Chapter 7, in turn, deals with the estimation of return and risk, and involves the important principles of Markowitz portfolio theory that all investors should understand as they choose portfolios of securities to hold for the future. Chapter 8 continues the discussion of portfolio theory, explaining how an efficient portfolio is selected. Chapter 9 discusses capital market theory.

Nine chapters of the text, involving Parts III, IV, and V, are devoted to evaluating the primary financial assets, stocks and bonds, and explaining the basics of asset valuation. Common stocks are analyzed in Part III. For both stocks and bonds, valuation techniques are discussed in the first of the two chapters, and analysis and management in the second. For stocks, a chapter on market efficiency is included, because this important concept affects the strategies followed in selecting and managing stocks.

Because of the complexity of common stocks, four additional chapters are needed to describe the basics of security analysis, the most popular method for analyzing stocks. Part IV is purposefully sequenced from market to industry to company analysis, followed by a discussion of technical analysis.

Part V covers bonds, using the same format as Part III. Chapter 17 covers the principles of bond valuation, and Chapter 18 covers the analysis and management of bonds.

Part VI contains a complete basic analysis of alternative investment opportunities involving derivative securities. Separate chapters cover options and futures.

Part VII contains two chapters involving the portfolio management process. Chapter 21 describes the process that investors or managers should follow in managing portfolios. The text concludes with the logical capstone to a study of investments, the measurement of portfolio performance, in Chapter 22.

Summary

▶ An investment is the commitment of funds to one or more assets that will be held over some future period. The field of Investments involves the study of the investment process.

▶ The investment opportunities considered in this text consist primarily of a wide array of financial assets (primarily marketable securities), which are financial claims on some issuer.

▶ The basic element of all investment decisions is the trade-off between expected return and risk. Financial assets are arrayed along an upward sloping expected return-risk trade-off, with the risk-free rate of return as the vertical axis intercept.

▶ Expected return and risk are directly related; the greater (smaller) the expected return, the greater (smaller) the risk.

▶ Investors seek to maximize expected returns subject to constraints, primarily risk.

▶ Risk is defined as the chance that the actual return on an investment will differ from its expected return.

▶ Rational investors are risk averse, meaning that they are unwilling to assume risk unless they expect to be adequately compensated. The study of Investments is based on the premise that investors act rationally.

▶ For organizational purposes, the investment decision process has traditionally been divided into two broad steps: security analysis and portfolio management.

▶ Security analysis is concerned with the valuation of securities. Valuation, in turn, is a function of expected return and risk.

▶ Portfolio management encompasses building an optimal portfolio for an investor. Considerations include initial portfolio construction, revision, and the evaluation of portfolio performance.

▶ Major factors affecting the decision process include uncertainty in investment decisions, the global na-

ture of investing, the changing nature of the economy, the increasing importance of the Internet, and the role of institutional investors in the marketplace. As they study investments, evaluate information and claims, and make decisions, investors should consider these factors carefully.

Key Words

Active investment strategy
Chartered Financial Analyst (CFA)
Efficient Market Hypothesis (EMH)
Emerging markets
Expected return
Financial assets
Institutional investors

Investment
Investments
Marketable securities
Passive investment strategy
Portfolio
Portfolio management
Real assets

Realized return
Risk
Risk-averse investor
Risk-free rate of return
Security analysis

Questions

1-1 Define the term *investments*.

1-2 Describe the broad two-step process involved in making investment decisions.

1-3 Is the study of investments really important to most individuals?

1-4 Distinguish between a financial asset and a real asset.

1-5 Carefully describe the risk-return trade-off faced by all investors.

1-6 In terms of Figure 1-1, when would an investor expect to earn the risk-free rate of return?

1-7 "A risk-averse investor will not assume risk." Do you agree or disagree with this statement?

1-8 Summarize the basic nature of the investment decision in one sentence.

1-9 Distinguish between expected return and realized return.

1-10 Define risk. How many specific types can you think of?

1-11 What other constraints besides risk do investors face?

1-12 Are all rational investors risk averse? Do they all have the same degree of risk aversion?

1-13 What external factors affect the decision process? Which do you think is the most important?

1-14 What are institutional investors? How are individual investors likely to be affected by institutional investors?

1-15 What is meant by the expression *efficient market*?

1-16 Of what significance is an efficient market to investors?

1-17 Why should the required rate of return be different for a corporate bond and a Treasury bond?

1-18 Discuss some reasons why U.S. investors should be concerned with international investing. Do you think the exchange rate value of the dollar will have any effect on the decision to invest internationally?

1-19 What is meant by the distinction between the Old Economy and the New Economy?

Web Resources

For additional resources visit our dynamic Web site located at **www.wiley.com/college/jones**.

☐ Career Options—A career choice is a major investment decision with considerable uncertainty about the future. In the case, a finance major investigates his employment alternatives in the investments field and learns about the requirements for the Chartered Financial Analyst and Certified Financial Planner designations.

☐ Internet Exercises—This chapter is an introduction to the subject of Investments. The exercises for this chapter will introduce some of the Web sites that provide information that is useful for investors.

☐ Multiple Choice Self Test

Selected References

An interesting book that has generated much interest because of sharp market corrections in 2000 and 2001 is:

Shiller, Robert J. *Irrational Exuberance*. Princeton University Press, 2000.

A perspective on Wall Street and the monetary system in general can be found in:

Kaufman, Henry. *On Money and Markets: A Wall Street Memoir*. McGraw-Hill, 2000.

An interesting discussion that possibly predicted the stock market declines in 2000 to 2001 and has useful information on how investors can protect themselves can be found in:

Smithers, Andrew and Stephen Wright. *Valuing Wall Street: Protecting Wealth in Turbulent Markets*. McGraw-Hill, 2000.

Appendix 1-A
THE CHARTERED FINANCIAL ANALYST (CFA®) PROGRAM

The Association for Investment Management and Research (AIMR) is a nonprofit professional organization of investment practitioners and academics formed in 1990 from a merger of the Financial Analysts Federation and the Institute of Chartered Financial Analysts (ICFA). AIMR, an autonomous, self-regulatory organization, seeks to maintain a professional organization with high ethical, professional, and educational standards for the investment community, broadly defined. More than 50,000 members in over 100 countries make up this global nonprofit organization.

Since 1963 the ICFA has offered a study and examination program involving a body of knowledge that encompasses a range of topics important to those in the investment business. This program is designed for investment professionals or those who wish to become investment professionals. Candidates enrolled in the CFA Program must show that they have mastered important material in Economics, Quantitative Analysis, Ethical and Professional Standards, Financial Accounting, Fixed Income Securities, Equity Securities Analysis, and Portfolio Management. Candidates must successfully complete three examinations, referred to as Level I, Level II, and Level III, in order to be awarded a CFA designation.

The basis of the CFA Study and Examination Program is a Body of Knowledge (BOK). The BOK is organized along functional rather than topical lines and is structured around the investment decision-making process. The BOK functional areas are Ethics and Professional Standards, Investment Tools, Asset Valuation, and Portfolio Management.

For each level of the exam, the curriculum is organized around a functional area:

Level I study program—emphasizes tools and inputs
Level II study program—emphasizes asset valuation
Level III study program—emphasizes portfolio management

Ethical and Professional Standards are considered to be an integral part of all three functional areas and are covered at all levels of the curriculum.

These six-hour examinations have traditionally been given throughout the United States and around the world once a year, approximately on June 1, and must be completed sequentially. Starting in 2003, the Level I exam will be given twice a year.

As of 2002, more than 55,000 charters had been awarded. In 2002, more than 100,000 candidates from over 150 countries enrolled for one of the CFA examinations. Also in 2002, more than 50 percent of CFA candidates were from outside North America, which indicates the global nature of investments and the importance of this designation worldwide. A substantial percentage of CFA candidates are female.

What does it mean to be a CFA charterholder? Increasingly, employers are recognizing the value of this designation and the potential benefits that an employee with this designation can offer to a company. The CFA charter represents a combination of academic achievement and professional experience along with a commitment to a stringent code of professional and ethical standards. CFAs must annually renew their pledge to abide by the code, and violations of the code can carry severe sanctions.

The investments profession, like many others, involves life-long learning. After receiving the CFA designation, investment professionals can participate in the CFA Accreditation Program in order to remain current on investment issues. This program allows them to earn continuing education credits through a variety of means, including workshops, seminars, and reading on their own.

AIMR has done an outstanding job of fostering a professional environment for investment practitioners and academics and is the professional organization for investment professionals. Similarly, the CFA professional designation is the designation for serious investment professionals committed to the highest standards of professionalism in investing activities and to the highest possible standards of ethical and professional conduct. All individuals interested in a serious career in the investments field should investigate the possibility of being awarded a CFA charter.

Complete information about AIMR and its programs, as well as the CFA program, can be found at the AIMR Web site, www.aimr.org.

chapter 2

Investment Alternatives

Chapter 2 explains the most important investment alternatives available to investors, ranging from money market securities to capital market securities—primarily bonds and stocks—to derivative securities. The emphasis is on the basic features of these securities, providing the reader with the necessary knowledge to understand the investment opportunities of interest to most investors. Recent trends such as securitization are considered, as is international investing.

AFTER READING THIS CHAPTER YOU WILL BE ABLE TO:

▶ Identify money market and capital market securities and understand the important features of these securities.

▶ Recognize key terms such as asset-backed securities, stock splits, bond ratings, and ADRs.

▶ Understand the basics of two derivative securities, options and futures, and how they fit into the investor's choice set.

This chapter's purpose is to organize the types of financial assets available in the money and capital markets and provide the reader with a good understanding of the securities that are of primary interest to most investors, particularly bonds and stocks. Although our discussion is as up-to-date as possible, changes in the securities field occur so rapidly that investors are regularly confronted with new developments. Investors in the twenty-first century have a wide variety of investment alternatives available, and it is reasonable to expect that this variety will only increase. However, if investors understand the basic characteristics of the major existing securities, they will likely be able to understand new securities as they appear.

Organizing Financial Assets

The emphasis in this chapter (and in the text in general) is on *financial assets*, which, as explained in Chapter 1, are financial claims on the issuers of the *securities*. These claims are marketable securities that are saleable in various marketplaces, as discussed in Chapter 4.

Direct Investing
Investors buy and sell securities themselves, typically through brokerage accounts

This chapter concentrates on investment alternatives available through **direct investing**, which involves securities that investors not only buy and sell themselves (typically using their brokerage accounts), primarily capital market securities and derivative securities, but also have direct control over. In Chapter 3, we examine **indirect investing**. Rather than invest directly in securities and manage them, investors can purchase some type of fund that holds various types of securities on behalf of its shareowners. Indirect investing is a very important alternative for all investors to consider, and it has become tremendously popular in the last few years with individual investors.

Indirect Investing The buying and selling of the shares of investment companies, which in turn hold portfolios of securities

Investors who invest directly in financial markets, either using a broker or by other means, have a wide variety of assets from which to choose. Nonmarketable investment opportunities, such as savings accounts at thrift institutions, are discussed briefly at the beginning of the chapter, since investors often own, or have owned, these assets and are familiar with them. Henceforth, we will consider only marketable securities, which may be classified into one of three categories: the money market, the capital market, and the derivatives market.

Investors should understand money market securities, particularly Treasury bills, but they typically will not own these securities directly, choosing instead to own them through the money market funds explained in Chapter 3. Within the capital market, securities can be classified as either fixed-income or equity securities. Finally, investors may choose to use derivative securities in their portfolios. The market value of these securities is derived from an underlying security such as common stock.

Exhibit 2-1 organizes the types of financial assets to be analyzed in this chapter and in Chapter 3 using the above classifications. Although for expositional purposes we cover direct investing and indirect investing in separate chapters, it is important to understand that investors can do both, and often do, investing directly through the use of a brokerage account and investing indirectly in one or more investment companies. Furthermore, brokerage accounts that accommodate the ownership of investment company shares are becoming increasingly popular, thereby combining direct and indirect investing into one account.

AN INTERNATIONAL PERSPECTIVE

As noted in Chapter 1, investors should adopt an international perspective in making their investment decisions. The investment alternatives analyzed in this chapter, in particular some money market assets, bonds, and stocks, are available from many foreign

Exhibit 2-1

Major types of financial assets.

	DIRECT INVESTING
Nonmarketable	• Savings deposits
	• Certificates of deposit
	• Money market deposit accounts
	• U.S. savings bonds
Money market	• Treasury bills
	• Negotiable certificates of deposit
	• Commercial paper
	• Eurodollars
	• Repurchase agreements
	• Banker's acceptances
Capital market	• *Fixed income*
	Treasuries
	Agencies
	Municipals
	Corporates
	• *Equities*
	Preferred stock
	Common stock
Derivatives market	• Options
	• Future contracts
	INDIRECT INVESTING
Investment companies	• Unit investment trust
	• *Open end*
	Money market mutual fund
	Stock, bond, and income funds
	• Closed end
	• Exchange traded funds

markets to U.S. investors. Thus, the characteristics of these basic securities are relevant whether investors limit themselves to domestic or foreign stocks or both. Furthermore, assets traditionally thought of as U.S. assets are, in reality, heavily influenced by global events. Investors should understand that, in many instances, they own securities heavily influenced by international events.

Example 2-1

Coca-Cola is justifiably famous for its brandname and its marketing skills. Its success, however, is heavily dependent upon what happens in the foreign markets it has increasingly penetrated. If foreign economies slow, Coke's sales may be hurt. Furthermore, Coke must be able to convert its foreign earnings into dollars at favorable rates and repatriate them. Therefore, investing in Coke involves betting on a variety of foreign events.

U.S. investors typically invest internationally by investing indirectly through investment company shares. Most U.S. investors invest internationally by turning funds over to a professional investment organization, the investment company, which makes all decisions on behalf of investors who own shares of the company. We will discuss details of doing this in Chapter 3.

Nonmarketable Financial Assets

We begin our discussion of investment alternatives by mentioning those that are nonmarketable simply because most individuals will own one or more of these assets regardless of what else they do in the investing arena. For example, approximately 15 percent of the total financial assets of U.S. households is in the form of deposits, including checkable deposits (and currency) and time and savings deposits. Furthermore, these assets represent useful contrasts to the marketable securities we will concentrate on throughout the text.

A distinguishing characteristic of these assets is that they represent personal transactions between the owner and the issuer. That is, you as the owner of a savings account at a bank must open the account personally, and you must deal with the bank in maintaining the account or in closing it. In contrast, marketable securities trade in impersonal markets—the buyer (seller) does not know who the seller (buyer) is and does not care.

These are "safe" investments, occurring at (typically) insured financial institutions or issued by the U.S. government. At least some of these assets offer the ultimate in **liquidity**, which can be defined as the ease with which an asset can be converted to cash. An asset is liquid if it can be disposed of quickly, and typically with no loss of principal, assuming no new information in the marketplace. Thus, we know we can get all of our money back from a savings account or a money market deposit account very quickly.

> **Liquidity** The ease with which an asset can be bought or sold quickly with relatively small price changes

Exhibit 2-2 describes the four primary nonmarketable assets held by investors. Note that new innovations are occurring in this area. For example, the Treasury now offers *I bonds*, or inflation-indexed savings bonds. The yield on these bonds is a combination of a fixed rate of return and a semiannual inflation rate.[1]

Exhibit 2-2 Important Nonmarketable Financial Assets

1. *Savings accounts.* Undoubtedly the best-known type of investment in the United States, savings accounts are held at commercial banks or at "thrift" institutions such as savings and loan associations and credit unions. Savings accounts in insured institutions (and your money should not be in a noninsured institution) offer a high degree of safety on both the principal and the return on that principal. Liquidity is taken for granted and, together with the safety feature, probably accounts substantially for the popularity of savings accounts. Historically, the rate of interest paid on these accounts has been regulated by various government agencies. As of April 1, 1986, the interest rate ceiling on all deposit accounts was removed.

2. *Nonnegotiable certificates of deposit.* Commercial banks and other institutions offer a variety of savings certificates known as certificates of deposit (CDs). These certificates are available for various maturities, with higher rates offered as maturity increases. (Larger deposits may also command higher rates, holding maturity constant.) In effect, institutions are free to set their own rates and terms on most CDs. Because of competition for funds, the terms on CDs have been liberalized. Although some CD issuers have now reduced the stated penalties for early withdrawal, and even waived them, penalties for early withdrawal of funds can be imposed.

3. *Money market deposit accounts (MMDAs).* Financial institutions offer money market deposit accounts (MMDAs) with no interest rate ceilings. Money market "investment" accounts have a required minimum deposit to open, pay competitive money market rates and are insured up to $100,000 by the Federal Deposit Insurance Corporation (FDIC), if the bank is insured. Six preauthorized or automatic transfers are allowed each month, up to three of which can be by check. As many withdrawals as desired can be made in person or through automated teller machines (ATMs), and there are no limitations on the number of deposits.

    Financial institutions also offer NOW (Negotiable Order of Withdrawal) accounts, that pay interest at the so-called NOW interest rate. NOW accounts pay a relatively low rate of interest while permitting unlimited check-writing privileges. A "Super NOW account" combines unlimited check-writing privileges with money market rates of interest (which typically will be higher than rates paid in a regular NOW account).

4. *U.S. government savings bonds.* The nontraded debt of the U.S. government, savings bonds, are nonmarketable, nontransferable, and nonnegotiable, and cannot be used for collateral. They are purchased from the Treasury, most often through banks and savings institutions. Series EE bonds are sold at 50 percent of face value, with denominations of $50, $75, $100, $200, $500, $1,000, $5,000, and $10,000. Investors receive interest on Series EE bonds in a lump sum only at redemption, which can occur anytime beginning six months from the issue date. When held for at least five years, an investor will receive the higher of a market-based rate or a guaranteed minimum rate (4 percent since March 1993). The market-based rate of interest is calculated as 85 percent of the average return during that time on Treasury securities with a five-year maturity.

    Rates on savings bonds are reset every six months; therefore, depending on how long the bond is held and the prevailing interest rates, investors receive more or less than the face amount at redemption. Based on a 4-percent interest rate, savings bonds would reach their face value in 18 years. They can continue to earn interest for 30 years, and federal tax can be deferred until the bond is redeemed. The interest is exempt from state and local taxes.

---

[1] *I bonds* are purchased at face value. Earnings grow inflation-protected for maturities up to 30 years. Face values range from $50 to $10,000. Federal taxes on earnings are deferred until redemption.

Money Market Securities

Money Market   The market for short-term, highly liquid, low-risk assets such as Treasury bills and negotiable CDs

Money markets include short-term, highly liquid, relatively low-risk debt instruments sold by governments, financial institutions, and corporations to investors with temporary excess funds to invest. This market is dominated by financial institutions, particularly banks, and governments. The size of the transactions in the money market typically is large ($100,000 or more). The maturities of money market instruments range from one day to one year and are often less than 90 days.

Some of these instruments are negotiable and actively traded, and some are not. Investors may invest directly in some of these securities, but more often they do so indirectly through money market mutual funds (discussed in Chapter 3), which are investment companies organized to own and manage a portfolio of securities and which in turn are owned by investors. Thus, many individual investors own shares in money market funds that in turn own one or more of these money market certificates.

Treasury Bill   A short-term money market instrument sold at discount by the U.S. government

Another reason a knowledge of these securities is important is the use of the **Treasury bill** (T-bill) as a benchmark asset. Although in some pure sense there is no such thing as a risk-free financial asset, on a practical basis the Treasury bill is risk free on a nominal basis (not accounting for inflation). There is no practical risk of default by the U.S. government. The Treasury bill rate, denoted RF, is used throughout the text as a proxy for the nominal (today's dollars) *risk-free rate of return* available to investors (e.g., the RF shown and discussed in Figure 1-1).

Investors purchase Treasury bills at weekly auctions at a discount from face value, which is a minimum $10,000. T-bills are redeemed at face value, thereby providing investors with their return. Obviously, the less investors pay for these securities, the larger their return. Convention in the United States for many years is to state the yield on bills with six month maturities or less on a **discount yield** basis, using a 360-day year. The discount yield is calculated as follows Pur. Price = Purchase Price:

Discount Yield
Conventional method for stating yields on Treasury bills with six month maturities or less

$$\text{Discount yield} = \left[\frac{(\text{Face Value} - \text{Pur. Price})}{\text{Face Value}} \right] \times \left[\frac{360}{\text{maturity of the bill in days}} \right]$$

Investment Yield
Method for calculating yields on Treasury bills using the purchase price of the bill

The discount yield understates the investor's actual yield because it uses a 360-day year and divides by the face value instead of the purchase price. The **investment yield** method (also called the bond equivalent yield and the coupon equivalent rate) can be used to correct for these deficiencies, and for any given Treasury bill the investment yield will be greater than the discount yield. It is calculated as follows:

$$\text{Investment yield} = \left[\frac{(\text{Face Value} - \text{Pur. Price})}{\text{Pur. Price}} \right] \times \left[\frac{365}{\text{maturity of the bill in days}} \right]$$

(Note in this equation a leap year would involve 366 days; in both equations, a 3-month T-bill uses 91 days and a 6-month T-bill uses 182 days).

In summary, money market instruments are characterized as short-term, highly marketable investments, with an extremely low probability of default. Because the minimum investment (i.e., the face value of the instrument) is generally large, money market securities are typically owned by individual investors indirectly in the form of investment companies known as money market mutual funds or, as they are usually called, money market funds.

Money market rates tend to move together, and most rates are very close to each other for the same maturity. Treasury bill rates are less than the rates available on other money market securities, approximately one-third of a percentage point, because of their risk-free nature.

Exhibit 2-3 describes the major money market securities of most interest to individual investors. (Other money market securities exist, such as federal funds, but most individual investors will never encounter them.)

Exhibit 2-3 Important Money Market Securities

1. *Treasury bills.* The premier money market instrument, a fully guaranteed, very liquid IOU from the U.S. Treasury. They are sold on an auction basis every week at a discount from face value in denominations starting at $10,000; therefore, the discount determines the yield. The greater the discount at time of purchase, the higher the return earned by investors. Typical maturities are 13 and 26 weeks. New bills can be purchased by investors on a competitive or noncompetitive bid basis. Outstanding (i.e., already issued) bills can be purchased and sold in the secondary market, an extremely efficient market where government securities dealers stand ready to buy and sell these securities.

2. *Negotiable certificates of deposit* (CDs). Issued in exchange for a deposit of funds by most American banks, the CD is a marketable deposit liability of the issuer, who usually stands ready to sell new CDs on demand. The deposit is maintained in the bank until maturity, at which time the holder receives the deposit plus interest. However, these CDs are negotiable, meaning that they can be sold in the open market before maturity. Dealers make a market in these unmatured CDs. Maturities typically range from 14 days (the minimum maturity permitted) to one year. The minimum deposit is $100,000.

3. *Commercial paper.* A short-term, unsecured promissory note issued by large, well-known, and financially strong corporations (including finance companies). Denominations start at $100,000, with a maturity of 270 days or less. Commercial paper is usually sold at a discount either directly by the issuer or indirectly through a dealer, with rates comparable to CDs. Although a secondary market exists for commercial paper, it is weak and most of it is held to maturity. Commercial paper is rated by a rating service as to quality (relative probability of default by the issuer).

4. *Eurodollars.* Dollar-denominated deposits held in foreign banks or in offices of U.S. banks located abroad. Although this market originally developed in Europe, dollar-denominated deposits can now be made in many countries, such as those of Asia. Eurodollar deposits consist of both time deposits and CDs, with the latter constituting the largest component of the eurodollar market. Maturities are mostly short term, often less than six months. The eurodollar market is primarily a wholesale market, with large deposits and large loans. Major international banks transact among themselves with other participants including multinational corporations and governments. Although relatively safe, eurodollar yields exceed those of other money market assets because of the lesser regulation for eurodollar banks.

5. *Repurchase agreement* (RPs). An agreement between a borrower and a lender (typically institutions) to sell and repurchase U.S. government securities. The borrower initiates an RP by contracting to sell securities to a lender and agreeing to repurchase these securities at a prespecified price on a stated data. The effective interest rate is given by the difference between the two prices. The maturity of RPs is generally very short, from three to 14 days, and sometimes overnight. The minimum denomination is typically $100,000.

6. *Banker's acceptance.* A time draft drawn on a bank by a customer, whereby the bank agrees to pay a particular amount at a specified future date. Banker's acceptances are negotiable instruments because the holder can sell them for less than face value (i.e., discount them) in the money market. They are normally used in international trade. Banker's acceptances are traded on a discount basis, with a minimum denomination of $100,000. Maturities typically range from 30 to 180 days, with 90 days being the most common.

Fixed-Income Securities

Capital Market The market for long-term securities such as stocks and bonds

Capital **markets** encompass fixed-income and equity securities with maturities greater than one year. Risk is generally much higher than in the money market because of the time to maturity and the very nature of the securities sold in the capital markets. Marketability is poorer in some cases. The capital market includes both debt and equity securities, with equity securities having no maturity date.

Fixed-Income Securities Securities with specified payment dates and amounts, primarily bonds

We begin our review of the principal types of capital market securities typically owned directly by individual investors with **fixed-income securities**. All of these securities have a specified payment schedule. In most cases, such as with a traditional bond, the amount and date of each payment are known in advance. Some of these securities deviate from the traditional bond format, but all fixed-income securities have a specified payment or repayment schedule—they must mature at some future date.

BONDS

Bonds Long-term debt instruments representing the issuer's contractual obligation

Bonds can be described simply as long-term debt instruments representing the issuer's contractual obligation, or IOU. The buyer of a newly issued coupon bond is lending money to the issuer who, in turn, agrees to pay interest on this loan and repay the principal at a stated maturity date.

Bonds are *fixed-income securities* because the interest payments (for coupon bonds) and the principal repayment for a typical bond are specified at the time the bond is issued and fixed for the life of the bond. At the time of purchase, the bond buyer knows the future stream of *cash flows* to be received from buying and holding the bond to maturity. Barring default by the issuer, these payments will be received at specified intervals until maturity, at which time the principal will be repaid. However, if the buyer decides to sell the bond before maturity, the price received will depend on the level of interest rates at that time.

Par Value (Face Value)
The redemption value paid at maturity, typically $1,000

Bond Characteristics The par value (face value) of most bonds is $1,000, and we will use this number as the amount to be repaid at maturity.[2] The typical bond matures (terminates) on a specified date and is technically known as a *term bond*.[3] Most bonds are coupon bonds, where *coupon* refers to the periodic interest that the issuer pays to the holder of the bonds.[4] Interest on bonds is typically paid semiannually.

Example 2-2

A 10-year, 10-percent coupon bond has a dollar coupon of $100 (10 percent of $1,000); therefore, knowing the percentage coupon rate is the same as knowing the coupon payment in dollars.[5] This bond would pay interest (the coupons) of $50 on a specified date every six months. The $1,000 principal would be repaid 10 years hence on a date specified at the time the bond is issued. Note that all the characteristics of the bond are specified exactly when the bond is issued.

Zero Coupon Bond A bond sold with no coupons at a discount and redeemed for face value at maturity

A radical innovation in the format of traditional bonds is the zero **coupon bond**, which is issued with no coupons, or interest, to be paid during the life of the bond. The purchaser pays less than par value for zero coupons and receives par value at maturity. The difference in these two amounts generates an effective interest rate, or rate of return. As in the case of Treasury bills, which are sold at discount, the lower the price paid for the coupon bond, the higher the effective return.

Issuers of zero coupon bonds include corporations, municipalities, government agencies, and the U.S. Treasury. In 1985, the Treasury created its STRIPS, or Separate Trading of Registered Interest and Principal of Securities. Under this program, all new Treasury bonds and notes with maturities greater than 10 years are eligible to be "stripped" to create zero coupon Treasury securities that are direct obligations of the Treasury.

Bond prices are quoted as a percentage of par value. By convention, corporations and treasuries use 100 as par rather than 1,000. Therefore, a price of 90 represents $900 (90 percent of the $1,000 par value), and a price of 55 represents $550 using the normal assumption of a par value of $1,000. Each "point," or a change of "1," represents 1 percent of $1,000, or $10. The easiest way to convert quoted bond prices to actual prices is to remember that they are quoted in percentages, with the common assumption of a $1,000 par value.

Example 2-3

A closing price of 101 3/8 on a particular day for an IBM bond represents 101.375 percent of $1,000, or $1,013.75.

---

[2] The par value is almost never less than $1,000, although it easily can be more.
[3] The phrase *term-to-maturity* denotes how much longer the bond will be in existence. In contrast, a serial bond has a series of maturity dates. One issue of *serial bonds* may mature in specified amounts year after year, and each specified amount could carry a different coupon.
[4] The terms *interest income* and *coupon income* are interchangeable.
[5] The coupon rate on a traditional, standard bond is fixed at the bond's issuance and cannot vary.

Example 2-3 suggests that an investor could purchase the IBM bond for $1,013.75 on that day. Actually, bonds trade on an *accrued interest* basis. That is, the bond buyer must pay the bond seller the price of the bond as well as the interest that has been earned (accrued) on the bond since the last semiannual interest payment. This allows an investor to sell a bond anytime between interest payments without losing the interest that has accrued. Bond buyers should remember this additional "cost" when buying a bond, because prices are quoted in the newspaper without the accrued interest.[6]

The price of the IBM bond in example 2-3 is above 100 (i.e., $1,000) because market yields on bonds of this type declined after this bond was issued. The coupon on this particular bond became more than competitive with the going market interest rate for comparable newly issued bonds, and the price increased to reflect this fact. At any point in time, some bonds are selling at *premiums* (prices above par value), reflecting a decline in market rates after that particular bond was sold. Others are selling at *discounts* (prices below par value of $1,000), because the stated coupons are less than the prevailing interest rate on a comparable new issue. So, always remember that although a bond will be worth exactly its face value (typically $1,000) on the day it matures, its price will fluctuate around $1,000 until then depending on what interest rates do. Interest rates and bond prices move inversely.

Call Provision Gives the issuer the right to call in a security and retire it by paying off the obligation

The **call provision** gives the issuer the right to "call in" the bonds, thereby depriving investors of that particular fixed-income security.[7] Exercising the call provision becomes attractive to the issuer when market interest rates drop sufficiently below the coupon rate on the outstanding bonds for the issuer to save money.[8] Costs are incurred to call the bonds, such as a "call premium" and administrative expenses. However, issuers expect to sell new bonds at a lower interest cost, thereby replacing existing higher interest–cost bonds with new, lower interest–cost bonds.[9]

Investments Intuition

The call feature is a disadvantage to investors who must give up the higher yielding bonds. The wise bond investor will note the bond issue's provisions concerning the call, carefully determining the earliest date at which the bond can be called and the bond's yield if it is called at the earliest date possible. (This calculation is shown in Chapter 17.) Some investors have purchased bonds at prices above face value and suffered a loss when the bonds were unexpectedly called in and paid off at face value.[10]

Some bonds are not callable. Most Treasury bonds cannot be called, although some older Treasury bonds can be called within five years of the maturity date.[11]

---

[6] The *invoice price*, or the price the bond buyer must pay, will include the accrued interest.

[7] Unlike the call provision, the *sinking fund* provides for the orderly retirement of the bond issue during its life. The provisions of a sinking fund vary widely. For example, it can be stated as a fixed or variable amount and as a percentage of the particular issue outstanding or the total debt of the issuer outstanding. Any part or all of the bond issue may be retired through the sinking fund by the maturity date. One procedure for carrying out the sinking fund requirement is simply to buy the required amount of bonds on the open market each year. A second alternative is to call the bonds randomly. Again, investors should be aware of such provisions for their protection.

[8] There are different types of call features. Some bonds can be called any time during their life, given a short notice of 30 or 60 days. Many callable bonds have a "deferred call" feature, meaning that a certain time period after issuance must expire before the bonds can be called. Popular time periods in this regard are 5 and 10 years.

[9] The call premium often equals one year's interest if the bond is called within a year; after the first year, it usually declines at a constant rate.

[10] A bond listed as "nonrefundable" for a specified period can still be called in and paid off with cash in hand. It cannot be refunded through the sale of a new issue carrying a lower coupon.

[11] Treasury bonds issued after February 1985 cannot be called.

A bond has certain legal ramifications. Failure to pay either interest or principal on a bond constitutes default for that obligation. Default, unless quickly remedied by payment or a voluntary agreement with the creditor, leads to bankruptcy. A filing of bankruptcy by a corporation initiates litigation and involvement by a court, which works with all parties concerned.

TYPES OF BONDS

There are four major types of bonds in the United States based on the issuer involved (U.S. government, federal agency, municipal, and corporate bonds), and variations exist within each major type.

Federal Government Securities   The U.S. government, in the course of financing its operations through the Treasury Department, issues numerous notes and bonds with maturities greater than one year.[12] The U.S. government is considered to be the safest credit risk because of its power to print money; therefore, *for practical purposes, investors do not consider the possibility of risk of default for these securities*. An investor purchases these securities with the expectation of earning a steady stream of interest payments and with full assurance of receiving the par value of the bonds when they mature.

Treasury Bonds A long-term bond sold by the U.S. government

Treasury bonds traditionally have maturities of 10 to 30 years, although a bond can be issued with any maturity.[13] Like Treasury bills, they are sold at competitive auctions; unlike bills, they are sold at face value, with investors submitting bids on yields. Interest payments (coupons) are paid semiannually. Face value denominations are $1,000, $5,000, $10,000, $100,000, $500,000, and $1 million.

In the fall of 2001, the Treasury announced that it would cease to issue 30-year Treasury bonds, which had been used as a benchmark in the bond market. The 10-year Treasury bond is now used as a benchmark measure of interest rates.

Treasury Inflation-Indexed Securities (TIPS) Bonds that protect investors against losses resulting from inflation

Since 1997 the Treasury has sold **Treasury Inflation-Indexed Securities (TIPS)** which protects investors against losses resulting from inflation. Based on the consumer price index (CPI), the value of the bond is adjusted upward every six months by the amount of inflation. The interest paid each six months is based on the increasing value of the principal. Maturities range from 2 to 29 years. Taxes must be paid each year on both the interest and the inflation adjustments, although the actual cash is not received until maturity. Therefore, many investors may prefer to hold these securities in a retirement account.

Are TIPS a good bet? Many investors these days think so. Effectively, holding other things constant, TIPS yield 1.7 percentage points less than a comparable Treasury bond. Therefore, over the life of the bond, if inflation exceeds 1.7 percent a year, a TIPS bond will do better than the regular Treasury. As we shall see in Chapter 6, the long-term annual average CPI has been higher than this, approximately 3 percent.

The Treasury also sells Series I savings bonds, which are inflation indexed. These I bonds are more suitable for taxable accounts, because the earnings on them are not taxable until the bonds are sold.

Government Agency Securities Securities issued by federal credit agencies (fully guaranteed) or by government-sponsored agencies (not guaranteed)

Government Agency Securities   Since the 1920s, the federal government has created various federal agencies designed to help certain sectors of the economy through either direct loans or guarantee of private loans. These various credit agencies compete for funds in the marketplace by selling **government agency securities**.

---

[12] Through 1982, Treasury securities were sold in bearer form, meaning they belong to the bearer (whoever possesses them). Most federal, state and local, and corporate bonds issued after January 1, 1983, must be registered in the owner's name (unless the maturity is one year or less).

[13] U.S. securities with maturities greater than 1 year and less than 10 years technically are referred to as Treasury notes. See www.publicdebt.treas.gov for information about Treasury bonds, including inflation-indexed bonds.

There are two types of federal credit agencies: federal agencies and federally sponsored credit agencies. Legally, federal agencies are part of the federal government and their securities are fully guaranteed by the Treasury. The most important "agency" for investors is the Government National Mortgage Association (often referred to as "Ginnie Mae").

In contrast to federal agencies that are officially a part of the government, federally sponsored credit agencies are privately owned institutions that sell their own securities in the marketplace in order to raise funds for their specific purposes. Although these agencies have the right to draw on Treasury funds up to some approved amount, their securities are not guaranteed by the government as to principal or interest. Nevertheless, the rapidly growing agency market is dominated by these federally sponsored credit agencies, which include the Federal National Mortgage Association, the Federal Home Loan Mortgage Corporation, the Federal Home Loan Bank, the Farm Credit System, and the Student Loan Marketing Association.

Example 2-4

A well-known federally sponsored agency is the Federal National Mortgage Association (FNMA, typically referred to as "Fannie Mae"), which is designed to help the mortgage markets. Although government sponsored, it is now a privately owned corporation, and its securities are not a direct obligation of the U.S. government. A variety of Fannie Mae issues are available, with maturities ranging from short term to long term.

Mortgage-Backed Securities Pools of securities based on mortgages packaged together in portfolios

The Federal National Mortgage Association, the Government National Mortgage Association, and the Federal Home Loan Mortgage Corporation (Freddie Mac) issue and guarantee securities backed by conventional mortgages bought from lenders. These **mortgage-backed securities** are part of the rapidly growing market of fixed-income securities known as asset-backed securities, which are discussed separately below.

Investments Intuition

Federal agency securities can be thought of as an alternative to U.S. Treasury securities from the investor's standpoint. The feeling in the marketplace seems to be that the Treasury would not stand by and permit a government-sponsored agency to default; however, they have to be viewed as having slightly greater default risk. Also, longer term issues may trade less frequently than comparable Treasury bonds. Together, these two factors cause these securities to carry slightly higher yields than Treasury securities of comparable maturity.

Municipal Bonds Securities issued by political entities other than the federal government and its agencies, such as states and cities

Municipal Securities Bonds sold by states, counties, cities, and other political entities (e.g., airport authorities, school districts) other than the federal government and its agencies are called **municipal bonds**. There are roughly 50,000 different issuers with roughly 1.5 million different issues outstanding and credit ratings ranging from very good to very suspect. Thus, risk varies widely, as does marketability. Overall, however, the default rate on municipal bonds has been quite favorable compared to corporate bonds.

Two basic types of municipals are *general obligation bonds*, which are backed by the "full faith and credit" of the issuer, and *revenue bonds*, which are repaid from the revenues generated by the project they were sold to finance (e.g., a toll road or airport improvement).[14] In the case of general obligation bonds, the issuer can tax residents to pay for the bond interest and principal. In the case of revenue bonds, the project must generate enough revenue to service the issue.

---

[14] Municipalities also issue short-term obligations. Some of these qualify for money market investments because they are short term and of high quality.

Most long-term municipals are sold as *serial bonds*, which means that a specified number of the original issue matures each year until the final maturity date. For example, a 10-year serial issue might have 10 percent of the issue maturing each year for the next 10 years.

In 2002, approximately 60 percent of municipals sold were insured by one of the four major municipal bond insurers. By having the bonds insured, the issuers achieve a higher rating for the bond, and therefore a lower interest cost. The insurer often charges about half of the interest rate savings; for example, if a higher bond rating reduced the interest cost to the issuer by 30 basis points, the insurer captures about half of this amount. Although investors gain protection this way, they give up some of the higher yield that would have been paid on a lower rated bond. Furthermore, although defaults on municipals do occur, they are rare.

The distinguishing feature of most municipals is their exemption from federal taxes. Because of this feature, the stated rate on these bonds will be lower than that on comparable nonexempt bonds. The higher an investor's tax bracket, the more attractive municipals become. To make the return on these bonds comparable to those of taxable bonds, the *taxable equivalent yield* (TEY) can be calculated. The TEY shows the interest rate on taxable bonds necessary to provide an after-tax return equal to that of municipals. The TEY for any municipal bond return and any marginal tax bracket can be calculated using the following formula:

$$\text{Taxable equivalent yield} = \frac{\text{Tax-exempt municipal yield}}{1 - \text{Marginal tax rate}} \qquad \textbf{(2-1)}$$

Example 2-5

An investor in the 28-percent marginal tax bracket who invests in a 5-percent municipal bond would have to receive

$$\frac{0.05}{1 - 0.28} = 6.94\%$$

from a comparable taxable bond to be as well off.[15]

In some cases, the municipal bondholder can also escape state and/or local taxes. For example, a North Carolina resident purchasing a bond issued by the state of North Carolina would escape all taxes on the interest received. To calculate the TEY in these cases, first determine the *effective state rate*:

Effective state rate = Marginal state tax rate × (1 − Federal marginal rate)

Then, calculate the *combined effective federal/state tax rate* as

Combined tax rate = Effective state rate + Federal rate

Use Equation 2-1 to calculate the combined TEY, substituting the combined effective tax rate for the federal marginal tax rate shown in Equation 2-1.

Corporate Bonds
Long-term debt securities of various types sold by corporations

Corporates Most of the larger corporations, several thousand in total, issue **corporate bonds** to help finance their operations. Many of these firms have more than one issue outstanding. AT&T, for example, has several different issues of bonds listed on the "New York Exchange Bonds" page of *The Wall Street Journal*. Although an investor can find a wide

[15] As a result of tax reform, municipal bonds used to finance nonessential government functions are now taxable—specifically, private-purpose municipal bonds issued after August 7, 1986. Some of these bonds are fully taxable to all investors, whereas others are taxable only to investors subject to the alternative minimum tax.

range of maturities, coupons, and special features available from corporates, the typical corporate bond matures in 20 to 40 years, pays semiannual interest, is callable, carries a sinking fund, and is sold originally at a price close to par value, which is almost always $1,000.

Senior Securities
Securities, typically debt securities, ahead of common stock in terms of payment or in case of liquidation

Corporate bonds are **senior securities**. That is, they are senior to any preferred stock and to the common stock of a corporation in terms of priority of payment and in case of bankruptcy and liquidation. However, within the bond category itself there are various degrees of security. The most common type of unsecured bond is the **debenture**, a bond backed only by the issuer's overall financial soundness.[16] Debentures can be subordinated, resulting in a claim on income that stands below (subordinate to) the claim of the other debentures.

Debenture An unsecured bond backed by the general creditworthiness of the firm

In an attempt to make bonds more accessible to individuals, high credit–quality firms have begun selling **direct access notes (DANs)**. These notes eliminate some of the traditional details associated with bonds by being issued at par ($1,000), which means no discounts, premiums, or accrued interest. Coupon rates are fixed, and maturities range from 9 months to 30 years. The company issuing the bonds typically "posts" the maturities and rates it's offering for one week, allowing investors to shop around. Currently, some companies are acting as wholesalers of the bonds to their own extensive network of brokerage firms from which investors would buy the bonds. The brokerage firm buys the notes from the wholesaler at a discount and pays the broker's commission.

Direct Access Notes (DANs) Notes issued at par that have no discounts, premiums, or accrued interest

One potential disadvantage of DANs is that they are best suited for the buy-and-hold investor. A seller has no assurance of a good secondary market for the bonds, and therefore no assurance as to the price that would be received.

Convertible Bonds
Bonds that are convertible, at the holder's option, into shares of common stock of the same corporation

Convertible bonds have a built-in conversion feature. The holders of these bonds have the option to convert whenever they choose. Typically, the bonds are turned in to the corporation in exchange for a specified number of common shares, with no cash payment being required. Convertible bonds are two securities simultaneously: a fixed-income security paying a specified interest payment and a claim on the common stock that will become increasingly valuable as the price of the underlying common stock rises. Thus, the prices of convertibles may fluctuate over a fairly wide range depending on whether they currently are trading like other fixed-income securities or are trading to reflect the price of the underlying common stock.

Investments Intuition

Investors should not expect to receive the conversion option free. The issuer sells convertible bonds at a lower interest rate than would otherwise be paid, resulting in a lower interest return to investors.

Bond Ratings Letters of the alphabet assigned to bonds by rating agencies to express the relative probability of default

Corporate bonds, unlike Treasury securities, carry the risk of default by the issuer. Three rating agencies, Standard & Poor's (S&P) Corporation, Moody's Investors Service Inc., and Fitch Inc. provide investors with **bond ratings**; that is, current opinions on the *relative* quality of most large corporate and municipal bonds, as well as commercial paper. As independent organizations with no vested interest in the issuers, they can render objective judgments on the relative merits of their securities. By carefully analyzing the issues in great detail, the rating firms, in effect, perform the *credit analysis* for the investor.

Standard & Poor's bond ratings consist of letters ranging from AAA, AA, A, BBB, and so on, to D. (Moody's corresponding letters are Aaa, Aa, A, Baa, etc., to D.) Plus or

---

[16] Bonds that are "secured" by a legal claim to specific assets of the issuer in case of liquidation are called *mortgage bonds*.

minus signs can be used to provide more detailed standings within a given category.[17] Exhibit 2-4 shows Standard & Poor's rating definitions and provides a brief explanation of the considerations on which the ratings are based.

The first four categories, AAA through BBB, represent *investment-grade* securities. AAA securities are judged to have very strong capacity to meet all obligations, whereas BBB securities are considered to have adequate capacity. Typically, institutional investors must confine themselves to bonds in these four categories. Other things being equal, bond ratings and bond coupon rates are inversely related.

Bonds rated BB, B, CCC, and CC are regarded as speculative securities in terms of the issuer's ability to meet its contractual obligations. These securities carry significant uncertainties, although they are not without positive factors. Bonds rated C are currently not paying interest, and bonds rated D are in default.

Junk Bonds High-risk, high-yield bonds carrying ratings of BB (S&P) or Ba (Moody's) or lower, with correspondingly higher yields

Junk bonds are high-risk, high-yield bonds that carry ratings of BB (S&P) or Ba (Moody's) or lower, with correspondingly higher yields. An alternative, and more reassuring, name used to describe this area of the bond market is the *high-yield debt market*. Default rates on junk bonds vary each year. The default rate in 2001 was almost 9 percent, the highest level since 1991. It was over 6 percent in 2000. Higher default rates would be expected during periods of economic difficulty, and the United States experienced a recession beginning in 2001.

Of the large number of corporate bonds outstanding, traditionally more than 80 percent have been rated A or better (based on the value of bonds outstanding). Traditionally, utilities and finance companies have the fewest low-rated bonds, and transportation companies the most (because of problems with bankrupt railroads).[18]

Despite their widespread acceptance and use, bond ratings have some limitations. The two agencies may disagree on their evaluations. Furthermore, because most bonds

Exhibit 2-4 Standard & Poor's debt-rating definitions.

AAA	Extremely strong capacity to pay interest and repay principal
AA	Strong capacity to pay interest and repay principal
A	Strong capacity to pay interest and repay principal but more vulnerable to an adverse change in conditions than in the case of AA
BBB	Adequate capacity to pay interest and repay principal. Even more vulnerable to adverse change in conditions than A-rated bonds
	Debt rated BB and below is regarded as having predominantly speculative characteristics.
BB	Less near-term risk of default than lower rated issues. These bonds are exposed to large ongoing uncertainties or adverse change in conditions
B	A larger vulnerability to default than BB but with the current capacity to pay interest and repay principal
CCC	A currently identifiable vulnerability to default and dependent on favorable conditions to pay interest and repay principal
CC	Applied to debt subordinated to senior debt rated CCC
C	Same as CC
D	A debt that is in default
+ or −	May be used to show relative standings within a category

---

[17] Moody's uses numbers (i.e., 1, 2, and 3) to designate quality grades further. For example, bonds could be rated Aa1 or Aa2. Major rating categories for Moody's include Aaa, Aa, A, Baa, Ba, B, Caa, Ca, and C.

[18] Less is known about the ratings of state and local government bonds, but the majority apparently are rated in the top three categories based on value. We do know that approximately 70 percent of newly issued *insured* municipal bonds carry a rating of A or better, and that less than 1 percent of all outstanding insured municipals have ratings that have declined below investment grade.

are in the top four categories, it seems safe to argue that not all issues in a single category (such as A) can be equally risky. It is extremely important to remember that *bond ratings are a reflection of the relative probability of default*, which says little or nothing about the absolute probability of default. Finally, it is important to remember that, like most people and institutions in life, rating agencies aren't perfect. Sometimes, for various reasons, they really miss the boat.

Example 2-6

In December 2001, Enron was rated investment grade on a Friday. On Sunday, it filed for bankruptcy. S&P continued to rate Tyco bonds as investment grade (BBB), although the market clearly priced Tyco bonds in the junk category. And by the time the rating services downgraded WorldCom to junk status, the market had reflected that fact for some time.

ASSET-BACKED SECURITIES

The money and capital markets are constantly adapting to meet new requirements and conditions. This has given rise to new types of securities that were not previously available.

Securitization refers to the transformation of illiquid, risky individual loans into more liquid, less risky securities referred to as **asset-backed securities (ABS)**. Another name for securitization is "structured finance." As of mid-2002, this was a $7 trillion dollar industry.

Asset-Backed Securities (ABS) Securities issued against some type of asset-linked debts bundled together, such as credit card receivables or mortgages

The best example of this process, the *mortgage-backed securities* issued by the federal agencies mentioned above, such as Ginnie Mae, are securities representing an investment in an underlying pool of mortgages.[19] The federal agencies discussed earlier purchase mortgages from banks and thrift institutions, repackage them in the form of securities, and sell them to investors as mortgage pools.

Investors in mortgage-backed securities are, in effect, purchasing a piece of a mortgage pool, taking into consideration such factors as maturity and the spread between the yield on the mortgage security and the yield on 10-year Treasuries (considered a benchmark in this market). Investors in mortgage-backed securities assume little default risk, because most mortgages are guaranteed by one of the government agencies. However, these securities present investors with uncertainty, because they can receive varying amounts of monthly payments depending on how quickly homeowners pay off their mortgages. Although the stated maturity can be as long as 40 years, the average life of these securities to date has been much shorter.

Ginnie Mae issues are well known to investors. This wholly owned government agency issues fully backed securities (i.e., they are full faith and credit obligations of the U.S. government) in support of the mortgage market. The GNMA *pass-through securities* have attracted considerable attention in recent years, because the principal and interest payments on the underlying mortgages used to collateralize them are "passed through" to the bondholder monthly as the mortgages are repaid.[20]

[19] In the area of mortgage-backed securities, **collateralized mortgage obligations (CMOs)** have been created to offer investors an alternative mortgage security. CMOs are bonds backed by a trust created to hold Ginnie Mae and other government-guaranteed mortgages. They are issued by brokerage firms. Shorter maturities are typically purchased by institutions, whereas individual investors often purchase the longer term issues known as "companion" CMOs. One advantage of CMOs is their lower minimum investment of $1,000 compared to $25,000 for Ginnie Maes. Yields are higher than for Ginnie Maes, perhaps one-half percentage point, presumably because of their lower liquidity. CMOs can be redeemed by random calls by the trust as the principal accumulates in a redemption fund. Like Ginnie Maes, investors in CMOs face the risk of early redemption as a result of mortgage refinancings.

[20] A related mortgage-backed security is "Freddie Mac," issued by the Federal Home Loan Mortgage Corporation. This is a *participation certificate* paying a monthly return. Unlike Ginnie Mae, Freddie Mac is not guaranteed by the U.S. government itself. Fannie Mae also issues passthroughs called mortgage-backed securities. These also are not guaranteed by the U.S. government; however, payment of interest and principal is guaranteed by Fannie Mae.

As a result of the trend to securitization, asset-backed securities have proliferated as financial institutions have rushed to securitize various types of loans. ABS are created when an underwriter, such as a bank, bundles some type of asset-linked debt (typically consumer oriented) and sells to investors the right to receive payments made on that debt.

Example 2-7

Citicorp, a major bank, has a large Visa operation. It regularly takes the cash flows from the monthly payments that customers make on their Visa accounts, securitizes them, and sells the resulting bonds to investors.

Marketable securities have been backed by car loans, credit card receivables, railcar leases, small business loans, photocopier leases, aircraft leases, and so forth. The assets that can be securitized seem to be limited only by the imagination of the packagers, as evidenced by the fact that by 1996 new asset types included royalty streams from films, student loans, mutual fund fees, tax liens, monthly electric utility bills, and delinquent child support payments.

Why do investors like these asset-backed securities? The attractions are relatively high yields and relatively short maturities (often five years) combined with investment-grade credit ratings.[21] Securities are subdivided into "tranches," which are priced according to the degree of risk. Institutional investors such as pension funds and life insurance companies became increasingly attracted to ABS because of the higher yields, and foreign investors are now buying these securities more often. Note, however, that the Enron scandal and the recession have been a severe setback to the industry. S&P has downgraded a number of these securities, and investors are more wary than they were before.

As for risks, securitization works best when packaged loans are homogeneous, so that income streams and risks are more predictable. This is clearly the case for home mortgages, for example, which must adhere to strict guidelines. This is not the case for some of the newer loans being considered for packaging, such as loans for boats and motorcycles; the smaller amount of information results in a larger risk from unanticipated factors.

RATES ON FIXED-INCOME SECURITIES

Interest rates on fixed-income securities fluctuate widely over the years as inflationary expectations change as well as demand and supply conditions for long-term funds. As we would expect on the basis of the return-risk trade-off explained in Chapter 1, corporate bond rates exceed Treasury rates because of the possible risk of default, and lower rated corporates yield more than do higher rated bonds. The municipal bond rate as reported is below all other rates, but we must remember that this is an after-tax rate. To make it comparable, municipal bond yields should be adjusted to a taxable equivalent yield using Equation 2-1. When this is done, the rate will be much closer to the taxable rates. Investors can obtain daily information on the rates available on fixed-income securities in the "Credit Markets" section of *The Wall Street Journal*.

Equity Securities

Unlike fixed-income securities, equity securities represent an ownership interest in a corporation. These securities provide a residual claim—after payment of all obligations to fixed-income claims—on the income and assets of a corporation. There are two forms of equities, preferred stock and common stock. Investors are primarily interested in common stocks.

[21] To date, some 75 percent of ABS have been rated AAA.

PREFERRED STOCK

Preferred Stock An equity security with an intermediate claim (between the bondholders and the stockholders) on a firm's assets and earnings

Although technically an equity security, **preferred stock** is known as a hybrid security, because it resembles both equity and fixed-income instruments. As an equity security, preferred stock has an infinite life and pays dividends. Preferred stock resembles fixed-income securities in that the dividend is fixed in amount and known in advance, providing a stream of income very similar to that of a bond. The difference is that the stream continues forever unless the issue is called or otherwise retired (most preferred stock is callable). The price fluctuations in preferreds often exceed those in bonds.[22]

Preferred stockholders are paid after the bondholders but before the common stockholders in terms of priority of payment of income and in case the corporation is liquidated. However, preferred stock dividends are not legally binding but must be voted on each period by a corporation's board of directors. If the issuer fails to pay the dividend in any year, the unpaid dividend(s) will have to be paid in the future before common stock dividends can be paid if the issue is cumulative. (If noncumulative, dividends in arrears do not have to be paid.)[23]

A large amount of the total preferred stock outstanding is variable-rate preferred; that is, the dividend rate is tied to current market interest rates. Other trends in preferred stocks include auction-rate preferred, a type of floating-rate preferred where the dividend is established by auction every 49 days. More than one-third of the preferred stock sold in recent years is convertible into common stock at the owner's option. A recent innovation is mandatory convertible preferreds, which automatically convert to the common stock in a few years at a ratio specified at time of issuance. These mandatory convertibles pay above-market yields, for which investors give up roughly 20 percent of any upside potential.

A new trend in this area is a hybrid security combining features of preferred stock and corporate bonds. These hybrid securities are available from brokerage houses under various acronyms, such as MIPS (*monthly income preferred securities*) and QUIPS (*quarterly income preferred securities*), issued by Goldman Sachs, and TOPrS, or *trust originated preferred security*, originated by Merrill Lynch. For individual investors, these securities are an alternative to corporate bonds and traditional preferred stocks.

Most of the new hybrids are traded on the New York Stock Exchange (NYSE), offer fixed monthly or quarterly dividends considerably higher than investment-grade corporate bond yields, are rated as to credit risk, and have maturities in the 30- to 49-year range. Hybrids are sensitive to interest rate changes and can be called, although a fixed dividend is paid for five years.[24]

COMMON STOCK

Common Stock An equity security representing the ownership interest in a company

Common stock represents the ownership interest of corporations, or the equity of the stockholders, and we can use the term *equity securities* interchangeably. If a firm's shares are held by only a few individuals, the firm is said to be "closely held." Most companies choose to "go public"; that is, they sell common stock to the general public. This action is taken primarily to enable the company to raise additional capital more easily. If a corporation meets certain requirements, it may, if it chooses to, be listed on one or more ex-

---

[22] Corporations are the largest buyer of preferreds because of a unique tax advantage: 70 percent of the dividends are not taxed, resulting in an effective tax rate of only 10.2 percent (assuming the maximum marginal corporate tax rate of 34 percent).

[23] In the event of omitted dividends, preferred stock owners may be allowed to vote for the directors of the corporation.

[24] Unlike a traditional preferred stock, hybrids can suspend dividend payments no longer than five years.

changes. Otherwise, it will be listed in the over-the-counter market (this process is discussed in Chapter 4).

As a purchaser of 100 shares of common stock, an investor owns $100/n$ percent of the corporation (where n is the number of shares of common stock outstanding). As the residual claimants of the corporation, stockholders are entitled to income remaining after the fixed-income claimants (including preferred stockholders) have been paid; also, in case of liquidation of the corporation, they are entitled to the remaining assets after all other claims (including preferred stock) are satisfied.[25]

As owners, the holders of common stock are entitled to elect the directors of the corporation and vote on major issues.[26] Each owner is usually allowed to cast votes equal to the number of shares owned for each director being elected. Such votes occur at the annual meeting of the corporation, which each shareholder is allowed to attend.[27] Most stockholders vote by *proxy*, meaning that the stockholder authorizes someone else (typically management) to vote his or her shares. Sometimes proxy battles occur, whereby one or more groups unhappy with corporate policies seek to bring about changes.

Stockholders also have *limited liability*, meaning that they cannot lose more than their investment in the corporation. In the event of financial difficulties, creditors have recourse only to the assets of the corporation, leaving the stockholders protected. This is perhaps the greatest advantage of the corporation and the reason why it has been so successful.

Characteristics of Common Stocks   The *par value* (stated or face value) for a common stock, unlike a bond or preferred stock, is generally not a significant economic variable. Corporations can make the par value any number they choose; for example, the par value of Coca-Cola is $0.25 per share. An often-used par value is $1. Some corporations issue no-par stock. New stock is usually sold for more than par value, with the difference being recorded on the balance sheet as "capital in excess of par value."

Book Value   The accounting value of the equity as shown on the balance sheet

The **book value** of a corporation is the accounting value of the equity as shown on the books (i.e., balance sheet). It is the sum of common stock outstanding, capital in excess of par value, and retained earnings. Dividing this sum, or total book value, by the number of common shares outstanding produces the *book value per share*. In effect, book value is the accounting value of the stockholders' equity. Although book value per share plays a role in making investment decisions, market value per share is the critical item of interest to investors.

Example 2-8   The Coca-Cola Company, an international soft drink company, reported $11.8 billion as total stockholders' equity for fiscal year-end 2002. This is the book value of the equity. Based on average shares outstanding of 2.478 billion for that year (a figure typically obtained for a company from its annual report), the book value per share was $4.76.

The market value (i.e., price) of the equity is the variable of concern to investors. The *aggregate market value* for a corporation, calculated by multiplying the market price

---

[25] The *preemptive right* in a corporation's charter grants existing stockholders the first right to purchase any new common stock sold by the corporation. The "right" is a piece of paper giving each stockholder the option to buy a specified number of new shares, usually at a discount, during a specified short period of time. Because of this, rights are valuable and can be sold in the market.

[26] The *voting rights* of the stockholders give them legal control of the corporation. In theory, the board of directors controls the management of the corporation, but in many cases the effective result is the opposite. Stockholders can regain control if they are sufficiently dissatisfied.

[27] Most shareholders do not attend, often allowing management to vote their proxy. Therefore, although technically more than 50 percent of the outstanding shares are needed for control of a firm, effective control can often be exercised with considerably less, because not all of the shares are voted.

per share of the stock by the number of shares outstanding, represents the total value of the firm as determined in the marketplace. The market value of one share of stock, of course, is simply the observed current market price. At the time the observation for Coca-Cola's book value was recorded, the market price was in the $45 range.

Dividends Cash payments declared and paid quarterly by corporations to stockholders

Dividends are the only cash payments regularly made by corporations to their stockholders. They are decided upon and declared by the board of directors and can range from zero to virtually any amount the corporation can afford to pay (typically up to 100 percent of present and past net earnings). Although roughly three-fourths of the companies listed on the NYSE pay dividends, *the common stockholder has no specific promises to receive any cash from the corporation, since the stock never matures, and dividends do not have to be paid.* Therefore, common stocks involve substantial risk, because the dividend is at the company's discretion and stock prices typically fluctuate sharply, which means that the value of investors' claims may rise and fall rapidly over relatively short periods of time.

The following two dividend terms are important:

Dividend Yield Dividends divided by current stock price

Payout Ratio Dividends divided by earnings

- ❑ The **dividend yield** is the income component of a stock's return stated on a percentage basis. It is one of the two components of total return, which is discussed in Chapter 6. Dividend yield typically is calculated as the most recent 12-month dividend divided by the current market price.
- ❑ The **payout ratio** is the ratio of dividends to earnings. It indicates the percentage of a firm's earnings paid out in cash to its stockholders. The complement of the payout ratio, or (1.0 − payout ratio), is the *retention ratio*, and it indicates the percentage of a firm's current earnings retained by it for reinvestment purposes.

Example 2-9

Coca-Cola's 2002 earnings were $1.23 per share, and it paid an annual dividend per share that year of $0.80. Based on a price for Coca-Cola of $45, the dividend yield would be 1.8 percent. The payout ratio was $0.80/$1.23, or 65 percent.

Dividends traditionally are declared and paid quarterly, although some firms (such as Disney, McDonald's, and Waste Management) are now moving to annual dividend payments. To receive a declared dividend, an investor must be a *holder of record* on the specified date that a company closes its stock transfer books and compiles the list of stockholders to be paid. However, to avoid problems, the brokerage industry has established a procedure of declaring that the right to the dividend remains with the stock until four days before the holder-of-record date. On this fourth day, the right to the dividend leaves the stock; for that reason this date is called the *ex-dividend* date.

Stock Dividend A payment by a corporation in shares of stock rather than cash

Example 2-10

Assume that the board of directors of Coca-Cola meets on May 24 and declares a quarterly dividend payable on July 2. May 24 is called the *declaration date*. The board will declare a *holder-of-record date*—say, June 7. The books close on this date, but Coke goes *ex-dividend* on June 5. To receive this dividend, an investor must purchase the stock by June 4. The dividend will be mailed to the stockholders of record on the *payment date*, July 2.

Stock Split Issuance by a corporation of shares of common stock in proportion to existing shares outstanding

Stock dividends and stock splits attract considerable investor attention. A **stock dividend** is a payment by the corporation in shares of stock instead of cash. A **stock split** involves the issuance of a larger number of shares in proportion to the existing shares outstanding. With a stock split, the book value and par value of the equity are changed; for example, each would be cut in half with a two for one split. However, on a practical basis, there is little difference between a stock dividend and a stock split.

Example 2-11 A 5-percent stock dividend would entitle an owner of 100 shares of a particular stock to an additional five shares. A two for one stock split would double the number of shares of the stock outstanding, double an individual owner's number of shares (e.g., from 100 shares to 200 shares), and cut the price in half at the time of the split.

The NYSE reported 101 stock distributions in 2001, consisting of 54 stock dividends and 47 stock splits (almost all of which were two for one to two and one-half for one). The total number of such distributions in recent years ranged from a high of 260 in 1997 to a low of 101 in 2001.

Stock data, as reported to investors in most investment information sources and in the company's reports to stockholders, typically are adjusted for all stock dividends and stock splits. Obviously, such adjustments must be made when stock splits or stock dividends occur in order for legitimate comparisons to be made for the data.

The important question to investors is the value of the distribution whether a dividend or a split. It is clear that the recipient has more shares (i.e., more pieces of paper), but has anything of real value been received? Other things being equal, these additional shares do not represent additional value, because proportional ownership has not changed. Quite simply, the pieces of paper, stock certificates, have been repackaged. For example, if you own 1,000 shares of a corporation that has 100,000 shares of stock outstanding, your proportional ownership is 1 percent; with a two for one stock split, your proportional ownership is still 1 percent, because you now own 2,000 shares out of a total of 200,000 shares outstanding. If you were to sell your newly distributed shares, however, your proportional ownership would be cut in half.

Regardless of the above, some evidence does suggest that the stock price receives a boost following a split. For example, David Ikenberry finds that such stocks tend to outperform the market in the first year following a split by an average 8 percentage points and that the effect continues for some three years following the split. According to S&P data, split shares tend to outperform the market for some 18 months following the split. One S&P study of 359 NYSE stocks with two for one or more stock splits for the period 1995 to 1997 found that these stocks did four times as well as the S&P Index on the day of the split, and even better in the 20 days prior to the execution dates; however, this particular study found that these stocks trailed in the Index in the next 12 months. In contrast, a study by Merrill Lynch found for a 12-year period that each year the group that split enjoyed superior performance over the next 12 months.[28]

Typically, the dividend is raised at the time of the split, which would have a positive effect by itself. If the above findings are indeed correct, it suggests that management signals with splits and dividends that they are confident about future prospects, which in turn should boost investor confidence.

P/E Ratio (Earnings Multiplier) The ratio of stock price to earnings, using historical, current, or estimated data

The **P/E ratio**, also referred to as the *earnings multiplier*, is typically calculated as the ratio of the current market price to the firm's earnings. It is an indication of how much the market as a whole is willing to pay per dollar of earnings.

It is standard investing practice to refer to stocks as selling at, say, 10 times earnings, or 15 times earnings. Investors have traditionally used such a classification to categorize stocks. Growth stocks, for example, have typically sold at high multiples, compared to the average stock, because of their expected higher earnings growth.

The P/E ratio is a widely reported variable appearing in daily newspapers carrying stock information, in brokerage reports covering particular stocks, in magazine articles recommending various companies, and so forth. As reported daily in newspapers, and in most other sources, it is an *identity*, because it is calculated simply by dividing the current price

---

[28] See Michelle DeBlasi, "Go Forth and Multiply," *Bloomberg Personal Finance*, March 1999, pp. 18–19.

by the latest 12-month earnings. However, variations of this ratio are often used in the valuation of common stocks. In fact, the P/E ratio in its various forms is one of the best-known and most often–cited variables in security analysis and is familiar to almost all investors.[29]

Example 2-12
The price of a Coca-Cola share in early March, 2003 was $45. The most recent 12-month earnings per share for the company at that time was $1.23. The P/E ratio, therefore, was 36.6 using the previous year's earnings.

Investing Internationally in Equities Foreign firms can also arrange to have their shares traded on an exchange or a market in another country. In the United States, two alternatives are available for trading internationally listed foreign securities. One is for the shares to be traded directly exactly like a U.S. company.

American Depository Receipts (ADRs)
Securities representing an ownership interest in the equities of foreign companies

The second alternative is via **American Depository Receipts (ADRs)**, which have existed since 1927. ADRs represent indirect ownership of a specified number of shares of a foreign company.[30] These shares are held on deposit in a bank in the issuing company's home country, and the ADRs are issued by U.S. banks called depositories. Examples of well-known companies that trade as ADRs include De Beers Consolidated, Toyota, Volvo, Sony, and Glaxo. The prices of ADRs are quoted in dollars, and dividends are paid in dollars.

In effect, ADRs are tradable receipts issued by depositories that have physical possession of the foreign securities through their foreign correspondent banks or custodian.[31] The securities are to be held on deposit as long as the ADRs are outstanding. The bank (or its correspondent) holding the securities collects the dividends, pays any applicable foreign withholding taxes, converts the remaining funds into dollars, and pays this amount to the ADR holders. Holders can choose to convert their ADRs into the specified number of foreign shares represented by paying a fee.

ADRs are an effective way for an American investor to invest in specific foreign stocks without having to worry about currency problems. The only realistic alternative for many Americans is to purchase investment companies (mutual funds or closed-end funds) specializing in foreign securities as discussed in the next section.

Derivative Securities

Derivative Securities
Securities that derive their value in whole or in part by having a claim on some underlying security

We will focus our attention here on the two types of derivative securities that are of interest to most investors. Options and futures contracts are **derivative securities**, so named because their value is derived from their connected underlying security. Numerous types of options and futures are traded in world markets. Furthermore, there are different types of options other than the puts and calls discussed here. For example, a **warrant** is a corporate-created long-term option on the underlying common stock of the company. It gives the holder the right to buy the stock from the company at a stated price within a stated period of time, typically several years.

Warrant A corporate-created option to purchase a stated number of common shares at a specified price within a specified time (typically several years)

Options and futures contracts share some common characteristics. Both have standardized features that allow them to be traded quickly and cheaply on organized ex-

---

[29] In calculating P/E ratios, on the basis of either the latest reported earnings or the expected earnings, problems can arise when comparing P/E ratios among companies if some of them are experiencing, or are expected to experience, abnormally high or low earnings. To avoid this problem, some market participants calculate a *normalized* earnings estimate. Normalized earnings are intended to reflect the "normal" level of a company's earnings; that is, transitory effects are presumably excluded, thus providing the user with a more accurate estimate of "true" earnings.

[30] It is not unusual for an ADR issue to represent several of the foreign issuer's underlying shares. Therefore, it is important to know the terms attached.

[31] ADRs are initiated by the depository bank, assuming the corporation does not object.

changes. In addition to facilitating the trading of these securities, the exchange guarantees the performance of these contracts and its clearinghouse allows an investor to reverse his or her original position before maturity. For example, a seller of a futures contract can buy the contract and cancel the obligation that the contract carries. The exchanges and associated clearinghouses for both options and futures contracts have worked extremely well.

Options and futures contracts are important to investors because they provide a way for investors to manage portfolio risk. For example, investors may incur the risk of adverse currency fluctuations if they invest in foreign securities, or they may incur the risk that interest rates will adversely affect their fixed-income securities. Options and futures contracts can be used to limit some, or all, of these risks, thereby providing risk-control possibilities.

Options and futures contracts have important differences in their trading, the assets they can affect, their riskiness, and so forth. Perhaps the biggest difference to note now is that a futures contract is an obligation to buy or sell, but an options contract is only the right to do so, as opposed to an obligation. The buyer of an option has limited liability, but the buyer of a futures contract does not.

OPTIONS

Options Rights to buy or sell a stated number of shares of stock within a specified period at a specified price

Put An option to sell a specified number of shares of stock at a stated price within a specified period

Call An option to buy a specified number of shares of stock at a stated price within a specified period

LEAPS Puts and calls with longer maturity dates of up to two years

In today's investing world, the word **options** refers to **puts** and **calls**. Options are created not by corporations but by investors seeking to trade in claims on a particular common stock. A call (put) option gives the buyer the right, but not the obligation, to purchase (sell) 100 shares of a particular stock at a specified price (called the exercise price) within a specified time. The maturities on most new puts and calls are available up to several months away, although a new form of puts and calls called **LEAPS** has maturity dates up to two and one-half years. Several exercise prices are created for each underlying common stock, giving investors a choice in both the maturity and the price they will pay or receive. Equity options are available for many individual stocks, but LEAPS are available for only about 450 stocks.

Buyers of calls are betting that the price of the underlying common stock will rise, making the call option more valuable. Put buyers are betting that the price of the underlying common stock will decline, making the put option more valuable. Both put and call options are written (created) by other investors who are betting the opposite of their respective purchasers. The sellers (writers) receive an option premium for selling each new contract, whereas the buyer pays this option premium.

Once the option is created and the writer receives the premium from the buyer, it can be traded repeatedly in the secondary market. The premium is simply the market price of the contract as determined by investors. The price will fluctuate constantly, just as the price of the underlying common stock changes. This makes sense, because the option is affected directly by the price of the stock that gives it value. In addition, the option's value is affected by the time remaining to maturity, current interest rates, the volatility of the stock, and the price at which the option can be exercised.

Puts and calls allow both buyers and sellers (writers) to speculate on the short-term movements of certain common stocks. Buyers obtain an option on the common stock for a small, known premium, which is the maximum that the buyer can lose. If the buyer is correct about the price movements on the common, gains are magnified in relation to having bought (or sold short) the common because a smaller investment is required. However, the buyer has only a short time in which to be correct. Writers (sellers) earn the premium as income, based on their beliefs about a stock. They win or lose depending on whether their beliefs are correct or incorrect.

Box 2-1 describes the pros and cons of using LEAPS as an alternative to buying the stock itself. The principles discussed in Box 2-1 pertain to puts and calls as well as to LEAPS.

BOX 2-1

Take Your Time

Option Buying is a battle between leverage and time decay. Leveraged gains from purchasing options can be achieved only if the underlying stock moves rapidly enough in the right direction to overcome the accelerating decay in the option premium as expiration approaches. Time decay usually wins, but when leverage prevails, the gains can be spectacular. To earn those gains, you must develop precision timing and be prepared to experience more losing trades than winning ones. You can make it easier on yourself—though you may reduce potential rewards—by avoiding out-of-the-money options with a few days or weeks before expiration in favor of in-the-money contracts with several weeks or months until they expire (see "A Comfortable Call" in the November 1998 issue). To better insulate yourself from the vagaries of time decay, you might stick with in-the-money LEAPS. Long-term equity anticipation securities are options with expirations ranging from nine months to three years. In buying them, you move further out of the realm of option-like behavior toward the realm of stock-like behavior.

In fact, buying in-the-money LEAPS can be an attractive alternative to a stock purchase, reducing your dollar exposure while retaining nearly all the appreciation potential. Of course, these benefits come at a cost, but many investors will find it very reasonable. Say you believe that the situation with Microsoft will ultimately be resolved in a positive manner for the company and its shareholders. But you are concerned that, if you buy the shares at $80 and your assessment is wrong, you could sustain a major dollar loss. The stock might decline from $80 to $40 or less in the worst-case scenario.

You can limit your loss exposure while retaining a major portion of the profit potential with in-the-money LEAPS. Say you buy the January 2002 LEAPS call with a strike price of $70. This gives you the right to buy 100 shares of Microsoft at $70 until January 2002. In return, you pay a premium of $24 for a total cost of $2,400. The premium is composed of two parts. One is the option's intrinsic value, or the difference between the strike and the current market price of the stock. Since Microsoft is trading at about $80, the intrinsic value of the LEAPS is $10. The $14 difference between this and the $24 premium represents the "time value," or premium you pay for the benefit of reducing your dollar-loss exposure while retaining most of the appreciation potential. As option expiration nears, and the stock has less time to move substantially from its current level, the option time value deteriorates at an accelerating rate, reaching zero at expiry.

Say Microsoft has doubled in price, to $160, at option expiration in January 2002 (see table). Someone who bought the stock at $80 will have achieved a profit of $80 a share. The LEAPS, meanwhile, will have attained an intrinsic value of $90 ($160 minus $70). So you would have a profit of $66 ($90 minus $24), or 82.5 percent of what the stock buyer realized.

Now assume the stock has declined 50 percent, to $40, at expiration. The buyer of 100 shares would have lost $4,000, but you can never lose more than $2,400. This is true whether the stock falls to $40 or $30 or even $20. So by buying the LEAPS, you limit your loss to the premium no mater how terribly the stock might perform.

Note that all the illustrations in the table assume you have sought the same exposure to Microsoft through LEAPS that you would have gotten through stock—for each 100 shares you would have purchased, you bought one LEAPS contract instead. Many investors who are new to options make the mistake of placing the same dollar amount at risk as they would have in the stock, leveraging both their potential losses and potential gains. Say that for each 100 shares of Microsoft at $80, you decided to buy 3 LEAPS contracts at $24, for a total of $7,200—as close as you can get to the stock cost. Should Microsoft close at $80 or below at option expiration, you would lose the entire $7,200 you invested in the LEAPS, versus just $1,000 from buying the stock.

TAKING LEAPS OF FAITH

The table shows how purchasing Microsoft stock at $80 fares compared with buying LEAPS (with a strike price of $70) at $24, for different stock closing prices.

	Value at Option Expiration in January 2002								
MSFT	$20	40	56	70	80	94	120	160	240
Stock gain/loss	−$60	−40	−24	−10	0	14	40	80	160
January 2002 LEAPS call	$0	0	0	0	10	24	50	90	170
LEAPS gain/loss	−$24	−24	−24	−24	−14	0	26	66	146

SOURCE: Schaeffer's Investment Research

That's the riskiest approach. The safest is to invest the $2,400 in the LEAPS and put your $5,600 "savings" from the share price of $8,000 into the money market. A middle way would be to invest the $5,600 in LEAPS on two or three other companies about which you are bullish. You mitigate the added risk of being totally invested in LEAPS by spread-ing your money among several underlying stocks. In this case, you would be exploiting LEAPS' relative cheapness in a diversification strategy rather than in a risk-reduction one.

SOURCE: Bernie Schaeffer, "Take Your Time," *Bloomberg Personal Finance*, October 2000, pp. 32 and 34. Reprinted by permission.

Options can be used in a variety of strategies, giving investors opportunities to manage their portfolios in ways that would be unavailable in the absence of such instruments. For example, since the most a buyer of a put or call can lose is the cost of the option, the buyer is able to truncate the distribution of potential returns. That is, after a certain point, no matter how much the underlying stock price changes, the buyer's position does not change.

FUTURES CONTRACTS

Futures Contract
Agreement providing for the future exchange of a particular asset at a currently determined market price

Futures contracts have been available on commodities such as corn and wheat for a long time. Recently, they have also become available on several financial instruments, including stock market indexes, currencies, Treasury bills, Treasury bonds, bank certificates of deposit, and GNMAs.

A **futures contract** is an agreement that provides for the future exchange of a particular asset between a buyer and a seller. The seller contracts to deliver the asset at a specified delivery date in exchange for a specified amount of cash from the buyer. Although the cash is not required until the delivery date, a "good faith deposit," called the margin, is required to reduce the chance of default by either party. The margin is small compared to the value of the contract.

Most futures contracts are not exercised. Instead, they are "offset" by taking a position opposite to the one initially undertaken. For example, a purchaser of a May Treasury bill futures contract can close out the position by selling an identical May contract before the delivery date, whereas a seller can close out the same position by purchasing that contract.

Most participants in futures are either hedgers or speculators. Hedgers seek to reduce price uncertainty over some future period. For example, by purchasing a futures contract, a hedger can lock in a specific price for the asset and be protected from adverse price movements. Similarly, sellers can protect themselves from downward price movements. Speculators, on the other hand, seek to profit from the uncertainty that will occur in the future. If prices are expected to rise (fall), contracts will be purchased (sold). Correct anticipations can result in very large profits, because only a small margin is required.

One of the newest innovations in financial markets is options on futures. Calls on futures give the buyer the right, but not the obligation, to assume the futures position.

Summary

► Important investment alternatives for investors include nonmarketable assets, money market instruments, capital market securities (divided into fixed-income and equity securities), derivative securities, and indirect investments in the form of investment company shares.

► Nonmarketable financial assets, widely owned by investors, include savings deposits, nonnegotiable certificates of deposit, money market deposit accounts, and U.S. savings bonds.

► Money market investments, characterized as short-term, highly liquid, very safe investments, include (but are not limited to) Treasury bills, negotiable certificates of deposit (CDs), commercial paper, eurodollars, repurchase agreements, and banker's acceptances. The first three are obligations (IOUs) of the federal government, banks, and corporations, respectively.

► Capital market investments have maturities in excess of one year.

► Fixed-income securities, one of the two principal types of capital market securities, have a specified payment and/or repayment schedule. They include four types of bonds: U.S. government, federal agency, municipal, and corporate bonds.

► Equity securities include preferred stock and common stock.

► Preferred stock, although technically an equity security, is often regarded by investors as a fixed-income type of security because of its stated (and fixed) dividend. Preferred has no maturity date but may be retired by call or other means.

► Common stock (equity) represents the ownership of the corporation. The stockholder is the residual claimant in terms of both income and assets.

► Derivative securities include options and futures.

► Options allow both buyers and sellers (writers) to speculate on and/or hedge the price movements of stocks for which these claims are available. Calls (puts) are multiple-month rights to purchase (sell) a common stock at a specified price.

► Futures contracts provide for the future exchange of a particular asset between a buyer and a seller. A recent innovation is options on futures.

Key Words

American Depository Receipts (ADRs)	Direct access notes (DANs)	Par value (face value)
Asset-backed securities (ABS)	Direct investing	Payout ratio
Bonds	Dividends	P/E ratio
Bond ratings	Dividend yield	Preferred stock
Book value	Government agency securities	Puts
Calls	Fixed-income securities	Senior securities
Call provision	Futures contract	Stock dividend
Capital market	Indirect investing	Stock split
Collateralized mortgage obligations (CMOs)	Junk bonds	Treasury bill
Common stock	LEAPS	Treasury bond
Corporate bonds	Liquidity	Treasury Inflation-Indexed Securities (TIPS)
Debenture	Money markets	Warrant
Derivative securities	Mortgage-backed securities	Zero coupon bond
	Municipal bonds	
	Options	

Questions

2-1 Outline the classification scheme for marketable securities used in the chapter. Explain each of the terms involved.

2-2 What is the difference between a savings deposit and a certificate of deposit?

2-3 How do money market deposit accounts at banks and thrifts differ from the other investment opportunities they offer investors?

2-4 What does it mean for Treasury bills to be sold at a discount?

2-5 Distinguish between a negotiable certificate of deposit and the certificate of deposit discussed in the section "Nonmarketable Securities."

2-6 Name the four issuers of bonds discussed in this chapter. Which do you think would be most risky as a general proposition?

2-7 From an issuer standpoint, what is the distinction between Fannie Mae and Ginnie Mae?

2-8 Name and explain the difference between the two types of municipal securities.

2-9 What does it mean to say that investors in Ginnie Maes face the risk of early redemption?

2-10 What are the advantages and disadvantages of Treasury bonds?

2-11 Is there any relationship between a savings bond and a U.S. Treasury bond?

2-12 Why is preferred stock referred to as a "hybrid" security?

2-13 Why is the common stockholder referred to as a "residual claimant"?

2-14 Do all common stocks pay dividends? Who decides?

2-15 What is meant by the term *derivative security*?

2-16 What is meant by the term *securitization*?

2-17 Give at least two examples of asset-backed securities.

2-18 Distinguish between a serial bond and a term bond.

2-19 What is meant by "indirect" investing?

2-20 Why should we expect six-month Treasury bill rates to be less than six-month CD rates or six-month commercial paper rates?

2-21 Why is the call provision on a bond generally a disadvantage to the bondholder?

2-22 Is a typical investor more likely to hold zero coupon bonds in a taxable account or a nontaxable account? Why?

2-23 What are the potential advantages and disadvantages of DANs (Direct Access Notes) to investors compared to conventional bonds?

2-24 What is an ADR? What advantages do they offer investors?

2-25 Of what value to investors are stock dividends and splits?

2-26 What are the advantages and disadvantages of being a holder of the common stock of IBM as opposed to being a bondholder?

2-27 Assume that a company in whose stock you are interested will pay regular quarterly dividends soon. Looking in *The Wall Street Journal*, you see a dividend figure of $3.20 listed for this stock. The board of directors has declared the dividend payable on September 1, with a holder-of-record date of August 15. When must you buy the stock to receive this dividend, and how much will you receive if you buy 150 shares?

Problems

2-1 Assuming an investor is in the 15-percent tax bracket, what taxable equivalent must be earned on a security to equal a municipal bond yield of 9.5 percent?

2-2 Assume an investor is in the 35-percent tax bracket. Other things being equal, after taxes are paid would this investor prefer a corporate bond paying 12.4 percent or a municipal bond paying 8.0 percent?

2-3   Assume an investor is in the 28-percent federal tax bracket and faces a 7-percent marginal state tax rate. What is the combined TEY for a municipal bond paying 6 percent?

Web Resources

For additional resources visit our dynamic Web site located at www.wiley.com/college/jones.

❏   *How Risky Is Your Parking Lot?*—The case considers the cash asset allocation decision and the start of the investment decision process. The case decision-maker compares the characteristics of three different money market mutual funds with a direct investment in Treasury bills through the *TreasuryDirect* online system.

❏   Alternate Case:

❏   *Deadman Funds*—The case is an opportunity to study mutual funds as an investment when there is a near-term need for liquidity. Costs and performance issues are the focus as well as the difficult decision to liquidate an underperforming asset.

❏   Internet Exercises—This chapter explains the important investment alternatives available to investors, and explores some recent trends in investing, such as international investment and securitization. The Web site exercises will present specific securities and allow the student to explore some of their distinctive characteristics.

Exercise 1: Provides you with current Web sites that discuss the basic characteristics of different financial securities.

Exercise 2: Introduces some innovative securities that have been created in a non-commercial context.

Exercise 3: Asks the reader to evaluate returns ex-post and to think about some simple investment strategies.

Exercise 4: Introduces the reader to international exchanges

❏   Multiple Choice Self Test

Selected References

The best sources of information about the financial assets available to investors, changes in their characteristics, and new financial assets that become available are the financial press, including:

> *The Wall Street Journal*
> *Business Week*
> *Financial World*
> *Forbes*
> *Fortune*
> *Kiplinger's Personal Finance Magazine*
> *Money*
> *Smart Money*
> *Worth*

Appendix 2-A
TAXES AND INVESTING

Tax laws were changed again in 2003. The four top marginal tax rates are now 25, 28, 33, and 35 percent. Any state (or city) income taxes also must be considered and could easily raise the effective marginal tax rate several percentage points.

Capital assets include property of all types. Gains can be unrealized (the asset has not been sold) or realized (the asset has been sold). Until an actual sale occurs, the gain or loss is not "realized," and therefore no tax is due.

The basis is the actual cost of an asset purchased. The capital gain or loss realized when an asset is sold is the difference between the value received and the asset's basis. Special rules on basis apply when the asset is received as a gift or from an inheritance.

Investors must distinguish between short-term and long-term capital gains. The holding period to become a long-term capital gain or loss is one year or more. A special lower rate now applies to holding periods of five years or more. Investors first aggregate all short-term gains and losses together to obtain either a net short-term gain or loss. They do the same with long-term gains and losses.

Long-term capital gains can be offset with long-term capital losses on a dollar-for-dollar basis, and the same is also true for short-term gains and losses. Finally, offsetting net long-term gains with net short-term losses produces the net capital gains referred to above. Up to $3,000 of net capital loss can be used for the current tax year to offset ordinary income, and the balance can be carried forward.

Aggregate short-term gains for assets held less than one year are taxed at the investor's ordinary income rate (one of the brackets above). If the holding period is 12 months or more, the aggregate gain generally is taxed at a rate of 15 percent. For lower-bracket taxpayers, the rate on dividends and capital gains for 2003–2007 is 5 percent, and zero in 2008.

Under the 2003 revision, dividend income is taxed at 15 percent. Municipal bond interest is generally exempt from federal taxes but may be subject to state taxes. Treasury securities are exempt from state taxes but are subject to federal income taxes.

Most investment income will be subject to taxes at some time, although various procedures such as tax-deferred retirement plans can delay that date for a long time. Investors do have the ability to control the realization of capital gains and losses by choosing when to sell the asset.

Taxes have a significant impact on investor returns and should be carefully considered in making investment decisions. For example, the 10 largest equity mutual funds returned an average annualized total return of 14.9 percent for the five years ending in 1993. After taxes, the return was 10.8 percent, a 28 percent difference (assuming reinvestment of distributions after taxes were paid at the highest federal rates in effect at the time, and the sale of shares and payment of capital gains taxes at the end of the period).

In recognition of this situation, the Vanguard Group, an investment company, now offers *Vanguard Tax-Managed Fund*, the first series of no-load portfolios specifically designed to minimize the impact of taxes on investment returns. To do this, the Fund seeks to minimize portfolio turnover (which limits capital gains distributions), uses a disciplined sell selection method that sells securities with the highest original cost and realizes capital losses, and expressly encourages long-term investors through the use of a redemption fee. Three different portfolios are available: Growth and Income, Capital Appreciation, and Balanced.

chapter 3

Indirect Investing

Chapter 2 was primarily concerned with direct investing whereby investors make decisions to buy various securities, typically in a brokerage account, and eventually they sell them. The investor makes the decisions and controls the actions involving the investments. Chapter 3, in contrast, discusses the very important alternative of indirect investing used by many investors—buying and selling mutual funds and closed-end funds, and a closely related product, exchange-traded funds.

All three types of investment companies are considered, with primary emphasis being on mutual funds where both money market funds and bond and stock funds are analyzed. The newer form of indirect investing, exchange-traded funds, is also discussed in some detail. The key point about indirect investing is that the investor turns his or her funds over to someone else to make decisions and manage the portfolio for better or for worse. In contrast, an investor with a portfolio of 10 stocks in his or her brokerage account can decide exactly how long to hold each one before selling, what to do with any dividends generated by the portfolio, and so forth.

AFTER READING THIS CHAPTER YOU WILL BE ABLE TO:

▶ Appreciate the importance of indirect investing (the use of investment companies and exchange-traded funds) to individual investors.

▶ Distinguish between unit investment trusts, closed-end funds, and mutual funds.

▶ Evaluate key features of mutual funds, such as the sales charge, the management fee, and the net asset value.

▶ Understand exchange-traded funds, a bridge between direct and indirect investing.

New York Stock Exchange (NYSE) survey data indicate that tens of millions of individual investors now own stocks either directly or indirectly.[1] According to the *1998 Survey of Consumer Finances* published by the Federal Reserve Board, 84 million individuals owned stock by 1998. This number had increased dramatically during the 1990s. For example, between 1989 and 1998 the number of shareholders increased by 32 million, and even between 1995 and 1998 the increase was 15 million. When we add in mutual fund assets representing *indirect ownership* of stocks, individuals accounted for ownership of more than 50 percent of all outstanding stocks.[2]

According to the above survey, the number of shareholders as a percentage of the adult population is at all time high. Furthermore, 45 percent of all investors own non-U.S. companies, which shows the importance of the global marketplace to investors in today's world.[3]

Basically, households have three choices with regard to savings options:

1. Hold the liabilities of traditional intermediaries, such as banks, thrifts, and insurance companies. This means holding savings accounts, MMDAs, NOW accounts (all discussed in Chapter 2), and so forth.
2. Hold securities directly, such as stocks and bonds, purchased directly through brokers and other intermediaries. This option can also include self-directed retirement plans involving IRAs, 401(k)s, Keoghs, and so forth.
3. Hold securities indirectly, through mutual funds and pension funds.

A pronounced shift occurred in these alternatives following World War II. Households turned away from the direct holding of securities and of the liabilities of traditional intermediaries and toward indirect holdings of assets through pension funds and mutual funds. In other words, investors increasingly opted for indirect investing.

Households own a large, and growing, amount of pension fund reserves, and they are actively involved in the allocation decisions of more than $1 trillion of pension funds through 401(k) plans and other defined contribution plans. Most of this amount is being invested by pension funds, on behalf of households, in equity and fixed-income securities. As we noted in Chapter 2, these are the primary securities of interest to most individual investors. Pension funds (both public and private) are the largest single institutional owner of common stocks, accounting for roughly 25 percent of corporate equity holdings.

The assets of mutual funds, the most popular type of investment company, grew 10-fold in the 1980s to $1 trillion, and by January 2001 approximated $7 trillion. As of March 2003, assets totaled $6.3 trillion. Mutual funds had the highest growth rate of any financial intermediary over much of the recent past. The dramatic growth in mutual fund assets, clearly demonstrated in Figure 3-1, has been the most important trend affecting the average household with regard to their investing activities and programs.

The following facts about mutual funds illustrate their importance to investors:

- ❏ Half of all U.S. households owned mutual funds as of early-2003.
- ❏ Individual ownership amounted to 95 million people.
- ❏ One-third of U.S. households hold mutual funds in employer-sponsored retirement plans.
- ❏ More than one-third of U.S. households own mutual funds outside employer-retirement plans.

---

[1] These data are discussed on the NYSE Web site, www.nyse.com.
[2] Furthermore, some newer evidence indicates that households were not so much active sellers of stock as simply beneficiaries of the retirement of stocks by mergers and buybacks.
[3] Discussed on the NYSE Web site, www.nyse.com

Figure 3-1

Assets of mutual funds for selected years.

SOURCE: Federal Reserve and ICI data.

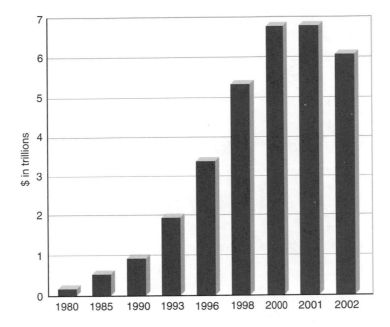

■ Mutual funds owned almost 19 percent of all U.S. stocks by the beginning of 2001, and since they are simply intermediaries between households and equities, this represents a significant household investment in equities.

Investors now rely heavily on investing through mutual funds and other similar alternatives. As we saw in Chapter 1, the 401(k) plan has become the most popular type of defined-contribution plan, and mutual funds at the end of 2002 had 45 percent of the 401(k) market. At the end of 2002, mutual funds held about 46 percent of the total assets in IRAs. Clearly, the fact that so many people choose to invest through mutual funds demonstrates that investors need to pay them careful attention.

Investing Indirectly

Indirect investing in this discussion usually refers to the buying and selling of the shares of investment companies that, in turn, hold portfolios of securities. Most of our attention is focused on investment companies, and mutual funds in particular, because of their importance to investors. However, we will conclude the chapter with a discussion of Exchange-Traded Funds (ETFs), which represent a bridge between direct and indirect investing. Investors buy ETFs like any other stock, but many ETFs can be compared to index mutual funds.

The decision of whether to invest directly or indirectly is an important one that all investors should think about carefully. Because each alternative has possible advantages and disadvantages, it is not necessarily easy to choose one over the other. Investors can be active investors, investing directly, or passive investors, investing indirectly. Of course, they can do both at the same time, and many individuals do exactly that!

An investment company such as a mutual fund is a clear alternative for an investor seeking to own stocks and bonds. Rather than purchase securities and manage a portfolio, investors can, in effect, indirectly invest by turning their money over to an investment company which will do all the work and make all the decisions (for a fee, of course). Investors who purchase shares of a particular portfolio managed by an investment company

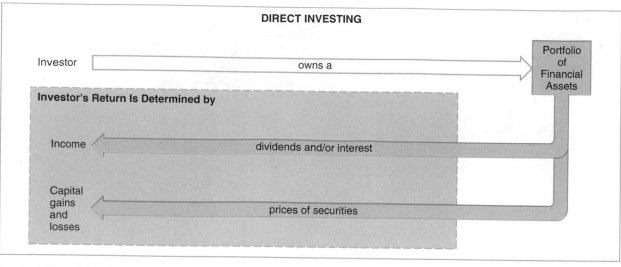

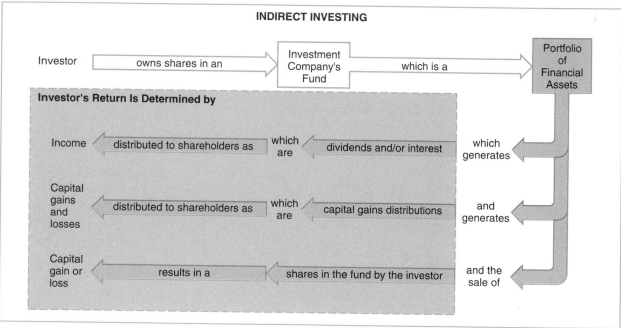

Figure 3-2

Direct vs. indirect investing.

are purchasing an ownership interest in that portfolio of securities and are entitled to a *pro rata* share of the dividends, interest, and capital gains generated. Shareholders must also pay a *pro rata* share of the company's expenses and its management fee, which will be deducted from the portfolio's earnings as it flows back to the shareholders. In other words, shareholders pay the costs of running a mutual fund or similar portfolio, and share the benefits or losses derived from the portfolio.

The contrast between direct and indirect investing is illustrated in Figure 3-2 using investment companies, which shows that indirect investing essentially accomplishes the same thing as direct investing. The primary difference is that the investment company stands between the investors and the portfolio of securities. Although technical qualifications exist, the point about indirect investing is that investors gain and lose through the investment company's activities in the same manner that they would gain and lose from holding a portfolio directly. The differences are the costs (any sales charges plus the management fee) and the benefits, which consist of additional services gained from the investment company, such as recordkeeping and check-writing privileges.

The line between direct and indirect investing is becoming blurred. For example, investors can invest indirectly by investing directly—that is, they can buy various mutual funds through their brokerage accounts. This is explained at the end of the chapter when we discuss fund "supermarkets." And, as noted above, ETFs have characteristics of both direct and indirect investing.

What Is an Investment Company?

Investment Company
A financial company that sells shares in itself to the public and uses these funds to invest in a portfolio of securities

An **investment company** is a financial service organization that sells shares in itself to the public and uses the funds it raises to invest in a portfolio of securities such as money market instruments or stocks and bonds. By pooling the funds of thousands of investors, a widely diversified portfolio of financial assets can be purchased and the investment company can offer its owners (shareholders) a variety of services.

Example 3-1

Fidelity Investments traditionally has been the largest mutual fund company in the United States, offering over 100 equity funds and over 100 bond and money market funds to investors. Fidelity manages among its 200+ funds the Equity-Income Fund, and we will use this fund throughout the chapter to illustrate mutual funds (the major type of investment company). In total, Fidelity had $750 billion under management in mid-2003.

A regulated investment company can elect to pay no federal taxes on any distribution of dividends, interest, and realized capital gains to its shareholders. The investment company acts as a conduit, "flowing through" these distributions to stockholders who pay their own marginal tax rates on them. In effect, fund shareholders are treated as if they held the securities in the fund's portfolio. Shareholders pay the same taxes they would pay if they owned the shares directly.[4]

Fund taxation is unique, with income taxed only once when it is received by its shareholders. A fund's short-term gains and other earnings are taxed to shareholders as ordinary income, whereas its long-term capital gains are taxed to shareholders as long-term capital gains. Tax-exempt income received by a fund is generally tax exempt to the shareholder.

Investment companies are required by the Investment Company Act of 1940 to register with the Securities and Exchange Commission (SEC).[5] This detailed regulatory statute contains numerous provisions designed to protect shareholders.[6] (The SEC and the Investment Company Act of 1940 are discussed in Chapter 5.) Both federal and state laws require appropriate disclosures to investors.[7]

---

[4] To qualify as a regulated investment company, a fund must earn at least 90 percent of all income from security transactions and distribute at least 90 percent of its investment company taxable income each year. Furthermore, the fund must diversify its assets. For at least 50 percent of the portfolio, no more than 5 percent of the fund's assets can be invested in the securities of any one issuer, and a position in any one security cannot exceed 25 percent of the fund's assets.

[5] The 1940 act was amended in 1970. These amendments, among other things, prohibited the charging of excessive commissions to share purchasers and the payment of excessive fees to investment company advisors.

[6] Investment companies are also regulated under the Securities Acts of 1933, the Securities Exchange Act of 1934, and the Investment Advisers Act of 1940. These acts are discussed in Chapter 5.

[7] Most states also regulate investment companies selling shares within the state.

It is important to note that investment companies are not insured or guaranteed by any government agency or by any financial institution from which an investor may obtain shares. These are risky investments, losses to investors can and do occur (just think 2000 to 2002), and investment companies' promotional materials state this clearly.

Example 3-2 Fidelity states on the cover of its prospectus for Equity-Income Fund: "Mutual fund shares are not deposits or obligations of, or guaranteed by, any depository institution. Shares are not insured by the FDIC, Federal Reserve Board, or any other agency, and are subject to investment risks, including possible loss of principal account invested."

Types of Investment Companies

All investment companies begin by selling shares in themselves to the public. The proceeds are then used to buy a portfolio of securities. Most investment companies are managed companies, offering professional management of the portfolio as one of the benefits. One less well-known type of investment company is unmanaged. We begin here with the unmanaged type and then discuss the two types of managed investment companies. After we consider each of the three types, we focus on mutual funds, the most popular type of investment company by far for the typical individual investor.

UNIT INVESTMENT TRUSTS

Unit Investment Trust
An unmanaged form of investment company, typically holding fixed-income securities, offering investor diversification and minimum operating costs

An alternative form of investment company that deviates from the normal managed type is the **unit investment trust** (UIT), which typically is an unmanaged, fixed-income security portfolio put together by a sponsor and handled by an independent trustee. Redeemable trust certificates representing claims against the assets of the trust are sold to investors at net asset value plus a small commission. All interest (or dividends) and principal repayments are distributed to the holders of the certificates. Most unit investment trusts hold either equities or tax-exempt securities.[8] The assets are almost always kept unchanged, and the trust ceases to exist when the bonds mature, although it is possible to redeem units of the trust.[9]

In general, unit investment trusts are designed to be bought and held, with capital preservation as a major objective. They enable investors to gain diversification, provide professional management that takes care of all the details, permit the purchase of securities by the trust at a cheaper price than if purchased individually, and ensure minimum operating costs. If conditions change, however, investors lose the ability to make rapid, inexpensive, or costless changes in their positions. Deposits of UITs totaled only about $745 million in April 2003, a very small part of total investment company assets.

CLOSED-END INVESTMENT COMPANIES

Closed-End Investment Company An investment company with a fixed capitalization whose shares trade on exchange markets

One of the two types of *managed* investment companies, the **closed-end investment company**, usually sells no additional shares of its own stock after the initial public offering. Therefore, their capitalizations are fixed unless a new public offering is made.

---

[8] An innovation in the 1990s is the *stock trust* designed for small investors. Typical initial investment is $1,000, and a typical projected holding period is one to five years. Like a bond trust, these trusts intend to keep their positions basically unchanged, selling an individual stock only in the event of major problems with the company.

[9] The sponsor makes a market in these certificates for those who wish to sell, with the units generally being sold back at the net asset value. It is also possible to find secondary markets for unit trusts among brokers and dealers.

Table 3-1 Example of the Data Available Weekly for the Closed-End Funds

Closed-End Funds
NAV and Price Data
[Traded on the NYSE (N), ASE (A), Nasdaq (O),
Chicago (C), and Toronto (T) Exchanges]

Selected General Equity Funds	Exchange	NAV	Mk. Price	Dis/Prem %
Adams Express	N	31.80	27.75	−12.7
Engex	A	11.05	10.25	−7.2
Gabelli Equity	N	11.65	11.75	+0.1
MFS Special Value	N	14.32	16.5	+15.2
Royce Micro Cap	O	9.95	8.625	−13.3
Tri-Continental	N	34.75	29.75	−14.4

NAV = net asset value of the fund

Mk.Price = current market price

Dis/Prem % = (NAV − Mk. Price)/NAV = percentage discount or premium

The shares of a closed-end fund trade in the secondary markets (e.g., on the exchanges) exactly like any other stock.[10] To buy and sell, investors use their brokers, paying (receiving) the current price at which the shares are selling plus (less) brokerage commissions.

Table 3-1 shows an example of typical closed-end data. Such data appear every Monday in *The Wall Street Journal*. Shown here is only one classification, "General Equity Funds." Other classifications shown in the weekly compilations include specialized equity funds, world equity funds, investment-grade bond funds, national municipal bond funds, single-state municipal bond funds, and several others. The information shown in Table 3-1 also includes the stock exchange where traded, the NAV (explained below), and the market price (price and NAV data are hypothetical).

Because shares of closed-end funds trade on stock exchanges, their prices are determined by the forces of supply and demand. Interestingly, however, the market price is seldom equal to the actual per-share value of the closed-end shares. We examine the issue of closed-end discounts and premiums later in the chapter. These discounts and premiums can be seen in Table 3-1.

Closed-end funds have been around for a long time; in fact, they were a popular investment before the great stock market crash of 1929. After the crash, they lost favor and were relatively unimportant until they started to attract significant investor interest again following the crash of 1987. As of January 2003, there were approximately 560 closed-end stock and bond funds that trade daily with total assets that approximated $156 billion. Municipal bond funds account for more than half of all closed-end funds. This small number is a result of several factors such as most sold at discounts for much of the 1990s. Perhaps more importantly, the exchange-traded funds (discussed below) are having a large negative impact on closed-end funds.

OPEN-END INVESTMENT COMPANIES (MUTUAL FUNDS)

Open-End Investment Company An investment company whose capitalization constantly changes as new shares are sold and outstanding shares are redeemed

Mutal Funds The popular name for open-end investment companies

Open-end investment companies, the most familiar type of managed company, are popularly referred to as **mutual funds** and continue to sell shares to investors after the initial sale of shares that starts the fund. The capitalization of an open-end investment

---

[10] A special type of closed-end fund is the dual-purpose fund, which has a limited life and sells two classes of shares to investors.

company is continually changing—that is, it is open-ended—as new investors buy additional shares and some existing shareholders cash in by selling their shares back to the company.

Mutual funds typically are purchased either:

1. Directly from a fund company, using mail or telephone, or at the company's office locations;
2. Indirectly from a sales agent, including securities firms, banks, life insurance companies, and financial planners.

Mutual funds may be affiliated with an underwriter, which usually has an exclusive right to distribute shares to investors. Most underwriters distribute shares through broker/dealer firms.

Mutual funds are either corporations or business trusts typically formed by an investment advisory firm that selects the board of trustees (directors) for the company. The trustees, in turn, hire a separate management company, normally the investment advisory firm, to manage the fund. The management company is contracted by the investment company to perform necessary research and to manage the portfolio, as well as to handle the administrative chores, for which it receives a fee.

Example 3-3   As stated in its prospectus (which is designed to describe a particular fund's objectives, policies, operations, and fees), "Equity-Income is a mutual fund: an investment that pools shareholders' money and invests it toward a specified goal. . . . The fund is governed by a Board of Trustees, which is responsible for protecting the interests of shareholders. . . . The fund is managed by FMR, which chooses the fund's investments and handles its business affairs."

Given the economies of scale in managing portfolios, expenses rise as assets under management increase, but not at the same rate as revenues. Because investment managers can oversee various amounts of money with few additional costs, management companies seek to increase the size of the fund(s) being managed. Many operate several different funds simultaneously. Investors can now choose from more than 400 mutual *fund complexes* (a fund complex is a group of funds under substantially common management). Thus, Fidelity, Vanguard, Janus, and T. Rowe Price are all fund companies (complexes), each of which manages multiple mutual funds.

Mutual funds are the most popular form of investment company for the typical investor. They are aggressively marketed and discussed in the popular press, and they offer numerous conveniences and services. For example, the minimum investment requirements for most funds are small, as Figure 3-3 shows. Almost two-thirds of all funds require $1,000 or less for investors to get started, and 83 percent require $5,000 or less. For IRA and other retirement accounts, the minimum required is often lower.

Example 3-4   A minimum investment of $2,500 is required to open an account in the Equity-Income Fund (only $500 for Fidelity retirement accounts). Minimum balances are $2,000. Minimums to add to the account are $250 in either case, or $100 through an automatic investment plan.

Owners of fund shares can sell them back to the company (redeem them) any time they choose; the mutual fund is legally obligated to redeem them. Investors purchase new

Figure 3-3

Minimum investment requirements for mutual funds.

SOURCE: *2003 Mutual Fund Fact Book*. Copyright © 2003 by the Investment Company Institute (*www.ici.org*). Reprinted by permission.

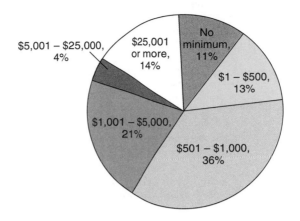

Net Asset Value (NAV)
The total value of the securities in an investment company's portfolio divided by the number of investment company fund shares currently outstanding

shares and redeem their existing shares at the **net asset value (NAV)**, which for any investment company share is computed daily by calculating the total market value of the securities in the portfolio, subtracting any trade payables, and dividing by the number of investment company fund shares currently outstanding.[11]

Example 3-5

Using Equity-Income Fund numbers for the year 2002, the NAV was calculated as:[12]

NAV, year-end 2002		$53.91
Income from investment operations		
net investment income	$ .71	
net realized and unrealized gain	(4.53)	
Total from investment operations	$(3.82)	
Less Distributions		
from net investment income	(.76)	
from net realized gain	(1.18)	
Total distribution	(1.94)	
NAV, end of period		$48.15

As this example shows, the net asset value is the per share value of the portfolio of securities held by the investment company. It changes during the year as the value of the securities held changes, and as income from the securities held is received and paid out. Notice that for this fiscal year, the Equity-Income Fund's NAV declined because the market performed poorly during this period and because the fund continued to make distributions to the shareholders. In the previous year, the NAV increased about $3 per share.

Major Types of Mutual Funds

Figure 3-4 shows the general range of mutual funds arrayed along a return-risk spectrum. As we can see, money market funds are on the lower end, and bond funds and balanced funds (which hold both bonds and stocks) are in the middle. Stock funds are on the upper-end of the risk-return spectrum.

---

[11] Total market value of the portfolio is equal to the product of each security's current market price multiplied by the number of shares of that security owned by the fund.

[12] Equity-Income data are based on January 31 as the year end.

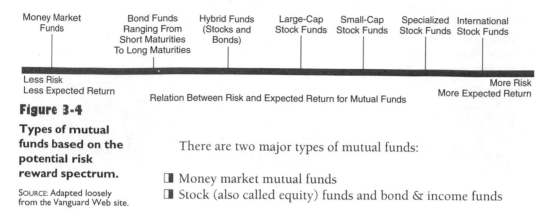

Figure 3-4

Types of mutual funds based on the potential risk reward spectrum.

SOURCE: Adapted loosely from the Vanguard Web site.

There are two major types of mutual funds:

❑ Money market mutual funds
❑ Stock (also called equity) funds and bond & income funds

These types of funds parallel our discussion in Chapter 2 of money markets and capital markets. Money market funds concentrate on short-term investing by holding portfolios of money market assets, whereas stock funds and bond & income funds concentrate on longer term investing by holding mostly capital market assets. (Of course, an investor can buy a stock or bond fund and hold it only a short time before selling.) We will discuss each of these two types of mutual funds in turn.

MONEY MARKET FUNDS

Money Market Fund (MMF) A mutual fund that invests in money market instruments

A major innovation in the investment company industry has been the creation, and subsequent phenomenal growth, of **money market funds** (**MMFs**), which are open-end investment companies whose portfolios consist of money market instruments. Created in 1974, when interest rates were at record-high levels, MMFs grew rapidly as investors sought to earn these high short-term rates. However, with the deregulation of the thrift institutions, competition has increased dramatically for investors' short-term savings. Money market deposit accounts (MMDAs) (as discussed in Chapter 2) pay competitive money market rates and are insured, and therefore have attracted large amounts of funds. Nevertheless, in August 2002, money market mutual fund assets approximated $2.3 trillion.

Money market funds can be divided into taxable funds and tax-exempt funds. Approximately 85 percent of these assets are in taxable funds. Investors in higher tax brackets should carefully compare the taxable equivalent yield on tax-exempt money market funds (see Chapter 2) with that available on taxable funds because the tax-exempt funds often provide an edge.

Taxable MMFs hold assets such as Treasury bills, negotiable certificates of deposit (CDs), and prime commercial paper. Some funds hold only bills, whereas others hold various mixtures. Commercial paper typically accounts for 40 to 50 percent of the total assets held by these funds, with Treasury bills, government agency securities, domestic and foreign bank obligations, and repurchase agreements rounding out the portfolios. The average maturity of money market portfolios ranges from approximately one to two months. SEC regulations limit the maximum average maturity of money funds to 90 days.

Example 3-6   Vanguard, one of the largest investment companies, has a taxable money market fund, the Prime Money Market fund. In December 2002, this fund had $55 billion in assets, with an average maturity of 56 days. Certificates of deposit accounted for 20 percent of assets, commercial paper 33 percent of assets, U.S. government and agency securities 44 percent of assets, and miscellaneous 3 percent of assets. The minimum investment was $3,000 ($1,000 in an IRA), and the expense ratio was 0.33 percent.

Tax-exempt money market funds consist of *national funds*, which invest in short-term municipal securities of various issuers, and *state tax-exempt money market funds*, which invest only in the issues of a single state, thereby providing additional tax benefits. These classifications are explained in Exhibit 3-1 and discussed below.

Investors in money market funds pay neither a sales charge nor a redemption charge, but they do pay a management fee (unless temporarily waived to attract business). Interest is earned and credited daily. The shares can be redeemed at any time by phone or wire. Note that by convention the shares of money market funds are held at $1—therefore, there are no capital gains or losses on money market shares under normal circumstances. Many funds offer check-writing privileges for checks of $250 or more, with the investor earning interest until the check clears.[13]

Money market funds (MMFs) provide investors with a chance to earn the going rates in the money market while enjoying broad diversification and great liquidity. The rates have varied as market conditions changed. The important point is that their yields corresponded to current market conditions. Although investors may assume little risk because of the diversification and quality of these instruments, money market funds are not insured. Banks and thrift institutions have emphasized this point in competing with money market funds for the savings of investors.

STOCK FUNDS AND BOND & INCOME FUNDS

The board of directors (trustees) of an investment company must specify the objective that the company will pursue in its investment policy. The companies try to follow a consistent investment policy according to their specified objective. Investors purchase mutual funds on the basis of their objectives.

Example 3-7   "Equity-Income seeks reasonable income by investing mainly in income-producing equity securities. In selecting investments, the fund also considers the potential for capital appreciation."

The Investment Company Institute, a well-known organization that represents the investment company industry, uses multiple major categories of investment objectives, most of which are for equity and bond & income funds (the remainder are for money market funds as previously explained).

As Exhibit 3-1 shows investors in equity and bond & income funds have a wide range of investment objectives from which to choose. Traditionally, investors often opted for *growth funds*, which seek capital appreciation, or *balanced funds*, which seek both income and capital appreciation. Now investors can choose from *global funds*, either bonds or stocks, *precious metal funds*, *municipal bond funds*, and so forth. In terms of the number of funds available, long-term municipal bond funds rank first, followed by growth funds.

These types of categories based on investment objectives such as "growth" and "growth and income" may change in the future. Some believe it is more important to describe a fund's *investment style* and actual portfolio holdings rather than state that the fund is seeking "growth of capital," which could be accomplished in several different ways. As part of this new trend, Morningstar, Inc., a Chicago mutual fund research firm discussed in Appendix 3-A, decided at the end of 1996 to use only nine categories for U.S.

---

[13] Shareholders have made only limited use of the check-writing privilege, however, indicating that they regard money market funds primarily as a way to save.

EXHIBIT 3-1

Mutual Fund Investment Objectives

The Investment Company Institute classifies mutual funds into 33 investment objective categories.

Equity Funds

Capital Appreciation Funds seek capital appreciation; dividends are not a primary consideration.

- *Aggressive growth funds* invest primarily in common stocks of small, growth companies.
- *Growth funds* invest primarily in common stocks of well-established companies.
- *Sector funds* invest primarily in companies in related fields.

Total Return Funds seek a combination of current income and capital appreciation.

- *Growth-and-income funds* invest primarily in common stocks of established companies.
- *Income-equity funds* invest primarily in equity securities and seek income more than capital appreciation.

World Equity Funds invest primarily in stocks of foreign companies.

- *Emerging market funds* invest primarily in companies based in developing regions of the world.
- *Global equity funds* invest primarily in equity securities traded worldwide, including those of U.S. companies.
- *International equity funds* invest primarily in equity securities of companies located outside the United States.
- *Regional equity funds* invest in companies based in a specific part of the world.

Hybrid Funds

Hybrid Funds may invest in a mix of equities, fixed-income securities, and derivative instruments.

- *Asset allocation funds* seek high total return by maintaining precise weightings in asset classes.
- *Balanced funds* invest in a mix of equity securities and bonds with the three-part objective of conserving principal, providing income, and achieving long-term growth of both principal and income.
- *Flexible portfolio funds* invest in common stocks, bonds, other debt securities, and money market securities to provide high total return.
- *Income-mixed funds* invest in a variety of income-producing securities, including equities and fixed-income instruments.

Taxable Bond Funds

Corporate Bond Funds seek current income by investing in high-quality debt securities issued by U.S. corporations.

- *Corporate bond funds—general*
- *Corporate bond funds—intermediate term*
- *Corporate bond funds—short term* (average maturity of one to five years)

High-Yield Funds invest two-thirds or more of their portfolios in lower rated U.S. corporate bonds (Baa or lower by Moody's and BBB or lower by Standard and Poor's rating services).

World Bond Funds invest in debt securities offered by foreign companies and governments. They seek the highest level of current income available worldwide.

- *Global bond funds—general* invest in worldwide debt securities with no stated average maturity or an average maturity of five years or more. These funds may invest up to 25 percent of assets in companies located in the United States.
- *Global bond funds—short term* invest in debt securities worldwide with an average maturity of one to five years. These funds may invest up to 25 percent of assets in companies located in the United States.
- *Other world bond funds*—two-thirds of the portfolio must be invested outside the United States.

Government Bond Funds invest in U.S. government bonds of varying maturities. They seek high current income.

- *Government bond funds—general*
- *Government bond funds—intermediate term*
- *Government bond funds—short term*
- *Mortgage-backed funds* invest two-thirds or more of their portfolios in pooled mortgage-backed securities.

Strategic Income Funds invest in a combination of U.S. fixed-income securities to provide a high level of current income.

Tax-Free Bond Funds

State Municipal Bond Funds invest primarily in municipal bonds issued by a particular state. These funds seek high after-tax income for residents of individual states.

- *State municipal bond funds—general* invest primarily in single-state municipal bonds with an average maturity of greater than five years or no specific stated maturity. The income from these funds is largely exempt from federal as well as state income tax for residents of the state.
- *State municipal bond funds—short term* invest primarily in single-state municipal bonds with an average maturity of one to five years. The income of these funds is largely exempt from federal as well as state income tax for residents of the state.

National Municipal Bond Funds invest primarily in the bonds of various municipal issuers in the United States. These funds seek high current income free from federal tax.

- *National municipal bond funds—general* invest primarily in municipal bonds with an average maturity of more than five years or no specific stated maturity.
- *National municipal bond funds—short-term* invest primarily in municipal bonds with an average maturity of one to five years.

Money Market Funds

Taxable Money Market Funds invest in short-term, high-grade money market securities and must have average maturities of 90 days or less.

- *Taxable money market funds—government*
- *Taxable money market funds—nongovernment*

Tax-Exempt Money Market Funds invest in short-term municipal securities and must have average maturities of 90 days or less.

- *National tax-exempt money market funds*
- *State tax-exempt money market funds*

SOURCE: Excerpted from the *2003 Mutual Fund Fact Book*. Copyright © 2003 by the Investment Company Institute (*www.ici.org*). Used with permission.

stock funds. These categories, such as "large cap," "mid cap," "small cap," "value," and "growth," are intended to describe investment styles.[14]

Figure 3-5 shows the investment style for Equity-Income Fund as shown in their prospectus, and as supplied by Morningstar. This fund concentrates on large-cap stocks using a value approach.

Lipper Inc., a well-known tracker of mutual funds since 1973, announced a new classification system for U.S. diversified equity mutual funds, effective mid-1999, to replace its "General Equity Investment Objectives." Funds are assigned to one of five investment

---

[14] "Cap" refers to capitalization, or market value for a company, calculated as the price of the stock times the total number of shares outstanding. A mutual fund that invests in stocks with a median market cap of $5 billion or more would be considered to be a large-cap fund, whereas a small-cap fund is one with a median market cap of $1 billion or less.

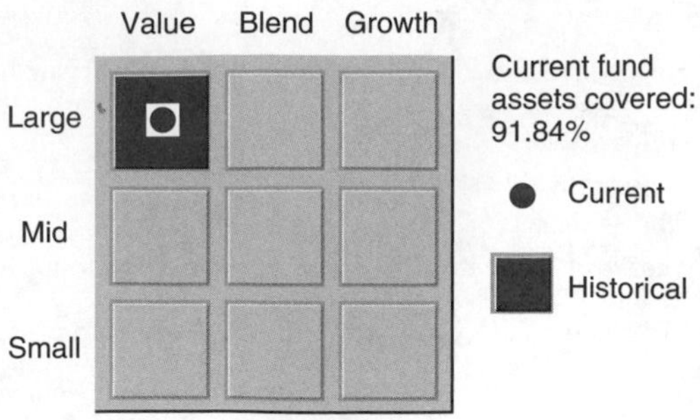

Figure 3-5

Investment style for Fidelity's Equity-Income Fund.

SOURCE: On-line Prospectus for Equity-Income Fund; with permission of Morningstar, Inc.

objectives: aggressive equity, growth equity, general equity, value equity, and income equity. The market capitalization of the funds is also recognized—for example, large-cap funds— and a special size category, flexible-cap range, was created for the roughly 1,500 funds that do not fit regularly into size categories. Lipper indexes for mutual fund categories are carried daily in *The Wall Street Journal*.

Most stock funds can be divided into two categories based on their approach to selecting stocks, *value funds* and *growth funds*. A value fund generally seeks to find stocks that are cheap on the basis of standard fundamental analysis yardsticks, such as earnings, book value, and dividend yield. Growth funds, on the other hand, seek to find companies that are expected to show rapid future growth in earnings even if current earnings are poor or, possibly, nonexistent.

Value funds and growth funds tend to perform well at different times, because value stocks and growth stocks perform well at different times, each having its own cycle. Therefore, value fund investors will have a run when they do well, and growth fund investors will have similar runs.[15]

Example 3-8

In the late 1990s, growth funds had a big run. With the emphasis on dot.coms and technology stocks, value funds performed poorly. Some growth funds had triple-digit returns, and some value managers quit the business. The situation reversed in 2000, however, with the average equity value fund gaining almost 10 percent for the year, whereas the average growth fund lost almost 12 percent.

A more risk-averse investor worrying about a market decline may wish to emphasize value funds, whereas more aggressive investors seeking good performance in an expected market rise would probably favor growth funds. Given the evidence on efficient markets, the best strategy is probably to buy both types of funds.

An analysis of the portfolio composition of the equity funds, bond funds, and hybrid funds indicates that equities (both common and preferred) represented about 65 percent of total net assets for these funds at the beginning of 2003. Municipal and corporate bonds and U.S. government securities constituted about 30 percent of total assets.

THE GROWTH IN MUTUAL FUNDS

As stated earlier, the growth in mutual funds and their assets has been one of the important stories in recent years. The number of mutual funds has grown rapidly in recent

[15] Some well-known mutual fund groups that tend to emphasize value investing include Gabelli, Lindner, Merrill Lynch, Neuberger & Berman, and Templeton. Some well-known fund groups that tend to emphasize growth stocks include Janus, Kemper, IDS, Phoenix, and Twentieth Century Investors.

Figure 3-6

Approximate distribution of total net mutual fund assets by type of fund.

SOURCE: Constructed by the author from data from the Investment Company Institute and popular press announcements.

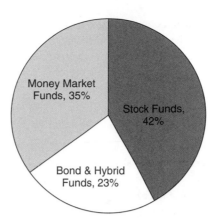

Money Market Funds, 35%

Stock Funds, 42%

Bond & Hybrid Funds, 23%

years. In 1980, there were 564 funds; at the beginning of 1990, there were approximately 2,900 funds, and at the beginning of 2003, there were approximately 8,250 mutual funds in the United States (according to the Investment Company Institute).

Quite dramatic is the change in the distribution of assets held by type of fund. In the 1950s and 1960s, mutual funds were generally thought of in terms of equity investments, with some bond holdings as a stabilizer. During the mid-1980s, however, money market funds accounted for about 40 percent of total assets as a result of relatively high, and rising, interest rates, and relatively low stock prices. Equity funds accounted for only about 20 percent of total assets. By the beginning of 2003, the situation had changed significantly. Equity funds accounted for 42 percent of total assets, and bond & hybrid funds another 23 percent, for a total of roughly 65 percent. Figure 3-6 shows the distribution of total net assets by type of fund.

The Mechanics of Investing Indirectly

Investors transact indirectly via investment companies by buying, holding, and selling shares of closed-end funds and mutual fund shares (as well as unit investment trusts). In this section, we analyze some of the details involved in these transactions.

CLOSED-END FUNDS

Historically, the market prices of closed-ends have varied widely from their net asset values (NAVs). A *discount* refers to the situation in which the closed-end fund is selling for less than the NAV. If the market price of the fund exceeds the NAV, as it sometimes does for some closed-end funds, the fund is said to be selling at a *premium*. That is,

If NAV > market price, the fund is selling at a discount.

If NAV < market price, the fund is selling at a premium.

Although several studies have addressed the question of why these funds sell at discounts and premiums, no totally satisfactory explanation has been widely accepted by all market observers. Some explanations that have been cited to explain discounts in various closed-end funds include illiquidity, either for the fund's holdings or in the fund's shares themselves, high expenses, poor performance, and unrealized capital gains. Another of these explanations—antitakeover provisions—would prevent investors from taking over the fund and liquidating it in order to realize the full NAV. Regardless of the reason, over a recent five-year period, closed-end funds sold for an average discount of about 11 percent.

By purchasing a fund at a discount, an investor is actually buying shares in a portfolio of securities at a price below their market value. Therefore, even if the value of the portfolio remains unchanged, an investor can gain or lose if the discount narrows or widens over time. It is important to remember that the portfolio's return is calculated based on net asset values, whereas the shareholder's return is calculated on the basis of closing prices. Historical discounts can be found at Morningstar.com and closed-endfunds.com.

Example 3-9   The John Hancock Bank & Thrift Opportunity Fund had an average discount of about 13.5 percent over a recent five-year period. At one point, the fund sold for a discount of 18 percent. Therefore, an investor could buy $1 worth of securities in this fund for $0.82. If the discount narrowed to its five-year average of 13.5 percent, the investor would make money even if the portfolio value (its NAV) remained unchanged.

Funds trade at premiums as well as discounts across time, and the variance between funds is great. As of the beginning of 2001, such well-known closed-end funds as Adams Express and Tri-Continental were trading at discounts of approximately 9 and 17 percent, respectively, whereas the Thai Capital Fund was trading at a 55 percent premium. In other words, investors buying the shares of Thai Capital were willing to pay about 55 percent more than the net asset value of the fund to obtain the shares.

Some Practical Advice

Initial public offerings (the first time shares are sold to the public) of closed-end funds typically involve brokerage commissions of 6 or 7 percent. Brokers often support the price in the after market temporarily, but then the price drops to NAV or below. Many small investors would do well not to purchase the initial public offerings (IPOs) of closed-end funds.

Finally, investors should note that the average expenses charged by closed-end funds are often less than those charged by open-end funds.

MUTUAL FUNDS

Some mutual funds use a sales force to reach investors, with shares being available from brokers, insurance agents, and financial planners. In an alternative form of distribution called direct marketing, the company uses advertising and direct mailing to appeal to investors. About 60 percent of all stock, bond, and income fund sales are made by funds using a sales force.

Mutual funds can be subdivided into:

❏ Load funds (those that charge a sales fee)
❏ No-load funds (those that do not charge a sales fee)

Load Funds   Funds that charge investors a sales fee for the costs involved in selling the fund to the investor are known as load funds. This front-end sales fee, added to the fund's NAV, currently ranges up to approximately 6 percent, but the average maximum load fee has averaged approximately 5.2 percent for a number of years. On a $1,000 purchase of a load mutual fund, with a 5.2-percent load fee, an investor would pay $52 "commission," acquiring only $948 in shares. Many load funds now charge less than the maximum they could charge because of market conditions or competition.

The load or sales charge goes to the marketing organization selling the shares, which could be the investment company itself or brokers. The fee is split between the salesperson and the company employing that person. The load fee percentage usually declines with the size of the purchase. The old adage in the investment company business is that "mutual fund shares are sold, not bought," meaning that the sales force aggressively sells the shares to investors. However, the percentage of stock and bond funds with the full 8.5-percent sales fee that was charged for a number of years declined from almost one-third of all such funds in 1980 to only about 5 percent of all such funds by the beginning of 1990. The typical maximum load charge total is 5.75 percent.

Example 3-10 American Funds is one of the largest mutual fund organizations. Rather than advertise extensively as does Fidelity, the no-load and low-load giant, American sells funds through brokers at a maximum sales charge (load charge) of 5.75 percent, a decrease in 1988 from the 8.5 percent charged previously. Despite the sales charges, American's funds, such as Investment Company of America and Washington Mutual Investors Fund, have attracted large amounts of money from investors.

A relatively recent fee is an annual fee known as the *12b-1 fee*, named after the Securities and Exchange Commission ruling allowing such a fee to be charged. The 12b-1 fee is of importance to investors, because roughly half of all mutual funds now impose it. It is a "distribution fee," covering a fund's cost of distribution, marketing, and advertising. The rationale for imposing it is that existing shareholders should benefit by paying such a fee that helps to attract new shareholders, thereby spreading the overhead. This fee is a fraction of a percent of the fund's average assets, and for some funds it has ranged as high as 1 percent.

Example 3-11 MFS Massachusetts Investors Growth Stock has a maximum sales load of 6.1 percent. These "A" shares (explained below) carry an annual distribution fee of 0.35 percent. The Class B and C shares carry an annual distribution fee of 1.0 percent.

In the 1990s, brokers began to emphasize a new trend in mutual fund sales whereby they offer several classes of shares of a fund, each with a different combination of front-end load (sales charge), annual or 12b-1 fee, and redemption fee. The idea is that if investors are reluctant to pay higher sales charges when they buy shares of a fund, for example, the brokers can do as well by charging less up front and more in annual and redemption fees. All fees must be stated in the prospectus. Investors should carefully read a fund's prospectus before investing.

Note carefully with regard to mutual fund share classes there is only one portfolio of securities and one investment adviser. Each class constitutes the same claim on the portfolio, so investors are not treated any differently in that respect. The difference comes about in how the mutual fund charges investors fees and expenses.

Class A shares are, in effect, the traditional type of load-fund shares, because this class (typically) charges a front-end sales charge. Class A shares are what most investors traditionally thought of when they purchased mutual funds with a load fee—they knew they were going to pay a fee upfront. Class A shares may also impose an annual 12b-1 distribution fee that is typically smaller than the distribution fee for other share classes.

Class B shares (typically) do not charge a front-end sales charge. Instead, Class B shares impose a redemption fee which declines over time and will disappear if the shares are held long enough (typically, five or six years). When the redemption fee period is over, Class B shares are often converted into Class A shares. This is typically an advantage to the investor, because the annual distribution fee is lower for the A shares than for the B shares, as we see above in the Hartford example.

Although 100 percent of an investor's funds goes to work for him or her when Class B shares are purchased, these shares are not no-load shares. The sales charge is simply being deferred against the possibility of early redemption.

The distribution fee (12b-1) is higher in the case of Class B shares—typically, 1 percent of assets. Also, the expense ratio charged investors for operating the fund may be larger under this alternative relative to the Class A shares. Annual operating expenses are an important cost to investors, and investors pay less with the Class A shares.

Class C shares, like Class B shares, do not impose a front-end sales charge at time of purchase. A small charge may be imposed if the shares are sold within a short period—typically a year. The difference is that these shares charge the same higher distribution fee, 1 percent of assets, as do Class B shares, and these shares do not eventually convert to Class A shares. Therefore, the distribution fee is not subsequently reduced as it is with Class B shares but continues on and on. The broker receives a larger part of the annual distribution fee than is the case with the Class B shares. Furthermore, the annual expense ratio is typically higher with Class C shares than for Class A shares, matching that of the Class B shares or even exceeding it.

Example 3-12 Consider the three classes of shares for the MFS Massachusetts Investors Growth Stock fund, A, B, and C. Each has a different combination of loads, fees and total annual expenses as follows:

	Class A	Class B	Class C
Sales Load	6.1%	None	None
Redemption Fee	None	4.2%	1.0%
Annual Distri. Fee	0.35%	1.0%	1.0%
Total Annual Expenses	0.85%	1.50%	1.50%

A single investment company—for example, Fidelity Investments—may simultaneously offer both no-load and low-load funds.

Example 3-13 Fidelity offers numerous no-load funds, such as its High Yield Bond Fund and its Balanced Stock Fund as well as the Equity-Income Fund discussed throughout the chapter. It also offers some load-low funds (with a 3 percent load charge), including its sector and industry funds.

No-load Funds In contrast to the load funds, *no-load funds* are bought at net asset value directly from the fund itself. No sales fee is charged, because there is no sales force to compensate. Investors must seek out these funds by responding to advertisements in the financial press and purchase and redeem shares by mail, wire, or telephone. Perhaps this explains why even in the 1990s approximately 60 percent of all mutual funds were still sold through brokers with load fees.

Some of the giants of the mutual fund industry, such as Fidelity, Vanguard, and T. Rowe Price, advertise no-load funds aggressively in the major financial publications such as *The Wall Street Journal*.

Example 3-14   Equity-Income Fund has no sales charge on purchases, no deferred sales charge on redemptions, no exchange fee, and no 12b-1 fee.

The Vanguard Group operates a well-known family of mutual funds, all of which are no-load. Vanguard advertises some of its funds virtually each day in *The Wall Street Journal*. Investors interested in no-load funds such as these can send in the coupon provided in the newspaper or call 24 hours a day. Vanguard also has a Web site.

A question that is often asked is, "If the no-load funds charge no sales fee, how is the investment company compensated?" The answer is that all funds, open-end and closed-end, load funds and no-load funds, charge the shareholders an expense fee for operating expenses. This fee is paid out of the fund's income, derived from the dividends, interest, and capital gains earned during the year and is typically stated as a percentage of average net assets. The annual expense fee consists of management fees, overhead, and 12b-1 fees, if any.

Typical annual management fees begin at 0.5 percent of the fund's total market value (in other words, 50 cents per year per $100 of assets under management). The average operating expense for all mutual funds is around 1.25 percent of assets, whereas the average for stock funds is approximately 1.5 percent of assets. The median expense ratio for bond funds is 1.04 percent, for growth and income stock funds, 1.11 percent, and for equity funds, 1.6 percent (an all-time high for equity funds).

Example 3-15   The Equity-Income Fund has an operating expense of 0.69 percent, consisting of a management fee of 0.48 percent and other expenses of 0.21 percent. The Fund calculates that if the annual return is 5 percent and its operating expenses are 0.69 percent, for every $10,000 invested, an investor would pay $70, $221, $384, and $859 if the account was closed after 1, 3, 5, and 10 years, respectively.

How do sales of load and no-load funds compare? In 1998, the share of new sales accounted for by no-load funds was about 56 percent, and in 2001 it was about 58 percent.

Using the Internet

Investors can access many Web sites for information about investment companies. For example, www.morningstar.net provides investors with extensive information about both the market and various funds. It includes a free section as well as a premium section. Www.quicken.com has a separate section for mutual funds, offering quotes on funds, screening criteria for fund selection, and more. Investors can search a database of more than 8,000 funds at www.bloomberg.com. Investors can find extensive information on mutual funds at CBS's Market-Watch—http://cbs.marketwatch.com.

Investment Company Performance

Few topics in investments are as well reported on a regular basis as is the performance of investment companies, and in particular mutual funds. *Business Week, Forbes, Money Magazine, U.S. News & World Report*, and *The Wall Street Journal*, among other popular press publications, regularly cover the performance of mutual funds, emphasizing their returns and risks. Appendix 3-A has a more detailed discussion of the major sources of information on mutual fund performance available to investors in both the popular press and specialized services.

We will discuss the calculation of investment returns in much more detail in Chapter 6, but the primary focus in that chapter is on individual securities or indices of securities and the actual mechanics involved. Furthermore, we will discuss the evaluation of portfolio performance in Chapter 22, and therefore we do not consider the evaluation of mutual fund performance in detail now. Nevertheless, it is instructive at this point to consider some of the basic points about mutual fund returns and risk and overall mutual fund performance.

MEASURES OF FUND PERFORMANCE

Throughout this text we will use *total return* (explained in detail in Chapter 6) to measure the return from any financial asset, including a mutual fund. Total return for a mutual fund includes reinvested dividends and capital gains, and therefore includes all of the ways investors make money from financial assets. It is stated as a percentage or a decimal, and can cover any time period—one month, one year, or multiple years.

A *cumulative total return* measures the actual cumulative performance over a stated period of time, such as the past 3, 5 and 10 years. This allows the investor to assess total performance over some stated period of time.

Example 3-16

For fiscal periods ended July 31, 2002, the cumulative total returns for the Equity-Income Fund as well as the Russell 3000, a comprehensive measure of large and small company equity returns, were:

	Past 1 Year	Past 5 Years	Past 10 Years
Equity-Income Fund	−17.68%	9.81%	183.18%
Russell 3000	−16.41	16.32%	197.26

Using these data, an investor who invested in Equity-Income Fund on January 31, 1992, experienced a 183 percent cumulative return over the next 10 years, or $18,318 dollars. Obviously, this was less than the performance for the Russell 3000, which was 197 percent over the same period. The contrast between the 1-year performance numbers and the 10-year performance numbers speaks for itself, and once again shows the risky nature of common stocks for specified periods of time.

Note that the cumulative total return numbers do not include the initial investment in the fund. We can use this number to determine terminal wealth over a period (including the starting amount) by doing the following, using the 10-year performance for Equity-Income as an example: Convert the 183.18 percent to a decimal, 1.8318, and add 1.0 to obtain 2.8318. Multiply this result by the beginning dollar investment for the period. Thus, $10,000 invested for 10 years would have resulted in $28,318 terminal wealth (this number includes the beginning investment).

Average Annual Return The compound average rate of return for a fund for a specified period of time

Standard practice in the mutual fund industry is to calculate and present the **average annual return**, a hypothetical rate of return that, if achieved annually, would have produced the same cumulative total return if performance had been constant over the entire period. The average annual return is a geometric mean (discussed in Chapter 6) and reflects the compound rate of growth at which money grew over time. As noted in the Equity-Income prospectus, "Average annual total returns smooth out variations in performance; they are not the same as actual year-by-year results."

Example 3-17

The average annual total returns for the Equity-Income Fund and the Russell 3000 Index for fiscal periods ended July 31, 2002, were:

	Past 1 Year	Past 5 Years	Past 10 Years
Equity-Income Fund	−17.68%	1.89%	10.97%
Russell 3000 Index	−16.41	3.07	11.51

Therefore, investing $10,000 in the Equity-Income Fund and compounding at the rate of 10.97 percent each year for 10 years would produce a final wealth of $28,318. To make the calculation, convert 10.97 percent to a decimal, add 1.0, and raise 1.1097 to the 10th power. Finally, multiply this result, 2.8318, by the $10,000 (and round) to obtain $28,318. Note that if we subtract the initial investment of $10,000 from the $28,318, we have $18,318, which corresponds to the cumulative total return of 183.18 percent above.

Average annual total returns allow investors to make direct comparisons among funds as to their performance, assuming they do so legitimately, as explained in Chapter 22 when we discuss the evaluation of performance. This means that the risk of the funds being compared should be equivalent, and the funds should have the same general objectives. We expect, on average, for equity funds to outperform bond funds and money market funds.

There is more to the issue of fund performance than simply looking at total return. The question of tax efficiency has become an important issue in recent years. Shareholders can end up paying significant taxes in a particular year regardless of the performance of the fund. In fact, performance can be negative although shareholders received large distributions on which they must pay taxes.

Example 3-18

Janus Venture Fund, an equity fund with strong performance over the last several years, had a return of −45 percent for the year 2000. In addition, it paid out $16.38 per share as a result of selling securities which had previously appreciated substantially. Therefore, shareholders in this fund faced a significant tax liability for 2000 at the same time they suffered a 45-percent loss in the value of their shares.

MORNINGSTAR RATINGS

One of the best-known assessments of mutual fund performance among investors today is the rating system developed by Morningstar, the well-known provider of information about mutual funds. Morningstar uses a five-star rating system, with five stars being the highest rating and one star the lowest rating. Many mutual fund companies run advertisements to tout any funds they manage that achieve high ratings, particularly five stars. The "star" system has become very well known among investors.[16]

Morningstar ratings are widely used by investors as a quick screening device when searching for a fund to buy. They feel that such a rating is a likely predictor of future success. However, it is important to note that this rating system is measuring historical risk-adjusted performance for funds that have at least a three-year history. The ratings take into account both a fund's risk relative to its category as a whole and its returns, taking out the sales charge on a monthly basis.

---

[16] Morningstar ratings and other information about mutual funds can be found at www.morningstar.com.

When both the risk and return measure are put together, a rating can be determined for all funds in a set. The top 10.0 percent receive five stars, the next 22.5 percent receive four stars, and the middle 35.0 percent receive three stars.

Based on weaknesses that became more and more recognized, Morningstar revamped its rating system in 2002. Previously, the system assigned funds to four broad categories, such as all U.S. stock funds. The result was that the funds invested in those sectors that were currently popular with investors generally received the most stars. Subsequently, these sectors fell out of favor just as many investors were purchasing the funds based on their high star ratings. Under the new system, Morningstar ranks funds against comparable funds in approximately 50 categories. This means that large-company value funds are ranked against other large-company value funds, and so forth.

Note that the Morningstar ranking system takes into account a fund's load charges by calculating a load-adjusted return. Because each share class of a fund with share classes has to be rated separately, one class of shares can have a different rating than another class of shares although the same mutual fund is being evaluated.

Example 3-19

Consider the PIMCO Total Return Fund with A, B, and C shares as well as a share class for institutional investors with a $5 million minimum. Its institutional share class receives a five-star ranking from Morningstar because of its performance and low expenses and no load (sales) charge. On the other hand, the PIMCO Total Return A share class receives only a three-star rating because Morningstar calculates a fund's star rating based on its load-adjusted return. This lower ranking is a result of the 4.5% sales charge and the higher annual expense ratio of 0.90% that apply to the A shares.

The Morningstar ranking system, using one to five stars, remains a popular measure of mutual fund performance. Although not perfect even now, it is a sound, well-regarded tool for investors if used properly. Morningstar itself has always urged investors to use its star system of rankings as a starting point in selecting funds, not as the bottom line. This is good advice to heed.

BENCHMARKS

Investors need to relate the performance of a mutual fund to some benchmark in order to judge relative performance with (hopefully) a comparable investment alternative. Fidelity's Equity-Income Fund, presented above, was compared to the S&P 500 Composite Index. Other firms make different comparisons and claims, as one will quickly discover by looking at their ads. For example, T. Rowe Price notes that its Dividend Growth Fund has a five-star Morningstar rating for overall risk-adjusted performance, and compares its fund to the Lipper Growth & Income Funds Average. As mentioned earlier, Lipper Inc. is a well-known provider of fund rankings and performance. The Kaufmann Fund, on the other hand, a well-known small company aggressive growth fund, compares its performance to the Russell 2000, an index of small companies and (in one ad) only for a 10-year period.

HOW IMPORTANT ARE EXPENSES?

An important issue for all fund investors is that of expenses. Should they be overly concerned about the load charges given the large number of no-load funds? What about annual operating expenses? Investors need to pay attention to fund expenses, because net performance can be dramatically affected. The annual expenses deducted for operating the fund can have a big impact on an investor's net return.

Example 3-20   The State Street High Income Fund has share classes. The B shares have no up-front sales charge. This fund had a return of 2.6 percent in 2002. The expense ratio was 2.17 percent. Therefore, before expenses, the owner of the B shares earned 4.77 percent, but after expenses, this share class, with no up-front charge for a new buyer, would have netted an owner only 2.6 percent for the year.

Consider the following evidence. *Mutual Funds*, a leading magazine covering mutual funds, reported in one issue that over the previous five years, the 25 top-performing domestic diversified growth funds returned 207 percent, while averaging only 1.09 percent in operating expenses. In contrast, the 25 worst-performing funds appreciated only 26 percent over that period, and averaged 3.25 percent in operating costs. According to this source, "Inefficient portfolio management and inefficient cost management are highly correlated."[17]

CONSISTENCY OF PERFORMANCE

Given the returns numbers above, widely available for mutual funds, can they help investors choose this year's, or next year's, winner? The consistency of performance of mutual funds has long been a controversy, and this continues to be true. Earlier studies tended to find a lack of consistency of fund performance, while some recent studies find some persistence in fund performance. For example, in the 1990s, Grinblatt and Titman found persistence in differences between funds over time, and more recently Elton, Gruber, and Blake and Gruber found evidence that performance differences persist.[18]

Malkiel has also found such evidence, although he found period effects, with differences persisting in the 1970s but not in the 1980s.[19] Malkiel, famous for many years as a strong believer in market efficiency, would have a difficult time saying past performance matters in selecting a fund. However, Malkiel's evidence on this subject suggests that investors may gain when selecting funds by relying on recent good performance. There are no guarantees when investing, of course, but a possible advantage is to be appreciated.

Before you get your hopes up on selecting funds based on their records, consider some recent work by Droms and Walker, who examined the 151 funds in existence for the entire 20 years ended in 1990. Only 40 of these funds beat a well-known market index in more than 10 of these 20 years, and no funds beat the market index in all four of the five-year subperiods of the 20-year stretch. Funds that did well in the first 10 years were no more likely than other funds to do well in the next 10 years.[20]

Index Funds   Passive funds with very low expenses designed to replicate some market index

Results such as these led a number of years ago to **index funds**, which are funds designed to replicate a market index such as the Standard & Poor's 500 Composite Index. The first index fund was started in 1976 by John Bogle (former CEO of Vanguard), and since that time index funds have become quite popular—one of the two largest mutual funds in terms of assets is Vanguard's S&P Index 500. By the beginning of 2003, there were 320+ index funds with $300 billion in assets.

[17] See "Fund World: Expensive Funds Aren't Worth It," *Mutual Funds*, March 1999, p. 20.
[18] See Mark Grinblatt and Sheridan Titman, "The Persistence of Mutual Fund Performance," *The Journal of Finance*, December 1992, pp. 1977–1984; Edwin Elton, Martin J. Gruber, and Christopher Blake, "The Persistence of Risk-Adjusted Mutual Fund Performance," *Journal of Business*, April 1996, pp. 133–157; and Martin J. Gruber, "Another Puzzle: The Growth in Actively Managed Mutual Funds," *The Journal of Finance*, July 1996, pp. 783–809.
[19] Burton G. Malkiel, "Returns From Investing in Equity Mutual Funds: 1971 to 1991," *The Journal of Finance*, June 1995, pp. 549–572.
[20] See Jonathan Clements, "By the Numbers: What the Researchers Are Digging Up on Fund Performance," *The Wall Street Journal*, December 24, 1996, p. C1.

Index funds have lower expenses, because they are "unmanaged" funds seeking only to duplicate the chosen index. Whereas the typical equity fund has operating expenses of almost 1.5 percent of assets annually, the typical index fund has expenses of only 0.56 percent, and Vanguard's Index 500 has an amazingly low expense rate of 0.18 percent.

How have index funds fared in recent years? Over the 10-year period ending in 1998, index funds outperformed 80 percent of the actively managed funds on a compound return basis. Of the actively managed funds in operation since 1976 when the first index fund was created, only one in three has managed to outperform Vanguard's S&P 500 fund.

Some Practical Advice

There are numerous index funds today, and expenses vary widely. Investors need to do due diligence when selecting an index fund to be sure that the expenses are reasonable. After all, if the Vanguard fund can match the S&P 500 Index with an expense ratio of 0.18 percent, why pay 0.50 percent or 0.70 percent to do the same thing? Fees for index funds can be amazingly large. For example, the Morgan Stanley S&P 500 Index Fund has an expense ratio of 0.69 and also charges a 5.25 percent load charge. To accomplish the same thing as Vanguard's S&P 500 fund, why would you give up 5.25 percent of your money off the top, and pay an annual expense ratio also four times as large as Vanguard's. Makes you wonder!

Investing Internationally Through Investment Companies

The mutual fund industry has become a global industry. Open-end funds around the world have grown rapidly, including emerging market economies. Worldwide assets as of mid-2002 were approximately $11.6 trillion. About 42 percent of worldwide mutual fund assets were invested in equity funds and another 26 percent in money market funds.

Aggregate mutual fund assets in Europe amount to about one-third of the world total. In Latin America, roughly one of every 200 people owns a mutual fund (compared to one in three in the United States). In Japan, mutual fund assets approximate one-half trillion dollars. In early 1999, there were more than 41,000 funds worldwide.

U.S. investors can invest internationally by buying and selling both mutual funds or closed-end funds whose shares are traded on exchanges. Funds that specialize in international securities have become both numerous and well known in recent years.

International Funds Mutual funds that concentrate primarily on international stocks

Global Funds Mutual funds that keep a minimum 25 percent of their assets in U.S. securities

- ❏ So-called **international funds** tend to concentrate primarily on international stocks. In one recent year, Fidelity Overseas Fund was roughly one-third invested in Europe and one-third in the Pacific Basin, whereas Kemper International had roughly one-sixth of its assets in each of three areas, the United Kingdom, Germany, and Japan.
- ❏ **Global funds** tend to keep a minimum of 25 percent of their assets in the United States. For example, in one recent year, Templeton World Fund had over 60 percent of its assets in the United States and small positions in Australia and Canada.
- ❏ Most mutual funds that offer "international" investing invest primarily in non-U.S. stocks, thereby exposing investors to foreign markets, which may behave differently from U.S. markets. However, investors may also be exposed to currency risks. An alternative approach to international investing is to seek international exposure by investing in U.S. companies with strong earnings abroad, which is a natural extension of the globalization concept. Based on a belief that the best-managed global companies tend to be based in the United States, this is a safer strategy. The Papp America-Abroad Fund is an example of this strategy.

Single-Country Funds
Investment companies, primarily closed-end funds, concentrating on the securities of a single country

❑ Another alternative in indirect investing, the **single-country funds**, concentrates on the securities of a single country. These funds traditionally have been closed-end, with a fixed number of shares outstanding. Like their domestic counterparts, international closed-end funds typically sell at either a discount or a premium to their net asset value as do their domestic counterparts. For example, during one recent year, the Brazil Fund sold at a discount of more than 40 percent, whereas the Spain Fund sold at a premium of more than 120 percent.

U.S. fund managers are now expanding globally by setting up foreign funds for sale in foreign markets. Such funds are tailored to meet the needs of the particular country. These separate foreign management subsidiaries both sponsor and advise foreign funds.

One of the potential problems with international investing is the higher costs involved. According to Morningstar, the costs of international index mutual funds average almost 2.3 percent when sales, redemption, and marketing charges are included. One solution to these costs is the exchange-traded fund, which we consider next.

Exchange-Traded Funds (ETFs)

Exchange-Trade Funds (ETFs)   Index funds holding a diversified portfolio of securities, priced and traded on public exchanges

A new investing trend of increasing importance is the **exchange-traded funds** (ETFs). These new financial assets have some characteristics of index mutual funds, closed-end funds, and even individual stocks.

An ETF is a basket of stocks that tracks a particular sector, investment style, geographical area, or the market as a whole. As of August 2002, there were approximately 125 ETFs, with perhaps $100 billion in assets. Although this is tiny compared to the assets in mutual funds, the growth rate in assets for ETFs has been impressive, as more and more investors discover them.

Like an index mutual fund, ETFs to date are passive portfolios (although actively managed ETFs are under consideration) that simply hold a basket of stocks. Unlike a mutual fund, however, and like a stock or a closed-end fund, an ETF trades on an exchange throughout the day, and can be bought on margin and sold short (both concepts are explained in Chapter 5). And like a closed-end fund, ETFs can trade at discounts and premiums, but to date, the differences between NAV and price have been tiny, and this will almost certainly continue to be the case because of the unique mechanisms that were developed to create and liquidate ETF shares.[21]

Let's consider some ETFs. Probably the best-known ETF is the "Spider" (Standard & Poor's Depositary Receipts, SPDRs), which was introduced in 1993 to reflect the S&P 500 Index. SPDRs are traded on the Amex, and priced continuously during the day. Other ETFs include "Diamonds" (the DJIA), "Cubes" (Nasdaq-100 Index Tracking Stock), and "iShares" (S&P 500 as well as other S&P indexes for small cap, mid-cap, and growth and value indexes, various Russell Indexes, various Dow Jones Sector funds, and various country funds). There are 77 different iShare ETFs. Vanguard, the investment company, created VIPERs to track the entire stock market.

---

[21] Recall that many closed-end funds sell at discounts, meaning the price of the shares is less than the NAV of the fund. ETFs, in turn, have devised an unusual process to ensure that the shares always sell for approximately the value of the portfolio holdings. This "in-kind" feature is accomplished by granting special trading rights to institutional investors interacting with the ETF company. ETF companies include the Bank of New York, Merrill Lynch, Barclays Global Investors, State Street, and Vanguard.

If the ETF share price is less than the actual value of the underlying assets, an institutional investor can buy the ETF shares and turn them in to the sponsoring company for an equivalent amount of the underlying stocks, which the institution then sells for an immediate profit. If the ETF share price is greater than the underlying assets, the process is reversed. This unique process essentially ensures that the price of the ETF shares will approximate very closely the value of the underlying assets.

Example 3-21   One of Vanguard's VIPERs, Vanguard Total Stock Market VIPERs, seeks to provide long-term growth of capital and income by matching the Wilshire 5000 Index, the most comprehensive measure of stocks in the United States. Its portfolio contains more than 3,700 stocks which attempt to match the index. These shares are available only through a broker, and carry a 0.15 percent expense ratio.

Merrill Lynch created HOLDRs, which are somewhat different. HOLDRs consist of groups of hand-picked stocks that focus on an industry or a theme (e.g., semiconductors). The original group of stocks selected does not change, and is not rebalanced, and therefore HOLDRs are not subject to SEC rules about how many stocks to hold for diversification purposes as are mutual funds. They typically begin with 20 stocks, but mergers and bankruptcies can reduce this number.

Until summer 2002, all ETFs involved equity securities. Now, several iShares are available covering debt securities. Some cover Treasury bond indexes and some cover corporate indexes.

In mid-2002, 34 of the 130 ETFs concentrated on foreign country and international indexes. Together they offered exposure to various foreign sectors, regions, countries, and global benchmarks. For example, investors could choose ETFs concentrating on the global energy sector; the Pacific region, countries such as Austria, South Korea, Italy and Japan; and indexes such as the Nikkei 225 index. Note that international ETFs are unhedged for currency risk, and therefore U.S. investors benefit when the foreign currency appreciates relative to the dollar. This happened in 2002 with the euro, for example, and with the South Korean won.

So why buy an ETF when you could buy an index mutual fund? After all, as one example, Vanguard offers the S&P 500 Index Fund, with operating expenses of perhaps 0.18%. For one thing, an investor can buy ETFs, or sell them, anytime during the trading day at the current price. Mutual funds are priced once a day, and you can only enter and exit accordingly. Furthermore, ETFs can be bought on margin (borrowed funds) or sold short if prices are expected to decline.

ETFs offer investors targeted diversification. It is possible to focus on a sector, style, or geographical region with a basket of stocks. Furthermore, ETFs have management fees that are actually lower than index mutual funds. For example, the S&P 500 iShare charges half of the Vanguard fund, or an amazing 0.09 percent annually. ETFs concentrating on the international side have expense ratios ranging from 0.40 to 1.0 percent, which are considerably less than many foreign-oriented mutual funds. On the other hand, investors must pay regular brokerage fees each time an ETF is bought or sold, whereas many index mutual funds do not charge for purchases and sales.

What happens when an investor wishes to sell his or her ETF? The shares are simply sold to another investor, thereby having no direct effect on the fund.

When investors sell their mutual fund shares back to the company, the fund may have to sell securities to purchase the shares. If enough redemptions occur, the fund could generate a capital gains liability for the remaining shareholders. In contrast, redemptions do not involve the ETF at all, but rather one investor selling to another. The ETF manager does not have to sell shares to pay for redemptions; therefore, redemptions do not create capital gains which must be distributed to the shareholders. Thus, although both index funds offered by an investment company and ETFs can avoid capital gains as a result of no active trading, the ETF also avoids redemptions and the capital gains that could result from this activity.

A particularly appealing feature of ETFs to many investors is their tax efficiency. Many ETFs report little or no capital gains over the years. Shareholders in mutual funds, in contrast, have no control over the amount of distributions their fund may make in a

BOX 3-1

Invest With An Edge

Tax-efficient investing is possibly the most overcovered topic in the financial press. So why pile on? First, because a very important development has been ignored. Second, because discussion has been misfocused on tax efficiency rather than the more important issue of after-tax return.

The Tax Advantage Mutual funds are thought of as tax-disadvantaged compared with individual stocks, because with stocks no tax is due until you sell appreciated shares. But when you buy into a fund, stocks it owns have usually risen above their purchase price. When the manager sells those shares, the tax liability on the entire gain flows through to you even though you don't benefit from appreciation before you bought the fund. This isn't as bad as it sounds, because when you sell your fund shares, your taxable profit is adjusted to reflect the fact that you already paid tax on gains you didn't really earn. The disadvantage, then, is in paying some capital gains taxes *sooner than later.*

But the bear market has turned this issue on its head. As prices cratered, many funds sold holdings at losses. For 2002, realized losses significantly exceeded realized gains, leaving the funds with a stash of losses that can be used to offset future gains and thereby forestall taxable payouts to shareholders. Many of these same funds also have unrealized losses on stocks still in their portfolios. These stocks have room to appreciate without generating a tax liability.

A number of excellent funds possess a combination of losses to carry forward and unrealized losses large enough to make it unlikely they will distribute any capital gains for a couple of years or longer even if they generate fairly strong returns. In other words, you have an opportunity to invest in funds whose gains will be taxed *later rather than sooner.* Not surprisingly, growth funds Brandywine, Harbor Capital Appreciation, and TCW Galileo Select Equities are most prominent on our list because they have been the hardest hit. But other opportunities exist for investors who want to defer their taxable gains. Similarly positioned core stock funds are Rainier Core Equity and Selected American Shares. In the undervalued-stocks camp is Oakmark fund. Artisan International and Harbor International Growth (the latter with a new manager as of late 2001) are global funds with big loss carryovers. Happy investing, everyone.

Efficiency Versus Results Typically, the discussion on funds and taxes focuses on "tax efficiency." This refers to the ability of funds to deliver after-tax returns that aren't much lower than their pretax returns. For example, if a fund returned an annualized 10% on a pretax basis over the past three years and 9% after figuring in the tax liability generated by its distributions, the fund would have a tax efficiency of 90%. But consider another fund that was 98% tax efficient but returned 1% after taxes. Or a third fund: 70% tax efficient but with an after-tax return of 12%.

Given these choices, investors should go with the least tax-efficient fund, because it delivered the highest after-tax return. So it's too simplistic to focus only on tax efficiency.

Our approach is first to identify funds likely to generate above-average pretax returns, because they are run by skilled stock pickers. As part of this process, we investigate whether a manager is a "tax-aware" investor who tries to maximize the after-tax return without penalizing the pretax return. This can be done through a variety of techniques if the manager is paying attention. In the list above, Oakmark and Selected American Shares are both run by tax-aware managers, although the funds are not considered to be "tax-managed."

SOURCE: Ken Gregory and Steve Savage, "Invest With An Edge," *Kiplinger's Personal Finance*, February 2003, p. 60. Reprinted by permission.

given year. In 2000, for example, many mutual funds made large distributions to shareholders, based on previous results, just as the stock market was declining sharply. In 2001, these shareholders had to pay large tax bills while looking at the sharply lowered prices of their mutual fund shares. Note, however, that capital gains distributions can occur. Also, ETFs holding the shares of companies that pay dividends do distribute some dividends to their shareholders. Regardless of these exceptions, in general, ETFs are highly tax efficient, and are being appreciated more and more by investors for this reason.

The "in-kind" feature described earlier, involving special trading rights for institutions, also leads to some tax efficiency. We know that index funds have much lower operating expenses than do actively managed funds, because they are passively managed. ETFs have even lower expenses. Whereas the average domestic stock index fund charges about 0.50 percent a year, the average ETF charges about 0.34 percent. This results from the investment company being responsible for the index fund and sending investors statements, whereas a brokerage firm does that in the case of ETFs, leaving the fund itself with very low expenses.

ETFs may not be suitable for all investors. Regular purchases will incur ongoing brokerage fees. Trading ETFs on a short-term basis leads to short-term capital gains taxed at the highest marginal rates.

Using the Internet

A good source of information about ETFs is Morningstar.com, perhaps the best-known provider of information about mutual funds. Click on ETFs on the left, choosing one of the topics provided. For general information about ETFs as well as information on more than 70 funds, go to iShares.com. Very detailed information about each ETF can be found at etfconnect.com. Details about all index mutual funds as well as ETFs can be found at www.indexfunds.com.

DISTINGUISHING AMONG ETFS, CLOSED-END FUNDS, AND MUTUAL FUNDS

The rise of the ETFs causes some confusion between the typical investment company products—IUTs, closed-end funds, and mutual funds—and this new innovation. It is worthwhile to remember the following:

1. Both closed-end funds and ETFs trade all day on exchanges, can be bought on margin, and can be shorted. Mutual funds, on the other hand, are bought and sold at the end of the trading day when the NAV is calculated. Thus, an investor urgently wanting to buy or sell such assets during the day would be out of luck with the typical mutual fund.
2. Closed-end funds and most mutual funds (exceptions are index funds) are actively managed for better or for worse. ETFs, in contrast, are currently passive in nature, following an index, a sector, an investment style, or a geographical region.
3. Mutual funds trade at NAV (although buyers of load funds pay a sales charge). Closed-end funds typically trade at discounts and premiums, with discounts predominating in many years. ETFs can trade at discounts or premiums, but their mechanics are such that they are very likely to trade close to their NAV.

ETFs offer an important advantage over funds with regard to flexibility on taxes. Mutual fund managers may have to sell shares to pay people who want to leave the fund, thereby generating capital gains. Market makers in ETFs, in contrast, are paid for ETFs with a swap of the underlying shares. In these transactions, no capital gains occur that must be passed on to shareowners.

The Future Of Indirect Investing

Fund Supermarkets A mechanism by which investors can buy, own, and sell funds of various mutual fund families through one source (e.g., a brokerage firm)

A popular trend concerning indirect investing is the mutual fund "supermarket"—indeed, a number of observers feel that fund supermarkets are the future of mutual funds sold directly to investors. **Fund supermarkets** are a mechanism by which investors can buy, own, and sell the funds of various mutual fund families through one source, such as a brokerage firm. "Supermarket" refers to the fact that an investor has hundreds of choices available through one source, and does not have to go to each mutual fund company separately to buy one of their funds.

The discount brokerages of Schwab, Fidelity, and Jack White have been pioneers in making funds available to investors through brokerage accounts offered by them. Schwab (www.schwab.com), with $84 billion in its OneSource no-fee supermarket at the beginning of 2003, offers about 3,500 funds, whereas Fidelity (www.fidelity.com) offers more than 4,000. Schwab and Fidelity are the two largest supermarkets by far, but many other discount brokerage firms and fund firms have smaller programs.

Fund supermarkets have two tracks, or "aisles": a no-fee aisle, where investors can buy various mutual funds without paying a sales charge or transaction fee, and a transaction-fee aisle, where they do pay a fee. For example, Schwab offers more than 1,700 funds at no-fee, and Fidelity offers more than 1,100 at no fee. The mutual funds participating in the fund supermarket which want to offer their shares with no fees to investors pay the supermarkets an annual charge of 0.35 percent of the assets that the fund has acquired at the supermarket.[22] As a result, the typical new fund being sold without fees will establish expense charges that are enough to cover the supermarket fees.

Investors are now using the web to access these supermarkets, with both Schwab and Fidelity reporting about 60 percent of mutual fund trades done on-line.

The Internet will have a substantial impact on investors who buy and sell mutual funds. Already, the major investment companies such as Fidelity and Vanguard offer extensive Web sites with much information. More than 400 fund companies had Web sites offering information by the start of 2001.

There is another potentially important change occurring that will negatively affect mutual funds. So-called "managed accounts" have existed for years for high-net-worth investors. Large brokerage firms, independent financial planners, and some firms on the Internet are now offering these services to smaller investors with, say, $250,000 (or sometimes less) to invest. These firms offer a single investment style and/or manager for average fees of less than 2 percent of assets. Investors receive customization and some ability to time gains and losses.

Example 3-22 Schwab offers managed accounts. On the Web, managerlink.com, wrapmanager.com, and mymoneypro.com all offer various managers for account minimums of $100,000, and with fees of roughly 1 to 2 percent of assets.

Summary

▶ As an alternative to purchasing financial assets themselves, all investors can invest indirectly, which involves the purchase of shares of an investment company or an ETF.

▶ Investment companies are financial intermediaries that hold a portfolio of securities on behalf of their shareholders.

▶ Investment companies are classified as either open end or closed end depending on whether their own capitalization (number of shares outstanding) is constantly changing or fixed.

▶ Open-end investment companies, commonly called mutual funds, can be divided into two categories: money market funds and stock, bond, and income funds.

▶ Money market mutual funds concentrate on portfolios of money market securities, providing investors with a way to own these high–face value securities indirectly.

[22] Participating mutual funds do not know the names of the new shareholders and cannot communicate with them directly because the supermarkets keep client lists secret. On the other hand, the funds do not have the costs of recordkeeping and mailing account statements to investors using the supermarkets.

▶ Stock, bond, and income funds own portfolios of stocks and/or bonds, allowing investors to participate in these markets without having to purchase these securities directly.

▶ Investors transacting indirectly in closed-end funds encounter discounts and premiums, meaning that the price of these funds is unequal to their net asset values.

▶ Mutual funds can be load funds, low-load funds, or no-load funds, where the load is a sales charge calculated as a percentage of the amount invested in the fund.

▶ All investment companies charge an expense fee to shareholders for running the fund to pay for the operating costs and the management fee.

▶ Total return for a mutual fund includes reinvested dividends and capital gains. A cumulative total return measures the actual performance over a stated period of time, such as the past 3, 5, or 10 years. The average annual return is a hypothetical rate of return that, if achieved annually, would have produced the same cumulative total return if performance had been constant over the entire period.

▶ International funds tend to concentrate primarily on international stocks, whereas global funds tend to keep a minimum of 25 percent of their assets in the United States.

▶ Single-country funds, which traditionally have been closed-end funds, concentrate on the securities of a single country.

▶ Exchange-traded funds (ETFs) bundle together a basket of stocks based on some index and trade as one security on an exchange. They resemble closed-end funds but generally sell close to NAV and have certain tax advantages.

Key Words

Average annual return	International funds	Net asset value (NAV)
Closed-end investment company	Investment company	Open-end investment companies
Exchange-traded fund (EFT)	Money market funds (MMFs)	Single-country funds
Global funds	Mutual funds	Unit investment trust
Index funds		

Questions

3-1 What is meant by "indirect" investing?

3-2 What is an investment company? Distinguish between an open-end and a closed-end company.

3-3 What is a money market fund? Why would it appeal to investors?

3-4 It has been said that many closed-end funds are "worth more dead than alive." What is meant by this expression?

3-5 What does it mean for an investment company to be regulated?

3-6 List the benefits of a money market fund for investors. List the disadvantages. What alternative investment is a close substitute?

3-7 What is meant by an investment company's "objective"? What are some of the objectives pursued by equity, bond, and income fund?

3-8 How does a unit investment trust holding municipal bonds differ from a mutual fund holding municipal bonds?

3-9 How is the net asset value for a mutual fund calculated?

3-10 What is meant by the term *pure intermediary*?

3-11 List some reasons an investor might prefer a closed-end fund to an open-end fund.

3-12 Distinguish between a global fund and an international fund.

3-13 What is the difference between the average annual return for a fund and the cumulative total return?

3-14 Distinguish between a value fund and a growth fund.

3-15 Why are unit investment trusts considered to be passive investments?

3-16 Distinguish between the direct and indirect methods by which mutual fund shares are typically purchased.

3-17 How would the owner of some shares of Fidelity's Equity-Income Fund "cash out" when he or she was ready to sell the shares?

3-18 How have investor preferences with regard to mutual fund investing changed over time?

3-19 Who owns a mutual fund? Who determines investment policies and objectives?

3-20 What does it mean when someone says, "Mutual funds involve investment risk"?

3-21 What is the difference between a load fund and a no-load fund? What is a low-load fund?

3-22 What are passively managed country funds? Give an example.

3-23 What is meant by the exchange privilege within a "family of funds"?

Web Resources

For additional resources visit our dynamic Web site located at www.wiley.com/college/jones.

- *Deadman Funds*—The case is an opportunity to study mutual funds as an investment when there is a near-term need for liquidity. Costs and performance issues are the focus as well as the difficult decision to liquidate an underperforming asset.
- Alternate Case:
- *Active Struggle*—The case examines the difference between passive and active stock investment strategies implemented through mutual funds. The case develops and applies cost-adjusted total returns to help decide between investment strategies.
- Internet Exercises—This chapter discusses an indirect investment strategy—the use of mutual funds. The exercises will take you to the Web sites of some of the larger mutual funds, and help you to work through the advantages and disadvantages of mutual funds.
  Exercise 1: Introduces the reader to some mutual fund sites.
  Exercise 2: Asks the reader to get information on different kinds of funds and their characteristics.
  Exercise 3: Leads the reader to consider the short-term and long-term performance of mutual funds
  Exercise 4: Asks the reader to look at the statistical characteristics of fund returns.
  Exercise 5: Introduces ETFs and some relevant Web sites.
  Exercise 6: Compares ETFs and Index-funds.
  Exercise 7: Asks the reader to compare the tracking performance of different ETFs.

- Multiple Choice Self Test
- Appendix 3-A—Obtaining Information on Investment Companies

Selected References

One of the best sources of information about mutual funds has been written by the chairman of the Vanguard Group of Investment Companies:

Bogle, John C. *Bogle on Mutual Funds*. Homewood, Ill.: Richard D. Irwin, 1994.

A basic discussion of the pros and cons of mutual funds can be found in:

Jones, Charles P. *Mutual Funds: Your Money, Your Choice*. Financial Times/Prentice Hall, 2002.

chapter 4

Securities Markets

C hapter 4 outlines the structure of the markets where investors buy and sell securities. Although primary markets, including the role of investment bankers, are considered, the emphasis is on secondary markets. Bond markets, equity markets, and derivative markets are covered, with emphasis on secondary markets where most investors are active. Changes in the securities markets are considered, including the globalization that is occurring.

AFTER READING THIS CHAPTER YOU WILL BE ABLE TO:

▶ Distinguish between primary and secondary markets.
▶ Describe where the three major types of securities discussed in Chapter 2—bonds, equities, and derivatives—are traded.
▶ Understand how the equity markets, where stocks are traded, are organized, how they operate, and how they differ from each other.
▶ Recognize the various stock market indexes typically encountered by investors.
▶ Follow changes that are occurring in the financial markets based on your understanding of what has happened in the past.

This chapter outlines the structure of the securities markets, with primary emphasis on markets in the United States, because they will be of most interest to U.S. investors. However, global market issues are increasingly important and are also covered here. We focus mainly on stocks and to a lesser extent on bonds and derivative securities, because these are the securities investors most often buy and sell. The factors involving other securities are discussed in the chapters dealing specifically with each security.

The structure and operating mechanisms of the securities markets in the United States have changed drastically in the last 20 years. Accordingly, this chapter concludes with a look at some of these changes and what the future may hold.

The Importance of Financial Markets

In order to finance their operations as well as expand, business firms must invest capital in amounts that are beyond their capacity to save in any reasonable period of time. Similarly, governments must borrow large amounts of money to provide the goods and services that the people demand of them. The financial markets permit both business and government to raise the needed funds by selling securities. Simultaneously, investors with excess funds are able to invest and earn a return, enhancing their welfare.

Financial markets are absolutely vital for the proper functioning of capitalistic economies, since they serve to channel funds from savers to borrowers. Furthermore, they provide an important allocative function by channeling the funds to those who can make the best use of them—presumably, the most productive. In fact, the chief function of a capital market is to allocate resources optimally.[1]

The existence of well-functioning secondary markets, where investors come together to trade existing securities, assures the purchasers of primary securities that they can quickly sell their securities if the need arises. Of course, such sales may involve a loss, because there are no guarantees in the financial markets. A loss, however, may be much preferred to having no cash at all if the securities cannot be sold readily.

In summary, in the United States, secondary markets are indispensable to the proper functioning of the primary markets. The primary markets, in turn, are indispensable to the proper functioning of the economy.

The Primary Markets

Primary Market The market for new issues of securities, typically involving investment bankers

A **primary market** is one in which a borrower issues new securities in exchange for cash from an investor (buyer). New sales of Treasury bills, or IBM stock, or North Carolina bonds all take place in the primary markets. The issuers of these securities—the U.S. government, IBM, and the state of North Carolina, respectively—receive cash from the buyers of these new securities, who in turn receive financial claims that previously did not exist.

Note that in all three of these examples, some amount of these securities is outstanding before the new sales occur. Sales of common stock of a publicly traded company are called *seasoned new issues*.

Initial Public Offering (IPO) Common stock shares of a company being sold for the first time

If the issuer is selling securities for the first time, these are referred to as **initial public offerings (IPOs)**. Once the original purchasers sell the securities, they trade in secondary markets. New securities may trade repeatedly in the secondary market, but the original issuers will be unaffected in the sense that they receive no additional cash from these transactions.

---

[1] A securities market with this characteristic is said to be *allocationally efficient*. An *operationally efficient* market, on the other hand, is one with the lowest possible prices for transactions services.

The year 2000 set a record for equity issuance of $223 billion in U.S. common stock underwriting vs. $175 billion in 1999. In 2000, 391 IPOs raised $61 billion. In 2001, there were only 107 IPOs, with $39 billion being raised, and in 2002, the number dropped to 97 domestic IPOs, with approximately $27 billion being raised.

When the IPO market is very active, and investors are clamoring for shares of new companies, the price of these stocks often soars on the first day of trading. Those investors lucky enough to receive an initial allocation of these stocks at the price set by the investment banker can see the value of their shares increase dramatically in a short time. The average investor typically cannot receive any of the initial allocation, because the investment bankers reward favored clients with shares.

IPOs tend to run in cycles of investor interest, often soaring in price on the day of sale and also rising strongly thereafter for some period of time when the IPO market is very active, such as in the late 1990s. However, conditions can change, and some studies indicate that investors holding IPOs for several months tend not to do well with them.

Example 4-1

Unlike the late 1990s, when IPOs tended to soar indefinitely, in 2000 they often did well on the first day but suffered thereafter. Almost 70 percent of IPOs traded below their issue price at the end of the year.

THE INVESTMENT BANKER

Investment Banker
Firm specializing in the sale of new securities to the public, typically by underwriting the issue

In the course of selling new securities, issuers often rely on an **investment banker** for the necessary expertise as well as the ability to reach widely dispersed suppliers of capital. Along with performing activities such as helping corporations in mergers and acquisitions, *investment banking firms* specialize in the design and sale of securities in the primary market while operating simultaneously in the secondary markets. For example, Merrill Lynch offers investment banking services while operating a large retail brokerage operation throughout the country. Salomon Smith Barney is another well-known investment banker, as are JP Morgan, Goldman Sachs, and Lehman Brothers. Other large financial institutions such as Banc of America Securities and Deutsche Bank are also active.

Investment bankers act as intermediaries between issuers and investors. The issuer sells its securities to investment bankers, who in turn sell the securities to investors. For firms seeking to raise long-term funds, the investment banker can provide important advice to their clients during the planning stage preceding the issuance of new securities. This advice includes providing information about the type of security to be sold, the features to be offered with the security, the price, and the timing of the sale.

Underwriting The process by which investment bankers purchase an issue of securities from a firm and resell it to the public

Investment bankers often **underwrite** new issues by purchasing the securities (once the details of the issue have been negotiated) and assuming the risk of reselling them to investors. Investment bankers provide a valuable service to the issuers at this stage. The issuer receives its check and can spend the proceeds for the purposes for which the funds are being raised. The investment bankers own the securities until they are resold. Although many issues are sold out quickly (e.g., the first day they are offered to the public), others may not be sold for days or even weeks. Investment bankers are compensated by a spread, which is the difference between what they pay the issuer for the securities and what they sell them for to the public (i.e., the securities are purchased from the issuer at a discount).

In addition to having expertise in these matters and closely scrutinizing any potential issue of securities, investment bankers can protect themselves by forming a *syndicate*, or group of investment bankers. This allows them to diversify their risk. One investment banker acts as the managing underwriter, overseeing the underwriting syndicate. This syndicate becomes part of a larger group that sells the securities.

Figure 4-1

A primary offering of securities.

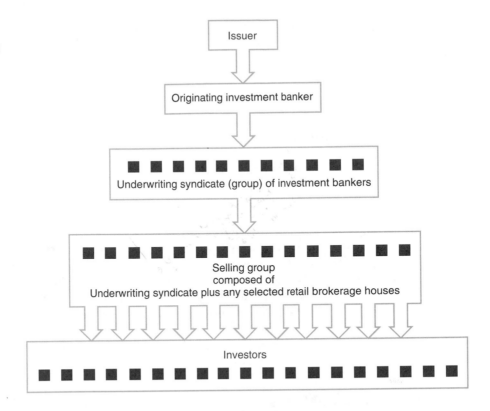

Figure 4-1 illustrates a primary offering of securities through investment bankers, a process referred to as a syndicated offering. The issuer (seller) of the securities works with the originating investment banker in designing the specific details of the sale.[2] A prospectus, which summarizes this information, offers the securities for sale officially.[3] The underwriter forms a syndicate of underwriters who are willing to undertake the sale of these securities once the legal requirements are met.[4] The selling group consists of the syndicate members and, if necessary, other firms affiliated with the syndicate. The issue may be fully subscribed (sold out) quickly, or several days (or longer) may be required to sell it.[5]

Securities and Exchange Rule 415 (the shelf rule) permits qualified companies to file a "short form registration" and to "place on the shelf" securities to be sold. The issuing company can sell the new securities over time by auctioning pieces of the issue to the lowest cost bidder, providing flexibility and savings.

GLOBAL INVESTMENT BANKING

The global perspective now in place allows companies in various countries to raise new capital in amounts that would have been impossible only a few years earlier, because these companies often were limited to selling new securities in their own domestic mar-

Prospectus Provides information about an initial public offering of securities to potential buyers

Shelf Rule Permits qualified companies to file a short form registration and "place on the shelf" securities to be sold over time under favorable conditions

---

[2] All documents are prepared to satisfy federal laws. In particular, the issuer files a registration statement, which contains financial and other information about the company, with the appropriate government agency.

[3] However, the selling group can send out a preliminary prospectus to investors describing the new issue. No offering date or price is shown, and the prospectus is identified clearly as an informational sheet and not a solicitation to sell the securities. For this reason, the preliminary prospectus is often referred to as a "red herring."

[4] New issues must be registered with the SEC at least 20 days before being publicly offered. Upon approval from the SEC, the selling group begins selling the securities to the public.

[5] During this time, the underwriting manager can legally elect to stabilize the market by placing purchase orders for the security at a fixed price. Underwriters believe that such stabilization is sometimes needed to provide for an orderly sale (thereby helping the issuer) and reduce their risk (thereby helping themselves).

kets. The global equity offering has changed all that. An important new development in investment banking is the emphasis on managing the global offerings of securities. A lead investment banker can act as a "global coordinator," linking separate underwriting syndicates throughout the world in selling equity issues.

U.S. firms now sell bonds in the new euro market. Although bonds denominated in dollars account for one-third to one-half of all new bond issues, more companies are selling bonds in Europe. The appeal for U.S. firms is that bond yields in the new euro market can be lower than in the United States. U.S. firms with foreign operations can also raise foreign currency in the form of euros by directly selling bonds in that market, thereby saving the costs of converting dollars to euros.

PRIVATE PLACEMENTS

In recent years, an increasing number of corporations have executed *private placements* whereby new securities issues (typically, debt securities) are sold directly to financial institutions, such as life insurance companies and pension funds, bypassing the open market. One advantage is that the firm does not have to register the issue with the SEC, thereby saving both time and money.[6] Investment bankers' fees also are saved, because they are not typically used in private placements, and even if they are used, the underwriting spread is saved. The disadvantages of private placements include a higher interest cost, because the financial institutions usually charge more than would be offered in a public subscription and possible restrictive provisions on the borrower's activities.[7]

The Secondary Markets

Secondary Markets
Markets where existing securities are traded among investors

Once new securities have been sold in the primary market, an efficient mechanism must exist for their resale if investors are to view securities as attractive opportunities. Secondary markets provide investors with a mechanism for trading existing securities.

Secondary markets exist for the trading of common and preferred stock, warrants, bonds, and puts and calls. Figure 4-2 diagrams the structure of the secondary markets, which is discussed below in the following order: equities, bonds, and derivative securities.

U.S. Securities Markets for the Trading of Equities

Equities trade in the United States in three major markets: The New York Stock Exchange (NYSE), the American Stock Exchange (Amex), and the Nasdaq Stock Market (Nasdaq). In addition, there are regional stock exchanges in several cities.

What about companies not listed on any market? In most cases, these companies fail to qualify for trading on an exchange or market, but in some cases, they simply choose not to apply for listing for whatever reason. These securities are considered to be *over-the-counter* (OTC) *securities*, a term which refers to an equity security not listed or traded on a national securities exchange or market.

Finally, investors increasingly trade on Electronic Communications Networks (ECNs). This is an important new venue for investor trading.

Each of these marketplaces is discussed below.

[6] The savings in time can sometimes be important, as market conditions can change rapidly between the time an issue is registered and sold.
[7] In addition, a lack of marketability exists, because the issue is unregistered. Therefore, the buyer may demand additional compensation from the lender in the form of a higher yield.

Figure 4-2

Structure of the secondary markets

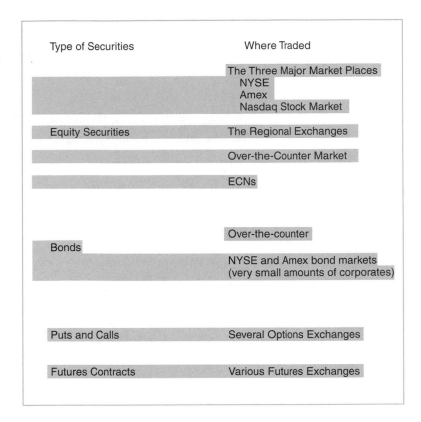

Type of Securities	Where Traded
	The Three Major Market Places NYSE Amex Nasdaq Stock Market
Equity Securities	The Regional Exchanges
	Over-the-Counter Market
	ECNs
Bonds	Over-the-counter
	NYSE and Amex bond markets (very small amounts of corporates)
Puts and Calls	Several Options Exchanges
Futures Contracts	Various Futures Exchanges

THE THREE MAJOR MARKETPLACES

As noted, the three major markets for the trading of U.S. securities are the NYSE, the Amex, and Nasdaq. Each of these markets involves the trading of listed securities. Companies that issue stock for public trading must choose where their shares will be listed for trading and then apply for listing in one of these three markets. They must also meet the listing requirements of the respective marketplace and agree to abide by the investor protection rules of that market. Additionally, each listing company must pay a listing fee to the market where their securities are traded.

The NYSE and Amex are auction markets involving physical locations in New York, whereas the Nasdaq stock market is an electronic market of dealers who make a market in each of the Nasdaq stocks. In either case, investors are represented by **brokers**, intermediaries who represent both buyers and sellers and attempt to obtain the best price possible for either party in a transaction. Brokers collect commissions for their efforts and generally have no vested interest in whether a customer places a buy order or a sell order or, in most cases, in what is bought or sold (holding constant the value of the transaction).

New York Stock Exchange Tracing its history back to 1792, the New York Stock Exchange (NYSE) is the oldest and most prominent secondary market in the United States. The NYSE typically is regarded as the best-regulated exchange in the world and has proven its ability to function in crisis. For example, on Black Monday in October 1987, this exchange handled some 600 million shares when other marketplaces discussed below were experiencing significant problems.

The NYSE is a not-for-profit corporation with member firms who own seats. Member firms are the only ones allowed to buy and sell securities on the trading floor.

Broker An intermediary who represents buyers and sellers in securities transactions and receives a commission

New York Stock Exchange (NYSE) The major secondary market for the trading of equity securities

The number of seats has remained constant at 1,366 for 50 years.[8] Most of the members are partners or directors of stockbrokerage houses.[9] Members may transfer seats, by sale or lease, subject to the approval of the exchange. The price of a seat has varied sharply over the years, ranging from less than $100,000 in the mid-1970s to a peak in February 1998 of $2,000,000. In March 2003, a seat was going for approximately $1.5 million.

The NYSE has specific listing requirements that companies must meet in order to be listed (i.e., accepted for trading). In considering an application to be listed, the NYSE pays particular attention to the degree of national interest in the company, its relative position and stability in the industry, and its prospects for maintaining its relative position. Requirements include specified amounts of earning power and net tangible assets, $40,000,000 market value of publicly traded shares, and a total of 1,100,000 common shares publicly held. New companies are added and dropped each year.

In early 2003, there were approximately 2,800 companies listed on the NYSE compared to 3,085 companies in mid-2000. The value of these companies was about $13.5 trillion.

Exhibit 4-1 contains some basic facts about the NYSE, which remains in many ways the premier secondary stock exchange in the world.

What can the NYSE offer investors who trade securities? According to the NYSE itself, this exchange is unique, because it offers an auction on the trading floor every day. The NYSE states, "Buy and sell orders for each listed security meet directly on the trading floor in assigned locations. Prices are determined through supply and demand." By having orders come through this one single location, according to the NYSE, investors are ensured that, "no matter how big or small," the investor is "exposed to a wide range of buyers and sellers." The exchange promises to see that each investor receives the best possible price.

EXHIBIT 4-1

Some Basic Facts About the NYSE

The New York Stock Exchange At Year-End 2002

⇒ had approximately 2,800 listed companies

  ⇒ worth about 13.5 trillion in global market capitalization
  ⇒ non-U.S. companies accounted for $4.9 trillion of the market capitalization total
  ⇒ 350 billion shares listed and available for trading

⇒ over 2/3 of the companies have listed within the last 14 years
⇒ number of newly listed companies for the year = 151

⇒ 473 non-U.S. companies are listed, representing more than 50 countries

⇒ number of warrants listed = 7

⇒ Average Daily Stock Volume in 2002 = 1.441 billion shares

⇒ Average price per share traded in 2002 = $28.39, compared to $42 in 2000

---

[8] The other 55 individuals paid an annual fee to have access to the trading floor. The number of seats has remained constant since 1953.

[9] For example, Merrill Lynch, the largest retail stockbrokerage firm, owns over 20 seats.

Specialist   A member of
an organized exchange
who is charged with
maintaining an orderly
market in one or more
stocks by buying or
selling for his or her own
account

There are approximately 400 member firms of the NYSE, and about 3,000 people working on the trading floor. Investors are most directly affected by brokers and specialists. We will discuss brokers in more detail in Chapter 5.

Specialists, who own roughly 33 percent of all the seats on the NYSE, are assigned to each trading post on the floor of the NYSE, where they handle one or more of the stocks traded at that post. Some specialists firms are part of well-known brokerage operations, whereas many others are virtually unknown to the public.

Example 4-2

Specialists of well-known institutions include Merrill Lynch Specialists, which handles the trading in Coca-Cola and Johnson & Johnson, and Bear Stearns Hunter Specialists, which handles Texas Instruments and Alcoa. Examples of specialists firms not known to the public include the largest specialist firm, Spear, Leeds & Kellogg, which handles more than 200 stocks, including IBM and Mobil, or the second largest firm, JJC Specialists, which handles Sears and General Electric, among other companies.

Specialist firms are, of course, affected by market conditions and the volume of trading. The market decline of 2000 to 2002, with lower trading volume and plunging stock prices, impacted their profits, as did the move to decimalization of stock prices.

Exhibit 4-2 contains a discussion of the roles that brokers and specialists play on the NYSE, as described by the NYSE itself. It is important for investors to understand the role of brokers in the investing process and the ultimate impact of specialists in the buying and selling of securities.

A specialist (firm) is assigned to each stock traded on the NYSE. Specialists are required to post bid and ask quotes at all times for the stocks(s) they are assigned to handle. The same is true of market makers on the Nasdaq Stock Market (explained below). The **bid quote** is what some buyer is currently willing to pay for a specified (or up to this) amount of a stock. The **ask quote** is what some seller is trying to sell some specified (or up to this) amount of stock for at the current time. These bid and ask quotes are constantly changing as new buyers and sellers emerge or existing buyers and sellers change their quotes.

Bid Quote   The price at
which a specialist or
dealer offers to buy
shares

Ask Quote   The price at
which a specialist or
dealer offers to sell
shares

Exhibit 4-3 illustrates bid-ask quotes for Cisco stock at one point in time. The spread between the two numbers can be lower or higher than illustrated. The important point to note is simply that at any time, bid and ask quotes exist for stocks traded on the three major markets, whether for Cisco on Nasdaq or GE on the NYSE.

In 2002, the NYSE had an aggregate share volume of over 363 billion shares compared to year 2000 share volume of 262 billion shares and 1995 volume of 87 billion shares. Daily trading volume averaged 1.441 billion shares in 2002.

Blocks   Transactions
involving at least 10,000
shares

Institutional investors often trade in large **blocks**, which are defined as transactions involving at least 10,000 shares. The average size of a trade on the NYSE has grown sharply over the years, as has institutional participation by block volume on both the NYSE and the Nasdaq National Market. A record 6.3 million block transactions were traded on the NYSE in 2002, accounting for almost 161 billion shares, or 44 percent of NYSE volume.

Program Trading
Involves the use of
computer-generated
orders to buy and sell
securities based on
arbitrage opportunities
between common stocks
and index futures and
options

Program trading is defined by the NYSE as the purchase or sale of a basket of 15 stocks or more and valued at $1 million or more. It is used to accomplish certain trading strategies, such as arbitrage against futures contracts and portfolio accumulation and liquidation strategies. By 2002, program trading volume accounted for 32 percent of total NYSE volume, double the figure from five years earlier—furthermore, in some weeks in 2002, it accounted for 40 percent or more of the volume.

EXHIBIT 4-2

The Broker and the Specialist on the NYSE

Broker An agent representing customer orders to buy or sell.

There are two main types of floor brokers: commission brokers and independent floor brokers. Individual firms called brokerage houses that are members of the NYSE employ commission brokers. Darting from booth to trading post, these highly trained men and women buy and sell securities for the general public. In return, they earn salaries and commissions.

Independent floor brokers are brokers who work for themselves. They handle orders for brokerage houses that do not have full-time brokers or whose brokers are off the floor or too busy to handle a specific order. Independent floor brokers are often still referred to as "$2 brokers," a term coined back in the days when they received $2 for every 100 shares they traded.

The public places its orders through sales personnel (or stockbrokers) of a brokerage house. These sales professionals are also called "registered representatives," since they must pass a qualifying examination and are registered with the NYSE and the Securities and Exchange Commission. Investor orders are transmitted from a branch office of a brokerage house to the NYSE Trading Floor through sophisticated electronic communications and order-processing systems.

Specialists Specialists are critical to the auction process. They perform a role that could be compared to that of an air traffic controller. Just as controllers maintain order among aircraft aloft, specialists maintain a fair and orderly market in the securities assigned to them.

They manage the auction process, providing a conduit of information—electronically quoting and recording current bid and asked prices for the stocks assigned to them. This enables current price information to be transmitted worldwide, keeping all market participants informed to the total supply and demand for any particular NYSE-listed stock.

Specialists act as agents, executing orders entrusted to them by a floor broker—orders to be executed if and when a stock reaches a price specified by a customer. In instances when there is a temporary shortage of buyers or sellers, NYSE specialists will buy or sell for their own accounts against the trend of the market. They are not, however, required to fund all the liquidity for the market at any time. These transactions serve to manage volatility and represent a small portion of trading. The vast majority of NYSE volume is a result of public order meeting public order—individuals, institutions and member firms interacting directly with each other.

Each stock listed on the NYSE is allocated to a specialist, a broker who trades only in specific stocks at a designated location. All buying and selling of a stock occurs at that location, called a trading post. Buyers and sellers—represented by the floor brokers—meet openly at the trading post to find the best price for a security.

The people who gather around a specialist's post are referred to as the trading crowd. Bids to buy and offers to sell are made by open outcry to provide interested parties with an opportunity to participate, enhancing the competitive determination of prices. When the highest bid meets the lowest offer, a trade is executed.

To a large degree the specialist is responsible for maintaining the market's fairness, competitiveness and efficiency. Specifically, the specialist performs five vital functions.

Act as Agents One of the specialist's jobs is to execute orders for floor brokers in their assigned stocks. A floor broker may get an order from a customer who only wants to buy a stock at a price lower than the current market price—or sell it at a price higher than the current market price. In such cases, the broker may ask the specialist to hold the order and execute it if and when the price of the stock reaches the level specified by the customer. In this role the specialist acts as an agent for the broker.

Act as Catalysts Specialists serve as the contact point between brokers with buy and sell orders in the NYSE's two-way auction market. In this respect, the specialists act as catalysts, bringing buyers and sellers together, so that offers to buy can be matched with offers to sell.

Act as Auctioneers At the start of each trading day, the specialists establish a fair market price for each of their stocks. The specialists base that price on the supply and demand for the stock. Then during the day, the specialist quote the current bids and offers in their stocks to other brokers.

Stabilize Prices Specialists are also called upon to maintain "orderly markets" in their assigned stocks. That is, they ensure that trading in the stocks moves smoothly throughout the day with minimal fluctuation in price.

Provide Capital Finally, if buy orders temporarily outpace sell orders in a stock—or if sell orders outpace buy orders—the specialist is required to use his firm's own capital to minimize the imbalance. This is done by buying or selling against the trend of the market, until a price is reached at which public supply and demand are once again in balance. In this role the specialist acts as a principal or dealer. Specialists participate in only about 10 percent of all shares traded. The rest of the time, public order meets public order, without specialist participation.

Source: NYSE Web site. Reprinted by permission.

EXHIBIT 4-3

Bid and Ask Quotes in the Marketplace

Assume Cisco stock's last trade is at $13.80.

The following information is available at this moment on Cisco
(Prices typically are changing constantly, as are bid and ask quotes)

Bid price $13.79   Bid size: 5,000
Ask price $13.80   Ask size: 3,000

Given that the last reported trade for Cisco was at $13.80, and with these bid and ask prices:

Currently, the best bid is $13.79, which means someone is willing to pay $13.79 for up to 5,000 shares of Cisco. The first seller willing to accept this price who wanted to sell immediately could sell up to 5,000 shares of Cisco at $13.79

Currently, the best ask price (or offer price) is $13.80, which means someone is trying to sell up to 3,000 shares of Cisco at $13.80. The first buyer willing to pay this price to buy immediately could buy up to 3,000 shares of Cisco for $13.80.

The difference between the bid and ask price is called the bid-ask spread. It is part of the cost of trading stocks.

American Stock Exchange The Amex is the only other national organized exchange. Its organization and procedures resemble those of the NYSE, most notably in being a specialist-based system. Relative to the NYSE, the Amex is smaller (membership is limited to 807 regular members) and fewer companies are listed there (approximately 760). The listing requirements are less stringent for stocks on the Amex than for stocks on the NYSE.

Share volume for 2002 amounted to approximately 2 percent of the total shares traded for the year on the Amex, NYSE, and Nasdaq combined. Typically, the NYSE does more trading in the first hour than the Amex does during the entire day. However, the Amex has been innovative in its trading, pioneering the trading of exchange-traded funds (ETFs). Its Standard & Poor's Depository Receipts (SPDRs), Cubes, and Diamonds, which are ETFs and were explained in Chapter 3, have proven to be quite popular. It does a large business in options and derivative securities, with almost 30 percent of the market in stock-option trading. Initiated in 2002, the Amex now trades some 135 Nasdaq-listed stocks.

Regardless of the lower level of activity on the Amex, some companies choose to be listed on the Amex.

Example 4-3

Metromedia International, following its restructuring, chose to be listed on the Amex, citing lower listing costs and the right to choose its own specialist, which the Amex allows firms to do.

In 1998, the NASD (explained below) and the Amex completed their announced merger, thereby creating the first financial marketplace to combine the central auction specialist and multiple market maker systems. Nasdaq (explained below) and Amex operate as separate markets under the management of the Nasdaq-Amex Market Group. Nasdaq-Amex intends to build a globally linked marketplace that provides investment choices to all investors worldwide, although this project has had some setbacks, as discussed later in the chapter.

Dealer An individual (firm) who makes a market in a stock by buying from and selling to investors

Nasdaq Stock Market (Nasdaq) The automated quotation system for the over-the-counter market, showing current bid-ask prices for thousands of stocks

National Association of Securities Dealers (NASD) A self-regulating body of brokers and dealers

The Nasdaq Stock Market In contrast to auction markets, the Nasdaq Stock Market is a competing dealer market consisting of a network of **dealers (market makers)** who make a market by standing ready to buy and sell securities at specified prices. Unlike brokers, dealers have a vested interest in the transaction, because the securities are bought from them and sold to them, and they earn a profit in these trades by the spread, or difference, between the two prices.

Most of the actively traded stocks not on the NYSE or Amex are part of the **Nasdaq Stock Market (Nasdaq)**. Thus, most investors think of stocks as trading on the NYSE, the Amex, or Nasdaq. More correctly, stocks are listed on one of these three markets (two of which are exchanges), but may also trade on other venues such as the electronic communications networks (ECNs).

Note that the NYSE and Amex trade only in stocks listed on their respective exchanges. However, stock listed on either also trade on the Nasdaq Intermarket, on a regional exchange, or the new Archipelago (ArcaEx) discussed below.

Figure 4-3 shows a comparison of Nasdaq companies with NYSE and Amex companies. As we can see, there are approximately 2,800 NYSE companies and approximately 3,800 Nasdaq companies. The Amex is completely dwarfed in these comparisons, having less than 700 companies listed.

Nasdaq was originally developed by the **National Association of Security Dealers (NASD)**, a self-regulating body of brokers and dealers. The NASD

1. Licenses brokers when they successfully complete a qualifying examination.
2. Provides for on-site compliance examinations of member firms. Violation of the fair practices prescribed by the NASD are grounds for censure, fine, suspension, or expulsion for both firms and principals in the firms. This self-regulating function of the NASD serves to protect the public as well as the interest of its members.
3. Provides automated market surveillance.
4. Reviews member advertising and underwriting arrangements.
5. Provides a mechanism for the arbitration of disputes between member firms and investors.

Nasdaq is now a private (for profit) corporation owned by its shareholders (primarily major financial service firms). It is expected to have an IPO and go public.

Figure 4-3

Number of companies listed at year-end 2002 on the NYSE, AMEX, and Nasdaq.

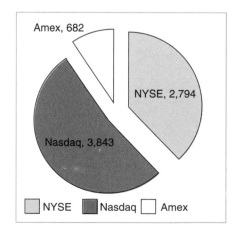
Amex, 682; NYSE, 2,794; Nasdaq, 3,843. NYSE, Nasdaq, Amex

Unlike the NYSE, Nasdaq does not have a specific location. Rather it is a fully computerized market consisting of many market makers who compete freely with each other through an electronic network of terminals rather than on the floor of an exchange. These dealers conduct transactions directly with each other and with customers. Nasdaq takes an "open architecture" approach, meaning there is no fixed number of participants. Any firm meeting the basic requirements of the organization can join, be a part of Nasdaq, and compete for business. In effect, what Nasdaq does is link together all of the liquidity providers for a particular stock, which allows them to compete efficiently with each other.

Each Nasdaq company has a number of competing market makers, or dealers, who make a market in the stock, with a minimum of 2 and an average of 11 dealers. (Some large Nasdaq companies have 40 or more dealers.) Market makers provide liquidity for stocks, because they stand ready to buy and sell. Market makers are required to post their bid and ask prices on the Nasdaq system.

Nasdaq features an electronic trading system as the centerpiece of its operations. This system provides instantaneous transactions as Nasdaq market makers compete for investor orders. *SelectNet* is used by market participants such as market makers, ECNs, day traders, and specialists, to transact electronically. It is an order delivery and negotiation system.

Nasdaq operates two distinct market segments:

Nasdaq National Market System A combination of the competing market makers in over-the-counter stocks and the up-to-the-minute reporting using data almost identical to that shown for the NYSE and Amex

- ❑ The **Nasdaq National Market** is a combination of competing market makers and the up-to-the-minute reporting of trades. The system uses data similar to data shown for the NYSE and Amex (specifically, high, low, and closing quotations, volume, and the net change from one day to the next). The vast majority of the roughly 4,000 companies listed on Nasdaq trade as national market system (NMS) securities. Included here are numerous well known stocks such as Cisco, Intel, and Dell. On a volume basis, NMS issues account for 90 percent of all Nasdaq volume.
- ❑ The Nasdaq SmallCap Market involves smaller stocks that have not yet reached a size suitable for the Nasdaq National Market. Alternatively, stocks that have traded on the Nasdaq National Market but failed to continue to qualify for trading there typically move to the SmallCap Market. The primary requirement that these companies fail to meet is a minimum bid price of $1 per share for the stock for 30 consecutive trading days. More than 800 stocks trade in the SmallCap Market.

Example 4-4 In October 2002, Corvis Corporation, a provider of optical networking solutions, announced that it was transferring the listing of its common stock from the Nasdaq National Market to the Nasdaq SmallCap Market. The company noted that it could be eligible to transfer back to the National Market if its bid price maintained the $1 minimum requirement for 30 consecutive trading days.

The Nasdaq has been a major player in the securities markets, ultimately having many more stocks listed than the NYSE and having a trading volume that exceeded the volume for the NYSE. However, the sharp market decline of 2000 to 2002 changed this market dramatically. The Nasdaq index went from an all-time high of 5048 in March 2000 to levels such as 1200 in 2002, and trading in technology stocks, a prominent feature of Nasdaq, plunged sharply. For example, the telecommunications companies such as Global Crossing and WorldCom were completely devastated, and many technology/internet companies went bankrupt.

Consider the following facts about the Nasdaq:

1. Share volume in July 2002 amounted to 47.5 billion shares compared to 41.5 billion shares on the NYSE.
2. For July 2002, dollar volume was $618 billion compared to $1.1 trillion on the NYSE.
3. There were three IPOs on both Nasdaq and the NYSE in July 2002.
4. The average price per share traded for July 2002 on Nasdaq was $13.01, whereas for the NYSE, it was $27.

When we think of the Nasdaq market we typically think of it as a network of market makers. However, in today's world, the Nasdaq network connects other trading systems, such as:

- ATSs/ECNs (Alternative Trading Sytems/Electronic Communications Networks)— these systems allow investors to trade electronically with each other at preset prices. No market maker is involved, as these systems are simply order-matching systems. ECNs are explained below.
- The Primex Auction System—in this system, any Nasdaq participant (market maker, ATSs/ECNs, and others) can expose an order to a crowd of bidders by, in effect, replicating a competitive trading crowd electronically.
- Nasdaq InterMarket connects Nasdaq market participants to the Intermarket Trading System used by the NYSE and the regional exchanges to direct orders between exchanges. This system provides a mechanism for the off-floor trading of exchange-listed stocks. The ITS is discussed later in the chapter.

SuperMontage A new Nasdaq system displaying its order book in more detail, showing multiple orders to buy and sell; in effect, it has features similar to the ECNs

Because of the inroads made into its business, Nasdaq in 2002 received Securities and Exchange Commission (SEC) clearance for a new trading platform called **SuperMontage**. This system, which better organizes buy and sell orders and provides more information to investors, is an attempt to win back business for Nasdaq lost by its failure to develop a completely electronic market with equal access for all investors. All stocks listed on Nasdaq now trade on this new system.

The SuperMontage system displays Nasdaq's order book in more detail, showing multiple orders to buy and sell—in effect, it has features similar to the ECNs discussed below. Investors with large orders are able to transact anonymously if they choose.

Using the Internet

Information, primarily factual, on the **NYSE** can be obtained at www.nyse.com. This site has extensive historical data as well as information about the NYSE and its companies. Information on the Amex and Nasdaq can be obtained at www.nasdaq-amex.com, which offers quotes, news, market activity, and portfolio tracking. The Nasdaq-Amex Newsroom[SM] at www.nasdaq-amexnews.com offers numerous press releases and key reports. By going to www.nasdaqnews.com and accessing "Nasdaq© Backgrounder," an interested individual can call up numerous reports on how this market functions, the companies traded, Nasdaq indexes, listing standards, and so forth.

REGIONAL EXCHANGES

The United States has several regional exchanges, including the Boston, Chicago, Cincinnati, Pacific, and Philadephia exchanges.[10] Regional exchanges list small companies that

[10] Stock exchanges existed in many cities years ago to meet the needs of local investors. Modern communications equipment negates the usefulness of most of these exchanges.

may have limited geographical interest ("local" stocks). Most of their activity is devoted to trading active NYSE and Nasdaq-listed stocks. This allows local brokerage firms that are not members of a national exchange to purchase a seat on a regional exchange and trade in these more active securities. Regional exchanges accounted for only a small percent of total share volume in 2002.

Some of the regional exchanges have physical trading floors, but in today's world, they more closely resemble the Nasdaq market makers. This means that the specialists on these exchanges are really acting as dealers. The SEC approved a new exchange in 2001, the Archipelago Exchange, which involves a combination of an ECN (explained later in the chapter) and the Pacific Exchange. The new exchange, called ArcaEx, will be a regulated facility of the Pacific Exchange.[11]

OVER-THE-COUNTER STOCKS

Although many investors associate the term "over-the-counter" with small stocks in general and Nasdaq in particular, in today's world, better distinctions need to be made. The Nasdaq Stock Market trades listed securities. **Over-the-counter (OTC) securities**, on the other hand, are not listed and traded on an organized exchange or market.

Over-the-counter securities typically are traded in one of two ways.[12] First, companies that file registration statements with the Securities and Exchange Commission (SEC) can be traded on the *OTC Bulletin Board®* (OTCBB). The OTCBB consists of a group of market makers who enter quotes and trade reports using a closed computer network. Although operated by Nasdaq, this system is completely separate from the Nasdaq market.

Second, companies not registered with the SEC can be traded through the Pink Sheets LLC, a privately owned company. This company provides an Internet-based, real-time quotation system for these OTC equities. There are more than 3,000 stocks traded here. Hundreds of these companies are financially sound and have been in business for many years. Some are "penny" stocks, and some are financially distressed. In many cases, corporate financial information is scarce, and analyst opinions on these stocks are almost nonexistent.

Recently, some well-known companies joined the ranks of the Pink Sheet companies because of well-publicized financial problems. This list includes Enron, WorldCom, and Kmart as well as Global Crossing. Thus, Enron went from being one of the largest corporations in the United States, widely admired as a prototype of the New Economy, to a virtually bankrupt entity traded on the Pink Sheets.

ELECTRONIC COMMUNICATIONS NETWORKS (ECNs)

Increasingly, the traditional ways of trading equity securities—agency auction markets and the fully computerized Nasdaq market—are being changed by new advances in electronic trading. **Electronic communications networks (ECNs)** are clearly having an effect on the traditional markets such as Nasdaq and the NYSE. There are now several ECNs within the Nasdaq market competing for customers with the more traditional Nasdaq market makers.

An ECN is a computerized trading network that matches buy and sell orders that come from their own subscribers as well as customer orders routed from other brokerage firms.[13] Each order received is displayed by the ECN in its computer system. Paying

Over-the-Counter (OTC) Market A network of securities dealers linked together to make markets in securities

Electronic Communications Network (ECN) A computerized trading network for institutions and large traders

[11] This discussion is based on "Market Mechanics: A Guide to U.S. Stock Markets," release 1.2, *Nasdaq Educational Foundation*, 2002.
[12] Ibid.
[13] Ibid.

subscribers can see the entire order book, and ECNs display their best bid and ask quotes in the Nasdaq quotation system for all market participants to see. An investor wishing to transact at one of the prices displayed on the computer system electronically submits an order to the ECN. The role of the ECN is to match buy and sell orders, thereby completing trades. Since ECNs simply match orders, they earn their fees from those who trade on their systems.

ECNs offer automation, lower costs, and anonymity as to who is doing the buying or selling. There are no spreads, or conflicts of interest with a broker (as explained in Chapter 5). Costs are about 1¢ a share.

**Instinet (Institutional
Network)**   An electronic
trading network, one of
the ECNs

Instinet (Institutional Network), owned by Reuters, is the original electronic trading network, started in 1969 long before the term ECN, which is a recent innovation. It is a system offering equity transactions and research services for brokers, dealers, exchange specialists, institutional fund managers, and plan sponsors who pay commissions of about 1¢ a share and receive free proprietary terminals. It has now started accepting retail clients. Instinet is always open for trading stocks on any of the exchanges worldwide to which Instinet belongs.

Instinet offers anonymous trading, allowing large traders to bypass brokers with their often attendant leaks on who is transacting. Trades are often less than 10,000 shares each, and an institution can do multiple trades to get into or out of a position in a stock without others knowing.

The prospect is for these electronic networks to grow and also to consolidate. By percentage of share volume, Instinet and Island are the two largest ECNs and merged in 2002. As of April 1999, ECNs are allowed to register as exchanges under SEC rules.[14]

As of August 2002, the ECNs share of Nasdaq trading had risen to 45 percent, whereas Nasdaq's own share of Nasdaq-traded stocks was about 30 percent (in-house brokerage order matching accounted for the other 25 percent). By providing additional ways for investors to trade, such as after exchange hours, ECNs may have increased the overall volume of trading.

The NYSE has been frustrated by its inability to attract the hot Internet and technology companies, such as Cisco, Dell, Intel, and Microsoft. Because the ECNs are getting some of the business for these companies, the NYSE has explored how it might link up with them. As of early 2003, ECNs had made relatively little headway in trading NYSE stocks despite attempts to do so. The NYSE's share of trading in its own stocks is about 85 percent.

After-Hours Trading   Normal stock exchange hours are 9:30 AM to 4 PM. ECNs allow investors to trade after–exchange hours, which primarily means 4 to 8 PM EST, and sometimes early in the morning. However, Instinet, one of the largest ECNs, usually operates around the clock.

On-line brokerage firms offer their clients access to this trading using the computerized order-matching systems of the ECNs. It is important to note that such trading is completely independent from the standard trading during market hours. Investors must, in effect, find someone willing to fill their orders at an acceptable price. Liquidity may be thin, although heavily traded NYSE stocks are good candidates for trading as are most Nasdaq 100 stocks. Limitations exist on the types of orders that can be placed and the size of the orders. As of the beginning of 2001, less than half of on-line brokerage firms allowed customers this option.

---

[14] As noted earlier Archipelago has been approved for exchange status.

IN-HOUSE TRADING

Along with the electronic networks, a new trend that has significant implications for the NYSE is the internal trading, or *in-house trading*, by fund managers without the use of a broker or an exchange. At a large institution with several funds or accounts, traders agree to buy and sell in-house, or cross trade, perhaps at the next closing price. For example, at a large bank with several pension fund accounts, the manager of Account A might wish to buy IBM at the same time that the manager of Account B is selling a position in IBM.

Example 4-5

Fidelity Investments, the largest mutual fund company, operates an in-house trading system for its own funds because of the tremendous amount of buying and selling it does every day. In addition, it has set up the *Investor Liquidity Network*, which is now used by other brokerage firms and institutional clients. This electronic routing system is said to handle 5 percent of the NYSE's volume, and Fidelity's in-house trading accounts for at least that much more.

FOREIGN MARKETS

As noted, investors have become increasingly interested in equity markets around the world, because the United States now accounts for only about one-third of the world's stock market capitalization. Many equity markets exist. Examples in the developed countries include the United Kingdom, France, Germany, Italy, Switzerland, Japan, Hong Kong, and Canada. Investors are also interested in *emerging markets* such as Mexico, Brazil, and Indonesia.[15] Because of the large number and variety of foreign markets, we will consider only a few highlights here.

Western Europe has several mature markets, including in addition to those mentioned above Belgium, Finland, Spain, and Sweden. U.S. investors sent more money to Britain in the last few years than any other country in the world. The London Stock Exchange (LSE) is an important equity market, handling both listed equities and bonds as well as unlisted securities. Germany has continental Europe's largest stock market. Switzerland is home to some of the largest global companies in the world, including Nestle (food and beverage) and Hoffman La Roche (drug manufacturer).

Interestingly, analysts now refer to Europe's emerging markets. These include the Czech Republic, Hungary, and Poland where potential profits are large, but risks are also large: illiquidity is great, corporate information is difficult to obtain, and political risk of a type unknown to U.S. investors still exists. Turkey is another example of an emerging market.

The Far East is the fastest growing region in the world, with growth rates twice that of the United States; U.S. investors have been particularly active in the Far Eastern markets. These markets also have been very volatile, with large gains and losses because of illiquidity (a scarcity of buyers at times) as well as currency risks and political risks.

Japan, the dominant Asian economic power, has one of the largest stock markets in the world, although the Japanese markets have been severely battered since 1989. Although Japan has eight stock exchanges, the Tokyo Stock Exchange (TSE) dominates that country's equity markets even more than the NYSE dominates the U.S. markets. Both domestic and foreign stocks are listed on the TSE, and among domestic issues, a relatively few are traded on the floor of the exchange; the rest (as well as foreign stocks) are handled by computer.

[15] There is no precise definition of an *emerging market*, but generally it involves a stable political system, fewer regulations, and less standardization in trading activity.

Other Asian markets include Hong Kong, which next to Japan is the largest Asian market in terms of market capitalization, India, Indonesia, Japan, South Korea, Malaysia, Pakistan, the Philippines, Singapore, Sri Lanka, Taiwan, and Thailand. Of course, some of these markets are quite small. The "Four Dragons"—Hong Kong, Singapore, South Korea, and Taiwan—dominate these markets when Japan is excluded.

The big unknown in Asian markets is, of course, China, an emerging economy of potentially great importance. China is booming as an economy but with great risks, for politics strongly affects investments in China. Its financial markets are still tiny by other countries' standards. Chinese companies do trade on the Hong Kong exchange as well as on exchanges in China such as Shanghai.

Latin America is the remaining emerging marketplace that has been of great interest to investors recently. The markets in Latin America include Argentina, Brazil, Chile, Colombia, Mexico, Peru, and Venezuela. Mexico's market is the largest, followed by Brazil, with the others being small by comparison in terms of market capitalization. As we would expect in emerging markets, profit potentials are large, but so are risks—volatile prices, liquidity problems, and political risks such as the assassination of Mexico's leading presidential candidate in 1994. In early 1999, Brazil suffered a severe financial crisis.

COMPARISONS OF EQUITY MARKETS

Figure 4-4 shows annual share volume comparisons for the major domestic markets for one recent year. Significantly, in 2002, Nasdaq accounted for 62 percent of total volume compared to 36 percent for the NYSE and only 2 percent for the Amex.

STOCK MARKET INDEXES

The most popular question asked about stock markets is probably, "What did the market do today?" To answer this question, we need a composite report on market performance, which is what stock market averages and indices are designed to provide. Because of the large number of equity markets, both domestic and foreign, there are numerous stock market indicators. In this section, we outline some basic information on these averages and indices, with subsequent chapters containing more analysis and discussion as needed. Appendix 4-A provides additional details on these indicators, including composition and construction details.

It is important to note in the discussion below the difference between a stock index, measuring prices only, and a total return index. For example, the Dow Jones Industrial

Figure 4-4

Number of shares traded for the NYSE, Amex, and Nasdaq, 2002.

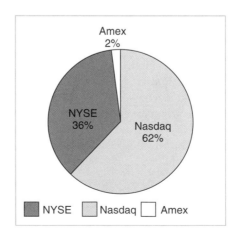

Average, like all major stock indexes, measures only the change in prices of a defined group of stocks over some period of time. Such indexes ignore dividend payments, which as we shall see in Chapter 6 constitute the other part of the total return for a common stock. Dividend payments can often make total returns much larger than the price change component alone. Thus, stock market indexes generally understate the total returns to investors from owning common stocks.

Dow Jones Industrial Average (DJIA) A price-weighted series of 30 industrial stocks used as a measure of stock market activity

Blue-Chip Stocks Stocks with long records of earning and dividends—well-known, stable mature companies

The Dow Jones Averages The best known average in the United States is the **Dow Jones Industrial Average (DJIA)**, probably because it has always been affiliated with Dow Jones & Company, publishers of *The Wall Street Journal*.[16] It is the oldest market measure, originating in 1896 and modified over the years.[17] The DJIA is computed from 30 leading stocks chosen somewhat arbitrarily by Dow Jones & Company to represent different industries. This average is said to be composed of **blue-chip stocks**, meaning large, well-established, and well-known companies. Dow Jones & Company also computes, and the *Journal* publishes, a transportation average and a public utility average.

It is important to note that the DJIA is a *price-weighted series*, which is unusual. Because it gives equal weight to equal dollar changes, high-priced stocks carry more weight than low-priced stocks. A 10-percent change in the price of stock A at $200 will have a much different impact on the DJIA from that of a 10-percent change in stock B at $20. This also means that as high-priced stocks split and their prices decline, they lose relative importance in the calculation of the average, whereas nonsplit stocks increase in relative importance. This bias against growth stocks, which are the most likely stocks to split, can result in a downward bias in the DJIA.

It is important to note that because of the adjustments in the divisor of the DJIA over time, to account for stock splits and stock dividends, one point on the Dow is not equal to $1. In early 2003, the divisor was 0.14585278; therefore, a change in the DJIA, given a one-point change in only one stock in the index and this divisor, amounts to 1/0.14585278 or 6.86 points. Furthermore, using this divisor, a movement of 30 points in the DJIA results in an *average* movement in each of the component stocks of only $0.1459. Of course, the divisor will continue to drop as more stock splits and stock dividends occur.

Example 4-6

On January 22, 1999, the DJIA fell 143.41 points, which most people would consider a large decline. The divisor at the time was 0.24272, which produces a point multiplier of 4.12. IBM, one of the 30 Dow stocks, declined $17.31, which accounted for 4.12(17.31) or 71.32 points of the Dow's decline, which is almost exactly half.

Investors need to distinguish between point changes in the DJIA and percentage changes. When the index is at a level such as 10,000 or 11,000, a 300-point change in one day can't mean as much as the same point change when the index was at 5000. Therefore, we need to be careful to put such changes in perspective:

---

[16] There are three other Dow Jones Averages: the transportation, the public utility, and the composite. The first two encompass 20 and 15 stocks, respectively, and the composite consists of these two groups plus the DJIA (i.e., 65 stocks). Each average is calculated similarly to the DJIA, with changes being made in the divisor to adjust for splits and other factors. Daily information on these averages can be found in *The Wall Street Journal* and other newspapers.

[17] The first average of U.S. stocks was created by Charles Dow in 1884 and consisted of 11 stocks, mostly railroads. The Dow Industrial Average, first published in 1896, consisted of 12 industrial companies.

Example 4-7 On March 18, 2000, the Dow gained approximately 500 points to close at 10,630.6. This was a percentage gain of 4.94 percent. In contrast, on October 21, 1987, the Dow gained 186.84 points to close at 2027.85, which represented a percentage gain of 10.15 percent, because the base was much lower. On July 24, 2002, the Dow gained about 489 points to close at 8191.29, a gain of 6.35 percent. (All calculations are done using the opening level of the index that day.)

Like any index, the level of the DJIA simply reflects the decisions that have been made on which stocks to include in the index. There have been 52 changes in the composition of the DJIA in 74 years. In March 1999, the DJIA closed for the first time above 10,000, and it later went above 11,000. In November 1999, Chevron, Goodyear, Union Carbide, and Sears were removed from the index and replaced by Intel, Microsoft, Home Depot, and SBC Communications. Had different stocks been selected for the index, these events may or may not have occurred, and the timing would have been different.

The DJIA has been criticized because of its use of only 30 stocks to reflect what the overall market is doing, and because it is price weighted (rather than value weighted). Furthermore, one can argue it is no longer an "industrial" index, because two-thirds of its weighting comes from sectors involving consumer products, financial services companies, and technology companies. Nevertheless, it is the oldest continuous measure of the stock market, and it remains the most prominent measure of market activity for many investors. Regardless of its problems, the DJIA remains relevant, because it is so widely reported and cited.

The DJIA does fulfill its role as a measure of market activity for stocks such as those on the NYSE. Furthermore, a recent study sheds even more light on the use of the DJIA as a measure of stock market activity, finding that[18]

1. Contrary to popular belief among its critics, price weighting has not caused the DJIA to be significantly different from what it would have been had it been calculated using market capitalization weights. Although market value weights are theoretically superior, they would not have made much difference in fact for the DJIA.
2. At the end of 1999, the value of the DJIA trailed the broader indexes, but not dramatically. The hypothesis that the mean monthly return for the DJIA is the same as the mean monthly return for value-weighted indexes such as the S&P 500 (explained below) could not be rejected.

Standard & Poor's Stock Price Indexes The Standard & Poor's Corporation, which publishes financial data for investors, also publishes five market indices, including a 400-stock Industrial Average, a 40-stock Utility Average, a 20-stock Transportation Average, a 40-stock Financial Average, and finally all of these combined into the well-known and widely cited 500-stock Composite Index.[19] The Composite Index is carried in the popular press such as *The Wall Street Journal*, and investors often refer to it as a "good" measure of what the overall market is doing, at least for large NYSE stocks. The S&P 500 is typically the measure of the market preferred by institutional investors when comparing their performance to that of the market.

---

[18] See John B. Sloven and Clemens Sialm, "The Dow Jones Industrial Average: The Impact of Fixing its Flaws," *The Journal of Wealth Management*, Winter 2000, pp. 9–18.

[19] Standard & Poor's also publishes indices for various groupings of stocks, covering specific industries, low-priced stocks, high-grade stocks, and so on.

Unlike the Dow Jones Industrial Average, the **Standard & Poor's 500 Composite Index (S&P 500)** is a market value index or capitalization-weighted index. It is expressed in relative numbers with a base value arbitrarily set to 10 (1941 to 1943). All stock splits and dividends are automatically accounted for in calculating the value of the index, because the number of shares currently outstanding (i.e., after the split or dividend) and the new price are used in the calculation. Unlike the Dow Jones Average, each stock's importance is based on relative total market value instead of relative per-share price.

Table 4-1 illustrates how a market value, or capitalization-weighted, index is constructed. For each stock, the share price is multiplied by the number of shares outstanding to obtain the current market value of the stock. A base value has to be set by construction—in Table 4-1, the value at the end of the first year is set at 100. At the end of the second year, market value is calculated the same way. Notice in Table 4-1 that stock ABD has a two-for-one stock split in the second year, and this is automatically adjusted for, because we are multiplying share price by number of shares to obtain market value. The new index value is 114.29, because the total market value of the stocks in this index has increased by that amount.

The S&P 500 is obviously a much broader measure than the Dow, and it should be more representative of the general market. However, it consists primarily of NYSE stocks, and it is clearly dominated by the largest corporations.[20] Like any index, the S&P 500 is affected by the performance of the individual stocks in the index.

In July 2002, the committee at Standard & Poor's that handles the S&P 500 Index decided that henceforth foreign corporations would no longer be included in the index. This resulted in dropping seven foreign-based firms, including Royal Dutch Petroleum and Unilever. They were replaced with, among others, eBay and UPS.

Nasdaq Indexes The National Association of Security Dealers produces several indexes. Separate Nasdaq indexes cover industrials, banks, transportation, insurance, other finance, biotechnology, telecommunications, and computers. All of these together comprise the Composite Index. The base period January 1971 is assigned a value of 100 for the Composite Index and the Industrial Index, and monthly data are available from January 1971.

Table 4-1 Illustration of How a Value-Weighted Index is Constructed and Calculated

	Stock	Price	Number of Shares	Market Value (price × shares)
Year-end 2002				
	ABD	$10	10,000,000	$ 100,000,000
	TWE	20	15,000,000	300,000,000
	CWF	40	25,000,000	1,000,000,000
			Total Market Value =	$1,400,000,000
Base Value of Index = 100 (by construction)				
Year-end 2003				
	ABD	$ 7	20,000,000*	$ 140,000,000
	TWE	14	15,000,000	210,000,000
	CWF	50	25,000,000	1,250,000,000
			Total Market Value =	$1,600,000,000

New Value of Index = $1,600,000,000 / $1,400,000,000 × 100 = 1.1429 × 100 = 114.29

*ABD splits two-for-one during the year 2001.

[20] The S&P 500 contains some stocks from the Nasdaq Stock Market.

In addition to these, the Nasdaq 100 and the Nasdaq Financial 100 consists of the 100 largest market-capitalized firms in each category. There are also indexes covering the Nasdaq National Market Composite and the Nasdaq National Market Industrials.

The Nasdaq indexes of most interest to investors, the Composite Index and the 100 Index, are widely available daily.

The Nasdaq Composite Index suffered the most horrific declines of all the major U.S. indexes during the period 2000 to 2002. After reaching a record level of about 5000 in 2000, it closed at 1240 on July 25, 2002, falling about 4 percent on that day alone. At that point, it had declined about 75 percent from its record high and 36 percent in 2002 alone up to that point in time.

The Nasdaq Composite Index is heavily dominated by the technology stocks such as Cisco, Dell, Microsoft, Oracle, and Intel. Therefore, this index is going to be affected significantly by what technology stocks are doing. In the 1990s, such stocks soared, but in 2000 to 2002, these stocks collapsed. The index reflected both events.

Other Indexes There are numerous other indexes available to investors, some of which are explained in Appendix 4-A. For example, both the NYSE and the Amex have Composite Indexes.

The Russell indexes are well known. The *Russell 1000 Index* is closely correlated with the S&P 500, because it consists primarily of "large-cap" stocks. These 1000 stocks make up about 90% of the total market value of the Russell 3000. The *Russell 2000* consists of the remaining 10% of the Russell 3000. These "small caps" have an average market capitalization of about $200 million compared to $4 billion for the Russell 1000. The Russell 2000 is often cited as an index of small common stocks.

The Dow Jones Equity Market Index is capitalization weighted. It consists of 700 stocks covering about 80% of the U.S. equity market. It correlates closely with the S&P 500 and the Russell 1000.

The *Equity Market Index*, unlike the DJIA, is an index similar to the S&P 500. Unlike the DJIA, which gives equal weight to each stock, this index weights each stock by its relative importance in the market based on its capitalization. Stock splits are automatically adjusted for, and stocks with the largest market values have the greatest effect on the index. It has a base of 100 set at June 30, 1982.

Relationships Between Domestic Stock Indexes As the previous discussion indicates, numerous measures of the "market," ranging from the DJIA to the broadest measure of the market, the Wilshire Index (discussed in Appendix 4-A), are available. It is obvious that the overall market is measured and reported on in several different ways.

The following observations about the various market indexes can be made:

1. Although the DJIA contains only 30 stocks and has often been criticized because of this small number and the manner in which the average is computed, it parallels the movements of the broader market value–weighted indexes involving NYSE stocks—specifically, the NYSE Composite Index (discussed in Appendix 4-A) and the S&P 500 Composite Index. The correlation between the price changes for the three indexes (S&P, NYSE, and DJIA) traditionally has been very high: on the order of 0.90.
2. Regardless of the close relationships among the indexes over long periods, the DJIA will show significantly different percentage changes over shorter intervals of time, such as a year.

Example 4-8   In 1995, the DJIA showed a total return of 36.53 percent and the S&P 500 showed a very similar return, 37.11 percent. However, for 1998, the Dow showed a return of 18.01 percent, whereas the S&P 500 showed a return of 28.34 percent. The same was true for 1997: 24.75 percent for the Dow and 33.10 percent for the S&P 500.

3. The greatest divergence in market indexes often occurs when comparisons are made between those indexes that involve only NYSE stocks and those that cover other exchanges, or NYSE stocks plus stocks from other exchanges. The Amex Index (described in Appendix 4-A) and the Nasdaq Composite can perform quite differently in certain years relative to indexes such as the S&P 500.

Example 4-9   For 1999, the DJIA gained about 25 percent, whereas the Nasdaq Composite Index gained about 86 percent.

Investors should use the correct index for the purpose at hand:

1. To measure how large stocks are doing, use the S&P 500, the Russell 1000, or the Dow Jones Equity Market Index. Alternatively, use the DJIA but be aware of its potential problems.
2. To measure how Amex or Nasdaq stocks are doing, use the corresponding index.
3. To measure small capitalization stocks, "small-cap" stocks, use the Russell 2000 Index.
4. To measure "mid-cap" stocks, use the S&P 400 Index.
5. To measure the U.S. stock markets in the broadest sense, use the Wilshire 5000 Index (which actually contains 6,500+ stocks)
6. To measure international stocks as broadly as possible, use the Dow Jones World Stock Index. We consider foreign stock market indicators next.

Foreign Stock Market Indicators Stock market indices are available for most foreign markets, but the composition, weighting, and computational procedures vary widely from index to index. This makes it difficult to make comparisons. To deal with these problems, some organizations have constructed their own set of indices on a consistent basis. Certain international indices also are regularly computed.

EAFE Index The Europe, Australia, and Far East Index, a value-weighted index of the equity performance of major foreign markets

A well-known index of foreign stocks is the **EAFE Index**, or the Europe, Australia, and Far East Index. This index, compiled by Morgan Stanley Capital International, is in effect a non-American world index.

Dow Jones World Stock Index A capitalization-weighted index designed to be a comprehensive measure of worldwide stock performance

The **Dow Jones World Stock Index** covers the Pacific Region, Europe, Canada, Mexico, and the United States. It is designed to be a comprehensive measure, and represents approximately 80 percent of the world's stock markets. Unlike the DJIA, the World Stock Index is a capitalization-weighted index. *The Wall Street Journal* calculates and reports the DJ World Stock Index as part of its "Dow Jones Global Indexes" carried daily in the *Journal*. Stock market indexes for all of the major foreign markets are also shown on this page in the *Journal*.

BOND MARKETS

Just as stockholders need good secondary markets to be able to trade stocks and thus preserve their flexibility, bondholders need a viable market in order to sell before maturity.

Otherwise, many investors would be reluctant to tie up their funds for up to 30 years. At the very least, they would demand higher initial yields on bonds, which would hinder raising funds by those who wish to invest productively.

Investors can purchase either new bonds being issued in the primary market or existing bonds outstanding in the secondary market. Yields for the two must be in equilibrium. If IBM's bonds are trading in the secondary market to yield 12 percent over a 20-year period, for example, comparable new IBM bonds will be sold with approximately the same yield.

A few thousand bonds are traded on the NYSE and a very few on the Amex; the prices of many of these bonds can be seen daily in *The Wall Street Journal*. The reported bond volume (par value) for 2002 on the NYSE was approximately $3.7 billion, virtually the same as 1998 volume.

The NYSE has the largest centralized bond market of any exchange. This order-driven bond market features an *Automated Bond System (ABS)*, a fully automated trading system that allows subscribing firms directly to enter and execute bond orders from their own computer terminals. Approximately 92 percent of NYSE bond volume is in nonconvertible debt. All NYSE bonds trade through this Automated Bond System.

Despite the 2,100 bond issues traded on the NYSE and its impressive ABS, *the secondary bond market is primarily an OTC market*, with a large network of dealers making markets in the various bonds. The volume of bond trading in the OTC market dwarfs that of all the exchanges combined.

Investors can buy and sell bonds through their brokers, who in turn trade with bond dealers. Certain features of the bond markets should be noted.

Treasury Bonds U.S. Treasury notes and bonds are widely purchased, held, and traded. The Federal Reserve conducts open-market operations with Treasury securities, resulting in a broad and deep market, with a volume of transactions exceeding that of any other security.[21] Many large banks act as dealers (make markets) in particular issues. Although larger investors can transact directly with these dealers, most investors use their banks and brokers and pay commissions on the order of $30 to $50 per purchase or sale.

Agency Bonds Federal agency securities trade in good secondary markets, with basically the same dealer market and procedures used as in the case of Treasury securities. Larger issues are more easily traded than smaller issues, and recently issued securities are usually more actively traded than those that have been in existence for some time.

Municipal Bonds Despite the fact that the municipal bond market is a $1 trillion plus market in size, municipal securities often have a relatively thin market, with only moderate activity in the secondary market. This is because most bonds are held to maturity and therefore are traded infrequently. Probably fewer than 5 percent of all securities firms maintain an active municipal bond operation.

When individual investors are ready to sell, it may be difficult to find a buyer for just a few bonds unless significant price concessions are made. Investors with less than $50,000 to put into municipals are sometimes advised to buy a unit investment trust, an indirect investing method.[22]

---

[21] The Treasury bond market consists of selected market makers who trade with the open-market desk of the Federal Reserve Bank of New York. These large dealers include the bond departments of several banks.

[22] These are fixed, diversified portfolios of bonds sold in multiples of $1,000 each (with a sales charge of about 4 percent) which pay interest monthly. They are discussed in Chapter 3.

Corporate Bonds Most corporate bonds are traded off the exchanges
dealing in round lots of at least 250 bonds and often larger amounts. This
market behaves independently of the bond trading on the exchanges, where a
collects bids to buy and offers to sell from around the country and executes a trade
a match is made. Although a substantial number of corporate bonds are listed on the
changes, exchange trading in corporate bonds is only a very small part of this market.
Liquidity is not always good for these small transactions, with delays occurring in the
trade, and price concessions often have to be made.

The Changing Bond Market Traditionally, the bond market has not been
friendly to individual investors. Brokerage firms act as dealers and quote a net price to
investors, making it difficult to know if the price is "fair." Bonds do not trade with commissions, since a net price is quoted, and therefore there are no discount bond brokerage
houses. Some discount brokerage firms such as Fidelity and Schwab do carry bond inventories for sale to investors. They collect a fee for bond transactions, but in actuality
they also are collecting a spread between what they paid for the bonds and what they sell
them for.

It has always been difficult for investors to compare bond prices or verify the fairness of the price being paid, because information was not available to do so. The Internet
has changed this situation dramatically, so that investors now have considerable access
to bond information and quotes. In addition to research on bonds and the bond market
(interest rates, yield curves, and so forth), investors can obtain current bond prices for
comparison. Furthermore, investors can now purchase bonds directly. This progress
in the bond market will presumably continue, providing even more access to individual
investors.

Using the Internet

At www.bondsonline.com investors can access over 12,000 current bond offerings of several types, and at www.bondagent.com, investors can access over 10,000 corporate, Treasury, and municipal bonds. At www.ebondtrade.com, investors can purchase mu- nicipals on-line and have them delivered to their bro- kerage account. Investors can trade bonds of all types and buy and sell certificates of deposit (CDs) at www.bondpage.com.

DERIVATIVES MARKETS

We discuss the details of derivatives markets in their respective chapters. At this point,
however, we can note that options trade on the floor of exchanges, such as the Chicago
Board Options Exchange, using a system of market makers. A bid and asked price is
quoted by the market maker, and floor brokers can trade with the market maker or with
other floor brokers.

In contrast, futures contracts are traded on exchanges in designated "pits," using as
a trading mechanism an open-outcry process. Under this system, the pit trader offers to
buy or sell contracts at an offered price and other pit traders are free to transact if they
wish. This open-outcry system is unique in securities trading. There are few sights in the
financial system that can rival frenzied trading activity in a futures market pit.

---

[23] For example, on a typical day, some two-thirds of the issues on the NYSE's bond board do not trade at all, and
a typical trade is less than 15 bonds.

...IES MARKETS

ding of Equities   105

by institutions
nstitutional
omputer
when
...3

...ecurities Markets

...ast 15 to 20 years, the securities markets have been changing rapidly, with many ...anges being expected over the coming years. At least two factors explain why ... underwent such rapid changes. First, institutional investors have different re...nts and often different views from individual investors, and their emergence as ...inant force in the market necessitated significant changes in market structure and ...n. Large-block activity on the NYSE is an indicator of institutional participation.

...e indication of the impact of institutional investors on trading power can be seen ...ining only one institutional investor, mutual funds. In 1985, mutual fund trading was the equivalent of about 15 percent of NYSE volume on a dollar basis. For the last several years, mutual funds have accounted for about 45 percent of the dollar volume traded on the NYSE.

The second factor stimulating a change in our markets was the passage of the Securities Acts Amendments in 1975. This act sought to promote a fully competitive national system of securities trading. Specifically, it called for a **national market system (NMS)**, but it left its final form undefined. The result was the evolution toward some type of national market, but its final form is not mandated and remains undetermined.

Brokers have a legal obligation to obtain the best possible execution for a customer's trades. One aspect of a national market, a central order-routing system, is designed to help investors obtain the best executions possible. This objective is accomplished by electronically routing orders to whatever market is offering the best price to a buyer or a seller. Such a system promotes competition and should lower spreads, because the dealers with the most attractive prices would automatically receive the orders. Brokerage houses, in particular Merrill Lynch, now have electronic systems that search out the best market for a customer's order and send the order to that market quickly.

The **Intermarket Trading System (ITS)** is an electronic communications network for trading shares across markets. It links the NYSE with the Amex, Nasdaq, and several other markets, allowing market professionals to interact whenever the nationwide Consolidated Quotation System shows a better price.[24] In fact, every market in the United States trading listed stocks is subject to the rules governing the ITS. For example, the "trade-through" rule states that ITS members cannot trade a stock at an inferior price if another market has a better price available at that time.

At the end of 2002, 4,718 issues were eligible for trading on ITS. Volume in 2002 increased to 9.5 billion shares.

Nasdaq participants are linked through the Nasdaq InterMarket[SM] with each other and with ITS. This allows them to enter and execute trades in all exchange-listed securities. Customers can choose to send an order directly to the market maker or to an ECN/alternative trading system rather than send orders directly to the exchanges for execution when transacting in exchange-listed securities.

Where do we go from here? More changes will occur, but the final structure of the securities market cannot yet be predicted. The Nasdaq National Market System (NMS) discussed earlier has had a big impact with its system of trading OTC stocks with competitive multiple market makers reporting last-sale data continuously (i.e., real-time trade reporting). Both individual and institutional investors are attracted by the increased visibility of the securities traded in this manner.

ECNs likely will have a big impact on investor trading. As a part of Nasdaq's open architecture, they already account for a significant percentage of Nasdaq trades. However,

National Market System (NMS) The market system for U.S. Securities called for, but left undefined, by the Securities Acts Amendments of 1975

Intermarket Trading System (ITS) A form of a central routing system consisting of a network of terminals linking together several stock exchanges

---

[24] The nine markets are the New York, American, Boston, Chicago, Cincinnati, Pacific, and Philadelphia exchanges, the Chicago Board Options Exchange, and the NASD.

the ECNs have themselves experienced a shakeout, with several mergers occurring because there was not enough order flow to support several ECNs. Instinet and Island now have the bulk of this business. After-hours trading has been slow to develop, and liquidity remains a problem.

An important issue that remains controversial is the role of the NYSE, the dominant secondary market in the United States. Of special concern to many is the nearly 200-year-old specialist system, which the NYSE continues to defend and justify, whereas others criticize it as a system not attuned to the needs of the modern market. The NYSE defends the specialist system vigorously, citing such evidence as the 1987 market crash, when the specialists stayed at their posts to handle orders while many OTC dealers refused to answer the phone.

The Globalization of Securities Markets

As the 1990s began, the move toward around-the-clock trading, which many expected to be the wave of the future, continued, although slowly. The Nasdaq International Market started in 1991, trading OTC stocks early in the morning during regular trading hours in London. Evening sessions for futures trading were started on the Chicago Board of Trade. In mid-1991, the NYSE began two after-hour "crossing sessions," which last from 4:15 PM to 5:30 PM. One session is for individual stocks and the other is for baskets of stocks.

Nasdaq set out to establish international links and build a global market. In the 1990s, it set up Nasdaq Japan on the Osaka Stock Exchange, expecting a growing business there. Unfortunately, the Japanese market sank further in 2000 to 2002 as the technology bust hit worldwide. In mid-2002, following several years of losses, Nasdaq announced the closing of Nasdaq Japan.

Nasdaq still envisions a global stock market with 24-hour trading. Such a market will link Asia, Europe, and the United States. When market conditions improve worldwide, Nasdaq hopes to develop this global market concept further.

Instinet, mentioned earlier in the chapter, is an electronic trading mechanism allowing large investors (primarily institutions) to trade with each other electronically at any hour.[25] This system offers such investors privacy—traders' transactions involve much less disclosure—and low trading costs, because regular brokerage fees do not have to be paid. In addition, institutions are able to negotiate prices electronically with each other.

Through such sources as Instinet, stock prices can change quickly, although the exchanges themselves are closed. The after-hours trading is particularly important when significant news events occur, or when an institutional investor simply is anxious to trade a position. Such activity could, in a few years, lead to the 24-hour trading for stocks such as that which already exists for currencies.

What about bonds? In today's world, bonds increasingly are being traded at all hours around the globe, more so than stocks. The emergence of global offerings means that bonds are traded around the clock and around the world. The U.S. Treasury securities market in particular has become a 24-hour a day marketplace. The result of this global trading in bonds is that bond dealers and investors are having to adopt to the new demands of the marketplace, being available to react and trade at all hours of the day and night. This includes new employees in various locales, expanded hours, and computer terminals in the home.

---

[25] Instinet also offers the Crossing Network, which allows large investors to trade blocks of stock at daily closing prices.

Foreign markets are changing rapidly. Stock markets in London, Frankfurt, and elsewhere in Europe have formed alliances. This is being done to reduce costs and attract business, because electronic trading costs are lower than those on an exchange. The British and French stock markets are almost totally computerized, and other countries are moving in that direction.

Summary

▶ Financial markets include primary markets, where new securities are sold, and secondary markets, where existing securities are traded.

▶ Primary markets involve investment bankers who specialize in selling new securities. They offer the issuer several functions, including advisory, underwriting, and marketing services.

▶ Alternatives to the traditional public placements include private placements.

▶ Secondary markets consist of equity markets, bond markets, and derivative markets.

▶ The three major equity markets are the NYSE and the Amex (both exchanges) and Nasdaq (an electronic market). Brokers act as intermediaries, representing both buyers and sellers; dealers make markets in securities, buying and selling for their own account.

▶ On the New York Stock Exchange (NYSE), which is still the premier secondary market, specialists act to provide a continuous market for NYSE stocks.

▶ The Amex, on which fewer and generally smaller stocks trade, resembles the NYSE in its operations. Several regional exchanges around the country list small companies of limited interest as well as securities traded on the NYSE and Amex.

▶ The Nasdaq Stock Market trades listed securities. Over-the-counter securities are not traded or listed on an organized exchange or market.

▶ The Nasdaq Stock Market is an electronic network of terminals linking together hundreds of market makers who compete for investor orders by buying and selling for their own account.

▶ The Nasdaq National Market System (NMS) offers multiple market makers and up-to-the-minute price information in a format similar to that on the organized exchanges.

▶ Instinet, a network for trading among institutions and brokers, has become the largest computerized brokerage in the world. It offers anonymous trading on any of 16 exchanges worldwide for commissions of about 1¢ per share.

▶ A new trend that has significant implications for the NYSE is internal trading at large institutions with several funds or accounts without the services of a broker.

▶ Investors have become increasingly interested in equity markets around the world, because the United States now accounts for only about one-third of the world's stock market capitalization. Many equity markets exist.

▶ The best-known stock market indicator in the United States is the Dow Jones Industrial Average (DJIA), which is computed from 30 leading industrial stocks. Standard & Poor's 500-stock Composite Index is carried in the popular press, and investors often refer to it as a "good" measure of what the overall market is doing, at least for large NYSE stocks. The National Association of Security Dealers produces 11 indexes in total.

▶ Although some bonds are traded on the NYSE (and to a lesser extent on the Amex) most bond trading occurs in the OTC market (a network of dealers).

▶ Although Treasury bonds and federal agency bonds enjoy broad markets, the markets for municipal bonds and corporate bonds are often less liquid.

▶ Derivatives markets involve options and futures contracts. Puts and calls are traded on option exchanges using market makers, whereas futures contracts are traded in pits using an open-outcry system.

▶ The securities markets are changing rapidly, stimulated by the demands of institutional investors and by the mandate of the Securities Acts Amendments of 1975 to create a national market system (NMS).

▶ Although the exact form NMS might take remains unknown, changes in the securities markets will continue.

▶ Securities markets increasingly are linked globally.

Key Words

Ask quote	Initial public offerings (IPOs)	Over-the-counter (OTC) securities
Auction markets	Instinet (Institutional Network)	Primary market
Blocks	Intermarket Trading System (ITS)	Program trading
Blue-chip stocks	Investment banker	Prospectus
Brokers	Market makers	Secondary market
Dealers (market makers)	Nasdaq Stock Market^{SM} (Nasdaq)	Shelf rule
Dow Jones Industrial Average (DJIA)	Nasdaq National Market	Specialist
Dow Jones World Stock Index	National Association of Securities	Standard & Poor's 500 Composite
EAFE Index	Dealers (NASD)	Index (S&P 500)
Electronic Communications	National market system (NMS)	SuperMontage
Network (ECN)	New York Stock Exchange (NYSE)	Underwrite

Questions

4-1. Discuss the importance of the financial markets to the U.S. economy. Can primary markets exist without secondary markets?

4-2. Discuss the functions of an investment banker.

4-3. Outline the process for a primary offering of securities involving investment bankers.

4-4. Outline the structure of equity markets in the United States. Distinguish between auction markets and negotiated markets.

4-5. In what way is an investment banker similar to a commission broker?

4-6. Explain the role of the specialists, describing the two roles they perform. How do they act to maintain an orderly market?

4-7. Do you think that specialists should be closely monitored and regulated because of their limit books?

4-8. Is there any similarity between an over-the-counter dealer and a specialist on an exchange?

4-9. Explain the difference between NASD and Nasdaq.

4-10. What is an Electronic Communications Network (ECN)? Give an example.

4-11. What are two primary factors accounting for the rapid changes in U.S. securities markets?

4-12. Why role does the Intermarket Trading System (ITS) play in the trading of stocks?

4-13. Outline recent international developments that relate to U.S. financial markets.

4-14. How does the Nasdaq/NMS differ from the conventional OTC market? What are its implications for the future?

4-15. What is the Dow Jones Industrial Average? How does it differ from the S&P 500 Composite Index?

4-16. What is meant by the term *blue-chip stocks*? Cite three examples.

4-17. What is the EAFE Index?

4-18. What is meant by block activity on the NYSE? How important is it on the NYSE?

4-19. What is the NYSE's current situation in terms of global trading?

4-20. What is Instinet? How does it affect the over-the-counter market?

4-21. What is meant by in-house trading? Who is likely to benefit from this activity?

4-22. What is meant by the statement, "The bond market is primarily an OTC market?"

4-23. How is the DJIA biased against growth stocks?

4-24. How has the role of institutional investors as participants in the Nasdaq market changed?

4-25. What does it mean to say an IPO has been underwritten by Merrill Lynch?

Web Resources

For additional resources visit our dynamic Web site located at www.wiley.com/college/jones.

- *A Financial Market Where?*—The focus is on the operations of a low-cost, yet real financial market in Iowa—the Iowa Electronic Markets. Those with limited cash can take advantage of their beliefs in a variety of different delayed delivery contracts.
- Internet Exercises—This chapter discusses the structure of various securities markets. The exercises will take you to the websites of some of the stock exchanges. The exercises will familiarize you with the major stock indices and their construction.
  Exercise 1: Takes the reader to securities exchanges and asks him/her to consider the nature of these markets.
  Exercise 2: Asks the reader to compare traditional securities markets and the non-commercial markets discussed in the Chapter 2 exercises.
  Exercise 3: Takes the reader to some good IPO sites.
  Exercise 4: Discusses the question of how the market reacts to IPOs.
  Exercise 5: Explores the relationships between indices and their component securities.
  Exercise 6: Looks at the weighting of component stocks in the Dow Jones Index.
  Exercise 7: Explores the special nature of the Dow with respect to stock splits.
  Exercise 8: Asks the reader to correlate different indexes.
  Exercise 9: Asks the reader to consider an electronic stock exchange.
  Exercise 10: Introduces ECNs.
  Exercise 11: Asks the reader to explore the SEC website in order to understand the connection between ECNs and fragmentation

- Multiple Choice Self Test
- Appendix 4-A—Stock Market Indexes

Selected References

Factual information concerning major secondary markets can be found in:

NASD Fact Book. Annual. Washington, D.C.: National Association of Securities Dealers, Inc.

New York Stock Exchange, Fact Book. Annual. New York: New York Stock Exchange, Inc. Available on the Web site www.nyse.com.

chapter 5

How Securities Are Traded

Chapter 5 discusses the mechanics of trading securities, which is critical information for every investor. Brokerage firms and their activities are analyzed, as are the types of orders to buy and sell securities and the handling of these orders. The regulation of the securities markets is discussed. Finally, the various aspects of trading securities that investors often encounter are considered.

AFTER READING THIS CHAPTER YOU WILL BE ABLE TO:

▶ Explain brokers' roles and how brokerage firms operate.

▶ Appreciate the changing nature of the securities business.

▶ Understand how orders to buy and sell securities work in the various marketplaces.

▶ Assess the role of regulation in the securities markets.

▶ Understand how margin trading and short selling contribute to investor opportunities.

In Chapter 4, we considered how securities markets are organized. In this chapter, we learn the mechanics of trading securities which investors must know in order to operate successfully in the marketplace. The details of trading, like the organization of securities markets, continue to evolve, although the basic procedures remain the same.

Brokerage Transactions

BROKERAGE FIRMS

In general, it is quite easy for any responsible person to open a brokerage account. An investor selects a broker or brokerage house by personal contact, referral, reputation, and so forth. Member firms of the New York Stock Exchange (NYSE) are supposed to learn certain basic facts about potential customers, but only minimal information is normally required. Actually, personal contact between broker and customer seldom occurs, with transactions being carried out by telephone or by computer.

Customers can choose the type of broker they wish to use. They can be classified according to the services offered and fees charged.

Full-Service Broker A brokerage firm offering a full range of services, including information and advice

Full-Service Brokers Traditionally, brokerage firms offered a variety of services to investors, particularly information and advice. Today, investors can still obtain a wide variety of information on the economy, particular industries, individual companies, and the bond market from **full-service brokers**, including Merrill Lynch, Paine Webber, Morgan Stanley Dean Witter, Salomon Smith Barney, and Prudential. These large retail brokerage firms execute their customers' orders, provide advice and recommendations about securities, and send them publications about individual stocks, industries, bonds, and so forth.

Today's full-service stockbrokers go by different titles, such as financial consultants or investment executives (or simply registered representatives). This change in title reflects the significant changes that have occurred in the industry. Full-service brokerage firms now derive only a small percentage of their revenues from commissions paid by individual investors, a significant change from the past. And the typical full-service stockbroker, whatever he or she is called, now derives less than 50 percent of his or her income from customer commissions. This is why firms such as Merrill Lynch are trying to encourage their brokers to become more like fee-based professionals and less like salespeople.

How do brokers earn the rest of their income? One alternative is to sell mutual funds owned by their own firms. These funds carry a load or sales charge, and the broker selling shares in these funds earns part of this sales charge.

Another alternative involves "principal transactions," or brokerage firms trading for their own accounts. When these firms end up owning shares they really do not want, brokers are often encouraged to sell these securities to their customers, with some additional financial incentives provided. Smart investors, when given a recommendation to buy a security by their broker, ask if the firm has issued a public buy recommendation or if the broker is being compensated to sell this security.

Yet another source of income is the sale of new issues of securities (IPOs), discussed in Chapter 4. Underwriting new issues is generally a profitable activity for brokerage firms, and brokers may have an incentive to steer their customers into the new issues.

Other sources of revenue today that were nonexistent or much smaller in the past include administrative fees resulting from imposing charges on customer accounts. For example, inactive-account, transfer, and maintenance fees may be imposed on customers. By one estimate, Merrill Lynch has earned over $100 million a year in handling fees.

Commissions on products sold by brokers will vary depending on the product. Treasury securities carry a commission of less than 1 percent, whereas a complicated limited partnership carries a commission of 8 percent or more. In some cases, the commission is "transparent" to the investor. For example, with many bonds the commission traditionally is built in, and as a result the investor does not realize that the commission is included. (As noted in Chapter 4, the Internet is changing bond trading for individual investors.)

Example 5-1 A $10,000 purchase of bonds may require an even $10,000 payment by the customer; however, a "spread" of perhaps 2 percent is built into this transaction. The result is that a sale of the same security immediately would net only $9,800.

How much does a typical full-service stockbroker earn? Obviously, annual compensation varies depending on market conditions that lead to more trading or less trading. For example, in one recent year, the average pay was about $117,000, which was actually a drop of 9 percent from the previous year for the approximately 93,000 active brokers. However, this average can be misleading because of the small number of superbrokers who earn $1 million or more. The median brokerage income in the same year, representing the point at which half are above and half are below, was $72,600, a decline of some 19 percent from the previous year. Because of Internet trading, the future may be very different. Meanwhile, severely depressed markets affect brokers' earnings.

Discount Broker A brokerage firm offering execution services at prices typically significantly less than full-line brokerage firms

Discount Brokers Investors can choose to use a **discount broker** who will provide virtually all of the same services except they offer less (or no) advice and publications and will charge less for the execution of trades.[1] Smart investors choose the alternative that is best for them in terms of their own needs. Some investors need and want personal attention and detailed research publications, and are willing to pay in the form of higher brokerage commissions. Others, however, prefer to do their own research, make their own decisions, and pay only for order execution.

Prominent discount brokers include Charles Schwab, Quick & Reilly, and Fidelity Investments. They advertise aggressively, have offices scattered around the country, and are very familiar to many investors. An early 2003 survey of discount brokers by *AAII Journal* (American Association of Individual Investors) reported on 76 discount brokers, 62 of which conducted business on-line.[2] This survey found the following about discount brokers:

1. Commissions vary widely by amount and the manner in which they are determined (e.g., dollar value of the transaction vs. number of shares traded). Those brokers who were primarily on-line brokers tended to charge a flat rate.
2. Some discount brokers offer research information and investment recommendations. The research is typically supplied by an outside source, but some research is done in-house.
3. Many of these firms offer no-load mutual funds to their customers, most of the time at a fee. However, some discounters offer a limited number of funds at no charge to the customer.
4. Many of these firms offer a touch-tone phone system for receiving information and placing trades.
5. Sixty-two of these firms offer on-line trading through the Internet.

---

[1] Some discount brokers do provide research information. This includes standard information supplied to the brokerage from outside sources and customized information generated in-house.
[2] See Jean Henrich, "Discount Broker Survey," *AAII Journal,* January 2003, pp. 15–23.

Example 5-2   Fidelity Investments is one of the largest discount brokers. Fidelity is listed in the survey as primarily an on-line broker, but it also features brokers for investors to speak with as well as a touch-tone phone system.

On-Line Discount Brokers Obviously, in this age of the Internet, an important option for many investors is the on-line discount broker. At the beginning of 2003, according to the survey mentioned above, 62 discount brokers offered trading through the Internet.[3] Of that number, 37 considered themselves primarily on-line firms. Note that the total number of 62 includes the well-known discount brokers such as Schwab, Fidelity, and E*Trade, lesser-known brokerages offering no touch-tone or live broker services (on-line services only), and the on-line component of full-service brokerages such as Merrill Lynch Direct.

Using the Internet

Investors can access a wide range of brokerage firms on the Internet. Fidelity Investments, the giant mutual fund company, offers extensive brokerage services at **www.fidelity.com**. Schwab advertises extensively and can be reached at **www.schwab.com**, and E*Trade can be reached at **www.etrade.com**. An annual survey of discount brokers and the services they offer, as well as net addresses and phone numbers, can be found in the January issue of *AAII Journal*, a very useful publication intended for average individual investors. See **www.aaii.org**. On-line brokers are rated by type of investor at **www.money.com**, and still other ratings are provided at **www.kiplinger.com**. The ratings and information at **www.smartmoney.com** allow investors to select a broker based on the criteria of most importance to them.

Cash Account The most common type of brokerage account in which a customer may make only cash transactions

Obviously, there are employment opportunities in the financial services industry, including brokers, financial services sales agents, financial planners, and so forth. See Box 5-1 for a description of these positions and what they involve.

TYPES OF BROKERAGE ACCOUNTS

Margin Account An account that permits margin trading, requiring $2,000 to open

The most basic type of account is the **cash account**, whereby the customer pays the brokerage house the full price for any securities purchased. Many customers open a **margin account**, which allows the customer to borrow from the brokerage firm to purchase securities. (*Margin* is explained in some detail later in this chapter.) The NYSE requires a minimum margin deposit of $2,000 to open this type of account (regardless of the transaction contemplated).

Asset Management Account Brokerage accounts offering various services for investors, such as investment of cash balances and check-writing privileges

Asset management accounts require a minimum balance to open (from $1,000 to $25,000) and the payment of an annual fee (from zero in the case of a discount brokerage such as Schwab to $100 or more in the case of some of the full-service brokerage firms). All offer automatic reinvestment of the account holders' free credit balances in shares of a money market fund (taxable or nontaxable) or other fund, such as a government securities fund. Money is typically swept daily into such funds, although a minimum balance of $500 or $1,000 may be required.

---

[3] This discussion is based on Jean Henrich, op. cit. "*AAII Computerized Investing*," January/February 2001, pp. 9–21.

BOX 5-1

Would You Like to Work in the Financial Services Industry?

- A college degree and good sales ability are among the most important qualifications for this profession.
- Employment is expected to grow much faster than average due to increasing investment in securities and other financial products.
- Many beginning securities and commodities sales representatives leave the occupation, because they are unable to establish a sufficient clientele; once established, however, these workers have a very strong attachment to their occupation because of high earnings and the considerable investment in training.

Securities and commodities sales representatives, also called brokers, stockbrokers, registered representatives, account executives, or financial consultants, perform a variety of tasks depending on their specific job duties. The most important part of a sales representative's job is finding clients and building a customer base. Thus, beginning securities and commodities sales representatives spend much of their time searching for customers—relying heavily on telephone solicitation.

Financial services sales representatives sell banking and related services. They contact potential customers to explain their services and to ascertain customers' banking and other financial needs. In doing so, they discuss services such as deposit accounts, lines of credit, sales or inventory financing, certificates of deposit, cash management, or investment services. They may also solicit businesses to participate in consumer credit card programs. As banks offer more and increasingly complex financial services—for example, securities brokerage and financial planning—financial services sales representatives assume greater importance.

Also included in this occupation are financial planners, who use their knowledge of tax and investment strategies, securities, insurance, pension plans, and real estate to develop and implement financial plans for individuals and businesses. Planners interview clients to determine their assets, liabilities, cash flow, insurance coverage, tax status, and financial objectives. They then analyze this information and develop a financial plan tailored to each client's needs. Planners may also sell financial products, such as stocks, bonds, mutual funds, and insurance, or refer clients to other resources.

Most securities and commodities sales representatives work in offices under fairly stressful conditions. They have access to "quote boards" or computer terminals that continually provide information on the prices of securities. When sales activity increases, perhaps due to unanticipated changes in the economy, the pace can become very hectic.

Established securities and commodities sales representatives usually work a standard 40-hour week. Beginners who are seeking customers may work longer hours. New brokers spend a great deal of time learning the firm's products and services and studying for exams to qualify them to sell other products, such as insurance and commodities. Most securities and commodities sales representatives accommodate customers by meeting with them in the evenings or on weekends.

A growing number of securities and commodities sales representatives, employed mostly by discount brokerage firms, work in call center environments. In these centers, hundreds of representatives spend much of the day on the telephone taking orders from clients or offering advice and information on different securities. Often these call centers operate 24 hours a day, requiring representatives to work in shifts.

Financial services sales representatives normally work 40 hours a week in a comfortable, less stressful office environment. They may spend considerable time outside the office meeting with present and prospective clients, attending civic functions, and participating in trade association meetings. Some financial services sales representatives work exclusively inside banks, providing service to "walk-in" customers.

Financial planners work in offices or out of their homes. They usually work standard business hours, but they often have to visit clients in the evenings or on weekends. Many teach evening classes or put on seminars in order to bring in more clients.

Many employers consider personal qualities and skills more important than academic training. Employers seek applicants who have considerable sales ability, good interpersonal and communication skills, and a strong desire to succeed. Some employers also make sure that applicants have a good credit history and a clean record. Self-confidence and an ability to handle frequent rejections are also important ingredients for success.

Because maturity and the ability to work independently are important, many employers prefer to hire those who have achieved success in other jobs. Some firms prefer candidates with sales experience, particularly those who have worked on commission in areas such as real estate or insurance. Therefore, most entrants to this occupation transfer from other jobs. Some begin working as securities and commodities sales representatives following retirement from other fields.

(continued)

Before beginners can qualify as registered representatives, they must pass the General Securities Registered Representative Examination (Series 7 exam), administered by the NASD, and be an employee of a registered firm for at least 4 months. Most states require a second examination—the Uniform Securities Agents State Law Examination.

Banks and other credit institutions prefer to hire college graduates for financial services sales jobs. A business administration degree with a specialization in finance or a liberal arts degree including courses in accounting, economics, and marketing serves as excellent preparation for this job.

In contrast to securities brokers, financial services sales representatives primarily learn their jobs through on-the-job training under the supervision of bank officers. Outstanding performance can lead to promotion to managerial positions.

There are no formal educational or licensure requirements for becoming a financial planner, but a license is required to offer advice or sell specific securities, mutual funds, or insurance products. And although a college education is not necessary to become a financial planner, the vast majority of planners have a bachelor's or master's degree. Courses in accounting, business administration, economics, and finance are particularly helpful.

Many planners also find it worthwhile to obtain a Certified Financial Planner (CFP) or Chartered Financial Consul-

tant (ChFC) designation. These designations demonstrate to potential customers that a planner has extensive training and competency in the area of financial planning.

Even in good times, turnover is relatively high for beginning brokers who are unable to establish a sizable clientele. Once established, though, securities and commodities sales representatives have a very strong attachment to their occupation because of high earnings and the considerable investment in training. Competition is usually intense, especially in larger companies, with more applicants than jobs. Opportunities for beginning brokers should be better in smaller firms.

The number of financial services sales representatives in banks will increase faster than average as banks attempt to become a "one-stop-shop" for investing. Deregulation will allow banks to offer an increasing array of services, such as stocks and insurance, that they have been prevented from offering in the past. Financial planners can also be expected to grow faster than average as an increasingly wealthy population seeks advice on tax and estate planning, retirement planning, and investing.

Source: Excerpted from the U.S. Department of Labor, Bureau of Labor Statistics, *Occupational Outlook Handbook*, as shown on the Web site of the Department of Labor, www.bls.gov.

Account holders are issued bank checks and a bank card. Checks can be written against the account's assets, and the checking account is no minimum, no fee. In addition, instant loans based on the marginable securities in the account can be obtained for virtually any purpose, not just securities transactions, at the current broker's call money rate plus 0.75 to 2.25 percent. For example, if you write a check for $10,000 against your account and your money market fund contains only $5,000, you will automatically borrow the other $5,000. Each month the customer receives a comprehensive summary statement.

Wrap Accounts Brokers can act as middlemen, matching clients with independent money managers. Using the broker as a consultant, the client chooses an outside money manager from a list provided by the broker. Under this **wrap account**, all costs—the cost of the broker-consultant and money manager, all transactions costs, custody fees, and the cost of detailed performance reports—are wrapped in one fee. For stocks, the fee is 1 to 3 percent of the assets managed.[4] For so-called "consultant wraps" involving the placement of client funds with institutional money managers, the average annual fee is 2.1 percent.

Large brokerage houses such as Merrill Lynch pioneered wrap accounts for investors with a minimum of $100,000 to commit. Merrill Lynch now offers five different types of wrap programs ranging from the traditional consultant wrap to a program where the investor makes the buy and sell decisions and can have unlimited no-commission

Wrap Account A newer type of brokerage account in which all costs are wrapped in one fee

---

[4] Fees are lower for bond portfolios or combinations of stocks and bonds.

trading. Because of their popularity, other financial companies such as bank trusts have begun offering these accounts.

A newer variation of wrap programs is the mutual fund wrap account involving an investment in various mutual funds. Minimum account size requirements are more modest at $10,000 to $100,000. A few mutual fund companies such as Fidelity participate in this market directly. Fees average 1.1 to 1.4 percent of assets. Mutual fund wrap accounts are based on an asset-allocation model that is updated quarterly to account for market conditions and client needs. The adviser may decide, for example, to shift some funds from bonds to stocks.

COMMISSIONS

For most of its long history, the NYSE required its members to charge fixed (and minimum) commissions.[5] Although this requirement was a source of bitter contention and gave rise to the third market, or off-the-market trading, little changed until 1975, when Congress, as part of the Securities Acts Amendments of 1975, eliminated all fixed commissions. Fees are supposed to be negotiated, with each firm free to act independently. Customers are free to shop around, and smart ones do so, because according to a survey by the National Council of Individual Investors, the difference in commissions among major firms can exceed 600 percent.

Brokerage costs for individual investors have changed rapidly because of competition and the rise of the Internet. Commissions charged by full-service brokers will presumably reflect the more extensive services offered by them. Commissions charged by discount brokers can vary from $10 or so to $30 or so depending on the type of trade (market order or limit order), how the order is placed, and other details.

Negotiated rates are the norm for institutional customers, who deal in large blocks of stock. The rates charged institutional investors have declined drastically from an average of 25¢ a share in 1975 to an average of only a very few cents a share for exchange-listed stocks. Institutional investors also receive a better deal when trading in over-the-counter (OTC) stocks.

INVESTING WITHOUT A BROKER

Dividend Reinvestment Plan (DRIP) A plan offered by a company whereby stockholders can reinvest dividends in additional shares of stock at no cost

Many companies now offer **dividend reinvestment plans (DRIPs)**. For investors enrolled in these plans, the company uses the dividends paid on shares owned to purchase additional shares, either full or fractional. Typically, no brokerage or administrative fees are involved. The advantages of such plans include dollar cost averaging, whereby more shares are purchased when the stock price is low than when it is high.

In order to be in a company's DRIP, investors often buy the stock through their brokers, although some companies sell directly to individuals. On becoming stockholders, investors can join the dividend reinvestment program and invest additional cash at specified intervals.

DRIPs are starting to resemble brokerage accounts. Investors can purchase additional shares by having money withdrawn from bank accounts periodically, and shares can even be redeemed by phone at many companies.

It is possible to invest in the market without a stockbroker or a brokerage account in the traditional sense. As an outgrowth of their DRIPs, a number of companies now offer *direct stock purchase plans* (DSPPs) to first-time investors.

---

[5] Technically, this is price fixing and therefore illegal, but the NYSE was exempted from prosecution under the antitrust laws.

Example 5-3 Exxon permits investors to buy up to $8,000 a month worth of Exxon stock from the company itself with no commissions. Investors can open a direct-purchase account with Exxon with as small an investment in Exxon stock as $250. Other companies that offer similar plans include Texaco, Mobil, Kroger, Sears, Procter & Gamble, and Home Depot.

Investors make their initial purchase of stock directly from the company for purchase fees ranging from zero to about 7¢ a share. The price paid typically is based on the closing price of the stock on designated dates, and no limit orders are allowed. The companies selling stock by this method view it as a way to raise capital without underwriting fees and as a way to build goodwill with investors.

Treasury bond buyers can also avoid brokers by using the *Treasury Direct Program*. Investors can buy or sell Treasuries by phone or Internet, check account balances, reinvest Treasuries as they mature, and get the forms necessary to sell Treasuries. Investors eliminate brokerage commissions, but some fees are involved ($34 per security sold and, in some cases, a $25 account fee).[6]

Using the Internet

See www.dripcentral.com for complete information on DRIP plans and the companies offering them. Also see www.netstockdirect.com for specifics on companies offering plans. The Motley Fool has information on DRIPs.

How Orders Work

ORDERS ON THE ORGANIZED EXCHANGES

The NYSE is often called an agency auction market. That is, agents represent the public at an auction where the interactions of buyers and sellers determine the price of stocks traded on the NYSE. Brokers and specialists are necessary for the trading of securities on the organized exchanges.

Example 5-4 Assume an investor places an order to buy or sell shares of an NYSE-listed company and that the brokerage firm transmits the order to the NYSE trading floor. The Common Message Switch/SuperDot system used by the NYSE will transmit the order to either a broker's booth or directly to the specialist assigned to that stock. Having received the order, the firm's floor broker would take the order to the trading post, compete for the best price, and make the trade. The specialist will expose the order and make the trade, and will seek the best price for the customer. Upon completion of the trade, a report is sent back to the originating brokerage firm and to the Consolidated Tape Displays worldwide. The brokerage firm processes the transaction electronically, settling the investor's account.

NYSE trades appear on the NYSE consolidated tape, which prints transactions for all NYSE-listed securities on participating markets. This involves several stock exchanges (in

---

[6] Treasury Direct can be reached at 800–943–6864 or www.publicdebt.treas.gov.

addition to the NYSE), Nasdaq, and Instinet. Daily papers such as *The Wall Street Journal* report the high and low prices for each stock wherever they occur.[7]

The role of the specialist is critical on an auction market such as the NYSE. Also referred to as NYSE-assigned dealers by the NYSE and representing a system nearly 200 years old on the NYSE, specialists are expected to maintain a fair and orderly market in those stocks assigned to them. They act as both brokers and dealers.

- As brokers, specialists maintain the limit book, which records all limit orders, or orders that investors have placed to buy or sell a security at a specific price (or better) and that will not be executed until that price is reached. The commission brokers leave the limit orders with the specialist to be filled when possible; therefore, the specialist receives part of the broker's fee.
- As dealers, specialists buy and sell shares of their assigned stock(s) to maintain an orderly market. The stock exchanges function essentially as a continuous market, assuring investors that they can almost always buy and sell a particular security at some price. Assuming that public orders do not arrive at the same time so that they can be matched, the specialist will buy from commission brokers with orders to sell and will sell to those with orders to buy, hoping to profit by a favorable spread between the two sides.

Since specialists are charged by the NYSE with maintaining a continuous, orderly market in their assigned stocks, they often must go "against the market," which requires adequate capital. The NYSE demands that specialists be able to assume a position of 5,000 shares in their assigned stocks.[8] However, the NYSE does not require specialists to fund all the liquidity for the market at a particular time, and these stabilization trades are only a small part of total trading.

Most of the NYSE volume results from public orders interacting directly with other public orders. Using NYSE data, in 2002 specialist participation, measured as the total shares bought and sold by specialists divided by twice total volume accounted for about 15 percent of the share volume traded. This implies that 85 percent of share volume resulted from public and member firm orders meeting directly in the NYSE market.[9] It is important to note that specialists are not on both sides of any trade.

How well does the system work? According to NYSE figures, in 2002, some 98.9 percent of all transactions occurred with no change in price or within the minimum change permissible on the NYSE. The quotation spread between bid and asked prices was 25 cents or less in 98 percent of NYSE quotes. As an indication of market depth, for volume of 3,000 shares or more, the average stock price showed no change, or one-eighth point change, 91 percent of the time.[10]

---

[7] An investor needs to realize that a limit order placed to sell a stock at, say, 101.25 may not have been executed, although the quotes from yesterday's trading in today's paper show a price of 101.25 as the high. This will happen if the investor's broker placed the order on the NYSE, but the stock's high was reached on the Pacific Stock Exchange, for example.

[8] Specialists must be approved by the Board of Governors of the NYSE and must have experience, ability as dealers, and specified minimum capital.

[9] According to the *NYSE Fact Book*, no more than 45 percent of NYSE volume involved a member firm as principal in one recent year.

[10] A recent study suggests that NYSE specialists regularly choose not to inform traders on the exchange about the highest bids and lowest offers that have been received. According to a study by Robert Wood and Thomas McInish of Memphis State University, approximately half of the time specialists opted not to announce this information on the consolidated tape, which is relied on by traders of the NYSE. Specialists are not required to announce the best bids and offers on the tape. Because traders on the floor of the NYSE can learn this additional information by talking with the specialists, some believe that traders on the regional exchanges and other outsiders are at a disadvantage. See Robert Steiner and Kevin G. Salwen, "Stock Specialists Often Keep Best Quotes to Themselves," *The Wall Street Journal*, May 8, 1992, p. C1.

SuperDot An electronic order-routing system for NYSE-listed securities

Automation of the NYSE Given the volume of shares handled by the NYSE, trading must be highly automated.[11] About 93 percent of orders and almost half of the volume are handled electronically. An electronic system matches buy and sell orders entered before the market opens, setting the opening price of a stock. **SuperDot** is the electronic order-routing system for NYSE-listed securities. Member firms send orders directly to the specialist post where the securities are traded, and confirmation of trading is returned directly to the member firm over the same system. The system's peak capacity has been increased to an order-processing capability of 2 billion shares per day.

As part of SuperDot, the *Opening Automated Report Service (OARS)* automatically and continuously scans the member firms' preopening buy and sell orders, pairing buy and sell orders and presenting the imbalance to the specialist up to the opening of a stock. This helps the specialist to determine the opening price. OARS handles preopening market orders up to 30,099 shares.

SuperDot also includes a postopening market order system designed to accept postopening market orders of up to 3 million shares. These market orders are executed and reported back to the member firm sending the order within 17 second on average.

The specialist's volume-handling and volume-processing capabilities have been enhanced electronically by creating the Specialist's Display Book, which is yet another part of the SuperDot system. This database system assists in recording and reporting limit and market orders. Not only does it help to eliminate paperwork and processing errors, but also it now handles about 98 percent of all SuperDot orders.[12]

The NYSE now allows large institutional investors to avoid trading on the floor of the exchange under certain conditions. The "clean-cross" rule now permits brokers to arrange trades of 25,000 shares or more between customers without considering orders at the same price from other investors on the NYSE floor. However, orders at a better price would have to be accepted.

Financial markets are changing as new techniques and processes are developed. Electronic Communications Networks (ECNs) are an obvious example. Long-standing institutions such as the NYSE must also change, and it is doing so.

Using the Internet

You can obtain a good understanding of the NYSE trading floor at **www.nyse.com/floor/floor.html**. Click on "The Trading Floor" and try the various segments to see how an order is handled.

ORDERS IN THE NASDAQ STOCK MARKET

Market makers (dealers) match the forces of supply and demand, with each market maker making a market in certain securities. They do this by standing ready to buy a particular security from a seller or to sell it to a buyer. As explained in Chapter 4, market makers quote bid and asked prices for each security. The dealer profits from the spread between these two prices.

Assume you place an order for a Nasdaq stock. The brokerage firm will forward it to one of several market maker firms for that stock (Nasdaq averages about 11 market makers per security). These market makers are constantly buying and selling shares and earning the spread, which is the compensation for acting as a middleman. In effect, they are

---

[11] The same is true for the Amex.
[12] This information is based on various *NYSE Fact Books* (New York: New York Stock Exchange).

being paid to make the market. Although market makers are expected to execute each order at the best available market price, they are not required to do so.[13]

Actual Order Trading Although the trading of securities is extremely smooth and in general works very well, some troubling practices remain.[14] A Securities and Exchange Commission (SEC) rule requires Nasdaq brokers to post limit orders within 30 seconds, which could help to narrow spreads. But evidence indicates this rule is often violated and that regulators lack the data to determine the compliance rate. Thus, "price improvement" often does not occur, because orders are not posted for all to see.

A more disturbing practice is that of "payment for order flow," whereby brokerage firms are paid to send orders to particular clearing firms. This practice is not prohibited by the SEC. Thus, a broker can charge an investor $8 or $10, a seemingly low fee, but route the order to a market maker who does not have the best quotes, thereby costing the investor. On-line brokerage firms in particular depend upon this practice to make money. Even worse, firms are paid more for market orders than for limit orders, and in turn will charge customers more to place a limit order. Most on-line brokers will not release data on this practice, so investors don't know how often they receive a better or worse price.

Another tactic that may not favor the investor occurs when brokers execute orders in-house rather than on the open market. Although meeting any specified prices from investors, this may prevent investors from receiving even better prices on the open market.

The bottom line is that investors using U.S. financial markets enjoy very good markets with excellent execution, but improvements could be made. As it stands, orders may be executed by exchanges, by market makers, by ECNs, or even internally by the brokerage firm, and investors will not know if they could have received a better price. Brokers pay for order flow, and do not always post prices as required.

DECIMALIZATION OF STOCK PRICES

For its entire history up to 2001, the exchanges and Nasdaq traded stocks based on prices in eighths and sixteenths. This was a tradition that originated in early stock trading and simply continued. It also provided a comfortable spread between bid and ask prices of at least one-eighth of a point, or 12.5 cents. Investors felt that if stocks were traded in decimals, as they are virtually everywhere else in the world, spreads could narrow and they would benefit.

Market Order An order to buy and sell at the best price when the order reaches the trading floor

The NYSE completed the transition to decimals for all securities trading on the NYSE by the end of January 2001. Nasdaq completed its transition the same year. Investors should remember that if they read articles about stocks or see quotes for stocks going back in time, the prices will in all likelihood be in eighths, whereas today's stock prices are in cents. In 2002, the average NYSE volume-weighted spread was 5 cents.

Limit Order An order to buy or sell at a specified (or better) price

TYPES OF ORDERS

Stop Order An order specifying a certain price at which a market order takes effect

Investors use three basic types of orders: **market orders**, **limit orders**, and **stop orders**. Each of these orders is explained in Exhibit 5-1. Today, investors are often advised to enter limit orders whenever possible in order to avoid the range of prices that may result from a market order.

---

[13] Market makers often share some of the profits from the spread with brokerage firms supplying the orders. This is called "payment for order flow."

[14] Some of this information is based on Neil Weinberg and Daniel Kruger, "Death by a Thousand Orders," *Forbes*, December 11, 2000, pp. 262–272.

EXHIBIT 5-1

Types of Orders Used by Investors

1. *Market orders*, the most common type of order, instruct the broker to buy or sell the securities immediately at the best price available. As a representative of the buyer or seller, it is incumbent upon the broker to obtain the best price possible. A market order ensures that the transaction will be carried out, but the exact price at which it will occur is not known until its execution and subsequent confirmation to the customer.

2. *Limit orders* specify a particular price to be met or bettered. They may result in the customer obtaining a better price than with a market order or in no purchase or sale occurring because the market price never reaches the specified limit. The purchase or sale will occur only if the broker obtains that price, or betters it (lower for a purchase, higher for a sale). Limit orders can be tried immediately or left with the broker for a specific time or indefinitely. In turn, the broker leaves the order with the specialist who enters it in the limit book.

   EXAMPLE: Assume the current market price of a stock is $50. An investor might enter a buy limit order at $47; if the stock declines in price to $47, this limit order, which is on the specialist's book, will be executed at $47 or less. Similarly, another investor might enter a sell limit order for this stock at $55; if the price of this stock rises to $55, this investor's shares will be sold.

3. *Stop orders* specify a certain price at which a market order takes effect. For example, a stop order to sell at $50 becomes a market order to sell as soon as the market price reaches (declines to) $50. However, the order may not be filled exactly at $50 because the closest price at which the stock trades may be 49.95. The exact price specified in the stop order is therefore not guaranteed and may not be realized.

   EXAMPLE 1: A sell stop order can be used to protect a profit in the case of a price decline. Assume, for example, that a stock bought at $32 currently trades at $50. The investor does not want to limit additional gains, but may wish to protect against a price decline. To lock in most of the profit, a sell stop order could be placed at $47.

   EXAMPLE 2: A buy stop order could be used to protect a profit from a short sale. Assume an investor sold short at $50, and the current market price of the stock is $32. A buy stop order placed at, say, $36 would protect most of the profit from the short sale.

Investors can enter limit orders as day orders, which are effective for only one day, or as good-until-canceled orders or open orders, which remain in effect for six months unless canceled or renewed.[15] There is no guarantee that all orders will be filled at a particular price limit when that price is reached, because orders are filled in a sequence determined by the rules of the various exchanges. Limit orders for more than one share can be filled in whole or in part until completed (involving more than one trading day) unless the order is specified as *all or none* (fill the whole order or no part of it), *immediate or cancel* (fill the whole order or any part immediately, canceling the balance), or *fill or kill* (fill the entire order immediately or cancel it).

Stop orders are used to buy and sell after a stock reaches a certain price level. A buy stop order is placed above the current market price, whereas a sell stop order is placed below the current price. A stop limit order automatically becomes a limit order when the stop limit price is reached.

A standard order is a round lot, which is 100 shares or a multiple of 100; an odd lot is any number of shares between 1 and 99. Odd lots are now executed by the NYSE directly by computer, and the overall volume of such transactions is small. Some large brokerage firms now handle their own odd lots, and most investors who transact in odd lots are actually transacting with a dealer.

CLEARING PROCEDURES

Most securities are sold on a regular way basis, meaning the settlement date is three business days after the trade date. On the settlement date, the customer becomes the legal owner of any securities bought, or gives them up if sold, and must settle with the brokerage firm by that time. Most customers allow their brokerage firm to keep their securities in a **street name**; that is, the name of the brokerage firm. The customer receives a monthly statement showing his or her position as to cash, securities held, any funds borrowed from the broker, and so on.

Street Name   When customers' securities are held by a brokerage firm in its name

---

[15] A market order remains in effect only for the day.

Use of stock certificates as part of the settlement is dying out in the United States. The Depository Trust Company (DTC) has helped to eliminate their use by placing these transactions on computers. Members (brokers and dealers) who own certificates (in street name) deposit them in an account and can then deliver securities to each other in the form of a bookkeeping entry. This book-entry system, as opposed to the actual physical possession of securities in either registered or "bearer" form, is essential to minimize the tremendous amount of paperwork that would otherwise occur with stock certificates.

Investor Protection in the Securities Markets

Investors should be concerned that securities markets are properly regulated for their protection. Our financial system depends heavily on confidence in that system. In the late nineteenth and early twentieth centuries, significant abuses in securities trading did occur; at the same time, there was a lack of information disclosure and trading procedures were not always sound. The market crash in 1929 and the Great Depression served as catalysts for reforms, which effectively began in the 1930s.

Investor protection can be divided into government regulation, primarily federal, and self-regulation by the industry. Although states also regulate securities transactions, the primary emphasis is on federal regulation, and so we will concentrate on that.

GOVERNMENT REGULATION

Federal Legislation Much of the legislation governing the securities markets and industry was enacted during the Great Depression. Many fraudulent and undesirable practices occurred in the 1920s, and the markets as a whole were shattered in the crash of 1929. Congress subsequently sought to improve the stability and viability of the securities markets, enacting the basis of all securities regulation in the 1930s. Additional acts have been legislated over the last 50 years. Exhibit 5-2 contains a brief description of the major legislation affecting securities markets.

EXHIBIT 5-2

Major Legislation Regulating the Securities Markets

1. The Securities Act of 1933 (the Securities Act) deals primarily with new issues of securities. The intent was to protect potential investors in new securities by requiring issuers to register an issue with full disclosure of information. False information is subject to criminal penalties and lawsuits by purchasers to recover lost funds.

2. The Securities Exchange Act of 1934 (SEA) extended the disclosure requirements to the secondary market and established the SEC to oversee registration and disclosure requirements. Organized exchanges are required to register with the SEC and agree to be governed by existing legislation.

3. The Maloney Act of 1936 extended SEC control to the OTC market. It provides for the self-regulation of OTC dealers through the National Association of Securities Dealers (NASD), which licenses and regulates members of OTC firms. The SEC has authority over the NASD, which must report all its rules to the SEC.

4. The Investment Company Act of 1940 requires investment companies to register with the SEC and provides a regulatory framework within which they must operate. Investment companies are required to disclose considerable information and to follow procedures designed to protect their shareholders. This industry is heavily regulated.

5. The Investment Advisors Act of 1940 requires individuals or firms who sell advice about investments to register with the SEC. Registration connotes only compliance with the law. Almost anyone can become an investment advisor because the SEC cannot deny anyone the right to sell investment advice unless it can demonstrate dishonesty or fraud.

6. The Securities Investor Protection Act of 1970 established the Securities Investor Protection Corporation (SIPC) to act as an insurance company in protecting investors from brokerage firms that fail. Assessments are made against brokerage firms to provide the funds with backup government support available.

7. The Securities Act Amendments of 1975 was a far-reaching piece of legislation, calling for the SEC to move toward the establishment of a national market. This act abolished fixed brokerage commissions.

The Justice Department can investigate alleged abuses in the financial markets. For example, an important development occurred in late 1994 concerning bid and asked prices on Nasdaq. Two professors discovered that actively traded Nasdaq stock spreads were typically quoted in quarters rather than eighths. This finding caused quite an uproar, with the Justice Department looking into the issue of alleged price fixing among brokerage firms on the Nasdaq market. Settlements of such cases vary widely.

Example 5-5

In July 1996, the Justice Department settled a civil agreement whereby the 24 firms involved did not have to admit any violations but did have to agree to obey the law in the future and establish trade-monitoring systems at a cost of $100 million. The Justice Department claims that spreads have narrowed on many of the most actively traded Nasdaq stocks.

The Securities and Exchange Commission In 1934 Congress created the **Securities and Exchange Commission** (SEC) as an independent, quasijudicial agency of the U.S. government. Its mission is to administer laws in the securities field and to protect investors and the public in securities transactions. The commission consists of five members appointed by the president for five-year terms. Its staff consists of lawyers, accountants, security analysts, and others divided into divisions and offices (including nine regional offices). The SEC has approximately 200 examiners.

In general, the SEC administers all securities laws. Thus, under the Securities Act of 1933, the SEC ensures that new securities being offered for public sale are registered with the commission, and under the 1934 act, it does the same for securities trading on national exchanges. The registration of securities in no way ensures that investors purchasing them will not lose money. Registration means only that the issuer has made adequate disclosure. In fact, the SEC has no power to disapprove securities for lack of merit.

Under the two acts of 1940—the Investment Company Act and the Investment Advisors Act—investment companies and investment advisors must register with the SEC and disclose certain information. The SEC ensures that these two groups will meet the requirements of the laws affecting them. One problem, however, is that the number of registered investment advisors increased fourfold in the 1980s to over 16,000 and the number of investment companies increased to some 3,500. The SEC has a staff of only a few hundred to deal with these two groups.

The SEC is required to investigate complaints or indications of violations in securities transactions. As mentioned above, the Justice Department began an antitrust investigation of the Nasdaq Stock Market. The focus was particularly on the spreads—the difference between what buyers pay for a stock and what they sell it for. The SEC launched its own investigation of this and related issues. It forced the National Association of Securities Dealers (NASD) into significant reforms, such as becoming a holding company with two units, the Nasdaq market itself and a separate unit for regulation called NASD Regulation Inc. SEC actions are designed to help investors.

Securities and Exchange Commission (SEC) An agency of the federal government established by the Securities Exchange Act of 1934 to protect investors

Example 5-6

In August 1996, the SEC instituted some new procedures to better protect investors trading in the Nasdaq market. The new rules require dealers to give customers the better prices quoted on such electronic markets as Instinet, discussed in Chapter 4, and to ensure that all investors are fully informed of the best prices offered by market makers.

A well-known illustration of SEC activity involves "insider trading," which has been a primary enforcement emphasis of the SEC. "Insiders" (officers and directors of corporations) are prohibited from misusing (i.e., trading on) corporate information that is not generally available to the public and are required to file reports with the SEC showing their equity holdings.

Several major insider-trading "scandals" have been reported over the years. In the 1980s, Dennis Levine, a key member of the mergers and acquisitions department of Drexel Burnham Lambert, Inc., was charged with insider trading in a major case with many repercussions. Also, a well-known arbitrageur, Ivan Boesky, was fined $100 million by the SEC in a highly publicized insider-trading case. Although questions remain about exactly what constitutes insider trading, small investors can, and are, charged with possessing "material, nonpublic information."

Smaller insider-trading cases occur regularly, primarily as a result of mergers and takeovers. The individuals involved are charged with the use of inside information to trade the stock of a company about to be acquired.

Example 5-7 In 1996, the SEC accused four individuals of gaining illegal profits by trading on inside information in early 1995.[16] The case involved Affymax NV, which at that time was involved in a secret proposed acquisition by Glaxo PLC. One of the accused was the legal assistant to the general counsel of the company and the others were acquaintances or family. Following a typical pattern, at the time of the report, one of the individuals had agreed to settle the charges without admission of guilt by repaying profits plus interest.

Using the Internet

The SEC maintains a well-known database called "EDGAR" (electronic data gathering and retrieval). The SEC requires all filings made by public domestic companies as of May 6, 1996, to be placed in EDGAR, and the SEC posts filings within 24 hours of receipt. Investors can search for companies in multiple ways (e.g., by ticker symbol, type of business, SIC code) at www.sec.gov/edgarhp.htm.

SELF-REGULATION

Regulation of the Stock Exchange Stock exchanges regulate and monitor trading for the benefit of investors and the protection of the financial system. The NYSE in particular has a stringent set of self-regulations and declares that it "provides the most meaningful market regulation in the world." The NYSE regulates itself as part of a combined effort involving the SEC (already discussed) itself and member firms (discussed below). Together, this triad enforces federal legislation and self-regulation for the benefit of the investing public.

During a typical trading day, the NYSE continuously monitors all market participants. It also closely monitors the performance of specialists in their responsibility for maintaining a fair and orderly market in their assigned stocks. NYSE rules and regulations are self-imposed and approved by the SEC.

In response to the market crash in 1987 and a smaller decline in 1989, the NYSE has instituted several measures to reduce market volatility and serve the investors' best interests. Because of the strong rise of the market in 1995 and 1996, the NYSE agreed in late

---

[16] "See Californians Accused of Insider Trading in Purchase of Affymax," *The Wall Street Journal*, September 16, 1996, p. B7.

1996 to revise the trigger points. These safeguards are referred to as "circuit-breakers" and include:

- ❏ Trading Halts. Trading halts occur based on trigger levels of 10, 20, and 30 percent of the Dow Jones Industrial Average (DJIA) using average closing values for the prior month. The halts vary according to conditions and range from 30 minutes to the remainder of the day.
- ❏ Sidecar. A five-minute "sidecar" period occurs when the Standard & Poor's 500 Composite Index (S&P 500) futures contract declines 12 points from the previous day's close. All program trading market orders are sent to a separate file for five minutes, after which buy and sell orders are paired off and are eligible for execution. Trading in a stock is halted if orderly trading cannot resume. The sidecar rule does not apply in the last 35 minutes of trading.
- ❏ Rule 80A. If the DJIA moves 50 points or more from the previous day's close, index arbitrage orders in stocks comprising the S&P 500 Index are subject to a tick test. In down- (up-)markets sell (buy) orders can be executed only on a plus or zero-plus (minus or zero-minus) tick, which was revised in 1999.

The National Association of Securities Dealers (NASD) The National Association of Securities Dealers (NASD) is a trade association established to enhance the self-regulation of the securities industry.[17] Virtually all securities firms are members. The NASD regulates brokers and dealers, thereby protecting investors. All brokers must register with the NASD in order to trade securities, and the NASD keeps records of disciplinary actions taken against stockbrokers and securities firms.[18] Information on individual brokers is available if the broker is currently licensed with the NASD (or was within the last two years). Such information includes employment information, where the broker is licensed to do business, and disclosures involving judgments, investigations, regulatory actions, criminal events, consumer complaints, arbitration proceedings, and so forth. (An investor can also obtain a complete record of customer complaints by calling the state securities board where the broker does business.)

Some Practical Advice

Conflicts between brokers and customers are inevitable, and investors should take steps to protect themselves. Investors can go to nasdr.com (Web site for the NASD) and click on "Check Broker/Advisor Info." under Broker/Advisor Information. State regulators can provide Central Registration Depository reports which offer more disciplinary details than provided by the NASD. Links to state regulators can be found at nasaa.org (Web site for the North American Securities Administrators Association).

Exactly what can the NASD do to members who are suspected of dubious dealings? First, it can bar the individual from association with any NASD member, although having done so, the NASD has no jurisdiction over the individual. Second, the NASD can fine an individual; in one case involving penny stocks, one person was fined almost $2 million. However, these penalties can be appealed to the SEC, which suspends the monetary penalties until resolution.

---

[17] The SEC can revoke the NASD's registration, giving the SEC power over this organization comparable to its powers over exchanges.

[18] Some examples of such actions against both firms and individuals include failing to honor arbitration awards and to maintain minimum required net capital, conducting trades at excessive markups and markdowns, receiving funds from investors without depositing them in an escrow account, and engaging in stock manipulation schemes.

OTHER INVESTOR PROTECTIONS

Insured Brokerage Accounts The Securities Investor Protection Corporation (SIPC), a nonprofit, membership corporation, insures each customer account of member brokers against brokerage firm failure. Each account is covered for as much as $500,000. (Coverage of cash is limited to $100,000.)[19] From its creation by Congress in 1970 through December 2001, SIPC states that it has advanced $513 million in order to make possible the recovery of $13.9 billion in assets for an estimated 622,000 investors. SIPC's figures indicate that more than 99 percent of eligible investors have been made whole in the failed brokerage firm cases that it has handled to date.

Mediation and Arbitration Investors who have disputes with their brokers generally cannot seek relief in court. When they open an account, investors pledge to resolve disputes through mediation or arbitration rather than go to court. When investors have problems, there are three stages of possible resolution.

First, investors can try to solve the problem with the brokerage firm. It is important to file a written claim (not an email), providing as much documentation as possible. Also, the claim should be sent to NASDR (the regulatory arm of the NASD), as well as the investor's state securities regulator (which licenses brokers in a state).

The second stage, particularly where compensation or damages is being sought, is mediation, which is voluntary. NASDR maintains a list of mediators and can appoint one if requested (investors have veto power over the choice of mediator). Mediation decisions are nonbinding.

The last stage is arbitration, which is a binding process that can determine damages. Arbiters can be a person or panel which examines the evidence and makes a ruling. Arbitration is not free, and investors should probably hire a lawyer.

In general, arbitration ruling cannot be appealed. The few exceptions (such as bias by the arbitrator) must be appealed within three months. Finally, litigation is possible, but difficult because of the arbitration clause investors sign. An example of when this might occur would be cases alleging broker fraud. Suit must be filed within one year of the alleged incident.

Margin

As previously noted, investor accounts at brokerage houses can be either cash accounts or margin accounts. Opening a margin account requires some deposit of cash or marginable securities. The NYSE requires that member firms establish a minimum deposit of $2,000 or its equivalent in securities for customers opening a margin account, but individual firms may require more. For example, Fidelity Investments requires a customer to have a minimum equity of $5,000 in cash or marginable securities.

With a margin account, the customer can pay part of the total amount due and borrow the remainder from the broker, who in turn typically borrows from a bank to finance customers. The bank charges the broker the "broker call rate," and the broker in turn charges the customer a "margin interest rate," which is the broker call rate plus a percentage added on by the brokerage firm.[20]

---

[19] In addition, many brokerage firms carry additional insurance, often for several million dollars, to provide even more protection for customers.

[20] One large discount brokerage firm adds 2 percent for margin loans up to $10,000, 1.5 percent for loans up to $25,000, 1 percent for loans up to $50,000, and 0.50 percent for loans above $50,000.

A margin account can be used to:

1. Purchase additional securities by leveraging the value of the eligible shares to buy more.[21]
2. Borrow money from a brokerage account for personal purposes. The margin interest rate is comparable to a bank's prime rate.
3. Provide overdraft protection in amounts up to the loan value of the marginable securities for checks written (or debit card purchases).

Investments Intuition

The traditional appeal of margin trading to investors is that it magnifies any gains on a transaction by the reciprocal of the margin requirement (i.e., 1/margin percentage; for example, with a margin of 40 percent, the magnification is 1/0.4 = 2.50). Unfortunately, the use of margin also magnifies any losses. Regardless of what happens, the margin trader must pay the interest costs on the margin account. An investor considering a margined stock purchase should remember that the stock price can go up, remain the same, or go down. In two of these three cases, the investor loses. Even if the stock rises, the breakeven point is higher by the amount of the interest charges.

Margin That part of a transaction's value that a customer has as equity in the transaction

Margin is that part of a transaction's value that a customer has as equity in the transaction; that is, it is that part of the total value of the transaction that is not borrowed from the broker. Cash has 100 percent loan value, and stock securities have 50 percent loan value. Other securities have differing amounts.

Initial Margin That part of a transaction's value the customer must pay to initiate the transaction, with the other part being borrowed from the broker

The Board of Governors of the Federal Reserve System (Fed), using Regulation T, has the authority to specify the **initial margin**, which is used as a policy device to influence the economy. Historically, the initial margin for stocks has ranged between 40 and 100 percent, with a current level of 50 percent since 1974.[22] The initial margin can be defined as:

$$\text{Initial margin} = \frac{\text{Amount investor puts up}}{\text{Value of the transaction}} \tag{5-1}$$

Example 5-8

If the initial margin requirement is 50 percent on a $10,000 transaction (100 shares at $100 per share), the customer must put up $5,000, borrowing $5,000 from the broker.[23] The customer could put up $5,000 in cash or by depositing $10,000 in marginable securities.

Maintenance Margin The percentage of a security's value that must be on hand as equity

All exchanges and brokers require a **maintenance margin** below which the actual margin cannot go. The NYSE requires an investor to maintain an equity of 25 percent of the market value of any securities held (and in practice brokers usually require 30 percent or more) on long positions.

As the stock price changes, the investor's equity changes. This is calculated as the market value of the collateral stock minus the amount borrowed. The market value of the stock is equal to the current market price multiplied by the number of shares.

---

[21] Starting in 1990, brokers can extend credit on certain foreign equity and corporate debt securities.
[22] Exchanges and brokerage houses can require more initial margin than that set by the Fed if they choose.
[23] With a 60 percent requirement, the customer must initially put up $6,000.

If the investor's equity exceeds the initial margin, the excess margin can be withdrawn from the account, or more stock can be purchased without additional cash. Conversely, if the investor's equity declines below the initial margin, problems can arise depending on the amount of the decline. It is at this point that the maintenance margin must be considered.

Example 5-9

Assume that the maintenance margin is 30 percent, with a 50 percent initial margin, and that the price of the stock declines from $100 to $90 per share. Equation 5-2 is used to calculate actual margin.[24]

$$\text{Actual margin} = \frac{\text{Current value of securities} - \text{Amount borrowed}}{\text{Current value of securities}} \qquad \textbf{(5-2)}$$

$$44.44\% = (\$9,000 - \$5,000)/\$9,000$$

The actual margin is now between the initial margin of 50 percent and the maintenance margin of 30 percent. This could result in a restricted account, meaning that additional margin purchases are prohibited, although the customer does not have to put additional equity (cash) into the account.

Margin Call A demand from the broker for additional cash or securities as a result of the actual margin declining below the maintenance margin

Brokerage houses calculate the actual margin in their customers' accounts daily to determine whether a margin call is required. This is known as having the brokerage accounts marked to market.

A **margin call** (maintenance call or "house call") occurs when the market value of the margined securities less the debit balance (amount owed) of the margin account declines below the maintenance requirement set by the brokerage house (typically 30 percent on stocks). This type of call is payable on demand, and the brokerage house may reserve the right to take action without notice if market conditions are deteriorating badly enough.

Example 5-10

Assume in the previous example that the maintenance margin is 30 percent. If the price of the stock drops to $80, the actual margin will be 37.5 percent [($8,000 − $5,000)/$8,000]. Because this is above the maintenance margin, there is no margin call. However, if the price of the stock declines to $66.66, the actual margin will be 25 percent [($6,666 − $5,000)/$6,666]. This results in a maintenance call to restore the investor's equity to the minimum maintenance margin.

The price at which a margin call (MC) will be issued can be calculated as:

$$\text{MC price} = \frac{\text{Amount borrowed}}{\text{Number of shares } (1 - \text{maintenance margin percentage})} \qquad \textbf{(5-3)}$$

where the MC price equals the price of the stock that triggers a margin call.

Example 5-11

Using the above data, for 100 shares, $5,000 borrowed, and a maintenance margin of 30 percent, a margin call (MC) will be issued when the price is:

$$\text{MC price} = \frac{\$5,000}{100 \,(1 - 0.30)}$$

$$= \$71.43$$

---

[24] The difference between the market value of the securities and the amount borrowed is the investor's equity.

Appendix 5-A contains detailed examples of margin calculations. Included are examples of what happens when an investor is on margin as well as examples of satisfying a margin call.

Although the initial margin requirement for common stocks and convertible bonds is 50 percent, it is only 30 percent (or less) of market value for "acceptable" municipal and corporate bonds.[25] U.S. government securities and Government National Mortgage Associations (GNMAs) require an initial margin of only 8 to 15 percent, whereas Treasury bills may require only 1 percent of market value.

Although the initial margin requirement for common stocks is 50 percent, and that is how virtually all investors think of it, the margin option does not have to be fully employed. That is, investors could limit their borrowing to one-third of their account, in which case, the value of the account could decline 50 percent before a margin call was issued. With borrowing limited to 20 percent of the account, the value of the account could decline 70 percent before a margin call occurred. Particularly in the latter situation, an investor would have an extremely low probability of ever encountering a margin call.

Short Sales

The purchase of a security technically results in the investor being "long" the security.

- ❏ Normal transaction (long the position)—A security is bought and owned because the investor believes the price is likely to rise. Eventually, the security is sold and the position is closed out. First you buy, then you sell.
- ❏ Reverse the transaction (short the position)—What if the investor thinks that the price of a security will decline? If he or she owns it, it might be wise to sell. If the security is not owned, the investor wishing to profit from the expected decline in price can sell the security short. A **short sale** involves selling a security because of a belief that the price will decline, and buying back the security later to close the position. First you sell, then you buy. Having sold first, and before you repurchase, you are "short" the position.

Short Sale The sale of a stock not owned but borrowed in order to take advantage of the expected decline in the price of the stock

How can an investor sell short, which is to say sell something he or she typically does not own? Not owning the security to begin with, the investor will have to borrow from a third party. The broker, on being instructed to sell short, will make these arrangements for this investor by borrowing the security from those held in street name margin accounts and, in effect, lending it to the short seller.[26] Therefore, short selling is simply borrowing a stock, selling it, and replacing it later (hopefully when the price has declined). After all, when you borrow someone's lawnmower or power tools, you are expected to bring them back and replace them.

The short seller's broker sells the borrowed security in the open market, exactly like any other sale, to some investor who wishes to own it. The short seller expects the price of the security to decline. Assume that it does. The short seller instructs the broker to repurchase the security at the currently lower price and cancel the short position (by replacing the borrowed security). The investor profits by the difference between the price at which the borrowed stock was sold and the price at which it was repurchased.

The process of short selling is spelled out in steps in Exhibit 5-3.

---

[25] This may also be stated as a percentage of principal—for example, 10 percent for nonconvertible corporates and 15 percent for municipals.

[26] The securities could be borrowed from another broker. If the lending firm calls back the stock loan, the broker may be forced to close the short position. Also, individuals sometimes agree to lend securities to short sellers in exchange for interest-free loans equal to the collateral value of the securities sold short. Collateral value equals the amount of funds borrowed in a margin transaction.

EXHIBIT 5-3

How Short Selling Works

1. An investor believes that IBM is overpriced at $60 a share and will decline. This investor does not own IBM stock but wishes to profit if her beliefs are correct and the price goes down.

2. You instruct your brokerage firm to short 100 shares of IBM for you, a transaction valued at $6,000 (ignore brokerage costs). The brokerage firm does this by borrowing the 100 shares from another investor's account, lending them to this investor, and selling the shares at the current market price of $6,000.

3. The sale proceeds of $6,000 are credited to your margin account because you sold the stock. The investor must put up 50 percent of the borrowed amount, or $3,000, as initial margin. The investor who sold short is now responsible for paying back 100 shares of IBM stock to replace the 100 shares that were borrowed.

4. Assume the price of IBM goes to $40 three months later. The investor is now ahead $2,000 because she can buy back 100 shares of IBM for $4,000 on the open market and replace the 100 shares she borrowed.

5. Having closed out the short sale, the investor regains access to the $3,000 margin she had to put up.

6. Should the price of IBM rise, the investor has two choices. One, buy the stock back and close out the position, taking a loss. For example, buying back at $70 would result in a loss of $1,000. Two, continue to hold the position and hope the price eventually drops. In the case of a rising stock price for a short position, the investor may face a margin call requiring cash or equivalents equal to 25 to 30 percent of the stock's value. Exact maintenance margin requirements vary by firm.

Example 5-12   Assume an investor named Helen believes that the price of General Motors (GM) will decline over the next few months and wants to profit if her assessment is correct. She calls her broker with instructions to sell 100 shares of GM short (she does not own GM) at its current market price of $50 per share. The broker borrows 100 shares of GM from Kellie, who has a brokerage account with the firm and currently owns GM ("long"). The broker sells the borrowed 100 shares at $50 per share, crediting the $5,000 proceeds (less commissions, which we will ignore for this example) to Helen's account.[27] Six months later, the price of GM has declined, as Helen predicted, and is now $38 per share. Satisfied with this drop in the price of GM, she instructs the broker to purchase 100 shares of GM and close out the short position. Her profit is $5,000 minus $3,800, or $1,200 (again, ignoring commissions). The broker replaces Kellie's missing stock with the just-purchased 100 shares, and the transaction is complete.[28]

Several technicalities are involved in a short sale; these are outlined in Exhibit 5-4. For example, there is no time limit on how long an investor can remain short in a stock, and any dividends paid on the stock during the time the seller is short must be covered by the seller.

Keep in mind that to sell short an investor must be approved for a margin account, because short positions involve the potential for margin calls. Using our earlier example of Fidelity Investments, we see that the initial minimum equity to open a margin account required by Fidelity would be $5,000, the initial margin requirement would be 50 percent of the short sale, and the maintenance margin would be 30 percent of market value (the absolute minimum to open a margin account is $2,000 in cash or securities). Should the

---

[27] Note that Kellie knows nothing about this transaction, nor is she really affected. Kellie receives a monthly statement from the broker showing ownership of 100 shares of GM. Should Kellie wish to sell the GM stock while Helen is short, the broker will simply borrow 100 shares from Elizabeth, a third investor who deals with this firm and owns GM stock, to cover the sale. It is important to note that all of these transactions are book entries and do not typically involve the actual stock certificates.

[28] Notice that two trades are required to complete a transaction, or "round trip." Investors who purchase securities plan to sell them eventually. Investors who sell short plan to buy back eventually; they have simply reversed the normal buy-sell procedure by selling and then buying.

EXHIBIT 5-4

The Details of Short Selling

1. Dividends declared on any stock sold short must be covered by the short seller. After all, the person from whom the shares were borrowed still owns the stock and expects all dividends paid on it.

2. Short sellers must have a margin account to sell short and must put up margin as if they had gone long. The margin can consist of cash or any restricted securities held long.

3. The net proceeds from a short sale, plus the required margin, are held by the broker; thus, no funds are immediately received by the short seller. The lender must be fully protected. To do this, the account is marked-to-the-market (as mentioned earlier in connection with margin accounts). If the price of the stock declines as expected by the short seller, he or she can withdraw the difference between the sale price and the current market price. If the price of the stock rises, however, the short seller will have to put up more funds.

4. There is no time limit on a short sale. Short sellers can remain short indefinitely. The only protection arises when the lender of the securities wants them back. In most cases the broker can borrow elsewhere, but in some situations, such as a thinly capitalized stock, this may not be possible.

5. Short sales are permitted only on rising prices, or an uptick. A short seller can sell short at the last trade price only if that price exceeded the last different price before it. Otherwise, they must wait for an uptick. Although the order to the broker can be placed at any time, it will not be executed until an uptick occurs.

---

price of the security shorted rise, an investor will be required by the broker to put more cash in the account or sell some securities.[29]

Example 5-13

Using the numbers that Fidelity requires, assume an investor shorts 100 shares of Merck at $100 per share. The investor must have $5,000 in the account (initial margin of 50 percent). If Merck rises to $180, the investor must have 30 percent of that, or $5,400 in equity in the account, requiring an additional cash deposit.

Short sellers argue that short sales help the overall market. For example, short sells provide liquidity, and can help smooth out the highs and lows in stock prices. And, of course, there have been long periods in the stock market when prices did not rise but instead fell. During such periods, short selling might be a good strategy for some investors.

Example 5-14

The DJIA was approximately 1000 in 1966. Sixteen years later, in 1982, the Dow was at 800.

How popular are short sales? In 2002, short sales accounted for about 10 percent of all reported volume. NYSE members accounted for about two-thirds of short sales on the NYSE, and the public accounted for the remainder. Specialists, who often sell short to meet public buy orders, accounted for about 40 percent of the members' total.[30]

Short-Interest Ratio
The ratio of total shares sold short to average daily trading volumes.

The **short-interest ratio** is an important possible indicator of how bearish investors are about a stock. It is calculated for a stock by dividing the amount of shares sold short by the average daily trading volume. It indicates the number of days it would take for short sellers to buy back (cover) all of the shares sold short.

---

[29] It is possible for investors to get caught in a "short squeeze." As a stock continues to rise in price, short sellers start buying to cover their positions, pushing the price even higher. Short sellers can actually create significant runups in the stock price, thereby causing the opposite of what they are trying to achieve. Brokers, in turn, may force the short sellers to cover their short positions if the price is rising dramatically. One way for short sellers to protect themselves against this is to use a buy stop-loss order.

[30] Specialists, in their role of maintaining an orderly market, must often sell short to meet an inflow of buy orders.

The short-interest ratio can be interpreted two ways. First, of course, it indicates how bearish investors are about a stock. The higher the ratio, the more bearish they are. On the other hand, a high short-interest ratio is viewed by some as bearish, because it says that more shares must ultimately be repurchased. Nevertheless, a study of the monthly short-interest positions for all NYSE and Amex companies over an 18-year period concluded that there was a strong negative relationship between short interest and subsequent stock returns.[31] This relationship persists over the entire period, and the abnormal returns are even more negative for firms which are heavily shorted for more than one month. This study is clear—short interest conveys negative information.

Why sell short instead of using puts (a derivative security explained in Chapter 2 and in more detail in Chapter 19)? Most stocks do not have publicly traded puts on them, and therefore this is not a possibility. Furthermore, options are a wasting asset—investors must not only be right in their predictions of the movement of the stock price, they must be right in a short period of time. With a short sale, the position can remain open indefinitely.

Although individual investors have often bypassed short selling in the OTC market, this is changing as short selling has become more accessible to them.

Furthermore, investors increasingly recognize that a portfolio consisting of both long and short positions can dampen volatility while still producing good returns. According to one study, a portfolio holding positions that are 65 percent long and 35 percent short is half as volatile as a portfolio that is 100 percent long.[32]

If you are interested in selling stocks short, how do you go about obtaining short-sale recommendations? Investors can do their own analysis or use investment advisory services. As in other areas of investing, the results of those who provide recommendations vary over a wide range.

Summary

- Brokerage firms consist of full-service brokers, discount brokers, and deep-discount brokers.

- Full-service stockbrokers earn their incomes from a variety of sources including individuals' trades, in-house mutual fund sales, principal transactions, new issues, and fees.

- With a cash brokerage account, the customer pays in full on the settlement date, whereas with a margin account money can be borrowed from the broker to finance purchases.

- Asset management accounts offering a variety of services are commonplace, and wrap accounts, where all costs are wrapped in one fee, are increasingly popular.

- Brokerage commissions are negotiable. Full-line brokerage houses charge more than discount brokers but offer recommendations. Some Internet-only discount brokers charge the least.

- Investors can invest without a broker through dividend reinvestment plans. Some companies sell shares directly to investors.

- Most orders sent to the exchanges involve a specialist and are highly automated. Specialists on the NYSE are charged with maintaining a continuous, orderly market in their assigned stocks.

- The NYSE is highly automated, with its SuperDot electronic order-routing system handling much of the routine trading.

- Market orders are executed at the best price available, whereas limit orders specify a particular price to be met or bettered.

---

[31] Paul Asquith and Lisa Meulbroek, An Empirical Investigation of Short Interest, 1999, working paper.
[32] This study is discussed in Pamela Black, "Upside-Down Investing," *Individual Investor*, Special Issue, January 2001, pp. 91–93.

▶ Stop orders specify a certain price at which a market order is to take over.

▶ Investor protection includes government regulation, primarily federal, and self-regulation by the industry. The SEC administers the securities laws.

▶ The NYSE has a stringent set of self-regulations. The NASD regulates brokers and dealers and has significantly improved the functioning of the OTC market.

▶ Margin is the equity an investor has in a transaction. The Federal Reserve sets an initial margin, but all exchanges and brokers require a maintenance margin. The appeal of margin to investors is that it can magnify any gains on a transaction, but it can also magnify losses.

▶ An investor sells short if a security's price is expected to decline. The investor borrows the securities sold short from the broker, hoping to replace them through a later purchase at a lower price.

Key Words

Asset management account

Cash account

Discount broker

Dividend reinvestment plan (DRIP)

Full-service broker

Initial margin

Limit order

Maintenance margin

Margin account

Margin call

Market order

Securities and Exchange Commission (SEC)

Short interest ratio

Short sale

Stop order

Street name

SuperDot

Wrap account

Questions

5-1 Discuss the advantages and disadvantages of a limit order versus a market order. How does a stop order differ from a limit order?

5-2 What is meant by selling securities on a "regular way" basis?

5-3 What are the advantages and disadvantages of using a street name?

5-4 Explain the margin process, distinguishing between initial margin and maintenance margin. Who sets these margins?

5-5 What conditions result in an account being "restricted"? What prompts a margin call?

5-6 How can an investor sell a security that is not currently owned?

5-7 What conditions must be met for an investor to sell short?

5-8 Explain the difference, relative to the current market price of a stock, between the following types of orders: sell limit, buy limit, buy stop, and sell stop.

5-9 What is the margin requirement for U.S. government securities?

5-10 What is a wrap account? How does it involve a change in the traditional role of the broker?

5-11 Distinguish between a large discount broker such as Fidelity and an Internet-only discount broker.

5-12 How can investors invest without a broker?

5-13 Explain the role of a specialist on the NYSE. How can specialists act as both brokers and dealers?

5-14 What is the role of SuperDot on the NYSE?

5-15 What is the difference between a day order and an open order?

5-16 What is the role of the SEC in the regulation of securities markets?

5-17 Who regulates brokers and dealers? What types of actions can be taken against firms and individuals?

5-18 Why are investors interested in having margin accounts? What risk do such accounts involve?

5-19 How popular are short sales relative to all reported sales?

5-20 Explain the basis of regulation of mutual funds. How successful has this regulation been?

5-21 What assurances does the Investment Advisors Act of 1940 provide investors in dealing with people who offer investment advice?

5-22 How could a "circuit-breaker" lead to a trading halt on the NYSE?

5-23 Given the lower brokerage costs charged by discount brokers and deep-discount brokers, why might an investor choose to use a full-service broker?

5-24 What assurances as to the success of a company does the SEC provide investors when an IPO is marketed?

5-25 Contrast the specialist system used on the NYSE and Amex with the dealer system associated with the OTC market.

Problems

5-1   a. Consider an investor who purchased a stock at $100 per share. The current market price is $125. At what price would a limit order be placed to assure a profit of $30 per share?

b. What type of stop order would be placed to ensure a profit of at least $20 per share?

5-2   Assume an investor sells short 200 shares of stock at $75 per share. At what price must the investor cover the short sale in order to realize a gross profit of $5,000? $1,000?

5-3   Assume that an investor buys 100 shares of stock at $50 per share and the stock rises to $60 per share. What is the gross profit, assuming an initial margin requirement of 50 percent? 40 percent? 60 percent?

5-4   Assume an initial margin requirement of 50 percent and a maintenance margin of 30 percent. An investor buys 100 shares of stock on margin at $60 per share. The price of the stock subsequently drops to $50.

a. What is the actual margin at $50?

b. The price now rises to $55. Is the account restricted?

c. If the price declines to $49, is there a margin call?

d. Assume that the price declines to $45. What is the amount of the margin call? At $35?

5-5   You open a margin account at Charles Pigeon, a discount broker. You subsequently short Exciting.com at $286, believing it to be overpriced. This transaction is done on margin, which has an annual interest rate cost of 9 percent. Exactly one year later, Exciting has declined to $54 a share, at which point you cover your short position. You pay brokerage costs of $20 on each transaction you make.

a. Assume the margin requirement is 55 percent. Calculate your dollar gain or loss on this position, taking into account both the margin interest and the transaction costs.

b. Calculate the percentage return on your investment (the amount of money you put up initially, counting the brokerage costs to buy).

5-6   Using your same brokerage account as in Problem 5-5 (same margin rate and transaction costs), assume you buy IBM at $156 a share, on 60 percent margin. During the year IBM pays a dividend of $1.30 per share. One year later you sell the position at $233.

a. Calculate the dollar gain or loss on this position.

b. Calculate the percentage return on your investment.

Web Resources

For additional resources visit our dynamic Web site located at www.wiley.com/college/jones.

- *What's DRIPping?*—The decision-maker learns about direct investing in stocks without paying fees and commissions to brokers. The case is an introduction to direct stock purchase plans and helps the reader understand various plan differences.
- Alternate Case:
- *Lost Coast Investment Club*—The case examines the differences between on-line brokerage accounts and highlights the importance of transaction costs in achieving investment objectives. Website links also help the reader understand brokerage issues and characteristics.
- Internet Exercises—This chapter discusses the mechanics of trading securities and the regulation of securities. Accordingly, the web exercises will engage you in exercises related to issues such as short-selling and trading on margin, as well as the role of the regulator.
  Exercise 1: Introduces the reader to how the NYSE works.
  Exercise 2: Gets the reader to play a NASDAQ market simulation game and introduces concepts about the bid-ask spread.
  Exercise 3: Asks the reader to consider the difference between NASDAQ and NYSE quotes.
  Exercise 4: Discusses the determinants of the bid-ask spread.
  Exercise 5: Introduces short selling.
  Exercise 6: Introduces online discount brokers and asks the reader to compare them by price and by research offerings.
- Multiple Choice Self Test

Selected References

Information on the mechanics of trading appears in most popular press magazines and newspapers, including:

Barron's
Business Week
Forbes
Fortune
Money Magazine
Smart Money
The Wall Street Journal
Worth

Appendix 5-A
THE DETAILS
OF MARGIN ACCOUNTS

We illustrate here the effects of margin using a balance sheet approach. We start with the purchase of 1,000 shares of Merck at $100 a share, a total cost of $100,000. With an initial margin requirement of 50 percent, $50,000 cash is deposited into the account and $50,000 is borrowed from the broker at a rate of 8 percent. The maintenance margin is 30 percent.

I.   The Effects of Being on Margin

DAY 0—The initial balance sheet at the time of purchase is:

Stocks	$100,000	Debt	$50,000
		Equity	$50,000

DAY 1—Assume Merck declines in price from $100 to $90 the next day. The actual margin is now 44.44 percent, calculated using Equation 5-2.

$$\text{Actual margin} = \frac{\text{Market value of securities} - \text{Amount borrowed}}{\text{Market value of securities}}$$

$$= (\$90,000 - \$50,000) / \$90,000 = 44.44\%$$

Because the actual margin of 44.44 percent is greater than the maintenance margin of 30 percent, no action by the investor is required.

The balance sheet on day 1 is:

Stocks	$90,000	Debt	$50,000
		Equity	$40,000

DAY 2—Assume now it is day 2 and Merck drops again, this time to $70. The actual margin is now 28.57 percent [($70,000 − $50,000) / $70,000].

A margin call is issued in this case because the actual margin is now below the maintenance margin of 30 percent.

The balance sheet is now:

Stocks	$70,000	Debt	$50,000
		Equity	$20,000

II.   Methods for Satisfying a Margin Call

Continuing with the example above, assume that the price of Merck is now $70. There are three ways to satisfy the margin call that would be issued.

A. ADD CASH TO THE ACCOUNT AND LEAVE IT IN THE FORM OF CASH

Solve Equation 5-2 to determine the amount of cash needed, based on a 30 percent maintenance margin.

$$30\% = \frac{(\text{cash} + \$70,000) - \$50,000}{\text{Cash} + \$70,000}$$

$$= \$1,428.58$$

Check: ($71,428.58 − $50,000) / $71,428.58 = 30%

The balance sheet is now:

Stocks	$70,000	Debt	$50,000
Cash	$ 1,429	Equity	$21,429

B. ADD CASH TO THE ACCOUNT AND USE IT TO REPAY SOME OF THE LOAN

Solve Equation 5-2 by determining how much to reduce the loan to bring the maintenance margin back to 30 percent.

$$30\% = \frac{\$70,000 - (\$50,000 - \text{cash})}{\$70,000}$$

$$= \$1,000$$

Check: ($70,000 − $49,000) / $70,000 = 30%

The balance sheet is now:

Stocks	$70,000	Debt	$49,000
Cash		Equity	$21,000

C. SELL SHARES AND REPAY A PORTION OF THE LOAN

An investor could sell some of the Merck shares and apply the proceeds to the loan, thereby bringing the maintenance margin back to 30 percent. Once again, solve Equation 5-2.

$$30\% = \frac{(\$70,000 - \text{cash}) - (\$50,000 - \text{cash})}{\$70,000 - \text{cash}}$$

$$= \$3,333.34$$

(48 shares would need to be sold, calculated as $3,333.34 / $70 = 48 [rounded])

Check: ($66,666.66 − $46,666.66) / $66,666.66 = 30%

The balance sheet is now:

Stocks	$66,667	Debt	$46,667
Cash	0	Equity	$20,000

chapter 6

The Returns and Risks from Investing

Chapter 6 analyzes the returns and risks from investing. We learn how well investors have done in the past investing in the major financial assets. Investors need a good understanding of the returns and risk that have been experienced to date before attempting to estimate returns and risk, which they must do as they build and hold portfolios for the future.

AFTER READING THIS CHAPTER YOU WILL BE ABLE TO:

▶ Calculate the return and risk for financial assets using the formulation appropriate for the task.

▶ Use key terms involved with return and risk, including geometric mean, cumulative wealth index, inflation-adjusted returns, and currency-adjusted returns.

▶ Discuss the historical returns on major financial assets.

▶ Understand clearly the returns and risk investors have experienced in the past, an important step in estimating future returns and risk.

The field of Investments traditionally has been divided into security analysis and portfolio management. Parts III, IV, and V discuss security analysis for equity and fixed-income securities. The heart of security analysis is the valuation of financial assets. Value, in turn, is a function of return and risk. These two concepts are, therefore, very important in the study of Investments. In fact, they are the foundation of investment decisions.

Return and risk are described, measured, and estimated throughout the text. Particular forms of these concepts will be used when needed, but before beginning an analysis of the various securities, it is extremely valuable to obtain a working knowledge of return and risk. Therefore, we must consider these concepts and learn how to analyze and measure them. In this chapter, we concentrate on the measurement of *realized* return and risk. In Chapter 7, we consider *expected* return and risk, which leads us into basic portfolio theory.

As we learned in Chapter 1, *realized return* is what the term implies; it is *ex post* (after the fact) return, or return that was or could have been earned. Realized return has occurred and can be measured with the proper data. *Expected return*, on the other hand, is the estimated return from an asset that investors anticipate (expect) they will earn over some future period. As an estimated return, it is subject to uncertainty and may or may not occur.

As explained in Chapter 1, the investment decision can be described as a trade-off between risk and expected return. We will consider this trade-off, which describes the future, in detail in subsequent chapters. Before doing so, however, it is very important to have a perspective on realized returns and risks from investing. How would investors have fared, on average, over the past by investing in the major marketable securities? What are the returns and risk from investing based on the historical record? We answer questions such as these in this chapter.

Although there is no guarantee that the future will be exactly like the past, a knowledge of historical risk-return relationships is a necessary first step for investors in making investment decisions for the future. Furthermore, there is no reason to assume that *relative* relationships will differ significantly in the future. Thus, if stocks have returned more than bonds, and Treasury bonds more than Treasury bills over the entire financial history available, there is every reason to assume that such relationships will continue over the long-run future. Therefore, it is very important for investors to understand what has occurred in the past.

Return

In Chapter 1, we learned that the objective of investors is to maximize expected returns, although they are subject to constraints, primarily risk. Return is the motivating force in the investment process. It is the reward for undertaking the investment.

Returns from investing are crucial to investors; they are what the game of investments is all about. The measurement of realized (historical) returns is necessary for investors to assess how well they have done or how well investment managers have done on their behalf. Furthermore, the historical return plays a large part in estimating future, unknown returns.

THE COMPONENTS OF RETURN

Return on a typical investment consists of two components:

Yield   The income component of a security's return

- ❑ **Yield**: The basic component that usually comes to mind when discussing investing returns is the periodic cash flows (or income) on the investment, either interest or dividends. The distinguishing feature of these payments is that the issuer makes the payments in cash to the holder of the asset.

■ **Yield** measures relate these cash flows to a price for the security, such as the purchase price or the current market price.

Capital Gain (Loss)
The change in price of a security over some period of time

■ **Capital gain (loss):** The second component is also important, particularly for common stocks but also for long-term bonds and other fixed-income securities. This component is the appreciation (or depreciation) in the price of the asset, commonly called the **capital gain (loss)**. We will refer to it simply as the price change. In the case of a long position, it is the difference between the purchase price and the price at which the asset can be, or is, sold; for a short position, it is the difference between the sale price and the subsequent price at which the short position is closed out. In either case, a gain or a loss can occur.[1]

Given the two components of a security's return, we need to add them together (algebraically) to form the total return, which for any security is defined as:

Total return = Yield + Price change   (6-1)

where: the yield component can be 0 or +

the price change component can be 0, +, or −

Example 6-1

A bond purchased at par ($1,000) and held to maturity provides a yield in the form of a stream of cash flows or interest payments but no price change. A bond purchased for $800 and held to maturity provides both a yield (the interest payments) and a price change: in this case a gain. The purchase of a nondividend-paying stock, such as Dell Computer, that is sold six months later produces either a capital gain or a capital loss but no income. A dividend-paying stock, such as IBM, produces both a yield component and a price change component (a realized or unrealized capital gain or loss).

Equation 6-1 is a conceptual statement for the total return for any security. The important point here is that any security's total return consists of the sum of two components: yield and price change. Investors' returns from financial assets can come only from these two components—an income component (the yield) and/or a price change component regardless of the asset. Investors sometimes focus on the yield component of their investments rather than the total return, and mistakenly assume they are achieving acceptable performance when they are not.

Example 6-2

Consider the following example based on actual market performance. At the beginning of 2001, a $500,000 portfolio was invested 50 percent in stocks (the Wilshire 5000 index) and half in bonds (the Lehman Aggregate Bond Index). At the end of the year, this portfolio had yielded about $19,000 in dividends and interest. However, because of the declining stock market, the value of the portfolio at the end of the year was about $475,000. Therefore, the capital loss exceeded the yield, resulting in a negative total return.

[1] This component involves only the difference between the beginning price and the ending price in the transaction. An investor can purchase or short an asset and close out the position one day, one hour, or one minute later for a capital gain or loss. Furthermore, gains can be realized or unrealized. See Appendix 2-A for more discussion on capital gains and losses and their taxation.

Risk

It is not sensible to talk about investment returns without talking about risk, because investment decisions involve a trade-off between the two—*return and risk are opposite sides of the same coin*. Investors must constantly be aware of the risk they are assuming, know what it can do to their investment decisions, and be prepared for the consequences.

Risk was defined in Chapter 1 as the chance that the actual outcome from an investment will differ from the expected outcome. Specifically, most investors are concerned that the actual outcome will be less than the expected outcome. The more variable the possible outcomes that can occur (i.e., the broader the range of possible outcomes), the greater the risk.

Investors should be willing to purchase a particular asset if the expected return is adequate to compensate for the risk, but they must understand that their expectation about the asset's return may not materialize. If not, the realized return will differ from the expected return. In fact, realized returns on securities show considerable variability—sometimes they are larger than expected, and other times they are smaller than expected, or even negative. Although investors may receive their expected returns on risky securities on a long-run average basis, they often fail to do so on a short-run basis.

Investments Intuition

It is important to remember how risk and return go together when investing. An investor cannot reasonably *expect* larger returns without being willing to assume larger risks. Consider the investor who wishes to avoid any practical risk on a nominal basis. Such an investor can deposit money in an insured savings account, thereby earning a guaranteed return of a known amount. However, this return will be fixed, and the investor cannot earn more than this rate. Although risk is effectively eliminated, the chance of earning a larger return is also removed. To have the opportunity to earn a return larger than the savings account provides, investors must be willing to assume risks—and when they do so, they may gain a larger return, but they may also lose money.

SOURCES OF RISK

What makes a financial asset risky? Traditionally, investors have talked about several sources of total risk, such as interest rate risk and market risk, which are explained below, because these terms are used so widely. Following this discussion, we will define the modern portfolio sources of risk, which will be used later when we discuss portfolio and capital market theory.

Interest Rate Risk   The variability in a security's returns resulting from changes in the level of interest rates is referred to as **interest rate risk**. Such changes generally affect securities inversely; that is, other things being equal, security prices move inversely to interest rates.[2] Interest rate risk affects bonds more directly than common stocks, but it affects both and is a very important consideration for most investors.

Market Risk   The variability in returns resulting from fluctuations in the overall market—that is, the aggregate stock market—is referred to as **market risk**. All securities are exposed to market risk, although it affects primarily common stocks.

Interest Rate Risk   The variability in a security's returns resulting from changes in interest rates

Market Risk   The variability in a security's returns resulting from fluctuations in the aggregate market

---

[2] The reason for this movement is tied up with the valuation of securities and will be explained in later chapters.

Market risk includes a wide range of factors exogenous to securities themselves, including recessions, wars, structural changes in the economy, and changes in consumer preferences.

Inflation Risk A factor affecting all securities is purchasing power risk, or the chance that the purchasing power of invested dollars will decline. With uncertain inflation, the real (inflation-adjusted) return involves risk even if the nominal return is safe (e.g., a Treasury bond). This risk is related to interest rate risk, since interest rates generally rise as inflation increases, because lenders demand additional inflation premiums to compensate for the loss of purchasing power.

Business Risk The risk of doing business in a particular industry or environment is called business risk. For example, AT&T, the traditional telephone powerhouse, faces major changes today in the rapidly changing telecommunications industry.

Financial Risk Financial risk is associated with the use of debt financing by companies. The larger the proportion of assets financed by debt (as opposed to equity), the larger the variability in the returns, other things being equal. Financial risk involves the concept of financial leverage, which is explained in managerial finance courses.

Liquidity Risk Liquidity risk is the risk associated with the particular secondary market in which a security trades. An investment that can be bought or sold quickly and without significant price concession is considered to be liquid. The more uncertainty about the time element and the price concession, the greater the liquidity risk. A Treasury bill has little or no liquidity risk, whereas a small over-the-counter (OTC) stock may have substantial liquidity risk.

Exchange Rate Risk
The variability in returns on securities caused by currency fluctuations

Exchange Rate Risk All investors who invest internationally in today's increasingly global investment arena face the prospect of uncertainty in the returns after they convert the foreign gains back to their own currency. Unlike the past when most U.S. investors ignored international investing alternatives, investors today must recognize and understand **exchange rate risk**, which can be defined as the variability in returns on securities caused by currency fluctuations. Exchange rate risk is sometimes called *currency risk*.

For example, a U.S. investor who buys a German stock denominated in marks must ultimately convert the returns from this stock back to dollars. If the exchange rate has moved against the investor, losses from these exchange rate movements can partially or totally negate the original return earned.

Obviously, U.S. investors who invest only in U.S. stocks on U.S. markets do not face this risk, but in today's global environment where investors increasingly consider alternatives from other countries, this factor has become important. Currency risk affects international mutual funds, global mutual funds, closed-end single-country funds, American Depository Receipts, foreign stocks, and foreign bonds.

Country Risk Country risk, also referred to as political risk, is an important risk for investors today—probably more important now than in the past. With more investors investing internationally, both directly and indirectly, the political, and therefore economic, stability and viability of a country's economy need to be considered. The United States arguably has the lowest country risk, and other countries can be judged on a relative basis using the United States as a benchmark. Examples of countries that needed careful monitoring in the 1990s because of country risk included the former Soviet Union and Yugoslavia, China, Hong Kong, and South Africa. In the early part of the twenty-first century, several countries in South America, Turkey, Russia, and Hong Kong, among others, require careful attention.

TYPES OF RISK

Thus far, our discussion has concerned the total risk of an asset, which is one important consideration in investment analysis. However, modern investment analysis categorizes the traditional sources of risk identified previously as causing variability in returns into two general types: those that are pervasive in nature, such as market risk or interest rate risk, and those that are specific to a particular security issue, such as business or financial risk. Therefore, we must consider these two categories of total risk. The following discussion introduces these terms. We discuss these two sources of risk in more detail in other chapters.

Dividing total risk into its two components, a general (market) component and a specific (issuer) component, we have systematic risk and nonsystematic risk, which are additive:

$$\text{Total risk} = \text{General risk} + \text{Specific risk} \qquad \text{(6-2)}$$

$$= \text{Market risk} + \text{Issuer risk}$$

$$= \text{Systematic risk} + \text{Nonsystematic risk}$$

These two types of risk will be discussed in more detail in Chapters 8 and 9. We will consider them only briefly here.

Systematic Risk   As shown in later chapters, an investor can construct a diversified portfolio and eliminate part of the total risk, the diversifiable or nonmarket part. What is left is the nondiversifiable portion or the market risk. Variability in a security's total returns that is directly associated with overall movements in the general market or economy is called **systematic (market) risk**.

Virtually all securities have some systematic risk, whether bonds or stocks, because systematic risk directly encompasses the interest rate, market, and inflation risks. The investor cannot escape this part of the risk, because no matter how well he or she diversifies, the risk of the overall market cannot be avoided. If the stock market declines sharply, most stocks will be adversely affected; if it rises strongly, as in the last few months of 1982, most stocks will appreciate in value. These movements occur regardless of what any single investor does. Clearly, market risk is critical to all investors.

Nonsystematic Risk   The variability in a security's total returns not related to overall market variability is called the **nonsystematic (nonmarket) risk**. This risk is unique to a particular security and is associated with such factors as business and financial risk as well as liquidity risk. Although all securities tend to have some nonsystematic risk, it is generally connected with common stocks.

> Systematic (Market) Risk   Risk attributable to broad macro factors affecting all securities
>
> Nonsystematic (Nonmarket) Risk   Risk attributable to factors unique to the security

Measuring Returns

TOTAL RETURN

> Total Return (TR)   Percentage measure relating all cash flows on a security for a given time period to its purchase price

A correct returns measure must incorporate the two components of return, yield and price change, as discussed earlier. Returns across time or from different securities can be measured and compared using the total return concept. Formally, the **total return (TR)** for a given holding period is a decimal (or percentage) number relating all the cash flows received by an investor during any designated time period to the purchase price of the asset. Total return is defined as

$$TR = \frac{\text{Any cash payments received} + \text{Price changes over the period}}{\text{Price at which the asset is purchased}} \quad (6\text{-}3)$$

All the items in Equation 6-3 are measured in dollars. The dollar price change over the period, defined as the difference between the beginning (or purchase) price and the ending (or sale) price, can be either positive (sales price exceeds purchase price), negative (purchase price exceeds sales price), or zero. The cash payments can be either positive or zero. Netting the two items in the numerator together and dividing by the purchase price results in a decimal return figure that can easily be converted into percentage form. Note that in using the TR, the two components of return, yield and price change, have been measured.[3]

The general equation for calculating TR is

$$TR = \frac{CF_t + (P_E - P_B)}{P_B} = \frac{CF_t + PC}{P_B} \quad (6\text{-}4)$$

where

CF_t = cash flows during the measurement period t
P_E = price at the end of period t or sale price
P_B = purchase price of the asset or price at the beginning of the period
PC = change in price during the period, or P_E minus P_B

The cash flow for a bond comes from the interest payments received, and that for a stock comes from the dividends received. For some assets, such as a warrant or a stock that pays no dividends, there is only a price change. Part A of Exhibit 6-1 illustrates the calculation of TR for a bond, a common stock, and a warrant. Although one year is often used for convenience, the TR calculation can be applied to periods of any length.

In summary, the total return concept is valuable as a measure of return, because it is all inclusive, measuring the total return per dollar of original investment. Total Return is *the* basic measure of the actual return earned by investors on any financial asset for any specified period of time. It facilitates the comparison of asset returns over a specified period whether the comparison is of different assets, such as stocks versus bonds, or different securities within the same type, such as several common stocks. Remember that using this concept does not mean that the securities have to be sold and the gains or losses actually realized— that is, the calculation applies to unrealized gains or realized gains (see Appendix 2-A).

Table 6-1 shows corrected estimates of the Standard & Poor's (S&P) 500 Stock Composite Index for the years 1920 through 2002 (a total of 83 years, because the data start on January 1, 1920). Included in the table are end-of-year values for the Index, from which capital gains and losses can be computed, and dividends on the Index, which constitute the income component.[4]

---

[3] This can be seen more easily by rewriting Equation 6-3 to show specifically its income and price change components.

$$TR = \frac{\text{Cash payments received}}{\text{Purchase price}} + \frac{\text{Price change over the period}}{\text{Purchase price}}$$

The first term is a yield component, whereas the second term measures the price change. An alternative name for total return is holding period return.

[4] Note that these are simple end-of-year values—the annual dividend for the year is added to the end-of-year price. When we analyze total returns later in the chapter, we assume monthly reinvestment of dividends.

EXHIBIT 6-1

Examples of Total Return and Price Relative Calculations

A. Total Return (TR) Calculations

I. Bond TR

$$\text{Bond TR} = \frac{I_t + (P_E - P_B)}{P_B} = \frac{I_t + PC}{P_B}$$

I_t = the interest payment(s) received during the period
P_B and P_E = the beginning and ending prices, respectively
PC = the change in price during the period

Example   Assume the purchase of a 10-percent-coupon Treasury bond at a price of $960, held one year, and sold for $1,020. The TR is

$$\text{Bond TR} = \frac{100 + (1020 - 960)}{960} = \frac{100 + 60}{960} = 0.1667 \text{ or } 16.67\%$$

II. Stock TR

$$\text{Stock TR} = \frac{D_t + (P_E - P_B)}{P_B} = \frac{D_t + PC}{P_B}$$

D_t = the dividend(s) paid during the period

Example   100 shares of DataShield are purchased at $30 per share and sold one year later at $26 per share. A dividend of $2 per share is paid.

$$\text{Stock TR} = \frac{2 + (26 - 30)}{30} = \frac{2 + (-4)}{30} = -0.0667 \text{ or } -6.67\%$$

III. Warrant TR

$$\text{Warrant TR} = \frac{C_t + (P_E - P_B)}{P_B} = \frac{C_t + PC}{P_B} = \frac{PC}{P_B}$$

where C_t = any cash payment received by the warrant holder during the period. Because warrants pay no dividends, the only return to an investor from owning a warrant is the change in price during the period.

Example   Assume the purchase of warrants of DataShield at $3 per share, a holding period of six months, and the sale at $3.75 per share.

$$\text{Warrant TR} = \frac{0 + (3.75 - 3.00)}{3.00} = \frac{0.75}{3.00} = 0.25, \text{ or } 25\%$$

B. Return Relative Calculations

The return relative for the preceding bond example shown is

$$\text{Bond return relative} = \frac{100 + 1020}{960} = 1.1667$$

The return relative for the stock example is

$$\text{Stock return relative} = \frac{2 + 26}{30} = 0.9333$$

The return relative for the warrant example is

$$\text{Warrant return relative} = \frac{3.75}{3.00} = 1.25$$

To convert from a return relative to a TR, subtract 1.0 from the return relative.

Table 6-1 Historical Composite Stock Price Index, Based on Standard & Poor's Estimates, Dividends in Index Form, and Total Returns (TRs), 1920–2002. Values are End-of-Year.

Year	Index Val	Div	TR%	Year	Index Val	Div	TR%
1919	10.34			1961	71.55	2.02	26.60
1920	7.98	0.56	−17.38	1962	63.10	2.13	−8.83
1921	8.35	0.51	10.99	1963	75.02	2.28	22.50
1922	10.30	0.56	30.04	1964	84.75	2.50	16.30
1923	9.99	0.58	2.63	1965	92.43	2.72	12.27
1924	11.97	0.61	25.97	1966	80.33	2.87	−9.99
1925	14.59	0.67	27.42	1967	96.47	2.92	23.73
1926	15.03	0.75	8.20	1968	103.86	3.07	10.84
1927	19.15	0.81	32.76	1969	92.06	3.16	−8.32
1928	25.61	0.84	38.14	1970	92.15	3.14	3.51
1929	22.05	0.95	−10.18	1971	102.09	3.07	14.12
1930	15.31	0.90	−26.48	1972	118.05	3.15	18.72
1931	7.89	0.76	−43.49	1973	97.55	3.38	−14.50
1932	6.80	0.46	−8.01	1974	68.56	3.60	−26.03
1933	10.19	0.36	55.34	1975	90.19	3.68	36.92
1934	10.10	0.40	3.00	1976	107.46	4.05	23.64
1935	13.91	0.41	41.79	1977	95.10	4.67	−7.16
1936	17.60	0.68	31.38	1978	96.11	5.07	6.39
1937	11.14	0.78	−32.29	1979	107.94	5.65	18.19
1938	13.60	0.52	26.70	1980	135.76	6.16	31.48
1939	13.19	0.59	1.31	1981	122.55	6.63	−4.85
1940	11.51	0.67	−7.63	1982	140.64	6.87	20.37
1941	9.59	0.75	−10.24	1983	164.93	7.09	22.31
1942	10.45	0.64	15.67	1984	167.24	7.53	5.97
1943	12.59	0.64	26.71	1985	211.28	7.90	31.06
1944	14.33	0.68	19.18	1986	242.17	8.28	18.54
1945	18.87	0.67	36.43	1987	247.08	8.81	5.67
1946	17.08	0.77	−5.44	1988	277.72	9.73	16.34
1947	16.74	0.92	3.43	1989	353.40	11.05	31.23
1948	16.11	1.05	2.45	1990	330.22	12.10	−3.14
1949	18.11	1.14	19.48	1991	417.09	12.20	30.00
1950	21.94	1.40	28.92	1992	435.71	12.38	7.43
1951	24.98	1.35	19.99	1993	466.45	12.58	9.94
1952	26.94	1.37	13.34	1994	459.27	13.18	1.29
1953	25.85	1.41	1.17	1995	615.93	13.79	37.11
1954	36.73	1.49	47.87	1996	740.74	14.90	22.68
1955	43.89	1.68	24.06	1997	970.43	15.50	33.10
1956	46.30	1.82	9.65	1998	1229.23	16.38	28.36
1957	39.99	1.87	−9.59	1999	1469.25	16.48	20.88
1958	55.21	1.75	42.44	2000	1320.28	15.97	−9.05
1959	59.89	1.83	11.79	2001	1148.08	15.71	−11.85
1960	58.11	1.95	0.28	2002	879.82	16.07	−22.10

Some Practical Advice

As you analyze and consider common stocks, never forget the important role that dividends historically have played in the TR shown for common stocks. For example, for the 46 years ending in 1991, for the Dow Jones Industrials, the price appreciation per year averaged 6.1 percent, but the TR per year averaged 11.2 percent.[5] Dividends made up the rest, and obviously were an important component of the total return. However, in the 1990s, the dividend yield on the major stock indexes continued to decline, and reached levels of about 1.5 percent in 2001 and 2002. As you estimate TRs on stocks for the future, you must take into consideration this dramatic, and unprecedented, decline in dividend yields. Clearly, if all other things remained equal, TRs on common stocks would have to decline relative to the past because of the significant decreases in the dividend yield.

Example 6-3

The TRs for each year as shown in Table 6-1 can be calculated as shown in Equation 6-4. As a demonstration of these calculations, the TR for 2000 is −9.07 percent, calculated as:

$$[1320.28 - 1469.25 + 15.69]/1469.25 = -.0907 \text{ or } -9.07\%$$

In contrast, in 1995, the same market index showed a TR of 37.113 percent, calculated as:

$$[615.93 - 459.27 + 13.79]/459.27 = .3711 \text{ or } 37.11\%$$

RETURN RELATIVE

It is often necessary to measure returns on a slightly different basis than TRs. This is particularly true when calculating either a cumulative wealth index or a geometric mean, both of which are explained below, because negative returns cannot be used in the calculation. The **return relative** (RR) solves this problem by adding 1.0 to the total return.

Return Relative The total return for an investment for a given time period stated on the basis of 1.0

❑ RR = TR in decimal form + 1.0
❑ TR in decimal form = RR − 1.0

Although return relatives may be less than 1.0, they will be greater than zero, thereby eliminating negative numbers.

Example 6-4

A TR of 0.10 for some holding period is equivalent to a return relative of 1.10, and a TR of −9.07%, as calculated in Example 6-3, is equivalent to a return relative of 0.9093.

Equation 6-4 can be modified to calculate return relatives directly by using the price at the end of the holding period in the numerator rather than the change in price, as in Equation 6-5.

$$\text{Return relative} = \text{RR} = \frac{CF_t + P_E}{P_B} \qquad (6\text{-}5)$$

Examples of return relative calculations for the same three assets as the preceding are shown in Part B of Exhibit 6-1.

---

[5] See A. Gary Shilling, "Dividends Back in Style," *Forbes*, May 27, 2002, p. 170.

Example 6-5   The return relative for 1995 (Example 6-3) is

$$(615.93 + 13.79)/459.27 = 1.3711$$

CUMULATIVE WEALTH INDEX

Return measures such as TRs measure changes in the level of wealth. At times, however, it is more desirable to measure levels of wealth (or prices) rather than changes. In other words, we measure the cumulative effect of returns over time given some stated beginning dollar amount invested, which typically is shown as $1 for convenience. Having calculated ending wealth (cumulative wealth) over some period on the base of a beginning $1, it is simple enough to multiply by the actual beginning amount, such as $10,000 or $100,000 or whatever the number is. The value of the **cumulative wealth index**, CWI_n, is computed as:

Cumulative Wealth Index   Cumulative wealth over time, given an initial wealth and a series of returns on some asset

$$CWI_n = WI_0 (1 + TR_1) (1 + TR_2) \ldots (1 + TR_n) \qquad (6\text{-}6)$$

where

CWI_n = the cumulative wealth index as of the end of period n
WI_0 = the beginning index value, typically $1
$TR_{1,n}$ = the periodic TRs in decimal form (when added to 1.0 in Equation 6-6, they become return relatives)

Example 6-6   For the S&P total returns in Table 6-1, the cumulative wealth index for the decade of the 1990s, the 10-year period 1990 to 1999, would be, using return relatives:

$$CWI_{90-99} = 1.00(0.969)(1.30)(1.0743)(1.0994)(1.0129)$$

$$(1.3711)(1.2268)(1.331)(1.2834)(1.2088)$$

$$= 5.2342$$

Thus, $1 (the beginning index value arbitrarily chosen) invested at the end of 1989 (the beginning of 1990) would have been worth $5.2342 by the end of 1999. Obviously, any beginning wealth value can be used to calculate cumulative wealth. For example, $10,000 invested under the same conditions would have been worth $52,342 at the end of 1999, and $37,500 invested under the same conditions would have been worth $196,282.50.

Note that the values for the cumulative wealth index can be used to calculate the rate of return for a given period, using Equation 6-7.

$$TR_n = \frac{CWI_n}{CWI_{n-1}} - 1 \qquad (6\text{-}7)$$

where

TR_n = the total return for period n
CWI = the cumulative wealth index

Example 6-7   Using the TRs illustrated above for the years 1990 to 1999, we can make the following calculations.

$$CWI_{90-99} = 1.00(0.969)(1.30)(1.0743)(1.0994)(1.0129)$$
$$(1.3711)(1.2268)(1.331)(1.2834)(1.2088)$$
$$= 5.2342$$

$$CWI_{90-98} = 1.00(0.969)(1.30)(1.0743)(1.0994)(1.0129)$$
$$(1.3711)(1.2268)(1.331)(1.2834)$$
$$= 4.3301$$

$$TR_{1999} = (5.2342/4.3301) - 1$$
$$= .2088 \text{ (rounded) or } 20.88\%$$

Thus, the TR for 1999 was 20.88 % (rounded), which agrees with Table 6-1.

Taking a Global Perspective

As noted in Chapter 1, international investing offers potential return opportunities and potential reduction in risk through diversification. Based on the historical record, investments in certain foreign markets would have increased investor returns during certain periods of time. However, investors need to understand how these returns are calculated and the risk they are taking.

INTERNATIONAL RETURNS AND CURRENCY RISK

When investors buy and sell assets in other countries, they must consider exchange rate risk or currency risk. This risk can convert a gain from an investment into a loss or a loss from an investment into a gain. We need to remember that international stocks are priced in local currencies—for example, a Swiss stock is priced in Swiss francs and a Japanese stock is priced in yen. For a U.S. investor, the ultimate return to him or her in spendable dollars depends upon the rate of exchange between the foreign currency and the dollar, and this rate typically changes daily. **Currency risk** is the risk that the changes in the value of the dollar and the foreign currency involved will be unfavorable; however, like risk in general, currency risk can work to the investor's favor, enhancing the return that would otherwise be received.

An investment denominated in an appreciating currency relative to the investor's domestic currency will experience a gain from the currency movement, whereas an investment denominated in a depreciating currency relative to the investor's domestic currency will experience a decrease in the return because of the currency movement. Said differently, when you buy a foreign asset, you are selling the dollar, and when you cash in by selling the asset, you are buying back the dollar.

Currency (Exchange Rate) Risk   The risk that the changes in the value of the dollar and the foreign currency involved will be unfavorable to one country's investors

- ❑ If the foreign currency strengthens while you hold the asset, you will be able to buy back more dollars, because the now stronger foreign currency buys more. Your dollar-denominated return will increase.
- ❑ If the dollar strengthens while you hold the asset, when you cash in you will only be able to buy back fewer dollars, thereby decreasing your dollar-denominated return.

Example 6-8   In 1999, the Brazilian market was up about 150 percent, but the currency adjustment was negative (83 percent), leaving a U.S. dollar return for the year of 67 percent. On the other hand, the Japan market enjoyed a 47 percent return, and the currency adjustment was positive, 15 percent, resulting in a U.S. dollar return of approximately 62 percent for the year.

To calculate the return from an investment in a foreign country, we use Equation 6-8. The foreign currency is stated in domestic terms; that is, the amount of domestic currency necessary to purchase one unit of the foreign currency.

$$\text{Total return in domestic terms} = \left[RR \times \frac{\text{Ending value of foreign currency}}{\text{Beginning value of foreign currency}} \right] - 1.0 \qquad \textbf{(6-8)}$$

Example 6-9   Consider a U.S. investor who invests in WalMex at 175.86 pesos when the value of the peso stated in dollars is $0.29. One year later, WalMex is at 195.24 pesos, and the stock did not pay a dividend. The peso is now at $0.27, which means that the dollar appreciated against the peso.

Return relative for WalMex = 195.24/175.86 = 1.11

Total return to the U.S. investor *after currency adjustment* is

$$\text{TR denominated in \$} = \left[1.11 \times \frac{\$0.27}{\$0.29} \right] - 1.0$$

$$= [1.11 \times 0.931] - 1.0$$

$$= 1.0334 - 1.0$$

$$= .0334 \text{ or } 3.34\%$$

In this example, the U.S. investor earned an 11-percent total return denominated in Mexican currency but only 3.34 percent denominated in dollars, because the peso declined in value against the U.S. dollar. With the strengthening of the dollar, the pesos received when the investor sells WalMex buy less U.S. dollars, pushing down the 11-percent return a Mexican investor would earn to only 3.34 percent for a U.S. investor.

How much difference can currency adjustments make to investors? It can make a substantial difference for selected periods of time. Consider one example—three selected periods for European stocks when the change in the value of the dollar was substantial, ranging from 17 to 37 percent (March 1971 to June 1973; October 1976 to October 1978; February 1985 to February 1990). The performance of European stocks in local currency was good, ranging from 6 to 28 percent. Given the dollar's performance, however, the dollar-denominated performance was outstanding, ranging from 33 to 50 percent.[6]

The U.S. dollar was extremely strong from 1994 through October 2000. It remained strong for months thereafter even as the stock market and the economy declined. However, the dollar began a decline in early 2002, dropping against the new euro and against the yen. As the dollar fell, foreign investors owning U.S. stocks suffered from the declining stock market and an unfavorable currency movement.

---

[6] This example is based on William Hester, "A Boost From Abroad," *Bloomberg Personal Finance*, June 2002, p. 16.

SUMMARY STATISTICS FOR RETURNS

The total return, return relative, and wealth index are useful measures of return for a specified period of time. Also needed in investment analysis are statistics to describe a series of returns. For example, investing in a particular stock for 10 years or a different stock in each of 10 years could result in 10 TRs, which must be described by one or more statistics. Two such measures used with returns data are described below.

Arithmetic Mean The best known statistic to most people is the arithmetic mean. Therefore, when someone refers to the *mean return* they usually are referring to the arithmetic mean unless otherwise specified. The arithmetic mean, customarily designated by the symbol $\overline{X}$(X-bar), of a set of values is calculated as:

$$\overline{X} = \frac{\Sigma X}{n}$$

(6-9)

or the sum of each of the values being considered divided by the total number of values n.

Example 6-10   Based on data from Table 6-1 for the 10 years of the 1990s ending in 1999, the arithmetic mean is calculated in Table 6-2.

$$X = [-3.14 + 30.00 + \ldots + 20.88]/10$$
$$= 187.63/10$$
$$= 18.76\%$$

Geometric Mean The arithmetic mean return is an appropriate measure of the central tendency of a distribution consisting of returns calculated for a particular time period, such as 10 years. However, when percentage changes in value over time are

Table 6-2 Calculation of the Arithmetic and Geometric Mean for the Years 1990–1999 for the S&P 500 Stock Composite Index

Year	S&P 500 TRs (%)	S&P 500 Return Relative
1990	−3.14	0.9687
1991	30.00	1.30001
1992	7.43	1.07432
1993	9.94	1.09942
1994	1.29	1.01286
1995	37.11	1.37113
1996	22.68	1.22683
1997	33.10	1.33101
1998	28.34	1.28338
1999	20.88	1.2088

Arithmetic Mean $= [-3.14 + 30.00 + \ldots + 20.88] / 10$
$= 18.76\%$

Geometric Mean $= [(0.9687)(1.30001)(1.07432)(1.09942)(1.01286)$
$(1.37113)(1.22683)(1.33101)(1.28338)(1.2088)]^{1/10} - 1$
$= 1.18 - 1$
$= 0.18$, or 18%

involved, as a result of compounding, the arithmetic mean of these changes can be misleading. A different mean, the geometric mean, is needed to describe accurately the "true" average rate of return over multiple periods.

The geometric mean return measures the compound rate of growth over time. It is often used in investments and finance to reflect the steady *growth rate* of invested funds over some past period; that is, the uniform rate at which money actually grew over time per period. Therefore, it allows us to measure the realized change in wealth over multiple periods.

Geometric Mean The compound rate of return over time

The **geometric mean** is defined as the *nth* root of the product resulting from multiplying a series of return relatives together, as in Equation 6-10.[7]

$$G = [(1 + TR_1)(1 + TR_2) \ldots (1 + TR_n)]^{1/n} - 1 \qquad \text{(6-10)}$$

where TR is a series of total returns in decimal form. Note that adding 1.0 to each total return produces a return relative. Return relatives are used in calculating geometric mean returns, because TRs, which can be negative, cannot be used.

Example 6-11

Continuing the example from Table 6-2, consisting of the 10 years of data ending in 1999 for the S&P 500, we find that the geometric mean would be as shown in Table 6-2:

$$G = [(0.969)(1.30)(1.0743)(1.0994)(1.0129)$$

$$(1.3711)(1.2268)(1.331)(1.2834)(1.2088)]^{1/10} - 1$$

$$= 1.1800 - 1 = 0.18, \text{ or } 18\%$$

The geometric mean reflects compound, cumulative returns over more than one period. Thus, $1 invested in the S&P 500 Composite Index would have compounded at an average annual rate of 18 percent over the period January 1, 1990, through December 31, 1999 (10 years), producing a cumulative ending wealth of $5.2342. Notice that this geometric average rate of return is lower than the arithmetic average rate of return of 18.76 percent, because it reflects the variability of the returns.

The geometric mean will always be less than the arithmetic mean unless the values being considered are identical. The spread between the two depends on the dispersion of the distribution: the greater the dispersion, the greater the spread between the two means.

Arithmetic Mean Versus Geometric Mean When should we use the arithmetic mean and when should we use the geometric mean to describe the returns from financial assets? The answer depends on the investor's objective:

- ▪ The arithmetic mean is a better measure of average (typical) performance over single periods. It is the best estimate of the expected return for next period.
- ▪ The geometric mean is a better measure of the change in wealth over the past (multiple periods). It is a backward-looking concept, measuring the realized compound rate of return at which money grew over a specified period.

---

[7] An alternative method of calculating the geometric mean is to find the log of each return relative, sum them, divide by *n*, and take the antilog.

Example 6-12 As an illustration of how the arithmetic mean can be misleading in describing returns over multiple periods, consider the data in Table 6-3, which show the movements in price for two stocks over two successive holding periods. Both stocks have a beginning price of $10. Stock A rises to $20 in period 1 and then declines to $10 in period 2. Stock B falls to $8 in period 1 and then rises 50 percent to $12 in period 2. For stock A, the indicated annual average arithmetic rate of change in price is 25 percent. This is clearly not sensible, because the price of stock A at the end of period 2 is $10, the same as the beginning price. The geometric mean calculation gives the correct annual average rate of change in price of 0 percent per year.

For stock B, the arithmetic average of the annual percentage changes in price is 15 percent. However, if the price actually increased 15 percent each period, the ending price in period 2 would be $10 (1.15) (1.15) = $13.23. We know that this is not correct, because the price at the end of period 2 is $12. The annual geometric rate of return, 9.54 percent, produces the correct price at the end of period 2: $10 (1.0954)(1.0954) = $12.

As this simple example demonstrates, over multiple periods the geometric mean shows the true average compound rate of growth that actually occurred—that is, the rate at which an invested dollar has grown.

On the other hand, we should use the arithmetic mean to represent the likely or typical performance for a single period. Consider the TR data for the S&P Index for the years 1990 to 1999 as described earlier. Our best representation of any one year's performance would be the arithmetic mean of 18.76 percent, because it was necessary to average this rate of return for a particular year, given the spread in the yearly numbers, in order to realize an actual annual compound growth rate of 18 percent after the fact.

INFLATION-ADJUSTED RETURNS

All of the returns discussed above are *nominal returns*, or money returns. They measure dollar amounts or changes but say nothing about the purchasing power of these dollars. To capture this dimension, we need to consider *real returns*, or inflation-adjusted returns.

To calculate inflation-adjusted returns, we divide 1 + nominal total return by 1 + the inflation rate as shown in Equation 6-11. This calculation is sometimes simplified by subtracting rather than dividing, producing a close approximation.

$$TR_{IA} = \frac{(1 + TR)}{(1 + IF)} - 1 \tag{6-11}$$

where

TR_{IA} = the inflation-adjusted total return
IF   = the rate of inflation

This equation applies to both individual years and average total returns.

Table 6-3 Contrasting the Arithmetic and Geometric Means

Stock	Period 1	Period 2	Annual Arithmetic Rate of Return	Annual Geometric Rate of Return
A	$20	$10	[100% + (−50%)]/2 = 25%	$[2.0(0.5)]^{1/2} - 1 = 0\%$
B	$ 8	$12	[−20% + (50%)]/2 = 15%	$[0.8(1.5)]^{1/2} - 1 = 9.54\%$

Example 6-13   The total return for the S&P 500 Composite Index in 1998 was 28.5731 percent (assuming monthly reinvestment of dividends). The rate of inflation was 1.6119 percent. Therefore, the real (inflation-adjusted) total return for large common stocks in 1998, as measured by the S&P 500, was:

$$1.2857/1.0161 = 1.2653$$

$$1.2653 - 1.0 = .265 \text{ or } 26.5\%$$

Example 6-14   Now consider the entire period 1920 to 2002. The geometric mean for the S&P 500 Composite Index for the entire period was 10.05 percent, and for inflation, 2.54 percent. Therefore, the real (inflation-adjusted) geometric mean rate of return for large common stocks for the period 1920 to 2002 was:

$$1.1082/1.0254 = 1.0807$$

$$1.0807 - 1.0 = 0.0807 \text{ or } 8.07\%$$

The Consumer Price Index (CPI) typically is used as the measure of inflation. When nominal total returns are adjusted for inflation, the result is real or constant purchasing-power terms.

The compound annual rate of inflation over the period 1920 to 2002 was 2.54 percent. This means that a basket of consumer goods purchased at the beginning of 1920 would cost approximately \$8.02 at year-end 2002. This is calculated as $(1.0254)^{83}$, because there are 83 years from the beginning of 1920 through the end of 2002.[8]

Measuring Risk

Risk is often associated with the dispersion in the likely outcomes. Dispersion refers to variability. Risk is assumed to arise out of variability, which is consistent with our definition of risk as the chance that the actual outcome of an investment will differ from the expected outcome. If an asset's return has no variability, in effect it has no risk. Thus, a one-year Treasury bill purchased to yield 10 percent and held to maturity will, in fact, yield (a nominal) 10 percent. No other outcome is possible, barring default by the U.S. government, which is not considered a reasonable possibility.

Consider an investor analyzing a series of returns (TRs) for the major types of financial assets over some period of years. Knowing the mean of this series is not enough; the investor also needs to know something about the variability in the returns. Relative to the other assets, common stocks show the largest variability (dispersion) in returns, with small common stocks showing even greater variability. Corporate bonds have a much smaller variability and therefore a more compact distribution of returns. Of course, Treasury bills are the least risky. The dispersion of annual returns for bills is compact.

In order to appreciate the range of outcomes for major financial asset classes, consider Figure 6-1. It shows the range of outcomes, and the mean (given by the circle) for each of the following asset classes for the period 1920 through 2002, in order from left to right: inflation, Treasury bills, Treasury bonds, corporate bonds, large common stocks (S&P 500 Composite Index), mid-cap stocks, and smaller common stocks.

---

[8] To determine the number of years in a series such as this, subtract the beginning year from the ending year and add 1.0. For example, 1998 − 1920 = 78, and we add 1.0 to account for the fact that 1920 is a full year of data.

Figure 6-1

Graph of spread in returns for major asset classes for the period 1920–2002.

SOURCE: Jack W. Wilson and Charles P. Jones, North Carolina State University.

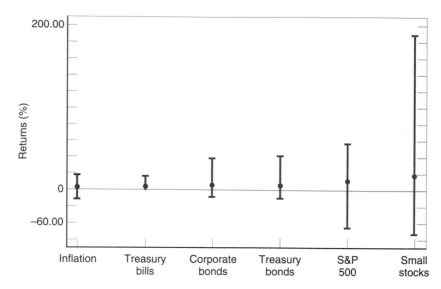

As we can see from Figure 6-1, stocks have a much wider range of outcomes than do bonds and bills. Smaller common stocks have a wider range of outcomes than do large common stocks. Given this variability, investors must be able to measure it as a proxy for risk. They often do so using the standard deviation.

STANDARD DEVIATION

The risk of distributions can be measured with an absolute measure of dispersion, or variability. The most commonly used measure of dispersion over some period of years is the **standard deviation**, which measures the deviation of each observation from the arithmetic mean of the observations and is a reliable measure of variability, because all the information in a sample is used.[9]

Standard Deviation A measure of the dispersion in outcomes around the expected value

The standard deviation is a measure of the total risk of an asset or a portfolio. It captures the total variability in the asset's or portfolio's return, whatever the source(s) of that variability. The standard deviation can be calculated from the variance, which is calculated as:

$$\sigma^2 = \frac{\sum_{i=1}^{n} (X - \overline{X})^2}{n - 1}$$

$\qquad\qquad$ (6-12)

where

σ^2 = the variance of a set of values
X = each value in the set
$\overline{X}$ = the mean of the observations
n = the number of returns in the sample
σ = $(\sigma^2)^{1/2}$ = standard deviation

Knowing the returns from the sample, we can calculate the standard deviation quite easily.

---

[9] The variance is the standard deviation squared. The variance and the standard deviation are similar and can be used for the same purposes; specifically, in investment analysis, both are used as measures of risk. The standard deviation, however, is used more often.

Example 6-15   The standard deviation of the 10 TRs for the decade of the 1970s, 1970 to 1979, for the Standard & Poor's 500 Index can be calculated as shown in Table 6-4.

In summary, the standard deviation of return measures the total risk of one security or the total risk of a portfolio of securities. The historical standard deviation can be calculated for individual securities or portfolios of securities using TRs for some specified period of time. This *ex post* value is useful in evaluating the total risk for a particular historical period and in estimating the total risk that is expected to prevail over some future period.

The standard deviation, combined with the normal distribution, can provide some useful information about the dispersion or variation in returns. For a *normal distribution*, the probability that a particular outcome will be above (or below) a specified value can be determined. With one standard deviation on either side of the arithmetic mean of the distribution, 68.3 percent of the outcomes will be encompassed; that is, there is a 68.3 percent probability that the actual outcome will be within one (plus or minus) standard deviation of the arithmetic mean. The probabilities are 95 and 99 percent that the actual outcome will be within two or three standard deviations, respectively, of the arithmetic mean.

RISK PREMIUMS

Risk Premium   The additional compensation for assuming risk

A **risk premium** is the additional return investors expect to receive, or did receive, by taking on increasing amounts of risk. It measures the payoff for taking various types of risk. Such premiums can be calculated between any two classes of securities.

Equity Risk Premium   The difference between the return on stocks and the risk-free rate

An often-discussed risk premium is the **equity risk premium**, defined as the difference between the return on stocks and a risk-free rate (proxied by the return on Treasury bills). The equity risk premium measures the additional compensation for assuming risk, since Treasury bills have no practical risk (on a nominal basis). Obviously, common stock investors care whether the expected risk premium is 5 percent, or 8 percent, because that affects what they earn on their investment in stocks. Holding interest rates constant, a narrowing of the equity risk premium implies a decline in the rate of return on stocks, because the amount earned beyond the risk-free rate is reduced.

Table 6-4 Calculating the Historical Standard Deviation for the Period 1970–1979

Year	TR (%), X	$X - \bar{X}$	$(X - \bar{X})^2$
1970	3.51	−3.87	14.98
1971	14.12	6.74	45.43
1972	18.72	11.34	128.6
1973	−14.50	−21.88	478.73
1974	−26.03	33.41	1116.23
1975	36.92	29.54	872.61
1976	23.64	16.26	264.39
1977	−7.16	14.54	211.41
1978	6.39	−0.99	0.98
1979	18.19	10.81	116.86

$\bar{X} = 7.38$ $\sum(X - \bar{X})^2 = 3250.22$

$$\sigma^2 = \frac{3250.22}{9} = 361.14$$

$$\sigma = (361.14)^{1/2} = 19.00\%$$

There are alternative ways to calculate the equity risk premium, involving arithmetic means, geometric means, Treasury bonds, and so forth. In order to maintain consistency with our other series, historical risk premiums are measured here as the geometric differences between pairs of return series (remember, other approaches are often used). Therefore, we calculate the risk premium as:

$$ERP = \frac{(1 + TR_{CS})}{(1 + RF)} - 1 \tag{6-13}$$

where

$\quad$ ERP $\;=$ the equity risk premium
$\quad$ $TR_{CS}=$ the total return on stocks
$\quad$ RF $\quad=$ the risk-free rate (the Treasury bill rate)

Example 6-16 Using data from Table 6-5, large common stocks had a geometric mean return over the period 1920 to 2002 of 10.0466 percent, and Treasury bills had a geometric mean return of 4.0358 percent. The historical equity risk premium was:

$$ERP_{1920-2002} = \frac{1.100466}{1.040358} - 1.0 = 0.0578 = 5.78\%$$

The equity risk premium is an important concept in finance, but one that remains misunderstood and controversial. There is a measurement problem, as noted. Furthermore, there are actually two different equity risk premiums. What we are discussing here is the realized equity risk premium based on rates of return that actually occurred. However, there is also an expected (or required) equity risk premium, which refers to what investors expect to earn in order to be willing to hold stocks relative to safe assets.

The equity risk premium affects several important issues, and has become an often-discussed topic in Investments. The amount of the risk premium is controversial, with varying estimates as to the actual risk premium in the past as well as the prospective risk premium in the future.

We know that historically the equity risk premium (based on the S&P 500 Index) was approximately 7 percent (estimates vary depending upon exactly how it is calculated). New research by Arnott and Bernstein argues that going forward, the equity risk premium may be around zero, or possibly negative.[10] They base this argument on the dramatic decline in dividend yields to less than 2 percent, the likely low rate of growth in real earnings per share, and the likelihood that the P/E ratio will, if anything, decline rather than increase from its recent lofty levels. All of these factors, according to Arnott and Bernstein, will result in a TR on large common stocks, inflation adjusted, of around 3.5 percent. A comparable return has been available on inflation-indexed Treasury bonds. Therefore, effectively, there is little or no risk premium to be expected.

Other risk premiums can also be calculated. For example, the *bond default premium* is measured by the difference between the return on long-term corporate bonds and the return on long-term government bonds. This premium reflects the additional compensation for investing in risky corporate bonds, which have some probability of default, rather than government bonds, which do not.

---

[10] See Robert Arnott and Peter L. Bernstein, "What Risk Premium Is Normal," *Financial Analysts Journal*, Vol. 58, March/April 2002, pp. 64–85.

Realized Returns and Risks from Investing

We are now in a position to examine the returns and risks from investing in major financial assets that have occurred in the United States. We also will see how the preceding return and risk measures are typically used in presenting realized return and risk data of interest to virtually all financial market participants.

Table 6-5 shows the average annual geometric and arithmetic returns, as well as standard deviations, for major financial assets for the period 1920 to 2002 (83 years). Included are both nominal returns and real returns. These data are comparable to those produced and distributed by Ibbotson Associates on a regular basis. The Ibbotson Associates data are widely available on a commercial basis. This is simply an alternative series reconstructed by Jack Wilson and Charles Jones that provides basically the same information for a slightly longer time period.

TOTAL RETURNS AND STANDARD DEVIATIONS

Table 6-5 indicates that common stocks, as measured by the well-known Standard & Poor's 500 Composite Index, had a geometric mean annual return over this 83-year period of 10.05 percent (rounded). Hence, $1 invested in the market index at the beginning of 1920 would have grown at an average annual compound rate of 10.05 percent over this very long period. In contrast, the arithmetic mean annual return for stocks was 11.94 percent. The best estimate of the "average" return for stocks in any one year, using only this information, would be 11.94 percent, based on the arithmetic mean, and not the 10.05 percent based on the geometric mean return.

Table 6-5 Summary Statistics of Annual Total Returns for Major Financial Assets for 83 Years, January 1, 1920, through December 31, 2002, Nominal and Inflation-Adjusted

Nominal Total Returns Summary			
	Arithmetic Mean	Std.Dev.	Geometric Mean
S&P 500 Composite	11.9377%	19.4181%	10.0466%
S&P Industrial	12.4099	21.7209	10.2038
S&P Utility	11.1037	20.3498	9.1868
SmallCap Stocks (S&P 600)*	18.1124	38.3213	12.2567
Aaa 20-year Corporate Bond	6.3561	8.6387	6.0267
US 15-year Treasury Bond	5.7288	8.9254	5.3804
Treasury bill	4.0852	3.2583	4.0358
Inflation	2.6319	4.4571	2.5353
Inflation-Adjusted Total Returns Summary			
	Arithmetic Mean	Std.Dev.	Geometric Mean
S&P 500 Composite	9.2110%	19.7573%	7.3256%
S&P Industrial	9.6618	21.5710	7.4790
S&P Utility	8.4732	20.5415	6.4870
SmallCap Stocks (S&P 600)*	14.8220	37.2315	9.1569
Aaa 20-year Corporate Bond	3.8725	10.0521	3.4052
US 15-year Treasury Bond	3.2545	10.2275	2.7748
Treasury bill	1.5690	4.6516	1.4635

* 1926–2002, price change only.

SOURCE: Jack W. Wilson and Charles P. Jones, North Carolina State University.

The difference between these two means is related to the variability of the stock return series. Given the data in Table 6-5, the linkage between the geometric mean and the arithmetic mean is approximated by Equation 6-14:

$$(1 + G)^2 \approx (1 + A.M.)^2 - (S.D.)^2 \qquad (6\text{-}14)$$

where

G = the geometric mean of a series of asset returns
A.M. = the arithmetic mean of a series of asset returns
S.D. = the standard deviation of the arithmetic series of returns

Example 6-17

Using the data in Table 6-5 for 1920 to 2002 for the S&P 500 Index:

$$(1.1005)^2 \approx (1.1194)^2 - (0.194)^2$$

$$1.2111 \approx 1.2531 - 0.0376$$

$$1.2111 \approx 1.2155$$

Thus, if we know the arithmetic mean of a series of asset returns and the standard deviation of the series, we can approximate the geometric mean for this series. As the standard deviation of the series increases, holding the arithmetic mean constant, the geometric mean decreases.

Table 6-5 also shows that "small" company stocks (as measured by the S&P 600 Index) had a geometric mean return of 12.257 percent and an arithmetic mean of 18.112 percent, the highest numbers recorded in this data set (these data are for the years 1926 to 2002, and do not include dividends). The spread between these two numbers reflects the even greater variability of this series—the standard deviation for small stocks is 38.32 percent. With such a large standard deviation, the geometric mean will be significantly smaller than the arithmetic mean.

Corporate and Treasury bonds had geometric means that were roughly 50 to 60 percent of the S&P 500 Composite Index, but the risk was considerably smaller. Standard deviations for the bond series were only about 40 percent as large as that for the S&P 500 Composite.[11]

Finally, as we would expect, Treasury bills had the smallest returns of any of the major assets shown in Table 6-5, as well as the smallest risk (as measured used annual returns).

The standard deviations for each of the major financial assets in Table 6-5 reflect the dispersion of the returns over the 83-year period covered. The standard deviations clearly show the wide dispersion in the returns from common stocks compared with bonds and Treasury bills. Furthermore, smaller common stocks can logically be expected to be riskier than the S&P 500 stocks, and the standard deviation indicates a much wider dispersion.

CUMULATIVE WEALTH INDEXES

Figure 6-2 shows the cumulative wealth indexes for the major financial assets and the corresponding index number for inflation from the data in Table 6-5. The series starts at the beginning of 1920 and shows the cumulative results of starting with $1 in each of

---

[11] The reason for the distribution of Treasury bonds and Treasury bills, which have no practical risk of default, is that this is a distribution of annual returns, where negative numbers are possible. Thus, a Treasury bond purchased at $1,000 on January 1 could decline to, say, $900 by December 31, resulting in a negative TR.

these series and going through the end of 2002. Note that the vertical axis of Figure 6-2 is a log scale.[12]

As Figure 6-2 shows, the cumulative wealth for stocks, as measured by the S&P 500 Composite Index, completely dominated the returns on corporate bonds over this period—$2,823.97 versus $128.67. Note that we use the geometric mean from Table 6-5 to calculate cumulative ending wealth for each of the series shown in Figure 6-2 by raising (1 + the geometric mean as a decimal) to the 83rd power.

Example 6-18   The ending wealth value of $2,823.97 for common stocks in Figure 6-2 is the result of compounding at 10.0466 percent for 83 years, or

$$CWI_{2000} = WI_0(1.100466)^{83} = \$1.00(2,823.97) = \$2,823.97$$

The large cumulative wealth index value for stocks shown in Figure 6-2 speaks for itself. Remember, however, that the variability of this series is considerably larger than that for bonds or Treasury bills, as shown by the standard deviations in Table 6-5.

Inflation-Adjusted Cumulative Wealth   On an inflation-adjusted basis, the cumulative ending wealth for any of the series can be calculated as

$$CWI_{IA} = \frac{CWI}{CI_{INF}} \qquad\qquad (6\text{-}15)$$

where

CWI_{IA} = the cumulative wealth index value for any asset on inflation-adjusted basis
CWI = the cumulative wealth index value for any asset on a nominal basis
CI_{INF} = the ending index value for inflation, calculated as $(1 + \text{geometric rate of inflation})^n$, where n is the number of periods considered

Figure 6-2

Wealth indices of investments in U.S. stocks, bonds bills, and cumulative inflation, 1920–2002.

SOURCE: Jack W. Wilson and Charles P. Jones, North Carolina State University.

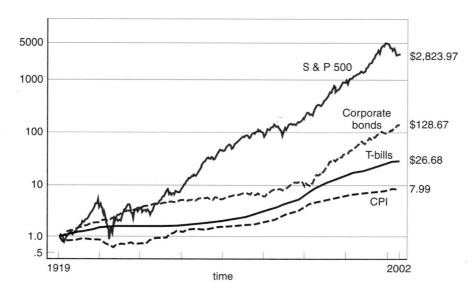

Example 6-19   For the period 1920 to 2002, the cumulative wealth index for the S&P 500 Composite Index was $2,823.97. Inflation had a total index value of 7.989. Therefore, the real cumulative wealth index, or inflation-adjusted cumulative wealth for the period 1920 to 2002, was:

$$\$2,823.97/7.989 = \$353.48$$

Alternatively, we can calculate real cumulative wealth by raising the geometric mean for inflation-adjusted returns to the appropriate power:

$$(1.073256)^{83} = \$353.49 \text{ (rounding error accounts for the difference)}$$

The Components of Cumulative Wealth   The cumulative wealth index (CWI) is equivalent to a cumulative total return index and, as such, can be decomposed into the two components of total return, the dividend component and the price change component. Because the CWI is a multiplicative relationship, these two components are multiplicative. To solve for either one, we divide the CWI by the other, as in Equation 6-16.

$$CPC = \frac{CWI}{CYI} \tag{6-16}$$

$$CDY = \frac{CWI}{CPC} \tag{6-17}$$

where

    CPC = the cumulative price change component of total return
    CWI = the cumulative wealth index or total return index for a series
    CDY = the cumulative dividend yield component of total return

Example 6-20   The CWI for common stocks (S&P 500) for 1920 to 2002 (83 years) was $2,823.97, based on a geometric mean of 10.0466 percent for that period. The cumulative price change index for the S&P 500 for that period was $85.087, which represents a geometric average annual return of

$$(\$85.087)^{1/83} - 1.0 = 0.0550 \text{ or } 5.50\%$$

The CDY for common stocks, therefore, is

$$CDY = \$2823.97/\$85.087$$

$$= \$33.189$$

The compound annual average rate of return for the yield component of total return is

$$(\$33.189)^{1/83} - 1.0 = 0.0431 \text{ or } 4.31\%$$

Note that the annual average geometric mean return relative for common stocks is the product of the corresponding geometric mean return relatives for the two components:
    For the period 1920 to 2002, an 83-year period

$$G_{TR} = G_{DY} \times G_{PC} \tag{6-18}$$

$$1.1005 = (1.0431)(1.055)$$

$$1.1005 - 1.0 = 0.1005 \text{ or } 10.053\%$$

Compounding and Discounting Of course, the single most striking feature of Figure 6-2 is the tremendous difference in ending wealth between stocks and bonds. This difference reflects the impact of compounding substantially different mean returns over long periods of time, which produces almost unbelievable results. The use of compounding points out the importance of this concept and of its complement, discounting. Both are important in investment analysis and are used often. *Compounding* involves future value resulting from compound interest—earning interest on interest. As we saw, the calculation of wealth indexes involves compounding at the geometric mean return over some historical period.

Present value (discounting) is the value today of a dollar to be received in the future. Such dollars are not comparable because of the time value of money. In order to be comparable, they must be discounted back to the present. Present value concepts are used extensively in Chapters 10 and 17 and in other chapters as needed.

Tables are readily available for both compounding and discounting, and calculators and computers make these calculations a simple matter. These tables are available at the end of this text.

Summary

▶ Return and risk go together in investments; indeed, these two parameters are the underlying basis of the subject. Everything an investor does, or is concerned with, is tied directly or indirectly to return and risk.

▶ The term *return* can be used in different ways. It is important to distinguish between realized (*ex post*, or historical) return and expected (*ex ante*, or anticipated) return.

▶ The two components of return are yield and price change (capital gain or loss).

▶ The total return is a percentage return concept that can be used to correctly measure the return for any security.

▶ The return relative, which adds 1.0 to the total return, is used when calculating the geometric mean of a series of returns.

▶ The cumulative wealth index (total return index) is used to measure the cumulative wealth over time given some initial starting wealth—typically, $1—and a series of returns for some asset.

▶ Return relatives, along with the beginning and ending values of the foreign currency, can be used to convert the return on a foreign investment into a domestic return.

▶ The geometric mean measures the compound rate of return over time. The arithmetic mean, on the other hand, is simply the average return for a series and is used to measure the typical performance for a single period.

▶ Inflation-adjusted returns can be calculated by dividing 1 + the nominal return by 1 + the inflation rate as measured by the CPI.

▶ Risk is the other side of the coin: risk and expected return should always be considered together. An investor cannot reasonably expect to earn large returns without assuming greater risks.

▶ The primary components of risk have traditionally been categorized into interest rate, market, inflation, business, financial, and liquidity risks. Investors today must also consider exchange rate risk and country risk.

▶ Each security has its own sources of risk, which we will discuss when we discuss the security itself.

▶ Historical returns can be described in terms of a frequency distribution and their variability measured by use of the standard deviation.

▶ The standard deviation provides useful information about the distribution of returns and aids investors in assessing the possible outcomes of an investment.

▶ Common stocks over the period 1920 to 2002 had an annualized geometric mean total return of 10.05 percent, compared to 5.38 percent for long-term Treasury bonds.

▶ Over the period 1920 to 2002, common stocks had a standard deviation of returns of approximately 20 percent, a little more than twice that of long-term government and corporate bonds and about six times that of Treasury bills.

Key Words

Capital gain (loss)	Interest rate risk	Standard deviation
Cumulative wealth index	Market risk	Systematic (market) risk
Equity risk premium	Nonsystematic (nonmarket) risk	Total return (TR)
Exchange rate risk (currency risk)	Return relative	Yield
Geometric mean	Risk premium	

Questions

6-1   Distinguish between historical return and expected return.

6-2   How long must an asset be held to calculate a TR?

6-3   Define the components of total return. Can any of these components be negative?

6-4   Distinguish between TR and holding period return.

6-5   When should the geometric mean return be used to measure returns? Why will it always be less than the arithmetic mean (unless the numbers are identical)?

6-6   When should the arithmetic mean be used in talking about stock returns?

6-7   What is the mathematical linkage between the arithmetic mean and the geometric mean for a set of security returns?

6-8   What is an equity risk premium?

6-9   According to Table 6-5, common stocks have generally returned more than bonds. How, then, can they be considered more risky?

6-10   Distinguish between market risk and business risk. How is interest rate risk related to inflation risk?

6-11   Classify the traditional sources of risk as to whether they are general sources of risk or specific sources of risk.

6-12   Explain what is meant by country risk. How would you evaluate the country risk of Canada and Mexico?

6-13   Assume that you purchase a stock on a Japanese market, denominated in yen. During the period you hold the stock, the yen weakens relative to the dollar. Assume you sell at a profit on the Japanese market. How will your return, when converted to dollars, be affected?

6-14   Define risk. How does use of the standard deviation as a measure of risk relate to this definition of risk?

6-15   Explain verbally the relationship between the geometric mean and a cumulative wealth index.

6-16   As Table 6-5 shows, the geometric mean return for stocks over a long period has been around 10 percent. The returns on Treasury bonds for some recent years have been extremely good, leading some to recommend that investors avoid stocks and purchase bonds because the returns can be very attractive and the risk is far less. Critique this argument.

6-17   Explain how the geometric mean annual average inflation rate can be used to calculate inflation-adjusted stock returns over the period 1920 to 2002.

6-18   Explain the two components of the cumulative wealth index for common stocks. If we know one of these components on a cumulative wealth basis, how can the other be calculated?

6-19   Common stocks have returned slightly less than twice the compound annual rate of return for corporate bonds. Does this mean that common stocks are about twice as risky as corporates?

6-20   What does it mean if the cumulative wealth index for government bonds over a long period is 0.85?

The following question was asked on the 1990 CFA Level I examination:

CFA
6-21   Fundamental to investing is the control of investment risk while maximizing total investment return. **Identify** *four* primary *sources* of risk faced by investors, and **explain** the possible impact on investment returns.

Demonstration Problems

6-1   Calculation of Arithmetic Mean and Geometric Mean:

IBM DATA

Year(t)	(1) End-of-Year Price (P_t)	(2) Calendar-Year Dividends (D_t)	TR%
19X0	$ 74.60	$2.88	—
19X1	64.30	3.44	− 9.2%
19X2	67.70	3.44	10.6%
19X3	56.70	3.44	−11.2%
19X4	96.25	3.44	75.8%
19X5	122.00	3.71	30.6%

The arithmetic mean of the total returns for IBM, 19X1–19X5:

$$\frac{\Sigma(\text{TR}\%)}{n} = \frac{96.6}{5} = 19.32\%$$

The *geometric* mean in this example is the fifth root of the product of the $(1 + r)$ version of the TR percent. We formed the TR percent by multiplying the decimal by 100 to get r percent. Now back up to the $(1 + r)$:

Year	TR% = r%	r	(1 + r)
19X1	− 9.2%	−0.092	0.908
19X2	10.6%	0.106	1.106
19X3	−11.2%	−0.112	0.888
19X4	75.8%	0.758	1.758
19X5	−30.6%	0.306	1.306

The geometric mean is GM = $[(1 + r_1)(1 + r_2) \ldots (1 + r_n)]^{1/n} - 1$. Therefore, take the fifth root of the product

$$(0.908)(1.106)(0.888)(1.758)(1.306) = 2.047462654, \text{ and}$$

$$(2.047462654)^{1/5} = 1.1541 = (1 + r), r = 0.1541, r\% = 100r = 15.41\%$$

6-2   **The Effects of Reinvesting Returns:** The difference in meaning of the arithmetic and geometric mean, holding IBM stock over the period January 1, 19X1 through December 31, 19X5 for two different investment strategies, is as follows:

Strategy A—keep a fixed amount (say, $1,000) invested and do not reinvest returns.
Strategy B—reinvest returns and allow compounding.

First, take IBM's TRs and convert them to decimal form (r) for Strategy A, and then to $(1 + r)$ form for Strategy B.

Jan. I Year	Strategy A Amount Invested $\times$	r	$=$ Return	Jan. I Year	Strategy B Amt. Inv. $\times$ $(1 + r)$		$=$ Terminal Amt.
19X1	$1000	−0.092	−$92.00	19X1	$1000	0.908	$ 908.00
19X2	1000	0.106	106.00	19X2	908.00	1.106	1004.25
19X3	1000	−0.112	−112.00	19X3	1004.25	0.888	891.77
19X4	1000	0.758	758.00	19X4	891.77	1.758	1567.74
19X5	1000	0.306	306.00	19X5	1567.74	1.306	2047.46
19X6	1000			19X6	2047.46		

Using Strategy A, keeping $1,000 invested at the beginning of the year, total returns for the years 19X1 to 19X5 were $966, or $193.20 per year average ($966/5), which on a $1,000 investment is $193.20/1000 = 0.1932, or 19.32 percent per year—the same value as the arithmetic mean in Demonstration Problem 6-1 earlier.

Using Strategy B, compounding gains and losses, total return was $1,047.46 (the terminal amount $2,047.46 minus the initial $1,000). The average annual rate of return in this situation can be found by taking the nth root of the terminal/initial amount:

$$[2047.46/1000]^{1/5} = (2.04746)^{1/5} = 1.1541 = (1 + r), r\% = 15.41\%$$

which is exactly the set of values we ended up with in Demonstration Problem 6-1 when calculating the geometric mean.

6-3 **Calculating the Standard Deviation:** Using the TR values for IBM for the five years 19X1 to 19X5, we can illustrate the calculation of the standard deviation.

The numerator for the formula for the variance of these Y_t values is $\Sigma(Y_t - \overline{Y})^2$, which we will call SS_y, the sum of the squared deviations of the Y_t around $\overline{Y}$. Algebraically, there is a simpler alternative formula.

$$SS_y = \Sigma(Y_t - \overline{Y})^2 = \Sigma Y_t^2 - \frac{(\Sigma Y)_t^2}{n}$$

Using IBM's annual total returns, we will calculate the SS_y both ways. $\overline{Y} = 19.32\%$.

Year	$Y_t = $ TR	$(Y_t - \overline{Y})$	$(Y_t - \overline{Y})^2$	Y_t^2
19X1	− 9.2%	28.52	813.3904	84.64
19X2	10.6%	− 8.72	76.0384	112.36
19X3	−11.2%	−30.52	931.4704	125.44
19X4	75.8%	56.48	3189.9904	5745.64
19X5	30.6%	11.28	127.2384	936.36
Sum	96.6%	-0-	5138.1280	7004.44

$$\overline{Y} = 19.32\%$$

$$SS_y = \Sigma(Y_y - \overline{Y})^2 = 5138.128, \text{ and also}$$

$$SS_y = \Sigma Y^2 - \frac{(\Sigma Y)^2}{n} = 7004.44 - \frac{(96.6)^2}{5} = 5138.128$$

The variance is the "average" squared deviation from the mean:

$$\sigma^2 = \frac{SS_y}{n - 1} = \frac{5138.128}{4} = 1284.532 \text{ "squared percent"}$$

The standard deviation is the square root of the variance:

$$\sigma = (\sigma^2)^{1/2} = (1284.532)^{1/2} = 35.84\%$$

The standard deviation is in the same units of measurement as the original observations, as is the arithmetic mean.

6-4   **Calculation of Cumulative Wealth Index and Geometric Mean:** By using the geometric mean annual average rate of return for a particular financial asset, the cumulative wealth index can be found by converting the TR on a geometric mean basis to a return relative by adding 1.0, and raising this return relative to the power representing the number of years involved. Consider the geometric mean of 12.8 percent for small common stocks for the period January 1926 to December 1998, a total of 73 years ([1998 − 1926] + 1). The cumulative wealth index, using a starting index value of $1, is

$$\$1(1.128)^{73} = \$6585.13$$

Conversely, if we know the cumulative wealth index value, we can solve for the geometric mean by taking the nth root and subtracting out 1.0.

$$(\$6585.13)^{1/73} - 1.0 = 1.128 - 1.0 = 12.8\%$$

6-5   **Calculation of Inflation-Adjusted Returns:** Knowing the geometric mean for inflation for some time period, we can add 1.0 and raise it to the nth power. We then divide the cumulative wealth index on a nominal basis by the ending value for inflation to obtain inflation-adjusted returns. For example, given a cumulative wealth index of $3,741.37 for common stocks for January 1920 to December 1998, and a geometric mean inflation rate of 2.62 percent, the inflation-adjusted cumulative wealth index for this 79-year period ([1998 − 1920] + 1) is calculated as

$$\$3741.37/(1.0262)^{79} = \$3741.37/\ 7.715 = \$484.95$$

6-6   **Analyzing the Components of a Cumulative Wealth Index:** Assume that we know that for the period January 1920 to December 1998 the yield component for common stocks was 4.46 percent, and that the cumulative wealth index was $3,741.37. The cumulative wealth index value for the yield component was

$$(1.0446)^{79} = 31.41$$

The cumulative wealth index value for the price change component was

$$\$3,741.37/31.41 = 119.11$$

The geometric mean annual average rate of return for the price change component for common stocks was

$$(119.11)^{1/79} = 1.0624$$

The geometric mean for common stocks is linked to its components by the following

$$1.0446\ (1.0624) = 1.1098$$

The cumulative wealth index can be found by multiplying together the individual component cumulative wealth indexes (rounding errors account for differences).

$$\$119.11\ (\$31.41) = \$3,741.25$$

Problems

6-1 Using the data for IBM from Demonstration Problem 6-1, calculate the capital gain (loss) and total return for the years 19X1 to 19X5 and confirm the 19X3 and 19X4 TRs.

6-2 Assume that an investor in a 28-percent marginal tax bracket buys 100 shares of a stock for $40, holds it for five months, and sells it at $50. What tax, in dollars, will be paid on the gain?

6-3 Calculate the TR and the return relative for the following assets:
a. A preferred stock bought for $70 per share, held one year during which $5 per share dividends are collected, and sold for $63.
b. A warrant bought for $11 and sold three months later for $13.
c. A 12-percent bond bought for $870, held two years during which interest is collected, and sold for $930.

6-4 Calculate the future value of $100 at the end of 5, 10, 20, and 30 years, given an interest rate of 12 percent. Calculate the present value of $1 to be received at the end of those same periods, given the same interest rate.

6-5 Calculate, using a calculator, the arithmetic and geometric mean rate of return for the Standard & Poor 500 Composite Index (Table 6-1) for the years 1980 to 1985.

6-6 Calculate, using a calculator, the standard deviation of TRs (from Table 6-1) for the years 1980 through 1985.

6-7 Calculate the index value for the S&P 500 (Table 6-1) assuming a $1 investment at the beginning of 1980 and extending through the end of 1989. Using only these index values, calculate the geometric mean for these years.

6-8 Calculate cumulative wealth for common stocks for the period 1920 through December 1998 (79 years of data), assuming the geometric mean was 10.98 percent.

6-9 Calculate cumulative wealth for corporate bonds for the period 1920 to 2002, using data in Table 6-5 (83 years).

6-10 Calculate the cumulative wealth index for government bonds for the period 1926 to 1993, assuming a geometric mean annual average rate of return of 5 percent.

6-11 Given a cumulative wealth index for corporate bonds of $95.84 for the period 1920 to 1998, calculate the geometric mean annual average rate of return.

6-12 Given an inflation rate of 3.00 percent over the period 1926 to 1998 (geometric mean annual average), calculate the inflation-adjusted cumulative wealth index for "small" common stocks as of year-end 1998, assuming that the nominal cumulative wealth index for this asset class was $13,293.14. There are 73 years of data in this situation.

6-13 If a basket of consumer goods cost $1 at the beginning of 1920 and $9 at the end of 2002, calculate the geometric mean annual average rate of inflation over this period.

6-14 Assume that over the period 1920–2002 the yield index component of common stocks had a geometric mean annual average of 1.0446. Calculate the cumulative wealth index for this component as of year-end 2002. Using this value, calculate the cumulative wealth index for the price change component of common stocks using information in Figure 6-2.

6-15 Assume that the yield component of the total return for small common stocks was 1 percent (geometric mean) for the period 1920 to 1998. Also assume that the cumulative wealth index for the price change component for this series was $6056.65. Calculate the cumulative wealth index for small common stocks for this period.

6-16 Assume that over the period 1920 to 2002 the geometric mean annual average rate of return for Treasury bonds was 5.38 percent. The corresponding number for the rate of inflation was 2.54 percent. Calculate, two different ways, the cumulative wealth index for Treasury bonds at the end of 2002, on an inflation-adjusted basis.

6-17 Using the TRs for the years 1926 to 1931 from Table 6-1, determine the geometric mean for this period. Show how the same result can be obtained from the ending wealth index value for 1931 of 0.79591.

6-18 Using data for three periods, construct a set of TRs that will produce a geometric mean equal to the arithmetic mean.

6-19 According to Table 6-5, the standard deviation for all common stocks for the period 1920 to 2002 was 19.42 percent. Using data from Table 6-1, calculate the standard deviation for the years 1981 to 1991 and compare your results.

6-20 Verify that the standard deviation calculated in Table 6-4 is correct. Change the 1975 TR from 36.92 to 26.92 and recalculate the standard deviation. What happened, and why?

Questions 6-21 through 6-32 are part of a comprehensive problem set using the information on rates of return for the period 1920 through 1998 (79 years) as given below:

	Geometric Mean	Arithmetic Mean	Std. Dev.
Common stocks	11.0%	12.8%	20.7%
Small company stocks	12.8	18.9	39.5
Long-term corporates	5.9	6.3	8.1
Long-term governments	5.5	5.6	8.1
Treasury bills	4.0	4.1	3.2
Inflation	2.6	2.7	4.6

6-21 Calculate the cumulative wealth index from an investment of $1 in common stocks from the beginning of 1920. There are 79 years involved.

6-22 Compare this with the corresponding ending wealth for long-term corporates.

6-23 Calculate the cumulative wealth index from an investment of $1 in small common stocks at the end of 1919. How do you explain the large difference in ending wealth between common stocks (the S&P 500) and small common stocks given only the roughly 2 percentage point difference in the geometric means?

6-24 According to the data, the capital appreciation index for common stocks amounted to 119.11 by the end of 1998. Explain what this number means relative to
a. the beginning point—the first day of 1920.
b. the cumulative index for common stocks of 3741.37.

6-25 Given the cumulative wealth index of 3741.37 and the capital appreciation index of 119.11:
a. What is the other component of total return for common stocks?
b. Calculate both the ending wealth index and the geometric mean annual rate of return for this component.
c. What do the two components of total return on an annual average basis imply about the relative importance of each?

6-26 Assume that the wealth index for common stocks was 675.592 for 1991 and 517.449 for 1990. What was the annual rate of return for common stocks for 1991?

6-27 Assume that for long-term governments, the capital appreciation index was 0.87 for the entire period.
a. Calculate the cumulative wealth index for long-term governments based on the table above.
b. Calculate the geometric mean annual average rate of return for the capital appreciation component.
c. What does this say about the income component of total return for long-term governments?

6-28 Calculate the ending index number for inflation as of 1998. How can this value be interpreted?

6-29 Now consider real returns—that is, inflation-adjusted returns. Based on the previous numbers given for the cumulative wealth index for common stocks and the ending index number for inflation, calculate the real (inflation-adjusted) cumulative wealth index for common stocks at the end of 1998.

6-30 Calculate the geometric mean annual average real return for stocks.

6-31 Given a geometric mean inflation-adjusted corporate bond annual return of 3.2 percent, calculate the cumulative wealth index for corporate bonds and compare this number to that of stocks.

6-32 Compare the arithmetic and geometric means in the table above. What factor(s) do you think account for the difference between the two for any given asset, such as for stocks or government bonds? Assume you could invest in a new category of high-risk common stocks with an expected arithmetic mean annual return over the next few years of 15 percent, with a standard deviation of 50 percent. Estimate the geometric mean rate of return for this new category of stocks.

Questions 6-33 through 6-38 are part of a comprehensive problem set using the information on closed-end funds as given below:

Consider total return data for some closed-end investment companies (discussed in Chapter 3). Exactly like mutual funds, various types of closed-end funds invest in portfolios of securities on behalf of their own shareholders. Some invest in stocks (domestic, foreign, or both) and some in bonds (taxable, nontaxable, foreign, and so forth). The following data are available from a variety of sources:

INA Investment Securities, classified as a general corporate bond fund. This fund seeks income, with capital appreciation a secondary objective; 90 percent of funds must be invested in debt and preferred stock of issuers within the highest four debt ratings. (See Chapter 2 for a discussion of bond ratings.)

Adams Express, classified as a domestic equity fund. One of the oldest closed-end funds, Adams Express has as its major objective the preservation of capital, with income and capital appreciation secondary objectives. It holds no bonds, but it may have a small percentage of assets in convertibles.

Bergstrom Capital, classified as a domestic equity fund. However, unlike Adams Express, this fund has as its objective long-term capital appreciation. There are no limits on the types of securities it can invest in.

The following hypothetical TRs are available for 1991 to 2003:

	INA Investment Securities	Adams Express	Bergstrom Capital	S&P 500 Index
1991	− 2.18%	42.51%	62.44%	31.48%
1992	− 0.48	5.97	− 7.83	− 4.85
1993	28.24	34.46	40.79	20.37
1994	10.25	14.48	22.16	22.31
1995	15.28	4.39	25.42	5.97
1996	24.61	30.09	42.61	31.06
1997	13.55	23.14	15.74	18.54
1998	− 2.26	− 4.72	− 10.75	5.67
1999	10.26	11.39	16.54	16.34
2000	10.66	20.30	50.75	31.23
2001	− 3.79	5.41	− 1.32	− 3.13
2002	29.94	40.76	107.32	30.00
2003	5.43	14.08	10.68	7.48

6-33 Based on the discussion of return and risk in general, and on the stated objective of each of these funds, rank these funds from highest (1) to lowest (3) on the basis of both the return and risk (standard deviation) that would typically be expected from these types of funds over time.

6-34 Without doing any calculations, and using 2003 as the last year, rank the funds in the table below on the basis of likely performance with regard to arithmetic mean total return for the last 3, 5, and 10 years. The 1-year ranking for 2003 is shown in the table below.

	INA Investment	Adams Express	Bergstrom Capital
1-year perf.	3	1	2
3-year avg.			
5-year avg.			
10-year avg.			

6-35 Using a spreadsheet or appropriate tools, calculate the arithmetic mean return, standard deviation, and geometric mean for these funds and for the S&P 500 for the years 1991 to 2003.

6-36 Is the S&P 500 the correct benchmark to use for INA Investment? Which of the two stock funds would you expect to be more closely related to the return on the S&P 500?

6-37 Determine the cumulative wealth index over the period 1991 to 2003 from investing $1 in each of the three funds.

6-38 Compare the geometric mean annual return for the two stock funds for this period to the S&P 500 for the same period and to the S&P 500 for the overall period 1920 to 2002. What conclusions can you draw from this analysis?

Web Resources

For additional resources visit our dynamic Web site located at www.wiley.com/college/jones.

- *Ray and Gladys*—A finance major gives investment advice to her grandparents to help make their retirement funds go as far as possible. She must analyze the retirement funds available and suggest the most appropriate types of securities for reinvestment.

- Internet Exercises—This chapter analyzes the returns and risks from investing. Obviously, a first step is measuring these quantities. The Web exercises will address the measurement of returns, and of risk.
  Exercise 1: Asks the reader to compute return statistics for individual stocks and portfolios.
  Exercise 2: The reader is asked to compute return statistics for the NYSE indices and for T-bills; s/he is the asked to compare average returns and volatilities.
  Exercise 3: Discusses the arithmetic and geometric means.

- Multiple Choice Self Test

Selected Reference

The best-known source for the returns and risk of major financial assets is:

Ibbotson Associates, Inc. *Stocks, Bonds, Bills and Inflation: Yearbook*. Annual. Chicago: Ibbotson Associates.

chapter 7

Portfolio Theory

$\mathbf{C}$hapter 7 analyzes *expected* return and risk, the two key components needed to construct portfolios. The critically important principle of Markowitz diversification is explored, focusing primarily on the concepts of the correlation coefficient and covariance as applied to security returns. In Chapter 8, we will complete the basics of Markowitz portfolio theory.

AFTER READING THIS CHAPTER YOU WILL BE ABLE TO:

▶ Understand the meaning and calculation of expected return and risk measures for an individual security.

▶ Recognize what it means to talk about modern portfolio theory.

▶ Understand portfolio return and risk measures as formulated by Markowitz.

▶ Understand what the efficient frontier is and its importance to investment analysis.

As stated in Chapter 1, this text is concerned primarily with investing in marketable securities. An investment in financial assets represents the current commitment of an investor's funds (wealth) for a future period of time in order to earn a flow of funds that compensates for two factors: the time the funds are committed and the risk involved. In effect, investors are trading a known present value (the purchase price of the asset) for some *expected* future value—that is, one not known with certainty.

When we invest, we defer current consumption in order to increase our future consumption. We are concerned with the increase in wealth from our investments, and this increase is typically measured as a rate of return in order to adjust for differing dollar amounts of investment.

As noted in Chapter 1, risk is the chance that the actual return from an investment will differ from its expected return. In an uncertain world, risk is the opposite side of the coin from return. Investors are concerned primarily with how to achieve the highest possible returns without bearing unacceptable risk.

In this chapter, we outline the nature of risk and return as it applies to investment decisions. Unlike Chapter 6, we are talking about the future, which involves *expected returns*, and not the past, which involves *realized returns*. Investors must estimate and manage the returns and risk from their investments. They reduce risk to the extent possible without affecting returns by building diversified portfolios. Therefore, we must be concerned with the investor's total portfolio and analyze investment risk accordingly. As we shall see, diversification is the key to effective risk management.

At the conclusion of this analysis, we will be able to understand the two key characteristics of every investment decision—its expected return and risk—on both an individual security basis and, more importantly, on a portfolio basis. We will also understand the basic principles of Markowitz portfolio theory, a very well-known investments concept.

Dealing with Uncertainty

In Chapter 6, we discussed the average returns, both arithmetic and geometric, that investors have experienced over the years from investing in the major financial assets available to them. We also considered the risk of these asset returns as measured by the standard deviation. Analysts often refer to the realized returns for a security, or class of securities, over time using these measures as well as other measures such as the cumulative wealth index.

Realized returns are important for several reasons. For example, investors need to know how their portfolios have performed. Realized returns also can be particularly important in helping investors to form expectations about future returns, because investors must concern themselves with their best estimate of return over the next year, or six months, or whatever. How do we go about estimating returns, which is what investors must actually do in managing their portfolios?

First of all, note that we will use the return and risk measures developed in Chapter 6. The total return measure, TR, is applicable whether one is measuring realized returns or estimating future (expected) returns. Because it includes everything the investor can expect to receive over any specified future period, the TR is useful in conceptualizing the estimated returns from securities.

Similarly, the variance, or its square root, the standard deviation, is an accepted measure of variability for both realized returns and expected returns. We will calculate both the variance and the standard deviation below and use them interchangeably as the situation dictates. Sometimes it is preferable to use one and sometimes the other. In Chapter 9 we will consider another measure of risk, beta, which relates to the systematic risk of an asset.

To estimate the returns from various securities, investors must estimate the cash flows these securities are likely to provide. The basis for doing so for bonds and stocks will be covered in their respective chapters. For now, it is sufficient to remind ourselves of the uncertainty of estimates of the future, a problem emphasized at the beginning of Chapter 1.

USING PROBABILITY DISTRIBUTIONS

The return an investor will earn from investing is not known; it must be estimated. Future return is an *expected* return and may or may not actually be realized. An investor may expect the TR on a particular security to be 0.10 for the coming year, but in truth this is only a "point estimate." Risk, or the chance that some unfavorable event will occur, is involved when investment decisions are made. Investors are often overly optimistic about expected returns.

Probability Distributions To deal with the uncertainty of returns, investors need to think explicitly about a security's distribution of probable TRs. In other words, investors need to keep in mind that, although they may expect a security to return 10 percent, for example, this is only a one-point estimate of the entire range of possibilities. Given that investors must deal with the uncertain future, a number of possible returns can, and will, occur.

In the case of a Treasury bond paying a fixed rate of interest, the interest payment will be made with 100-percent certainty barring a financial collapse of the economy. The probability of occurrence is 1.0, because no other outcome is possible.

With the possibility of two or more outcomes, which is the norm for common stocks, each possible likely outcome must be considered and a probability of its occurrence assessed. The probability for a particular outcome is simply the chance that the specified outcome will occur. The result of considering these outcomes and their probabilities together is a *probability distribution* consisting of the specification of the likely outcomes that may occur and the probabilities associated with these likely outcomes.

Probabilities represent the likelihood of various outcomes and are typically expressed as a decimal. (Sometimes fractions are used.) The sum of the probabilities of all possible outcomes must be 1.0, because they must completely describe all the (perceived) likely occurrences.

How are these probabilities and associated outcomes obtained? In the final analysis, investing for some future period involves uncertainty, and therefore subjective estimates. Although past occurrences (frequencies) may be relied on heavily to estimate the probabilities, the past must be modified for any changes expected in the future.

Probability distributions can be either discrete or continuous. With a discrete probability distribution, a probability is assigned to each possible outcome. In Figure 7-1a, five possible TRs are assumed for a stock for next year. Each of these five possible outcomes has an associated probability, with the sum of the probabilities being equal to 1.0.

With a continuous probability distribution, as shown in Figure 7-1b, an infinite number of possible outcomes exist. Because probability is now measured as the area under the curve in Figure 7-1b, the emphasis is on the probability that a particular outcome is within some range of values.

The most familiar continuous distribution is the normal distribution depicted in Figure 7-1b. This is the well-known bell-shaped curve often used in statistics. It is a two-parameter distribution in that the mean and the variance fully describe it.

Figure 7-1

(*a*) **A discrete probability distribution.** (*b*) **A continuous probability distribution.**

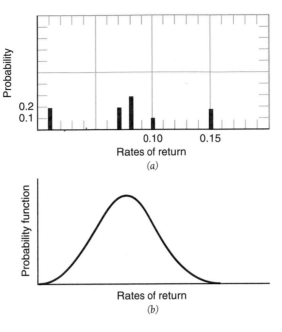

CALCULATING EXPECTED RETURN FOR A SECURITY

To describe the single most likely outcome from a particular probability distribution, it is necessary to calculate its *expected value*. The expected value is the weighted average of all possible return outcomes, where each outcome is weighted by its respective probability of occurrence. Since investors are interested in returns, we will call this expected value the *expected rate of return*, or simply **expected return**, and for any security, it is calculated as

Expected Return The *ex ante* return expected by investors over some future holding period

$$E(R) = \sum_{i=1}^{m} R_i pr_i \tag{7-1}$$

where

$E(R)$ = the expected return on a security
R_i = the *i*th possible return
pr_i = the probability of the *i*th return R_i
m = the number of possible returns

Example 7-1   The expected return for the discrete probability distribution in Figure 7-1*a* is 0.08.

CALCULATING RISK FOR A SECURITY

Investors must be able to quantify and measure risk. To calculate the total risk associated with the expected return, the variance or standard deviation is used. As we know from Chapter 6, the variance and its square root, standard deviation, are measures of the spread or dispersion in the probability distribution; that is, they measure the dispersion of a random variable around its mean. The larger this dispersion, the larger the variance or standard deviation.

To calculate the variance or standard deviation from the probability distribution, first calculate the expected return of the distribution using Equation 7-1. Essentially, the same procedure used in Chapter 6 to measure risk applies here, but now the probabilities associated with the outcomes must be included, as in Equation 7-2.

$$\text{the variance of returns} = \sigma^2 = \sum_{i=1}^{m} [R_i - E(R)]^2 pr_i \qquad \textbf{(7-2)}$$

and

$$\text{the standard deviation of returns} = \sigma = (\sigma^2)^{1/2} \qquad \textbf{(7-3)}$$

where all terms are as defined previously.

Example 7-2   The variance and standard deviation for the hypothetical stock shown in Figure 7-1a are calculated in Table 7-1.

Calculating a standard deviation using probability distributions involves making subjective estimates of the probabilities and the likely returns. However, we cannot avoid such estimates, because future returns are uncertain. The prices of securities are based on investors' expectations about the future. The relevant standard deviation in this situation is the *ex ante* standard deviation and not the *ex post* based on realized returns.

Although standard deviations based on realized returns are often used as proxies for *ex ante* standard deviations, investors should be careful to remember that the past cannot always be extrapolated into the future without modifications. *Ex post* standard deviations may be convenient, but they are subject to errors when used as estimates of the future.

One important point about the estimation of standard deviation is the distinction between individual securities and portfolios. Standard deviations for well-diversified portfolios are reasonably steady across time, and therefore historical calculations may be fairly reliable in projecting the future. Moving from well-diversified portfolios to individual securities, however, makes historical calculations much less reliable. Fortunately, the number one rule of portfolio management is to diversify and hold a portfolio of securities. Investors should always diversify in order to deal with the uncertainty involved when investing. Therefore, we need to consider the expected return and risk for a portfolio.

Portfolio Return and Risk

When we analyze investment returns and risks, we must be concerned with the total portfolio held by an investor. Individual security returns and risks are important, but it is the return and risk to the investor's total portfolio that ultimately matters, because invest-

Table 7-1   Calculating the Standard Deviation Using Expected Data

(1) Possible Return	(2) Probability	(3) (1) × (2)	(4) $R_i - E(R)$	(5) $(R_i - E(R))^2$	(6) $(R_i - E(R))^2 pr_i$
0.01	0.2	0.002	−0.070	0.0049	0.00098
0.07	0.2	0.014	−0.010	0.0001	0.00002
0.08	0.3	0.024	0.000	0.0000	0.00000
0.10	0.1	0.010	0.020	0.0004	0.00004
0.15	0.2	0.030	0.070	0.0049	0.00098
	1.0	0.080 = E(R)			0.00202

$\sigma = (0.00202)^{1/2} = 0.0449 = 4.49\%$

ment opportunities can be enhanced by packaging them together to form portfolios. As we learned in Chapter 1, an investor's portfolio is his or her combination of assets.

As we will see, portfolio risk is a unique characteristic and not simply the sum of individual security risks. A security may have a large risk if it is held by itself but much less risk when held in a portfolio of securities. Since the investor is concerned primarily with the risk to his or her total wealth, as represented by his or her portfolio, individual stocks are risky only to the extent that they add risk to the total portfolio.

PORTFOLIO EXPECTED RETURN

Portfolio Weights
Percentages of portfolio funds invested in each security, summing to 1.0

The expected return on any portfolio is easily calculated as a weighted average of the individual securities' expected returns. The percentages of a portfolio's total value that are invested in each portfolio asset are referred to as **portfolio weights**, which we will denote by w. The combined portfolio weights are assumed to sum to 100 percent of total investable funds, or 1.0, indicating that all portfolio funds are invested. That is,

$$w_1 + w_2 + \ldots + w_n = \sum_{i=1}^{n} w_i = 1.0 \qquad (7\text{-}4)$$

Example 7-3

With equal dollar amounts in three securities, the portfolio weights are 0.333, 0.333, and 0.333. Under the same conditions with a portfolio of five securities, each security would have a portfolio weight of 0.20. Of course, dollar amounts do not have to be equal. A five-stock portfolio could have weights of 0.40, 0.10, 0.15, 0.25, and 0.10, or 0.18, 0.33, 0.11, 0.22, and 0.16.

The expected return on any portfolio p can be calculated as

$$E(R_p) = \sum_{i=1}^{n} w_i \, E(R_i) \qquad (7\text{-}5)$$

where

$E(R_p)$ = the expected return on the portfolio
w_i = the portfolio weight for the ith security
Σw_i = 1.0
$E(R_i)$ = the expected return on the ith security
n = the number of different securities in the portfolio

Example 7-4

Consider a three-stock portfolio consisting of stocks G, H, and I with expected returns of 12 percent, 20 percent, and 17 percent, respectively. Assume that 50 percent of investable funds is invested in security G, 30 percent in H, and 20 percent in I. The expected return on this portfolio, using Equation 7-5, is:

$$E(R_p) = 0.5(12\%) + 0.3(20\%) + 0.2(17\%) = 15.4\%$$

Regardless of the number of assets held in a portfolio, or the proportion of total investable funds placed in each asset, the expected return on the portfolio is always a weighted average of the expected returns for individual assets in the portfolio. This is a very important principle that should always be kept in mind.

PORTFOLIO RISK

The remaining computation in investment analysis is that of the risk of the portfolio. Risk is measured by the variance (or standard deviation) of the portfolio's return, exactly as in the case of each individual security. Typically, portfolio risk is stated in terms of standard deviation which is simply the square root of the variance.

It is at this point that the basis of modern portfolio theory emerges, which can be stated as follows: Although the expected return of a portfolio is a weighted average of its expected returns, portfolio risk (as measured by the variance or standard deviation) is *not* a weighted average of the risk of the individual securities in the portfolio. Symbolically,

$$E(R_p) = \sum_{i=1}^{n} w_i E(R_i) \tag{7-6}$$

But

$$\sigma_p^2 \neq \sum_{i=1}^{n} w_i \sigma_i^2 \tag{7-7}$$

Precisely because Equation 7-7 is an inequality, investors can reduce the risk of a portfolio beyond what it would be if risk were, in fact, simply a weighted average of the individual securities' risk. In order to see how this risk reduction can be accomplished, we must analyze portfolio risk in detail.

Analyzing Portfolio Risk

RISK REDUCTION—THE INSURANCE PRINCIPLE

To begin our analysis of how a portfolio of assets can reduce risk, assume that all risk sources in a portfolio of securities are independent. As we add securities to this portfolio, the exposure to any particular source of risk becomes small. According to the *Law of Large Numbers*, the larger the sample size, the more likely it is that the sample mean will be close to the population expected value. Risk reduction in the case of independent risk sources can be thought of as the *insurance principle*, named for the idea that an insurance company reduces its risk by writing many policies against many independent sources of risk.

We are assuming here that rates of return on individual securities are statistically independent such that any one security's rate of return is unaffected by another's rate of return. In this situation, the standard deviation of the portfolio is given by

$$\sigma_p = \frac{\sigma_i}{n^{1/2}} \tag{7-8}$$

As Figure 7-2 shows, the risk of the portfolio will quickly decline as more securities are added. Notice that no decision is to be made about which security to add, because all have identical properties. The only issue is how many securities are added.

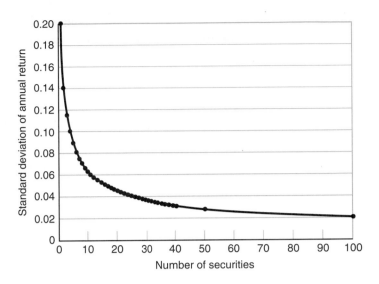

Figure 7-2

Risk reduction when returns are independent.

Example 7-5 Figure 7-2 shows how risk declines given that the risk of each security is 0.20. The risk of the portfolio will quickly decline as more and more of these securities are added. Equation 7-8 indicates that for the case of 100 securities the risk of the portfolio is reduced to 0.02:

$$\sigma_p = \frac{0.20}{100^{1/2}}$$
$$= 0.02$$

Figure 7-2 illustrates the case of independent risk sources. As applied to investing, all risk in this situation is firm specific. Therefore, the total risk in this situation can continue to be reduced. Unfortunately, the assumption of statistically independent returns on stocks is unrealistic in the real world. Going back to the definition of market risk in Chapter 6, we find that most stocks are positively correlated with each other; that is, the movements in their returns are related.

Most stocks have a significant level of comovement with the overall market of stocks, as measured by such indexes as the Standard & Poor's (S&P) 500 Composite Index. In Chapter 6, we identified this risk as systematic (market) risk. Although total risk can be reduced, it cannot be eliminated, because common sources of risk (systematic risk) affect all firms and cannot be diversified away. For example, a rise in interest rates will affect most firms adversely, because most firms borrow funds to finance part of their operations.

DIVERSIFICATION

The insurance principle illustrates the concept of attempting to diversify the risk involved in a portfolio of assets (or liabilities). In fact, diversification is the key to the management of portfolio risk, because it allows investors significantly to lower portfolio risk without adversely affecting return. Throughout our discussion in both this chapter and Chapter 8, we will be focusing on the diversification principle. We begin with random diversification and move to efficient diversification.

Random Diversification *Random* or *naive diversification* refers to the act of randomly diversifying without regard to relevant investment characteristics such as expected return and industry classification. An investor simply selects a relatively large number of securities randomly—the proverbial "throwing a dart at *The Wall Street Journal* page showing stock quotes." For simplicity, we assume equal dollar amounts are invested in each stock.

Table 7-2 uses actual data for domestic stocks from a number of years ago to illustrate naive diversification. As we can see, for randomly selected portfolios, average portfolio risk was reduced to approximately 19 percent. As we add securities to the portfolio, the total risk associated with the portfolio of stocks declines rapidly. The first few stocks cause a large decrease in portfolio risk. Based on these actual data from the past, 51 percent of portfolio standard deviation is eliminated as we go from 1 to 10 securities.

One of the long-standing tenets of portfolio theory is that part of the total risk of stocks can be eliminated by diversification—the company-specific risk, which is also

Table 7-2 Expected Standard Deviations of Annual Portfolio

Number of Stocks in Portfolio	Expected Standard Deviation of Annual Portfolio Returns	Ratio of Portfolio Standard Deviation to Standard Deviation of a Single Stock
1	49.236	1.00
2	37.358	0.76
4	29.687	0.60
6	26.643	0.54
8	24.983	0.51
10	23.932	0.49
12	23.204	0.47
14	22.670	0.46
16	22.261	0.45
18	21.939	0.45
20	21.677	0.44
25	21.196	0.43
30	20.870	0.42
35	20.634	0.42
40	20.456	0.42
45	20.316	0.41
50	20.203	0.41
75	19.860	0.40
100	19.686	0.40
200	19.423	0.39
300	19.336	0.39
400	19.292	0.39
450	19.277	0.39
500	19.265	0.39
600	19.247	0.39
700	19.233	0.39
800	19.224	0.39
900	19.217	0.39
1000	19.211	0.39
Infinity	19.158	0.39

SOURCE: Meir Statman, "How Many Stocks Make a Diversified Portfolio?" *Journal of Financial and Quantitative Analysis* (September 1987), p. 355.

called idiosyncratic risk. Although it is recognized that the other component of risk, systematic or market risk, cannot be diversified away, investors have expected to achieve significant portfolio benefits by diversifying their stock holdings across industries and sectors, thereby reducing or possibly eliminating the company-specific risk.

Unfortunately, the benefits of random diversification do not continue as we add more securities. As additional stocks are added, the marginal risk reduction is small. Nevertheless, adding one more stock to the portfolio continued to reduce the risk, although the amount of the reduction becomes smaller and smaller.

Example 7-6   Based on the data in Table 7-2, going from 10 to 20 securities eliminated an additional 5 percentage points of the portfolio standard deviation, whereas going from 20 to 30 securities eliminated only an additional 2 percentage points of the standard deviation.

An important point illustrated by the data in Table 7-2 is that the benefits of diversification kick in immediately—two stocks are better than one, three stocks are better than two, and so on. However, diversification cannot eliminate the risk in a portfolio. Furthermore, and very important to note, recent studies suggest that it takes far more securities to diversify properly than has traditionally been believed to be the case (this point is discussed in detail in Chapter 8).

Some Practical Advice

The stock market decline of 2000 to 2002 dramatically illustrates the importance of diversification. Holding portfolios of tech stocks turned out to be a disaster. However, true diversification involves more than simply the number, or type, of stocks you hold; instead, it should be considered in a much broader context. For young people, the biggest asset they have is their ability to earn an income. Many workers have much of their 401(k) funds invested in their employer's stock, because they often think this stock is safer than a diversified portfolio. Being invested in industries that are highly correlated with the one you are employed in is not good diversification strategy. Also, consider that the typical American family has 60 percent of its wealth tied up in a house. Smart diversification principles would lead people not to invest heavily in industries that dominant their area, because if they were to fail, it could have an effect on housing values.

Modern Portfolio Theory (MPT)

Now that we understand the importance of diversification, we need to be more sophisticated and take advantage of information that we can calculate, such as the expected return and risk for individual securities and measures of how stock returns move together. This will allow us to understand the true nature of portfolio risk and why Equation 7-7 is an inequality. It will also allow us to optimize our diversification, achieving the maximum portfolio risk reduction possible in a given situation.

In the 1950s, Harry Markowitz, considered the father of modern portfolio theory (MPT), developed the basic portfolio principles that underlie modern portfolio theory. His original contribution was published in 1952, making portfolio theory 50+ years old. Over time, these principles have been widely adopted by the financial community, with the result that the legacy of MPT is very broad today.[1] Nevertheless, the primary impact of MPT is on portfolio management, because it provides a framework for the systematic selection of portfolios based on expected return and risk principles. Most portfolio managers today are aware of the basic principles of MPT.

Think of MPT as an investment process, or a theory of portfolio selection. It is sometimes referred to as mean-variance analysis or mean-variance optimization, because portfolios are built on the basis of optimizing the expected return-risk tradeoff.

Markowitz Portfolio Theory Before Markowitz, investors dealt loosely with the concepts of return and risk. Investors have known intuitively for many years that it is smart to diversify; that is, not to "put all of your eggs in one basket." Markowitz, however, was the first to develop the concept of portfolio diversification in a formal way—he quantified the concept of diversification. He showed quantitatively why and how portfolio diversification works to reduce the risk of a portfolio to an investor.

Markowitz sought to organize the existing thoughts and practices into a more formal framework and to answer a basic question: Is the risk of a portfolio equal to the sum of the risks of the individual securities comprising it? Markowitz was the first to develop a specific measure of portfolio risk and to derive the expected return and risk for a portfolio based on covariance relationships. We consider covariances in detail in the discussion below.

Portfolio risk is *not* simply a weighted average of the individual security risks. Rather, as Markowitz first showed, we must account for the interrelationships among security returns in order to calculate portfolio risk, and in order to reduce portfolio risk to its minimum level for any given level of return. The reason we need to consider these interrelationships is that in any one time period, poor performance by some securities may be offset by strong performance in other securities. Therefore, we now consider how to measure these interrelationships, or comovements, among security returns.

In order to remove the inequality sign from Equation 7-7 and develop an equation that will calculate the risk of a portfolio as measured by the variance or standard deviation, we must account for two factors:

1. Weighted individual security risks (i.e., the variance of each individual security, weighted by the percentage of investable funds placed in each individual security).
2. Weighted comovements between securities' returns (i.e., the covariance between the securities' returns, again weighted by the percentage of investable funds placed in each security).

Measuring Comovements in Security Returns

As explained below, covariance is an absolute measure of the comovements between security returns used in the calculation of portfolio risk. We need the actual covariance between securities in a portfolio in order to calculate portfolio variance or standard deviation. Before considering covariance, however, we can easily illustrate how security returns move together by considering the correlation coefficient, a relative measure of association learned in statistics.

---

[1] See Frank J. Fabozzi, Francis Gupta, and Harry M. Markowitz, "The Legacy of Modern Portfolio Theory," *The Journal of Investing*, Fall, 2002, pp. 7–22.

Correlation Coefficient

A statistical measure of the extent to which two variables are associated

The Correlation Coefficient As used in portfolio theory, the **correlation coefficient** ρ_{ij} (pronounced "rho") is a statistical measure of the *relative* comovements between security returns. It measures the extent to which the returns on any two securities are related; however, it denotes only association, not causation. It is a relative measure of association that is bounded by $+1.0$ and -1.0, with

$$\rho_{ij} = +1.0$$

$$= \text{perfect positive correlation}$$

$$\rho_{ij} = -1.0$$

$$= \text{perfect negative (inverse) correlation}$$

$$\rho_{ij} = 0.0$$

$$= \text{zero correlation}$$

Figure 7-3

Returns for the years 1993–1998 on two stocks, A and B, and a portfolio consisting of 50 percent A and 50 percent B, when the correlation coefficient is $+1.0$.

With perfect positive correlation, the returns have a perfect direct linear relationship. Knowing what the return on one security will do allows an investor to forecast perfectly what the other will do. In Figure 7-3, stocks A and B have identical return patterns over the six-year period 1993 to 1998. When stock A's return goes up, stock B's does also. When stock A's return goes down, stock B's does also.

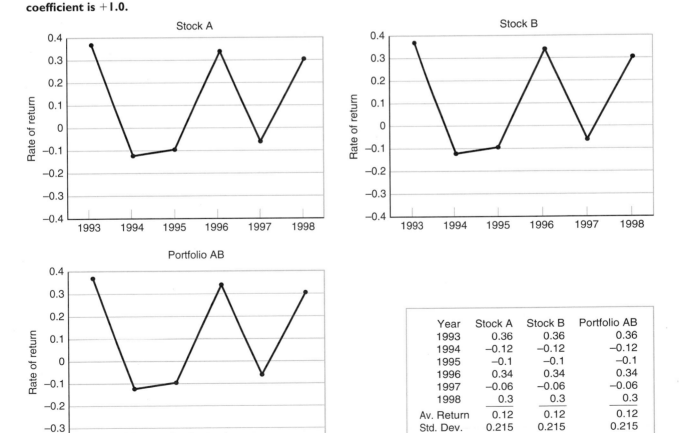

Year	Stock A	Stock B	Portfolio AB
1993	0.36	0.36	0.36
1994	−0.12	−0.12	−0.12
1995	−0.1	−0.1	−0.1
1996	0.34	0.34	0.34
1997	−0.06	−0.06	−0.06
1998	0.3	0.3	0.3
Av. Return	0.12	0.12	0.12
Std. Dev.	0.215	0.215	0.215

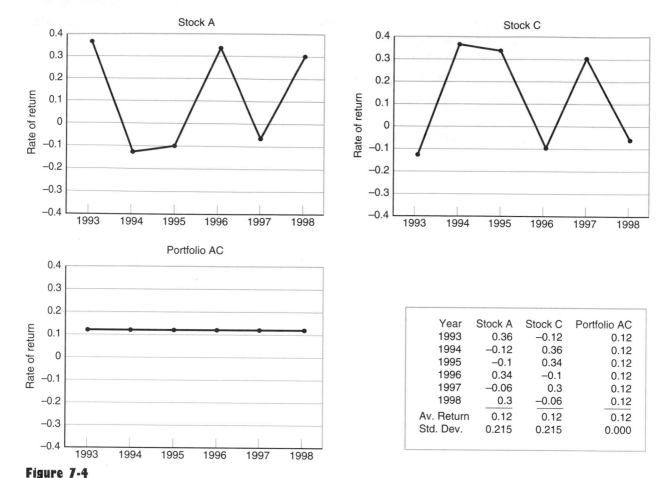

Year	Stock A	Stock C	Portfolio AC
1993	0.36	−0.12	0.12
1994	−0.12	0.36	0.12
1995	−0.1	0.34	0.12
1996	0.34	−0.1	0.12
1997	−0.06	0.3	0.12
1998	0.3	−0.06	0.12
Av. Return	0.12	0.12	0.12
Std. Dev.	0.215	0.215	0.000

Figure 7-4

Returns for the years 1993–1998 on two stocks, A and C, and a portfolio consisting of 50 percent A and 50 percent C, when the correlation coefficient is −1.0.

Consider the return and standard deviation information in Figure 7-3. Notice that a portfolio combining stocks A and B, with 50 percent invested in each, has exactly the same return as does either stock by itself, since the returns are identical. The risk of the portfolio, as measured by the standard deviation, is identical to the standard deviation of either stock by itself.

When returns are perfectly positively correlated, the risk of a portfolio is simply a weighted average of the individual risks of the securities.

On the other hand, with perfect negative correlation, the securities' returns have a perfect inverse linear relationship to each other. Therefore, knowing the return on one security provides full knowledge about the return on the second security. When one security's return is high, the other is low.

In Figure 7-4, stocks A and C are perfectly negatively correlated with each other. Notice that the information given for these two stocks states that each stock has exactly the same return and standard deviation. When combined, however, the deviations in the returns on these stocks around their average return of 12 percent cancel out, resulting in a portfolio return of 12 percent. This portfolio has no risk. It will earn 12 percent each year over the period measured, and the average return will be 12 percent.

With zero correlation, there is no linear relationship between the returns on the two securities. Combining two securities with zero correlation (statistical independence) with each other reduces the risk of the portfolio. If more securities with uncorrelated returns

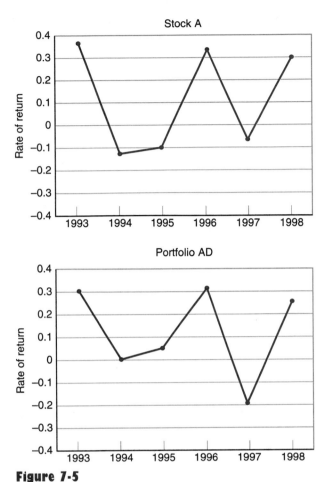

Year	Stock A	Stock D	Portfolio AD
1993	0.36	0.25	0.305
1994	−0.12	0.13	0.005
1995	−0.1	0.19	0.045
1996	0.34	0.28	0.31
1997	−0.06	−0.35	−0.205
1998	0.3	0.22	0.26
Av. Return	0.12	0.12	0.12
Std. Dev.	0.215	0.215	0.180

Figure 7-5

Returns for the years 1993–1998 on two stocks, A and D, and a portfolio consisting of 50 percent A and 50 percent D, when the correlation co-efficient is +0.55.

are added to the portfolio, significant risk reduction can be achieved. However, portfolio risk cannot be eliminated in this case.

Figure 7-5 illustrates the more normal case of stocks A and D positively correlated with each other at a level of $\rho = +0.55$. This is approximately the typical correlation of New York Stock Exchange (NYSE) stocks with each other, thereby representing a "normal" situation encountered by investors. Note that the standard deviation of each security is still 0.215, with an average return of 0.12, but when combined with equal weights of 0.50 into the portfolio, the risk is somewhat reduced to a level of 0.18. Any reduction in risk that does not adversely affect return has to be considered beneficial.

With positive correlation, risk can be reduced but it cannot be eliminated. Other things being equal, investors wish to find securities with the least positive correlation possible. Ideally, they would like securities with negative correlation or zero correlation, but they generally will be faced with positively correlated security returns.

Covariance   Given the significant amount of correlation among security returns, we must measure the actual amount of comovement and incorporate it into any measure of portfolio risk, because such comovements affect the portfolio's variance (or standard deviation). The covariance measure does this.

The covariance is an absolute measure of the degree of association between the returns for a pair of securities. **Covariance** is defined as the extent to which two random

Covariance   An absolute measure of the extent to which two variables tend to covary, or move together

variables covary (move together) over time. As is true throughout our discussion, the variables in question are the returns (TRs) on two securities. As in the case of the correlation coefficient, the covariance can be

1. Positive, indicating that the returns on the two securities tend to move in the same direction at the same time; when one increases (decreases), the other tends to do the same. When the covariance is positive, the correlation coefficient will also be positive.
2. Negative, indicating that the returns on the two securities tend to move inversely; when one increases (decreases), the other tends to decrease (increase). When the covariance is negative, the correlation coefficient will also be negative.
3. Zero, indicating that the returns on two securities are independent and have no tendency to move in the same or opposite directions together.

The formula for calculating covariance on an expected basis is

$$\sigma_{AB} = \sum_{i=1}^{m} [R_{A,i} - E(R_A)] \ [R_{B,i} - E(R_B)] \ pr_i \qquad (7\text{-}9)$$

where

σ_{AB} = the covariance between securities A and B
R_A = one possible return on security A
$E(R_A)$ = the expected value of the return on security A
m = the number of likely outcomes for a security for the period

Equation 7-9 indicates that covariance is the expected value of the product of deviations from the mean. The size of the covariance measure depends upon the units of the variables involved and usually changes when these units are changed. Therefore, the covariance primarily provides information about whether the association between variables is positive, negative, or zero because simply observing the number itself is not very useful.

Relating the Correlation Coefficient and the Covariance   The covariance and the correlation coefficient can be related in the following manner:

$$\rho_{AB} = \frac{\sigma_{AB}}{\sigma_A \sigma_B} \qquad (7\text{-}10)$$

This equation shows that the correlation coefficient is simply the covariance standardized by dividing by the product of the two standard deviations of returns.

Given this definition of the correlation coefficient, the covariance can be written as

$$\sigma_{AB} = \rho_{AB}\sigma_A\sigma_B \qquad (7\text{-}11)$$

Therefore, knowing the correlation coefficient, we can calculate the covariance because the standard deviations of the assets' rates of return will already be available. Knowing the covariance, we can easily calculate the correlation coefficient.

Calculating Portfolio Risk

Now that we understand the covariances that account for the comovements in security returns, we are ready to calculate portfolio risk. First, we will consider the simplest possible case, two securities, in order to see what is happening in the portfolio risk equation. We will then consider the case of many securities, where the calculations soon become too large and complex to analyze with any means other than a computer.

THE TWO-SECURITY CASE

The risk of a portfolio, as measured by the standard deviation of returns, for the case of two securities, 1 and 2, is

$$\sigma_P = [w_1^2\sigma_1^2 + w_2^2\sigma_2^2 + 2(w_1)(w_2)(\rho_{1,2})\sigma_1\sigma_2]^{\frac{1}{2}} \tag{7-12}$$

Equation 7-12 shows us that the risk for a portfolio encompasses not only the individual security risks but also the covariance between these two securities and that three factors, not two, determine portfolio risk:

- The variance of each security, as shown by σ_1^2 and σ_2^2 in Equation 7-12
- The covariance between securities, as shown by $\rho_{1,2}\sigma_1\sigma_2$ in Equation 7-12
- The portfolio weights for each security, as shown by the w_1's in Equation 7-12

Note the following about Equation 7-12:

- The covariance term contains two covariances—the (weighted) covariance between stock 1 and stock 2 and between stock 2 and stock 1. Since each covariance is identical, we simply multiply the first covariance by two. Otherwise, there would be four terms in Equation 7-12 rather than three.
- We first solve for the variance of the portfolio, and then take the square root to obtain the standard deviation of the portfolio.

Example 7-7 Consider the realized TRs between Coca-Cola and Duke Energy for the period 1992 to 2001. The summary statistics for these two stocks are as follows:

	Coca-Cola	Duke Energy
Mean	12.12	15.16
Standard Deviation	21.58	25.97
Correlation Coeff.	0.29	

Assume we place equal amounts in each stock; therefore, the weights are 0.5 and 0.5.

$$\sigma_P = [w_1^2\sigma_1^2 + w_2^2\sigma_2^2 + 2(w_1)(w_2)(\rho_{1,2})\sigma_1\sigma_2]^{\frac{1}{2}}$$

$$= [(0.5)^2(21.58)^2 + (0.5)^2(25.97)^2 + 2(0.5)(0.5)(0.29)(21.58)(25.97)]^{\frac{1}{2}}$$

$$= [116.42 + 168.61 + 81.26]^{\frac{1}{2}}$$

$$= 19.14$$

Alternatively,

$$\sigma_P = [w_1^2\sigma_1^2 + w_2^2\sigma_2^2 + (w_1)(w_2)(\rho_{1,2})\sigma_1\sigma_2 + (w_2)(w_1)(\rho_{2,1})\sigma_2\sigma_1]^{\frac{1}{2}}$$

$$= [(0.5)^2(21.58)^2 + (0.5)^2(25.97)^2 + (0.5)(0.5)(0.29)(21.58)(25.97)]^{\frac{1}{2}}$$

$$+ (0.5)(0.5)(0.29)(25.97)(21.58)]^{\frac{1}{2}}$$

$$= [116.42 + 168.61 + 40.63 + 40.63]^{\frac{1}{2}}$$

$$= 19.14$$

The standard deviation of the portfolio will be directly affected by the correlation between the two stocks. Portfolio risk will be reduced as the correlation coefficient moves from +1.0 downward, with everything else being constant.

Example 7-8

Assume we have some data for two companies, EG&G and GF, and that the estimated TRs are 26.3 and 11.6 percent, respectively, with standard deviations of 37.3 and 23.3 percent. The correlation coefficient between their returns is +0.15. To see the effects of changing the correlation coefficient, assume weights of 0.5 each—50 percent of investable funds is to be placed in each security. Summarizing the data in this example,

$$\sigma_{EG\&G} = 0.373$$

$$\sigma_{GF} = 0.233$$

$$w_{EG\&G} = 0.5$$

$$w_{GF} = 0.5$$

$$\rho_{EG\&G,GF} = 0.15$$

With these data, the standard deviation, or risk, for this portfolio, σ_p, is

$$\sigma_p = [(0.5)^2(0.373)^2 + (0.5)^2(0.233)^2 +$$

$$2(0.5)(0.5)(0.373)(0.233)\ _{\rho EG\&G,}G_F]^{\frac{1}{2}}$$

$$= [0.0348 + 0.0136 + 0.0435\ \rho_{EG\&G,}G_F]^{\frac{1}{2}}$$

since $2(0.5)(0.5)(0.373)(0.233) = 0.0435$.

The risk of this portfolio clearly depends heavily on the value of the third term, which in turn depends on the correlation coefficient between the returns for EG&G and GF. To assess the potential impact of the correlation, consider the following cases: a ρ of +1, +0.5, +0.15, 0, −0.5, and −1.0. Calculating portfolio risk under each of these scenarios produces the following portfolio risks:

If $\rho = +1.0$: $\sigma_p = [0.0348 + 0.0136 + 0.0435(1)]^{\frac{1}{2}} = 30.3\%$

If $\rho = +0.5$: $\sigma_p = [0.0348 + 0.0136 + 0.0435(0.5)]^{\frac{1}{2}} = 26.5\%$

If $\rho = +0.15$: $\sigma_p = [0.0348 + 0.0136 + 0.0435(0.15)]^{\frac{1}{2}} = 23.4\%$

If $\rho = 0.0$: $\sigma_p = [0.0348 + 0.0136]^{\frac{1}{2}} = 22.0\%$

If $\rho = -0.5$: $\sigma_p = [0.0348 + 0.0136 + 0.0435(-0.5)]^{\frac{1}{2}} = 16.0\%$

If $\rho = -1.0$: $\sigma_p = [0.0348 + 0.0136 + 0.0435(-1.0)]^{\frac{1}{2}} = 7.0\%$

These calculations clearly show the impact that combining securities with less than perfect positive correlation will have on portfolio risk. The risk of the portfolio steadily decreases from 30.3 to 7 percent as the correlation coefficient declines from +1.0 to −1.0. Note, however, that the risk has declined from 30.3 to only 22 percent as the correlation coefficient drops from +1 to 0, and it has only been cut in half (approximately) by the time ρ drops to −0.5.

We said earlier (Figure 7-4) that with a two-stock portfolio and perfect negative correlation the risk can be reduced to zero. Notice that this did not happen in Example 7-8 (the risk when $\rho = -1.0$ was 7 percent). The reason for this is that the weights for each stock were selected to be 0.50 for illustrative purposes. To reduce the risk to zero in this case, and to minimize risk in general, it is necessary to select optimal weights.

Let's consider the importance of the portfolio weights in the calculation of portfolio risk. The size of the portfolio weights assigned to each security has an effect on portfolio risk, holding the correlation coefficient constant.

Example 7-9 Using the same data as Example 7-8, let's consider the portfolio risk for these two securities assuming the correlation coefficient between the two is +0.15. For illustrative purposes, we will examine five different sets of weights, each of which sums to 1.0.

EG&G	GF	σ_p
0.9	0.1	34%
0.7	0.3	28%
0.5	0.5	23.4%
0.3	0.7	21.1%
0.1	0.9	21.8%

As we can see, in this two-stock portfolio example, holding the correlation coefficient constant at +0.15, the risk of the portfolio can vary quite widely as the weights for each of the assets changes. Of course, as the weights change, the expected return for the portfolio also changes, because expected return is simply a weighted average of the individual security expected returns.

Summarizing our findings, portfolio risk is affected both by the correlation between assets and by the percentages of funds invested in each asset.

THE n-SECURITY CASE

The two-security case can be generalized to the n-security case. Portfolio risk can be reduced by combining assets with less than perfect positive correlation. Furthermore, the smaller the positive correlation, the better.

Portfolio risk is a function of each individual security's risk and the covariances between the returns on the individual securities. Stated in terms of variance, portfolio risk is

$$\sigma_p^2 = \sum_{i=1}^{n} w_i^2 \sigma_i^2 + \sum_{i=1}^{n} \sum_{\substack{j=1 \\ i \neq j}}^{n} w_i w_j \sigma_{ij} \tag{7-13}$$

where

σ_p^2 = the variance of the return on the portfolio
σ_i^2 = the variance of return for security i
σ_{ij} = the covariance between the returns for securities i and j
w_i = the portfolio weights or percentage of investable funds invested in security i
$\sum_{i=1}^{n} \sum_{j=1}^{n}$ = a double summation sign indicating that n^2 numbers are to be added together (i.e., all possible pairs of values for i and j)

Although Equation 7-13 appears to be formidable, it states exactly the same message as Equation 7-12 for the two-stock portfolio. This message is portfolio risk is a function of:

❑ The weighted risk of each individual security (as measured by its variance)
❑ The weighted covariances among all pairs of securities

Note that three variables actually determine portfolio risk: variances, covariances, and weights.

We can rewrite Equation 7-13 into a shorter format:

$$\sigma_p^2 = \sum_{i=1}^{n} \sum_{j=1}^{n} w_i w_j \sigma_{ij} \qquad \qquad (7\text{-}14)$$

or, because $\sigma_{ij} = \rho_{ij} \sigma_i \sigma_j$,

$$\sigma_p^2 = \sum_{i=1}^{n} \sum_{j=1}^{n} w_i w_j \rho_{ij} \sigma_i \sigma_j$$

These equations account for both the variance and the covariances because when $i = j$, the variance is calculated; when $i \neq j$, the covariance is calculated.

The Importance of Covariance   One of Markowitz's real contributions to portfolio theory is his insight about the relative importance of the variances and covariances. When we add a new security to a large portfolio of securities, there are two impacts:

1. The asset's own risk, as measured by its variance, is added to the portfolio's risk
2. There is a covariance between the new security and every other security already in this large portfolio that is also added

As the number of securities held in a portfolio increases, the importance of each individual security's risk (variance) decreases, whereas the importance of the covariance relationships increases. In a portfolio of 150 securities, for example, the contribution of each security's own risk to the total portfolio risk will be extremely small; portfolio risk will consist almost entirely of the covariance risk between securities.[2]
We can state the following conclusion:

❑ When a new security is added to a large portfolio of securities, what matters most is its average covariance with the other securities in the portfolio

Simplfying the Markowitz Calculations   Equation 7-13 illustrates the problem associated with the calculation of portfolio risk using the Markowitz mean-variance analysis. In the case of two securities, there are two covariances, and we multiply the weighted covariance term in Equation 7-12 by two, since the covariance of A with B is the same as the covariance of B with A. In the case of three securities, there are six covariances; with four securities, 12 covariances; and so forth, based on the fact that the total number of covariances in the Markowitz model is calculated as $n(n-1)$, where n is the number of securities.
Table 7-3 shows the variance-covariance matrix associated with these calculations. For the case of two securities, there are n^2, or four, total terms in the matrix—two variances and two covariances. For the case of four securities, there are n^2, or 16 total terms in the matrix—four variances and 12 covariances. The variance terms are on the diagonal

---

[2] To see this, consider the first term in Equation 7-13:

$$\sum_{i=1}^{n} w_i^2 \sigma_i^2$$

Assume equal amounts are invested in each security. The proportions, or weights, will be $1/n$. Rewriting this term produces

$$\sum_{i=1}^{n} [(1/n)^2] \sigma_i^2 = 1/n \sum_{i=1}^{n} \sigma_i^2 / n$$

The term in brackets represents an average variance for the stocks in the portfolio. As n becomes larger, this average variance becomes smaller, approaching zero for large values of n. Therefore, the risk of a well-diversified portfolio will be largely attributable to the impact of the second term in Equation 7-13 representing the covariance relationships.

Table 7-3 The Variance-Covariance Matrix Involved in Calculating the Standard Deviation of a Portfolio

Two securities:

$$
\begin{array}{cc}
\sigma_{1,1} & \sigma_{1,2} \\
\sigma_{2,1} & \sigma_{2,2}
\end{array}
$$

Four securities:

$$
\begin{array}{cccc}
\sigma_{1,1} & \sigma_{1,2} & \sigma_{1,3} & \sigma_{1,4} \\
\sigma_{2,1} & \sigma_{2,2} & \sigma_{2,3} & \sigma_{2,4} \\
\sigma_{3,1} & \sigma_{3,2} & \sigma_{3,3} & \sigma_{3,4} \\
\sigma_{4,1} & \sigma_{4,2} & \sigma_{4,3} & \sigma_{4,4}
\end{array}
$$

of the matrix and, in effect, represent the covariance of a security with itself. Note that the covariance terms above the diagonal are a mirror image of the covariance terms below the diagonal; that is, each covariance is repeated twice, since COV_{AB} is the same as COV_{BA}.

The number of covariances grows quickly based on the calculation of $n(n - 1)$, where n is the number of securities involved. Because the covariance of A with B is the same as the covariance of B with A, there are $[n(n - 1)]/2$ unique covariances.

Example 7-10

An analyst considering 100 securities must estimate $[100(99)]/2 = 4{,}950$ unique covariances. For 250 securities, the number is $[250(249)]/2 = 31{,}125$ unique covariances.

Obviously, estimating large numbers of covariances quickly becomes a major problem for model users. Since many institutional investors follow as many as 250 or 300 securities, the number of inputs required may become an impossibility. In fact, until the basic Markowitz model was simplified in terms of the covariance inputs, it remained primarily of academic interest.

On a practical basis, analysts are unlikely to be able directly to estimate the large number of correlations necessary for a complete Markowitz analysis. In his original work, Markowitz suggested using an index to which securities are related as a means of generating covariances. One response was the famous Single Index Model.

The Single Index Model is considered in Chapter 8.

Obtaining the Data   To calculate portfolio risk using Equation 7-13, we need estimates of the variance for each security and estimates of the correlation coefficients or covariances. Both variances and correlation coefficients can be (and are) calculated using either *ex post* or *ex ante* data. If an analyst uses *ex post* data to calculate the correlation coefficient or the covariance and then uses these estimates in the Markowitz model, the implicit assumption is that the relationship that existed in the past will continue into the future. The same is true of the variances for individual securities. If the historical variance is thought to be the best estimate of the expected variance, it should be used. However, it must be remembered that an individual security's variance and the correlation coefficient between securities can change over time (and does), as can the expected return.

Efficient Portfolio   A portfolio with the highest level of expected return for a given level of risk or a portfolio with the lowest risk for a given level of return

Efficient Portfolios

Markowitz's approach to portfolio selection is that an investor should evaluate portfolios on the basis of their expected returns and risk as measured by the standard deviation. He was the first to derive the concept of an **efficient portfolio**, which is defined as one that

Figure 7-6

The attainable set and the efficient set of portfolios.

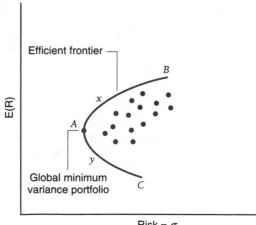

has the smallest portfolio risk for a given level of expected return or the largest expected return for a given level of risk. Investors can identify efficient portfolios by specifying an expected portfolio return and minimizing the portfolio risk at this level of return. Alternatively, they can specify a portfolio risk level they are willing to assume and maximize the expected return on the portfolio for this level of risk. Rational investors will seek efficient portfolios, because these portfolios are optimized on the two dimensions of most importance to investors, expected return and risk.

To begin our analysis, we must first determine the risk-return opportunities available to an investor from a given set of securities. Figure 7-6 illustrates the opportunities available from a given set of securities. A large number of possible portfolios exist when we realize that varying percentages of an investor's wealth can be invested in each of the assets under consideration. Is it necessary to evaluate all of the possible portfolios illustrated in Figure 7-6? Fortunately, the answer is no, because investors should be interested in only that subset of the available portfolios known as the efficient set.

The assets in Figure 7-6 generate the *attainable set* of portfolios, or the opportunity set. The attainable set is the entire set of all portfolios that could be found from a group of *n* securities. However, risk-averse investors should be interested only in those portfolios with the lowest possible risk for any given level of return. All other portfolios in the attainable set are *dominated*.

Using the inputs described earlier—expected returns, variances, and covariances—we can calculate the portfolio with the smallest variance, or risk, for a given level of expected return based on these inputs.[3] Given the minimum-variance portfolios, we can plot the *minimum-variance frontier* as shown in Figure 7-6. Point A represents the *global minimum-variance portfolio*, because no other minimum-variance portfolio has a smaller risk. The bottom segment of the minimum-variance frontier, AC, is dominated by portfolios on the upper segment, AB. For example, since portfolio X has a larger return than portfolio Y for the same level of risk, investors would not want to own portfolio Y.

The segment of the minimum-variance frontier above the global minimum-variance portfolio, AB, offers the best risk-return combinations available to investors from this particular set of inputs. This segment is referred to as the **efficient set** of portfolios. This efficient set is determined by the principle of dominance—portfolio X dominates portfolio Y if it has the same level of risk but a larger expected return or the same expected return but a lower risk.

Efficient Set (Frontier) The set of portfolios generated by the Markowitz portfolio model

---

[3] Each investor doing this may use a different set of inputs, and therefore the outputs will differ.

The solution to the Markowitz model revolves around the portfolio weights, or percentages of investable funds to be invested in each security.[4] Because the expected returns, standard deviations, and correlation coefficients for the securities being considered are inputs in the Markowitz analysis, the portfolio weights are the only variable that can be manipulated to solve the portfolio problem of determining efficient portfolios.

Think of efficient portfolios as being derived in the following manner. The inputs are obtained and a level of desired expected return for a portfolio is specified; for example, 10 percent. Then all combinations of securities that can be combined to form a portfolio with an expected return of 10 percent are determined, and the one with the smallest variance of return is selected as the efficient portfolio. Next, a new level of portfolio expected return is specified—for example, 11 percent—and the process is repeated. This continues until the feasible range of expected returns is processed. Of course, the problem could be solved by specifying levels of portfolio risk and choosing that portfolio with the largest expected return for the specified level of risk.

Summary

▶ The expected return from a security must be estimated. Since this is done under conditions of uncertainty, it may not be realized. Risk (or uncertainty) is always present in the estimation of expected returns for risky assets.

▶ Probability distributions are involved in the calculation of a security's expected return.

▶ The standard deviation or variance of expected return for a security is a measure of the risk involved in the expected return; therefore, it also incorporates the probabilities used in calculating the expected return.

▶ The expected return for a portfolio is the weighted average of the individual security expected returns.

▶ Portfolio weights, designated w_i, are the percentages of a portfolio's total funds that are invested in each security, where the weights sum to 1.0.

▶ Portfolio risk is not a weighted average of the individual security risks. To calculate portfolio risk, we must take account of the relationships between the securities' returns.

▶ The correlation coefficient is a relative measure of the association between security returns. It is bounded by +1.0 and −1.0, with zero representing no association.

▶ The covariance is an absolute measure of association between security returns and is used in the calculation of portfolio risk.

▶ Portfolio risk is a function of security variances, covariances, and portfolio weights.

▶ The covariance term captures the correlations between security returns and determines how much portfolio risk can be reduced through diversification.

▶ The risk of a well-diversified portfolio is largely attributable to the impact of the covariances. When a new security is added to a large portfolio of securities, what matters most is its average covariance with the other securities in the portfolio.

▶ The major problem with the Markowitz model is that it requires a full set of covariances between the returns of all securities being considered in order to calculate portfolio variance.

▶ The number of covariances in the Markowitz model is $n(n - 1)$; the number of unique covariances is $[n(n - 1)]/2$.

▶ An efficient portfolio is one with the maximum amount of return for a given level of risk, or the minimum risk for a given level of return.

▶ Having calculated the expected returns and standard deviations for a set of portfolios, the efficient set (or efficient frontier) can be determined.

▶ The expected returns, standard deviations, and correlation coefficients for the securities being considered are inputs in the Markowitz analysis. Therefore, the portfolio weights are the variable manipulated to determine efficient portfolios.

---

[4] Technically, the basic Markowitz model is solved by a complex technique called quadratic programming.

Key Words

Correlation coefficient   Efficient portfolio   Expected return
Covariance   Efficient set   Portfolio weights

Questions

7-1 Distinguish between historical return and expected return.

7-2 How is expected return for one security determined? For a portfolio?

7-3 Evaluate this statement: With regard to portfolio risk, the whole is not equal to the sum of the parts.

7-4 How many, and which, factors determine portfolio risk?

7-5 The Markowitz approach is often referred to as a mean-variance approach. Why?

7-6 When, if ever, would a stock with a large risk (standard deviation) be desirable in building a portfolio?

7-7 What is the relationship between the correlation coefficient and the covariance, both qualitatively and quantitatively?

7-8 Many investors have known for years that they should not "put all of their eggs in one basket." How does the Markowitz analysis shed light on this old principle?

7-9 How would the expected return for a portfolio of 500 securities be calculated?

7-10 What does it mean to say that portfolio weights sum to 1.0 or 100 percent?

7-11 What are the boundaries for the expected return of a portfolio?

7-12 What is meant by naive diversification?

7-13 How many covariance terms would exist for a portfolio of 10 securities using the Markowitz analysis? How many unique covariances?

7-14 How many total terms (variances and covariances) would exist in the variance-covariance matrix for a portfolio of 30 securities? How many of these are variances and how many covariances?

7-15 Evaluate the following statement: As the number of securities held in a portfolio increases, the importance of each individual security's risk decreases.

7-16 In explaining diversification concepts and the analysis of risk, why is the correlation coefficient more useful than the covariance?

7-17 Should investors expect positive correlations between stocks and bonds? Bonds and bills? Stocks and real estate? Stocks and gold?

7-18 Calculate the number of covariances needed for an evaluation of 500 securities using the Markowitz model.

CFA

7-19 Given the following:

Stock A standard deviation = 0.45

Stock B standard deviation = 0.32

If stock A and stock B have perfect positive correlation, which portfolio combination represents the minimum-variance portfolio?

a. 100% stock A
b. 50% stock A/50% stock B
c. 100% stock B
d. 30% stock A/70% stock B

7-20 Consider the following information for Exxon and Merck:

> Expected return for each stock is 15 percent.
> Standard deviation for each stock is 22 percent.
> Covariances with other securities vary.

Everything else being equal, would the prices of these two stocks be expected to be the same? Why or why not?

7-21 Select the **CORRECT** statement from among the following:

a. The risk for a portfolio is a weighted average of individual security risks.
b. Two factors determine portfolio risk.

c. Having established the portfolio weights, the calculation of the expected return on the portfolio is independent of the calculation of portfolio risk.

d. When adding a security to a portfolio, the average covariance between it and the other securities in the portfolio is less important than the security's own risk.

7-22 Select the **CORRECT** statement from among the following:

a. The risk of a portfolio of two securities, as measured by the standard deviation, would consist of two terms.

b. The expected return on a portfolio is usually a weighted average of the expected returns of the individual assets in the portfolio.

c. The risk of a portfolio of four securities, as measured by the standard deviation, would consist of 16 covariances and 4 variances.

d. Combining two securities with perfect negative correlation could eliminate risk altogether.

7-23 Select the **INCORRECT** statement from among the following:

a. Under the Markowitz formulation, a portfolio of 30 securities would have 870 covariances.

b. Under the Markowitz formulation, a portfolio of 30 securities would have 30 variances in the variance-covariance matrix.

c. Under the Markowitz formulation, a portfolio of 30 securities would have 870 terms in the variance-covariance matrix.

d. Under the Markowitz formulation, a portfolio of 30 securities would require 435 unique covariances to calculate portfolio risk.

7-24 Concerning the riskiness of a portfolio of two securities using the Markowitz model, select the **CORRECT** statements from among the following set:

a. The riskiness depends on the variability of the securities in the portfolio.

b. The riskiness depends on the percentage of portfolio assets invested in each security.

c. The riskiness depends on the expected return of each security.

d. The riskiness depends on the amount of correlation among the security returns.

e. The riskiness depends on the beta of each security.

7-25 Select the **CORRECT** statement from the following statements regarding the Markowitz model:

a. As the number of securities held in a portfolio increases, the importance of each individual security's risk also increases.

b. As the number of securities held in a portfolio increases, the importance of the covariance relationships increases.

c. In a large portfolio, portfolio risk will consist almost entirely of each security's own risk contribution to the total portfolio risk.

d. In a large portfolio, the covariance term can be driven almost to zero.

Problems

7-1 Calculate the expected return and risk (standard deviation) for General Foods for 2003, given the following information:

Probabilities: 0.15 0.20 0.40 0.10 0.15
Expected returns: 0.20 0.16 0.12 0.05 −0.05

7-2 Four securities have the following expected returns:

A = 15%, B = 12%, C = 30%, and D = 22%

Calculate the expected returns for a portfolio consisting of all four securities under the following conditions:

a. The portfolio weights are 25 percent each.

b. The portfolio weights are 10 percent in A, with the remainder equally divided among the other three stocks.

c. The portfolio weights are 10 percent each in A and B and 40 percent each in C and D.

7-3 Assume the additional information provided below for the four stocks in Problem 7-2.

		Correlations with			
	σ(%)	A	B	C	D
A	10	1.0			
B	8	0.6	1.0		
C	20	0.2	−1.0	1.0	
D	16	0.5	0.3	0.8	1.0

a. Assuming equal weights for each stock, what are the standard deviations for the following portfolios?

    A, B, and C
    B and C
    B and D
    C and D

b. Calculate the standard deviation for a portfolio consisting of stocks B and C, assuming the following weights: (1) 40 percent in B and 60 percent in C; (2) 40 percent in C and 60 percent in B.

c. In part a, which portfolio(s) would an investor prefer?

The following data apply to Problems 7-4 through 7-7.

Assume expected returns and standard deviations as follows:

	EG&G	GF
Return (%)	25	23
Standard deviation (%)	30	25
Covariance (%)	112.5	

The correlation coefficient, ρ, is +0.15.

		Proportion in		
EG&G w_i	GF w_j = (1 − w_i)	(1) Portfolio Expected Returns (%)	(2) Variance (%)	(3) Standard Deviation
1.0	0.0	25.0	900	30.0
0.8	0.2	24.6	637	25.2
0.6	0.4	24.2	478	21.9
0.2	0.8	23.4	472	21.7
0.0	1.0	23.0	625	25.0

7-4 Confirm the expected portfolio returns in column 1.

7-5 Confirm the expected portfolio variances in column 2.

7-6 Confirm the expected standard deviations in column 3.

7-7 On the basis of these data, determine the lowest risk portfolio.

Use the following expectations on stocks X and Y to answer Questions 7-8 through 7-10. (Round to the nearest percent.)

	Bear Market	Normal Market	Bull Market
Probability	0.2	0.5	0.3
Stock X	−20%	18%	50%
Stock Y	−15%	20%	10%

CFA

7-8 What is the expected return for stocks X and Y?

	Stock X	Stock Y
a.	18%	5%
b.	18%	12%
c.	20%	11%
d.	20%	10%

CFA

7-9 What is the standard deviation for returns on stocks X and Y?

	Stock X	Stock Y
a.	15%	26%
b.	20%	4%
c.	24%	13%
d.	28%	8%

CFA

7-10 Assume you invest your $10,000 portfolio into $9,000 in stock X and $1,000 in stock Y. What is the expected return on your portfolio?

a. 18%

b. 19%

c. 20%

d. 23%

CFA

7-11 Given $100,000 to invest, what is the expected risk premium in dollars of investing in equities versus risk-free T-bills (U.S. Treasury bills) based on the following table?

Action	Probability	Expected Return
Invest in equities	0.6	$50,000
	0.4	−$30,000
Invest in risk-free T-bill	1.0	$ 5,000

a. $13,000

b. $15,000

c. $18,000

d. $20,000

CFA

7-12 Based on the scenarios below, what is the expected return for a portfolio with the following return profile?

	Market Condition		
	Bear	Normal	Bull
Probability	0.2	0.3	0.5
Rate of return	−25%	10%	24%

a. 4%

b. 10%

c. 20%

d. 25%

7-13 Assume that RF is 7 percent, the estimated return on the market is 12 percent, and the standard deviation of the market's expected return is 21 percent. Calculate the expected return and risk (standard deviation) for the following portfolios:

a. 60 percent of investable wealth in riskless assets, 40 percent in the market portfolio
b. 150 percent of investable wealth in the market portfolio
c. 100 percent of investable wealth in the market portfolio

Web Resources

For additional resources visit our dynamic Web site located at www.wiley.com/college/jones.

❏ *Pick A Stock, Any Stock*—The case studies the effect of the addition of a stock on the return and total risk of a portfolio. Calculations based on Markowitz portfolio diversification and the implications of the single-index model of security returns are necessary to make a recommendation.

❏ Internet Exercises—In previous chapters of this text, you have been introduced to different kinds of instruments, and how they have performed over time. This chapter set us off on the road to understanding portfolio construction by introducing expected return and risk, the two key components necessary for this purpose. The corresponding exercises for Chapter Seven on the Jones Investments Web site address the following topics:

  ❏ Why stock prices change over time;
  ❏ Stock return and asset return distributions; and
  ❏ Domestic and International Diversification.

Exercise 1: This exercise explains the connection between individual stock returns and portfolio returns.

Exercise 2: There are also different kinds of securities whose returns derive from the same cashflows. The following exercise explores the relationship between stock returns and option returns.

Exercise 3: Often, it is necessary to go beyond the mean and standard deviation in describing return distributions. The following exercise expands on this.

Exercises on Diversification: An important advantage of holding portfolios consisting of several stocks over holding single stocks lies in the power of diversification. The following exercises can be used to explain this principle.

Exercises on Covariance: By this point, the students know that the extent of diversification that is possible depends on the covariance between the returns of pairs of stocks. The following exercises look more closely at what determines the covariance between the returns on different stocks.

❏ Multiple Choice Self Test

Selected References

A good discussion of the intricacies of portfolio theory can be found in:

Elton, Edwin J., Gruber, Martin J., Brown, Stephen J., and Goetzmann, William N., *Modern Portfolio Theory and Investment Analysis*, 6th ed. New York: John Wiley, 2002.

chapter 8

Portfolio Selection

C hapter 8 concentrates on portfolio selection. The Markowitz portfolio selection model, involving the important concept of efficient portfolios, is considered in some detail. We also analyze asset allocation decisions using the Markowitz analysis. Finally, we derive some important conclusions about portfolio risk that will be used in Chapter 9 to develop asset pricing models.

AFTER READING THIS CHAPTER YOU WILL BE ABLE TO:

► Appreciate the importance of the efficient frontier and understand how an optimal portfolio of risky assets is determined.
► Recognize the Single-Index Model.

► Apply the Markowitz optimization procedure to asset classes and understand the implications and significance of doing so.
► Understand how the total risk of a portfolio can be broken into two components.

In Chapter 7, we learned that risky assets should be evaluated on the basis of their expected returns and risk, as measured by the standard deviation, and that portfolio expected return and risk can be calculated based on these inputs and the covariances involved. Calculation of portfolio risk is the key issue. The complete Markowitz variance-covariance analysis can be used to calculate portfolio risk. Alternatively, the single-index model, explained later in this chapter, can be used to simplify the calculations subject to the assumptions of the model.

In Chapter 7, we analyzed basic portfolio principles such as diversification and determined that investors should hold portfolios of financial assets in order to reduce their risk when investing. Clearly, risk reduction through diversification is a very important concept. In fact, diversification is the number one rule of portfolio management and the key to optimal risk management. Every intelligent investor will diversify his or her portfolio of risky assets, because we invest under conditions of uncertainty.

Despite the importance of the diversification principle, our analysis is incomplete, because an infinite number of potential portfolios of risky assets exist. Even when we limit our analysis to efficient portfolios as determined by the Markowitz analysis, there are a large number of these. This chapter completes our portfolio analysis by analyzing how investors select optimal risky portfolios. In effect, we are analyzing the optimal trade-off that exists between risk and expected return.

Building a Portfolio Using Markowitz Principles

To select an optimal portfolio of financial assets using the Markowitz analysis, investors should:

1. Identify optimal risk-return combinations available from the set of risky assets being considered by using the Markowitz efficient frontier analysis. This step uses the inputs from Chapter 7, the expected returns, variances, and covariances for a set of securities.
2. Choose the final portfolio from among those in the efficient set based on an investor's preferences.

In Chapter 9, we examine how investors can invest in both risky assets and riskless assets and buy assets on margin or with borrowed funds. As we shall see, the use of a risk-free asset changes the investor's ultimate portfolio position from that derived under the Markowitz analysis.

USING THE MARKOWITZ PORTFOLIO SELECTION MODEL

As we saw in Chapter 7, even if portfolios are selected arbitrarily, some diversification benefits are gained. This results in a reduction of portfolio risk. However, to take the full information set into account, we use portfolio theory as developed by Markowitz. Portfolio theory is normative, meaning that it tells investors how they should act to diversify optimally. It is based on a small set of assumptions, including

1. A single investment period; for example, one year.
2. Liquidity of positions; for example, there are no transaction costs.
3. Investor preferences based only on a portfolio's expected return and risk, as measured by variance or standard deviation.

EFFICIENT PORTFOLIOS

Markowitz's approach to portfolio selection is that an investor should evaluate portfolios on the basis of their expected returns and risk as measured by the standard deviation. He was the first to derive the concept of an *efficient portfolio* (discussed in Chapter 7), defined as one that has the smallest portfolio risk for a given level of expected return or the largest expected return for a given level of risk. Rational investors will seek efficient portfolios, because these portfolios are optimized on the two dimensions of most importance to investors, expected return and risk.

Chapter 7 explained the basic details of how to derive efficient portfolios. In brief, based on inputs consisting of estimates of expected return and risk for each security being considered as well as the correlation between pairs of securities, an optimization program varies the weights for each security until an efficient portfolio is determined. This portfolio will have the maximum expected return for a given level of risk or the minimum risk for a given level of expected return.

Figure 8-1 shows the Markowitz efficient frontier. Note again that expected return is on the vertical axis, whereas risk, as measured by the standard deviation, is on the horizontal axis. There are many efficient portfolios on the arc AB in Figure 8-1. All of the efficient portfolios together are referred to as the Markowitz **efficient frontier** (equivalent to the efficient set discussed in Chapter 7).

Efficient Set (Frontier)
The set of portfolios generated by the Markowitz portfolio model

SELECTING AN OPTIMAL PORTFOLIO OF RISKY ASSETS

Once the efficient set of portfolios is determined using the Markowitz model, investors must select from this set the portfolio most appropriate for them. The Markowitz model does not specify one optimum portfolio. Rather it generates the efficient set of portfolios, all of which, by definition, are optimal portfolios (for a given level of expected return or risk).

In economics in general and finance in particular, we assume investors are risk averse. This means that investors, if given a choice, will not take a "fair gamble," defined as one with an expected payoff of zero and equal probabilities of a gain or a loss. In effect, with a fair gamble, the disutility from the potential loss is greater than the utility from the potential gain. The greater the risk aversion, the greater the disutility from the potential loss.

Indifference Curves
Curves describing investor preferences for risk and return

To select the expected return-risk combination that will satisfy an individual investor's personal preferences, **indifference curves** (which are assumed to be known for an investor) are used. These curves, shown in Figure 8-2 for a risk-averse investor, describe

Figure 8-1

The feasible set of portfolios and the efficient frontier.

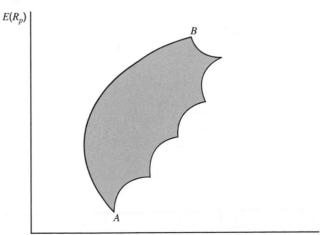

Figure 8-2

Indifference curves.

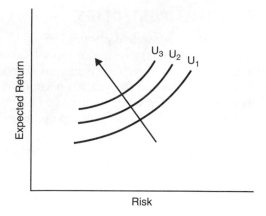

investor preferences for risk and return.[1] Each indifference curve represents the combinations of risk and expected return that are equally desirable to a particular investor (i.e., they provide the same level of utility).

A few important points about indifference curves should be noted. Indifference curves cannot intersect, since they represent different levels of desirability. Investors have an infinite number of indifference curves. The curves for all risk-averse investors will be upward sloping, but the shapes of the curves can vary depending on risk preferences. Higher indifference curves are more desirable than lower indifference curves. The greater the slope of the indifference curves, the greater the risk aversion of investors. Finally, the farther an indifference curve is from the horizontal axis, the greater the utility.

The optimal portfolio for a risk-averse investor is the one on the efficient frontier that is tangent to an investor's indifference curve that is highest in return-risk space. In Figure 8-3, this occurs at point 0. This portfolio maximizes investor utility, because the

Figure 8-3

Selecting a portfolio on the efficient frontier.

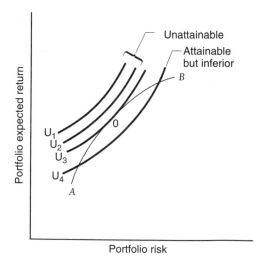

---

[1] Although not shown, investors could also be risk neutral (the risk is unimportant in evaluating portfolios) or risk seekers. A risk-seeking investor, given a fair gamble, will want to take the fair gamble, and larger gambles are preferable to smaller gambles.

indifference curves reflect *investor preferences*, whereas the efficient set represents *portfolio possibilities*.

❑ In selecting one portfolio from the efficient frontier, we are matching investor preferences (as given by his or her indifference curves) with portfolio possibilities (as given by the efficient frontier).

Notice that curves U2 and U1 are unattainable and that U3 is the highest indifference curve for this investor that is tangent to the efficient frontier. On the other hand, U4, though attainable, is inferior to U3, which offers a higher expected return for the same risk (and therefore more utility). If an investor had a different preference for expected return and risk, he or she would have different indifference curves, and another portfolio on the efficient frontier would be optimal.

Investments Intuition

Stated on a practical basis, conservative investors would select portfolios on the left end of the efficient set AB in Figure 8-3, because these portfolios have less risk (and, of course, less expected return). Conversely, aggressive investors would choose portfolios toward point B, because these portfolios offer higher expected returns (along with higher levels of risk). Since indifference curves are difficult to determine under the best of circumstances, investors end up subjectively selecting their optimal efficient portfolio based on their risk preferences.

THE GLOBAL PERSPECTIVE—INTERNATIONAL DIVERSIFICATION

Our discussion has implicitly assumed diversification in domestic securities such as stocks traded on the New York Stock Exchange (NYSE) and on Nasdaq. However, we now know the importance of taking a global approach to investing. The United States may be the world's largest market by far, but it still accounts for slightly less than half of the total market value of the world's stocks.

What effect would the addition of international stocks have on our diversification analysis? Considering only the potential for risk reduction and ignoring the additional risks of foreign investing, such as currency risk, we could reasonably conclude that if domestic diversification is good, international diversification must be better. And empirical studies have confirmed that at least historically, adding foreign stocks to a well-diversified portfolio reduced the overall volatility.

Bruno Solnik, a leading authority on international investing, has noted that as recently as 10 years ago country factors dominated stock prices and the correlation of country factors was weak.[2] This means equity markets around the world were in fact different, and because of the low correlations, investors could reduce the total variance of their portfolio by diversifying across countries. However, conditions changed dramatically in recent years as financial markets became more and more integrated. There is enormous growth in what is called cross-border mergers and acquisitions, which means, for example, that a British company wishing to grow will buy the same type of business in another country rather than buy another type of British company.

---

[2] These comments are based on Bruno Solnik, "Global Considerations for Portfolio Construction," in *AIMR Conference Proceedings: Equity Portfolio Construction*, Association for Investment Management and Research, Charlottesville, VA, 2002, pp. 29–35.

The bottom line is that correlations among country returns increased significantly starting in 1995, and the immediate benefits of risk reduction through combining assets with low correlations have been reduced. This is not surprising because of empirical evidence that the correlation between the Standard and Poor's (S&P) 500 Index and the EAFE Index has risen and fallen in a continuous cycle in the past, and is likely to do so again. It appears that events such as the technology stock craze in the late 1990s and the energy crisis in the early 1970s caused the increased correlation which is eventually reversed.

Although correlations between domestic and foreign stock indexes have recently been high, this does not mean that investors should ignore international diversification. Instead they need to look at it in a different manner. As Solnik puts it: "The very simplistic correlation-based argument of risk diversification is passé . . the question is . . . how can investors afford not to be global in all aspects of their investment management approach today?"[3]

Box 8-1 discusses the issue of diversifying internationally, pointing out, as noted above, that foreign markets have become more correlated with the U.S. markets in recent years. Nevertheless, there are good reasons to diversify internationally and preferred ways of doing so.

SOME IMPORTANT CONCLUSIONS ABOUT THE MARKOWITZ MODEL

Five important points must be noted about the Markowitz portfolio selection model:

1. Markowitz portfolio theory is referred to as a two-parameter model, because investors are assumed to make decisions on the basis of two parameters, expected return and risk.
2. The Markowitz analysis generates an entire set, or frontier, of efficient portfolios, all of which are equally "good." No portfolio on the efficient frontier, as generated, dominates any other portfolio on the efficient frontier.
3. The Markowitz model does not address the issue of investors using borrowed money along with their own portfolio funds to purchase a portfolio of risky assets; that is, investors are not allowed to use leverage. As we shall see in Chapter 9, allowing investors to purchase a risk-free asset increases investor utility and leads to a different efficient set on what is called the Capital Market Line.
4. In practice, different investors, or portfolio managers, will estimate the inputs to the Markowitz model differently. This will produce different efficient frontiers. This results from the uncertainty inherent in the security analysis part of investments as described in Chapter 1.
5. The Markowitz model remains cumbersome to work with because of the large variance-covariance matrix needed for a set of stocks. For example, using only 100 stocks, the variance-covariance matrix has 10,000 terms in it (although each covariance is repeated twice). This raises two issues, which we will deal with in turn below:
   a. Are there simpler methods for computing the efficient frontier?
   b. Can the Markowitz analysis be used to optimize asset classes rather than individual assets?

---

[3] Ibid., p. 35.

BOX 8-1

Does Diversifying Internationally Really Help?

You think the U.S. has problems? Japan's economy, with its many bankrupt banks and so-called zombie companies still operating, brings to mind *Night of the Living Dead.* After a 14-year bear market, Japan's leaders still can't summon the political will to enact needed reforms. And Germany is in danger of becoming the next Japan, with deflation looming and many of its banks in shambles. Despite high joblessness and slow growth on the Continent, the European Central Bank has been inexplicably tardy in lowering interest rates.

Given all this, you might wonder why you'd want to invest your money abroad. Plus, on top of these fundamental woes, foreign markets increasingly move in lock step with the U.S. stock market. That calls into question a basic argument for investing overseas: that diversifying with foreign stocks will smooth your investment ups and downs. Nowadays, when the Dow tumbles, the Dax will probably tank, too.

Not Entirely in Sync

Still, we think foreign stocks offer some diversity benefits. Although the main foreign-market indexes move in line with big U.S. stocks about 80% of the time, small foreign and emerging-markets stocks correlate much less closely with their U.S. counterparts. And if you invest only in U.S. stocks, "you're leaving out half the world," says Murdo Murchison, manager of Franklin Templeton Growth fund, which invests worldwide.

It helps to envision the U.S. as a growth company (albeit one that hasn't grown all that lustily lately) and to characterize the rest of the globe as an undervalued stock. The U.S. market sells for about 17 times estimated 2003 profits. European stocks trade at about 14 times 2003 earnings, and Asian stocks at about 13 times. U.S. stocks command richer prices because America's economy is more productive and adaptable than economies in Europe and Japan. Economist Ken Goldstein of the Conference Board predicts that the U.S. economy will grow 3.5% a year, after inflation, during the next decade. He sees Europe growing 2.5% a year, and Japan growing just 1.5%.

As Japan fades, China forges ahead. China just passed Japan as the largest non–North American exporter to the U.S. China's economy, sixth-largest in the world, is expected to grow 8% a year, after inflation, for at least the next few years. "China is becoming the production center of the world," says Rod Smyth, chief investment strategist for Wachovia Securities.

Risky Business

You could profit from China's growth by investing in Chinese or Hong Kong stocks, as well as in stocks from other Pacific Rim nations, such as Taiwan and South Korea. Or you could invest in China-only or Asian mutual funds. But we don't think you should invest directly in China or, for that matter, even in a diversified emerging-markets fund. While developing markets periodically deliver off-the-chart returns, their long-term records are uniformly dismal. Accounting practices in most of these countries are shabby, and governments and corporate insiders tend to treat shareholders poorly. And it's altogether possible for an economy to grow briskly while little dribbles down to the bottom line.

Instead, put the bulk of your overseas money in broad-based foreign funds. One of our longtime favorites, Oakmark International (symbol OAKIX; 800–625–6275), has about one-fourth of its assets invested in emerging markets. Managed by David Herro and Michael Welsh, Oakmark invests in bargain-priced stocks. Another favorite, Artisan International (ARTIX; 800–344–1770), invests in fast-growing companies, but manager Mark Yockey tries to buy them at reasonable prices. It has 10% of assets in emerging markets. William Blair International Growth N (WBIGX; 800-742-7272) has been in the top 10% of diversified overseas funds over the past five years. Manager George Greig, who invests in fast-growing companies, has about 20% of the fund in developing markets. Any one of these three funds—or Oakmark International in tandem with either the Artisan or William Blair fund—should give you an excellent window of the world.

SOURCE: Steven T. Goldberg, "Does Diversifying Internationally Really Help?" *Kiplinger's Personal Finance,* January 2003, p. 38. Reprinted by permission.

Alternative Methods of Obtaining the Efficient Frontier

The single-index model provides an alternative expression for portfolio variance, which is easier to calculate than in the case of the Markowitz analysis. This alternative approach can be used to solve the portfolio problem as formulated by Markowitz—determining the efficient set of portfolios. It requires considerably fewer calculations. Multi-index models have also been examined and evaluated.

THE SINGLE-INDEX MODEL

Single-Index Model A model that relates returns on a security to the returns on a market index

William Sharpe, following Markowitz, developed the **single-index model**, which relates returns on each security to the returns on a common index.[4] A broad market index of common stock returns is generally used for this purpose.[5] Think of the S&P 500 as this index.

The single-index model can be expressed by the following equation:

$$R_i = a_i + \beta_i R_M + e_i \tag{8-1}$$

where

R_i = the return (TR) on security i
R_M = the return (TR) on the market index
a_i = that part of security i's return independent of market performance
β_i = a constant measuring the expected change in the dependent variable, R_i, given a change in the independent variable, R_M
e_i = the random residual error

The single-index model divides a security's return into two components: a unique part, represented by a_i, and a market-related part represented by $\beta_i R_M$. The unique part is a *micro* event, affecting an individual company but not all companies in general. Examples include the discovery of new ore reserves, a fire, a strike, or the resignation of a key company figure. The market-related part, on the other hand, is a *macro* event that is broad based and affects all (or most) firms. Examples include a Federal Reserve announcement about the discount rate, a change in the prime rate, or an unexpected announcement about the money supply.

Given these values, the error term is the difference between the left-hand side of the equation, the return on security i, and the right-hand side of the equation, the sum of the two components of return. Since the single-index model is, by definition, an equality, the two sides must be the same.

Example 8-1

Assume the return for the market index for period t is 12 percent, the a_i = 3 percent, and the β_i = 1.5. The single-index model estimate for stock i is

$$R_i = 3\% + 1.5\,R_M + e_i$$

$$R_i = 3\% + (1.5)(12\%) = 21\%$$

If the market index return is 12 percent, the likely return for stock i is 21 percent.

[4] W. Sharpe, "A Simplified Model for Portfolio Analysis," *Management Science*, 9 (January 1963): 277–293.
[5] There is no requirement that the index be a stock index. It could be any variable thought to be the dominant influence on stock returns. This means that the model cannot be based on a consistent theoretical set of assumptions.

However, no model is going to explain security returns perfectly. The error term, e_i, captures the difference between the return that actually occurs and the return expected to occur given a particular market index return.

Example 8-2

Assume in Example 8-2 that the actual return on stock i for period t is 19 percent. The error term in this case is $19\% - 21\% = -2\%$.

This illustrates what we said earlier about the error term. For any period, it represents the difference between the actual return and the return predicted by the parameters of the model on the right-hand side of the equation. Figure 8-4, which depicts the single-index model, illustrates the difference between the actual return of Example 8-2, 19 percent, and the predicted return of 21 percent—the error term is -2 percent.

The β term, or beta, is important. It measures the sensitivity of a stock to market movements. To use the single-index model, we need estimates of the beta for each stock we are considering. Subjective estimates could be obtained from analysts, or the future beta could be estimated from historical data. We consider the estimation of beta in more detail in Chapter 9.

R_M and e_i are random variables. The single-index model assumes that the market index is unrelated to the residual error. One way to estimate the parameters of this model is with a time series regression. Use of this technique ensures that these two variables are uncorrelated.

We will use σ_{ei} to denote the standard deviation of the error term for stock i. The mean of the probability distribution of this error term is zero.

The single-index model also assumes that securities are related only in their common response to the return on the market. That is, the residual errors for security i are uncorrelated with those of security j; this can be expressed as COV $(e_i, e_j) = 0$. *This is the key assumption of the single-index model, because it implies that stocks covary together only because of their common relationship to the market index.* In other words, there are no influences on stocks beyond the market, such as industry effects. Therefore,

$$R_i = a_i + \beta_i R_M + e_i \text{ for stock } i$$

and

$$R_j = a_j + \beta_j R_M + e_j \text{ for stock } j$$

Figure 8-4

The single index model.

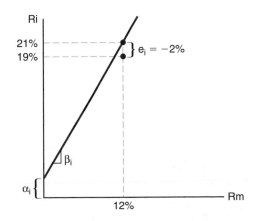

It is critical to recognize that this is a simplifying assumption. If this assumption is not a good description of reality, the model will be inaccurate.[6]

In the single-index model, all the covariance terms can be accounted for by stocks being related only in their common responses to the market index; that is, the covariance depends only on market risk. Therefore, the covariance between any two securities can be written as

$$\sigma_{ij} = \beta_i \beta_j \sigma_M^2 \tag{8-2}$$

Once again, this simplification rests on the assumption about the error terms being uncorrelated. An alternative is to consider more than one index.

In the Markowitz model, we need to consider all of the covariance terms in the variance-covariance matrix. The single-index model splits the risk of an individual security into two components; similar to its division of security return into two components. This simplifies the covariance and greatly simplifies the calculation of total risk for a security and for a portfolio. The total risk of a security, as measured by its variance, consists of two components: market risk and unique risk.

$$\sigma_i^2 = \beta_i^2 [\sigma_M^2] + \sigma_{ei}^2 \tag{8-3}$$

$$= \text{Market risk} + \text{company-specific risk}$$

The market risk accounts for that part of a security's variance that cannot be diversified away. This part of the variability occurs when the security responds to the market moving up and down. The second term is the security's residual variance and accounts for that part of the variability due to deviations from the fitted relationship between security return and market return.

This simplification also holds for portfolios, providing an alternative expression to use in finding the minimum variance set of portfolios.

$$\sigma_p^2 \quad = \quad \beta_p^2 [\sigma_M^2] \quad + \quad \sigma_{ep}^2 \tag{8-4}$$

Total		Portfolio		Portfolio
Portfolio	=	market	+	residual
Variance		risk		variance

MULTI-INDEX MODELS

As noted in the previous section, the single-index model assumes that stock prices covary only because of common movement with one index, specifically that of the market. Some researchers have attempted to capture some nonmarket influences by constructing multi-index models. Probably the most obvious example of these potential nonmarket influences is the industry factor.[7]

A multi-index model is of the form

$$E(R_i) = a_i + b_i R_M + c_i NF + e_i \tag{8-5}$$

where NF is the nonmarket factor and all other variables are as previously defined. Equation 8-5 could be expanded to include three, four, or more indexes.

---

[6] The use of regression analysis does not guarantee that this will be true. Instead, it is a specific simplifying assumption that, in fact, may or may not be true.

[7] In a well-known early study, Benjamin King found a common movement between securities, beyond the market effect, associated with industries. See B. King, "Market and Industry Factors in Stock Price Behavior," *Journal of Business,* 39 (January 1966): 139–190.

It seems logical that a multi-index model should perform better than a single-index model, because it uses more information about the interrelationships between stock returns. In effect, the multi-index model falls between the full variance-covariance method of Markowitz and Sharpe's single-index model.

How well do these models perform? Given the large number of possible multi-index models, no conclusive statement is possible. However, one well-known study, by Cohen and Pogue, found that the single-index model outperformed a multi-index model in that it produced more efficient portfolios.[8] This study, using industry classifications, found the single-index model not only was simpler but also led to lower expected risks.

It is worth noting that the multi-index model tested by Cohen and Pogue (and by Elton and Gruber as well) actually reproduced the *historical* correlations better than the single-index model.[9] However, it did not perform better *ex ante*, which is the more important consideration, because portfolios are built to be held for a future period of time.

Some Conclusions About the Single-Index Model   The single-index model greatly simplifies the calculation of the portfolio variance, and therefore the calculation of efficient portfolios.

Example 8-3   In the case of the Markowitz analysis, 250 stocks require 31,125 covariances and 250 variances. Using the single-index model, we would need $3n + 2$ estimates, or 752 numbers for 250 securities.[10]

However, this model makes a specific assumption about the process that generates portfolio returns—the residuals for different securities are uncorrelated. Thus, the accuracy of the estimate of the portfolio variance depends on the accuracy of the key assumption being made by the model. For example, if the covariance between the residuals for different securities is positive, not zero as assumed, the true residual variance of the portfolio will be underestimated.

The end objective of the single-index model is the same as that of the Markowitz analysis, tracing the efficient frontier (set) of portfolios from which an investor would choose an optimal portfolio. Its purpose is to simplify the calculations necessary to do this.

The single-index model is a valuable simplification of the full variance-covariance matrix needed for the Markowitz model. As discussed above, this model reduces by a large amount the number of estimates needed for a portfolio of securities.[11]

An obvious question to ask is how it performs in relation to the Markowitz model. In his original paper developing the single-index model, Sharpe found that two sets of efficient portfolios—one using the full Markowitz model and one using his simplification—generated from a sample of stocks were very much alike.[12] A later study also found that the Sharpe model did no worse than the Markowitz model in all tests conducted, and in tests using shorter time periods it performed better.[13]

---

[8] K. Cohen and J. Pogue, "An Empirical Evaluation of Alternative Portfolio Selection Models," *Journal of Business*, 46 (April 1967): 166–193.

[9] E. Elton and M. Gruber, "Estimating the Dependence Structure of Share Prices—Implications for Portfolio Selection," *Journal of Finance*, 5 (December 1973): 1203–1232.

[10] The single-index model requires $3n + 2$ total pieces of data to implement, where n is the number of securities being considered. In contrast, the full variance-covariance model of Markowitz requires $[n(n + 3)]/2$ estimates for n securities.

[11] The single-index model can be used to directly estimate the expected return and risk for a portfolio.

[12] Sharpe, "A Simplified Model."

[13] G. Frankfurter, H. Phillips, and J. Seagle, "Performance of the Sharpe Portfolio Selection Model: A Comparison," *Journal of Financial and Quantitative Analysis* (June 1976): 195–204.

Selecting Optimal Asset Classes—The Asset Allocation Decision

The Markowitz model is typically thought of in terms of selecting portfolios of individual securities; indeed, that is how Markowitz expected his model to be used. As we know, however, it is a cumbersome model to employ because of the number of covariance estimates needed when dealing with a large number of individual securities.

An alternative way to use the Markowitz model as a selection technique is to think in terms of asset classes, such as domestic stocks, foreign stocks of industrialized countries, the stocks of emerging markets, bonds, and so forth. Using the model in this manner, investors decide what asset classes to own and what proportions of the asset classes to hold.

Asset Allocation Decision   The allocation of a portfolio's funds to classes of assets, such as cash equivalents, bonds, and equities

The **asset allocation decision** refers to the allocation of portfolio assets to broad asset markets; in other words, how much of the portfolio's funds are to be invested in stocks, in bonds, money market assets, and so forth. Each weight can range from zero percent to 100 percent. Asset allocation is one of the most widely used applications of modern portfolio theory (MPT).

Examining the asset allocation decision globally leads us to ask the following questions:

1. What percentage of portfolio funds is to be invested in each of the countries for which financial markets are available to investors?
2. Within each country, what percentage of portfolio funds is to be invested in stocks, bonds, bills, and other assets?
3. Within each of the major asset classes, what percentage of portfolio funds is to be invested in various individual securities?

Many knowledgeable market observers agree that the asset allocation decision is the most important decision made by an investor. According to some studies, for example, the asset allocation decision accounts for more than 90 percent of the variance in quarterly returns for a typical large pension fund.[14]

The rationale behind this approach is that different asset classes offer various potential returns and various levels of risk, and the correlation coefficients between some of these asset classes may be quite low, thereby providing beneficial diversification effects. As with the Markowitz analysis applied to individual securities, inputs remain a problem, because they must be estimated. However, this will always be a problem in investing, because we are selecting assets to be held over the uncertain future.

SOME MAJOR ASSET CLASSES

Let's consider some of the major asset classes that investors can use in building a portfolio. Investment counselors have regularly recommended that investors diversify internationally by holding foreign securities. The rationale for this has been that such investing reduces the risk of the portfolio, because correlations are lower and potential opportunities in other markets may be greater than those available in the United States.

Historically, international diversification clearly provided some risk-reducing benefits because of some low positive correlations between asset returns in various countries. Numerous studies confirmed these lower correlations and led many in the investing busi-

---

[14] See Gary P. Brinson, L. Randolph Hood, and Gilbert L. Beebower, "Determinants of Portfolio Performance," *Financial Analysts Review* (July/August 1986).

ness to recommend foreign holdings as an asset class. Regardless of the previous studies showing how international diversification can lower portfolio risk, as we noted earlier, the benefits of international diversification have come under increasing criticism.

It is clear that many economies have become more integrated as a result of global mergers, rapid money flows around the world, a more integrated European community, and so forth. Therefore, we might reasonably expect that the correlation between U.S. stocks and some index of foreign stocks has increased over time, and this is exactly the case. By early 2002, the correlation between the S&P 500 Index and EAFE was 91 percent.[15] Ten years earlier, it was only 58 percent. Furthermore, the new, higher correlation between markets stays high when markets decline, thereby failing investors when they most need it.

Should investors give up on international diversification? In short, NO! As we know from Chapter 6, a weakening dollar increases dollar-denominated foreign returns to U.S. investors, and if a weakening dollar is anticipated, it might be a good time to invest internationally. Furthermore, valuation differences will still occur between U.S. companies and non-U.S. companies.

How easy is it to choose foreign markets to add to a domestic portfolio? History teaches us that the best-performing markets differ from year to year. Emerging markets may produce good returns for certain periods and very bad returns during other periods. The same is true of developed countries. Japan had great equity returns in the 1980s and disastrous returns in the 1990s and into the twenty-first century. History also teaches us that past returns are not accurate predictors of future returns. For the 10 years ending in 1994, the EAFE Index showed higher returns than did the broadest measure of U.S. stock returns. However, the five years starting in 1995 and ending in 1999 were the greatest consecutive five years in U.S. market history, and clearly where U.S. investors wanted to be at that time.

Bonds are an obvious choice as one of the asset classes to hold in a diversified portfolio. Traditionally, asset allocation was described as dividing one's funds between stocks, bonds, and Treasury bills. The average correlation between the returns on the S&P 500 Index and 15-year Treasury bonds over a very long period was about 0.20. In some time periods, such as 1951 to 1965, the correlation between these two asset classes was negative.[16]

Treasury Inflation-Protected Securities (TIPS) Treasury securities fully indexed for inflation

Treasury inflation-protected securities (TIPS) are a relatively new asset class of growing importance, because they are the only asset class to provide systematic protection against inflation risk. TIPS pay a base interest rate that is fixed at the time the bonds are auctioned. However, the principal value of the bonds is adjusted for inflation. Therefore, the fixed rate of interest is applied to the inflation-adjusted principal of the bonds rather than their par value. Malkiel has estimated that the correlation between the S&P 500 Index and TIPS has fluctuated around zero but would actually have often been negative during the last 20 years.[17] As we know, negative correlations provide significant risk-reducing possibilities.

Real estate is another obvious choice for portfolio diversification. Real estate is typically cited as an asset that has little or no correlation with stocks. Investors can easily hold real estate by buying real estate investment trusts (REITs). Malkiel reports that the correlation between the S&P 500 Index and the National Association of Real Estate Investment Trusts (NAREIT) Equity Index has in recent years been close to zero (although 10 or so years ago the correlation was quite high).[18]

---

[15] See Nicholas Stein, "Small world, after all," *Fortune*, July 22, 2002, p. 302.

[16] These data come from Charles P. Jones and Jack W. Wilson, "The Changing Nature of Stock and Bond Volatility," forthcoming, the *Financial Analysts Journal*.

[17] See Burton Malkiel, "How Much Diversification is Enough?" in *AIMR Conference Proceedings: Equity Portfolio Construction*, Association for Investment Management and Research, Charlottesville, VA, 2002, p. 23.

[18] Ibid., p. 22.

COMBINING ASSET CLASSES

As an indication of what can be accomplished using asset classes for an investment program, consider some evidence which suggests that investors can diversify across mutual funds to create a bearproof portfolio. Portfolio funds are spread across seven asset classes: blue-chip stocks, small-cap stocks, international equities, domestic bonds, international bonds, gold, and money markets. Such a portfolio is said to have outperformed the S&P 500 Index over a 22-year period by more than two percentage points annually, while avoiding every bear market during the period. Note that this analysis does not employ the Markowitz efficient frontier technique, because it simply uses equal portfolio weights for each of the seven asset classes. Presumably, Markowitz analysis could improve the results obtained from this strategy.

Programs exist to calculate efficient frontiers using asset classes. These programs allow for a variety of constraints, such as minimum yield and no short selling.

Table 8-1 shows an example of calculating efficient portfolios using the Markowitz optimization technique. It contains return and risk data for "traditional" asset allocation portfolios consisting of stocks (S&P 500 Index), Treasury bonds, and Treasury bills, as well as "nontraditional" portfolios which could also include real estate and TIPS. Notice that three different portfolios are shown: a low-risk portfolio with a standard deviation of 5 percent, a moderate-risk portfolio with a standard deviation of 10 percent, and a high-risk portfolio with a standard deviation of 15 percent.

The nontraditional portfolios can include all five assets as opposed to three for the traditional. As we can see in Table 8-1, the standard deviations are the same for each of the three risk levels: 5, 10, and 15 percent. But note that the expected returns are higher in each case for the nontraditional portfolios as compared to the traditional portfolios.

Table 8-1   Comparison of Traditional Portfolio and Nontraditional Portfolio, March 1991–September 2001

Characteristic	Low Risk	Moderate Risk	High Risk
Traditional			
Expected return (%)	9.13	12.98	14.51
Standard deviation (%)	5.00	10.00	15.00
Sharpe ratio	0.88	0.83	0.65
Efficient asset allocation			
S&P 500 Index (%)	22.80	56.54	92.34
U.S. long-term government bonds (%)	36.28	43.46	7.66
U.S. T-bills (%)	40.92	0.00	0.00
Nontraditional			
Expected return (%)	10.11	13.57	14.80
Standard deviation (%)	5.00	10.00	15.00
Sharpe ratio	1.08	0.89	0.67
Efficient asset allocation			
S&P 500 Index (%)	18.65	39.23	88.20
U.S. long-term government bonds (%)	26.47	26.93	0.00
U.S. T-bills (%)	0.00	0.00	0.00
TIPS (%)	41.53	0.00	0.00
NAREIT Equity Index (%)	13.08	33.85	11.80

Note: The average risk-free rate during the period was 4.71 percent.

Figure 8-5

Efficient frontiers of a traditional and a nontraditional portfolio, March 1991–September 2001.

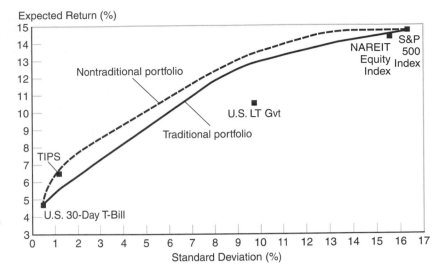

For the traditional portfolios, an investor seeking low risk (5 percent standard deviation) would place funds in each of the three major asset classes, ranging from 22.8 percent in stocks to 40.92 percent in Treasury bills. With a nontraditional portfolio, four of the five asset classes would be held for a low-risk position, with no funds in Treasury bills. In contrast, for the high-risk portfolio, funds are allocated only to stocks and bonds with the traditional portfolio and only to stocks and real estate for the nontraditional.

Figure 8-5 shows a plot of the efficient frontiers for the traditional and nontraditional portfolios. Note that the boundaries are Treasury bills on the low end and stocks on the high end. As we would expect, the nontraditional efficient frontier plots above the traditional efficient frontier. Thus, using the Markowitz analysis, investors can determine efficient portfolios by calculating the optimal allocations to each of the asset classes being considered.

Whether we use the Markowitz analysis for asset classes or individual securities, the end result is an efficient frontier of risky portfolios and the choice of an optimal risky portfolio based on investor preferences.

The Impact of Diversification on Risk

The Markowitz analysis demonstrates that the standard deviation of a portfolio is typically less than the weighted average of the standard deviations of the securities in the portfolio. Thus, diversification typically reduces the risk of a portfolio—as the number of portfolio holdings increases, portfolio risk declines.

SYSTEMATIC AND NONSYSTEMATIC RISK

Nonsystematic Risk
Risk attributable to factors unique to a security

The riskiness of the portfolio generally declines as more stocks are added, because we are eliminating the **nonsystematic risk**, or company-specific risk. This is unique risk related to a particular company. However, the extent of the risk reduction depends upon the degree of correlation among the stocks. As a general rule, correlations among stocks, at least domestic stocks and particularly large domestic stocks, are positive, although less than 1.0. Adding more stocks will reduce risk at first, but no matter how many partially correlated stocks we add to the portfolio, we cannot eliminate all of the risk.

Systematic Risk Risk attributable to broad macro factors affecting all securities

Variability in a security's total returns that is directly associated with overall movements in the general market or economy is called **systematic risk**, or market risk, or nondiversifiable risk. Virtually all securities have some systematic risk, whether bonds or stocks, because systematic risk directly encompasses interest rate risk, market risk, and inflation risk. We defined nonsystematic and systematic risk in Chapter 6.

After the nonsystematic risk is eliminated, what is left is the nondiversifiable portion, or the market risk (systematic part). This part of the risk is inescapable, because no matter how well an investor diversifies, the risk of the overall market cannot be avoided. If the stock market rises strongly, as it did in 1998 and 1999, most stocks will appreciate in value; if it declines sharply, as in 2000, 2001, and 2002, most stocks will be adversely affected. These movements occur regardless of what any single investor does.

Investors can construct a diversified portfolio and eliminate part of the total risk, the diversifiable, or nonmarket, part. Figure 8-6 illustrates this concept of declining nonsystematic risk in a portfolio of securities. As more securities are added, the nonsystematic risk becomes smaller and smaller, and the total risk for the portfolio approaches its systematic risk. Since diversification cannot reduce systematic risk, total portfolio risk can be reduced no lower than the total risk of the market portfolio.

Diversification can substantially reduce the unique risk of a portfolio. However, Figure 8-6 indicates that no matter how much we diversify, we cannot eliminate systematic risk. The declining total risk curve in Figure 8-6 levels off and at most becomes asymptotic to the systematic risk. Clearly, market risk is critical to all investors. It plays a central role in asset pricing, because it is the risk that investors can expect to be rewarded for taking.

HOW MANY SECURITIES ARE ENOUGH TO DIVERSIFY PROPERLY?

Table 7-2 showed that with 20 securities the standard deviation of annual returns had dropped to 21.7 percent, and going to 30 securities changed the standard deviation to only 20.9 percent, a very small difference. In fact, based on studies over the years, it has become commonplace for investors to believe that 15 or 20 stocks provide adequate diversification. This belief is now being revised.

Figure 8-6

Systematic and nonsystematic risk.

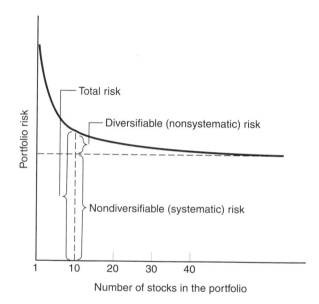

According to a new study by Campbell, Lettau, Malkiel, and Xu, between 1962 and 1997, the market's overall volatility did not change, whereas the volatility of individual stocks increased sharply.[19] Market volatility was found to be essentially trendless, whereas the volatility of individual stocks has risen. This study suggests that investors need more stocks in today's environment to adequately diversify.

In a separate article, Malkiel illustrates how today's situation differs from the past in terms of idiosyncratic (nonsystematic) risk and risk reduction.[20] Figure 8-7 shows how total risk declines based on the 1960s and the 1990s. Using the 1960s, which is the typical diagram traditionally shown to illustrate this, total risk declines rapidly as the idiosyncratic (labeled unsystematic in Figure 8-7) risk is eliminated. Twenty stocks diversified by sector could effectively eliminate the company-specific risk. In contrast, for the 1990s, even a 50-stock portfolio contains a significant amount of idiosyncratic risk. Malkiel goes on to say that in "today's market, a portfolio must hold many more stocks than the 20 stocks that in the 1960s achieved sufficient diversification."[21]

Based on the recent research done on diversification, it seems reasonable to state that approximately 50 securities are needed to ensure adequate diversification. It is possible that the number is even larger, but this appears to be a good working number.

The Implications of the Markowitz Portfolio Model

The construction of optimal portfolios and the selection of the best portfolio for an investor have implications for the pricing of financial assets. As we saw in the previous discussion, part of the riskiness of the average stock can be eliminated by holding a well-diversified portfolio. This means that part of the risk of the average stock can be eliminated and part cannot. Investors need to focus on that part of the risk that cannot be eliminated by diversification, because this is the risk that should be priced in the financial markets.

The relevant risk of an individual stock is its contribution to the riskiness of a well-diversified portfolio. The return that should be expected on the basis of this contribution can be estimated by the capital asset pricing model. We consider these topics in Chapter 9.

Figure 8-7

Diversification and the number of securities past and present.

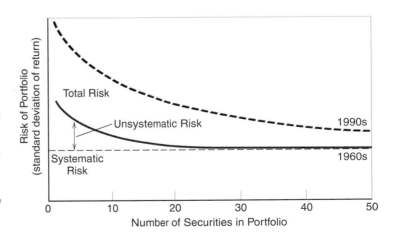

[19] See John Campbell, Martin Lettau, Burton Malkiel, and Yexiao Xu, "Have Individual Stocks Become More Volatile? An Empirical Exploration of Idiosyncratic Risk," *The Journal of Finance*, 56 (February 2001), pp. 1–43.

[20] Malkiel, op. cit., p. 19.

[21] Malkiel, op. cit., p. 19.

Summary

▶ Markowitz portfolio theory provides the way to select optimal portfolios based on using the full information set about securities.

▶ An efficient portfolio has the highest expected return for a given level of risk or the lowest level of risk for a given level of expected return.

▶ The Markowitz analysis determines the efficient set of portfolios, all of which are equally desirable. The efficient set is an arc in expected return–standard deviation space.

▶ The efficient frontier captures the possibilities that exist from a given set of securities. Indifference curves express investor preferences.

▶ The optimal portfolio for a risk-averse investor occurs at the point of tangency between the investor's highest indifference curve and the efficient set of portfolios.

▶ The single-index model provides an alternative expression for portfolio variance, which is easier to calculate than in the case of the Markowitz analysis. This alternative approach can be used to solve the portfolio problem as formulated by Markowitz.

▶ The single-index model relates returns on each security to the returns on a common index and can be expressed as:

$$R_i = a_i + \beta_i R_M + e_i$$

▶ The single-index model divides a security's return into two components: a unique part, represented by a_i, and a market-related part, represented by $\beta_i R_M$.

▶ The single-index model splits the risk of an individual security into two components. The total risk of a security, as measured by its variance, consists of market risk and unique risk. This simplifies the

covariance and greatly simplifies the calculation of total risk for a security and for a portfolio.

▶ The key assumption of the single-index model *is* that securities are related only in their common response to the return on the market. This implies that stocks covary together only because of their common relationship to the market index.

▶ The single-index model divides a security's return into two components: a unique part, represented by a_i, and a market-related part, represented by $\beta_i R_M$.

▶ Multi-index models reproduce the *historical* correlations better than the single-index model but may not perform better *ex ante*.

▶ The asset allocation decision refers to the allocation of portfolio assets to broad asset markets; in other words, how much of the portfolio's funds is to be invested in stocks, in bonds, money market assets, and so forth. Each weight can range from zero percent to 100 percent. Asset allocation is one of the most widely used applications of MPT.

▶ The Markowitz analysis can be applied to asset classes to determine optimal portfolios to hold. Efficient frontiers involving asset classes can be generated.

▶ Diversification can substantially reduce the unique risk of a portfolio. However, no matter how much we diversify, we cannot eliminate systematic risk. Therefore, systematic (market) risk is critical to all investors.

▶ New research indicates that it takes substantially more stocks to diversify adequately than has previously been thought. This number is at least 50, and could be more.

▶ The relevant risk of an individual stock is its contribution to the riskiness of a well-diversified portfolio.

Key Words

Asset allocation decision	Indifference curves	Systematic risk
Efficient set	Nonsystematic risk	Treasury inflation-indexed securities (TIPS)
Efficient frontier	Single-index model	

Questions

8-1 Calculate the number of covariances needed for an evaluation of 200 securities using the Markowitz model. Also, calculate the total number of pieces of information needed.

8-2 Using the Sharpe model, how many covariances would be needed to evaluate 200 securities? How many total pieces of information?

8-3 Consider a diagram of the efficient frontier. The vertical axis is _____? The horizontal axis is _____ as measured by the _____?

8-4 How many portfolios are on an efficient frontier? What is the Markowitz efficient set?

8-5 Why do rational investors seek efficient portfolios?

8-6 Using the Markowitz analysis, how does an investor select an optimal portfolio?

8-7 How is an investor's risk aversion indicated in an indifference curve? Are all indifference curves upward sloping?

8-8 With regard to international investing, how has the situation changed in recent years with regard to correlations among the stocks of different countries?

8-9 Given what has happened with regard to correlations among country returns, should U.S. investors give up, or decrease significantly, their positions in foreign securities?

8-10 What is the purpose of the single-index model?

8-11 The single-index model divides a security's returns into two components. What are they?

8-12 What is the key assumption of the single-index model?

8-13 How is the covariance between any two securities calculated with the single-index model?

8-14 With the single-index model, the risk of a security consists of two components. What are they?

8-15 A multi-index model has been found to reproduce the historical correlations better than the single-index model. Therefore, should we use a multi-index model rather than a single-index model to build portfolios?

8-16 What is meant by the asset allocation decision? How important is this decision?

8-17 When efficient frontiers are calculated using asset classes, what types of results are generally found?

8-18 As we add securities to a portfolio, what happens to the total risk of the portfolio?

8-19 How well does diversification work in reducing the risk of a portfolio? Are there limits to diversification? Do the effects kick in immediately?

8-20 What is the difference between traditional beliefs (starting in the 1960s) as to the number of securities needed to diversify properly, and the very recent evidence that has been presented by Malkiel and others?

8-21 Select the correct statement concerning the Markowitz model:
a. The Markowitz model determines the optimal portfolio for each investor.
b. The efficient frontier expresses preferences while indifference curves express possibilities.
c. All conservative investors would have the same optimal portfolio.
d. An investor's optimal portfolio can be found where his or her highest indifference curve is tangent to the efficient frontier.

CFA
8-22 Which *one* of the following portfolios cannot lie on the efficient frontier as described by Markowitz?

	Portfolio	Expected Return	Standard Deviation
a.	W	9%	21%
b.	X	5%	7%
c.	Y	15%	36%
d.	Z	12%	15%

CFA
8-23 Portfolio theory as described by Markowitz is most concerned with
a. The elimination of systematic risk
b. The effect of diversification on portfolio risk
c. Identifying one optimal portfolio for investors
d. Active portfolio management to enhance return

CFA
8-24 Which statement about portfolio diversification is correct?

a. Proper diversification can reduce or eliminate systematic risk.
b. The risk-reducing benefits of diversification do not occur meaningfully until at least 10 to 15 individual securities have been purchased.

c. Because diversification reduces a portfolio's total risk, it necessarily reduces the portfolio's expected return.
d. Typically, as more securities are added to a portfolio, total risk is expected to fall at a decreasing rate.

Problems

8-1 Given the following information for four securities:

Security	1	2	3	4
E(R) %	10	12	14	18
σ^2	300	350	400	450

$$r(1,2) = 0.2; r(1,3) = 0.4; r(1,4) = 0.6; r(2,3) = 0.1; r(3,4) = 0.9; r(2,4) = 0.5$$

Calculate five efficient portfolios using the Markowitz analysis, an upper boundary of 25 percent, and a lower boundary of 10 percent.

a. What is the highest expected return from these five portfolios?
b. What is the lowest standard deviation from these five portfolios?
c. Which portfolios involve short sales?
d. Which portfolio should be preferred by an investor?

8-2 Using the information in Problem 8-1, determine the effects of changing the correlation coefficient between securities 1 and 2 from 0.20 to −0.20.

a. What is the effect on the expected return of the portfolios?
b. What is the effect on the variance of the portfolios?

8-3 Based on the information in the table below, determine which of these portfolio(s) would constitute the efficient set.

Portfolio	Expected Return (%)	Standard Deviation (%)
1	10	20
2	12	24
3	8	16
4	6	12
5	9	21
6	20	40
7	18	36
8	8	15
9	11	19
10	12	22
11	14	26

8-4   Given the following information:

> Standard deviation for stock X = 12%
> Standard deviation for stock Y = 20%
> Expected return for stock X = 16%
> Expected return for stock Y = 22%
> Correlation coefficient between X and Y = 0.30

The covariance between stock X and Y is

a. 0.048
b. 72.00
c. 3.60
d. 105.6

8-5   Given the information in Problem 8-4 regarding risk, the expected return for a portfolio consisting of 50 percent invested in X and 50 percent invested in Y can be seen to be

a. 19%
b. 16%
c. less than 16%
d. more than 22%

8-6   Given the information in Problem 8-4, assume now that the correlation coefficient between stocks X and Y is +1.0. Choose the investment below that represents the minimum-risk portfolio.

a. 100% investment in stock Y
b. 100% investment in stock X
c. 50% investment in stock X and 50% investment in stock Y
d. 80% investment in stock Y and 20% investment in stock X

Web Resources

For additional resources visit our dynamic Web site located at www.wiley.com/college/jones.

❏ *It's a Four-letter Word*—The decision-maker struggles with the right balance between investment risk, return objectives, and his attitude toward risk. The case links to online risk tolerance assessments to help understand the investment decision-making process.

❏ Internet Exercises—This chapter discusses how one should go about constructing a portfolio, using the concepts learnt in the previous chapters.
Exercise 1: Takes the reader through the construction of an efficient frontier.
Exercise 2: Relates portfolio choice to risk aversion.
Exercise 3: Constructs an efficient portfolio of mutual funds.
Exercise 4: Uses the single-index model to compute the efficient frontier.

❏ Multiple Choice Self Test

Selected Reference

A good discussion of asset allocation strategies, as well as statistical concepts such as standard deviation, can be found in

Bernstein, William, *The Intelligent Asset Allocator*. New York: McGraw-Hill, 2000.

chapter 9

Asset Pricing Models

Chapter 9 analyzes the two best-known models used in the valuation of risky assets, the capital asset pricing model and arbitrage pricing theory. Both are equilibrium models used to predict the theoretical equilibrium price of an asset. These asset pricing models utilize portfolio theory as developed by Markowitz, and therefore are a natural follow-up to our discussion in Chapters 7 and 8.

Most of our discussion concerns capital market theory and the capital asset pricing model (CAPM), because many investors are familiar with these concepts. This chapter provides a solid basis for understanding and estimating the required rate of return based on the CAPM. When we discuss the valuation of common stocks in later chapters, the concept of the required rate of return will be important in that discussion.

AFTER READING THIS CHAPTER YOU WILL BE ABLE TO:

▶ Understand capital market theory as an extension of portfolio theory.

▶ Recognize the capital market line, which applies to efficient portfolios, and the security market line, which applies to all portfolios as well as individual securities.

▶ Understand and use the capital asset pricing model (CAPM) equation to calculate the required rate of return for a security.

▶ Recognize an alternative theory of how assets are priced, arbitrage pricing theory.

In Chapter 8, we discussed portfolio theory, which is normative, describing how investors should act in selecting an optimal portfolio of risky securities. In this chapter, we consider theories about asset pricing. What happens if all investors seek portfolios of risky securities using the Markowitz framework under idealized conditions? How will this affect equilibrium security prices and returns? In other words, how does optimal diversification affect the market prices of securities? Under these idealized conditions, what is the risk-return trade-off that investors face? In general, we wish to examine models that explain security prices under conditions of market equilibrium. These are asset pricing models, or models for the valuation of risky assets.

We devote most of our attention to capital market theory (CMT), which begins where portfolio theory ends. CMT provides a model for pricing risky assets.[1] Although CMT has its shortcomings, and Arbitrage Pricing Theory provides an important alternative, it remains the case that most investors are much more likely to encounter, and use, CMT in the form of the CAPM.

Capital Market Theory

Capital market theory is a positive theory in that it hypothesizes how investors do behave rather than how investors should behave, as in the case of Modern Portfolio Theory (MPT). It is reasonable to view capital market theory as an extension of portfolio theory, but it is important to understand that MPT is not based on the validity, or lack thereof, of capital market theory.

The equilibrium model of interest to many investors is known as the capital asset pricing model, typically referred to as the CAPM. It allows us to measure the relevant risk of an individual security as well as to assess the relationship between risk and the returns expected from investing. The CAPM is attractive as an equilibrium model because of its simplicity and its implications. Because of serious challenges to the model, however, alternatives have been developed. The primary alternative to the CAPM is arbitrage pricing theory, or APT, which allows for multiple sources of risk.

CAPITAL MARKET THEORY ASSUMPTIONS

Capital market theory involves a set of predictions concerning equilibrium expected returns on risky assets. It typically is derived by making some simplifying assumptions in order to facilitate the analysis and help us to understand the arguments without fundamentally changing the predictions of asset pricing theory.

Capital market theory builds on Markowitz portfolio theory. Each investor is assumed to diversify his or her portfolio according to the Markowitz model, choosing a location on the efficient frontier that matches his or her return-risk references. Because of the complexity of the real world, additional assumptions are made to make individuals more alike:

Homogeneous Expectations Identical investor expectations regarding the three inputs for the Markowitz portfolio model.

1. All investors can borrow or lend money at the risk-free rate of return (designated RF in this text).
2. All investors have identical probability distributions for future rates of return; they have **homogeneous expectations** with respect to the three inputs of the portfolio model explained in Chapter 7: expected returns, the variance of returns, and the correlation matrix. Therefore, given a set of security prices and a risk-free rate, all investors use the same information to generate an efficient frontier.

[1] Much of this analysis is attributable to the work of Sharpe. See W. Sharpe, "Capital Asset Prices: A Theory of Market Equilibrium under Conditions of Risk," *The Journal of Finance*, 19 (September 1964): 425–442. Lintner and Mossin developed a similar analysis.

3. All investors have the same one-period time horizon.
4. There are no transaction costs.
5. There are no personal income taxes—investors are indifferent between capital gains and dividends.
6. There is no inflation.
7. There are many investors, and no single investor can affect the price of a stock through his or her buying and selling decisions. Investors are price takers and act as if prices are unaffected by their own trades.
8. Capital markets are in equilibrium.

These assumptions appear to be unrealistic and often disturb investors encountering capital market theory for the first time. However, the important issue is how well the theory predicts or describes reality, and not the realism of its assumptions. If CMT does a good job of explaining the returns on risky assets, it is very useful, and the assumptions made in deriving the theory are of less importance.

Most of these assumptions can be relaxed without significant effects on the CAPM or its implications; in other words, the CAPM is robust.[2] Although the results from such a relaxation of the assumptions may be less clear-cut and precise, no significant damage is done. Many conclusions of the basic model still hold.

Finally, most investors recognize that all of the assumptions of CMT are not unrealistic. For example, some institutional investors are tax exempt, and brokerage costs today, as a percentage of the transaction, are quite small. Nor is it too unreasonable to assume that for the one-period horizon of the model, inflation may be fully (or mostly) anticipated and, therefore, not a major factor.

INTRODUCTION OF THE RISK-FREE ASSET

The first assumption of CMT listed above is that investors can borrow and lend at the risk-free rate. Although the introduction of a risk-free asset appears to be a simple step to take in the evolution of portfolio and CMT, it is a very significant step. In fact, it is the introduction of a risk-free asset that allows us to develop CMT from portfolio theory.

With the introduction of a risk-free asset, investors can now invest part of their wealth in this asset and the remainder in any of the risky portfolios in the Markowitz efficient set. It allows Markowitz portfolio theory to be extended in such a way that the efficient frontier is completely changed, which in turn leads to a general theory for pricing assets under uncertainty.

A risk-free asset can be defined as one with a certain-to-be-earned expected return and a variance of return of zero. (Note, however, that this is a nominal return and not a real return, which is uncertain, because inflation is uncertain.) Since variance = 0, the nominal risk-free rate in each period will be equal to its expected value. Furthermore, the covariance between the risk-free asset and any risky asset i will be zero.

The true risk-free asset is best thought of as a Treasury security, which has no risk of default, with a maturity matching the holding period of the investor. In this case, the amount of money to be received at the end of the holding period is known with certainty at the beginning of the period. The Treasury bill typically is taken to be the risk-free asset, and its rate of return is referred to here as RF.

---

[2] For a discussion of changing these assumptions, see E. Elton, M. Gruber, S. Brown, and W. Goetzmann, *Modern Portfolio Theory and Investment Analysis*, Sixth Edition (New York: John Wiley & Sons, 2003), Chapter 14.

Figure 9-1

The Markowitz efficient frontier and the possibilities resulting from introducing a risk-free asset.

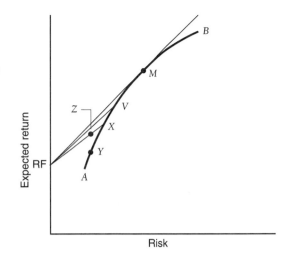

Risk-Free Borrowing and Lending Assume that the efficient frontier, as shown by the arc AB in Figure 9-1, has been derived by an investor. The arc AB delineates the efficient set of portfolios of risky assets as explained in Chapter 8. (For simplicity, assume these are portfolios of common stocks.) We now introduce a risk-free asset with return RF and $\sigma = 0$.

As shown in Figure 9-1, the return on the risk-free asset (RF) will plot on the vertical axis because the risk is zero. Investors can combine this riskless asset with the efficient set of portfolios on the efficient frontier. By drawing a line between RF and various risky portfolios on the efficient frontier, we can examine combinations of risk-return possibilities that did not exist previously.

In Figure 9-1, a new line could be drawn between RF and the Markowitz efficient frontier above point X, for example, connecting RF to point V. Each successively higher line will dominate the preceding set of portfolios. This process ends when a line is drawn tangent to the efficient set of risky portfolios, given a vertical intercept of RF. In Figure 9-1, we will call this tangency point M. The set of portfolio opportunities on this line (RF to M) dominates all portfolios below it.

The straight line from RF to the efficient frontier at point M, RF-M, dominates all straight lines below it and contains the superior *lending portfolios* given the Markowitz efficient set depicted in Figure 9-1. Lending refers to the purchase of a riskless asset such as Treasury bills, because by making such a purchase, the investor is lending money to the issuer of the securities, the U.S. government. We can think of this risk-free lending simply as *risk-free investing*.

What if we extend this analysis to allow investors to borrow money? The investor is no longer restricted to his or her wealth when investing in risky assets. Technically, we are short selling the riskless asset. One way to accomplish this borrowing is to buy stocks on margin, which has a current initial margin requirement of 50 percent. We will assume that investors can also borrow at the risk-free rate RF.[3] This assumption can be removed without changing the basic arguments.

Borrowing additional investable funds and investing them together with the investor's own wealth allows investors to seek higher expected returns while assuming

---

[3] Keep in mind that with lending the investor earns a rate RF, whereas with borrowing the investor pays the rate RF on the borrowed funds.

Figure 9-2

The efficient frontier when lending and borrowing possibilities are allowed.

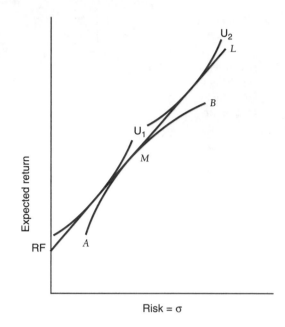

greater risk. These borrowed funds can be used to lever the portfolio position beyond point M, the point of tangency between the straight line emanating from RF and the efficient frontier AB. As in the lending discussion, point M represents 100 percent of an investor's wealth in the risky asset portfolio M. The straight line RF-M is now extended upward, as shown in Figure 9-2, and can be designated RF-M-L.

The Equilibrium Return-Risk Tradeoff

Given the previous analysis, we can now derive some predictions concerning equilibrium expected returns and risk. The CAPM is an equilibrium model that encompasses two important relationships. The first, the capital market line, specifies the equilibrium relationship between expected return and risk for efficient portfolios. The second, the security market line, specifies the equilibrium relationship between expected return and systematic risk. It applies to individual securities as well as portfolios.

THE CAPITAL MARKET LINE

The straight line shown in Figure 9-2, which traces out the risk-return trade-off for efficient portfolios, is tangent to the Markowitz efficient frontier at point M and has a vertical intercept RF. We now know that portfolio M is the tangency point to a straight line drawn from RF to the efficient frontier, and that this straight line is the best obtainable efficient-set line. All investors will hold portfolio M as their optimal risky portfolio, and all investors will be somewhere on this steepest trade-off line between expected return and risk, because it represents those combinations of risk-free investing/borrowing and portfolio M that yield the highest return obtainable for a given level of risk.

Capital Market Line (CML)   The trade off between expected return and risk for efficient protfolios

This straight line, usually referred to as the **capital market line (CML)**, depicts the equilibrium conditions that prevail in the market for *efficient portfolios* consisting of the optimal portfolio of risky assets and the risk-free asset. All combinations of the risk-free asset and the risky portfolio M are on the CML, and, in equilibrium, all investors will end up with portfolios somewhere on the CML.

Figure 9-3

The capital market line and the components of its slope.

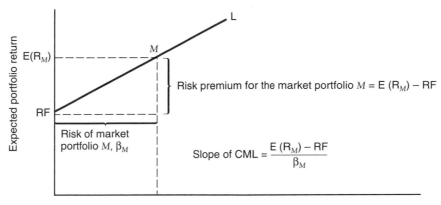

Consider the equation for the CML, which is shown as a straight line in Figure 9-3 without the now-dominated Markowitz frontier. We know that this line has an intercept of RF. If investors are to invest in risky assets, they must be compensated for this additional risk with a risk premium. The vertical distance between the risk-free rate and the CML at point M in Figure 9-3 is the amount of return expected for bearing the risk of the market portfolio; that is, the excess return above the risk-free rate. At that point, the amount of risk for the market portfolio is given by the horizontal dotted line between RF and σ_M.

Therefore,

$$\frac{E(R_M) - RF}{\sigma_M} = \text{Slope of the CML}$$

$$= \text{Expected return-risk trade-off for efficient portfolios}$$

The slope of the CML is the *market price of risk* for efficient portfolios. It is also called the equilibrium market price of risk.[4] It indicates the additional return that the market demands for each percentage increase in a portfolio's risk; that is, in its standard deviation of return.

Example 9-1

Assume that the expected return on portfolio M is 13 percent, with a standard deviation of 25 percent, and that RF is 7 percent. The slope of the CML would be

$$(0.13 - 0.07)/0.25 = 0.24$$

In our example, a risk premium of 0.24 indicates that the market demands this amount of return for each percentage increase in a portfolio's risk.

We now know the intercept and slope of the CML. Since the CML is the trade-off between expected return and risk for efficient portfolios, and risk is being measured by the standard deviation, the equation for the CML is

$$E(R_p) = RF + \frac{E(R_M) - RF}{\sigma_M} \sigma_p \qquad \textbf{(9-1)}$$

[4] The assumption throughout this discussion is that $E(R_M)$ is greater than RF. This is the only reasonable assumption to make, because the CAPM is concerned with expected returns (i.e., *ex ante* returns). After the fact, this assumption may not hold for particular periods; that is, over historical periods such as a year RF has exceeded the return on the market, which is sometimes negative.

where

$E(R_p)$ = the expected return on any efficient portfolio on the CML
RF   = the rate of return on the risk-free asset
$E(R_M)$ = the expected return on the market portfolio M
σ_M = the standard deviation of the returns on the market portfolio
σ_p = the standard deviation of the efficient portfolio being considered

In words, the expected return for any portfolio on the CML is equal to the risk-free rate plus a risk premium.

The following points should be noted about the CML:

1. Only efficient portfolios consisting of the risk-free asset and portfolio M lie on the CML. Portfolio M, the market portfolio of risky securities, contains all securities weighted by their respective market values—it is the optimum combination of risky securities. The risk-free asset has no risk. Therefore, all combinations of these two assets on the CML are efficient portfolios.

2. As a statement of equilibrium, the CML must always be upward sloping, because the price of risk must always be positive. Remember that the CML is formulated in a world of expected return, and risk-averse investors will not invest unless they expect to be compensated for the risk. The greater the risk, the greater the expected return.

3. On a historical basis, for some particular period of time such as a year or two, or four consecutive quarters, the CML can be downward sloping; that is, the return on RF exceeds the return on the market portfolio. This does not negate the validity of the CML; it merely indicates that returns actually realized differ from those that were expected. Obviously, investor expectations are not always realized. (If they were, there would be no risk.) Thus, although the CML must be upward sloping *ex ante* (before the fact), it can be, and sometimes is, downward sloping *ex post* (after the fact).

4. The CML can be used to determine the optimal expected returns associated with different portfolio risk levels. Therefore, the CML indicates the required return for each portfolio risk level.

Market Portfolio The portfolio of all risky assets, with each asset weighted by the ratio of its market value to the market value of all risky assets

The Market Portfolio Portfolio M in Figure 9-2 is called the **market portfolio** of risky securities. It is the highest point of tangency between RF and the efficient frontier and is *the* optimal risky portfolio. All investors would want to be on the optimal line RF-M-L, and, unless they invested 100 percent of their wealth in the risk-free asset, they would own portfolio M with some portion of their investable wealth or they would invest their own wealth plus borrowed funds in portfolio M. This portfolio is the optimal portfolio of risky assets.[5]

---

[5] All assets are included in portfolio M in proportion to their market value. For example, if the market value of IBM constitutes 2 percent of the market value of all risky assets, IBM will constitute 2 percent of the market value of portfolio M and, therefore, 2 percent of the market value of each investor's portfolio of risky assets. Therefore, we can state that security *i*'s percentage in the risky portfolio M is equal to the total market value of security *i* relative to the total market value of all securities.

In theory, the market portfolio should include all risky assets worldwide, both financial (e.g., bonds, options, futures) and real (e.g., gold, real estate), in their proper proportions. The global aspects of such a portfolio are important to note. By one estimate, the value of non-U.S. assets exceeds 60 percent of the world total. U.S. equities make up only about 10 percent of total world assets. Therefore, international diversification is clearly important.

A worldwide portfolio, if it could be constructed, would be completely diversified. Of course, the market portfolio is unobservable.

Why do all investors hold identical risky portfolios? Based on our assumptions above, all investors use the same Markowitz analysis on the same set of securities, have the same expected returns and covariances, and have an identical time horizon. Therefore, they will arrive at the same optimal risky portfolio, and it will be the market portfolio, designated M.

It is critical to note that although investors take different positions on the straight-line efficient set in Figure 9-2, all investors are investing in portfolio M, the same portfolio of risky assets. This portfolio will always consist of all risky assets in existence. The emergence of the market portfolio as the optimal efficient portfolio is the most important implication of the CAPM. In effect, the CAPM states that portfolio M is the optimal risky portfolio.

In equilibrium, all risky assets must be in portfolio M, because all investors are assumed to arrive at, and hold, the same risky portfolio. If the optimal portfolio did not include a particular asset, the price of this asset would decline dramatically until it became an attractive investment opportunity. At some point, investors will purchase it, and it will be included in the market portfolio. Because the market portfolio includes all risky assets, *portfolio M is completely diversified*. Portfolio M contains only market (systematic) risk which, even with perfect diversification, cannot be eliminated, because it is the result of macroeconomic factors that affect the value of all securities.

The market portfolio is often proxied by the portfolio of all common stocks, which in turn is proxied by a market index such as the Standard & Poor's 500 (S&P 500) Composite Index, which has been used throughout the text. Therefore, to facilitate this discussion, think of portfolio M as a broad market index such as the S&P 500 Index. The market portfolio is, of course, a risky portfolio, and its risk is designated σ_M.

The Separation Theorem We have established that each investor will hold combinations of the risk-free asset (either lending or borrowing) and the tangency portfolio from the efficient frontier, which is the market portfolio. Because we are assuming homogeneous expectations, in equilibrium all investors will determine the same tangency portfolio. Further, under the assumptions of CMT all investors agree on the risk-free rate. Therefore, the linear efficient set shown in Figure 9-2 now applies to all investors.

Borrowing and lending possibilities, combined with one portfolio of risky assets, M, offer an investor whatever risk-expected return combination he or she seeks; that is, investors can be anywhere they choose on this line depending on their risk-return preferences. An investor could:

1. Invest 100 percent of investable funds in the risk-free asset, providing an expected return of RF and zero risk.
2. Invest 100 percent of investable funds in risky-asset portfolio M, offering $E(R_M)$, with its risk σ_M.
3. Invest in any combination of return and risk between these two points; obtained by varying the proportion w_{RF} invested in the risk-free asset.
4. Invest more than 100 percent of investable funds in the risky-asset portfolio M by borrowing money at the rate RF, thereby increasing both the expected return and the risk beyond that offered by portfolio M.

Different investors will choose different portfolios because of their risk preferences (they have different indifference curves), but they will choose the same combination of risky securities as denoted by the tangency point in Figure 9-2, M. Investors will then borrow or lend to achieve various positions on the linear trade-off between expected return and risk.

Unlike the Markowitz analysis, it is not necessary to match each client's indifference curves with a particular efficient portfolio, because only one efficient portfolio is held by all investors. Rather each client will use his or her indifference curves to determine where along the new efficient frontier RF-M-L he or she should be. In effect, each client must determine how much of investable funds should be lent or borrowed at RF and how much should be invested in portfolio M. This result is referred to as a separation property.

The **separation theorem** states that the investment decision (which portfolio of risky assets to hold) is separate from the financing decision (how to allocate investable funds between the risk-free asset and the risky asset). The risky portfolio M is optimal for every investor regardless of that investor's utility function; that is, M's optimality is determined separately from knowledge of any investor's risk-return preferences and is not affected by investor risk preferences. All investors, by investing in the same portfolio of risky assets (M) and either borrowing or lending at the rate RF, can achieve any point on the straight line RF-M-L in Figure 9-2. Each point on that line represents a different expected return-risk trade-off. An investor with utility curve U1 will be at the lower end of the line, representing a combination of lending and investment in M. On the other hand, utility curve U2 represents an investor borrowing at the rate RF to invest in risky assets—specifically, portfolio M.

The concept of the riskless-asset–risky-asset (portfolio) dichotomy is an important one in investments, with several different applications. As we have seen, using the two in combination allows investors to achieve any point on the expected return-risk trade-off that all investors face. This is in sharp contrast to the traditional investing approach where investment firms and money managers "tailor" a portfolio of stocks to each individual client because of their unique preferences. For example, a retiree living off the income from a stock portfolio would be guided to a portfolio of relatively conservative stocks with an emphasis on their dividend yields. A 35-year-old investor doing well in his or her profession, on the other hand, might be guided to a portfolio of very different stocks with considerably more risk and expected return.

The separation theorem, given multiple clients or complete agreement by all concerned about the future prospects of securities, argues that this "tailoring" process is inappropriate. All investors should hold the same portfolio of risky assets and achieve their own position on the risk-return trade-off through borrowing and lending. The opportunity set (the portfolio of securities to hold) is the same—investors with different preferences can be accommodated with this same opportunity set.

The capital market line depicts the risk-return trade-off in the financial markets in equilibrium. However, it applies only to efficient portfolios and cannot be used to assess the equilibrium expected return on a single security. What about individual securities or inefficient portfolios? To relate expected return and risk for any asset or portfolio, efficient or inefficient, we need the expected return-beta form of the capital asset pricing model (CAPM).

THE SECURITY MARKET LINE

The capital market line depicts the risk-return trade-off in the financial markets in equilibrium. However, it applies only to efficient portfolios and cannot be used to assess the equilibrium expected return for a single security. What about individual securities or inefficient portfolios?

Under the CAPM all investors will hold the market portfolio, which is the benchmark portfolio against which other portfolios are measured. How does an individual security contribute to the risk of the market portfolio?

Investors should expect a risk premium for buying a risky asset such as a stock. The greater the riskiness of that stock, the higher the risk premium should be. If investors

Separation Theorem
The idea that the decision of which portfolio of risky assets to hold is separate from the decision of how to allocate investable funds between the risk-free asset and the risky asset

hold well-diversified portfolios, they should be interested in portfolio risk rather than individual security risk. Different stocks will affect a well-diversified portfolio differently. The relevant risk for an individual stock is its contribution to the riskiness of a well-diversified portfolio. And the risk of a well-diversified portfolio is market risk, or systematic risk, which is nondiversifiable.

Beta We now know that investors should hold diversified portfolios to reduce the portfolio risk. When an investor adds a security to a portfolio what matters is the security's average covariance with the other securities in the portfolio. We also now know that under CMT all investors will hold the same portfolio of risky assets, the market portfolio. Therefore, the risk that matters when we consider any security is its covariance with the market portfolio.

We could relate the expected return on a stock to its covariance with the market portfolio. However, it is more convenient to use a standardized measure of the systematic risk that cannot be avoided through diversification. Beta is a *relative measure* of risk—the risk of an individual stock relative to the market portfolio of all stocks. If the security's returns move more (less) than the market's returns as the latter changes, the security's returns have more (less) volatility (fluctuations in price) than those of the market. For example, a security whose returns rise or fall on average 15 percent when the market return rises or falls 10 percent is said to be an aggressive, or volatile, security.

Securities with different slopes have different sensitivities to the returns of the market index. If the slope of this relationship for a particular security is a 45-degree angle, as shown for security B in Figure 9-4, the beta is 1.0. This means that for every 1-percent change in the market's return, *on average*, this security's returns change 1 percent. The market portfolio has a beta of 1.0.

Example 9-2

In Figure 9-4, Security A's beta of 1.5 indicates that, *on average*, security returns are 1.5 times as volatile as market returns, both up and down. A security whose returns rise or fall on average 15 percent when the market return rises or falls 10 percent is said to be an aggressive, or volatile, security. If the line is less steep than the 45-degree line, beta is less than 1.0; this indicates that, on average, a stock's returns have less volatility than the market as a whole. For example, security C's beta of 0.6 indicates that stock returns move up or down, on average, only 60 percent as much as the market as a whole.

In summary, the aggregate market has a beta of 1.0. More volatile (risky) stocks have betas larger than 1.0, and less volatile (risky) stocks have betas smaller than 1.0. As a relative measure of risk, beta is very convenient. Beta is useful for comparing the relative sys-

Figure 9-4

Illustrative betas of 1.5 (A), 1.0 (B), and 0.6 (C).

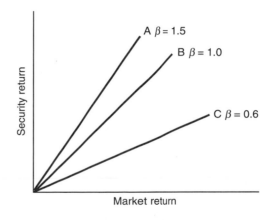

tematic risk of different stocks and, in practice, is used by investors to judge a stock's riskiness. Stocks can be ranked by their betas. Because the variance of the market is a constant across all securities for a particular period, ranking stocks by beta is the same as ranking them by their absolute systematic risk. Stocks with high (low) betas are said to be high (low) risk securities.

Security Market Line (SML)   The graphical depiction of the CAPM

The CAPM's Expected Return–Beta Relationship The security market line (SML) is the CAPM specification of how risk and required rate of return for any asset, security, or portfolio are related. This theory posits a linear relationship between an asset's risk and its required rate of return. This linear relationship, called the security market line (SML), is shown in Figure 9-5. Required rate of return is on the vertical axis and beta, the measure of risk, is on the horizontal axis. The slope of the line is the difference between the required rate of return on the market index and RF, the risk-free rate.

Investments Intuition

As we could (and should) expect, Figure 9-5 again demonstrates that if investors are to seek higher expected returns, they must assume a larger risk as measured by beta, the relative measure of systematic risk. The trade-off between *expected* return and risk must always be positive. In Figure 9-5, the vertical axis can be thought of as the expected return for an asset.

In equilibrium, investors require a minimum expected return before they will invest in a particular security. That is, given its risk, a security must offer some minimum expected return before a given investor can be persuaded to purchase it. Thus, in discussing the SML concept, we are simultaneously talking about the required and expected rate of return.

Capital Asset Pricing Market (CAPM)   Relates the required rate of return for any security with the risk for that security as measured by beta

The **capital asset pricing model (CAPM)** formally relates the expected rate of return for any security or portfolio with the relevant risk measure. The CAPM's expected return–beta relationship is the most-often cited form of the relationship. Beta is the relevant measure of risk that cannot be diversified away in a portfolio of securities and, as such, is the measure that investors should consider in their portfolio management decision process.

Figure 9-5

The security market line (SML).

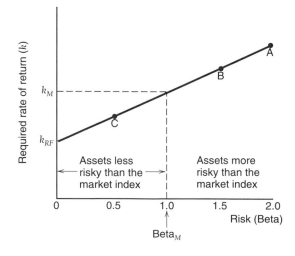

The CAPM in its expected return–beta relationship form is a simple but elegant statement. It says that the expected rate of return on an asset is a function of the two components of the **required rate of return**—the risk-free rate and the risk premium. Thus,

Required Rate of Return
The minimum expected rate of return necessary to induce an investor to purchase a security

$$k_i = \text{Risk-free rate} + \text{Risk premium} \tag{9-2}$$

$$= \text{RF} + \beta_i[\text{E}(R_M) - \text{RF}]$$

where

$$
\begin{aligned}
k_i &= \text{the required rate of return on asset } i \\
\text{E}(R_M) &= \text{the expected rate of return on the market portfolio} \\
\beta_i &= \text{the beta coefficient for asset } i
\end{aligned}
$$

Market Risk Premium
The difference between the expected return for the equities market and the risk-free rate of return

This relationship provides an explicit measure of the risk premium. It is the product of the beta for a particular security i and the **market risk premium**, $\text{E}(R_M) - \text{RF}$. Thus,

$$\text{Risk premium for security } i = \beta_i \text{ (market risk premium)}$$

$$= \beta_i[\text{E}(R_M) - \text{RF}]$$

Investments Intuition

Equation 9-2 indicates that securities with betas greater than the market beta of 1.0 should have larger risk premiums than that of the average stock and, therefore, when added to RF, larger required rates of return. This is exactly what investors should expect, since beta is a measure of risk, and greater risk should be accompanied by greater return. Conversely, securi- ties with betas less than that of the market are less risky and should have required rates of return lower than that for the market as a whole. This will be the indicated result from the **CAPM**, because the risk pre- mium for the security will be less than the market risk premium and, when added to RF, will produce a lower required rate of return for the security.

The CAPM's expected return–beta relationship is a simple but elegant statement about expected (required) return and risk for any security or portfolio. It formalizes the basis of investments, which is that the greater the risk assumed, the greater the expected (re- quired) return should be. This relationship states that an investor requires (expects) a re- turn on a risky asset equal to the return on a risk-free asset plus a risk premium, and the greater the risk assumed, the greater the risk premium.

Example 9-3

Assume that the beta for IBM is 1.15. Also assume that RF is 0.05 and that the expected return on the market is 0.12. The required return for IBM can be calculated as

$$k\text{I}_{BM} = 0.05 + 1.15(0.12 - 0.05)$$

$$= 13.05\%$$

The required (or expected) return for IBM is, as it should be, larger than that of the mar- ket because IBM's beta is larger—once again, the greater the risk assumed, the larger the required return.

Over- and Undervalued Securities The SML has important implications for security prices. In equilibrium, each security should lie on the SML, because the expected return on the security should be that needed to compensate investors for the systematic risk.

What happens if investors determine that a security does not lie on the SML? To make this determination, they must employ a separate methodology to estimate the expected returns for securities. In other words, a SML can be fitted to a sample of securities to determine the expected (required) return-risk trade-off that exists. Knowing the beta for any stock, we can determine the required return from the SML. Then, estimating the expected return from, say, fundamental analysis, an investor can assess a security in relation to the SML and determine whether it is under- or overvalued.

Example 9-4

In Figure 9-6, two securities are plotted around the SML. Security X has a high expected return derived from fundamental analysis and plots above the SML; security Y has a low expected return and plots below the SML. Which is undervalued?

Security X, plotting above the SML, is undervalued because it offers more expected return than investors require, given its level of systematic risk. Investors require a minimum expected return of $E(R_X)$, but security X, according to fundamental analysis, is offering $E(R_X')$. If investors recognize this, they will do the following:

> Purchase security X, because it offers more return than required. This demand will drive up the price of X, as more of it is purchased. The return will be driven down, until it is at the level indicated by the SML.

Now consider security Y. This security, according to investors' fundamental analysis, does not offer enough expected return given its level of systematic risk. Investors require $E(R_Y)$ for security Y, based on the SML, but Y offers only $E(R_Y')$. As investors recognize this, they will do the following:

> Sell security Y (or perhaps sell Y short), because it offers less than the required return. This increase in the supply of Y will drive down its price. The return will be driven up for new buyers, because any dividends paid are now relative to a lower price, as is any expected price appreciation. The price will fall until the expected return rises enough to reach the SML and the security is once again in equilibrium.

Estimating the SML

To implement the SML approach described here, an investor needs estimates of the return on the risk-free asset (RF), the expected return on the market index, and the beta for an individual security. How difficult are these to obtain?

Figure 9-6

Overvalued and undervalued securities using the SML.

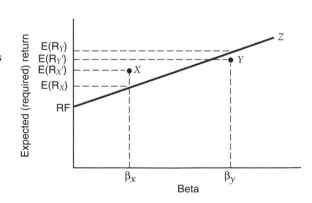

The RF should be the easiest of the three variables to obtain. In estimating RF, the investor can use as a proxy the return on Treasury bills for the coming period (e.g., a year).

Estimating the market return is more difficult, because the expected return for the market index is not observable. Furthermore, several different market indexes could be used. Estimates of the market return could be derived from a study of previous market returns (such as the Standard & Poor's data in Table 6-1). Alternatively, probability estimates of market returns could be made, and the expected value calculated. This would provide an estimate of both the expected return and the standard deviation for the market.

Finally, it is necessary to estimate the betas for individual securities. This is a crucial part of the CAPM estimation process. The estimates of RF and the expected return on the market are the same for each security being evaluated. Only beta is unique, bringing together the investor's expectations of returns for the stock with those for the market. Beta is the only company-specific factor in the CAPM; therefore, risk is the only asset-specific forecast that must be made in the CAPM.

ESTIMATING BETA

Market Model Relates the return on each stock to the return on the market, using a linear relationship with intercept and slope

A less restrictive form of the single-index model is known as the **market model**. This model is identical to the single-index model except that the assumption of the error terms for different securities being uncorrelated is not made.

The market model equation is the same as Equation 8-1 for the single-index model (again, without the restrictive assumption):

$$R_i = \alpha_i + \beta_i R_M + e_i \tag{9-3}$$

where

R_i = the return (TR) on security i
R_M = the return (TR) on the market index
α_i = the intercept term
β_i = the slope term
e_i = the random residual error

The market model produces an estimate of return for any stock.

To estimate the market model, the TRs for stock i can be regressed on the corresponding TRs for the market index. Estimates will be obtained of α_i (the constant return on security i that is earned regardless of the level of market returns) and β_i (the slope coefficient that indicates the expected increase in a security's return for a 1-percent increase in market return). This is how the estimate of a stock's beta is often derived.

Example 9-5

To illustrate the calculation of the market model, we use Total Return (TR) data for the Coca-Cola company (ticker symbol "KO"). Fitting a regression equation to 60 months of return data along with corresponding TRs for the S&P 500, the estimated equation is:

$$R_{KO} = 1.06 + 1.149 \, R_{S\&P500}$$

Characteristic Line A regression equation used to estimate beta by regressing stock returns on market returns

When the TRs for a stock are plotted against the market index TRs, the regression line fitted to these points is referred to as the **characteristic line**. Coca-Cola's characteristic line is shown in Figure 9-7.

The characteristic line is often fitted using *excess returns*. The excess return is calculated by subtracting out the risk-free rate, RF, from both the return on the stock and the return on the market.

Figure 9-7

The characteristic line for Coca-Cola, monthly data.

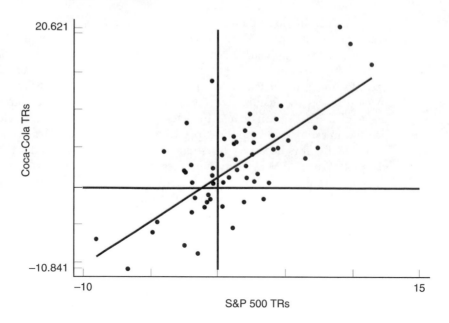

In excess return form, the same analysis as before applies. The alpha is the intercept of the characteristic line on the vertical axis and, in theory, should be zero for any stock. It measures the excess return for a stock when the excess return for the market portfolio is zero.

In excess return form, the beta coefficient remains the slope of the characteristic line. It measures the sensitivity of a stock's excess return to that of the market portfolio.

The variance of the error term measures the variability of a stock's excess return not associated with movements in the market's excess return. Diversification can reduce this variability.

Many brokerage houses and investment advisory services report betas as part of the total information given for individual stocks. For example, *The Value Line Investment Survey* reports the beta for each stock covered, as do such brokerage firms as Merrill Lynch. Both measures of risk discussed above, standard deviation and beta, are widely known and discussed by investors.

Whether we use the single-index model or the market model, beta can be estimated using regression analysis. However, the values of α_i and β_i obtained in this manner are estimates of the true parameters and are subject to error. Furthermore, beta can shift over time as a company's situation changes. A legitimate question, therefore, is how accurate are the estimates of beta?

As noted, beta is usually estimated by fitting a characteristic line to the data. However, this is an estimate of the beta called for in the CAPM. The market proxy used in the equations for estimating beta may not fully reflect the market portfolio specified in the CAPM. Furthermore, several points should be kept in mind:

1. We are trying to estimate the future beta for a security, which may differ from the historical beta.
2. In theory, the independent variable R_M represents the total of all marketable assets in the economy. This is typically approximated with a stock market index, which in turn is an approximation of the return on all common stocks.
3. The characteristic line can be fitted over varying numbers of observations and time periods. There is no one correct period or number of observations for calculating beta. As a result, estimates of beta will vary. For example, *The Value Line Investment Survey* calculates betas from weekly rates of return for five years, whereas other analysts often use monthly rates of return over a comparable period.

4. The regression estimates of α and β from the characteristic line are only estimates of the true α and β, and are subject to error. Thus, these estimates may not be equal to the true α and β.

5. As the fundamental variables (e.g., earnings, cash flow) of a company change, beta should change; that is, the beta is not perfectly stationary over time. This issue is important enough to be considered separately.

Blume found that in comparing nonoverlapping seven-year periods for 1, 2, 4, 7, 10, 21, and so on stocks in a portfolio, the following observations could be made[6]:

1. Betas estimated for individual securities are unstable; that is, they contain relatively little information about future betas.

2. Betas estimated for large portfolios are stable; that is, they contain much information about future betas.

In effect, a large portfolio (e.g., 50 stocks) provides stability because of the averaging effect. Although the betas of some stocks in the portfolio go up from period to period, others go down, and these two movements tend to cancel each other. Furthermore, the errors involved in estimating betas tend to cancel out in a portfolio. Therefore, estimates of portfolio betas show less change from period to period and are much more reliable than are the estimates for individual securities.

Researchers have found that betas in the forecast period are, on average, closer to 1.0 than the estimate obtained using historical data. This would imply that we can improve the estimates of beta by measuring the adjustment in one period and using it as an estimate of the adjustment in the next period. For example we could adjust each beta toward the average beta by taking half the historical beta and adding it to half of the average beta. Merrill Lynch, the largest brokerage firm, reports adjusted betas based on a technique such as this. Other methods have also been proposed, including a Bayesian estimation technique.

Tests of the CAPM

The conclusions of the CAPM are entirely sensible:

1. Return and risk are positively related—greater risk should carry greater return.

2. The relevant risk for a security is a measure of its effect on portfolio risk.

The question, therefore, is how well the theory works. After all, the assumptions on which capital market theory rest are, for the most part, unrealistic. To assess the validity of this or any other theory, empirical tests must be performed. If the CAPM is valid, and the market tends to balance out so that realized security returns average out to equal expected returns, equations of the following type can be estimated:

$$R_i = a_1 + a_2\beta_i \qquad\qquad (9\text{-}4)$$

where

R_i = the average return on security i over some number of periods
β_i = the estimated beta for security i

[6] See M. Blume, "Betas and Their Regression Tendencies," *The Journal of Finance*, 10 (June 1975): 785–795; and R. Levy, "On the Short-Term Stationarity of Beta Coefficients," *Financial Analysts Journal*, 27 (December 1971): 55–62.

When Equation 9-4 is estimated, a_1 should approximate the average risk-free rate during the periods studied, and a_2 should approximate the average market risk premium during the periods studied.

An extensive literature exists involving tests of capital market theory, in particular, the CAPM. Although it is not possible to summarize the scope of this literature entirely and to reconcile findings from different studies that seem to be in disagreement, the following points represent a reasonable consensus of the empirical results[7]:

1. The SML appears to be linear; that is, the trade-off between expected (required) return and risk is an upward-sloping straight line.
2. The intercept term, a_1, is generally found to be higher than RF.
3. The slope of the CAPM, a_2, is generally found to be less steep than posited by the theory.
4. Although the evidence is mixed, no persuasive case has been made that nonsystematic risk commands a risk premium. In other words, investors are rewarded only for assuming systematic risk.

The major problem in testing capital market theory is that it is formulated on an *ex ante* basis but can be tested only on an *ex post* basis. We can never know investor expectations with certainty. Therefore, it should come as no surprise that tests of the model have produced conflicting results in some cases, and that the empirical results diverge from the predictions of the model. In fact, it is amazing that the empirical results support the basic CAPM as well as they do. Based on studies of many years of data, it appears that the stock market prices securities on the basis of a linear relationship between systematic risk and return, with diversifiable (nonsystematic) risk playing little or no part in the pricing mechanism.

The CAPM has not been proved empirically, nor will it be. In fact, Roll has argued that the CAPM is untestable, because the market portfolio, which consists of all risky assets, is unobservable.[8] In effect, Roll argues that tests of the CAPM are actually tests of the mean-variance efficiency of the market portfolio. Nevertheless, the CAPM remains a logical way to view the expected return-risk trade-off.

Arbitrage Pricing Theory

Arbitrage Pricing Theory (APT) An equilibrium theory of expected returns for securities involving few assumptions about investor preferences

The CAPM is not the only model of security pricing. Another model that has received attention is based on **arbitrage pricing theory (APT)** as developed by Ross and enhanced by others. In recent years, APT has emerged as an alternative theory of asset pricing to the CAPM. Its appeal is that it is more general than the CAPM, with less restrictive assumptions. However, like the CAPM, it has limitations, and like the CAPM, it is not the final word in asset pricing.

Similar to the CAPM, or any other asset-pricing model, APT posits a relationship between expected return and risk. It does so, however, using different assumptions and procedures. Very importantly, APT is not critically dependent on an underlying market portfolio as is the CAPM, which predicts that only market risk influences expected returns. Instead, APT recognizes that several types of risk may affect security returns.

APT is based on the *law of one price*, which states that two otherwise identical assets cannot sell at different prices. APT assumes that asset returns are linearly related to a set

---

[7] For a discussion of empirical tests of the CAPM, see Elton, Gruber, Brown, and Goetzmann, *Modern Portfolio Theory.*

[8] See R. Roll, "A Critique of the Asset Pricing Theory's Tests; Part I: On Past and Potential Testability of the Theory," *Journal of Financial Economics*, 4 (March 1977): 129–176.

Arbitrage Pricing Theory   **237**

of indexes, where each index represents a factor that influences the return on an asset. Market participants develop expectations about the sensitivities of assets to the factors. They buy and sell securities so that, given the law of one price, securities affected equally by the same factors will have equal expected returns. This buying and selling is the arbitrage process, which determines the prices of securities.

APT states that equilibrium market prices will adjust to eliminate any arbitrage opportunities, which refer to situations where a *zero investment portfolio* can be constructed that will yield a risk-free profit. If arbitrage opportunities arise, a relatively few investors can act to restore equilibrium.

Unlike the CAPM, APT does not assume:

1. A single-period investment horizon
2. The absence of taxes
3. Borrowing and lending at the rate RF
4. Investors select portfolios on the basis of expected return and variance

APT, like the CAPM, does assume:

1. Investors have homogeneous beliefs
2. Investors are risk-averse utility maximizers
3. Markets are perfect
4. Returns are generated by a factor model.

Factor Model   Used to depict the behavior of security prices by identifying major factors in the economy that affect large numbers of securities

A **factor model** is based on the view that there are underlying *risk factors* that affect realized and expected security returns. These risk factors represent broad economic forces and not company-specific characteristics, and by definition they represent the element of surprise in the risk factor—the difference between the actual value for the factor and its expected value.

The factors must possess three characteristics[9]:

1. Each risk factor must have a pervasive influence on stock returns. Firm-specific events are not APT risk factors.
2. These risk factors must influence expected return, which means they must have nonzero prices. This issue must be determined empirically, by statistically analyzing stock returns to see which factors pervasively affect returns.
3. At the beginning of each period, the risk factors must be unpredictable to the market as a whole. This raises an important point. In our example above, we used inflation and the economy's output as the two factors affecting portfolio returns. The rate of inflation is *not* an APT risk factor, because it is at least partially predictable. In an economy with reasonable growth where the quarterly rate of inflation has averaged 3 percent on an annual basis, we can reasonably assume that next quarter's inflation rate is not going to be 10 percent. On the other hand, unexpected inflation—the difference between actual inflation and expected inflation—is an APT risk factor. By definition, it cannot be predicted, since it is unexpected.

What really matters are the *deviations* of the factors from their expected values. For example, if the expected value of inflation is 5 percent and the actual rate of inflation for a period is only 4 percent, this 1-percent deviation will affect the actual return for the period.

---

[9] See Michael A. Berry, Edwin Burmeister, and Marjorie B. McElroy, "Sorting Out Risks Using Known APT Factors," *Financial Analysts Journal* (March–April 1988): 29–42.

Example 9-6   An investor holds a portfolio of stocks that she thinks is influenced by only two basic economic factors, inflation and the economy's output. Diversification once again plays a role, because the portfolio's sensitivity to all other factors can be eliminated by diversification.

Portfolio return varies directly with output and inversely with inflation. Each of these factors has an expected value, and the portfolio has an expected return when the factors are at their expected values. If either or both of the factors deviates from expected value, the portfolio return will be affected.

We must measure the sensitivity of each stock in our investor's portfolio to changes in each of the two factors. Each stock will have its own sensitivity to each of the factors. For example, stock #1 (a mortgage company) may be particularly sensitive to inflation and have a sensitivity of 2.0, whereas stock #2 (a food manufacturer) may have a sensitivity to inflation of only 1.0.

Based on this analysis, we can now understand the APT model. It assumes that investors believe that asset returns are randomly generated according to a n-factor model, which for security i can be formally stated as:

$$R_i = E(R_i) + \beta_{i1}f_1 + \beta_{i2}f_2 + \cdots + \beta_{in}f_n + e_i \tag{9-5}$$

where

R_i = the actual (random) rate of return on security i in any given period t
$E(R_i)$ = the expected return on security i
f = the deviation of a systematic factor F from its expected value
β_i = sensitivity of security i to a factor
e_i = random error term, unique to security i[10]

It is important to note that the expected value of each factor, F, is zero. Therefore, the f's in Equation 9-5 are measuring the deviation of each factor from its expected value. Notice in Equation 9-5 that the actual return for a security in a given period will be at the expected or required rate of return if the factors are at expected levels [e.g., $F_1 - E(F_1) = 0$, $F_2 - E(F_2) = 0$, and so forth] and if the chance element represented by the error term is at zero.

A factor model makes no statement about equilibrium. If we transform Equation 9-5 into an equilibrium model, we are saying something about *expected* returns across securities. APT is an equilibrium theory of expected returns that requires a factor model such as Equation 9-5. The equation for expected return on a security is given by Equation 9-6.

$$E(R_i) = a_0 + b_{i1}\overline{F}_1 + b_{i2}\overline{F}_2 + \cdots + b_{in}\overline{F}_n \tag{9-6}$$

where

$E(R_i)$ = the expected return on security i
a_0 = the expected return on a security with zero systematic risk
$\overline{F}$ = the risk premium for a factor [e.g., the risk premium for F_1 is equal to $E(F_1) - a_0$]

With APT, risk is defined in terms of a stock's sensitivity to basic economic factors, whereas expected return is directly related to sensitivity. As always, expected return increases with risk.

----

[10] It is assumed that all covariances between returns on securities are attributable to the effects of the factors; therefore, the error terms are uncorrelated.

The expected return-risk relationship for the CAPM is:

$$E(R_i) = RF + \beta_i[\text{market risk premium}]$$

The CAPM assumes that the only required measure of risk is the sensitivity to the market. The risk premium for a stock depends on this sensitivity and the market risk premium (the difference between the expected return on the market and the risk-free rate).

The expected return-risk relationship for the APT can be described as:

$$E(R_i) = RF + b_{i1} \text{ (risk premium for factor 1) } +$$
$$b_{i2} \text{ (risk premium for factor 2) } + \cdots +$$
$$b_{in} \text{ (risk premium for factor n)}$$

Note that the sensitivity measures (β_i and b_i) have similar interpretations. They are measures of the relative sensitivity of a security's return to a particular risk premium. Also notice that we are dealing with risk premiums in both cases. Finally, notice that the CAPM relationship is the same as would be provided by APT if there were only one pervasive factor influencing returns. APT is more general than CAPM.

The problem with APT is that the factors are not well specified, at least *ex ante*. To implement the APT model, we need to know the factors that account for the differences among security returns. The APT makes no statements about the size or the sign of the F_i's. Both the factor model and these values must be identified empirically. In contrast, with the CAPM the factor that matters is the market portfolio, a concept that is well understood conceptually; however, as noted earlier, Roll has argued that the market portfolio is unobservable.

Early empirical work by Roll and Ross suggested that three to five factors influence security returns and are priced in the market.[11] Typically, systematic factors such as the following have been identified:

1. Changes in expected inflation
2. Unanticipated changes in inflation
3. Unanticipated changes in industrial production
4. Unanticipated changes in the default-risk premium
5. Unanticipated changes in the term structure of interest rates

These factors are related to the components of a valuation model. The first three affect the cash flows of a company, whereas the last two affect the discount rate.

According to APT models, different securities have different sensitivities to these systematic factors, and investor risk preferences are characterized by these dimensions. Each investor has different risk attitudes. Investors could construct a portfolio depending upon desired risk exposure to each of these factors. Knowing the market prices of these risk factors and the sensitivities of securities to changes in the factors, the expected returns for various stocks could be estimated.

Another study has suggested that an APT model that incorporates unanticipated changes in five macroeconomic variables is superior to the CAPM. These five variables are:[12]

1. Default risk
2. The term structure of interest rates
3. Inflation or deflation
4. The long-run expected growth rate of profits for the economy
5. Residual market risk

---

[11] R. Roll and S. Ross, "An Empirical Investigation of the Arbitrage Pricing Theory," *The Journal of Finance*, 35 (December 1980): 1073–1103.

[12] These factors are based on Berry et al.

USING APT IN INVESTMENT DECISIONS

Roll and Ross have argued that APT offers an approach to strategic portfolio planning. The idea is to recognize that a few systematic factors affect long-term average returns. Investors should seek to identify the few factors affecting most assets in order to appreciate their influence on portfolio returns. Based on this knowledge, they should seek to structure the portfolio in such a way as to improve its design and performance.

Some researchers have identified and measured, for both economic sectors and industries, the risk exposures associated with APT risk factors such as the five identified previously in the work of Berry, Burmeister, and McElroy. These "risk exposure profiles" vary widely. For example, the financial, growth, and transportation sectors were found to be particularly sensitive to default risk, whereas the utility sector was relatively insensitive to both unexpected inflation and the unexpected change in the growth rate of profits.

An analysis of 82 different industry classifications showed the same result—exposure to different types of risk varies widely. For example, some industries were particularly sensitive to unexpected inflation risk, such as the mobile home building industry, retailers, hotels and motels, toys, and eating places. The industries least sensitive to this risk factor included foods, tire and rubber goods, shoes, and breweries. Several industries showed no significant sensitivity to unexpected inflation risk, such as corn and soybean refiners and sugar refiners.

A portfolio manager could design strategies that would expose them to one or more types of these risk factors, or "sterilize" a portfolio such that its exposure to the unexpected change in the growth rate of profits matched that of the market as a whole. Taking an active approach, a portfolio manager who believes that he or she can forecast a factor realization can build a portfolio that emphasizes or deemphasizes that factor. In doing this, the manager would select stocks that have exposures to the remaining risk factors that are exactly proportional to the market. If the manager is accurate with the forecast—and remember that such a manager must forecast the unexpected component of the risk factor—he or she can outperform the market for that period.

Some Conclusions About Asset Pricing

The question of how security prices and equilibrium returns are established—whether as described by the CAPM or APT or some other model—remains open. Some researchers are convinced that the APT model is superior to the CAPM. For example, based on their research using the five factors discussed above, the authors concluded, "The APT model with these five risk factors is vastly superior to both the market model and the CAPM for explaining stock returns." The CAPM relies on the observation of the market portfolio which, in actuality, cannot be observed. On the other hand, APT offers no clues as to the identity of the factors that are priced in the factor structure.

In the final analysis, neither model has been proven to be superior. Both rely on expectations which are not directly observable. Additional testing is needed.

Summary

▶ Capital market theory, based on the concept of efficient diversification, describes the pricing of capital assets in the marketplace.

▶ Capital market theory is derived from several assumptions that appear to be unrealistic; however, the important issue is the ability of the theory to predict. Relaxation of most of the assumptions does not change the major implications of capital market theory.

▶ Risk-free borrowing and lending changes the efficient set to a straight line.

▶ Borrowing and lending possibilities, combined with one portfolio of risky assets, offer an investor whatever risk-expected return combination he or she seeks; that is, investors can be anywhere they choose on this line depending on their risk-return preferences.

▶ Given risk-free borrowing and lending, the new efficient frontier has a vertical intercept of RF and is tangent to the old efficient frontier at point M, the market portfolio. The new efficient set is no longer a curve, or arc, as in the Markowitz analysis. It is now linear.

▶ All investors can achieve an optimal point on the new efficient frontier by investing in portfolio M and either borrowing or lending at the risk-free rate RF.

▶ The new efficient frontier is called the capital market line, and its slope indicates the equilibrium price of risk in the market. In effect, it is the expected return-risk trade-off for efficient portfolios.

▶ *Ex ante*, the CML must always be upward sloping, although *ex post* it may be downward sloping for certain periods.

▶ In theory, the market value–weighted market portfolio, M, should include all risky assets, although in practice it is typically proxied by a stock market index such as the Standard & Poor's 500.

▶ The separation theorem states that the investment decision (what portfolio of risky assets to buy) can be separated from the financing decision (how much of investable funds should be put in risky assets and how much in the risk-free asset).

▶ Under the separation theorem, all investors should hold the same portfolio of risky assets and achieve their own position on the return-risk trade-off through borrowing and lending.

▶ Investors need to focus on that part of portfolio risk that cannot be eliminated by diversification because this is the risk that should be priced in financial markets.

▶ Total risk can be divided into systematic risk and nonsystematic risk. Nonsystematic risk, also called diversifiable risk, can be eliminated by diversification.

▶ Market risk cannot be eliminated by diversification and is the relevant risk for the pricing of financial assets in the market.

▶ Based on the separation of risk into its systematic and nonsystematic components, the security market line can be constructed for individual securities (and portfolios). What is important is each security's contribution to the total risk of the portfolio, as measured by beta.

▶ Using beta as the measure of risk, the SML depicts the trade-off between required return and risk for all securities and all portfolios.

▶ The market model can be used to estimate the alpha and beta for a security by regressing total returns for a security against total returns for a market index.

▶ The characteristic line is a graph of the regression involved in the market model.

▶ Beta, the slope of the characteristic line, is a relative measure of risk. It indicates the volatility of a stock.

▶ Betas for individual stocks are unstable while betas for large portfolios are quite stable.

▶ If the expected returns for securities can be estimated from security analysis, and plotted against the SML, undervalued and overvalued securities can be identified.

▶ Problems exist in estimating the SML; in particular, estimating the betas for securities. The stability of beta is a concern, especially for individual securities; however, portfolio betas tend to be more stable across time.

▶ Tests of the CAPM are inconclusive. An *ex ante* model is being tested with *ex post* data. It has not been proved empirically, nor is it likely to be, but its basic implications seem to be supported.

▶ Alternative theories of asset pricing, such as the arbitrage pricing theory, also exist but are unproved.

▶ APT is not critically dependent on an underlying market portfolio as is the CAPM, which predicts that only market risk influences expected returns. Instead, APT recognizes that several types of risk may affect security returns.

▶ A factor model recognizes risk factors that affect realized and expected security returns. These risk factors represent broad economic forces and not company-specific characteristics and by definition they represent the element of surprise in the risk factor.

▶ APT is more general than the CAPM. If only one factor exists, the two models can be shown to be identical.

▶ The problem with APT is that the factors are not well specified, at least *ex ante*.

▶ Most empirical work suggests that three to five factors influence security returns and are priced in the market.

Key Words

Arbitrage pricing theory (APT)

Capital asset pricing model (CAPM)

Capital market line (CML)

Characteristic line

Factor model

Homogeneous expectations

Market model

Market portfolio

Market risk premium

Required rate of return

Security market line (SML)

Separation theorem

Questions

9-1 How do lending possibilities change the Markowitz model? borrowing possibilities?

9-2 Why, under the CAPM, do all investors hold identical risky portfolios?

9-3 In terms of their appearance as a graph, what is the difference between the CML and the SML?

9-4 What is the market portfolio?

9-5 What is the slope of the CML? What does it measure?

9-6 Why does the CML contain only efficient portfolios?

9-7 How can we measure a security's contribution to the risk of the market portfolio?

9-8 How can the SML be used to identify over- and undervalued securities?

9-9 What happens to the price and return of a security when investors recognize it as undervalued?

9-10 What are the difficulties involved in estimating a security's beta?

9-11 What is the major problem in testing capital market theory?

9-12 How can the CAPM be tested empirically? What are the expected results of regressing average returns on betas?

9-13 What is "the law of one price"?

9-14 Why does Roll argue that the CAPM is untestable?

9-15 The CAPM provides required returns for individual securities or portfolios. What uses can you see for such a model?

9-16 What is the relationship between the CML and the Markowitz efficient frontier?

9-17 How does an investor decide where to be on the new efficient frontier represented by the CML?

9-18 The CML can be described as representing a trade-off. What is this trade-off? Be specific.

9-19 Draw a diagram of the SML. Label the axes and the intercept.
a. Assume the risk-free rate shifts upward. Draw the new SML.
b. Assume that the risk-free rate remains the same as before the change in (a) but that investors become more pessimistic about the stock market. Draw the new SML.

9-20 What common assumptions do the CAPM and APT share? How do they differ in assumptions?

9-21 What is a factor model?

9-22 What characteristics must the factors in a factor model possess?

9-23 Based on empirical work, how many factors are thought to influence security returns? Name some of these likely factors.

9-24 What does a factor model say about equilibrium in the marketplace?

9-25 How can APT be used in investment decisions?

9-26 What role does the market portfolio play in the APT model?

9-27 What is meant by an "arbitrage profit"? What ensures that investors could act quickly to take advantage of such opportunities?

9-28 Why is the standard deviation of a security's returns an inadequate measure of the contribution of that security to the risk of a portfolio that is well diversified?

9-29 Explain the separation theorem.

9-30 What does the separation theorem imply about the "tailored" approach to portfolio selection?

CFA
9-31 **Identify** and **briefly discuss** three criticisms of beta as used in the capital asset pricing model (CAPM).

CFA
9-32 **Briefly explain** whether investors should expect a higher return from holding portfolio A versus portfolio B under capital asset pricing theory (CAPM). Assume that both portfolios are fully diversified.

	Portfolio A	Portfolio B
Systematic risk (beta)	1.0	1.0
Specific risk for each individual security	High	Low

CFA
9-33 Capital Asset Pricing Theory asserts that portfolio returns are best explained by:

  a. diversification.
  b. systematic risk.
  c. economic factors.
  d. specific risk.

CFA
9-34 What is the expected return of a zero-beta security?

  a. Market rate of return
  b. Zero rate of return
  c. Negative rate of return
  d. Risk-free rate of return

CFA
9-35 Assume that both X and Y are well-diversified portfolios and the risk-free rate is 8 percent.

Portfolio	Expected Return	Beta
X	16%	1.00
Y	12%	0.25

In this situation, you would conclude that portfolios X and Y:

  a. are in equilibrium.
  b. offer an arbitrage opportunity.
  c. are both underpriced.
  d. are both fairly priced.

CFA
9-36 The Arbitrage Pricing Theory (APT) differs from the Capital Asset Pricing Model (CAPM) because the APT:

  a. places more emphasis on market risk.
  b. minimizes the importance of diversification.
  c. recognizes multiple unsystematic risk factors.
  d. recognizes multiple systematic risk factors.

Copyright, 1994, Association for Investment Management and Research. Reproduced and republished from *CFA® Program Materials* with permission from the Association for Investment Management and Research. All Rights Reserved.

CFA
9-37 You ask John Statdud, your research assistant, to analyze the relationship between the return on Coca-Cola Enterprises (CCE) common stock and the return on the market using the Standard & Poor's 500 Stock Index as a proxy for the market. The data include monthly returns for both CCE and the S&P 500 over a recent five-year period. The results of the regression are:

$$R_{CCE} = 0.59 + 0.94\,R_{S\&P500}$$

$$(3.10)$$

The numbers in parentheses are the *t*-statistics (the 0.1 critical value is 2.66). The coefficient of determination (R^2) for the regression is 0.215.

    Statdud wrote the following summary of the regression results:

1. The regression statistics indicate that during the five-year period under study, when the annual return on the S&P 500 was zero, CCE had an average annual return of 0.59 percent.

2. The alpha value of 0.59 is a measure of the variability of the return on the market.

3. The coefficient of 0.94 indicates CCE's sensitivity to the return on the S&P 500 and suggests that the return on CCE's common stock is less sensitive to market movements than the average stock.

4. The *t*-statistic of 3.10 for the slope coefficient indicates the coefficient is not statistically significant at the 0.01 level.

5. The R^2 for the regression of 0.215 indicates the average estimate deviates from the actual observation by an average of 21.5 percent.

6. There is no concern that the slope coefficient lacks statistical significance since beta values tend to be less stable (and therefore less useful) than alpha values.

7. The regression should be rerun using 10 years of data. This would improve the reliability of the estimated coefficients while not sacrificing anything.

Identify which of the seven statements made by Statdud are incorrect and justify your answer(s).

Demonstration Problems

9-1   CALCULATION OF THE CHARACTERISTIC LINE: Calculate the characteristic line for EG&G by letting Y be the annual TRs for EG&G and X be the TRs for the S&P 500 Index. The summary statistics are as follows:

$$n = 10$$

$$\Sigma Y = 264.5$$

$$\Sigma Y^2 = 19{,}503.65$$

$$\Sigma X = 84.5$$

$$\Sigma X^2 = 4{,}660.31$$

$$\Sigma XY = 6{,}995.76$$

$$SS_y = \Sigma(Y - \overline{Y})^2 = \Sigma Y^2 - \frac{(\Sigma Y)^2}{n} = 12{,}507.625$$

$$SS_x = \Sigma(X - \overline{X})^2 = \Sigma X^2 - \frac{(\Sigma X)^2}{n} = 3{,}946.285$$

$$SS_{xy} = \Sigma(X - \overline{X})^2 (Y - \overline{Y})^2 = \Sigma XY - \frac{(\Sigma X)(\Sigma Y)}{n} = 4{,}760.735$$

$$\hat{\beta} = \frac{SS_{xy}}{SS_x} = 1.206384$$

$$\hat{a} = \overline{Y} - \hat{\beta}\overline{X} = 16.256$$

$$\hat{Y} = 16.256 + 1.206X$$

Analysis of Variance Source (Risk)		Sum of Squares	No. of Observations	Variance
Total SS$_y$	=	12,507.625	$n - 1 = 9$	1,389.736 = Total variance
Systematic $\beta^2 SS_x$	=	5,743.275	$n - 1 = 9$	638.142 = Systematic variance
Nonsystematic	=	6,764.350	$n - 1 = 9$	751.594 = Nonsystematic variance

Problems

9-1 Given the following information show that the characteristic line for this company is

$$\hat{Y} = 5.055 + 0.776X$$

$$\Sigma X = 264.5$$

$$\Sigma X^2 = 4,660.31$$

$$\Sigma Y = 116.1$$

$$\Sigma Y^2 = 6,217.13$$

$$\Sigma XY = 4,042.23$$

$$SS_x = 3,946.285$$

$$SS_y = 4,869.209$$

$$SS_{xy} = 3,061.185$$

9-2 The expected return for the market is 12 percent, with a standard deviation of 21 percent. The expected risk free rate is 8 percent. Information is available for five mutual funds, all assumed to be efficient, as follows:

Mutual Funds	SD (%)
Affiliated	14
Omega	16
Ivy	21
Value Line Fund	25
New Horizons	30

a. Calculate the slope of the CML.
b. Calculate the expected return for each portfolio.
c. Rank the portfolios in increasing order of expected return.
d. Do any of the portfolios have the same expected return as the market? Why?

9-3 Given the market data in Problem 9-2, and the following information for each of five stocks:

Stock	Beta	R_i
1	0.9	12
2	1.3	13
3	0.5	11
4	1.1	12.5
5	1.0	12

a. Calculate the expected return for each stock.
b. With these expected returns and betas, think of a line connecting them—what is this line?
c. Assume that an investor, using fundamental analysis, develops the estimates labeled R_i for these stocks. Determine which are undervalued and which are overvalued.
d. What is the market's risk premium?

9-4   Given the following information:

> Expected return for the market, 12 percent
> Standard deviation of market return, 21 percent
> Risk-free rate, 8 percent
> Correlation coefficient between
> > Stock A and the market, 0.8
> > Stock B and the market, 0.6
> > Standard deviation for stock A, 25 percent
> > Standard deviation for stock B, 30 percent

a. Calculate the beta for stock A and stock B.
b. Calculate the required return for each stock.

9-5   Assume that the risk-free rate is 7 percent and the expected market return is 13 percent. Show that the security market line is

$$E(R_i) = 7.0 + 6.0\beta$$

Assume that an investor has estimated the following values for six different corporations:

Corporation	β_i	R_i (%)
GF	0.8	12
PepsiCo	0.9	13
IBM	1.0	14
NCNB	1.2	11
EG&G	1.2	21
EAL	1.5	10

Calculate the ER_i for each corporation using the SML, and evaluate which securities are overvalued and which are undervalued.

9-6   Assume that Exxon is priced in equilibrium. Its expected return next year is 14 percent, and its beta is 1.1. The risk-free rate is 6 percent.

a. Calculate the slope of the SML.
b. Calculate the expected return on the market.

CFA
9-7   Within the context of the Capital Asset Pricing Model (CAPM), assume:

> ❑ Expected return on the market = 15 percent
> ❑ Risk free rate = 8 percent
> ❑ Expected rate of return on XYZ security = 17 percent
> ❑ Beta of XYZ security = 1.25

Which *one* of the following is *correct?*

a. XYZ is overpriced.
b. XYZ is fairly priced.
c. XYZ's alpha is −0.25%.
d. XYZ's alpha is 0.25%.

Web Resources

For additional resources visit our dynamic Web site located at www.wiley.com/college/jones.

- *Systematic Reckoning*—The case builds on the single-index model of security valuation to estimate the beta of Abercrombie and Fitch equity shares. Case readers address issues in data analysis and differences in available beta estimates while learning spreadsheet functions.
- Internet Exercises—This chapter looks at the Capital Asset Pricing Model and the Arbitrage Pricing Theory. The Web exercises ask you to compute stock betas and to look at the relationship between expected returns and beta risk.
  Exercise 1: Looks at Diversifiable and Non-diversifiable risk.
  Exercise 2: Relates stock return volatility to news.
  Exercise 3: Compares stock return and beta risk characteristics across industries.
  Exercise 4: Asks the reader to examine the output of the beta regressions.
  Exercise 5: Pursues the same point as in the previous exercise, but makes it more obvious.
- Multiple Choice Self Test

Selected Reference

A good discussion of capital market theory can be found in:

Elton, Edwin and Gruber, Martin. *Modern Portfolio Theory and Portfolio Analysis*, Fifth Edition. New York: John Wiley & Sons, 1995.

chapter *10*

Common Stock Valuation

Chapter 10 concentrates on the valuation of common stocks. Discounted cash flow techniques are considered, in particular the dividend discount model, as well as relative valuation techniques because of their frequency of use. All of these approaches are used by investors in the valuation of stocks and their likely prospects for the future. Every serious investor should be comfortable with the principles of common stock valuation as presented in this chapter.

AFTER READING THIS CHAPTER YOU WILL BE ABLE TO:

▶ Understand the foundation of valuation for common stocks, discounted cash-flow techniques, and the concept of intrinsic value.

▶ Use the dividend discount model to estimate the prices of stocks.

▶ Understand the P/E ratio as well as the determinants of the P/E ratio.

▶ Analyze stocks on the basis of relative valuation techniques.

What determines the value of a common stock? What approaches are commonly used by investors interested in valuing and selecting stocks? These questions are answered in the next few chapters. Because of the complexity of common stocks and the related questions that are raised in their analysis, several chapters are needed to adequately describe the most frequently used analysis and selection processes.

Two basic approaches to valuing common stocks using fundamental security analysis are:

1. Discounted cash flow techniques
2. Relative valuation techniques

Discounted cash flow techniques attempt to estimate the value of a stock today using a present value analysis similar to the discounting process used for bonds (and explained in Chapter 17). For example, the future stream of dividends to be received from a common stock is discounted back to the present at an appropriate discount rate (i.e., the investor's required rate of return as discussed in Chapter 9). Alternative models discount such variables as free cash flow.

Relative valuation techniques such as the P/E ratio, the price/book value ratio and the price/sales ratio are typically more widely used by practicing security analysts. A stock is valued relative to other stocks on the basis of ratios such as these. The value of the relative valuation approach is that, unlike discounted cash flow techniques, an estimate of the stock's value (its intrinsic value) does not have to be made. Instead, the valuation variable used is compared to one or more benchmarks to decide if a stock is overvalued or undervalued.

Discounted Cash Flow Techniques

The classic method of calculating the estimated value of any security involves the use of discounted cash flow techniques, a present value analysis sometimes referred to as the *capitalization of income method*. The value of a security can be estimated by a present value process involving the capitalization (discounting) of expected future cash flows. That is, the estimated value of a security is equal to the discounted (present) value of the future stream of cash flows that an investor expects to receive from the security, as shown in Equation 10-1:

$$\text{Estimated value of any security} = V_0 = \sum_{t=1}^{n} \frac{\text{Cash flows}}{(1 + k)^t} \qquad \textbf{(10-1)}$$

where

k = the appropriate discount rate or required rate of return[1]

To use such a model, an investor must:

1. Estimate an appropriate required rate of return.
2. Estimate the amount and timing of the future stream of cash flows.
3. Use these two components in a present value model to estimate the value of the security, which is then compared to the current market price of the security.

---

[1] If all earnings are paid out as dividends, they will be accounted for as dividends. If earnings are retained by the corporation, they presumably will be reinvested, thereby enhancing future earnings and, ultimately, dividends. The present value analysis should not count the earnings reinvested currently and also paid later as dividends. If properly defined and separated, these two variables produce the same results. In addition to dividends and earnings, the variable referred to as "cash flow" (earnings after tax plus depreciation) has been suggested for these models.

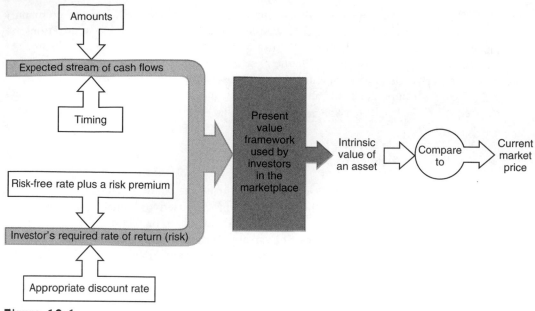

Figure 10-1

The present value approach to valuation.

Figure 10-1 summarizes the discounted cash flow process used in *fundamental analysis*. It emphasizes the factors that go into valuing common stocks. The exact nature of the present value process used by investors in the marketplace depends upon which cash flows are used to value the asset.

THE REQUIRED RATE OF RETURN

An investor who is considering the purchase of a common stock must assess its risk and, given its risk, the *minimum expected rate of return* that will be required to induce the investor to make the purchase.

▮ As we saw in Chapter 9 when we discussed the capital asset pricing model (CAPM), the *required rate of return* is the minimum expected rate of return necessary to induce an investor to buy a particular stock, given its risk.

The *required rate of return*, *capitalization rate*, and *discount rate* are interchangeable terms in valuation analysis. Regardless of which term is used, it is challenging to determine the numerical value to use for a particular stock. Although in theory we know what this variable is, in practice, it is not easy to determine a precise discount rate. Because of this complexity, we will generally assume that we know the discount rate and concentrate on the other issues involved in valuation, which are difficult enough. In the next chapter, we consider the required rate of return in more detail.

THE EXPECTED CASH FLOWS

The other component that goes into the present value framework is the expected stream of cash flows. Just as the value of a bond is the present value of any interest payments plus the present value of the bond's face value that will be received at maturity, the value of a common stock is the present value of all the cash flows to be received from the issuer (corporation). The questions that arise are:

1. What are the cash flows to use in valuing a stock?
2. What are the expected amounts of the cash flows?
3. When will the expected cash flows be received?

As we will see, there are different approaches to the valuation of a stock using discounted cash flow techniques. We will describe an alternative method later which has been popularized as a book. However, for our purposes in understanding how to value stocks, we will analyze the traditional, classic discounted cash-flow technique based on dividends.

To understand the basis of the dividend discount model, ask yourself the following question: If I buy a particular common stock and place it in a special trust fund for the perpetual benefit of myself and my heirs, what cash flows will be received? The answer is *dividends*, because this is the only *cash* distribution that a corporation actually makes to its stockholders. Although a firm's earnings per share (EPS) in any year belong to the stockholders, corporations generally do not pay out all their earnings to their stockholders; furthermore, EPS is an accounting concept, whereas dividends represent cash payments.

Stockholders may plan to sell their shares sometime in the future, resulting in a cash flow from the sales price. As shown later, however, even if investors think of the total cash flows from common stocks as a combination of dividends and a future price at which the stock can be sold, this is equivalent to using the stream of all dividends to be received on the stock.

What about earnings? Are they important? Can they be used in valuing a stock? The answer to both questions is yes. Dividends are paid out of earnings, so earnings are clearly important. And the second approach to fundamental analysis to be considered later, relative valuation techniques, uses as its best-known variant the P/E ratio, which has earnings in the denominator. Therefore, earnings are an important part of fundamental analysis; in fact, earnings receive more attention from investors than any other single variable when they are analyzing and considering stocks to buy and sell.

Because dividends are the only cash flow stream to be received directly by investors under normal conditions, it is appropriate to base a valuation model on dividends. We now consider such a model, the dividend discount model (DDM), which is the basis for understanding the fundamental valuation of common stocks using discounted cash flow techniques. *Therefore, whether you end up using this model very often or not, it is important to understand it in order really to understand the valuation of common stocks. In many respects, the DDM is the foundation to understanding the valuation of common stocks.*

THE DIVIDEND DISCOUNT MODEL

Since dividends are the only cash payment a stockholder receives directly from a firm, *they are the foundation of valuation using discounted cash-flow techniques.* In adapting Equation 10-1 specifically to value common stocks, the cash flows are the dividends *expected* to be paid in each future period. An investor or analyst using this approach carefully studies the future prospects for a company and estimates the likely dividends to be paid. In addition, the analyst estimates an appropriate required rate of return or discount rate based on the risk foreseen in the dividends and given the alternatives available. Finally, he or she discounts the entire stream of estimated future dividends, properly identified as to amount and timing. The derived present value is the estimated value of the stock.

Dividend Discount Model (DDM) A model for determining the estimated price of a stock by discounting all future dividends.

The present value approach to calculating the value of a common stock is conceptually no different from the approach used later to value bonds, or in Appendix 10-B to value preferred stock. Specifically, Equation 10-1, adapted for common stocks, where dividends are the cash flows, results in Equation 10-2. This equation, known as the **dividend discount model (DDM)**, states that the value (per share) of a stock today is the discounted value of all future dividends:

$$\begin{aligned} \text{Estimated value} \\ \text{of a stock} \end{aligned} = V_0 = \frac{D_1}{(1+k)} + \frac{D_2}{(1+k)^2} + \frac{D_3}{(1+k)^3} + \cdots + \frac{D_\infty}{(1+k)^\infty} \quad \textbf{(10-2)}$$

$$= \sum_{t=1}^{n} \frac{D_t}{(1+k)^t}$$

$$= \text{Dividend discount model}$$

where

$D_1, D_2, \ldots$ = the dividends expected to be received in each future period

k = the required rate of return for this stock, which is the discount rate applicable for an investment with this degree of riskiness (again, the opportunity cost of a comparable risk alternative)

Two immediate problems with Equation 10-2:

1. The last term in Equation 10-2 indicates that investors are dealing with infinity. They must value a stream of dividends that may be paid forever, since common stock has no maturity date.
2. The dividend stream is uncertain:
   a. There are no specified number of dividends, if in fact any are paid at all. Dividends must be declared periodically by the firm's board of directors. (Technically, they are declared quarterly, but conventional valuation analysis uses annual dividends.)
   b. The dividends for most firms are expected to grow over time; therefore, investors usually cannot simplify Equation 10-2 to a **perpetuity** as in the case of a preferred stock.[2] Only if dividends are not expected to grow can such a simplification be made. Although such a possibility exists, and is covered below, it is unusual.

Perpetuity A security without a maturity date

How are these problems resolved? The first problem, that Equation 10-2 involves an infinite number of periods and dividends, will be resolved when we deal with the second problem, specifying the expected stream of dividends. However, from a practical standpoint, the infinity problem is not as troublesome as it first appears. At reasonably high discount rates, such as 12, 14, or 16 percent, dividends received 40 or 50 years in the future are worth very little today, so that investors need not worry about them. For example, the present value of $1 to be received 50 years from now, if the discount rate is 15 percent, is only $0.0009.

The conventional solution to the second problem, that the dollar amount of the dividend is expected to grow over time, is to make some assumptions about the *expected growth rate* of dividends. That is, the investor or analyst estimates or models the expected *percentage* rate of growth in the future stream of dividends. To do this, he or she classifies

---

[2] Refer to Appendix 10-B for the valuation of preferred stock.

each stock to be valued into one of three categories based on the *expected growth rate in dividends*. In summary: *The dividend discount model is operationalized by estimating the expected growth rate(s) in the dividend stream.*

A time line will be used to represent the three alternative growth rate versions of the dividend discount model. All stocks that pay a dividend, or that are expected to pay dividends sometime in the future, can be modeled using this approach. It is critical to remember in using the DDM that an investor must account for all dividends from now to infinity by modeling the growth rate(s). As shown below, the mechanics of this process are such that we do not actually see all of these dividends, because the formulas reduce to a simplified form, but nevertheless we are accounting for all future dividends when we use the DDM.

It is necessary in using the DDM to remember that the dividend currently being paid on a stock (or the most recent dividend paid) is designated as D_0 and is, of course, known. Specifically, D_0 designates the current dividend being paid, or the most recent dividend paid. Investors must estimate the future dividends to be paid, starting with D_1, the dividend expected to be paid in the next period.

The three *growth rate models* for dividends are:

1. **The zero growth rate case**: A dividend stream with a zero growth rate resulting from a fixed dollar dividend equal to the current dividend, D_0, being paid every year from now to infinity.

$$\frac{D_0\ D_0\ D_0\ D_0\ +\cdots+D_0}{0\ \ \ 1\ \ \ 2\ \ \ 3\ +\cdots+\ \infty}\quad\begin{array}{l}\text{Dividend stream}\\ \text{Time period}\end{array}$$

2. **The constant (normal) growth rate case**: A dividend stream that is growing at a constant rate g, starting with D_0.

$$\frac{D_0\ D_0\,(1+g)^1\ D_0(1+g)^2\ D_0(1+g)^3\ +\cdots+\ D_0(1+g)^\infty}{0\qquad 1\qquad\quad 2\qquad\quad 3\qquad +\cdots+\qquad \infty}\quad\begin{array}{l}\text{Dividend stream}\\ \text{Time period}\end{array}$$

3. **The multiple growth rate case**: A dividend stream that is growing at variable rates; for example, g_1 for the first four years and g_2 thereafter.

$$\frac{D_0\ D_1=D_0(1+g_1)\ D_2=D_1(1+g_1)\ D_3=D_2(1+g_1)\ D_4=D_3(1+g_1)}{0\qquad 1\qquad\qquad 2\qquad\qquad 3\qquad\qquad 4}$$

$$\frac{D_5=D_4(1+g_2)\ +\cdots+\ D_\infty=D_{\infty-1}(1+g_2)}{5\qquad\quad +\cdots+\qquad\quad \infty}\quad\begin{array}{l}\text{Dividend stream}\\ \text{Time period}\end{array}$$

The Zero-Growth Rate Model   A zero growth rate equates to a fixed dollar dividend. For example, a firm pays a dividend of $1 a share annually, and has no plans to change this dollar amount. The zero growth rate dividend case reduces to a perpetuity. Assuming a constant *dollar* dividend, which implies a zero growth rate, Equation 10-2 simplifies to *the zero-growth rate model* shown as Equation 10-3.

$$\text{Estimated value of stock}=\frac{D_0}{k}=\begin{array}{l}\text{Zero-growth rate version}\\ \text{of the dividend discount model}\end{array}\qquad\text{(10-3)}$$

where D_0 is the constant dollar dividend expected for all future time periods and k is the opportunity cost or required rate of return for this particular common stock.

The no-growth rate case is equivalent to the valuation process for a preferred stock, because, exactly like a preferred stock, the dividend (numerator of Equation 10-3) remains unchanged. Therefore, a zero-growth rate common stock is a perpetuity and is easily valued once k is determined.

It is extremely important in understanding the valuation of common stocks using the DDM to recognize that in all cases considered an investor is discounting the future stream of dividends from now to infinity. This fact tends to be overlooked when using the perpetuity formula involved with the zero-growth rate case, because the discounting process is not visible. Nevertheless, we are accounting for all dividends from now to infinity in this case, as in all other cases. It is simply a mathematical fact that dividing a constant dollar amount by the discount rate, k, produces a result equivalent to discounting each dividend from now to infinity separately and summing all of the present values.

The Constant-Growth Rate Model The other two versions of the DDM indicate that to establish the cash flow stream of expected dividends, which is to be subsequently discounted, it is first necessary to compound some beginning dividend into the future. Obviously, the higher the growth rate used, the greater the future dollar amounts.

A well-known scenario in valuation is the case in which dividends are expected to grow at a constant growth rate over time. This *constant-* or *normal-growth rate model* is shown as Equation 10-4.

$$\text{Estimated value of stock} = \frac{D_0(1 + g)}{(1 + k_{cs})} + \frac{D_0(1 + g)^2}{(1 + k_{cs})^2} + \frac{D_0(1 +g)^3}{(1 + k_{cs})^3} + \cdots + \frac{D_0(1 + g)^\infty}{(1 + k_{cs})^\infty} \quad \text{(10-4)}$$

where D_0 is the current dividend being paid and growing at the constant-growth rate g, and k is the appropriate discount rate.

Equation 10-4 can be simplified to the following equation[3]:

$$\text{Estimated value of stock} = \frac{D_1}{k - g} = \begin{array}{l}\text{Constant-growth rate version of}\\ \text{the dividend discount model}\end{array} \quad \text{(10-5)}$$

where D_1 is the dividend expected to be received at the end of year 1.

Equation 10-5 is used whenever the *growth rate* of *future* dividends is expected to be more or less a constant. In actual practice, it is used quite often because of its simplicity, and because it is the best description of the expected dividend stream for a large number of companies, in particular large, stable companies and, in many instances, the market as a whole.

Example 10-1

Assume Summa Corporation is currently paying $1 per share in dividends and investors expect dividends to grow at the rate of 7 percent a year for the foreseeable future. For investments at this risk level, investors require a return of 15 percent a year. The estimated value of Summa is:

$$\text{Value of Summa} = \frac{D_1}{k - g}$$

$$= \frac{\$1.00(1.07)}{0.15 - 0.07} = \$13.38$$

Note that the current dividend of $1, ($D_0$), must be compounded one period, because *the constant-growth version of the DDM specifies the numerator as the dividend expected to be received one period from now, which is D_1.* In valuation terminology, D_0 represents the dividend currently being paid, and D_1 represents the dividend expected to be paid in the next period.

---

[3] Note that k must be greater than g, or nonsensical results are produced. Equation 10-4 collapses to Equation 10-5 as the number of periods involved approaches infinity.

Given D_0, which is known and observable, D_1 can always be determined[4]:

D_0 = Current dividend

$D_1 = D_0(1 + g)$

where g is the expected growth rate of dividends.

To understand completely the constant-growth model, which is widely used in valuation analysis, it is instructive to think about the process that occurs under constant growth. Appendix 10-A illustrates in more detail the process involved with the constant-growth version of the DDM.

Table 10A-1 in Appendix 10-A illustrates a very important point about these valuation models that was explained earlier. The constant-growth version of the DDM—Equation 10-5—takes account of all future cash flows from now to infinity, although this is not apparent from simply looking at the equation itself. Although Equation 10-5 has no summation or infinity sign, the results produced by this equation are equivalent to those that would be obtained if the dividend for each future period is determined and then discounted back to the present. In other words, the mathematics of the process involving a constant-growth rate to infinity reduces to a very simple expression, masking the fact that all dividends from now to infinity are being accounted for.

To understand fully the constant-growth rate version of the DDM, it is also important to realize that the model implies that the stock price for any one period is estimated to grow at the same rate as the dividends, which is g. In fact, holding the payout ratio (the ratio of dividends to earnings) constant, the constant-growth model implies that dividends, earnings, and stock price are all expected to grow at the expected constant growth rate, g.

Example 10-2   For Summa, the estimated value today is $13.38 and for the end of period 1, using D_2 in the numerator of Equation 10-5, it is:

$$\text{Estimated value of Summa} = \frac{(\$1.07)(1.07)}{0.15 - 0.07}$$

$$= \$14.31$$

This estimated value at the end of period 1 is 7 percent higher than the estimated value today of $13.38, or (rounding causes slight differences)

$$\text{Change in value} = \frac{\text{Ending value} - \text{Beginning value}}{\text{Beginning value}}$$

$$= (\$14.31 - \$13.38)/\$13.38 = 7\%$$

An examination of Equation 10-5 quickly demonstrates the factors affecting the value of a common stock, assuming the constant-growth version of the dividend discount model to be the applicable valuation approach:

1. If the market lowers the required rate of return for a stock, value will rise (other things being equal).
2. If investors decide that the expected growth in dividends will be higher as the result of some favorable development for the firm, value will also rise (other things being equal). Of course, the converse for these two situations also holds—a rise in the discount rate or a reduction in the expected growth rate of dividends will lower value.

---

[4] D_2 can be determined in the constant-growth model as $D_0(1 + g)^2$ or $D_1(1 + g)$.

One of the limitations of the DDM is that the model is not robust; that is, the estimated value is quite sensitive to the exact inputs used. The present value calculated from Equation 10-5 is quite sensitive to the estimates used by the investor in the equation. Relatively small variations in the inputs can change the estimated value by large percentage amounts.

Example 10-3 For Summa, assume the discount rate used, k, is 16 percent instead of 15 percent, with other variables held constant:

$$\text{Estimated value of Summa} = \frac{\$1(1.07)}{0.16 - 0.07} = \$11.89$$

In this example, a 1-percentage-point rise in k results in an 11.14-percent decrease in estimated value, from \$13.38 to \$11.89.

Example 10-4 Assume that for Summa the growth rate, g, is 8 percent instead of 7 percent, with other variables held constant:

$$\text{Estimated value of Summa} = \frac{\$1(1.08)}{0.15 - 0.08} = \$15.43$$

In this example, a 1-percentage-point decline in g results in a 15.3-percent increase in estimated value, from \$13.38 to \$15.43.

Example 10-5 Assume that for Summa the discount rate rises to 16 percent, and the growth rate declines to 4 percent:

$$\text{Estimated value of Summa} = \frac{\$1(1.04)}{0.16 - 0.04} = \$8.67$$

In this example, the estimated value declines from \$13.38 to \$8.67, a 35-percent change.

These differences suggest why stock prices constantly fluctuate as investors make their buy and sell decisions. Even if all investors use the constant-growth version of the dividend discount model to value a particular common stock, many different estimates of value will be obtained because:

1. Each investor has his or her own required rate of return, resulting in a relatively wide range of values of k.
2. Each investor has his or her own estimate of the expected growth rate in dividends. Although this range may be reasonably narrow in most valuation situations, small differences in g can produce significant differences in price, everything else held constant.

Thus, at any point in time for a particular stock, some investors are willing to buy, whereas others wish to sell, depending on their estimate of the intrinsic value of the stock. This helps to make markets active and liquid.

The Multiple-Growth Rate Model Many firms grow at a rapid rate (or rates) for a number of years and then slow down to an "average" growth rate. Other companies pay no dividends for a period of years, often during their early growth period. The constant-growth model discussed earlier is unable to deal with these situations; therefore, a model is needed that can. Such a variation of the DDM is the *multiple-growth rate model*.

Multiple growth is defined as a situation in which the expected future growth in dividends must be described using two or more growth rates (one of which could be zero). Although any number of growth rates is possible, most stocks can be described using two or possibly three different growth rates. It is important to remember that at least two different growth rates are involved; *this is the distinguishing characteristic of multiple-growth situations*.

A number of companies have experienced rapid growth that could not be sustained forever. During part of their lives, the growth rate exceeded that of the average company in the economy, but later the growth rate slowed. Examples from the distant past include McDonald's, Disney, Xerox, and IBM, and from the more recent past, Cisco, Intel, and Dell.

To capture the expected growth in dividends under this scenario, it is necessary to model the dividend stream during each period of different growth. It is reasonable to assume that at some future point the company's growth will slow down to that of the economy as a whole. At this future point in time, the company's growth can be described by the constant-growth rate model (Equation 10-5). What remains, therefore, is to model the dividend stream up to the point at which dividends slow to a constant-growth rate and to find the present value of all the components. This means we are doing the following:

$$\text{Estimated value} = \frac{\text{PV of the dividends during the period of unusual growth}}{\text{of the stock} + \text{PV of the estimated terminal price}}$$

A well-known multiple-growth rate model is the two-stage model. This model assumes near-term growth at a rapid rate for some period (typically, 2 to 10 years) followed by a steady long-term growth rate that is sustainable (i.e., a constant-growth rate as discussed earlier). This can be described in equation form as (we will use P_0 to represent the estimated value of a stock):

$$P_0 = \sum_{t=1}^{n} \frac{D_0(1 + g_s)^t}{(1 + k)^t} + \frac{D_n(1 + g_c)}{k - g} \frac{1}{(1 + k)^n} \tag{10-6}$$

where

P_0 = the estimated value of the stock today
D_0 = the current dividend
g_s = the supernormal (or subnormal) growth rate for dividends
g_c = the constant growth rate for dividends
k = required rate of return
n = the number of periods of supernormal (or subnormal) growth
D_n = the dividend at the end of the abnormal growth period

Notice in Equation 10-6 that the first term on the right side defines a dividend stream covering n periods, growing at a high (or low) growth rate of g_s and discounted at the required rate of return, k. This term covers the period of supernormal (or subnormal) growth, at which time the dividend is expected to grow at a constant rate forever. In effect, we must identify each of the dividends during this abnormal growth period, and then discount them back to the present using the required rate of return.

The second term on the right-hand side is the constant-growth version discussed earlier, which takes the dividend expected for the next period, $n + 1$, and divides by the difference between k and g.[5] Notice, however, that the value obtained from this calcula-

---

[5] The dividend at period $n + 1$ is equal to the dividend paid in period n compounded up by the new growth rate, g_c. The designation $n + 1$ refers to the first period after the years of abnormal growth.

tion is the value of the stock at the beginning of period $n + 1$ (or the end of period n), which we shall call P_n. It must be discounted back to time period zero by multiplying by the appropriate discount (present value) factor.

The valuation process outlined here is as stated above:

Estimated value = PV of the dividends during the period of unusual growth
+ PV of the terminal price (which is a function of all
dividends at the constant growth rate c)

Think about the second term in Equation 10-6 as representing a P_n, or the estimated price of the stock derived from the constant-growth model as of the end of period n. The constant-growth version of the dividend discount model is used to solve for estimated price at the end of period n, which is the beginning of period $n + 1$. Therefore,

$$P_n = \frac{D_{n+1}}{k - g_c}$$

Because P_n is the estimated price of the stock at the end of period n, it must be discounted back to the present. When it is added to the value of the discounted dividends from the first term, we have the estimated value of the stock today.

Example 10-6   Figure 10-2 illustrates the concept of valuing a multiple-growth rate company. In this example, the current dividend is $1 and is expected to grow at the higher rate (g_s) of 12 percent a year for five years, at the end of which time the new growth rate (g_c) is expected to be a constant 6 percent a year. The required rate of return is 10 percent.

The first step in the valuation process illustrated in Figure 10-2 is to determine the dollar dividends in each year of supernormal growth. This is done by compounding the beginning dividend, $1, at 12 percent for each of five years, producing the following:

$D_0 = \$1.00$

$D_1 = \$1.00(1.12) \quad = \$1.12$

$D_2 = \$1.00(1.12)^2 = \$1.25$

$D_3 = \$1.00(1.12)^3 = \$1.40$

$D_4 = \$1.00(1.12)^4 = \$1.57$

$D_5 = \$1.00(1.12)^5 = \$1.76$

Once the stream of dividends over the supergrowth period has been determined, they must be discounted to the present using the required rate of return of 10 percent. Thus,

$\$1.12(0.909) = \$1.02$

$\$1.25(0.826) = \$1.03$

$\$1.40(0.751) = \$1.05$

$\$1.57(0.683) = \$1.07$

$\$1.76(0.621) = \underline{\$1.09}$

$\qquad\qquad\qquad \$5.26$

Summing the five discounted dividends produces the value of the stock for its first five years only, which is $5.26. To evaluate years 6 on, when constant growth is expected, the constant-growth model is used.

$$P_n = \frac{D_{n+1}}{k - g_c}$$

$$= \frac{D_6}{k - g_c}$$

$$= \frac{D_5(1.06)}{k - g_c}$$

$$= \frac{1.76(1.06)}{0.10 - 0.06}$$

$$= \$46.64$$

Thus, $46.64 is the expected price of the stock at the beginning of year 6 (end of year 5). It must be discounted back to the present, using the present value factor for five years and 10 percent, 0.621. Therefore,

$$P_n \text{ discounted to today} = P_n \text{ (PV factor for 5 years, 10\%)}$$

$$= \$46.64(0.621)$$

$$= \$28.96$$

The last step is to add the two present values together:

$ 5.26 = present value of the first five years of dividends

28.96 = present value of the price at the end of Year 5, representing the discounted value of dividends from Year 6 to ∞

$34.22 = P_0, the value today of this multiple growth rate stock

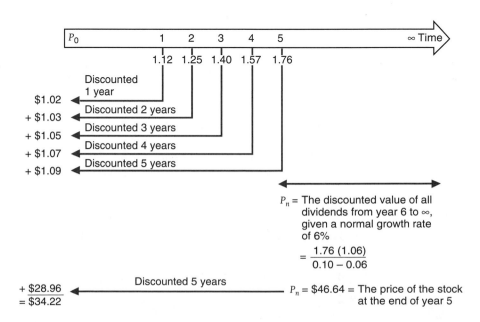

Figure 10-2

Valuing a multiple-growth rate company.

As mentioned previously, the DDM is subject to limitations, and these clearly apply to multiple-growth rate models. As before, this model is very sensitive to the inputs. Since a large part of the model involves a constant-growth rate calculation, changing one of the parameters will obviously impact the final estimate of value. Furthermore, determining the length of the abnormal growth period is quite difficult to do in practice. Will it last 5 years or 12 years? Also, the model as described above assumes an immediate transition from unusual growth to constant growth, whereas in reality the transition may not take place that quickly.

DIVIDENDS, DIVIDENDS—WHAT ABOUT CAPITAL GAINS?

In their initial study of valuation concepts, investors often are bothered by the fact that the dividend discount model contains only dividends, and an infinite stream of dividends at that. Although this is the correct formulation, many investors are sure that (1) they will not be here forever and (2) they really want capital gains. Dividends may be nice, but buying low and selling high is wonderful! Since so many investors are interested in capital gains, which by definition involves the difference between the price paid for a security and the price at which this security is later sold, a valuation model should seemingly contain a stock price somewhere. Thus, in computing present value for a stock, investors are interested in the present value of the estimated price two years from now, or six months from now, or whatever the expected, and finite, holding period is. How can price be incorporated into the valuation—or should it be?

Because of the construction of the DDM, investors need only be concerned with dividends. Expected price in the future is built into the dividend discount model in Equation 10-2—it is simply not visible. To see this, ask yourself at what price you can expect to sell your stock at some point in the future. Assume, for example, that you purchase the stock today and plan to hold it for three years. The price you receive three years from now will reflect the buyer's expectations of dividends from that point forward (at the end of years 4, 5, and so on). The estimated price today of the stock, P_0, is equal to

$$P_0 = \frac{D_1}{1+k} + \frac{D_2}{(1+k)^2} + \frac{D_3}{(1+k)^3} + \frac{P_3}{(1+k)^3} \qquad \text{(10-7)}$$

But P_3 (the estimated price of the stock at the end of year 3), is in turn equal to the discounted value of all future dividends from year 4 to infinity. That is,

$$P_3 = \frac{D_4}{(1+k)^4} + \frac{D_5}{(1+k)^5} + \cdots + \frac{D_\infty}{(1+k)^\infty} \qquad \text{(10-8)}$$

Substituting Equation 10-8 into 10-7 produces Equation 10-2, the basic DDM. Thus, in principle, investors obtain the same estimate of value today whether they

1. discount only the stream of dividends expected to be paid on the stock, or
2. a combination of dividends for some period and an expected terminal price

Since price at any point in the future is a function of the dividends to be received after that time, the price today for a common stock is best thought of as the discounted value of all future dividends.

INTRINSIC VALUE AND MARKET PRICE

After making careful estimates of the expected stream of dividends and the required rate of return for a common stock, the value of the stock today is estimated using the DDM.

Intrinsic Value   The
estimated or formula
value of a security

This value is often called the **intrinsic value** of the stock, which we denote as V_0. Note that *intrinsic value simply means an estimated value or a formula value*. This is the end objective of a discounted cash flow technique such as the DDM.

- What does intrinsic value imply? Again, it is simply the estimated value of the stock today, derived from estimating and discounting the future cash flows for a stock.
- How is it used? Traditionally, investors and analysts specify a relationship between the intrinsic value (which we shall call V_0) of an asset and its current stock price, P_0.

Specifically:

If $V_0 > P_0$, the asset is undervalued and should be purchased or held if already owned.

If $V_0 < P_0$, the asset is overvalued and should be avoided, sold if held, or possibly sold short.

If $V_0 = P_0$, this implies an equilibrium in that the asset is correctly valued.

Security analysis has traditionally been thought of as the search for undervalued or overvalued stocks. To do this, one can calculate the estimated or intrinsic value of the stock and compare this value to the current market price of the stock. Most investors believe that stocks are not always priced at their intrinsic values, thereby leading to buy and sell opportunities.

Important questions to ask at this point are, How exact is intrinsic value? How do I use it in actual practice?

First, always remember that security analysis, of which valuation is the heart, is an art and not a science—it has never been an exact process, and never will be. So when an investor calculates an intrinsic value, it is an estimate, no more and no less. It is always subject to error. However, the only intelligent way to make investment decisions in this context is to base them on price versus estimated value. If you estimate the value of Cisco at $20 per share and it is selling for $19 or $21.50, then it really doesn't matter too much. But if you do careful analysis and you estimate an intrinsic value for Cisco of $20 when it is selling for $10, then you should buy, because the stock is substantially undervalued. In a similar vein, if your careful analysis indicates an intrinsic value for Cisco of $14 when it is currently selling for $30, you should avoid the stock at all costs, or perhaps sell it short.

In actual daily practice, analysts often use a 15-percent rule in recognition of the fact that the estimation of a security's value is an inexact process. Thus, if the P_0 is not 15 percent or more on either side of the estimated value, no action is warranted.

Investments Intuition

A problem with intrinsic value is that it is derived from a present value process involving estimates of uncertain (future) cash flows and use of (varying) discount rates by different investors. Therefore, the same asset may have many intrinsic values at any point in time—it depends on who and how many are doing the valuing. This is why, for a particular asset on a particular day, some investors are willing to buy and some to sell. Because future benefits are uncertain and investors have differing required rates of return, the use of fundamental valuation models will result in varying estimates of the intrinsic value of an asset. The market price of an asset at any point in time is, in this sense, the consensus intrinsic value of that asset for the market.

The valuation process can establish justified prices for assets or indicate whether or not you can expect to earn your required rate of return on a prospective asset. Remember, however, that you are not assured of earning your required rate of return. Investment decisions always involve a forward-looking process. Estimates are made under uncertainty, being based on the best information available. But even the best estimates may not be realized. As discussed in Chapter 1, uncertainty will always be the dominant feature of the environment in which investment decisions are made. Furthermore, other factors are at play, including the psychology of the market. And with the rise of the Internet, and investors interacting with each other there, information, including false or misleading information, can be spread quickly, and prices affected accordingly.

THE DIVIDEND DISCOUNT MODEL IN PRACTICE

Many money managers and investment services firms, including a number of large Wall Street firms, use the DDM in various ways to estimate the intrinsic values of stocks. Regardless of who uses the model, and how it is used, estimates will always be involved. Investors should always remember this in using, or evaluating, output from these models. However, this also applies to any other valuation model that is used. All involve judgments and estimates, because all valuation models are dealing with the uncertain future.

In practice, investors may use the DDM in other ways to select stocks. This results from rearranging Equation 10-4 to solve for k, which we can think of as the expected rate of return on a stock.

$$k = D_1/P_0 + g \qquad\qquad (10\text{-}9)$$

Equation 10-9 says that the expected rate of a return on a constant growth stock, k, is the dividend yield plus the expected growth rate in dividends and price, g. The latter term can be thought of as the price change component or capital gains component. Therefore, an investor's expected rate of return from a stock is the sum of the income component and the price change component, which together constitute the total return from a stock as discussed in Chapter 6.

OTHER DISCOUNTED CASH-FLOW APPROACHES

The DDM is certainly not the only discounted cash-flow model used by investors and analysts. Others are being used and promoted. Regardless, all involve the same basic concepts—an estimation of future cash flows, discounted back to today using a discount rate to reflect the time value of money and the risk involved.

One cash-flow approach currently being promoted will illustrate the variations from the DDM. In a book titled *Streetsmart Guide to Valuing a Stock*, Gray, Cusatis, and Woolridge advocate the following discounted cash-flow (DCF) approach that any investor can employ by using a spreadsheet with no complex mathematics.

Step 1: Forecast Expected Cash Flows. In this model, estimates involve expected free cash flow to the firm. Free cash flow is defined as cash amounts available to be paid to both debtholders and stockholders.

Step 2: Estimate the Discount Rate. The appropriate discount rate in this model is the after-tax weighted average cost of capital.

Step 3: Calculate the Value of the Corporation. This step involves calculating the discounted value of the expected cash flows over a 10-year forecast horizon and then calculating the residual value of the company beyond this period. The total corporate value is the sum of the discounted free cash flow over the 10-year excess return period plus the present value of the residual value.

Step 4: Calculate Intrinsic Stock Value. Compute the total value to common equity by subtracting the market value of senior claims on the cash flows and dividing by shares outstanding to obtain an estimate of stock value per share.

In the book mentioned above, the authors outline the steps necessary to develop a valuation model based on DCF methods using any well-known spreadsheet. The model allows investors to perform scenario analysis, which means they can observe changes in stock values as expectations change.[6]

Example 10-7 At the website www.valuepro.net, entering the symbol for Coca-Cola in early March 2003 produced an estimate of intrinsic value of about $44.50 per share, at which time the market price was about $40.22. Some of the inputs underlying this calculation are shown along with this price. Users could accept this estimate, and decide that Coke was undervalued (current market price less than intrinsic value), or change some of the values used in this model to calculate intrinsic value.

It is not difficult to find other variations of the cash-flow model. For example, Standard & Poor's (S&P), the large investment advisory service, publishes a weekly service called *The Outlook* which makes stock recommendations and analyzes the stock market in general. Standard & Poor's uses a cash-flow model to estimate the intrinsic value of stocks, and it also uses relative valuation techniques (explained below) to do so. Although S&P's cash-flow model varies somewhat from the approach outlined above, the end product is the same—an estimate of intrinsic value based on S&P's estimate of future cash flows, discounted at a rate thought to be appropriate.

Example 10-8 In early January 2003, *The Outlook* carried a brief evaluation of Polaris Industries, a maker of recreational vehicles. After reviewing the company's operations and profit prospects, the analysis concluded with this statement: "Based on our discounted cash flow analysis, we estimate the intrinsic value of the shares is about $75." At that point in time, the shares were priced at $59.[7]

Relative Valuation Techniques

An alternative fundamental analysis approach to valuation often used by practicing security analysts is that of relative valuation techniques. Most analysts and knowledgeable investors recognize the underlying foundation and intuitive nature of the discounted cash-flow techniques, but they also recognize the difficulties of using these models in practice. Small differences in inputs result in large differences in estimates of intrinsic value, which in turn can easily lead to errors in determining if a stock is undervalued or overvalued.

The relative value concept is based on making comparisons in order to determine value. By calculating measures such as the P/E ratio and making comparisons to some benchmark(s), such as the market, an industry, or the stock's history over time, analysts

---

[6] The software is available for purchase at their Web site, http://www.valuepro.net, at which you can also value some stocks and try out this approach.
[7] Standard & Poor's, *The Outlook*, vol. 75, no. 1, January 8, 2003, p. 5.

can avoid having to estimate the g and k parameters of the DDM. Relative value investors use several different ratios in an attempt to assess value. We will discuss the better known measures.

THE P/E RATIO OR EARNINGS MULTIPLIER APPROACH

Earnings Multiplier

The P/E ratio for a stock

The P/E ratio or **earnings multiplier** approach is the best-known and most widely used valuation technique. Analysts are more comfortable talking about earnings per share (EPS) and P/E ratios, and this is how their reports are often worded. Talk about EPS and P/E ratios is the typical language of Wall Street. Without question, the P/E ratio is one of the most widely mentioned and discussed variables pertaining to a common stock, and will almost always appear in any report from an analyst or an investment advisory service. For this reason, we develop the P/E ratio in detail.

What is the P/E Ratio? *As a definition*, the P/E ratio is simply the number of times investors value earnings as expressed in the stock price. For example, a stock priced at $100, with most recent 12-month earnings of $5, is said to selling for a multiple of 20. In contrast, if another stock had earnings of $2.50 and was selling for $100, investors would be valuing the stock at 40 times earnings. Thus, the P/E ratio as reported daily in such sources as *The Wall Street Journal* is simply an identity calculated by dividing the current market price of the stock by the latest 12-month earnings. As such, it tells investors the price being paid for each $1 of most recent 12-month earnings.

Example 10-9

In March 2003, investors were willing to pay 36 times (the most recent 12-month) earnings for Bed, Bath & Beyond but only 10 times earnings for General Motors. Burlington Industries had no P/E, because it had no earnings.

It is true by definition that:

$$P_0 = \text{Current stock price} = E_0 \times P_0 / E_0 \qquad (10\text{-}10)$$

where:

P_0 = the current stock price
E_0 = the most recent 12-month earnings per share

It is worth emphasizing:

- Stock price is the product of two variables when using this type of approach:
  1. EPS
  2. The P/E multiple

Determinants of the P/E Ratio What variables affect the P/E ratio? To shed some light on this question, the P/E ratio can be derived from the dividend discount model, which, as we have seen, is the foundation of valuation for common stocks. Note, however, that *this process directly applies only for the case of constant growth*. If a multiple-period growth model is applicable to the stock being considered, a different formulation from the one presented here will be needed. In fact, using the P/E ratio for multiple-growth rate companies can be misleading and should be done with care.

Start with Equation 10-5, the estimated value of a stock today (which we shall call P to stay in the context of a P/E ratio) using the constant-growth version of the model.

$$P = \frac{D_1}{k-g} = \quad \text{Constant-growth version of the dividend discount model} \qquad \text{(10-5)}$$

Dividing both sides of Equation 10-5 by expected earnings, E_1,

$$P/E_1 = \frac{D_1/E_1}{k - g} \qquad \text{(10-11)}$$

Equation 10-11 indicates those factors that affect the estimated P/E ratio.

1. The *expected* dividend payout ratio, D_1/E_1
2. The required rate of return, which has to be estimated
3. The *expected* growth rate of dividends

The following relationships should hold, other things being equal:

1. The higher the expected payout ratio, the higher the P/E.
2. The higher the expected growth rate, g, the higher the P/E.
3. The higher the required rate of return, k, the lower the P/E.

It is important to remember the phrase "other things being equal," because usually other things are not equal and the preceding relationships do not hold by themselves. It is quite obvious, upon reflection, that if a firm could increase its estimated P/E ratio, and therefore its market price, by simply raising its payout ratio, it would be very tempted to do so. However, such an action would in all likelihood reduce future growth prospects, lowering g, and thereby defeating the increase in the payout. Similarly, trying to increase g by taking on particularly risky investment projects would cause investors to demand a higher required rate of return, thereby raising k. Again, this would work to offset the positive effects of the increase in g.

Variables 2 and 3 are typically the most important factors in the preceding determination of the P/E ratio, because a small change in either can have a large effect on the P/E ratio.

Example 10-10 Assume that the payout ratio is 60 percent. By varying k and g, and therefore changing the difference between the two (the denominator in Equation 10-11), investors can assess the effect on the P/E ratio as follows:

Assume $k = 0.15$ and $g = 0.07$	P/E = 0.60 / (0.15 − 0.07) = 7.5
Now assume $k = 0.16$ and $g = 0.06$	P/E = 0.60 / (0.16 − 0.06) = 6
Or that $k = 0.14$ and $g = 0.08$	P/E = 0.60 / (0.14 − 0.08) = 10

Think about each of these P/E ratios being used as a multiplier with an expected earnings for stock i for next year of $3. The possible prices for stock i would be $22.50, $18, and $30, respectively, which is quite a range, given the small changes in k and g that were made.

Understanding the P/E Ratio Most investors intuitively realize that the P/E ratio should be higher for companies whose earnings are expected to grow rapidly. However, how much higher is not an easy question to answer. The market will assess the degree of risk involved in the expected future growth of earnings—if the higher growth rate carries a high level of risk, the P/E ratio will be affected accordingly. Furthermore, the high-growth rate may be attributable to several different factors, some of which are more desirable than others. For example, rapid growth in unit sales owing to strong demand for a firm's products is preferable to favorable tax situations, which may change, or liberal accounting procedures, which one day may cause a reversal in the firm's situation.

P/E ratios reflect investors' expectations about the growth potential of a stock and the risk involved. These two factors can offset each other. Other things being equal, the greater the risk of a stock, the lower the P/E ratio; however, growth prospects may offset the risk and lead to a higher P/E ratio. The Internet companies that were so popular in the late 1990s were clearly very risky, but investors valued their potential very highly, and were willing to pay very high prices for these companies.

The P/E ratio reflects investor optimism and pessimism. It is related to the required rate of return. As the required rate of return increases, other things being equal, the P/E ratio decreases, as can be seen from Equation 10-11.

The required rate of return, in turn, is related to interest rates, which are the required returns on bonds. As interest rates increase, required rates of return on all securities, including stocks, also generally increase. As interest rates increase, bonds become more attractive compared to stocks on a current return basis.

Based on these relationships, an inverse relationship between P/E ratios and interest rates is to be expected. As interest rates rise (decline), other things being equal, P/E ratios should decline (rise). Table 10-1 shows interest rates (yields) on corporate, federal, and

Table 10-1 The Relationship Between Interest Rates and P/E Ratios, 1976–2002

Year	Aaa Industrial	30-Year Treasuries	High-grade municipals	P/E Ratio
2002	6.49	5.43	5.05	31.89*
2001	7.08	5.49	5.19	46.48
2000	7.62	5.94	5.77	26.00
1999	7.05	5.87	5.43	30.50
1998	6.53	5.58	5.12	32.60
1997	7.27	6.61	5.55	24.43
1996	7.37	6.71	5.75	19.13
1995	7.59	6.88	5.95	18.14
1994	7.97	7.37	6.19	15.00
1993	7.22	6.59	5.63	21.30
1992	8.14	7.67	6.41	22.81
1991	8.77	8.14	6.89	26.12
1990	9.32	8.61	7.25	15.47
1989	9.26	8.45	7.24	14.69
1988	9.71	8.96	7.76	11.68
1987	9.38	8.59	7.73	14.12
1986	9.02	7.78	7.38	16.52
1985	11.37	10.79	9.18	14.15
1984	12.71	12.41	10.15	9.95
1983	12.04	11.18	9.47	11.67
1982	13.79	12.76	11.57	11.13
1981	14.17	13.45	11.23	7.98
1980	11.94	11.27	8.51	9.16
1979	9.63	9.28	6.39	7.31
1978	8.73	8.49	5.90	7.79
1977	8.02	7.75	5.56	8.73
1976	8.43	6.78	6.49	10.84

* = preliminary

SOURCE: Federal Reserve Data, *Bond Yields and Interest Rates*

municipal bonds, and P/E ratios for the Standard & Poor's 500 Composite Index for recent years. Although Table 10-1 shows annual observations, the inverse relationship between the two can clearly be seen.

As interest rates rose from 1976 through 1981, the P/E ratio on the S&P 500 Composite Index declined. Conversely, as interest rates declined from 1994 through 1998, P/E ratios rose, reaching record levels. Interest rates started rising in 1999, and were higher in 2000 than in 1998, and P/E ratios declined. The P/Es in 2001 and 2002 reflect the much-lower earnings for the S&P 500 Index for those years.

VALUATION USING THE P/E RATIO

Equation 10-10 tells us what is true by definition, but it is not very useful for valuing a stock. To use the earnings multiplier model as a valuation model, investors must look ahead because valuation is always forward looking. They can do this by making a forecast of next year's earnings per share.

Assume that we are talking about a stock that has a constant growth rate. Expected earnings, E_1, can be found by taking this year's earnings, E_0, and compounding them up one period by the expected growth rate, g.

$$E_1 = E_0(1 + g)$$

Alternatively, investors can obtain estimates of next year's earnings from security analysts and investment advisory services such as *The Value Line Investment Survey* or Standard & Poor's *Outlook*.

By dividing current price, P_0, by the estimated earnings for the next year, we obtain a forward P/E ratio, P_0/E_1:

Forward P/E ratio $= P_0/E_1$, where E_1 is expected earnings for next year

In actual practice, analysts and investment advisory services often recommend stocks on the basis of this forward P/E ratio, or multiplier, by making a relative valuation judgment. For example, they make a judgment as to whether this forward P/E is lower than is justified by the stock's prospects. If it is, the stock is undervalued, and if it is higher than is justified by the prospects, it is overvalued.

Example 10-11 In its late January issue of *The Outlook* in 2003, Standard & Poor's said the following about Constellation Brands: "At less than 11 times our fiscal 2004 earnings estimate, the shares are trading at a discount to the S&P MidCap 400 index and to the stock of the company's peers. We recommend purchase."[8]

Relative P/E ratios remain an important valuation technique despite problems with accounting EPS and varying definitions of earnings. The simple point is that under normal conditions, P/E ratios tend to have boundaries and sooner or later they adjust if they vary from these boundaries too much.

Example 10-12 Consider the 80+ technology stocks in the S&P 500 Index. Based on forward 12-month earnings, the average P/E for these stocks had almost doubled by March 2000 from the average only two years earlier. The average P/E for these stocks was in the high 40s in March. As we now know, stocks peaked in March 2000 and declined sharply thereafter, particularly technology stocks. The P/Es for these stocks underwent a sharp drop from the high 40s.

[8] Standard & Poor's, *The Outlook*, vol. 75, no. 4, January 29, 2003, p. 10.

PRICE TO BOOK VALUE

Price to Book Value

The ratio of stock price to per share stockholders' equity

Price to book value is calculated as the ratio of price to stockholders' equity as measured on the balance sheet (and explained in Chapter 15). Book value, the accounting value of the firm as reflected in its financial statements, measures the actual values recorded under accounting conventions (typically on a historical cost basis). As such, book values have the advantages and disadvantages of accounting numbers. If the value of this ratio is 1.0, the market price is equal to the accounting (book) value. If the ratio is less than 1.0, price is less than book value.

Example 10-13 For 2002, General Motors, with a large amount of plant and equipment, had a price to book value ratio of 0.8. Coca-Cola, on the other hand, had a price to book value ratio of 9.3, whereas the same ratio for the S&P 500 was less than 3.0.

Investors obviously need to be careful when interpreting this ratio, like all valuation ratios. For example, how relevant is book value to the business? Firms with significant "intellectual property" may have a low book value. Banks, on the other hand, tend to have investments that are easily valued and close to book value, so their ratios tend to be close to 1.0. Other issues to consider are share repurchases by a company and restructurings, which would tend to raise the price to book ratio.

The price to book value ratio (or, as it is commonly stated, the book value to price [or market equity] ratio) has received support in empirical tests. For example, a study by Rosenberg et al. found that stocks with low price to book values significantly outperformed the average stock.[9] This variable got a major boost in 1992 with the publication of an article by Eugene Fama and Kenneth French, which found that two basic variables, size (market value of equity, or ME) and book to market equity (BV/ME), effectively combined to capture the cross-sectional variation in average stock returns during the period 1963 to 1990. Furthermore, the book to market equity ratio had a consistently stronger role in average returns.[10]

Several analysts recommend as a decision rule stocks with low price to book value ratios. To use this measure of relative value, comparisons should be made to the firm's own ratio over time as well as to its industry ratio and that of the market as a whole.

Standard & Poor's, in its weekly *Outlook*, recommends stocks to investors. Box 10-1 is an example of one of their stock analyses, in this case for Zions Bankcorp in early 2003. Note that the recommendation is based on the stock being attractive on the relative basis of its P/E ratio and its book value. As S&P notes, "Both figures are significantly below the comparable ratios for most other regional banks."[11]

PRICE/SALES RATIO (PRS)

Price/Sales Ratio (PSR)

A company's stock price divided by its sales per share

A valuation technique that has received increased attention recently is the **price/sales ratio (PSR)**. This ratio is calculated by dividing a company's current stock price by its revenues per share over the four most recent quarters (typically it may be easier to divide a company's total market value (price times number of shares) divided by its annual sales). In effect, it indicates what the market is willing to pay for a firm's revenues.

---

[9] See Barr Rosenberg, Kenneth Reid, and Ronald Lanstein, "Persuasive Evidence of Market Inefficiency," *The Journal of Portfolio Management* 11 (Spring 1985): pp. 9–17.
[10] See Eugene Fama and Kenneth French, "The Cross-Section of Expected Stock Returns," *The Journal of Finance* 47 (June 1992): pp. 427–465.
[11] Standard & Poor's, *The Outlook*, vol. 75, no.1, January 8, 2003, p. 9.

BOX 10-1

An Example of Relative Valuation Techniques in Practice

ZIONS, 40, Nasdaq ****; Quality ranking: A

Until 2002, the stock of this Utah-based community bank holding company commanded a premium to its peers, reflecting Zions' presence in rapidly growing markets in the western U.S. and strong growth prospects for its e-commerce businesses. But as the economic recovery disappointed, the company wrote off many of its technology investments and new lending slowed. These issues caused the shares to trade at a discount to their peers. We believe, however, that Zions has reacted well to the tough economy and the slowdown in revenues it precipitated. The company has reined in its costs and should generate healthy profit growth in 2003. We think Zions is particularly well posi-

tioned to benefit from an improving economy, which should fuel greater demand for commercial credit and improve the credit quality in its loan portfolio. We see 2003 profits climbing 18% to $4.10 per share from the $3.48 likely earned in 2002. We also think there's a good chance for P/E multiple expansion, as investors focus on Zions' above-average long-term prospects for loan and deposit growth. We recommend accumulation of the shares, which are trading at 10 times our 2003 estimate and 1.6 times book value. Both figures are significantly below the comparable ratios for most other regional banks.

SOURCE: Standard & Poor's, *The Outlook*, vol. 75, January 8, 2003, p. 9. Reprinted by permission of Standard & Poor's, a division of The McGraw-Hill Companies.

Example 10-14 In one recent year, General Mills had sales of $5,179 million. Based on an average of the high and low price for the year of $51, and 87 million shares outstanding, the total market value was $4,437 million. The PSR ratio, therefore, was 0.86. Thus, General Mills was selling at 86 percent of its annual sales.

Investors may be concerned about the P/E ratio because a company could have erratic earnings, or, perhaps, no earnings. Also, earnings can be defined different ways (e.g., with or without write-offs). In contrast, the PSR ratio can be used to value any public company and companies with no earnings. Furthermore, many believe that sales are much more unlikely to be "managed" by the company as opposed to earnings.

A 1996 book, *What Works on Wall Street*, by James O'Shaughnessy, gives new emphasis to the price/sales ratio. Using Compustat data back to 1951, he analyzed all of the basic investment strategies used to select common stocks, such as book value, cash flow, P/E, return on equity (ROE), yield, and so forth. O'Shaughnessy found that the 50 stocks with the lowest PSRs, based on an annual rebalancing of the portfolio, performed at an annual rate of 15.42 percent over the 40 years since 1954 through 1994 compared to 12.45 percent annually for his universe of stocks. Stocks with the highest PSRs earned only 4.15 percent annually. Furthermore, combining low PSR stocks (generally, a PSR of 1.0 or lower) with stocks showing *momentum* (the best 12-month price performance) produced results of 18.14 percent annually over the full 40-year period.[12]

An often-quoted rule of thumb is to say that a PSR of 1.0 is average for all companies, and therefore those with a PSR considerably less than 1.0, such as 0.5, are bargains. Such a simplistic approach is not likely to be suitable for reasons discussed below.

As with any other valuation technique, investors cannot simply accept all PSR numbers at face value, or rely on simple rules of thumb in all cases. For example, O'Shaughnessy found that this valuation technique worked best for large capitalization stocks, presumably because their market values tend to be more in line with their sales as a

---

[12] See James O'Shaughnessy, *What Works on Wall Street: A Guide to the Best-Performing Investment Strategies of All Time*. New York: McGraw-Hill, 1998.

general proposition. It is important to interpret the ratio within industry bounds. For example, retailers tend to have low price/sales ratios because of their low margins, whereas biotechnology companies tend to have high price/sales ratios. In addition, a firm's financing can play an important role in interpreting this ratio. There are quite a few companies selling at PSRs of less than 1.0 which have a large amount of debt and are not profitable. Some of these companies could go bankrupt.

Investors should make comparisons with industry averages, and also consider a company's PSR in relation to it historical average PSR. Comparing a company's PSR ratio to that of its competitors as well as its own history makes sense, because PSR is a relative valuation technique.

ECONOMIC VALUE ADDED

Economic Value Added
(EVA)   A technique for
focusing on a firm's
return on capital in
order to determine if
stockholders are being
rewarded

A new technique for evaluating stocks is to calculate the **economic value added**, or EVA.[13] In effect, EVA is the difference between operating profits and a company's true cost of capital for both debt and equity and reflects an emphasis on return on capital. If this difference is positive, the company has added value. Some studies have shown that stock price is more responsive to changes to EVA than to changes in earnings, the traditional variable of importance.[14]

Some mutual funds are now using EVA analysis as the primary tool for selecting stocks for the fund to hold. One recommendation for investors interested in this approach is to search for companies with a return on capital in excess of 20 percent, because this will in all likelihood exceed the cost of capital and, therefore, the company is adding value.

Which Approach to Use?

We have described the two most often used approaches in fundamental analysis—discounted cash-flow techniques and relative valuation techniques. Which should be used?

In theory, the discounted cash-flow approach is a correct, logical, and sound position. Conceptually, the best estimate of the current value of a company's common stock is the present value of the (estimated) cash flows to be generated by that company. However, some analysts and investors feel that this model is unrealistic. After all, they argue, with regard to the DDM, no one can forecast dividends into the distant future with very much accuracy. Technically, the model calls for an estimate of all dividends from now to infinity, which is an impossible task. Finally, many investors want capital gains and not dividends, so for some investors focusing solely on dividends is not desirable.

The previous discussion dealt with these objections that some raise about the dividend discount model. Can you respond to these objections based on this discussion?

Possibly because of the objections to the dividend discount model cited here, or possibly because it is easier to use, relative valuation techniques such as the earnings multiplier or P/E model remain a popular approach to valuation. They are less sophisticated, less formal, and more intuitive models. In fact, understanding the P/E model can help investors to understand the DDM. Because dividends are paid out of earnings, investors must estimate the growth in earnings before they can estimate the growth in dividends or dividends themselves.

---

[13] This term has been trademarked by Stern Stewart, a consulting firm that pioneered the use of this concept.
[14] This discussion is based on Maggie Topkis, "A New Way to Find Bargains," *Fortune*, December 6, 1996, pp. 265–266.

Regardless of which approach is used, it is important to remember that valuation employing fundamental analysis, or any other approach, is always subject to error. This is because we are dealing with the uncertain future. *No matter who does the analysis, or how it is done, mistakes will be made.*

❑ *Every valuation model and approach, properly done, requires estimates of the uncertain future.*

In the first three chapters of Part IV, we extensively utilize the overall logic of the fundamental valuation approach—namely, that the intrinsic value of a common stock, or the aggregate market, is a function of its expected returns and accompanying risk, as proxied by the required rate of return. The DDM and the P/E ratio model are used interchangeably to illustrate the fundamental valuation process.

Bursting the Bubble on New Economy Stocks— A Lesson in Valuation

At the end of the 1990s and into 2000, investors were caught up in a speculative bubble involving "New Economy" stocks, such as eToys and Dr.Koop.com. These new companies, involving the Internet, were thought to represent the wave of the future and to be more desirable than "Old Economy" stocks such as Gillette or Procter & Gamble. There seemed to be no upper limit as the prices of these stocks were bid higher and higher. Tremendous fortunes, mostly on paper, were being made.

Example 10-15 From the beginning of 1998, the *Amex Interactive Week Internet Index* rose to 689 in late March 2000 from a starting point of about 87 (split adjusted). Therefore, in just over two years, this index showed a gain of almost 700 percent.

Because these companies involved revolutionary new technology, many investors argued that they should be valued using revolutionary techniques, because the old methods no longer applied. As one of the leading Internet gurus at Merrill Lynch proclaimed in early 2000, "Valuation is often not a helpful tool in determining when to sell hypergrowth stocks." Other star analysts were talking about "usage metrics" when discussing these stocks, which basically means nonfinancial metrics such as customer loyalty, site hits, and "engaged shoppers." Many analysts and investors did not want to talk about such things as EPS, cash flows, and P/E ratios, and of course for many of these companies these variables did not exist. They had no profitability, and in many cases little hope of profitability for the foreseeable future.

In the past, companies had to show profitability, or the likely prospect thereof, to go public. In 1995, for example, about two-thirds of new companies going public were profitable at the time. In the first quarter of 2000, in contrast, less than 20 percent of companies going public were profitable at the time.

As we now know, the bubble started to burst in March 2000 and continued with horrific declines in early 2001. Many of the hot New Economy stocks dropped 80 percent or more, and hundreds of Internet companies went out of business. The aggregate dollar loss in the value of investor portfolios was staggering—roughly $4 trillion from March 2000 to March 2001. The index mentioned in Example 10-12 declined to about 280 by the end of 2000, a 60-percent loss, and declined even further in early 2001.

As of early 2001, it became apparent again to all but the most obtuse that the old metrics of valuation really do apply. To survive and succeed, companies sooner or later have to generate cash flows and be profitable. Investors no longer believe statements such as that of a major brokerage firm report which argued that cash burned by dot-com companies is "primarily an investor sentiment issue" and not a long-term risk for the sector.[15]

The bottom line here is that valuation standards apply, at least in part, to New Economy stocks, and stocks must be valued on a rational basis. Revenues and profits do matter, and so do P/E ratios when they get too far out of line.

Example 10-16 At the peak of the Nasdaq market rise, which occurred on March 10, 2000, Cisco had a P/E ratio of about 150, Yahoo about 650, and JDS Uniphase about 640. One year later, the same companies had P/E ratios of 31, 35, and 41.

Some Final Thoughts on Valuation

Valuing stocks is difficult under the best of circumstances. Judgments must be made and variables estimated. No one knows with precision which valuation model should be used for any particular stock. It is almost impossible to prove that an investor's calculations for a valuation model are correct or incorrect (although many calculations could be judged by most people to be "reasonable" or not "reasonable"). Valuation of stocks always has been, is, and will continue to be an art and not a science. Errors are to be expected.

In the final analysis, stocks are worth what investors pay for them. Valuations may appear out of line, but market prices prevail.

Summary

▶ Two primary approaches for analyzing and selecting common stocks are fundamental analysis and technical analysis. Efficient market considerations should be taken into account.

▶ Fundamental analysis seeks to estimate the intrinsic value of a stock, which is a function of its expected returns and risk. Two fundamental approaches to determining value are the present value approach and the earnings multiplier (P/E ratio) approach.

▶ The present value approach for common stocks is similar to that used with bonds. A required (minimum) expected rate of return must be determined based on the risk-free rate and a risk premium.

▶ As for expected returns, since dividends are the only cash flows directly paid by a corporation, they are the logical choice for a present value model.

▶ According to the dividend discount model, the value of a stock today is the discounted value of all future dividends. To account for an infinite stream of dividends, stocks to be valued are classified by their expected growth rate in dividends.

▶ If no growth is expected, the dividend discount model reduces to a perpetuity. If two or more growth rates are expected, a multiple-growth model must be used in which the future stream of dividends is identified before being discounted.

▶ The constant-growth version of the dividend discount model is used most often; it reduces to the ratio of the dividend expected next period to the difference between the required rate of return and the expected growth rate in dividends.

▶ The dividend discount model is sensitive to the estimates of the variables used in it; therefore, investors

---

[15]This statement and some of the thoughts in this section are based on Gretchen Morgenson, "How Did They Value Stocks? Count the Absurd Ways," *The New York Times*, March 18, 2001.

will calculate different prices for the same stock while using an identical model. This model implicitly accounts for the terminal price of a stock.

▶ The multiplier or P/E ratio approach is based on the identity that a stock's current price is the product of its actual earnings per share and the P/E ratio. It follows that the P/E ratio can be calculated by dividing the current price by the actual earnings per share.

▶ To implement the P/E ratio approach to estimate the value of a stock, we must estimate the earnings and the P/E ratio for next period.

▶ The P/E ratio itself is a function of the dividend payout ratio, the required rate of return, and the expected growth rate of dividends.

▶ Also, P/E ratios are inversely related to interest rates because interest rates are directly related to required rates of return.

▶ The relative value concept is based on making comparisons in order to determine value. By calculating measures such as the P/E ratio, and making comparisons to some benchmark(s), analysts can avoid having to estimate the g and k parameters of the DDM as well as one-point estimates of the value of a stock in the form of intrinsic values.

▶ Relative valuation techniques include, among others, the P/E ratio, P/B, and P/S. Like all valuation techniques, each has its strengths and weaknesses.

Key Words

Dividend discount model (DDM)
Earnings multiplier
Economic value added

Intrinsic value
Perpetuity

Price to book value
Price/sales ratio (PSR)

Questions

10-1 What is meant by "intrinsic value"? How is it determined?

10-2 Why is the required rate of return for a stock the discount rate to be used in valuation analysis?

10-3 Why can earnings not be used as readily as dividends in the present value approach?

10-4 What is the dividend discount model? Write this model in equation form.

10-5 What problems are encountered in using the dividend discount model?

10-6 Describe the three possibilities for dividend growth. Which is the most likely to apply to the typical company?

10-7 Since dividends are paid to infinity, how is this problem handled in the present value analysis?

10-8 Demonstrate how the dividend discount model is the same as a method that includes a specified number of dividends and a terminal price.

10-9 Assume that two investors are valuing General Foods Company and have agreed to use the constant-growth version of the dividend valuation model. Both use $3 a share as the expected dividend for the coming year. Are these two investors likely to derive different prices? Why or why not?

10-10 Once an investor calculates intrinsic value for a particular stock, how does he or she decide whether or not to buy it?

10-11 How valuable are the P/E ratios shown daily in *The Wall Street Journal*?

10-12 What factors affect the P/E ratio? How sensitive is it to these factors?

10-13 Some investors prefer the P/E ratio model to the present value analysis on the grounds that the latter is more difficult to use. State these alleged difficulties and respond to them.

10-14 Indicate the likely direction of change in a stock's P/E ratio if
a. The dividend payout decreases.
b. The required rate of return rises.
c. The expected growth rate of dividends rises.
d. The riskless rate of return decreases.

10-15 Assume you are trying To value a company using relative valuation techniques but the company has no earnings. Which techniques could you use?

10-16 List two advantages of using the Price/Sales ratio as a valuation technique. How is this ratio calculated without using per share numbers?

Demonstration Problems

10-1 Puglisi Pharmaceuticals is currently paying a dividend of $2 per share, which is not expected to change. Investors require a rate of return of 20 percent to invest in a stock with the riskiness of Puglisi. Calculate the intrinsic value of the stock.

Solution: The first step to solving a common stock valuation problem is to identify the type of growth involved in the dividend stream. The second step is to determine whether the dividend given in the problem is D_0, or is it D_1.

In this problem, it is clear that the growth rate is zero and that we must solve a zero-growth valuation problem (Equation 10-3). The second step is not relevant here, because all of the dividends are the same.

$$P_0 = \frac{D_0}{k}$$

$$= \frac{\$2.00}{0.20}$$

$$= \$10.00$$

10-2 Richter Construction Company is currently paying a dividend of $2 per share, which is expected to grow at a constant rate of 7 percent per year. Investors require a rate of return of 16 percent to invest in stocks with this degree of riskiness. Calculate the implied price of Richter.

Solution: Since dividends are expected to grow at a constant rate, we use the constant-growth version of the dividend discount model (Equation 10-5). Note carefully that this equation calls for D_1 in the numerator and that the dividend given in this problem is the current dividend being paid, D_0. Therefore, we must compound this dividend up one period to obtain D_1 before solving the problem.

$$D_1 = D_0 (1 + g)$$

$$= \$2.00(1.07)$$

$$= \$2.14$$

and

$$P = \frac{D_1}{k - g}$$

$$= \frac{\$2.14}{0.16 - 0.07}$$

$$= \$23.78$$

10-3 Baddour Legal Services is currently selling for $60 per share and is expected to pay a dividend of $3. The expected growth rate in dividends is 8 percent for the foreseeable future. Calculate the required rate of return for this stock.

Solution: To solve this problem, note first that this is a constant-growth model problem. Second, note that the dividend given in the problem is D_1, because it is stated as the dividend to be paid in the next period. To solve this problem for k, the required rate of return, we simply rearrange Equation 10-5:

$$k = \frac{D_1}{P_0} + g$$

$$= \frac{\$3.00}{\$60} + 0.08$$

$$= 0.13$$

Note that we could also solve for g by rearranging Equation 10-5 to solve for g rather than k.

10-4 O. M. Joy Golf Tours has been undergoing rapid growth for the last few years. The current dividend of $2 per share is expected to continue to grow at the rapid rate of 20 percent a year for the next three years. After that time Joy is expected to slow down, with the dividend growing at a more normal rate of 7 percent a year for the indefinite future. Because of the risk involved in such rapid growth, the required rate of return on this stock is 22 percent. Calculate the implied price for Joy Golf Tours.

Solution: We can recognize at once that this is a multiple-growth case of valuation because more than one growth rate is given. To solve for the value of this stock, it is necessary to identify the entire stream of future dividends from year 1 to infinity, and discount the entire stream back to time period zero. After the third year, a constant-growth model can be used which accounts for all dividends from the beginning of year 4 to infinity.

We first calculate the dividends for each individual year of the abnormal growth period, and we discount each of these dividends at the required rate of return.

$$D_1 = \$2.00(1 + 0.20) = \$2.40$$

$$D_2 = \$2.00(1 + 0.20)^2 = \$2.88$$

$$D_3 = \$2.00(1 + 0.20)^3 = \$3.46$$

$$\$2.40(0.820) = \text{present value of } D_1 = \$1.97$$

$$\$2.88(0.672) = \text{present value of } D_2 = \$1.94$$

$$\$3.46(0.551) = \text{present value of } D_3 = \$1.91$$

Present value of the first three years of dividends = $5.82

$$P_3 = \frac{\$3.46(1.07)}{0.22 - 0.07} = \$24.68, \text{ which is the}$$

Present value of the stock at the end of year 3

$$P_0 = \$24.68(0.551) = \$13.60, \text{ which is the}$$

Present value of P_3 at time period zero

$$\hat{P}_0 = \$5.82 + \$13.60 = \$19.42, \text{ which is the}$$

Present value of the stock at time period zero

Note that the price derived from the constant model is the price of the stock at the end of year 3, which is equivalent to the price of the stock at the beginning of year 4. Therefore, we discount it back three periods to time period zero. Adding this value to the present value of all dividends to be received during the abnormal growth period produces the intrinsic value of this multiple-growth period stock.

Problems

10-1   Billingsley Products is currently selling for $45 a share with an expected dividend in the coming year of $2 per share. If the growth rate in dividends expected by investors is 9 percent, what is the required rate of return for this stock?

10-2   Assume that Chance Industries is expected by investors to have a dividend growth rate over the foreseeable future of 8 percent a year and that the required rate of return for this stock is 13 percent. The current dividend being paid (D_0) is $2.25. What is the price of the stock?

10-3   Mittra Motors is currently selling for $50 per share and pays $3 in dividends ($D_0$). Investors require 15 percent return on this stock. What is the expected growth rate of dividends?

10-4   Howe Poultry pays $1.50 a year in dividends, which is expected to remain unchanged. Investors require a 15 percent rate of return on this stock. What is its price?

10-5   a. Given a preferred stock with an annual dividend of $3 per share and a price of $40, what is the required rate of return?
   b. Assume now that interest rates rise, leading investors to demand a required rate of return of 9 percent. What will the new price of this preferred stock be?

10-6   An investor purchases the common stock of a well-known house builder, DeMong Construction Company, for $25 per share. The expected dividend for the next year is $3 per share, and the investor is confident that the stock can be sold one year from now for $30. What is the implied required rate of return?

10-7   a. The current risk-free rate (RF) is 5 percent, and the expected return on the market for the coming year is 10 percent. Calculate the required rate of return for (1) stock A, with a beta of 1.0; (2) stock B, with a beta of 1.7; and (3) stock C, with a beta of 0.8.
   b. How would your answers change if RF in part (a) were to increase to 7 percent, with the other variables unchanged?
   c. How would your answers change if the expected return on the market changed to 12 percent, with the other variables unchanged? RF = 5 percent.

10-8   Rader Chocolate Company is currently selling for $60 and is paying a $3 dividend.
   a. If investors expect dividends to double in 12 years, what is the required rate of return for this stock?
   b. If investors had expected dividends to approximately triple in six years, what would the required rate of return be?

10-9   Wingler Company is currently selling for $36, paying $1.80 in dividends, and investors expect dividends to grow at a constant rate of 8 percent a year.
   a. If an investor requires a rate of return of 14 percent for a stock with the riskiness of Wingler Company, is it a good buy for this investor?
   b. What is the maximum an investor with a 14 percent required return should pay for Wingler Company? What is the maximum if the required return is 15 percent?

10-10 The Hall Dental Supply Company sells at $32 per share, and Randy Hall, the CEO of this well-known Research Triangle firm, estimates the latest 12-month earnings are $4 per share with a dividend payout of 50 percent. Hall's earnings estimates are very accurate.
   a. What is Hall's current P/E ratio?
   b. If an investor expects earnings to grow by 10 percent a year, what is the projected price for next year if the P/E ratio remains unchanged?
   c. Ray Parker, President of Hall Dental Supply, analyzes the data and estimates that the payout ratio will remain the same. Assume the expected growth rate of dividends is 10 percent, and an investor has a required rate of return of 16 percent, would this stock be a good buy? Why or why not?
   d. If interest rates are expected to decline, what is the likely effect on Hall's P/E ratio?

10.11 The required rate of return for Warr Industries is 15.75 percent. The stock pays a current dividend of $1.30, and the expected growth rate is 11 percent. Calculate the formula price.

10-12 In Problem 10-11, assume that the growth rate is 16 percent. Calculate the formula price for this stock.

10-13 McEnally Motorcycles is a rapidly growing firm. Dividends are expected to grow at the rate of 18 percent annually for the next 10 years. The growth rate after the first 10 years is expected to be 7 percent annually. The current dividend is $1.82. Investors require a rate of return of 19 percent on this stock. Calculate the intrinsic value of this stock.

10-14 Avera Software Products is currently paying a dividend of $1.20. This dividend is expected to grow at the rate of 30 percent a year for the next five years, followed by a growth rate of 20 percent a year for the following five years. After 10 years the dividend is expected to grow at the rate of 6 percent a year. The required rate of return for this stock is 21 percent. What is its intrinsic value?

10-15 In Problem 10-14, assume that the growth rate for the first five years is 25 percent rather than 30 percent. How would you expect the value calculated in Problem 10-14 to change? Confirm your answer by calculating the new intrinsic value.

10-16 Wansley Corporation is currently paying a dividend of $1.60 per year, and this dividend is expected to grow at a constant rate of 8 percent a year. Investors require a 16 percent rate of return on Wansley. What is its estimated price?

10-17 Carter and Carter Pharmaceuticals is expected to earn $2 per share next year. Carter has a payout ratio of 40 percent. Earnings and dividends have been growing at a constant rate of 10 percent per year, but analysts are estimating that the growth rate will be 7 percent a year for the indefinite future. Investors require a 15 percent rate of return on this company. What is its estimated price?

10-18 Bolster Industries is expected to pay a dividend of $0.60 next year, $1.10 the following year, and $1.25 each year thereafter. The required rate of return on this stock is 18 percent. How much should investors be willing to pay for this stock?

10-19 Dukes Power and Gas is currently paying a dividend of $1.80. This dividend is expected to grow at a rate of 6 percent in the future. Dukes Power is 10 percent less risky than the market as a whole. The market risk premium is 7 percent, and the risk-free rate is 5 percent. What is the estimated price of this stock?

10-20 Wilson Industries is currently paying a dividend of $1 per share, which is not expected to change in the future. The current price of this stock is $12. What is the expected rate of return on this stock?

10-21 Sigetich and Company is currently selling for $40. Its current dividend is $2, and this dividend is expected to grow at a rate of 7 percent a year. What is the expected rate of return for this stock?

10-22 Kish and Company is not expected to pay a dividend until five years have elapsed. At the beginning of year 6, investors expect the dividend to be $3 per share and to remain that amount forever. If an investor has a 25 percent required rate of return for this stock, what should he or she be willing to pay for Kish?

10-23 The Yur-Austin Coporation is currently selling for $50. It is expected to pay a dividend of $2 next period. If the required rate of return is 10 percent, what is the expected growth rate?

10-24 Poindexter Industries is expected to pay a dividend of $10 per year for 10 years and then increase the dividend to $15 per share for every year thereafter. The required rate of return on this stock is 20 percent. What is the estimated stock price for Poindexter?

10-25 Roenfeldt Components recently paid a dividend of $1 per share. This dividend is expected to grow at a rate of 25 percent a year for the next five years, after which it is expected to grow at a rate of 7 percent a year. The required rate of return for this stock is 18 percent. What is the estimated price of the stock?

10-26 BS Lee Software is expected to enjoy a very rapid growth rate in dividends of 30 percent a year for the next three years. This growth rate is then expected to slow to 20 percent a year for the next five years. After that time, the growth rate is expected to be 6 percent a year. D_0 is $2. The required rate of return is 20 percent. What is the estimated price of BS Lee stock?

10-27 Peterson Corporation makes advanced computer components. It pays no dividends currently, but it expects to begin paying $1 a share four years from now. The expected dividends in subsequent years are also $1 a share. The required rate of return is 14 percent. What is the estimated price for Peterson?

CFA
10-28 As a firm operating in a mature industry, Arbot Industries is expected to maintain a constant dividend payout ratio and constant growth rate of earnings for the foreseeable future. Earnings were $4.50 per share in the recently completed fiscal year. The dividend payout ratio has been a constant 55 percent in recent years and is expected to remain so. Arbot's return on equity (ROE) is expected to remain at 10 percent in the future, and you require an 11-percent return on the stock.

a. Using the constant-growth dividend discount model, calculate the current value of Arbot common stock. Show your calculations.

   After an aggressive acquisition and marketing program, it now appears that Arbot's earnings per share and ROE will grow rapidly over the next two years. You are aware that the dividend discount model can be useful in estimating the value of common stock even when the assumption of constant growth does not apply.

b. Calculate the current value of Arbot's common stock using the dividend discount model, assuming Arbot's dividend will grow at a 15-percent rate for the next two years, return in the third year to the historical growth rate, and continue to grow at the historical rate for the foreseeable future. Show your calculations.

CFA
10-29 The constant-growth dividend discount model can be used both for the valuation of companies and for the estimation of the long-term total return of a stock.

   Assume: $20 = the price of a stock today

   8% = the expected growth rate of dividends

   $0.60 = the annual dividend one year forward

a. Using *only* the above data, **compute** the expected long-term total return on the stock using the constant-growth dividend discount model. **Show** calculations.

b. **Briefly discuss** *three* disadvantages of the constant-growth dividend discount model in its application to investment analysis.

c. **Identify** *three* alternative methods to the dividend discount model for the valuation of companies.

CFA
10-30 Mulroney recalled from her CFA studies that the constant-growth discounted dividend model (DDM) was one way to arrive at a valuation for a company's common stock. She collected current dividend and stock price data for Eastover and Southampton, shown in Table 4.

a. Using 11 percent as the required rate of return (i.e., discount rate) and a projected growth rate of 8 percent, **compute** a constant-growth DDM value for Eastover's stock and **compare** the computed value for Eastover to its stock price indicated in Table 4. **Show** calculations.

Mulroney's supervisor commented that a two-stage DDM may be more appropriate for companies such as Eastover and Southampton. Mulroney believes that Eastover and Southampton could grow more rapidly over the next three years and then settle in at a lower but sustainable rate of growth beyond 1994. Her estimates are indicated in Table 5.

b. Using 11 percent as the required rate of return, **compute** the two-stage DDM value of Eastover's stock and **compare** that value to its stock price indicated in Table 4. **Show** calculations.

c. **Discuss** *two* advantages and *three* disadvantages of using a constant-growth DDM. **Briefly discuss** how the two-stage DDM improves upon the constant-growth DDM.

Table 4 Current Information

	Current Share Price	Current Dividends Per Share	1992 EPS Estimate	Current Book Value Per Share
Eastover (EO)	$ 28	$ 1.20	$ 1.60	$ 17.32
Southampton (SHC)	48	1.08	3.00	32.21
S&P 500	415	12.00	20.54	159.83

Table 5 Projected Growth Rates

	Next 3 Years (1992, 1993, 1994)	Growth Beyond 1994
Eastover (EO)	12%	8%
Southampton (SHC)	13%	7%

Web Resources

For additional resources visit our dynamic Web site located at www.wiley.com/college/jones.

- *Right for the Price*—Estimates of equity intrinsic value are required to find which of three stocks that is the best value at current prices. The problems and required assumptions of estimating intrinsic value for firms that may or may not pay dividends are central to the case analysis.

- Internet Exercises—This chapter presents the basic structure for the valuation of stocks. We will look at the market prices of stocks on the Internet and work on exercises that bring P/E ratios and models such as the dividend discount model to life.
  Exercise 1: Compares reported price-earnings ratios on different websites and asks the reader to relate them to firm characteristics.
  Exercise 2: Explores the use of the Zero-Growth model versus the Constant Growth and Multiple Growth models.

  Exercise 3: Looks at analysts' earning estimates for the different stocks.
  Exercise 4: Looks at comparative valuation techniques.

- Multiple Choice Self Test
- Appendix 10-B—The Analysis and Valuation of Preferred Stock

Selected References

A 4-step valuation approach that can be applied to almost any stock is explained in:

Gray, Gary, Cusatis, Patrick J. and Woolridge, J. Randall. *Valuing a Stock*. McGraw-Hill, 1999.

A book that examines 40 years of stock market data using various selection criteria:

O'Shaughnessy, James. *What Works on Wall Street: A Guide to the Best-Performing Investment Strategies of All Time*. McGraw-Hill, 1998.

A book by a well-known authority on valuation is:

Damodaran, Aswath. *Investment Valuation*. John Wiley & Sons, 1996.

Appendix 10-A
THE CONSTANT GROWTH VERSION OF THE DDM

Table 10A-1 illustrates the case of Summa's growth stock with a current dividend of $1 per share ($D_0$), an expected constant-growth rate of 7 percent, and a required rate of return, k, of 15 percent.

As Table 10A-1 shows, the expected dollar dividend for each period in the future grows by 7 percent. Therefore, $D_1 = \$1.07$, $D_2 = \$1.14$, $D_{10} = \$1.97$, and so forth. Only the first 60 years of growth are shown, at the end of which time the dollar dividend is $57.95. The last column of Table 10A-1 shows the discounted value of each of the first 60 years of dividends. Thus, the present value of the dividend for Period 1, discounted at 15 percent, is $0.93, while the present value of the actual dollar dividend in Year 60, $57.95, is only $0.01 today. Obviously, dividends received far in the future, assuming normal discount rates, are worth very little today.

Figure 10A-1 shows this growth in the dollar dividend for only the first 30 years in order to provide some scale to the process. Because k is greater than g, the present value of each future dividend is declining—for example, the present value of $D_1 = \$0.93$, the present value of $D_2 = \$0.87$, and the present value of $D_{10} = \$0.49$. Therefore, the present-value-of-dividends curve at the bottom of Figure 10A-1 is declining more rapidly than the growth-in-dividends-over-time curve above it is growing.

The estimated value of Summa, as illustrated in Table 10A-1 and Figure 10A-1, is the sum of the present values of each of the future dividends. Adding each of these present values together from now to infinity would produce the correct estimated value of the stock. Note from Table 10A-1 that adding the present values of the first 60 years of dividends together produces an estimated value of $13.20. The correct answer, as obtained from adding all years from now to infinity, or using Equation 10-5, is:

$$V_0 = \text{Estimated value} = \frac{\$1.07}{0.15 - 0.07} = \$13.38$$

Thus, years beyond 40 to 50 typically add very little to the estimated value of a stock. Adding all of the discounted dividends together for the first 60 years produces a present value, or estimated value for the stock, of $13.20, which is only $0.18 different from using Equation 10-5. Therefore, years 61 to infinity add a total value of $0.18 to the stock price.

Table 10A-1 Present Value of 60 Years of Dividends (Current Dividend = $1, g = 7%, k = 15%)

Period	Dollar Dividend	PV Factor	PV of Dollar Dividend	Period	Dollar Dividend	PV Factor	PV of Dollar Dividend
1	1.07	0.8696	0.93	31	8.15	0.0131	0.11
2	1.14	0.7561	0.87	32	8.72	0.0114	0.10
3	1.23	0.6576	0.81	33	9.33	0.0099	0.09
4	1.31	0.5718	0.75	34	9.98	0.0086	0.09
5	1.40	0.4972	0.70	35	10.68	0.0075	0.08
6	1.50	0.4323	0.65	36	11.42	0.0065	0.07
7	1.61	0.3759	0.60	37	12.22	0.0057	0.07
8	1.72	0.3269	0.56	38	13.08	0.0049	0.06
9	1.84	0.2843	0.52	39	13.99	0.0043	0.06
10	1.97	0.2472	0.49	40	14.97	0.0037	0.06
11	2.10	0.2149	0.45	41	16.02	0.0032	0.05
12	2.25	0.1869	0.42	42	17.14	0.0028	0.05
13	2.41	0.1625	0.39	43	18.34	0.0025	0.05
14	2.58	0.1412	0.36	44	19.63	0.0021	0.04
15	2.76	0.1229	0.34	45	21.00	0.0019	0.04
16	2.95	0.1069	0.32	46	22.47	0.0016	0.04
17	3.16	0.0929	0.29	47	24.05	0.0014	0.03
18	3.38	0.0808	0.27	48	25.73	0.0012	0.03
19	3.62	0.0703	0.25	49	27.53	0.0011	0.03
20	3.87	0.0611	0.24	50	29.46	0.0009	0.03
21	4.14	0.0531	0.22	51	31.52	0.0008	0.03
22	4.43	0.0462	0.20	52	33.73	0.0007	0.02
23	4.74	0.0402	0.19	53	36.09	0.0006	0.02
24	5.07	0.0349	0.18	54	38.61	0.0005	0.02
25	5.43	0.0304	0.16	55	41.32	0.0005	0.02
26	5.81	0.0264	0.15	56	44.21	0.0004	0.02
27	6.21	0.0230	0.14	57	47.30	0.0003	0.02
28	6.65	0.0200	0.13	58	50.61	0.0003	0.02
29	7.11	0.0174	0.12	59	54.16	0.0003	0.01
30	7.61	0.0151	0.11	60	57.95	0.0002	0.01

Sum of dividends = $870.47

Sum of 1st 60 years of discounted dividends = $13.20

Figure 10A-1

The constant-growth model: g = 7%; k = 15%.

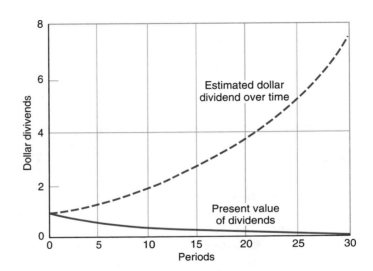

chapter 11

Common Stocks: Analysis and Strategy

Chapter 11 covers the analysis and strategy for selecting and holding common stocks. Similar to the passive approach to bonds, investors can follow a buy-and-hold strategy, or buy index funds that mimic some market index. Under the active approach, we analyze the primary alternatives of stock selection, sector rotation, and market timing, and consider the implications of the efficient market hypothesis. A framework for fundamental analysis is outlined, which forms the organization for Part IV.

AFTER READING THIS CHAPTER YOU WILL BE ABLE TO:

▶ Recognize the overall impact of the market on stocks and understand the importance of the required rate of return.

▶ Analyze the pros and cons of a passive approach to building a stock portfolio.

▶ Evaluate critically the well-known active strategies for stocks used by investors.

▶ Differentiate between technical analysis and fundamental analysis and understand the framework used in doing fundamental analysis.

In this chapter, we consider how investors should go about analyzing some important issues involving common stocks as well as the most common strategies available for selecting stocks. We begin by reviewing a key part of any analysis of common stocks, the impact of the overall stock market. Because of its importance in the analysis of common stocks, we analyze in some detail the required rate of return used in the valuation process.

In our discussion of analysis and strategy for both stocks and bonds, we will divide the strategies into two categories, passive and active. Common stock investors need carefully to consider whether they will follow an active approach, a passive approach, or a combination of the two. Within the active approach, they must decide what activity to concentrate on—selecting stocks, timing the market, and so forth.

We conclude by considering the two basic approaches typically used in security analysis. The fundamental approach, which ties in closely with the analysis of Chapter 10, is described first, followed by a brief description of technical analysis. We also analyze a framework for fundamental analysis. This discussion provides the reader with an overall view of security analysis and sets the stage for Part IV, which covers security analysis in detail with a complete discussion of both fundamental analysis and technical analysis.

Taking a Global Perspective

In today's investing world, investors cross borders more and more when they invest. And the investing is more sophisticated. Rather than start with a portfolio of U.S.-listed stocks and add selected foreign equities, investors today search for the truly "good" companies wherever they are—the industry giants, the innovative leaders, those with proven track records, and so forth. What matters today is being a world-class firm whether that is Pfizer in the United States or Nokia in Finland. When it comes to important sectors such as pharmaceuticals and telecommunications, globalization is the name of the game.

American investors have traditionally been myopic, focusing only on companies they are familiar with, such as IBM or Bank of America. Although this has paid off in recent years, this is not always the case. Although Standard & Poor's 500 Composite (S&P 500) Index outperformed many foreign equity markets in the 1990s, it underperformed a well-known foreign index in the 1980s, when Hong Kong, Germany, and Japan outperformed the U.S. year after year. Regardless, we are now in an age of globalization, and investors should take a global perspective. Many financial advisors regularly recommend to clients that some percentage of their overall portfolio be devoted to international investing.

Consider this—the S&P 500 index was up about 316 percent in the 1990s, whereas the rest of the world generally lagged behind. Emerging markets were often a disaster. Nevertheless, one study has shown that the Morgan Stanley EAFE Index of foreign stocks has outperformed the S&P 500 in 11 of 15 rolling 10-year periods since 1975. Many believe that foreign markets are ready to catch up even as the U.S. market showed a loss in 2000, 2001, and 2002.

How much of a U.S. investor's portfolio should be allocated to foreign securities? A general consensus among market observers is that a typical U.S. investor should have 10 to 20 percent of his/her portfolio in international markets. Of course, all foreign markets are not the same—emerging markets are generally much more risky than developed economies, and investors should probably not have more than 5 percent of their portfolio is emerging markets.

Analyzing Some Important Issues Involving Common Stocks

As we shall see in Chapter 17, bonds are analyzed in terms of interest rates because of the fundamental relationship between interest rates and bond prices. In a similar manner, we must consider the impact of market risk on common stock investors. The impact of the market on every investor in common stocks is pervasive and dominant, and must be fully appreciated by investors if they are to be successful.

We also consider the required rate of return in detail. This variable is important in any analysis of common stocks. As we saw in Chapter 10, the required rate of return is a very important component of the valuation process.

THE IMPACT OF THE OVERALL MARKET ON INDIVIDUAL STOCKS

Market risk is the single most important risk affecting the price movements of common stocks. Aggregate market movements remain the largest single factor explaining fluctuations in both individual stock prices and portfolios of stocks. When the market is going up strongly, as it did in the five-year period 1995 to 1999, most stocks appreciate significantly. It would almost be impossible for an investor with a diversified portfolio not to have earned very handsome returns during that period of time. Similarly, when the market declines sharply, as it did in 2000 to 2002, most stocks react accordingly. Few, if any, investors who owned stocks during this period, and whose positions were unhedged (which was true for most investors), escaped some degree of losses on their portfolios—the only question is how much did they lose?

A good demonstration of the impact of the overall market on stocks is shown in Figure 11-1, which covers the first quarter of 2001. This was the worst quarter for stock mutual funds in more than two decades (up to that time). Every category of stock funds, domestic and international, declined. The S&P 500 Index declined 12.45 percent, and the average diversified U.S. stock fund, which holds primarily S&P 500 stocks, declined

Figure 11-1

Performance of market indices and the average diversified U.S. equity fund for the first quarter of 2001.

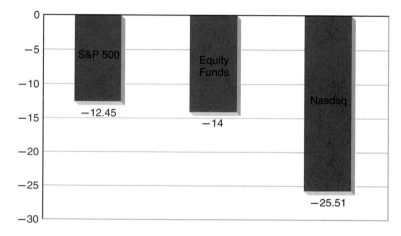

about 14 percent. As Figure 11-1 shows, Nasdaq declined even more, a dramatic 25.51 percent in one quarter alone. Can there be any doubt that most investors owning Nasdaq stocks during that quarter suffered a loss?

The impact of the market is particularly visible for a diversified portfolio of stocks. As we now know, the basic tenet of portfolio theory is to diversify into a number of securities (properly chosen). For adequately diversified portfolios, market effects can account for 90 percent and more of the variability in the portfolio's return. In other words, for a well-diversified portfolio, which each investor should hold, the market is the dominant factor affecting the variability of its return. Although any given portfolio may clearly outperform the market, it will usually be significantly influenced by what happens on an overall basis.

Example 11-1   Consider the performance of Fidelity's Magellan Fund over a recent nine-year period, as shown in Figure 11-2. This fund has often ranked as the largest mutual fund in the United States, and has a famous history, being well known among investors. Notice how this fund and the S&P 500 Index track very closely over this period, based on an initial investment of $10,000. At the end of 2000, the $10,000 investment would have grown to $38,105 in the Magellan Fund and $38,283 in the S&P 500 Index. Clearly, the market's performance explains most of the fund's performance for this time period.

The International Perspective   U.S. investors buying foreign stocks face the same issues when it comes to market risk. Some of these markets have performed very well, and some have performed poorly over specified periods of time. The investor fortunate enough to have invested in the Bolivian stock market in 2000 experienced a gain of more than 160 percent, whereas the South Korean market declined about 51 percent during the same period. Mexico, having suffered a meltdown in 1994 and recovered somewhat, was down approximately 21 percent in 2000.

Example 11-2   Perhaps the best foreign example of the impact of the overall market on investors is Japan, clearly an economic superpower in recent years. In the 1980s, Japan seemed invincible in its economic performance, and its stock market, as measured by the Nikkei stock index, reflected Japan's success with seemingly unending rises in stock prices. The Nikkei stock index peaked at the end of 1989 at a level of almost 39,000. By mid-1992, the index had declined below the 15,000 level, representing a staggering decline of some 60 percent. As one well-known magazine put it at the time, this was the "biggest erasure of wealth in history." Such is the impact of the overall market on investor wealth. The Japanese stock market for the year 2000 was down about 27 percent, and has already reached levels below 8,000 in the new century. Regardless of an investor's prowess, virtually no portfolio invested in Japanese stocks can hold up well in the face of such long and dramatic declines in the Japanese equity markets.

Figure 11-2

Performance of the Magellan Fund and the S&P 500 over 1992–2000.

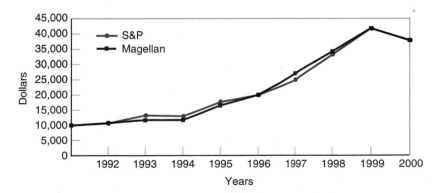

THE REQUIRED RATE OF RETURN

Required Rate of Return
The minimum expected rate of return necessary to induce an investor to purchase a security

The required rate of return was used in Chapter 10 as the discount rate for valuing common stocks. The **required rate of return** for a common stock, or any security, is defined as the minimum expected rate of return needed to induce an investor to purchase it. That is, given its risk, a security must offer some minimum expected return before a particular investor can be persuaded to buy it.

This discussion is directly related to the Capital Asset Pricing Model (CAPM) discussion in Chapter 9. The CAPM provides investors with a method of actually calculating a required (expected) rate of return for a stock, an industry, or the market as a whole. Our interest here is to think of the required rate of return on an overall basis as it affects the strategies that investors employ and the management of their portfolios.

What do investors require (expect) when they invest? First of all, investors can earn a riskless rate of return by investing in riskless assets such as Treasury bills. This *nominal* risk-free rate of return is designated RF throughout this text. It consists of a real risk-free rate of interest and an expected inflation premium.[1] In summary, as an approximation:[2]

$$\text{Risk-free rate of return} = \text{Real risk} = \text{free value} + \text{Expected Inflation} \qquad \textbf{(11-1)}$$

In addition to the risk-free rate of return available from riskless assets, rational risk-averse investors purchasing a risky asset expect to be compensated for this additional risk. Therefore, risky assets must offer **risk premiums** above and beyond the riskless rate of return. And the greater the risk of the asset, the greater the promised risk premium must be.

Risk Premium   That part of a security's return above the risk-free rate of return

The risk premium should reflect all the uncertainty involved in the asset. Thinking of risk in terms of its traditional sources, such components as the business risk and the financial risk of a corporation would certainly contribute to the risk premium demanded by investors for purchasing the common stock of the corporation. After all, the risk to the investor is that the expected income (return) will not be realized because of unforeseen events.

The particular business that a company is in will significantly affect the risk to the investor. One has only to look at the textile and steel industries in the last few years to appreciate business risk [which leads to an understanding of why industry analysis (Chapter 14) is important]. And the financial decisions that a firm makes (or fails to make) will also affect the riskiness of the stock.

Understanding the Required Rate of Return   The required rate of return for any investment opportunity can be expressed as Equation 11-2. This is, in effect, the CAPM model discussed in Chapter 9.

$$\text{Required rate of return} = \text{Risk-free rate} + \text{Risk premium} \qquad \textbf{(11-2)}$$

It is important to note that there are many financial assets and therefore many different required rates of return. The average required rate of return on bonds is different from the average required rate of return on preferred stocks, and both are different from the typical required rates of return for common stocks, warrants, or puts and calls. Furthermore, within a particular asset category such as common stocks, there are many required rates of return. Common stocks cover a relatively wide range of risk from conservative utility stocks to small, risky high-technology stocks.

[1] The real risk-free rate of interest (i.e., the real time value of money) is the basic exchange rate in the economy, or the price necessary to induce someone to forego consumption and save in order to consume more in the next period. It is defined within a context of no uncertainty and no inflation.
[2] The actual calculation involves adding 1.0 to both the real rate of return and the inflation premium, multiplying the two together, and subtracting the 1.0 from the product. For example, [(1 + 0.02)(1 + 0.05)] − 1.0 = 0.071, or 7.1 percent.

Figure 11-3

The trade-off between required rate of return and risk for common stocks.

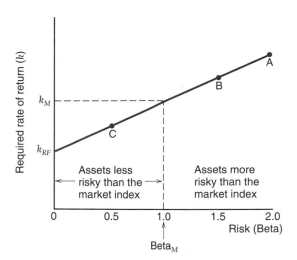

We know from Chapter 9 that the trade-off between the required rate of return and risk is linear and upward sloping, as shown in Figure 11-3; that is, the required rate of return increases as the risk, measured by beta, increases. The stock market taken as a whole has a beta of 1.0, indicated by point M in Figure 11-3. The required rate of return for all stocks is therefore k_M. A stock with a beta lower than 1.0 has a required rate of return below k_M, because its risk (beta) is less than that of the market. On the other hand, a stock with a beta greater than 1.0 has a required rate of return greater than that of the market.

It is also important to be aware that the level of required rates of return changes over time. For example, required rates of return change as inflationary expectations change, because the inflation premium is a component of the risk-free rate of return, which in turn is a component of the required rate of return. The level also changes as the risk premiums change. Investor pessimism will increase the risk premium and the required rate; investor optimism lowers both.

Building Stock Portfolios

We now consider how investors go about selecting stocks to be held in portfolios. Individual investors often consider the investment decision—based on objectives, constraints, and preferences—as consisting of two steps:

1. Asset allocation
2. Security selection

Asset Allocation
Allocating total portfolio funds to various asset classes

Asset allocation, which was discussed in Chapter 8, refers to allocating total portfolio wealth to various asset classes, such as stocks, bonds, and cash equivalents. The percentages add up to 100 percent, indicating that all portfolio funds have been allocated. A common asset allocation for a number of institutional investors is 60 percent equities and 40 percent bonds. Of course, many investors use several asset classes beyond these three, including foreign stocks, foreign bonds, real estate, and small-capitalization stocks. And some of these categories can be further divided—foreign stocks can be allocated by region, type of economy (developed vs. developing), and so forth.

In many respects, asset allocation is the most important decision an investor makes. Having made the portfolio allocation decision, the largest part of an investor's success or failure is locked in. For example, think of one investor allocating her portfolio as 90 percent Nasdaq stocks and 10 percent cash equivalents, and another investor doing the opposite, 90 percent cash equivalents and 10 percent Nasdaq stocks. Now imagine the Nasdaq market going down 60 percent, as it did in 2000 to 2001. Clearly, the results of these two portfolios will be vastly different regardless of the exact securities selected. Such is the importance of asset allocation.

Using the Internet

A good discussion of basic asset allocation guidelines is available in the "Education" section at Vanguard's site, www.vanguard.com. A detailed discussion is available under "How Can You Protect Yourself?", part of *SmartMoney University* at www.smartmoney.com.

We will assume that the asset allocation decision—what percentage of portfolio funds to allocate to each asset class such as stocks, bonds, and bills—has been made so that our focus is only on common stocks (asset allocation is discussed again in Chapter 21). The common stock portion could constitute 100 percent of the total portfolio or any other percentage an investor chooses.

In discussing strategies we consider the passive and active approaches separately for exposition purposes. These approaches are applicable to investors as they select and manage common stock portfolios, or select investment company managers who will manage such portfolios on their behalf. Which of these to pursue will depend on a number of factors, including the investor's expertise, time, and temperament, and, importantly, what an investor believes about the efficiency of the market, as discussed in Chapter 12. We will consider each of these two strategies in turn. It is important to realize that investors can, and often do, employ some combination of these strategies in their approach to investing.

The Passive Strategy

A natural outcome of a belief in efficient markets is to employ some type of passive strategy in owning and managing common stocks. If the market is highly efficient, impounding information into prices quickly and on balance accurately, no active strategy should be able to outperform the market on a risk-adjusted basis. The efficient market hypothesis (EMH) has implications for fundamental analysis and technical analysis, both of which are active strategies for selecting common stocks. That is why we consider the EMH in detail in Chapter 12.

Passive strategies do not seek to outperform the market but simply to do as well as the market. The emphasis is on minimizing transaction costs and time spent in managing the portfolio, because any expected benefits from active trading or analysis are likely to be less than the costs. Passive investors act as if the market is efficient and accept the consensus estimates of return and risk, recognizing current market price as the best estimate of a security's value.

An investor can simply follow a buy-and-hold strategy for whatever portfolio of stocks is owned. Alternatively, a very effective way to employ a passive strategy with common stocks is to invest in an indexed portfolio. We will consider each of these strategies in turn.

BUY-AND-HOLD STRATEGY

A buy-and-hold strategy means exactly that—an investor buys stocks and basically holds them until some future time in order to meet some objective. The emphasis is on avoiding transaction costs, additional search costs, and so forth. The investor believes that such a strategy will, over some period of time, produce results as good as alternatives that require active management whereby some securities are deemed not satisfactory, sold, and replaced with other securities. These alternatives incur transaction costs and involve inevitable mistakes.

Evidence to support this view comes from a study by Odean and Barber, who examined 60,000 investors. They found the average investor earned 15.3 percent over the period 1991 to 1996, whereas the most active traders (turning over about 10 percent of their holdings each month) averaged only 10 percent.[3]

Notice that a buy-and-hold strategy is applicable to the investor's portfolio whatever its composition. It may be large or small, and it may emphasize various types of stocks. Also note that an important initial selection must be made to implement the strategy. The investor must decide to buy stocks A, B, and C and not X, Y, and Z.

It is important to recognize that the investor will, in fact, have to perform certain functions while the buy-and-hold strategy is in existence. For example, any income generated by the portfolio may be reinvested in other securities. Alternatively, a few stocks may do so well that they dominate the total market value of the portfolio and reduce its diversification. If the portfolio changes in such a way that it is no longer compatible with the investor's risk tolerance, adjustments may be required. The point is simply that even under such a strategy investors must still take certain actions.

INDEX FUNDS

An increasing amount of mutual fund and pensions fund assets can be described as passive equity investments. These asset pools are designed to duplicate as precisely as possible the performance of some market index. An index fund (defined in Chapter 3) is an unmanaged fund designed to replicate as closely as possible (or practical) the performance of a specified index of market activity.

A stock-index fund may consist of all the stocks in a well-known market average such as the S&P 500 Index. No attempt is made to forecast market movements and act accordingly, or to select under- or overvalued securities. Expenses are kept to a minimum, including research costs (security analysis), portfolio managers' fees, and brokerage commissions. Index funds can be run efficiently by a small staff.

Example 11-3 The Vanguard Group of Investment Companies offers its Vanguard Index Trust portfolios, the largest selection of index funds in the industry, to allow investors to duplicate the broad market of all common stocks at a low cost. Investors can choose from among several portfolios in the trust.

1. *The Index Trust 500 Portfolio* consists of stocks selected to duplicate the S&P 500 and emphasizes large-capitalization stocks.
2. *The Extended Market Portfolio* consists of a statistically selected sample of the Wilshire 4500 Index and of medium- and small-capitalization stocks.

[3] Terrance Odean and Brad Barber, "Trading is Hazardous to Your Wealth: The Common Stock Investment Performance of Individual Investors," *Journal of Finance*, Vol. LV, No. 2 (April 2000): 773–806.

3. The *Total Stock Market Portfolio* seeks to match the performance of all (approximately 7000) publicly traded U.S. stocks.
4. The *Small Capitalization Stock Portfolio* seeks to match the performance of the Russell 2000 Small Stock Index, consisting of 2000 small-capitalization stocks.
5. The *Value Portfolio* seeks to match the investment performance of the S&P/BARRA Value Index, which consists of stocks selected from the S&P 500 Index with lower than average ratios of market price to book value.
6. The *Growth Portfolio* seeks to match the investment performance of the S&P 500/BARRA Growth Index, which consists of stocks selected from the S&P 500 Index with higher than average ratios of market price to book value.
7. *The Total International Portfolio* covers 31 countries across Europe, the Pacific, and emerging markets, and holds over 1500 stocks. The European Portfolio invests in Europe's 14 largest markets, whereas the Pacific Portfolio invests in the six most developed countries in the Pacific region. The Emerging Markets Portfolio invests in 14 of the most accessible markets in the less-developed countries.

There are no sales charges or exit charges of any kind. Total operating expenses for several of these funds is about 0.20 percent annually, which is extremely low.

Investments Intuition

Index funds arose in response to the large body of evidence concerning the efficiency of the market, and they have grown as evidence of the inability of mutual funds consistently, or even very often, to outperform the market continues to accumulate. If the market is efficient, many of the activities normally engaged in by funds are suspect; that is, the benefits are not likely to exceed the costs. The available evidence indicates that many investment companies have failed to match the performance of broad market indexes. For example, for the period 1986 to 1995, 78 percent of general equity mutual funds were outperformed by the S&P 500 Index, and 68 percent of international stock funds were outperformed by their comparative index.

How important are equity index funds in today's investing world? Vanguard's 500 Index fund had approximately $100 billion in assets by the beginning of 2001, placing it in the top two mutual funds in terms of assets in the United States. (Because of the market declines in 2001 and 2002, total assets decreased to about $63 billion in late fall 2002.) And the Vanguard Group is one of the two largest fund families (along with Fidelity) in the United States, based primarily on the amount of money in its index funds. Fidelity Investments, which has traditionally been the largest fund family, bases its prowess on actively managed equity funds. However, even Fidelity has increased its index offerings after publicly declaring some years ago it would not run index funds.

A significant advantage of index funds is their tax efficiency. Index funds basically buy and hold, selling shares only when necessary. Actively managed funds, on the other hand, do more frequent trading and generate larger tax bills, some of which may be short-term gains taxable at ordinary income tax rates. The tax issue really hit investors in 2001 when they went to pay their taxes for 2000—many funds made large, taxable distributions based on prior years of good returns, but the value of the fund shares themselves declined in 2000, many quite sharply.

One of the strongest cases for index funds has been made by Burton Malkiel, an Economics Professor at Princeton and author of the book *Earn More, Sleep Better: The*

Index Fund Solution. According to Malkiel, "On average, the typical actively managed fund underperforms the index by about two percentage points a year. And that calculation ignores the sales charges that are imposed by some actively managed funds and the extra taxes an investor pays on funds that turn over their portfolios rapidly."[4]

According to Malkiel, there are four reasons why indexing works:

1. Securities markets are extremely efficient in digesting information.
2. Indexing is cost efficient, with expenses much lower than actively managed funds.
3. Funds incur heavy trading expenses. Trading costs can amount to 0.5 to 1.0 percent per year.
4. Indexing has a tax advantage, deferring the realization of capital gains while earlier realization of capital gains reduces net returns significantly.

As for actual performance of equity index funds, consider the following. Morningstar, the mutual fund tracking company, defines nine "equity style boxes," consisting of large value, blend and growth, medium value, blend and growth, and small value, blend and growth. For the five-year period ending in 2000, indexing outperformed the comparable actively managed equity fund in eight of the nine categories. The only exception was the small-cap growth segment.[5]

According to John Bogle, founder of the Vanguard Group and a leading proponent of index funds, the S&P Index will outperform 70 percent of all actively managed equity funds over time. Consider the period 1992 to 2002 as one example. The Vanguard 500 Index fund outperformed approximately 73 percent of diversified U.S. stock funds.[6]

Investors can also purchase so-called "enhanced" index funds, which are index funds that are tweaked by their managers to be a little different. For example, an enhanced fund tracking the S&P 500 Index could have the same sector weighting in, say, technology stocks as the S&P 500 but hold somewhat different stocks, perhaps with lower P/E ratios. Or an enhanced fund can use futures and options to hold the S&P 500 Index and invest the remainder of the funds in bonds or other securities. The theory is that the manager can, by tweaking the fund slightly, outperform the index. The reality is, according to a study of 40 of these funds since their start dates, about half of the funds outperformed their benchmark and half did not.

The Active Strategy

Most of the techniques discussed in this text involve an active approach to investing. In the area of common stocks, the use of valuation models to value and select stocks indicates that investors are analyzing and valuing stocks in an attempt to improve their performance relative to some benchmark such as a market index. They assume or expect the benefits to be greater than the costs.

Pursuit of an active strategy assumes that investors possess some advantage relative to other market participants. Such advantages could include superior analytical or judgment skills, superior information, or the ability or willingness to do what other investors, particularly institutions, are unable to do. For example, many large institutional investors

[4] See Burton Malkiel, "The Case for Index Funds," *Mutual Funds Magazine*, February 1999, p. 72. This entire discussion involving Malkiel is based on this article, pp. 72–75.
[5] See "Indexing Knocks the Cover Off the Ball in 2000," *In The Vanguard*, The Vanguard Group, Winter 2001.
[6] This paragraph is based on Robert Frick, "The New Spin On Indexing," *Kiplinger's Personal Finance*, March 2003, p. 36.

COMMON STOCKS: ANALYSIS AND STRATEGY

cannot take positions in very small companies, leaving this field for individual investors. Furthermore, individuals are not required to own diversified portfolios and are typically not prohibited from short sales or margin trading as are some institutions.

Most investors still favor an active approach to common stock selection and management despite the accumulating evidence from efficient market studies and the published performance results of institutional investors. The reason for this is obvious—the potential rewards are very large, and many investors feel confident that they can achieve such awards even if other investors cannot.

There are numerous active strategies involving common stocks. We consider the most prominent ones below. Because of its importance, we then consider the implications of market efficiency for these strategies.

SECURITY SELECTION

The most traditional and popular form of active stock strategies is the selection of individual stocks identified as offering superior return-risk characteristics. Such stocks typically are selected using fundamental security analysis, but technical analysis is also used, and sometimes a combination of the two. Many investors have always believed, and continue to believe despite evidence to the contrary from the market efficiency literature, that they possess the requisite skill, patience, and ability to identify undervalued stocks.

We know from Chapter 1 that a key feature of the investments environment is the uncertainty that always surrounds investing decisions. Most stock pickers recognize the pervasiveness of this uncertainty and protect themselves accordingly by diversifying. Therefore, the standard assumption of rational, intelligent investors who select stocks to buy and sell is that such selections will be part of a diversified portfolio.

The Importance of Stock Selection How important is stock selection in the overall investment process? Most active investors, individuals or institutions, are, to various degrees, stock selectors. The majority of investment advice and investment advisory services is geared to the selection of stocks thought to be attractive candidates at the time. *The Value Line Investment Survey* (discussed in Chapters 12 and 15), the largest investment advisory service in terms of number of subscribers, is a good example of stock-selection advice offered to the investing public.

To gain some appreciation of the importance of stock selection, consider the cross-sectional variation in common stock returns. Latané, Tuttle, and Jones were the first to point out the widely differing performances of stocks in a given year using the interquartile range.[7] Examining data through 1972, they found a remarkable constancy from year to year in the spread between the performance of stocks in the upper quartile and the performance of stocks in the lower quartile.

A subsequent study by McEnally and Todd for the period 1946 to 1989 found that investors who successfully confined stock selection to the stocks in the highest quartile would have largely avoided losing years, and even the bad years showed only modest losses.[8] Conversely, for the bottom quarter, results were negative about 55 percent of the time, and about 25 percent of the time even the best stocks would have lost money despite generally favorable market conditions. The implication of these results is that "For

[7] See H. Latané, D. Tuttle, and C. Jones, *Security Analysis and Portfolio Management*, 2nd ed. (New York: Ronald Press, 1975), pp. 192–193. In an ordered set of numbers, the interquartile range is the difference between the value that cuts off the top quarter of these numbers and the value that cuts off the bottom quarter of these numbers. The interquartile range is an alternative measure of dispersion.

[8] See Richard McEnally and Rebecca Todd, "Cross-Sectional Variation in Common Stock Returns," *Financial Analysts Journal* (May/June 1992): 59–63. The quote is on p. 61 of this article.

those who do attempt to pick stocks, the rewards can be very high, but the risk and negative consequences of poor selection are substantial." An additional finding of this study is that cross-sectional variation of returns has been increasing steadily over the decades, making stock selection even more important in recent years.

The importance of stock selection cannot be overemphasized. Although we outline an approach to security analysis below that logically places company analysis last, its importance is obvious. As Peter Lynch, one of the most celebrated portfolio managers of recent years as former head of Fidelity's Magellan Fund, states: "If it's a choice between investing in a good company in a great industry, or a great company in a lousy industry, I'll take the great company in the lousy industry any day."[9] Lynch goes on to discuss what we can learn from the top 100 winners over the past decade. The basic lesson is that small stocks make big moves—the trick is identifying them. But as Lynch notes, "What do the great successes of the past 20 years tell us? It's the company, stupid."

Using the Internet

Screening stocks for possible selection, based on a set of criteria, is where a computer can really aid investors in making decisions. A good site is www.marketguide.com, which has considerable fundamental data available along with great screening tools. By going to www.financialweb.com, and selecting "Rapid Research," investors can use either a basic screen, with about six criteria, or an advanced screen, allowing about 27 criteria. In either case, screening can be done by exchange and by industry. www.quicken.com also has a stock screening section (go to "Investments" and then "Stock Search"). A large number of criteria can be specified, based on ranges for the values or minimum and maximum values. www.aol.com also provides stock screening for its subscribers, allowing up to 12 variables. StockTools Super Stock Screener, www.stocktools.com, offers both fundamental and technical screening. Investors can specify a number of technical criteria, such as historic trading price ranges and 52-week highs and lows as well as fundamental criteria such as growth rates, yield, and so forth. A well-known site with considerable content is MSN Moneycentral Investor, found at http://moneycentral.msn.com.

The Role of the Security Analyst Stocks are, of course, selected by both individual investors and institutional investors. Rather than do their own security analysis, individual investors may choose to rely on the recommendations of the professionals. An important part of the institutional side of stock selection and recommendation is the role of the security analyst (also called equity analyst or simply analyst) in the investment process. There are perhaps 4,000 "Wall Street" analysts, called **sell-side analysts**, covering, to various degrees, some 9,000 actively traded stocks in the United States (some stocks are heavily covered, whereas others are covered by only one or two analysts, and some stocks are not covered at all). On the other hand, there are more than 20,000 **buy-side analysts** employed by money management firms (such as pension funds, mutual funds, and investment advisers). These analysts search for equities for their firms to buy and hopefully profit from.

The typical sell-side security analyst works for an institution concerned with stocks and other financial assets, but the analyst's product is often available to the individual investor in the form of brokerage reports (primarily, full-service brokerage firms) and newsletters, reports from recommendation services, and so forth. Some analysts work for independent firms such as Value Line and Standard and Poor's. When considering stock selection, investors must understand the role of the analyst, and why there has been so much controversy concerning analysts.

Sell-Side Analysts
"Wall Street" analysts who cover stocks and make recommendations on them to investors

Buy-Side Analysts
Analysts employed by financial firms to search for equities for their firms to buy as investment opportunities

[9] See Peter Lynch, "The Stock Market Hit Parade," *Worth* (July/August 1994): p. 32.

A typical analyst report contains a description of the company's business, how the analyst expects the company to perform, earnings estimates, price estimates, or price targets for the year ahead, and recommendations as to buy, hold, or sell. Investors should be wary of any analyst report in which the analyst cannot satisfactorily explain what a company does. Analysts should do more than simply recommend companies expected to grow rapidly.

The central focus of the analysts' job is to attempt to forecast a specific company's price, growth rate, or return. Alternatively, it can involve the inputs to a valuation model such as those we considered in Chapter 10. Investors interested in stock selection use valuation models, and for inputs they can utilize their own estimates or, in many cases, use those provided by analysts. The most important part of what the analyst produces in this regard is the estimate of a company's earnings.

What sources of information do analysts use in evaluating common stocks for possible selection or selling? The major sources of information are presentations from the top management of the companies being considered, annual reports, and Form 10-K reports that must be filed by the companies with the Securities and Exchange Commission (SEC). According to surveys of analysts, they consistently emphasize the long term over the short term. Variables of major importance in their analysis include expected changes in earnings per share, expected return on equity (ROE), and industry outlook. An important point to note here is that the security analysis process used by financial analysts—in terms of information sources and processes—is the same one that we will learn in Part IV.

One of the most important responsibilities of an analyst is to forecast earnings per share for particular companies because of the widely perceived linkage between expected earnings and stock returns (explained in Chapter 15). Earnings are critical in determining stock prices, and what matters is a company's *expected* earnings (what is referred to on Wall Street as earnings estimates). Therefore, the primary emphasis in fundamental security analysis is on expected earnings, and analysts spend much of their time forecasting earnings. Regardless of the effort expended by analysts, investors should be cautious in accepting analysts' forecasts of earnings per share (EPS). Analysts' forecasts are typically overly optimistic. Errors can be large and occur often.

Interestingly, despite modern technology and advances in the understanding of stocks and financial markets, analysts' estimates have not become more accurate. David Dreman, a money manager and financial writer discussed below, has found that errors in analysts' forecasts are high across a wide range of industry groups. Using quarterly earnings estimates, Dreman found an average error of 44 percent on an annual basis. Less than one-third of the estimates were plus or minus 5 percent of the actual earnings announcements, and slightly less than half were within 10 percent plus or minus of the actual earnings announcements. This results in earnings surprises, a topic discussed later.

Empirical studies indicate that current expectations of earnings, as represented by the average of the analysts' forecasts, are incorporated into current stock prices. Perhaps more importantly, revisions in the average forecast for year-ahead earnings may have predictive ability concerning future stock returns. We will consider the related issues of consensus earnings estimates, "guidance" of forthcoming earnings by company management, preannouncements of earnings, whispers about earnings, and earnings surprises in Chapter 15.

Investors should carefully study a company's earnings, and estimates of earnings, before investing. Estimates are available at many major Web sites covering investing. Analyst estimates, for better or worse, are quite widely reported, and some aspects of their analysis are important despite the controversy about analysts explained in the next section. For example, in 2002, *Business Week* concluded in an article that analysts still have a major impact on the market, and therefore investors need to pay attention.[10] In connection with this article, StarMine (cited below) did an analysis that measures the impact that analysts have on stock prices when they change their recommendations.

Figure 11-4 shows the results of the StarMine analysis.[11] On the day of an upgrade by security analysts, stocks rise an average of 2.1 percent; following a downgrade, stocks decline an average of 5.4 percent. Downgrades are more prominent, because investors who trade stocks are more concerned with bad news. StarMine also reports that there is a continued drift in stock prices for several months following a change in recommendation. This suggests that investors can benefit by buying those stocks that are upgraded and shorting those that are downgraded.

Using the Internet

Consensus earnings estimates as well as brokerage recommendations can be found at **www.zacks.com** and at First Call, **www.firstcall.com**. Ratings of Wall Street analysts as to their earnings estimations and stock picking ability can be found at **www.bulldogresearch.com** and at **www.starmine. com**. Earnings estimates are easily available at many sites, including **www.quicken.com**, **www. bloomberg.com**, and **www.morningstar.com**.

The Controversy Surrounding Security Analysts In doing their job of analyzing and recommending companies, analysts supposedly present their recommendations in the form of "Buy," "Hold," and "Sell." However, until very recently investors who receive brokerage reports typically saw recommendations for specific companies as

Figure 11-4

Average percentage amount a stock moved in a single day following a change in analysts' recommendations, 1994–2002 (a) following an upgrade; (b) following a downgrade.

SOURCE: *StarMine Newsletter*, StarMine Web site, October 15, 2002. Reprinted by permission.

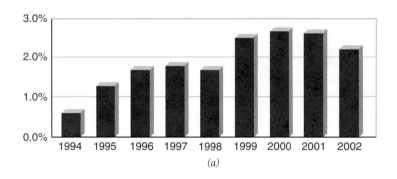

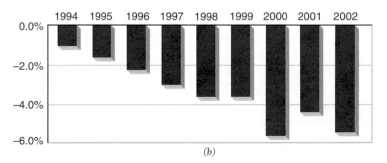

---

[10] "Don't Sell Street Analysts Short," *Business Week*, October 21, 2002.
[11] Based on information on the StarMine Web site, October, 2002.

either "buy" or "hold" or "speculative hold" or other words such as these. Traditionally, analysts were under great pressure to avoid the word "sell" from the companies they follow. One study reported that two-thirds of analysts surveyed felt that a negative recommendation on a company would severely impact their access to the company's management.

Analysts have also been under significant pressure from their own firms which are seeking to be the underwriter on lucrative stock and bond underwritings. The firms want the analyst to support the stock by making positive statements about it in the hopes of winning the investment banking business. This generates massive conflicts of interest, which have become widely discussed. Analysts lose their objectivity by being at least partly rewarded on the basis of investment banking business. Supposedly, reprisals by companies against brokerage firms, in terms of cutting off investment banking business, have often been widespread.

In 2001 to 2002, several articles appeared in the popular press that were less than flattering to analysts. The market declined sharply in 2000 and 2001, and investors discovered that analysts continued to recommend stocks even as their prices declined tremendously. Analysts rapidly became the focus of very intensive negative criticism because of the conflicts of interest with the investment banking side of their firms' business, and because their recommendations were found to be so faulty in many cases.

In mid-2002, the Attorney General of New York went to court to force Merrill Lynch, the nation's largest retail brokerage, to change the procedures followed by its analysts in rating stocks (some Merrill Lynch analysts reportedly sent email among themselves castigating some stocks that were being recommended by the firm to its clients). Merrill Lynch agreed to a $100 million fine to settle charges that its analysts were overly optimistic in their research recommendations in order to win investment banking business. Some other large firms followed suit in changing their practices, primarily because of this action.

Merrill Lynch in mid-2002 announced a new system of stock recommendations, with all stocks being rated either "buy," "neutral," or "sell." Its stock recommendations are to be tied to projections of total return and risk. The firm also intends to provide investors with more disclosure on when it changes the ratings on a company. At about the same time, Prudential Securities announced it was going to a system of "buy," "hold," and "sell." Other firms are expected to announce similar moves.

Merrill's changes were in line with new rules adopted by the New York Stock Exchange (NYSE) and Nasdaq in May 2002, having been approved by the SEC. These changes—forcing analysts to limit and disclose contacts with the investment banking side—were a direct result of the enormously negative criticism the brokerage industry has received as a result of the above-mentioned problems.

The SEC adopted new rules in 2002 that should allow investors to understand more thoroughly what analysts are saying and what conflicts of interest may still exist. These include:

- Clear indications of what analysts are saying, like "buy" or "sell"
- Reports must indicate the percentage of recommendations that are buy, hold, or sell
- Reports must show the author's track record
- Analysts must indicate for a stock when they initiated coverage and when they changed opinions
- Price targets for a stock are to be shown, and if changed, when
- Research must disclose any recent investment banking ties

Some Practical Advice

Despite all the negative criticism leveled at analysts recently, most of which is richly deserved, investors can use analysts' reports and information intelligently. Many analysts are quite good at analyzing industries, trends in the economy and various industries, and companies. They compile useful information, and often have good insights as to future prospects, because they have followed the industries and companies for years. Investors should use this information in conjunction with their own analysis. On the other hand, they should be skeptical of such items as earnings estimates, because analysts are typically overly optimistic, and they should ignore price targets and estimates of price one year from now, which are basically worthless.

It is now possible for investors to examine a free database, www.starmine.com, involving analysts and their stock recommendations. This site offers information that can help identify the best analysts for a stock or an industry based on their actual results.

It is also important to note that investors need not rely on Wall Street analysts for their recommendations and analysis. Some firms employ independent analysts to study companies, and the information from these firms is available to investors either by paid subscription, free in a library, or even free on a Web site. Three outstanding sources of independent information are:

- *The Value Line Investment Survey* (discussed in Chapter 15), one of the most famous sources of stock information for investors. Value Line has ranked stocks into five categories since 1965. It is available in printed and electronic format by subscription and widely available in libraries.
- Standard and Poor's *Outlook*, available by subscription and at libraries. A very informative weekly source of information.
- Morningstar, although best known for mutual funds, now analyzes and recommends individual stocks. Much information is available on its Web site.

SECTOR ROTATION

An active strategy that is similar to stock selection is group or sector rotation. This strategy involves shifting sector weights in the portfolio in order to take advantage of those sectors that are expected to do relatively better and avoid or deemphasize those sectors that are expected to do relatively worse. Investors employing this strategy are betting that particular sectors will repeat their price performance relative to the current phase of the business and credit cycle.

An investor could think of larger groups as the relevant sectors, shifting between cyclicals, growth stocks, and value stocks. It is quite standard in sector analysis to divide common stocks into four broad sectors: interest-sensitive stocks, consumer durable stocks, capital goods stocks, and defensive stocks. Each of these sectors is expected to perform differently during the various phases of the business and credit cycles. For example, interest-sensitive stocks would be expected to be adversely impacted during periods of high interest rates, and such periods tend to occur at the latter stages of the business cycle. As interest rates decline, the earnings of the companies in this sector—banks, finance companies, savings and loans, utilities, and residential construction firms—should improve.

Defensive stocks deserve some explanation. Included here are companies in such businesses as food production, soft drinks, beer, pharmaceuticals, and so forth that often are not hurt as badly during the down side of the business cycle as are other companies, because people will still purchase bread, milk, soft drinks, and so forth. As the economy worsens and more problems are foreseen, investors may move into these stocks for investment protection. These stocks often do well during the late phases of a business cycle.

Investors may view industries as sectors and act accordingly. For example, if interest rates are expected to drop significantly, increased emphasis could be placed on the interest-sensitive industries such as housing, banking, and the savings and loans. The defense industry is a good example of an industry in recent years that has experienced wide swings in performance over multiyear periods.

It is clear that effective strategies involving sector rotation depend heavily on an accurate assessment of current economic conditions. A knowledge and understanding of the phases of the business cycle are important, as is an understanding of political environments, international linkages among economies, and credit conditions both domestic and international. Obviously, an insight into the expected performance of various industries or sectors is also necessary.

Indirect Investing in Sectors   Investors can pursue the sector investing approach using mutual funds. For example, Invesco, a large mutual fund company, has offered sector funds for more than 12 years. Its sector funds now include worldwide communications, energy, financial services, technology, worldwide capital goods, environmental services, gold, health sciences, leisure, and utilities. Each sector fund contains 40 to 70 stocks, providing strong diversification within that sector. Invesco's Technology Sector Fund recorded an annualized 10-year average total return of 25.19 percent over the period 1990 to 1999.

There are now 600+ sector funds specializing in industry sectors. Real estate, utilities, and health care are three prominent sectors for funds. Morningstar, a provider of mutual fund information, has increased its coverage of sector listings. Sector funds are often at both the bottom and the top of the rankings for some period. For example, when technology was so hot, these sectors clearly dominated the list. However, the bottom performers also are often sector funds—for example, precious metal funds.

Sector investing in mutual funds offers the potential of large returns, but the risks are also large. It is also possible to construct a balanced mutual fund portfolio consisting solely of sector funds. For example, an investor could include blue chips, technology stocks, real estate stocks, financial stocks, natural resources, and utilities with six sector funds.

Industry Momentum and Sector Investing   Sector funds are particularly popular with momentum traders. **Momentum** in stock returns refers to the tendency of stocks that have performed well (poorly) to continue to perform well (poorly). Academic research has uncovered an intermediate (3 to 12 months) momentum in U.S. stock returns and attributed it to an industry effect. This suggests that strong (weak) industry performance is followed by strong (weak) industry performance over periods of months.

O'Neal has considered exploiting this momentum in stock prices by using actively-traded sector mutual funds.[12] He used Fidelity SelectPortfolios sector funds and found strong evidence of industry momentum. The difference between high and low portfolios averaged across 12 portfolio strategies was 8.6 percentage points on an annualized basis, and momentum appeared to be particularly strong for 12-month holding periods. These annualized differences in return support the evidence that industry momentum does exist.

Momentum   The tendency of stock prices to continue recent trends, up or down

Using the Internet

Sector performance can be found at www.smartmoney.com, using their "Sector Tracker." Different time periods can be specified.

[12] See Edward S. O'Neal, "Industry Momentum and Sector Mutual Funds," *Financial Analysts Journal*, 58, no. 4 (July/August 2000): pp. 37–49.

MARKET TIMING

Market timers attempt to earn excess returns by varying the percentage of portfolio assets in equity securities. One has only to observe a chart of stock prices over time to appreciate the profit potential of being in the stock market at the right times and being out of the stock market at the bad times.

When equities are expected to do well, timers shift from cash equivalents such as money market funds to common stocks. When equities are expected to do poorly, the opposite occurs. Alternatively, timers could increase the betas of their portfolios when the market is expected to rise and carry most stocks up, or decrease the betas of their portfolio when the market is expected to go down. One important factor affecting the success of a market timing strategy is the amount of brokerage commissions and taxes paid with such a strategy as opposed to those paid with a buy-and-hold strategy.

Mark Hulbert, publisher of a service that monitors the performance of investment advisory letters called the *Hulbert Financial Digest*, believes that the popularity of market timing follows a cycle of its own.[13] If the market is strongly up, market timing falls into disrepute, and buying and holding is the popular strategy. Following a severe market decline, however, market timing comes into vogue, and the buy-and-hold strategy is not popular.

Like many issues in the investing arena, the subject of market timing is controversial. Can some investors regularly time the market effectively enough to provide excess returns on a risk-adjusted basis? The only way to attempt to answer this question is to consider the available evidence on the subject, keeping in mind that market timing is a broad topic and that it is difficult to summarize all viewpoints.

Much of the empirical evidence on market timing comes from studies of mutual funds. A basic issue is whether fund managers increase the beta of their portfolios when they anticipate a rising market and reduce the beta when they anticipate a declining market. Several studies found no evidence that funds were able to time market changes and change their risk levels in response.

Chang and Lewellen examined the performance of mutual funds and found little evidence of any market timing ability. Furthermore, the average estimated down-market beta turned out to be slightly higher than the average estimated up-market beta. Overall, this study supported the conclusion that mutual funds do not outperform a passive investment strategy. This conclusion was also supported by Henriksson in a study of 116 mutual funds using monthly data. He found that mutual fund managers could not successfully employ strategies involving market timing, including those involving only large changes in the market.[14]

A well-known study of market timing was done by Sharpe in 1975, who showed that in switching between stocks and cash equivalents over a long period, a successful timer could certainly enhance returns, but the timer needed to be right seven times out of ten. A very recent study of the entire time period 1926 to 1999 concluded that for monthly market timing involving large-cap stocks or T-bills, "the investor would need to have a predictive accuracy, or average, of greater than 66 percent to outperform choices made from simply flipping a coin. As the holding period increases, the needed accuracy also increases."[15]

[13] See Mark Hulbert, "New Tool for Contrarians," *Forbes*, November 18, 1996, p. 298.

[14] Eric Chang and Wilbur Lewellen, "Market Timing and Mutual Fund Investment Performance," *Journal of Business*, 57, no. 1, part 1 (January 1984): 57–72. Roy D. Henriksson, "Market Timing and Mutual Fund Performance: An Empirical Investigation," *Journal of Business*, 57, no. 1, part 1 (January 1984): 73–96.

[15] Richard J. Bauer, Jr. and Julie R. Dahlquist, "Market Timing and Roulette Wheels," *Financial Analysts Journal*, 57, no. 1 (January/February 2001): 28–40. See also William F. Sharpe, "Likely Gains from Market Timing," *Financial Analysts Review*, 31, no. 2 (March/April 1975): 60–69.

As for recent evidence of market timing, newsletters that track money managers who use market timing to invest indicate that only about 40 percent of those tracked outperformed the S&P 500 Index in 2000.[16]

Considerable research now suggests that the biggest risk of market timing is that investors will not be in the market at critical times, thereby significantly reducing their overall returns. Investors who miss only a few key months may suffer significantly. For example, over a recent 40-year period, investors who missed the 34 best months for stocks would have seen an initial $1,000 investment grow to only $4,492 instead of $86,650. Even Treasury bills would have been a better alternative in this situation.

If you are still considering market timing as a strategy suitable for the average individual investor, think again, particularly after considering the following information. For the period 1986 to 1995, inclusive, returns on the S&P 500 Composite Index were:

Fully invested—annualized rate of return = 14.8 percent

Take out the 10 best days = 10.2 percent

Take out the 20 best days = 7.3 percent

Take out the 30 best days = 4.8 percent

Take out the 40 best days = 2.5 percent

According to another estimate, as Figure 11-5 shows, for the period 1980 to 2000, the value of $1 invested in the S&P 500 would have grown to $18.41. However, taking out the best 15 months of S&P performance, $1 would have grown to only $4.73, which would have been about the same return one could have earned from bonds yielding 8 percent a year. As one magazine summed up these statistics, "You gotta be in it to win it."[17]

Some Practical Advice

Available evidence today, as shown above, clearly suggests market timing will not work for most investors. Not only must you decide when to get out of stocks, you must also decide when to get back in stocks. Charles Ellis, in his well-known book about why investors are not likely to outperform the market, summed it up well: "Market timing is a wicked idea. Don't try it, ever."[18]

RATIONAL MARKETS AND ACTIVE STRATEGIES

One of the most significant developments in recent years is the proposition that securities markets are efficient and that rational asset–pricing models predominate. Investors are assumed to make rational, informed decisions on the basis of the best information available at the time. In a rational market, security prices accurately reflect investor expectations about future cash flows. This idea has generated considerable controversy concerning the analysis and valuation of securities because of its significant implications for investors. Regardless of how much (or how little) an investor learns about investments, and regardless of whether an investor ends up being convinced by the efficient markets literature, it is prudent to learn something about this idea early in one's study of investments.

Much evidence exists to support the basic concepts of market efficiency and rational asset pricing, and it cannot be ignored simply because one is uncomfortable with the idea or because it sounds too improbable. It is appropriate to consider this concept with

---

[16] See Carol Cropper, "It's Not All in the Timing," *Business Week*, March 5, 2001, p. 112.
[17] Statistics and quote are from John Curran, "The Money Fund Trap," *Mutual Funds*, April 2001, p. 14.
[18] See Charles Ellis, *Winning the Loser's Game*, McGraw-Hill, 3rd edition, 1998, p. 10.

Figure 11-5

Growth of $1.00 in the S&P 500 Index over the period 1980–2000 assuming investment during the entire period versus leaving out the best 15 months of performance.

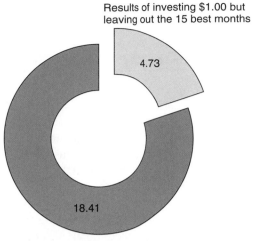

Results of investing $1.00 but leaving out the 15 best months

4.73

18.41

Results of investing $1.00 during the entire period

any discussion of active strategies designed to produce excess returns—that is, returns in excess of those commensurate with the risk being taken. After all, if the evidence suggests that active strategies are unlikely to be successful over time after all costs have been assessed, the case for a passive strategy becomes much more important.

As we will see in Chapter 12, the efficient market hypothesis is concerned with the assessment of information by investors. Security prices are determined by expectations about the future. Investors use the information available to them in forming their expectations. If security prices fully reflect all the relevant information that is available and usable, a securities market is said to be efficient. In the same vein, rational asset–pricing models use changes in valuation parameters to explain changes in equity valuations.

If the stock market is efficient, prices reflect their fair economic value as estimated by investors. Even if this is not strictly true, prices may reflect their approximate fair value after transaction costs are taken into account, a condition known as economic efficiency. In such a market, where prices of stocks depart only slightly from their fair economic value, investors should not employ trading strategies designed to "beat the market" by identifying undervalued stocks. Nor should they attempt to time the market in the belief that an advantage can be gained. Sector rotation also will be unsuccessful in a highly efficient market.

The implications of a rational market are extremely important for investors. They include one's beliefs about how to value securities in terms of the two approaches to selecting common stocks discussed below—the fundamental approach and the technical approach. This, in turn, encompasses questions about the time and effort to be devoted to these two approaches. Other implications include the management of a portfolio of securities. Again, in terms of the above discussion, should investors follow active or passive strategies in managing their equity portfolios? Efficient market proponents often argue that less time should be devoted to the analysis of securities for possible inclusion in a portfolio and more to such considerations as reducing taxes and transaction costs and maintaining the chosen risk level of a portfolio over time.

Suffice it to say that an intelligent investor must be aware of this issue and form some judgment about its implications if he or she is to formulate a reasonable investment strategy. A person's beliefs about market efficiency will have a significant impact on the type of stock strategy implemented. Investors are constantly being bombarded with reports of techniques and procedures that appear to offer above-average returns, thereby contradicting the idea that the market is so efficient that they should not attempt to outperform it. Intelligent investors examine such claims and strategies carefully before using them.

Approaches for Analyzing and Selecting Stocks

The two traditional and well-known approaches to analyzing and/or selecting common stocks are fundamental analysis and technical analysis. However, the significant amount of research in recent years on the concept of efficient markets has widespread implications for the analysis and valuation of common stock. Therefore, our discussion of common stocks is built around these approaches plus any implications from the efficient markets literature.

Traditionally, fundamental analysis has occupied the majority of resources devoted to the analysis of common stocks. All investors should understand the logic of, and rationale for, fundamental analysis. It deserves, and receives, careful consideration in Part IV, which is devoted to security analysis. The other approach to security analysis, technical analysis, is also analyzed in Part V. The efficient market concept has implications for both approaches as well as for portfolio management.

The two basic approaches, technical analysis and fundamental analysis, are described briefly here, followed by a consideration of efficient market concepts and implications. The fundamental approach is then developed in some detail in the remainder of this chapter, thereby setting the stage for Part IV (Chapters 13, 14, and 15), which analyze the fundamental approach in a specific, recommended order.

TECHNICAL ANALYSIS

One of the two traditional strategies long available to investors is technical analysis, which is examined in detail in Chapter 16. In fact, technical analysis is the oldest strategy and can be traced back to at least the late nineteenth century.

Technical Analysis
The search for identifiable and recurring stock price patterns

The term **technical analysis** refers to the methodology of forecasting fluctuations in securities prices. This methodology can be applied either to individual securities or to the market as a whole (e.g., forecasting a market index such as the Dow Jones Industrial Average).

The rationale behind technical analysis is that the value of a stock is primarily a function of supply and demand conditions. These conditions in turn are determined by a range of factors, from scientific to opinions and guesses. The market uses all of these factors in determining the changes in prices. These prices will move in trends that may persist, with changes in trends resulting from changes in supply and demand conditions. Technicians seek to detect, and act upon, changes in the direction of stock prices.

In its purest sense, technical analysis is not concerned with the underlying economic variables that affect a company or the market; therefore, the causes of demand and supply shifts are not important. The basic question to be asked can be stated as follows: Does excess demand or supply exist for a stock, and can such a condition be detected by studying either the patterns of past price fluctuations or the movements of certain technical indicators or rules? Technicians study the market using graphical charting of price changes, volume of trading over time, and a number of technical indicators.

Momentum Investing
Investing on the basis of recent movements in the price of stock

Momentum Strategies One of the most popular investing strategies relies heavily on price trends. **Momentum investing** involves buying companies whose earnings or stock prices are rising, with heavy emphasis on price momentum. The basic premise of momentum investing is that if a stock has outperformed the market over some recent period, it is likely to continue to do so. Momentum investing is a short-run approach. For example, stocks that are strong for the prior six months tend to outperform the market only over the next 6 to 12 months.

In today's market, managers have varied the technique to include buying (selling) companies with positive (negative) earnings surprises and earnings estimate revisions as part of a momentum strategy (and they may not use the term "momentum").

Example 11-4   Rite-Aid Corp. was a momentum stock, rising from $15 in 1996 to $50 in early 1999. At $37, in March 1999, Rite-Aid sold for a P/E of 48 (using trailing earnings). When Rite-Aid warned that its fourth quarter fiscal earnings would be significantly lower, it declined to $22.5 in one day. The momentum ride was over, and investors bailed out.[19]

According to a survey done by Merrill Lynch on fund managers' styles that covers a decade, momentum (in various forms) was the most popular style, with more than half the managers using estimate revision and earnings surprises forms and 40 percent using earnings momentum. Only 25 percent used price-to-book value.

The *Value Line Investment Survey*, the largest investment advisory service available to investors (and discussed in Chapter 15), ranks stocks on the basis of both price and earnings momentum, and *Value Line* has the best 15-year ranking in the *Hulbert Financial Digest*. According to Hulbert, the best-performing investment advisory letters over the last 10 and 5 years, respectively, rely heavily on price momentum.[20]

According to Hulbert, such an approach also seems to work with mutual funds. Investors should buy those funds showing the strongest relative strength or momentum. Hulbert notes that investment advisory letters that recommend those mutual funds with the greatest momentum have performed better than the market as a whole.

FUNDAMENTAL ANALYSIS

Fundamental Analysis
The study of a stock's
value using basic data
such as earnings, sales,
risk, and so forth

Fundamental analysis is based on the premise that any security (and the market as a whole) has an intrinsic value, or the true value as estimated by an investor. This value is a function of the firm's underlying variables, which combine to produce an expected return and an accompanying risk. By assessing these fundamental determinants of the value of a security, an estimate of its intrinsic value can be determined. This estimated intrinsic value can then be compared to the current market price of the security. Similar to the decision rules used for bonds in Chapter 17, decision rules are employed for common stocks when fundamental analysis is used to calculate intrinsic value.

In equilibrium, the current market price of a security reflects the average of the intrinsic value estimates made by investors. An investor whose intrinsic value estimate differs from the market price is, in effect, differing with the market consensus as to the estimate of either expected return or risk, or both. Investors who can perform good fundamental analysis and spot discrepancies should be able to profit by acting before the market consensus reflects the correct information.

BEHAVIORAL FINANCE IMPLICATIONS

Given the widespread discussion of market efficiency, investors sometimes overlook the issue of psychology in financial markets—that is, the role that emotions play. Particularly in the short run, investors' emotions affect stock prices, and markets, and those making investment decisions need to be aware of this.

---

[19] Information about Rite-Aid and the survey is based on Greg Ip, "Market Mass Times Velocity = Momentum," *The Wall Street Journal*, March 15, 1999, p. C1.
[20] See Mark Hulbert, "Mutual Momentum," *Forbes*, June 3, 1996, p. 178. This discussion of momentum investing is indebted to that article.

Behavioral Finance
The study of investment behavior, based on the belief that investors may act irrationally

Behavioral finance is a hot topic in investing today. Whereas traditional economics is built on the proposition that investors act rationally on the basis of utility theory, behavioral finance recognizes that investors can, and do, behave irrationally. Markets overreact, both up and down. Investors are motivated by numerous "irrational" forces, such as overconfidence, regrets about decisions, aversion to losses, and so forth. This means that careful attention to past trends and similar information can be beneficial. Unfortunately, despite several promising research findings, behavioral finance currently does not have a unifying theory that ties everything together.

Clear recognition of the impact of behavioral finance came in 2002 with the awarding of the Nobel prize in Economics to Daniel Kahneman, a Princeton psychologist, and to Vernon Smith of George Mason University, whose economic experiments are at odds with the efficient market hypothesis. Furthermore, the last two John Bates Clark medals in economics (awarded every two years) have gone to behavioralists.

David Dreman, a money manager and columnist for *Forbes*, has been a leading proponent of behavioral finance. He particularly espouses the "investor overreaction hypothesis," which states that investors overreact to events in a predictable manner, overvaluing the best alternatives and undervaluing the worst. Premiums and discounts are the result, and eventually these situations reverse as assets regress toward the mean or average valuation.

Contrarian Investing
Assuming investing positions currently out of favor

This behavior has led Dreman to his "**contrarian investing**" philosophy, which involves taking positions that are currently out of favor. For example, in 1998, growth investing was much more profitable than value investing (both concepts are explained below), but Dreman continued to recommend stocks that looked promising on a value basis on the assumption that value stocks would once again excel.[21] And Dreman is famous for recommending that investors buy the low P/E ratio stocks (which are often out of favor) rather than the often currently popular high P/E ratio stocks. We will discuss this strategy in Chapter 12.

A Framework for Fundamental Analysis

Under either of these fundamental approaches, an investor will obviously have to work with individual company data. Does this mean that the investor should plunge into a study of company data first and then consider other factors such as the industry within which a particular company operates or the state of the economy, or should the reverse procedure be followed? In fact, each of these approaches is used by investors and security analysts when doing fundamental analysis. These approaches are referred to as the "top-down" approach and the "bottom-up" approach.

BOTTOM-UP APPROACH TO FUNDAMENTAL ANALYSIS

Bottom-Up Approach
Approach to fundamental analysis that focuses directly on a company's fundamentals

With the **bottom-up approach**, investors focus directly on a company's basics, or fundamentals. Analysis of such information as the company's products, its competitive position, and its financial status leads to an estimate of the company's earnings potential and, ultimately, its value in the market.

Considerable time and effort are required to produce the type of detailed financial analysis needed to understand even relatively small companies. The emphasis in this ap-

---

[21] Dreman has published a book called *Contrarian Investment Strategies: The Next Generation*, by Simon and Schuster. He also started a new journal, *The Journal of Psychology and Financial Markets*.

proach is on finding companies with good long-term growth prospects, and making accurate earnings estimates. To organize this effort, bottom-up fundamental research is often broken into two categories, growth investing and value investing.

Value versus Growth   Growth stocks carry investor expectations of above-average future growth in earnings and above-average valuations as a result of high price/earnings ratios. Investors expect these stocks to perform well in the future, and they are willing to pay high multiples for this expected growth. Recent examples include Microsoft, Cisco Systems, and Intel.

Value stocks, on the other hand, feature cheap assets and strong balance sheets. Value investing can be traced back to the value-investing principles laid out by the well-known Benjamin Graham, who coauthored a famous book on security analysis in the 1930s that has been the foundation for many subsequent security analysts.

Example 11-5   David Dreman, mentioned above, is one of the best-known value investors. He emphasizes buying stocks with low P/E ratios, because such stocks represent good value. His P/E ratio approach is discussed in more detail in Chapter 12.

Growth stocks and value stocks tend to be in vogue over different periods, and the advocates of each camp prosper and suffer accordingly. For example, value investing dominated from 1981 through 1988, but lagged for the next three years through 1991 as growth stock investing returned to favor. Much of 1992, however, saw rough going for growth stocks. On the other hand, growth stock investing dominated value investing in 1998, and this continued in 1999, which was the worst year for value investing in many years. In 2000, on the other hand, dot-com and other technology stocks experienced very volatile periods, and value stocks made a strong comeback, completely dominating growth stocks, which collapsed.

In many cases, bottom-up investing does not attempt to make a clear distinction between growth and value. Many companies feature strong earnings prospects and a strong financial base or asset value, and therefore have characteristics associated with both categories. This may be quite appropriate in today's investing world, as Box 11-1 points out. It raises the issue of whether style (growth vs. value) really matters very much anymore.

TOP-DOWN APPROACH TO FUNDAMENTAL ANALYSIS

Top-Down Approach
Approach to
fundamental analysis
that proceeds from
market/economy to
industry/sector

The **top-down approach** is the opposite to the bottom-up approach. Investors begin with the economy and the overall market, considering such important factors as interest rates and inflation. They next consider future industry prospects, or sectors of the economy that are likely to do particularly well (or particularly poorly). Finally, having decided that macro factors are favorable to investing, and having determined which parts of the overall economy are likely to perform well, individual companies are analyzed.

There is no "right" answer to which of these two approaches to follow. However, fundamental analysis can be overwhelming in its detail, and a structure is needed. This text takes the position that the better way to proceed in fundamental analysis is the top-down approach: First, analyze the overall economy and securities markets to determine if now is a good time to commit additional funds to equities; second, analyze industries and sectors to determine which have the best prospects for the future; and finally, analyze in-

Growth vs. Value: Does Style Matter?

During the late '90s growth-stock bonanza, telecom-equipment maker Tellabs surged from $17 to $70 in less than a year and sold for more than 65 times earnings. Then came what CEO Michael Birck likes to call the telecom industry's "nuclear winter," and you could pick up shares of his company for $7. That's when things got really weird: Birck was invited to a New York conference to address a group of value investors.

Michael Birck, meet Marty Whitman. The fact that the venerable deep-value manager invited Birck to speak at his annual Third Avenue investors' conference is just the latest sign that the line between growth and value is starting to blur. Qwest, Lucent, and JDS Uniphase are now components of the S&P 500/Barra Value Index. Growth managers are snapping up shares of Berkshire Hathaway and Boeing, while top value manager Bill Nygren of Oakmark Select is buying troubled growth stocks such as AOL Time Warner.

Is style going out of style? Traditionally, value investments are stocks with low price/book ratios, and growth stocks are—well, it depends whom you ask. For disciplined growth investors, a good growth stock prospect might have a high P/E but an even higher growth rate. Since growth stock valuations returned from the late '90s stratosphere, however, that distinction has come to mean less and less. At the end of November, the price/book ratio for the Russell 3000 Growth index was 4.04, versus 1.83 for the value index. At its peak in August 2000, the growth index's price/book ratio was 12.3, while the Russell 3000 Value price/book stood at 3.01.

The result: Growth and value managers are stepping on each other's toes. Shares in Lehman Brothers are held by an equal number of growth and value funds, according to Morningside.

Citigroup is owned by 283 growth funds and 271 value funds, while IBM is owned by 189 growth funds and 172 value funds.

"Everything that was a growth company three years ago is now a value company," says John Carr, a vice president of research shop H.C. Wainwright & Co. Economics.

"But they're the same companies, and they have the same business."

Some fund managers say they wouldn't mind if growth and value labels were relegated to the great financial glossary in the sky. In many cases, managers don't claim to subscribe to one philosophy or the other, but they find themselves categorized—and then accused of "style drift" when they don't fit neatly in the box. The top-performing Fairholme fund, for example, "has changed categories a few times," says comanager Larry Pitkowsky, "but we don't spend a lot of time thinking about it. Our philosophy never changes, despite the fact that our style category changes." Investing is all about buying something for less than you think it's worth, he says, and growth and value are always part of the equation: "We're always trying to buy dollar bills for 50 cents." Chris Davis, a portfolio manager at the Davis Funds, recently wrote in a trade magazine that the growth/value distinction is an "unnecessary categorization" that deludes investors into believing they're diversified and needlessly limits fund managers to a narrow universe of stocks.

Of course, it's not likely the growth/value dichotomy will simply go away. Investors like the distinction for many reasons, including the hope that owning funds of both styles will help diversify their portfolios, as well as the simple fact that different philosophies appeal to different temperaments: Some people like the speed of Porsches, others like reliable Hondas. Many investors believe that, over the long term, value outperforms growth. In 1992, economists Eugene Fama and Kenneth French found that stocks with the lowest price/book ratios beat stocks with the highest ratios, without additional risk.

But Tim Loughran, a finance professor at the University of Notre Dame, says the Fama-French findings don't mean much for most investors. He argues that value stocks' strong showing in the study was due to their January performance. Thanks to tax-loss selling, the shares trade close to their bid prices in December and close to ask prices in January. Take this "January Effect" out of the equation and there's no statistically significant difference between value and growth. "If I remove one month, it shouldn't have an effect," Loughran says. "But it does." He says that for the largest 20 percent of firms, there's no difference in performance between value and growth with or without January.

Loughran's work may raise a few eyebrows at style-conscious fund shops, but it's not news to Warren Buffett. In 1992, Buffett wrote to Berkshire Hathaway shareholders, "Many investment professionals see any mixing of [value and growth] as a form of intellectual cross-dressing. We view this as fuzzy thinking. . . . In our opinion, the two approaches are joined at the hip."

That doesn't mean the growth/value distinction should be tossed altogether. The terms, Carr says, should be redefined. He believes stocks could be more usefully described in terms of cyclical versus defensive, variability of earnings, or degrees of financial leverage. "Cyclical stocks go up and down because of sensitivity to interest rates and monetary policy, and cyclical stocks are generally associated with value," Carr says. If a company's earnings are independent of the economy, that makes a stock more valuable and more associated with growth, he adds. "True growth stocks shouldn't depend on interest rates." This way, he argues, it's easier to find agreement on which category stocks belong in, and investors can avoid the confusion that results when value and growth investors lay claim to the same stock based on price/book "or some other random definition."

SOURCE: Eleanor Laise, "Growth vs. Value: Does Style Matter?" pp. 29–30. Reprinted by permission of *SmartMoney*. Copyright © 2003 by *SmartMoney*. *SmartMoney* is a joint publishing venture of Dow Jones & Company, Inc. and Hearst Communications, Inc. All rights reserved worldwide.

dividual companies. Using this structure, the valuation models presented in Chapter 10 can be applied successively at each of the three levels.

Thus, the preferred order for fundamental security analysis used here is (1) the economy and market, (2) the industry/sector, and (3) the company. This approach is used in Part IV, which explains fundamental security analysis in detail. Here we consider only the justification for this approach.

Economy/Market Analysis It is very important to assess the state of the economy and the outlook for primary variables such as corporate profits and interest rates. Investors are heavily influenced by these variables in making their everyday investment decisions. If a recession is likely, or under way, stock prices will be heavily affected at certain times during the contraction. Conversely, if a strong economic expansion is under way, stock prices will be heavily affected, again at particular times during the expansion. Thus, the status of economic activity has a major impact on overall stock prices. It is, therefore, very important for investors to assess the state of the economy and its implications for the stock market.

In turn, the stock market impacts each individual investor. Investors cannot very well go against market trends. If the market goes up (or down) strongly, most stocks are carried along. Company analysis is likely to be of limited benefit in a year such as 1974, when the stock market was down 25 percent. Conversely, almost all investors did well in 1995 regardless of their specific company analysis, because the market was up about 37 percent as measured by the S&P 500.

Example 11-6 Perhaps the best example of the importance of the market to investors is the period 1995 to 1999, the greatest five-year period of stock performance in U.S. history. The S&P returned an average of 28.7 percent a year, with each of the five years returning more than 20 percent. Nasdaq experienced even better performance, roughly 40 percent per year during this period. Many investors enjoyed tremendous growth in their portfolios, and in their wealth, during this astounding period of market performance.

Another indication of the importance of the economy/market on common stocks is the impact on the earnings for a particular company. Available evidence suggests that from one-fourth to one-half of the variability in a company's annual earnings is attributable to the overall economy (plus some industry effect).

The economy also significantly affects what happens to various industries. One has only to think of the effects of import quotas, record high interest rates, and so forth, to see why this is so. Therefore, economy analysis must precede industry analysis.

Industry/Sector Analysis After completing an analysis of the economy and the overall market, an investor can decide if it is a favorable time to invest in common stocks. If it is, the next step should be industry or sector market analysis. King identified an industry factor as the second component (after market movements) affecting the variability in stock returns.

Individual companies and industries tend to respond to general market movements, but the degree of response can vary significantly. Industries undergo significant movements over both relatively short and relatively long periods. Industries will be affected to various degrees by recessions and expansions. For example, the heavy goods industries will be severely affected in a recession. (Examples include the auto and steel industries in the 1981 to 1982 recession.) Consumer goods will probably be much less affected during such a contractionary period. During a severe inflationary period such as the late 1970s and very early 1980s, regulated industries such as utilities were severely hurt by their inability to pass along all price increases. Finally, new "hot" industries emerge from time to time and enjoy spectacular (if short-lived) growth. Examples include synthetic fuels and genetic engineering.

Company Analysis Although the first two steps are important and should be done in the indicated order, great attention and emphasis should be placed on company analysis. Security analysts are typically organized along industry lines, but the reports that they issue usually deal with one (or more) specific companies.

The bottom line for companies, as far as most investors are concerned, is earnings per share. There is a very close relationship between earnings and stock prices, and for this reason, most attention is paid to earnings. Dividends, after all, are paid out of earnings. The dividends paid by companies are closely tied to earnings, but not necessarily the current quarterly (or even annual) earnings.

A number of factors are important in analyzing a company. However, because investors tend to focus on earnings and dividends, we need to understand the relationship between these two variables and between them and other variables. We also need to consider the possibilities of forecasting earnings and dividends.

Because dividends are paid out of earnings, we will concentrate on earnings in our discussion of company analysis in Chapter 15. Earnings are the real key to the fundamental analysis of a common stock. A good understanding of earnings is vital if an investor is to understand, and perform, fundamental analysis.

THE FRAMEWORK FOR FUNDAMENTAL ANALYSIS IN PERSPECTIVE

It is useful to summarize the framework for fundamental analysis we are using because three chapters Part IV (Chapters 13, 14, and 15) are based on this framework.

Figure 11-6 depicts the fundamental valuation process. We should examine the economy and market first, then industries, and finally individual companies. Fundamental valuation is usually done within the context of a present value model, primarily the dividend discount model, or a multiplier (P/E ratio) model. In either case, the two components of the value of any security being examined are (1) the expected stream of benefits, either earnings or dividends, and (2) the required rate of return (discount rate)—alternatively, the multiplier or P/E ratio. Investors should concentrate on these two factors as they systematically proceed through the three levels of analysis: economy/market, industry/sector, and company.

Figure 11-6

A framework
for fundamental
security analysis.

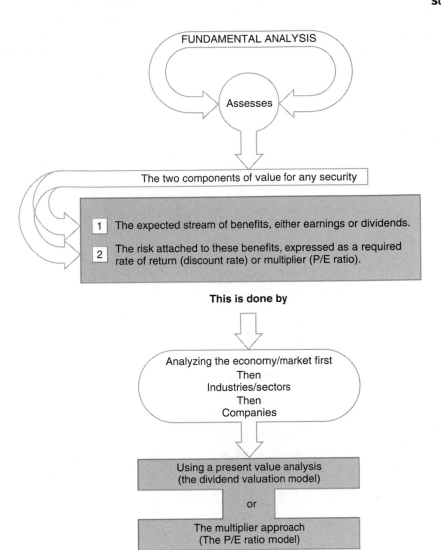

FUNDAMENTAL ANALYSIS

Assesses

The two components of value for any security

1 The expected stream of benefits, either earnings or dividends.

2 The risk attached to these benefits, expressed as a required
   rate of return (discount rate) or multiplier (P/E ratio).

This is done by

Analyzing the economy/market first
Then
Industries/sectors
Then
Companies

Using a present value analysis
(the dividend valuation model)

or

The multiplier approach
(The P/E ratio model)

Summary

▶ Market risk is the single most important risk affecting the price movements of common stocks.

▶ For well-diversified portfolios, market effects account for 90 percent and more of the variability in the portfolio's return.

▶ The required rate of return for a common stock, or any security, is defined as the minimum expected rate of return needed to induce an investor to purchase the stock.

▶ The required rate of return for any investment opportunity can be expressed as the sum of the risk-free rate of return and a risk premium.

▶ The trade-off between the required rate of return and risk is linear and upward sloping, which means that the required rate of return increases as the risk, measured by beta, increases.

▶ If the market is totally efficient, no active strategy should be able to beat the market on a risk-adjusted basis, and, therefore, a passive strategy may be superior.

▶ Passive strategies include buy-and-hold and the use of index funds.

▶ Pursuit of an active strategy assumes that investors possess some advantage relative to other market participants.

▶ Active strategies include stock selection, sector rotation, and market timing.

▶ The efficient market hypothesis, which states that current stock prices reflect information quickly and without bias, has implications for all stock investors.

▶ There are two traditional and well-known approaches to analyzing and/or selecting common stocks: fundamental analysis and technical analysis.

▶ The rationale behind technical analysis is that stock prices will move in trends that may persist and that these changes can be detected by analyzing the action of the market price itself.

▶ Momentum investing involves buying companies whose earnings or stock prices are rising, with heavy emphasis on price momentum.

▶ Fundamental analysis is based on the premise that any security (and the market as a whole) has an intrinsic value that is a function of the firm's underlying variables. This estimated intrinsic value can then be compared to the current market price of the security.

▶ Behavioral finance recognizes that investors can, and do, behave irrationally. Markets overreact, both up and down.

▶ Fundamental security analysis can be done following a bottom-up approach or a top-down approach.

▶ The bottom-up approach focuses directly on the individual company. Growth stocks carry investor expectations of above-average future growth in earnings and above-average valuations as a result of high price/earnings ratios. Value stocks, on the other hand, feature cheap assets and strong balance sheets.

▶ The approach used in Part IV, the top-down approach, considers, in order: (1) the economy/market, (2) the industry/sector, and (3) the company.

Key Words

Asset allocation	Fundamental analysis	Risk premium
Behavioral finance	Momentum	Sell-side analysts
Bottom-up approach	Momentum investing	Technical analysis
Buy-side analysts	Required rate of return	Top-down approach
Contrarian investing		

Questions

11-1 What impact does the market have on well-diversified portfolios? What does this suggest about the performance of mutual funds?

11-2 How does an investor in common stocks reconcile the large variability in stock returns, and the big drops that have occurred, with taking a prudent position in owning a portfolio of financial assets?

11-3 Given the drastic—some would say unprecedented—drop in the prices of Japanese stocks, how can U.S. investors justify owning foreign stocks?

11-4 What is meant by the required rate of return? Explain your answer in the context of an investor considering the purchase of IBM shares.

11-5 What are the two components of the required rate of return?

11-6 Is there one required rate of return? If not, how many are there?

11-7 What is the shape of the trade-off between the required rate of return for a stock and its risk? Must this shape always prevail?

11-8 What is the required rate of return on the overall market?

11-9 Outline the rationale for passive strategies.

11-10 Describe three active strategies involving common stocks.

11-11 What are the major sources of information used by security analysts in evaluating common stocks?

11-12 How does the cross-sectional variation in common stock returns relate to the issue of stock selection?

11-13 What is meant by sector rotation? What is the key input in implementing effective strategies in sector rotation?

11-14 What does the evidence cited on market timing suggest about the likelihood of success in this area?

11-15 What is the basic idea behind the efficient market hypothesis?

11-16 What are the implications of the efficient market hypothesis to both stock selectors and market timers?

11-17 Identify and differentiate the two traditional approaches to analyzing and selecting common stocks.

11-18 What is the recommended framework for fundamental analysis? Is this a top-down or bottom-up approach?

11-19 How does this recommended framework relate to the discussion about the impact of the market on investors?

11-20 What is the relationship between fundamental analysis and intrinsic value?

Web Resources

For additional resources visit our dynamic Web site located at **www.wiley.com/college/jones**.

- *Active Struggle*—The case examines the difference between passive and active stock investment strategies implemented through mutual funds. The case develops and applies cost-adjusted total returns to help decide between investment strategies.
- Internet Exercises—This chapter considers different approaches to building an equity portfolio. The Web exercises will help you evaluate the pros and cons of these different approaches, using actual stock prices off the Internet.
  Exercise 1: Looks at Passive versus Active strategies.
  Exercise 2: Evaluates Analysts' picks.
  Exercise 3: Examines Market timing.
- Multiple Choice Self Test

Selected References

Burton Malkiel's book on index investing is a good source of information about an important strategy available to all investors.

Richard Evans and Burton Malkiel, *Earn More, Sleep Better: The Index Fund Solution*, 1999, Simon & Schuster.

For those investors interested in behavioral finance from a practical level, and contrarian strategies:

David Dreman, *Contrarian Investment Strategies: The Next Generation*, 1998, Simon & Schuster.

A well-known and popular book that discusses why most investors are destined to achieve no more than average results, and is highly recommended for all interested readers, is:

Charles Ellis, *Winning the Loser's Game*, 4th ed., McGraw-Hill, 2002.

chapter *12*

Market Efficiency

Chapter 12 considers the question of how quickly and accurately information about securities is disseminated in financial markets. The efficient market hypothesis is considered in detail, including various tests of market efficiency. The implications of market efficiency to investors are analyzed. Chapter 12 concludes with a careful consideration of the well-known anomalies that constitute possible exceptions to market efficiency.

AFTER READING THIS CHAPTER YOU WILL BE ABLE TO:

▶ Analyze the efficient market hypothesis (EMH) and recognize its impact on all aspects of investing.

▶ Discuss the EMH in each of its three forms: weak, semistrong, and strong.

▶ Understand how the EMH is tested and what the evidence has shown.

▶ Recognize the anomalies (exceptions to market efficiency) that have been put forward, and be in a position to know when and how you might use this evidence in your own investment strategies.

"If the markets aren't completely efficient, they're close to it!!!" (A quotation in 2002 from a long-time, well-known developer of stock-selection techniques—exclamation points added for emphasis).[1]

Why should you as an investor care if the market is efficient, an issue that has been debated vigorously by academics for many years? In an informationally efficient market, many traditional investing activities are suspect at best and useless at worst. Why? Because in a truly efficient market, it should be impossible to discriminate between a profitable investment and an unprofitable one given currently available information. Therefore, you carefully need to consider your investing activities, particularly with regard to how active or passive you are as an investor. Furthermore, if you are interested in a job in the securities business, you need to consider what a truly efficient market would mean. Your expected probability of "beating" the market as a portfolio manager is small; futhermore the value of the product of a typical security analyst may be very small.

The idea of an efficient market has generated tremendous controversy over the years, which continues today, and a number of participants refuse to accept it, at least as it applies to them. This is not surprising in view of the enormous implications that an efficient market has for everyone concerned with securities. Some market participants' jobs and reputations are at stake, and they are not going to accept this concept readily. Think of the large number of highly paid portfolio managers of actively managed mutual funds as well as other institutional portfolios—how would you expect them to react to the notion that they are unlikely to add value because the market is efficient?

Because of its significant impact and implications, the idea that markets are efficient deserves careful thought and study. Beginning investors should approach it with an open mind. The fact that some well-known market observers and participants reject or disparage this idea does not reduce its validity. Furthermore, the argument that the stock market is efficient is not going to disappear, because too much evidence exists to support this argument regardless of the counterarguments and exceptions to market efficiency that apparently continue to remain unexplained. The intelligent approach for investors, therefore, is to learn about it and from it.

First, we consider what an efficient market is. Although the concept of market efficiency can apply to all financial markets, we concentrate on the equities market. Next, we will sample the evidence that has accumulated in support of the concept of market efficiency, as well as some evidence of possible market anomalies (i.e., inefficiencies). We also consider the implications of efficient markets for investors, because after all that is the bottom line.

The Concept of an Efficient Market

WHAT IS AN EFFICIENT MARKET?

Investors determine stock prices on the basis of the expected cash flows to be received from a stock and the risk involved. Rational investors should use all the information they have available or can reasonably obtain. This information set consists of both known information and beliefs about the future (i.e., information that can reasonably be inferred). Regardless of its form, *information is the key to the determination of stock prices and therefore is the central issue of the efficient markets concept.*

---

[1] This quote is from Samuel Eisenstadt, the major player in the development of Value Line's famed stock-ranking system which is 40+ years old. See Steven T. Goldberg, "Civil Warriors," *Kiplinger's Personal Finance*, August 2002, p. 39.

Efficient Market (EM)
A market in which prices of securities quickly and fully reflect all available information

An **efficient market (EM)** is defined as one in which the prices of all securities quickly and fully reflect all available information about the assets. This concept postulates that investors will assimilate all relevant information into prices in making their buy and sell decisions. Therefore, the current price of a stock reflects:

1. All known information, including:
   - ❑ Past information (e.g., last year's or last quarter's earnings)
   - ❑ Current information as well as events that have been announced but are still forthcoming (such as a stock split).
2. Information that can reasonably be inferred; for example, if many investors believe that the Federal Reserve (Fed) will cut interest rates at its meeting next week, prices will reflect this belief before the actual event occurs.

To summarize, a market is efficient relative to any information set if investors are unable to earn abnormal profits (returns beyond those warranted by the amount of risk) by using that information set in their investing decisions.

❑ When investors speak of efficient capital markets, they are referring to the proposition that security prices fully reflect all available information.

The early literature on market efficiency made the assumption that market prices incorporated new information instantaneously. The modern version of this concept does not require that the adjustment be literally instantaneous, only that it occur very quickly as information becomes known. Given the extremely rapid dissemination of information in the United States through electronic communications equipment, with the Internet widely accessible to most investors, information is spread very quickly, almost instantaneously, to market participants with access to these sources. For individual investors without this access, important information can be received daily on radio and television (including specialized cable TV programs) or, at the latest, the following day in such sources as *The Wall Street Journal*.

The widespread use of the Internet in today's investing world means that investors have quick and cheap access to information on a continual basis. Numerous Web sites offer updated information during the day about the economy, the financial markets, and individual companies. Clearly, the Internet has made the market more efficient in the sense of how widely and quickly data are disseminated.

The concept that markets are efficient does not claim, or require, a perfect adjustment in price following the new information. Rather the correct statement involved with this concept is that the adjustment in prices resulting from information is "unbiased" (this means that the expected value of the adjustment error is zero—sometimes too large and at other times too small, but on average balancing out and correct). The new price does not have to be the new equilibrium price, but only an unbiased estimate of the final equilibrium price that will be established after investors have fully assessed the input of the information.

Figure 12-1 illustrates the concept of market efficiency for one company for which a significant event occurs that has an effect on its expected profitability. The stock is trading at $50 on the announcement date of the significant event—Day 0 in Figure 12-1 is the announcement date for the event. If the market is fully efficient, the price of a stock always reflects all available information. Investors will very quickly adjust a stock's price to its intrinsic (fair) value. Assume that the new fair value for the stock is $52. In an efficient market, an immediate increase in the price of the stock to $52 will occur, as represented by the solid line in Figure 12-1. Since, in our example, no additional new information occurs, the price of the stock will continue at $52.

Figure 12-1

The adjustment of stock prices to information: (*a*) if the market is efficient; (*b*) one possibility if the market is inefficent.

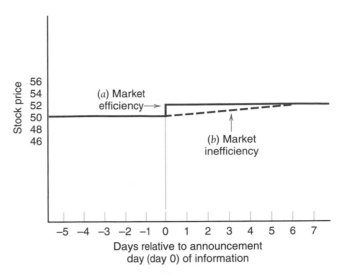

If the market adjustment process is inefficient, a lag in the adjustment of the stock prices to the new information will occur and is represented by the dotted line. The price eventually adjusts to the new fair value of $52 as brokerage houses disseminate the new information and investors revise their estimates of the stock's fair value. Note that the time it would take for the price to adjust is not known ahead of time—the dotted line is only illustrative.

WHY THE U.S. MARKET CAN BE EXPECTED TO BE EFFICIENT

If the type of market adjustment described above seems too much to expect, consider the situation from the following standpoint. It can be shown that an efficient market can exist if the following events occur:

1. A large number of rational, profit-maximizing investors exist who actively participate in the market by analyzing, valuing, and trading stocks. These investors are price takers; that is, one participant alone cannot affect the price of a security.
2. Information is costless and widely available to market participants at approximately the same time.
3. Information is generated in a random fashion such that announcements are basically independent of one another.
4. Investors react quickly and fully to the new information, causing stock prices to adjust accordingly.

These conditions may seem strict, and in some sense they are. Nevertheless, consider how closely they parallel the actual investments environment. There is no question that a large number of investors are constantly "playing the game." Both individuals and institutions follow the market closely on a daily basis, standing ready to buy or sell when they think it is appropriate. The total amount of money at their disposal at any one time is more than enough to adjust prices at the margin.

Although the production of information is not costless, for institutions in the investments business, generating various types of information is a necessary cost of business, and many participants receive it "free" (obviously, investors pay for such items indirectly in their brokerage costs and other fees). It is widely available to many participants at approximately the same time as information is reported on radio, television, and specialized communications devices now available to any investor willing to pay for such services.

Information is largely generated in a random fashion in the sense that most investors cannot predict when companies will announce significant new developments, when wars will break out, when strikes will occur, when currencies will be devalued, when important leaders will suddenly suffer a heart attack, and so forth. Although there is some dependence in information events over time, by and large announcements are independent and occur more or less randomly.

If these conditions are generally met in practice, the result is a market in which investors adjust security prices very quickly to reflect random information coming into the market. Prices reflect fully all available information. Furthermore, price changes are independent of one another and move in a random fashion. Today's price change is independent of the one yesterday because it is based on investors' reactions to new, independent information coming into the market today.

THE INTERNATIONAL PERSPECTIVE

A strong case can be made for U.S. financial markets being efficient based on the arguments above. What about foreign markets? Unlike the U.S. markets with its thousands of analysts, many foreign markets are much less analyzed. Information tends to be scarcer and less reliable in many cases. Of course, the large developed countries provide much information and tend to have companies that are well known and scrutinized. The less-developed countries have less-well developed flows of information, and the emerging markets may have significant gaps in information.

If there is less efficiency in the financial markets of other countries than in the United States, there should be some evidence of more success involving international investing. In fact, during the 1990s only 10 percent of U.S. mutual fund managers outperformed the Standard & Poor's (S&P 500) Composite Index, whereas 31 percent outperformed a European index, and during the last three years of the decade, about 51 percent outperformed an emerging markets index. As the managing partner of one investment firm stated, "There are greater inefficiencies in these markets, so we can take advantage of mispriced securities."[2]

Before leaping to the wrong conclusion, however, we should consider the lead and lag structure of market returns to see how markets are linked. Copeland and Copeland used the Dow Jones global industry indexes by region (the Americas, Europe, and the Pacific), by country, and by industry between 1972 and 1997 to examine the leads and lags among markets. They found strong contemporaneous relationships among regional exchanges that are open at the same time. They also found that the United States does have a statistically significant one-day lead over markets in Europe and Asia, but that no significant leads extend beyond one day—that is, all information adjustments occur within one day. The reason for the one-day lead by the United States presumably is that the driving information is generated in the Americas.[3]

FORMS OF MARKET EFFICIENCY

If, as discussed, the conditions necessary to produce market efficiency exist, exactly how efficient is the market and what does this imply for investors? We have defined an efficient market as one in which all information is reflected in stock prices quickly and fully.

---

[2] This information and quote are based on Harvey D. Shapiro, "Over There: The ABCs of Global Investing," *Individual Investor*, March 2000, p. 93.

[3] Maggie Copeland and Tom Copeland, "Leads, Lags, and Trading in Global Markets," *Financial Analysts Journal*, 54, No. 4 (July/August 1998): 70–80.

Thus, the key to assessing market efficiency is information. In a perfectly efficient market, security prices always reflect immediately all available information, and investors are not able to use available information to earn abnormal returns, because it already is impounded in prices. In such a market, every security's price is equal to its intrinsic (investment) value, which reflects all information about that security's prospects.

If some types of information are not fully reflected in prices or lags exist in the impoundment of information into prices, the market is less than perfectly efficient. In fact, the market is not perfectly efficient, and it is certainly not perfectly inefficient, so it is a question of degree. Therefore, we can think of market efficiency with respect to specific sets of information and ask if investors, on average, can earn abnormal returns using a set of information to buy and sell securities—in other words, exactly how efficient is the market?

Efficient Market Hypothesis (EMH) The idea that securities markets are efficient, with prices of securities reflecting their economic value

We define the major concept involved with efficient markets as the **efficient market hypothesis (EMH)**, which is simply the formal statement of market efficiency concerned with the extent to which security prices quickly and fully reflect available information. In 1970, Fama proposed dividing the hypothesis into three categories, and these have generally been used since that time in discussions of the EMH. These three classifications are illustrated in Figure 12-2.[4]

For purposes of our discussion, we will continue to follow these widely referred-to classifications. However, it should be noted that in a subsequent article some 20 years later, Fama refers to a "weaker and economically more sensible version of the efficiency hypothesis" which deals with prices reflecting information to the extent that it is not financially worthwhile to act on any information.[5] In this article, he changed the weak-form (described below) tests to be more general tests of return predictability, and he changed semistrong efficiency (described below) to studies of announcements, which is associated with what is often called event studies.

Market Data Primarily stock price and volume information

Weak Form That part of the efficient market hypothesis stating that prices reflect all price and volume data

1. Weak Form: One of the most traditional types of information used in assessing security values is **market data**, which refers to all past price (and volume) information. If security prices are determined in a market that is **weak-form** efficient, historical price and volume data should already be reflected in current prices and should be of no value in predicting future price changes. Since price data are the basis of technical analysis, technical analysis that relies on the past history of price information is of little or no value.

Figure 12-2

Cumulative levels of market efficiency and the information associated with each.

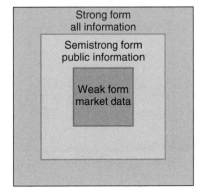

---

[4] See E. Fama, "Efficient Capital Markets: A Review of Theory and Empirical Work," *The Journal of Finance*, 25, no. 2 (May 1970): 383–417.
[5] See Eugene F. Fama, "Efficient Capital Markets: II," *The Journal of Finance*, 46 (December 1991): 1575–1617.

Tests of the usefulness of price data are called weak-form tests of the EMH. If the weak form of the EMH is true, past price changes should be unrelated to future price changes. In other words, a market can be said to be weakly efficient if the current price reflects all past market data. The correct implication of a weak-form efficient market is that the past history of price information is of no value in assessing future changes in price.[6]

2. Semistrong Form: A more comprehensive level of market efficiency involves not only known and publicly available market data, but all publicly known and available data, such as earnings, dividends, stock split announcements, new product developments, financing difficulties, and accounting changes. A market that quickly incorporates all such information into prices is said to show **semistrong-form** efficiency. Thus, a market can be said to be "efficient in the semistrong sense" if current prices quickly reflect all available information. Note that a semistrong efficient market encompasses the weak form of the hypothesis, because market data are part of the larger set of all publicly available information.

Tests of the semistrong EMH are tests of the speed of adjustment of stock prices to announcements of new information. In fact, most tests of the EMH are concerned with how quickly information is incorporated into security prices.

A semistrong efficient market implies that investors cannot act on new public information after its announcement and expect to earn above-average risk-adjusted returns. If lags exist in the adjustment of stock prices to certain announcements, and investors can exploit these lags and earn abnormal returns, the market is not fully efficient in the semistrong sense.

3. Strong Form: The most stringent form of market efficiency is the **strong form**, which asserts that stock prices fully reflect all information, public and nonpublic. The strong form goes beyond the semistrong form in considering the value of the information contained in announcements, whereas the semistrong form focuses on the speed with which information is impounded into stock prices. If the market is strong-form efficient, no group of investors should be able to earn, over a reasonable period of time, abnormal rates of return by using information in a superior manner.

A second aspect of the strong form has to do with private information—that is, information not publicly available because it is restricted to certain groups such as corporate insiders and specialists on the exchanges. At the extreme, the strong form holds that no one with private information can make money using this information. Needless to say, such an extreme belief is not held by many people.

Note that these three forms of market efficiency are cumulative. If one believes in semistrong-form efficiency, the weak form is also encompassed. Strong-form efficiency encompasses the weak and semistrong forms and represents the highest level of market efficiency.

Semistrong Form That part of the efficient market hypothesis stating that prices reflect all publicly available information

Strong Form That part of the efficient market hypothesis stating that prices reflect all information, public and private

Evidence on Market Efficiency

Because of the significance of the EMH to all investors, and because of the controversy that surrounds the EMH, we will examine some empirical evidence on market efficiency. Many studies have been done over the years and continue to be done. Obviously, we cannot begin to discuss them all, nor is it necessarily desirable to discuss several in detail. Our purpose here is to present an idea of how these tests are done, the scope of what has

[6] It is incorrect to state, as is sometimes done, that the best estimate of price at time $t + 1$ is the current (time t) price, because this implies an expected return of zero. The efficient market in no way implies that the expected return on any security is zero.

been done, and some results. The empirical evidence will be separated into tests of the three forms of market efficiency previously discussed.

The key to testing the validity of any of the three forms of market efficiency is the consistency with which investors can earn returns in excess of those commensurate with the risk involved based on the information set involved. Short-lived inefficiencies appearing on a random basis do not constitute evidence of market inefficiencies, at least in an economic (as opposed to a statistical) sense. Therefore, it makes sense to talk about an economically efficient market, where assets are priced in such a manner that investors cannot exploit any discrepancies and earn abnormal risk-adjusted returns after consideration of all transaction costs. In such a market, some securities could be priced slightly above their intrinsic values and some slightly below, and lags can exist in the processing of information, but again not in such a way that the differences can be profitably exploited after costs are considered.

Example 12-1

In the Copeland and Copeland study above, concerning how capital markets are linked, the authors examined a trading rule for one of the most significant lags found: Hong Kong versus the United States. Although much of the earnings adjustment occurred overnight, they found a statistically significant spread of up to 11.5 basis points that could be earned over and above a buy-and-hold strategy. They concluded that arbitrage might be possible if trading costs are lower than 11.5 basis points, but that this was not likely except for a trading house (and even that is not assured). Thus, these results suggest that although statistically significant differences may exist, the markets are probably economically efficient.

What about the time period involved? In the short run, investors may earn unusual returns even if the market is efficient. After all, you could buy a stock today and tomorrow a major discovery could be announced that would cause its stock price to increase significantly. Does this mean the market is inefficient? Obviously not; it means you are either very skillful or, more likely, very lucky. The question is can you and enough other investors do this a sufficient number of times in the long run to earn abnormal profits? Even in the long run, some people will be lucky given the total number of investors.

WEAK-FORM EVIDENCE

As noted, weak-form efficiency means that price data are incorporated into current stock prices. If prices follow nonrandom trends, stock-price changes are dependent; otherwise, they are independent. Therefore, weak-form tests involve the question of whether all information contained in the sequence of past prices is fully reflected in the current price.

The weak-form EMH is related to, but not identical with, an idea popular in the 1960s called the *random walk hypothesis*. If prices follow a random walk, price changes over time are random (independent).[7] The price change for today is unrelated to the price change yesterday, or the day before, or any other day. This is a result of the scenario described at the outset of the chapter. If new information arrives randomly in the market and investors react to it immediately, changes in prices will also be random.

One way to test for weak-form efficiency is statistically to test the independence of stock-price changes. If the statistical tests suggest that price changes are independent, the

---

[7] Technically, the random walk hypothesis is more restrictive than the weak-form EMH. Stock prices can conform to weak-form efficiency without meeting the conditions of a random walk. The random walk model specifies that successive returns are independent and are identically distributed over time.

implication is that knowing and using the past sequence of price information is of no value to an investor. In other words, trends in price changes, to the extent they exist, cannot be profitably exploited.

A second way to test for weak-form efficiency, after testing the pure statistical nature of price changes, is to test specific trading rules that attempt to use past price data. If such tests legitimately produce risk-adjusted returns beyond that available from simply buying a portfolio of stocks and holding it until a common liquidation date, after deducting all costs, it would suggest that the market is not weak-form efficient.

Statistical Tests of Price Changes Stock-price changes in an efficient market should be independent. Two simple statistical tests of independence are the serial correlation test and the signs test. The serial correlation test involves measuring the correlation between price changes for various lags, such as one day, two days, and so on, whereas the signs test involves classifying each price change by its sign, which means whether it was +, 0, or − (regardless of amount). Then the "runs" in the series of signs can be counted and compared to known information about a random series. If there are persistent price changes, the length of the runs will indicate it.

Fama studied the daily returns on the 30 Dow Jones industrial stocks and found that only a very small percentage of any successive price change could be explained by a prior change.[8] Serial correlation tests by other researchers invariably reached the same conclusion.

The signs test also supports independence. Although some "runs" do occur, they fall within the limits of randomness, since a truly random series exhibits some runs (several + or − observations in succession).

It should be noted that both tests produce some small positive relationships between yesterday's return and today's return. However, transaction costs tend to eliminate any potential profits that might exist.

Technical Trading Rules The statistical tests described above demonstrate that trends, other than those consistent with a random series, do not appear to exist in stock prices. However, technical analysts believe that such trends not only exist but can also be used successfully (technical analysis is discussed in Chapter 16). They argue that the statistical tests do not detect more sophisticated or realistic strategies. Because an almost unlimited number of possible technical trading rules exist, not all of them can be examined; however, if a sufficient number are examined and found to be ineffective, the burden of proof shifts to those who argue that such techniques have value. This is exactly the situation that prevails. Little evidence exists that a technical trading rule based solely on past price and volume data can, after all proper adjustments have been made, outperform a simple buy-and-hold strategy.

Again, it is important to emphasize the difference between statistical dependence and economic dependence in stock-price changes. The statistical tests discussed earlier detected some small amount of dependence in price changes. Not all of the series could be said to be completely independent statistically. However, they were economically independent in that one could not exploit the small statistical dependence that existed. After brokerage costs, excess returns disappear. After all, this is the bottom line for investors— can excess returns be earned with a technical trading rule after all costs are deducted?[9]

---

[8] E. Fama, "The Behavior of Stock Market Prices," *The Journal of Finance*, 38, No. 1 (January 1965): 34–105.
[9] Some studies have indicated that trading rules can produce profits after making the necessary adjustments. For a study that argues that trading rules may not be so readily implemented under actual conditions, see Ray Ball, S. P. Kothari, and Charles Wasley, "Can We Implement Research on Stock Trading Rules?" *The Journal of Portfolio Management* (Winter 1995): 54–63.

Weak-Form Contraevidence DeBondt and Thaler have tested an "overreaction hypothesis," which states that people overreact to unexpected and dramatic news events.[10] As applied to stock prices, the hypothesis states that, as a result of overreactions, "loser" portfolios outperform the market after their formation. DeBondt and Thaler found that over a half-century period, the loser portfolios of 35 stocks outperformed the market by an average of almost 20 percent for a 36-month period after portfolio formation. Winner portfolios earned about 5 percent less than the market. Interestingly, the overreaction seems to occur mostly during the second and third year of the test period. DeBondt and Thaler interpreted this evidence as indicative of irrational behavior by investors, or "overreaction."

This tendency for stocks that experience extreme returns to go through subsequent return reversals after portfolios are formed, and for the effect to be observed years after portfolio formation, has implications for market efficiency. Specifically, it indicates substantial weak-form inefficiencies, because DeBondt and Thaler are testing whether the overreaction hypothesis is predictive. In other words, according to their research, knowing past stock returns appears to help significantly in predicting future stock returns.

A recent study of the overreaction hypothesis, which adjusts for several potential problems, found an "economically important overreaction effect" even after adjusting for time variations in beta and for size effects.[11] Using five-year periods to form portfolios, the study revealed that extreme prior losers outperformed extreme prior winners by 5 to 10 percent per year over the following five years. The overreaction effect was considerably stronger for smaller firms (held predominantly by individuals) than for larger firms (held predominantly by institutions).

These studies present a challenge to the notion of market rationality, which was referred to in Chapter 11. However, these studies have also been challenged, and the final answers are not available.

SEMISTRONG-FORM EVIDENCE

Weak-form tests of both the statistical and the trading rule types are numerous and almost unanimous in their findings (after necessary corrections and adjustments have been made). Semistrong tests, on the other hand, are also numerous but more diverse in their findings. Although most of these studies support the proposition that the market adjusts to new public information very rapidly, some do not.

Semistrong-form tests are tests of the speed of price adjustments to publicly available information. The question is whether investors can use publicly available information to earn excess returns after proper adjustments. As noted earlier, Fama has changed the traditional notion of semistrong-form efficiencies to studies of announcements of various types, which involves event studies.

Event Study An empirical analysis of stock price behavior surrounding a particular event

This empirical research often involves an **event study**, which means that a company's stock returns are examined to determine the impact of a particular event on the stock price.[12] This methodology uses an index model of stock returns. An index model states that security returns are determined by a market factor (index) and a unique company factor. The single-index model from Chapter 8 is an example.

Company-unique returns are the residual error terms representing the difference between the security's actual return and that given by the index model. In other words,

[10] Werner F. M. DeBondt and Richard Thaler, "Does the Stock Market Overreact?" *The Journal of Finance* (July 1985): 793–805.
[11] See Navin Chopra, Josef Lakonishok, and Jay R. Ritter, "Measuring Abnormal Performance: Do Stocks Overact?" *The Journal of Financial Economics*, 31 (1992): 235–268.
[12] See Fama, "Efficient Capital Markets."

Abnormal Return
Return on a security
beyond that expected on
the basis of its risk

after adjusting for what the company's return should have been, given the index model, any remaining portion of the actual return is an **abnormal return** representing the impact of a particular event.

$$\text{Abnormal return} = AR_{it} = R_{it} - E(R_{it})$$

where

AR_{it} = the abnormal rate of return for security i during period t
R_{it} = the actual rate of return on security i during period t
$E(R_{it})$ = the expected rate of return for security i during period t based on the market model relationship

Cumulative Abnormal Return (CAR) The sum of the individual abnormal returns over the time period under examination

The **cumulative abnormal return (CAR)** is the sum of the individual abnormal returns over the period of time under examination and is calculated as

$$CAR_i = \sum_{t=1}^{n} AR_{it}$$

where

CAR_i = the cumulative abnormal return for stock i

Below we consider a sampling of often-cited studies of semistrong efficiency without developing them in detail. It is important to obtain a feel for the wide variety of information tested and the logic behind these tests. The methodology and a detailed discussion of the results are not essential for our purposes. At this point, we consider evidence that tends to support semistrong efficiency.

1. Stock splits. An often cited study of the long-run effects of stock splits on returns was done by Fama, Fisher, Jensen, and Roll (FFJR) and was the first event study.[13] A stock split adds nothing of value to a company and, therefore, should have no effect on the company's total market value. FFJR found that, although the stocks they studied exhibited sharp increases in price prior to the split announcement, abnormal (i.e., risk-adjusted) returns after the split announcement were very stable. Thus, the split itself did not affect prices. The results indicate that any implications of a stock split appear to be reflected in price immediately following the announcement, and not the event itself, which supports the semistrong form of market efficiency.[14]

Because some subsequent evidence produced conflicting results about stock splits, Byun and Rozeff reexamined the stock split issue in 2003. They used the most comprehensive sample to date—12,747 splits over the years 1927 to 1996—and two methods of measuring abnormal returns. Applied to splits 25 percent or larger, neither method found performance significantly different from zero. Based on their findings, the authors caution *against* abandoning the concept of market efficiency in favor of the view that "long-run abnormal performance pervades financial markets."

2. Dividend announcements. Several studies have examined the effects of dividend announcements. These studies are more difficult than some, because the dividend effects must be separated from other effects, and different approaches have been used to do this. For example, dividend announcements almost always appear with earnings announcements, which may contain earnings surprises.

[13] E. Fama, L. Fisher, M. Jensen, and R. Roll, "The Adjustment of Stock Prices to New Information," *International Economics Review*, 10, No. 1 (February 1969): 2–21.
[14] J. Byun and M. Rozeff, "Long-run Performance after Stock Splits: 1927 to 1996," *The Journal of Finance*, 58, No. 3 (June 2003): 1063–1086.

Several studies of dividend announcements have been done. The studies generally agree that the market appeared to adjust rapidly to new information.

3. Initial public offerings. A company that goes public creates an initial public offering, or IPO. Given the risk the underwriters face in trying to sell a new issue where the true price is unknown, the underwriters may be underpricing the new issue to ensure its rapid sale. The investors who are able to buy the IPO at its offering price may be able to earn abnormal profits, but if prices adjust quickly, investors buying the new issues shortly after their issuance should not benefit.

The evidence indicates that new issues purchased at their offering price yield abnormal returns to the fortunate investors who are allowed to buy the initial offering.[15] This is attributed to underpricing by the underwriters. Investors buying shortly after the initial offering, however, are not able to earn abnormal profits, because prices adjust very quickly to the "true" values.

4. Reactions to economic news. Investors are constantly given a wide range of information concerning both large-scale events and items about particular companies. Each of these types of announcements has been examined for the effects on stock prices.

One form of announcement involves economic news, such as money supply, real economic activity, inflation, and the Fed's discount rate. A study of these announcements found no impact on stock prices that lasted beyond the announcement day.[16] Even an analysis of hourly stock-price reactions to surprise announcements of money supply and industrial production found that any impact was accounted for within one hour.[17]

The "Heard on the Street" column in *The Wall Street Journal* is a daily feature highlighting particular companies and analysts' opinions on stocks. A study of public takeover rumors from the "Heard on the Street" column found that the market is efficient at responding to published takeover rumors.[18] Excess returns could not be earned on average by buying or selling rumored takeover targets at the time the rumor appeared. No significant excess returns occurred on the day the takeover rumor in *The Wall Street Journal* was published, although a positive cumulative excess return of approximately 7 percent occurs in the calendar month before the rumor appears in the "Heard on the Street" column.

STRONG-FORM EVIDENCE

The strong form of the EMH states that stock prices quickly adjust to reflect all information, including private information.[19] Thus, no group of investors has information that allows them to earn abnormal profits consistently, even those investors with monopolistic access to information. Note that investors are prohibited not from possessing monopolistic information, but from profiting from the use of such information. This is an important point in light of the studies of insider trading reported below.

One way to test for strong-form efficiency is to examine the performance of groups presumed to have access to "true" nonpublic information. If such groups can consistently earn above-average risk-adjusted returns, at least an extreme version of the strong form will not be supported. We will consider corporate insiders, a group that presumably falls into the category of having monopolistic access to information.

---

[15] For a review of this literature, see Roger Ibbotson, Jody Sindelar, and Jay Ritter, "Initial Public Offerings," *Journal of Applied Corporate Finance*, 1 (Summer 1988): 37–45.

[16] See Doug Pearce and Vance Roley, "Stock Prices and Economic News," *Journal of Business*, 59 (Summer 1985): 49–67.

[17] See Prom C. Jain, "Response of Hourly Stock Prices and Trading Volume to Economic News," *Journal of Business*, 61 (April 1988): 219–231.

[18] See John Pound and Richard Zeckhauser, "Clearly Heard on the Street: The Effect of Takeover Rumors on Stock Prices," *Journal of Business* (July 1990): 291–308.

[19] Fama, in his 1991 paper, refers to these tests as "tests for private information" instead of strong-form tests. See Fama, "Efficient Capital Markets."

Another aspect of the strong form is the ability of any investor to earn excess returns as a result of using information in a superior manner. In other words, can an investor, or group of investors, use the value of the information contained in an announcement to earn excess returns? If not, the market is strong-form efficient. This aspect of the strong form has been examined in several ways, including analyzing the returns of the professional money managers such as those of mutual funds and pension funds and examining the value of what security analysts do.

Corporate Insiders A corporate insider is an officer, director, or major stockholder of a corporation who might be expected to have valuable inside information. The Securities and Exchange Commission (SEC) requires insiders (officers, directors, and owners of more than 10 percent of a company's stock) to report their monthly purchase or sale transactions to the SEC by the tenth of the next month. This information is made public in the SEC's monthly publication, *Official Summary of Security Transactions and Holdings* (*Official Summary*).

Insiders have access to privileged information and are able to act on it and profit before the information is made public. This is logical and not really surprising. Therefore, it is not surprising that several studies of corporate insiders found they consistently earned abnormal returns on their stock transactions.[20] A recent study of insider trades by chairpersons, presidents, and other top officials of firms over the period 1975 to 1989 found that these groups substantially outperformed the market when they made large trades. Trades by top executives of 1,000 shares or more were "abnormally profitable" for insiders.[21] On the other hand, most insiders did only slightly better than a coin toss.

An even more recent study covering the period 1975 to 1995, by Lakonishok and Lee, found that companies with a high incidence of insider buying outperform those where insiders have done a large amount of selling.[22] The margin was almost 8 percentage points for the subsequent 12-month period. Interestingly, the largest differences occurred in companies with a market capitalization of less than $1 billion.

Profitable insider trading is a violation of strong-form efficiency, which requires a market in which no investor can consistently earn abnormal profits. Furthermore, successful use of this information by outsiders (the general public) would be a violation of semistrong efficiency. Investors without access to this private information can observe what the insiders are doing by studying the publicly available reports that appear in the Official Summary. Several investment information services compile this information and sell it to the public in the form of regularly issued reports, and it is available weekly in *Barron's* and *The Wall Street Journal*. Furthermore, such services as *The Value Line Investment Survey* report insider transactions for each company they cover.

Rozeff and Zaman used the typical abnormal return methodology of previous studies and found that outsiders can earn profits by acting on the publicly available information concerning insider transactions.[23] However, when they used an abnormal returns measure that takes into account size and earnings/price ratio effects, these profits decreased substantially and disappeared altogether when transactions cost of 2 percent are

[20] See, for example, J. Jaffe, "Special Information and Insider Trading," *Journal of Business*, 47 (July 1974): 410–428, and Ken Nunn, G. P. Madden, and Michael Gombola, "Are Some Investors More 'Inside' Than Others?" *Journal of Portfolio Management*, 9 (Spring 1983): 18–22.
[21] See Alexandra Peers, "Insiders Reap Big Gains from Big Trades," *The Wall Street Journal*, September 23, 1992, pp. C1 and C12.
[22] See Josef Lakonishok and Inmoon Lee, "Are Insider Trades Informative?" *Review of Financial Studies*, 14 (Spring 2001) 79–111.
[23] See Michael S. Rozeff and Mir A. Zaman, "Market Efficiency and Insider Trading: New Evidence," *Journal of Business* (January 1988): 25–45.

included. Furthermore, imposition of the 2-percent transactions cost on corporate insiders reduces their abnormal returns to an average of 3.0 to 3.5 percent per year. Therefore, this study reaffirms semistrong market efficiency with respect to insider trading, and also suggests that corporate insiders do not earn substantial profits from directly using insider information, which in effect supports strong-form efficiency.

There are several reasons why insider transactions can be very misleading or simply of no value as an indicator of where the stock price is likely to go. Selling shares acquired by option grants to key executives has become commonplace—they need the cash, and they sell shares acquired as part of their compensation. Similarly, acquiring shares through the exercise of options can simply represent an investment decision by the executive.

Using the Internet

Investors can obtain information on insider buying and selling at http://finance.yahoo.com and at http://insider.thompsonfn.com. The latter site, Thompson Financial, has a scoring system which rates insiders on the predictive nature of their past decisions (both buys and sells). Some observers recommend disregarding transactions of less than $100,000, and trying to determine when insiders make unusual transactions relative to what they have done in the past. Also, investors should focus on insiders directly involved in operating the business as opposed to outside directors.

CAN EXCESS RETURNS BE EARNED BY USING INFORMATION?

A number of studies have examined the information in analysts' forecasts, but most of these studies suffer from survivorship bias (some forecasts don't survive and are not reported) and from selection bias (access to forecasts are controlled, so an unbiased record cannot be observed). However, studies by Dimson and Marsh and by Elton, Gruber, and Grossman are free of these biases. Both studies find information in analysts' forecasts.[24] Looking at the consensus view across brokerage firms appears to offer valuable information that lasts at least for short periods of time.

Many studies have been done of the performance of mutual funds, because data are readily available. However, a number of these studies suffer from survivorship bias, because they exclude funds that went out of business during the time period examined; therefore, the studies are analyzing only funds that survived. Nevertheless, most of these studies find that mutual funds do not perform all that well on a risk-adjusted basis after expenses. Elton, Gruber, Das, and Hklarka corrected for the survivorship bias and found that managers of funds underperformed on a risk-adjusted basis after fees and expenses are taken into account.[25]

Implications of the Efficient Market Hypothesis

The nonexhaustive evidence on market efficiency presented here is impressive in its support of market efficiency. What are the implications to investors if this evidence is descriptive of the actual situation? How should investors analyze and select securities and manage their portfolios if the market is efficient?

---

[24] The discussion of the strong form and tests of the strong form has benefited significantly from Edwin Elton, Martin Gruber, Stephen Brown, and William Goetzmann, *Modern Portfolio Theory and Investment Analysis*, 6th Edition, John Wiley and Sons, 2003. For the studies about analysts, see Elroy Dimson and Paul Marsh, "An Analysis of Brokers' and Analysts' Unpublished Forecasts of UK Stock Returns," *The Journal of Finance*, 39 (December 1984), pp. 1257–1292, and Edwin Elton, Martin Gruber, and Seth Grossman, "Discreet Expectational Data and Portfolio Performance," *The Journal of Finance*, 41, (July 1986), pp. 699–712.

[25] See Edwin Elton, Martin Gruber, Sanjiv Das, and Matt Hklarka, "Efficiency with Costly Information: A Reinterpretation of Evidence from Managed Portfolios," Unpublished Manuscript, New York University, 1990.

FOR TECHNICAL ANALYSIS

As mentioned earlier, technical analysis and the EMH directly conflict with each other. Technicians believe that stock prices exhibit trends that persist across time, whereas the weak-form EMH states that price (and volume) data are already reflected in stock prices. EMH proponents believe that information is disseminated rapidly and that prices adjust rapidly to this new information. If prices fully reflect the available information, technical trading systems that rely on knowledge and use of past trading data cannot be of value.

Although technical analysis cannot be categorically refuted because of its many variations and interpretations, the evidence accumulated to date overwhelmingly favors the weak-form EMH and casts doubt on technical analysis. The evidence is such that the burden of proof has shifted to the proponents of technical analysis to demonstrate, using a properly designed test procedure (e.g., adjusting for transaction costs, risk, and any other factors necessary to make a fair comparison), that technical analysis outperforms a buy-and-hold strategy.

FOR FUNDAMENTAL ANALYSIS

The EMH also has implications for fundamental analysis, which seeks to estimate the intrinsic value of a security and provide buy or sell decisions depending on whether the current market price is less than or greater than the intrinsic value. If the semistrong form is true, no form of "standard" security analysis based on publicly available information will be useful. In this situation, since stock prices reflect all relevant publicly available information, gaining access to information others already have is of no value.

Given the evidence on market efficiency, clearly superior fundamental analysis becomes necessary. For example, an investor's estimates of future variables such as earnings must be better, or at least more consistent, than those of other investors. This investor must also derive more and better insights from information that is publicly available to all investors. There is no theoretical reason why an investor could not do a superior job of analysis and profit thereby. However, the EMH suggests that investors who use the same data and make the same interpretations as other investors will experience only average results.

FOR MONEY MANAGEMENT

What about money management activities? First, the evidence:

- For the $16\frac{1}{2}$-year period from August 1982 (start of the bull market) through 1998, the Vanguard 500 Index Fund had an annual average return of 19.7 percent, the average big-cap fund averaged 18.2 percent, and the average equity fund averaged 15.9 percent. Thus, this premier index fund clearly outperformed equity money managers.
- For the 10 years ending in 2002, the Vanguard 500 Index Fund outperformed almost three-fourths of all U.S. diversified stock funds (and this doesn't count poorly performing funds that simply disappeared during that period).

Assume for a moment that the market is efficient. What would this mean to the money management process; that is, to professional money managers? The most important effect would be a reduction in the resources devoted to assessing individual securities. For the manager to act in this respect, he or she would have to believe that an analyst had come up with some superior insights. Passive strategies would become the norm. Nevertheless, the portfolio manager would still have tasks to perform in this efficient market. These tasks would consist of at least the following:

1. Diversification: As we saw in Chapter 7, the basic tenet of good portfolio management is to diversify the portfolio. The manager would have to be certain that the correct amount of diversification had been achieved.
2. Portfolio risk: Depending on the type of portfolio being managed and its objectives, the manager must achieve a level of risk appropriate for that portfolio as well as maintain the desired risk level.
3. Taxes: Investors are interested in the amount of return they are allowed to keep after taxes. Accordingly, their tax situation should be kept in mind as investment alternatives are considered. Tax-exempt portfolios have their own needs and interests.
4. Transaction costs: Trading costs can have a significant impact on the final performance of the portfolio. Managers should seek to reduce these costs to the extent possible and practical. Index funds are one possibility.

FOR INDIVIDUAL INVESTORS

The EMH has important implications for individual investors making their own investing decisions. Equity portfolio management comes down to taking a passive or an active approach, as explained in Chapter 11. If an investor believes that the U.S. stock market is highly efficient, such an investor should opt for a passive approach. This approach takes a long-term view on a buy-and-hold basis. The investor will buy stocks and plan to hold them for the long run, or buy stocks with the intent of doing as well as a market index. Alternatively, some mutual funds or ETFs can be purchased.

Index funds assume particular importance in passive strategies. Indexing, discussed in Chapter 11, is a way to help ensure that an investor does as well as one or more market indexes, while minimizing the time and costs involved in investing. Numerous studies have shown that index funds held over multiple-year periods produce results that are superior to a majority of actively managed mutual funds, primarily because of the lower costs that index funds have.

If investors feel that the stock market has ongoing inefficiencies, they may wish to pursue an active strategy. Such an approach has as its objective to outperform some benchmark portfolio on a risk-adjusted basis. For example, an investor may believe that he or she can do better security analysis than most investors, or build better screening models for analyzing hundreds of stocks. Alternatively, an investor may believe he or she has special expertise in one or more areas that can profitably be put to use. Keep in mind that one must accurately account for all costs involved in pursuing an active strategy before deciding that it is worthwhile to do so.

Evidence of Market Anomalies

Market Anomalies
Techniques or strategies that appear to be contrary to an efficient market

Having considered the type of evidence supporting market efficiency, we now can appropriately consider some **market anomalies**. By definition, an anomaly is an exception to a rule or model. Thus, these market anomalies are in contrast to what would be expected in a totally efficient market, and constitute exceptions to market efficiency. To date, most of them have not been explained away, and until that happens, they remain anomalies or exceptions to market efficiency.

We will examine several anomalies that have generated much attention and have yet to be satisfactorily explained. However, investors must be cautious in viewing any of these anomalies as a stock-selection device guaranteed to outperform the market. There is no such guarantee, because empirical tests of these anomalies may not approximate actual trading strategies that could be followed by investors. Furthermore, even if anomalies exist and can be identified, investors should still hold a portfolio of stocks rather than concentrating on a few stocks identified by one of these methods. As we saw in Chapter 7, diversification is crucial for all investors—indeed, diversification is the number one rule of all portfolio management.

EARNINGS ANNOUNCEMENTS

The adjustment of stock prices to earnings announcements has been studied in several papers, opening up some interesting questions and possibilities. The information found in such announcements should, and does, affect stock prices. The questions that need to be answered are as follows:

1. How much of the earnings announcement is new information and how much has been anticipated by the market? In other words, how much of the announcement is a "surprise"?
2. How quickly is the "surprise" portion of the announcement reflected in the price of the stock? Is it immediate, as would be expected in an efficient market, or is there a lag in the adjustment process? If a lag occurs, investors have a chance to realize excess returns by quickly acting on the publicly available earnings announcements.

To assess the earnings announcement issue properly, we must separate a particular earnings announcement into an expected and an unexpected part. The expected part is that portion anticipated by investors by the time of announcement and that requires no adjustment in stock prices, whereas the unexpected part is unanticipated by investors and requires an adjustment in price.

Latané, Tuttle, and Jones studied quarterly earnings reports in 1968 and found them to be positively correlated with subsequent short-term price movements.[26] This finding indicated a lag in the adjustment of stock prices to the information in these reports. Following several papers that examined the value of quarterly earnings in stock selection, Henry Latané, Charles Jones, and Robert Rieke in 1974 developed the concept of **standardized unexpected earnings** (SUE) as a means of investigating the earnings surprises in quarterly data. SUE is defined as

$$\text{SUE} = \frac{\text{Actual quarterly earnings} - \text{Predicted quarterly earnings}}{\text{Standardization factor to adjust for size differences}}$$

$$= \text{Unexpected earnings/Standard error of the estimate}$$

Standardized Unexpected Earning (SUE)   A variable used in the selection of common stocks, calculated as the ratio of unexpected earnings to a standardization factor

The actual quarterly earnings are the earnings reported by the company and available on brokerage house wire services the same day as reported or in *The Wall Street Journal* the following day. Predicted earnings for a particular company are estimated from historical earnings data before the earnings are reported. As each company's earnings are announced, the SUE can be calculated and acted on. Companies with high (low) unexpected earnings are expected to have a positive (negative) price response.

---

[26] See H. A. Latané, Donald L. Tuttle, and Charles P. Jones, "E/P Ratios vs. Changes in Earnings in Forecasting Future Price Changes," *Financial Analysts Journal* (January–February 1969): 117–120, 123.

Latané and Jones documented the performance of SUE in a series of papers. SUE was shown to have a definite relationship with subsequent excess holding-period returns. In one paper, the authors documented the precise response of stock prices to earnings announcements using a large sample of stocks (over 1,400) for the 36 quarters covering mid-1971 to mid-1980.[27] Daily returns were used, allowing the exact response of stock prices to quarterly earnings announcements to be analyzed before, on, and after the day the earnings were announced.

Figure 12-3 shows a similar analysis for an updated period involving a sample size ranging from about 1,700 companies per quarter to almost 2,000 companies. SUEs are separated into 10 categories based on the size and sign of the unexpected earnings. Category 10 contains all SUEs larger than 4.0, and category 1 contains all SUEs smaller than −4.0; categories 5 and 6 contain the smallest unexpected earnings.

Excess returns are calculated for each security as the difference between a security's return for each day and the market's return for that day. These excess returns are cumulated for the period beginning 63 days before the announcement date of earnings through 63 days following the announcement date. (There are approximately 63 trading days in a quarter.) As Figure 12-3 shows, the SUE categories follow a monotonic discrimination, with category 10 performing the best and category 1 the worst. Categories 5 and 6 show virtually no excess returns after the announcement date of earnings, as would be expected from the smallest unexpected earnings.

Figure 12-3 indicates that, although a substantial adjustment to the forthcoming earnings announcement occurs before the actual announcement, a substantial adjustment

Figure 12-3

Cumulative excess returns surrounding the announcement date of quarterly earnings for 10 SUE categories.

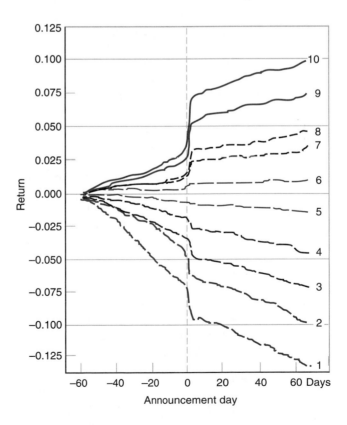

[27] See Charles P. Jones, Richard J. Rendleman, and Henry A. Latané, "Stock Returns and SUEs during the 1970s," *Journal of Portfolio Management* (Winter 1984): 18–22.

also occurs after the day of announcement. This is the unexplained part of the SUE puzzle. In an efficient market, prices should adjust quickly to earnings rather than with a lag.

By the mid-1980s, considerable evidence had been presented about the relationship between unexpected earnings and subsequent stock returns. Although such evidence is not in any way conclusive, it cannot be easily dismissed. Different researchers, using different samples and different techniques, have examined the unexpected earnings issue and have found similar results. It must be emphasized, however, that techniques such as SUE are not a guarantee of major success for investors. The relationships discussed are averages and do not necessarily reflect what any single investor would experience.

LOW P/E RATIOS

One of the more enduring concepts in investments concerns the price/earnings (P/E) ratio discussed earlier in the valuation chapters. A number of investors believe that low P/E stocks, on average, outperform high P/E stocks. The rationale for this concept is not explicit, but the belief persists.

Basu studied this issue by ranking stocks by their P/E ratios and comparing the results of the high–P/E ratio group with those of the low–P/E ratio group 12 months following purchase.[28] Since the P/E ratio is known information and is presumably reflected in price, a relationship between the P/E ratio and subsequent returns should not exist if the market is efficient. The results of Basu's study indicated that the low–P/E ratio stocks outperformed the high–P/E ratio stocks. Furthermore, risk was not a factor. After various adjustments for risk, the low–P/E stocks were still superior performers.

These results attracted considerable attention because of their implications for the concept of market efficiency and because the P/E ratio is an easy, well-known strategy to use in selecting stocks. Subsequently, questions about the validity of the P/E ratio were raised by other academic researchers in studies of the firm size effect, which is discussed later as another anomaly.

In response to the questions raised, Basu conducted a study to reexamine the relationship between the P/E ratio, the size effect, and returns on New York Stock Exchange (NYSE) stocks for the period 1963 to 1980.[29] He found that the stocks of low–P/E firms generally had higher risk-adjusted returns than firms with high–P/E ratios. Furthermore, this P/E ratio effect was significant even after adjustments were made for differences in firm size. Controlling for differences in both risk and P/E ratios, Basu found that the size effect virtually disappeared.

In view of some research suggesting that the P/E effect is confined to low–beta-risk securities, another study examined the P/E anomaly with respect to both total risk and systematic risk.[30] The results indicate that the P/E effect is not confined to low–beta-risk securities. Regardless of the risk measure used, low P/E securities provided significant positive excess returns across all risk levels.

The P/E ratio anomaly appears to offer investors a potential strategy for investing that could produce returns superior to many alternatives they may be using. Some well-known commentators continue to advocate investing in low–P/E stocks. For example, David Dreman (discussed in Chapter 11 in connection with contrarian analysis) recommends that investors ignore professional investment advice and select stocks with

[28] S. Basu, "Investment Performance of Common Stocks in Relation to Their Price-Earnings Ratios: A Test of the Efficient Market Hypothesis," *The Journal of Finance*, 32, No. 2 (June 1977): 663–682.
[29] S. Basu, "The Relationship Between Earnings' Yield, Market Value and Return for NYSE Common Stocks: Further Evidence," *Journal of Financial Economics*, 12 (June 1983): 129–156.
[30] See David Goodman and John Peavy, "The Risk Universal Nature of the P/E Effect," *The Journal of Portfolio Management* (Summer 1985): 14–17.

low–P/E ratios. His hypothesis is that low–P/E stocks may currently be unwanted, but if they have strong finances, high yields, and good earnings records, they almost always do well eventually.

According to Dreman, for the 20-year period through 1993, for a sample of 1,200 small stocks, low–P/E stocks outperform high–P/E stocks over long periods of time. The lowest P/E group returned 22.9 percent on an annual basis compared to 11.3 percent for the highest P/E group and 17.2 percent for the mean small-capitalization sample. Over the more recent 10 years, the smallest quintile outperformed the largest quintile by almost a three to one ratio.[31]

In Dreman's 1998 book (see Selected References—this discussion is based on the book), he examines the 1,500 largest companies (on Compustat) by market size for the period 1970 to 1996. Dividing the stocks into 44 industries, Dreman found that the lowest 20 percent of stocks as measured by the P/E ratio showed an average return of 17.7 percent annually over these 27 years, whereas the highest 20 percent showed returns of 12.2 percent annually. The S&P 500 return was 15.3 percent. Thus, the low–P/E ratio stocks outperformed the high–P/E ratio stocks by about 5.5 percentage points.

Investors need to be careful when following the low–P/E strategy. Although a diversified portfolio, as always, is critical, rigid adherence to a low–P/E strategy could result in an inadequately diversified portfolio. Dreman has indicated that he takes a minimum of 25 stocks in 15 to 18 industries and that "most [low-P/E stocks] have significant problems or very good reasons why you don't want to own them." Only about 1 in 10 candidates on the basis of low–P/E passes his additional screens, such as dividend yields higher than average and accelerating earnings growth over the past. Dreman also suggests an emphasis on large stocks as opposed to small-company stocks.

According to some evidence, the low–P/E strategy does well neither in turbulent markets nor in periods of slow economic growth. However, these stocks may perform well in a "full-blown" bear market because of their higher dividend yields. Overall, the low–P/E strategy should be viewed as a long-run strategy to be pursued through both good and bad markets.

THE SIZE EFFECT

Size Effect The observed tendency for smaller firms to have higher stock returns than large firms

A third potential anomaly that generated considerable attention is the firm **size effect**, referred to earlier. In a well-publicized study, Rolf Banz found that the stocks of small NYSE firms earned higher risk-adjusted returns than the stocks of large NYSE firms (on average).[32] This size effect appeared to have persisted for many years. Mark Reinganum, using a sample of both NYSE and Amex firms, also found abnormally large risk-adjusted returns for small firms.[33] Both of these researchers attributed the results to a misspecification of the capital asset pricing model (CAPM) rather than to a market inefficiency. Donald Keim found that roughly 50 percent of the return difference reported by Reinganum is concentrated in January.[34]

It is easy today to get confused about the size effect given all of the research findings and the various definitions of small caps. Many investors today generally accept the notion that small caps outperform large caps, based partly on results from the Ibbotson Associates data which show that "small" stocks have outperformed the S&P 500 Index by roughly

---

[31] See David Dreman, "Emotion Versus Logic," *Forbes*, November 7, 1994, p. 351.

[32] R. Banz, "The Relationship Between Returns and Market Value of Common Stocks," *Journal of Financial Economics*, 9 (March 1981): 3–18.

[33] M. Reinganum, "Misspecification of Capital Asset Pricing: Empirical Anomalies Based on Earnings Yield and Market Values," *Journal of Financial Economics*, 9 (March 1981): 19–46.

[34] These results, as well as a discussion of most of the anomalies, can be found in Donald B. Keim, "The CAPM and Equity Return Regularities," *Financial Analysts Journal* (May–June 1986): 19–34.

two percentage points on a compound annual average basis; however, "small" as used in this context means the bottom 20 percent of NYSE stocks based on market value.

From 1926 through 1979, small caps had a mean annualized return of 12.2 percent, whereas large caps showed 8.2 percent. From 1980 to 1996, small caps had a 13.3 percent return, whereas large caps showed 15.9 percent. Thus, by this measure, the small-cap "premium" has disappeared. Looking at the Ibbotson Associates data or comparable data from the beginning of 1979 through 1997, small caps and large caps have earned about the same compound annual rate of return. Dreman has argued that the size "myth" is based on stocks that trade thinly or not at all. James O'Shaughnessy, in his book *What Works on Wall Street* (see Selected References), argues that the returns associated with small stocks are mostly associated with micro-cap stocks which have very small capitalizations, and are not easily bought by individuals or even institutions because of large spreads and commissions.[35]

THE JANUARY EFFECT

Several studies in the past have suggested that seasonality exists in the stock market. Recent evidence of stock return seasonality has grown out of studies of the size anomaly explained in the previous section. Keim studied the month-to-month stability of the size effect for all NYSE and Amex firms with data for 1963 to 1979.[36] His findings again supported the existence of a significant size effect (a 30.5-percent small-size premium). However, roughly half of this size effect occurred in January, and more than half of the excess January returns occurred during the first five trading days of that month. The first trading day of the year showed a high small-firm premium for every year of the period studied. The strong performance in January by small-company stocks has become known as the **January effect**.[37]

January Effect The observed tendency for small-cap stocks to be higher in January than in other months

Another paper by Keim further documented the abnormal returns for small firms in January. Keim also found a yield effect—the largest abnormal returns tended to accrue to firms either paying no dividends or having high-dividend yields.[38]

Recent evidence on the January effect, as measured by the performance of the Nasdaq Composite Index for the month of January, is:

1985	+112.7%	1995	+ 0.4%
1986	+ 3.3%	1996	+ 0.7%
1987	+112.4%	1997	+ 6.9%
1988	+ 4.3%	1998	+ 3.1%
1989	+ 5.2%	1999	+14.2%
1990	− 8.6%	2000	− 3.2%
1991	+110.8%	2001	+12.2%
1992	+ 5.8%	2002	− 0.8%
1993	+ 2.9%	2003	− 1.1%
1994	+ 3.1%		

This simple evidence, which makes no comparisons or other judgments, suggests that the January effect has continued to exist in recent years, at least in the sense of a solid Janu-

---

[35] A more detailed discussion of this issue can be found in Marc R. Reinganum, "The Size Effect: Evidence and Potential Explanations," in *Investing in Small-Cap and Microcap Securities*, Association for Investment Management and Research, 1997.

[36] See Donald B. Keim, "Size-Related Anomalies and Stock Return Seasonality, *Journal of Financial Economics*, 12 (1983): 13–32.

[37] See Richard Roll, "Vas ist das? The Turn of the Year Effect and the Return Premium of Small Firms," *The Journal of Portfolio Management* (Winter 1983): 18–28. Roll also found a turn-of-the-year effect with abnormal returns for small firms on the last trading day in December.

[38] See Donald B. Keim, "Dividend Yields and the January Effect," *The Journal of Portfolio Management* (Winter 1986): 54–60.

ary performance for these stocks. As the data indicate, there were only three negative years through January, 2003. (Nasdaq includes a wide range of firms by size.)

The information about a possible January effect has been available for years and has been widely discussed in the press. The question arises, therefore, as to why a January effect would persist and recur again and again. Nevertheless, Haugen and Jorion find no evidence that the January effect has disappeared for NYSE stocks.[39] They detect no significant change in the magnitude of the effect, nor a trend that would suggest the January effect will disappear. As Haugen and Jorion indicate, "Because the anomaly can be inexpensively exploited, its persistence has implications for the theory of efficient markets and for the persistence of anomalies in general."[40]

Some Practical Advice

Abnormally high returns in January are most significant for micro-caps, which have gained about 8.6 percent in January on average compared to 1.9 percent for the market as a whole and 4.8 percent for small caps. For small-cap stocks overall, the January effect appears to be moving into December. Since 1980 the average return for small caps in December was 2.4 percent, and since 1990, 4.1 percent. For micro-caps, these numbers reversed—4.8 percent since 1990 versus 5.7 percent since 1980.[41]

THE VALUE LINE RANKING SYSTEM

The Value Line Investment Survey is the largest, and perhaps best-known, investment advisory service in the country.[42] *Value Line* ranks each of the roughly 1,700 stocks it covers from 1 (best) to 5 (worst) as to its "timeliness"—probable relative price performance within the next 12 months. These timeliness ranks, updated weekly, have been available since 1965.

The performance of the five rankings categories has been very strong based on *Value Line*'s calculations. For example, the complete record of *Value Line* rankings for timeliness from 1965 shows that the ranking system clearly discriminates in a monotonic order. That is, Group 1 stocks perform better than Group 2 stocks, which perform better than Group 3, and so on. Figure 12-4 shows the record for the *Value Line* ranks for the period 1965 to 2002 without allowing for changes in ranks each week (equal amounts are invested in each stock in each grouping at the beginning of the year and held for 12 months without allowing for subsequent changes in ranking).

Figure 12-4 presents *Value Line*'s total record over time, along with both the DJIA and the S&P 500 Index. According to *Value Line*, 2002 was only the fifth time in 38 years that the Group 1 stocks failed to outperform the Group 5 stocks—in other words, over the 38-year life of *Value Line* rankings Group 1 stocks have outperformed Group 5 stocks about 87 percent of the time.

Allowing for changes in ranks produced spectacular results. For the comparable period shown in Figure 12-4, Group 1 stocks showed a cumulative total return of 34,064

[39] See Robert A. Haugen and Phillipe Jorion, "The January Effect: Still There after All These Years," *Financial Analysts Journal* (January–February 1996): 27–31.

[40] A 1992 study of the January anomaly indicates that the previous studies of abnormal returns for small firms may be biased by incomplete consideration of a price effect and transaction costs. This study argues, on the basis of the years 1967 to 1986, that the January effect is a low-price phenomenon rather than a small-firm effect. Further tests indicated that, after adjusting for differential transaction costs, portfolios of lower price stocks almost always underperformed the market portfolio. Therefore, the large before-transaction-costs excess January returns observed on low-price stocks may be explainable by higher transaction costs and a bid-ask bias. The implication of this study is that the reported January anomaly is not persistent and is not likely to be exploitable by most investors. See Ravinder K. Bhardaj and Leroy D. Brooks, "The January Anomaly: Effects of Low Share Price, Transaction Costs, and Bid-Ask Bias," *The Journal of Finance*, 47 (June 1992): 553–575.

[41] See Daniel Coker, "Leap Into the New Year," *Bloomberg Personal Finance*, December 1998, p. 29.

[42] This investment advisory service is discussed in more detail in Chapter 15.

Figure 12-4

Record of *Value Line* ranks for timeliness without allowing for annual changes in rank, 1965–2002.

SOURCE: *"Value Line* Selection and Opinion," *The Value Line Investment Survey,* January 31, 2003, p. 3149. Reproduced with the permission of Value Line Publishing, Inc.

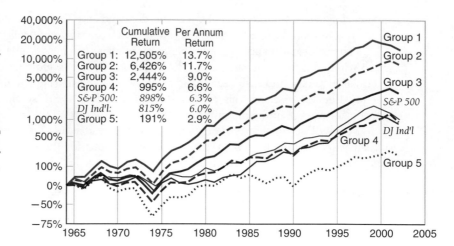

percent (down from 58,848 percent at the end of 2000) compared to the 12,505 percent (down from 15,915 percent at the end of 2000) shown in Figure 12-4. Performance was sharply negative during 2000 to 2002, particularly in 2001 and 2002, which lowered the cumulative results drastically from the peak reached by the end of 1999. Note that this procedure of allowing for changes in rank would have resulted in a prohibitive portfolio turnover rate, generating large transaction costs and short-term capital gains.

According to available evidence, for the period mid-1980 through 1993, Group 1 stocks showed an annualized return of 19.3 percent. According to Mark Hulbert, who tracks the performance of investment letters for his *Hulbert Financial Digest,* this made *Value Line* the best overall performer for this period of all the investment letters tracked.

The Value Line Investment Survey now regularly reports a comparison of the relative price performance of its Group 1 stocks with four other strategies: low P/E, low cap (small size), low price/book value, and low price/sales. These results provide some information on two of the strategies discussed earlier, low P/E and the size effect, as well as two valuation techniques, price/book value and price/sales, that are discussed in Chapter 10. These results are shown in Figure 12-5 for the same period, 1965 to 2002.

Figure 12-5 suggests that *Value Line's* Group 1 stocks outperformed the other four strategies by a significant amount. Interestingly, by this comparison, the small-cap stocks did better than the other strategies (other than *Value Line's* Group 1), with the low–P/E ratio strategy the next best. The low P/sales and low price/book did particularly poorly in this comparison. It is easy from Figure 12-5 to see why *Value Line* concluded, "The lesson is clear—stay with the Group 1s."

Several studies of the success of *Value Line's* rankings have been made. Not surprisingly, results vary somewhat depending on the exact study one examines. It appears that the rankings, and changes in the rankings, do contain useful information. However, there is evidence that the market adjusts quickly to this information (one or two trading days following the Friday release), and that true transaction costs can negate much of the price changes that occur as a result of adjustments to this information.[43]

A recent study by Choi examined *Value Line's* timeliness rankings from 1965 to 1996 based on both a statistical analysis and a comparison to benchmark portfolios that corresponded to the evaluated stocks' characteristics. Choi found some evidence of performance of these stocks beyond that expected on the basis of models of expected return.

---

[43] See Scott Stickel, "The Effect of *Value Line* Investment Survey Changes on Common Stock Prices," *Journal of Financial Economics,* 14 (March 1985): 121–143. A good review that attempts to reconcile the various findings about *Value Line* can be found in Gur Huberman and Shmuel Kandel, "Market Efficiency and *Value Line's* Record," *Journal of Business,* 63 (April 1990): 187–216.

Figure 12-5

Value Line **group 1 stocks vs. other strategies, 1966–2002.**

SOURCE: "*Value Line* Selection and Opinion," *The Value Line Investment Survey*, January 31, 2003, p. 3154. Reproduced with the permission of Value Line Publishing, Inc.

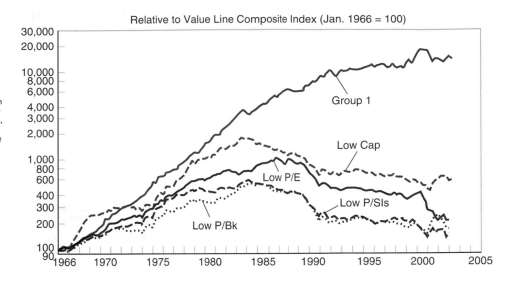

However, he also found that after transaction costs, it is doubtful that investors could have earned profitable abnormal returns.[44]

Strong support for the *Value Line* system comes from Mark Hulbert, who has monitored the performance of investing newsletters for 22 years. From January 1989 through the first three-fourths of 2002, Hulbert determined that *Value Line's* ranking system outperformed Standard & Poor's *Outlook*, which uses a five-tiered stock-ranking system based on S&P's stock analysts. Over this period, the average *Value Line* top-ranked stock outperformed the average S&P top-ranked stock by more than three percentage points on an annualized basis (13 compared to 9.7 percent). For comparison, the Wilshire 5000 produced a 10.2-percent annualized return.[45]

The Value Line Investment Survey is an important source of information for investors and is one of the most used investment advisory services available. We will refer to it again in Chapter 15.

OTHER ANOMALIES

The above list of anomalies is not exhaustive. Others have been reported and discussed, including in particular several calendar anomalies such as the day of the week, turn-of-the-month, day preceding a holiday, and so forth. One anomaly of interest, because it is consistent with the commonsense notion that market efficiency is most likely applied to the larger, well-known stocks as opposed to all stocks, is the neglected firm effect. Neglect in this case means that few analysts follow the stock or that few institutions own the stock. The area of neglected stocks would appear to be a good opportunity for small investors interested in security analysis and stock selection.

Using the Internet

An excellent source of information about the anomalies can be found by choosing "Anomalies" at **www.investorhome.com**. Most of the anomalies are discussed, and each discussion has links to both the original research and recent articles on the subject.

[44] See James J. Choi, "The *Value Line* Enigma: The Sum of Known Parts?" *Journal of Financial and Quantitative Analysis*, 35 (September 2000): 485–498.
[45] Web site, CBS MarketWatch, "Mark Hulbert: The main event—S&P vs. *Value Line* 'Machine' over 'man' in stock performance rankings," October 29, 2002.

SOME CONCLUSIONS ABOUT MARKET EFFICIENCY

Given all of the evidence about market efficiency discussed previously—the studies supporting it as well as the anomalies evidence—what conclusions can be drawn? In truth, no definitive conclusion about market efficiency can be stated. The evidence in support of market efficiency has convinced many market observers because of the large amount of research done over the years by numerous investigators. And almost certainly the widespread availability of information and data on the Internet, along with the investment tools offered there, has made the market even more efficient. Nevertheless, many technicians and fundamentalists are convinced that they can outperform the market, or at least provide more benefits than cost. Paradoxically, this belief helps to make the market efficient.

Investments Intuition

A paradox of efficient markets and active investors is that investors, in an attempt to uncover and use important information about security prices, help to make the market efficient. In other words, in the course of searching out undervalued and overvalued stocks, investors discover information and act on it as quickly as possible. If the information is favorable, the discoverers will buy immediately, and if unfavorable, they will sell immediately. As investors scramble for information and attempt to be the first to act, they make the market more efficient. If enough of this activity occurs, all information will be reflected in prices. Thus, the fact that a number of investors do not believe in the EMH results in actions that help to make the market efficient.

Some anomalies do seem to exist, and since the late 1970s the flow of research reporting on anomalies has accelerated. These anomalies require considerable work to document scientifically and do not represent a guarantee of investment riches. However, these anomalies appear to offer opportunities to astute investors. The reasons why these anomalies exist remain unsettled. The quantity and quality of the research in this area has undermined the extreme view that the market is so perfectly efficient that no opportunities for excess returns could possibly exist.

The anomalies that have been reported are not conclusive proof of market inefficiencies. It may be that better testing procedures and/or better data may explain some of these anomalies away. Furthermore, the size effect does not appear to have held up as originally believed and may not be an anomaly at all.

Data Mining The search for patterns in securities returns by exhaustively examining the data

In judging whether a market inefficiency has been uncovered that could be exploited, investors must guard against **data mining**. This terms refers to the search for patterns in security returns by examining various techniques applied to a set of data. With enough effort, patterns will be uncovered and investing rules and techniques can be found that appear to work in the sense of providing abnormal returns. In most cases, they do not stand up to independent scrutiny or application to a different set of data or time period. The rules and selection techniques resulting from data mining often have no theoretical basis, or rationale, for existing—they simply result from mining the data.

Example 12-2   The *Motley Fool* is a popular and well-known source of investment information and ideas for individual investors. Operating a Web site and also producing some books and other publications, this source has advocated that small investors can often do well in the market by applying simple principles. One technique advocated by the *Motley Fool* was the "Foolish Four," a system that involved taking the 30 Dow Jones Industrial Average stocks and calculating the ratio of the dividend yield to the square root of the share price. The stock with the highest ratio was ignored, and the next four highest became the Foolish Four. The founders of the *Motley Fool* claimed that the Foolish Four strategy, which would take only 15 minutes a year to implement, was so effective it would "crush your mutual funds." A *Money Magazine* columnist who criticized this technique was severely criticized by *Motley Fool* followers. Eventually, the founders had to admit this technique did not work, saying it was a result of faulty analysis of historical data resulting from "finding random correlations and considering them valid and repeatable."[46]

The earnings surprise evidence is particularly strong, and this technique is widely used. However, Eugene Fama, a long-time proponent of market efficiency, argues that the evidence on anomalies does not refute the EM proposition.[47] He believes that many of the studies showing anomalies contain statistical problems. He also believes that overreaction and underreaction are about equally likely to be found, which suggests that markets are efficient because this behavior can be attributable to chance. For example, the post announcement earnings drift observed in the SUE studies and similar work suggest underreaction to information. The poor performance of IPOs over five years is evidence of overreaction.

Interestingly, even Fama, in making these arguments, recognizes the validity of the work that has been done documenting the postannouncement drift that occurs following quarterly earnings announcements. The SUE results, and similar analyses showing a delayed reaction to earnings announcements, have never been satisfactorily refuted and stand today as a documented anomaly. Thus, although Fama may be correct in general, some exceptions do seem to exist. And others, such as Dreman, continue to make a strong case for other anomalies such as low–P/E ratio stocks.

In the final analysis, it is probably best to accept the idea that the market is quite efficient, but not totally. Most of the research done to date suggests that information is received and acted on quickly, and generally the correct adjustments are made. To outperform the market, fundamental analysis beyond the norm must be done. The fundamental analysis that is routinely done every day is already reflected in stock prices. The marginal value of one more investor performing the same calculations that have been done by other investors is zero. Until more evidence to the contrary is forthcoming, technical analysis remains questionable at best.

Simon Keane has argued that investors must choose between a belief in operational efficiency and operational inefficiency.[48] In an operationally efficient market, some investors with the skill to detect a divergence between price and semistrong value earn economic rents. For the majority of investors, however, such opportunities are not available. An operationally inefficient market, on the other hand, contains inefficiencies that the average investor can spot. The evidence to date suggests that investors face an operationally efficient market.[49]

One difficult problem for those who believe in efficient markets is the crash of October 1987. The S&P 500 Index lost over 20 percent in one day. Is it really reasonable to argue that investors, efficiently discounting information, decided in one day that the mar-

---

[46] This discussion is based on "Investing: Word on the Street," *Money Magazine*, February 2001 and on the *Motley Fool* Web site.

[47] See Eugene Fama, "Market Efficiency, Long-Term Returns, and Behavioral Finance," *Journal of Financial Economics* (September, 1998): 283–306.

[48] See Simon Keane, "The Efficient Market Hypothesis on Trial," *Financial Analysts Journal* (March–April 1986): 58–63. This article presents an excellent discussion of the typical debate on efficient markets.

[49] For evidence that the market is not perfectly efficient and therefore offers investors investment opportunities, see Robert F. Vandell and Robert Panino, "A Purposeful Stride Down Wall Street," *The Journal of Portfolio Management* (Winter 1986): 31–39.

ket should be valued some 20 percent less? Not many people, including efficient market proponents, are comfortable making this argument. Another recent example is the market bubble that burst in 2000, with the stock market declining sharply over the next two years. A strict interpretation of the EMH would say that a rational explanation should exist for what happened in the market in the late 1990s as stocks were bid up to higher and higher levels before ultimately collapsing. But most observers today accept the proposition that a bubble did occur, that it was not based on rational behavior, and that this is not in agreement with the efficient markets view.

In addition to the above challenges to the concept of market efficiency, mathematicians are helping a new kind of trader to justify the position that the market is not very efficient, using leading-edge ideas such as chaos theory, neural networks, and genetic algorithms.

The controversy about market efficiency remains. Every investor is still faced with the choice between pursuing an active investment strategy or a passive investment strategy, or some combination thereof. Making this choice depends heavily upon what the investor believes about efficient markets.

What about the behavioral finance view and its current ascendancy in finance thinking? On the one hand, this theory can easily accommodate the notion that some investors can perform better than the market given the irrationalities that exist. On the other hand, behavioral finance accepts that markets can remain out of kilter for extended periods of time, making it difficult for professionals who manage money to survive the effects of such a market—witness the flight from equities during the recent bear market. Therefore, most professional managers, such as mutual fund managers and hedge fund managers, do not beat the market.

A good close to this discussion is to quote from the same paragraph by Samuel Eisenstadt, which we used to begin the chapter. Eisenstadt was the primary force in the development of *Value Line's* famed ranking system for stocks, one of the best known and most successful systems ever developed for general investor use. Eisenstadt noted, ". . . beating the market is difficult and becoming even more so."[50]

Summary

▶ Investors must consider the implications of efficient markets for investment decisions.

▶ An efficient market is defined as one in which the prices of securities fully reflect all known information quickly and accurately.

▶ The conditions that guarantee an efficient market can be shown to hold to a large extent: many investors are competing, information is widely available and generated more or less randomly, and investors react quickly to this information.

▶ To assess market efficiency, three cumulative forms (or degrees) of efficiency are discussed: the weak form, the semistrong form, and the strong form. The weak form involves market data, whereas the semistrong and strong form involve the assimilation of all public and private information, respectively.

▶ The weak-form evidence, whether statistical tests or trading rules, strongly supports the hypothesis.

▶ Many tests of semistrong efficiency have been conducted, including such factors as stock splits, money supply changes, accounting changes, dividend announcements, and reactions to other announcements. Although all the studies do not agree, the majority support semistrong efficiency.

▶ Strong-form evidence takes the form of tests of the performance of groups presumed to have "private" information and of the ability of professional managers to outperform the market. Insiders apparently are able to do well, although the decisions of

[50] See Steven T. Goldberg, "Civil Warriors," *Kiplinger's Personal Finance*, August 2002, p. 39.

the managers of mutual funds have not been found to add value.

▶ Most knowledgeable observers accept weak-form efficiency, reject strong-form efficiency, and feel that the market is, to a large degree, semistrong efficient. This casts doubt on the value of both technical analysis and conventional fundamental analysis.

▶ Although the EMH does not preclude investors from outperforming the market, it does suggest that this is quite difficult to accomplish and that the investor must do more than the norm.

▶ Even if the market is efficient, money managers still have activities to perform, including diversifying the portfolio, choosing and maintaining some degree of risk, and assessing taxes and transaction costs.

▶ Several major "anomalies" that have appeared over the last several years have yet to be satisfactorily explained. These anomalies, which would not be expected in a totally efficient market, include the following:

1. Unexpected earnings, as represented by SUE: The market appears to adjust with a lag to the earnings surprises contained in quarterly earnings. SUE has been shown to be a monotonic discriminator of subsequent short-term (e.g., three-month) stock returns.
2. P/E ratios: Low–P/E stocks appear to outperform high–P/E stocks over annual periods even after adjustment for risk and size.
3. The size effect: Evidence suggests that small firms have outperformed large firms, on a risk-adjusted basis, over a period of many years.
4. The January effect: Much of the abnormal return for small firms occurs in the month of January, possibly because tax-induced sales in December temporarily depress prices, which then recover in January.
5. *Value Line*'s performance: The *Value Line* rankings for timeliness have performed extremely well over the period 1965 to 2002 and appear to offer the average investor a chance to outperform the averages.

Key Words

Abnormal return	Event study	Size effect
Cumulative abnormal return (CAR)	January effect	Standardized unexpected earnings (SUE)
Data mining	Market anomalies	Strong form
Efficient market (EM)	Market data	Weak form
Efficient market hypothesis (EMH)	Semistrong form	

Questions

12-1 What is meant by an efficient market?

12-2 Describe the three forms of market efficiency.

12-3 What are the conditions for an efficient market? How closely are they met in reality?

12-4 Why is a market that is weak-form efficient in direct opposition to technical analysis?

12-5 What do semistrong market efficiency tests attempt to test for?

12-6 Describe two different ways to test for weak-form efficiency.

12-7 Distinguish between economic significance and statistical significance.

12-8 If the EMH is true, what are the implications for investors?

12-9 Could the performance of mutual fund managers also be a test of semistrong efficiency?

12-10 Describe the money management activities of a portfolio manager who believes that the market is efficient.

12-11 What are market anomalies? Describe four.

12-12 If all investors believe that the market is efficient, could that eventually lead to less efficiency in the market?

12-13 What is the relationship between SUE and fundamental analysis?

12-14 What other types of events or information could be used in semistrong-form tests?

12-15 What are the benefits to society of an efficient market?

12-16 If the market moves in an upward trend over a period of years, would this be inconsistent with weak-form efficiency?

12-17 Do security analysts have a role in an efficient market?

12-18 Evaluate the following statement: "My mutual fund has outperformed the market for the last four years. How can the market be efficient?"

12-19 What are the necessary conditions for a scientific test of a trading rule?

12-20 Are filter rules related to timing strategies or stock-selection strategies? What alternative should a filter rule be compared with?

12-21 Assume that you analyze the activities of specialists on the NYSE and find that they are able to realize consistently above-average rates of return. What form of the EMH are you testing?

12-22 What are some possible explanations for the size anomaly?

12-23 How can data on corporate insiders be used to test both the semistrong and the strong forms of the EMH?

12-24 How can data on the performance of mutual funds be used to test both the semistrong and the strong forms of the EMH?

12-25 Assume that the price of a stock remains constant from time period 0 to time period 1, at which time a significant piece of information about the stock becomes available. Draw a diagram that depicts the situation if (a) the market is semistrong efficient and (b) there is a lag in the adjustment of the price to this information.

12-26 How is the SUE concept related to technical analysis?

12-27 What is meant by an operationally efficient market?

CFA
12-28 a. **List** and **briefly define** the three forms of the efficient market hypothesis.
   b. **Discuss** the role of a portfolio manager in a perfectly efficient market.

CFA
12-29 According to the efficient market hypothesis:
   a. high-beta stocks are consistently overpriced.
   b. low-beta stocks are consistently overpriced.
   c. positive alphas on stocks will quickly disappear.
   d. negative alpha stocks consistently yield low returns for arbitragers.

CFA
12-30 Assume that a company announces an unexpectedly large cash dividend to its shareholders. In an efficient market *without* information leakage, one might expect:
   a. an abnormal price change at the announcement.
   b. an abnormal price increase before the announcement.
   c. an abnormal price decrease after the announcement.
   d. no abnormal price change before or after the announcement.

CFA
12-31 Which *one* of the following would provide evidence *against* the semistrong form of the efficient market theory?
   a. About 50 percent of pension funds outperform the market in any year.
   b. All investors have learned to exploit signals about future performance.
   c. Trend analysis is worthless in determining stock prices.
   d. Low–P/E stocks tend to have positive abnormal returns over the long-run.

CFA
12-32 The weak form of the efficient market hypothesis contradicts:
   a. technical analysis, but supports fundamental analysis as valid.
   b. fundamental analysis, but supports technical analysis as valid.
   c. both fundamental and technical analysis.
   d. technical analysis, but is silent on the possibility of successful fundamental analysis.

Problem

12-1   Calculate the SUE for a stock with actual quarterly earnings of $0.50 per share and expected quarterly earnings of $0.30 per share. The standard error of estimate is 0.05. Is this a good buy?

Web Resources

For additional resources visit our dynamic Web site located at www.wiley.com/college/jones.

▢   *A Golden Opportunity*—Concepts of market efficiency are background for the decision to trade stocks based on on-line information. The decision-maker must decide if the hot tip is a once-in-a-lifetime opportunity or fool's gold.

▢   Internet Exercises—This chapter looks at how well market prices reflect relevant information. The Web exercises will ask you to evaluate different trading strategies with a view to getting a more informed opinion on the informational efficiency of financial markets.
Exercise 1: Evaluates random investment strategies against other active strategies.
Exercise 2: Evaluates the weak form of market efficiency—using historical return data to predict future prices.
Exercise 3: Looks at investment strategies using market-to-book ratios.

▢   Multiple Choice Self Test

Selected References

For a lively discussion of possible market inefficiencies and how to exploit them, see:

Haugen, Robert A. *The Inefficient Stock Market: What Pays Off and Why,* 2nd ed. Prentice-Hall, 2001.

For a comprehensive review of various techniques that may help the investor to do better than the market, see:

O'Shaughnessy, James P. *What Works on Wall Street: A Guide to the Best-Performing Investment Strategies of All Time.* McGraw-Hill, 1998.

Dreman's approach to contrarian investing, and the low–P/E strategy, can be found in:

Dreman, David N. *Contrarian Investment Strategies: The Next Generation: Beat the Market by Going Against the Crowd.* Simon & Schuster, 1998.

chapter 13

Economy/ Market Analysis

Chapter 13 begins our discussion of fundamental security analysis by considering the economy and the market. This is the first step in the top-down approach outlined in Chapter 11 because of the overall importance of the economy/market in impacting stock returns. A key issue here is the relationship between the economy and the stock market, since they do not move in lockstep.

AFTER READING THIS CHAPTER YOU WILL BE ABLE TO:

▶ Understand the relationship between the stock market and the economy.
▶ Analyze conceptually the determinants of the stock market.

▶ Make some basic forecasts of possible changes in the level of the market.

Ultimately, investors must make intelligent judgments about the current state of the financial markets as well as changes that have a high probability of occurring in the future. Are particular markets at unusually high or low levels, and what are they likely to do in the next year or five years?

A logical starting point in assessing any equity market is to analyze the economic factors that affect stock prices. Understanding the current and future condition of the economy is the first step in understanding what is happening and what is likely to happen to the market.

Based on a knowledge of the U.S. economy-market relationship, we apply our knowledge of valuation concepts discussed in Chapter 10 to understanding the stock market. In this chapter, we also consider forecasts of changes in the stock market. Although *investors cannot possibly hope to be consistently correct in their forecasts of the stock market*, they can reasonably expect to be able to make some intelligent inferences about major trends in the market. Because of the market's impact on investor success, all but the really long-term investor should consider the market's likely direction over some future period. On the other hand, the true long-term investor following a buy-and-hold strategy (discussed in Chapter 11) need not be directly concerned with the market's direction most of the time, because this investor will be making few changes in his or her portfolio.

Taking a Global Perspective

As noted throughout this text, investors must now think globally. U.S. investors can choose equities from some 50 countries, and these equities comprise slightly more than half of the world's market capitalization and two-thirds of the world's gross domestic product (GDP). Therefore, they should think about economies in other countries and parts of the world. For example, what is the euro currency doing, and how will expected movements in it affect securities?

The current trend worldwide is to open economies and deregulate industries. Multinational corporations are following the U.S. lead in restructuring traditional processes and embracing new technologies. Therefore, as a general rule, the analysis we consider in this chapter of the U.S. market and economy applies to other countries as well. Their equity markets are going to be driven by earnings growth and interest rate changes just as U.S. markets are. By understanding the U.S. equity markets, investors are in a better position to understand foreign equity markets despite the cultural, economic, and political differences.

Another reason why investors must consider the global perspective is currency changes. In 2002, the euro gained significantly against the dollar, achieving parity with it and even exceeding it at times. This continued into 2003, and by early March 2003, the euro was worth a record (at the time) of $1.10. A falling dollar helps the earnings of U.S. corporations. One estimate at the time was that a 15-percent additional fall in the dollar would add about 2.5 percentage points to the expected growth rate in corporate earnings in 2003.[1]

Using the Internet

A world equity index along with information about international indexes can be found at Morgan Stanley's site, www.msci.com. Peaks and troughs for both the business cycle and the growth rate cycle for the United States and 17 other economies can be found at www.businesscycle.com under the "International Cycle Chronologies" section.

---

[1] "The Declining Dollar: A Balm for Battered Profits," *Business Week*, August 12, 2002, p. 82.

Assessing the Economy

Gross Domestic Product (GDP) The market value of final goods and services produced by an economy for some time period

A basic measure of the economy is **Gross Domestic Product (GDP)**, defined as the market value of final goods and services produced by an economy for some time period (typically a year). GDP numbers are prepared quarterly and released a few weeks following the end of the quarter. These numbers constitute a basic measure of the economic health and strength of the economy.

We can measure and observe GDP on both a nominal and real (inflation-adjusted) basis. Figure 13-1 shows real GDP over the last quarter century (percent change from year earlier). The shaded areas indicate official periods of recession. Note the ups and downs up to about 1990 and the long upward movement from early 1991 into 2000, the greatest economic expansion in U.S. history. Following this, a recession officially started in March 2001.

GDP is revised twice in the first three months after its initial release.[2] The Bureau of Economic Analysis initially releases an advance estimate of quarterly GDP in the first month following quarter end. In the second month, it provides a preliminary estimate, and in the third month, it provides a final estimate (however, even this estimate is subject to annual revisions). The cycle then starts over again. Over the last 30+ years, the average revision of GDP growth from the advance to the final estimate has been about two-thirds of a percentage point. It should be noted that almost 90 percent of the time the advance estimate correctly predicts the direction of quarterly change in real GDP growth.

Of more immediate interest to investors, GDP ups and downs directly affect companies. The mechanism is relatively straightforward—if growth in GDP slows, as it did by the end of 2000, corporate revenues will slow, and profits will slow. The market, of course, reacts to this prospect negatively. While real GDP growth in 2000 was 3.8 percent, it was 0.3 percent in 2001, and 2.4 percent in 2002. A recession officially began in 2001, and the stock market suffered declines in 2001 and 2002.

For discussion purposes, think of the economy in terms of the activity that occurs over time. Investors are very concerned about whether the economy is experiencing an expansion or a contraction, because stock prices, interest rates, and inflation will clearly be affected. This recurring pattern of expansion and contraction is referred to as the **business cycle**.

Business Cycle The recurring patterns of expansion, boom, contraction, and recession in an economy

THE BUSINESS CYCLE

The business cycle reflects movements in economic activity as a whole, which comprises many diverse parts. The diversity of the parts ensures that business cycles are virtually unique, with no two parts being identical. However, cycles do have a common framework, with a beginning (they start from a trough), a peak, and an ending (a new trough). Thus, economic activity starts in depressed conditions, builds up in the expansionary

Figure 13-1

Percent change year-to-year in real gross domestic product (GDP), 1977–March 2003.

SOURCE: *National Economic Trends*, The Federal Reserve Bank of St. Louis, April 2003, p. 4.

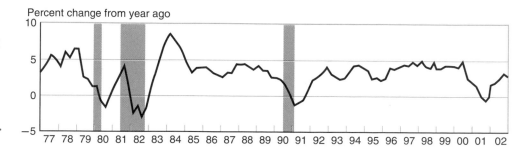

---

[2] This discussion is based on Abbigail J. Chiodo and Michael T. Owyang, "Subject to Revision," *National Economic Trends*, The Federal Reserve Bank of St. Louis, June 2002, p. 1.

phase, and ends in a downturn, only to start again (perhaps because of government stimulus). The word *trough* is used to indicate when the economy has hit bottom.

The typical business cycle in the United States seems to consist of an expansion averaging about 29 months if measured from 1854 through 1945, but almost 50 months if measured since the end of World War II. Contractions since World War II average slightly less than one year. Obviously, however, these are only averages, and we cannot rely on them exclusively to interpret current or future situations. For example, the expansion that began in March 1991 and ended in March 2001 was the longest peacetime expansion. Business cycles cannot be neatly categorized as to length and turning points at the time they are occurring; only in hindsight can such nice distinctions be made.

The National Bureau of Economic Research (NBER), a private nonprofit organization, measures business cycles and officially decides on the economic "turning points." The NBER's Business Cycle Dating Committee determines the turning points of the business cycle, which are the dates at which the economy goes from an expansion mode to a contraction mode and vice versa. These turning points typically are determined well after the fact, so that observers do not know on a current basis, at least officially, when a peak or trough has been reached.

It is possible to identify those components of economic activity that move at different times from each other. Such variables can serve as indicators of the economy in general. The Conference Board now provides these data.[3]

Composite Indexes of General Economic Activity Leading, coincident, and lagging indicators of economic activity

Standard practice is to identify leading, coincident, and lagging **composite economic indexes**. The leading indicators consist of variables such as stock prices, index of consumer expectations, money supply, and interest rate spread. The coincident indicators consist of four variables such as industrial production and manufacturing and trade sales, and the lagging indicators consist of seven variables such as duration of unemployment and commercial and industrial loans outstanding.

The composite indexes are used to indicate peaks and troughs in the business cycle. The intent of using all three is to summarize and reveal turning point patterns in economic data better. Note that a change in direction in a composite index does not automatically indicate a cyclical turning point. The movement must be of sufficient size, duration, and scope.[4]

Example 13-1

In March 2001, following the stock market plunge and weakening of the economy, it was reported that the index of leading economic indicators declined in February for the fourth time in five months. In November 2001, the NBER declared that a recession began in March 2001. In July 2003, the NBER declared it ended in November 2001.

Using the Internet

Business cycles dates can be found at www.nber.org. Information on the composite indexes can be found at http://www.tcb-indicators.org/. The late Geoffrey Moore is considered the father of the Leading Economic Indicators. His research firm, Economic Cycle Research Institute (ECRI), can be found at www.businesscycle.com. This site carries the Weekly Leading Index (WLI), which is updated weekly (available Friday afternoon) and provides the most current indicator of what's happening in the economy. It incorporates seven major economic indicators and gives a quick read on consumer confidence. It recorded a peak up to that time of 125.3 in June 2000 and then declined. The start of the recession is officially March 2001. ECRI also produces an inflation index they call the Future Inflation Gauge.

---

[3] The Conference Board, a business membership and research network founded in 1916, assumed the responsibility for computing the composite indexes from the Department of Commerce.
[4] All of this information is available at the Conference Board Web site, http://www.tcb-indicators.org/.

The Global Perspective The most recent downturn in economic activity in the United States occurred as other countries were experiencing the same thing. Thus, there was a synchronized global downturn, which has been the case for most recent recessions. As we noted in Chapter 1, economies around the world are now more integrated and linked to each other because of increased trade and capital flows among countries. However, the most important reason for synchronized recessions among many countries is a common shock that is felt around the world. For example, in the 1970s, there was an oil price shock, and it affected numerous countries. With the most recent recession, the collapse of the technology sector, and with it the technology stocks, was the common shock that occurred in several countries.

Has the Business Cycle Been Tamed? From the end of World War II through the end of the twentieth century, there were nine recessions. As of June 2000, the economy had been expanding for 114 months, and the bull market for equities that began in the fall of 1990 had become the longest running bull market on record (the previous record was 1921 to 1929). Some observers were asking if the business cycle is dead. This is based in part on the belief by some that slumps are not inevitable but rather are caused by accidents that happen. As one CEO noted, "We are in a global economy . . ." which "has changed the paradigm. . . . We don't see the cyclical events that characterized the past."[5]

The other side of the coin is that as the expansion continues, people tend to forget the lessons learned from prior recessions. As one researcher on business cycles noted, "Who can eliminate herding?," referring to the tendency of people getting collectively carried away. Expansions typically end for one of the following reasons: an overheating economy with rising inflation, forcing the Federal Reserve (Fed) to raise interest rates; an external shock, such as a sharp rise in oil prices; or a financial crash following a break in a speculative **bubble** (when speculation pushes asset prices to unsustainable highs). For example, the Japanese economic expansion of the 1980s was a speculative bubble that drove stock prices and land values to record levels, and the bubble burst at the end of the 1980s—the Japanese economy and market have yet to recover.

One can argue that a bubble occurred in U.S. stock markets in the late 1990s, peaking in March 2000.[6] Regardless of whether it did, and whether it caused a recession, the tenth recession since WW II officially began in March 2001, demonstrating once again that the business cycle is not dead. Although less frequent than they were even 30 years ago, given the great expansion of the 1990s, recessions still occur! Business cycles may be different than they used to be, but they still exist, and in all likelihood will continue to do so.

The Stock Market and the Business Cycle The stock market is, of course, a significant and vital part of the overall economy. Clearly, a strong relationship exists between the two. If the economy is doing badly, most companies will also be performing poorly, as will the stock market. Conversely, if the economy is prospering, most companies will also be doing well, and the stock market will reflect this economic strength.

The relationship between the economy and the stock market is interesting—stock prices generally lead the economy. Historically, it is the most sensitive indicator of the business cycle (as we saw, it is one of the leading indicators). Therefore, we must take into account this leading relationship when we are using the economy's condition to evaluate the market. The market and the economy are closely related, but stock prices typically turn before the economy.

Bubble When speculation pushes asset prices to unsustainable highs

---

[5] This quote and discussion is based on Jacob M. Schlesinger, "The Business Cycle Is Tamed, Many Say, Alarming Some Others," *The Wall Street Journal*, November 15, 1996, p. A1 and p. A16.

[6] For a discussion of whether the U.S. markets underwent a speculative bubble, see Robert J. Shiller, "Bubbles, Human Judgment, and Expert Opinion," *Financial Analysts Journal*, May/June 2002, pp. 18–26.

Why is the market a leading indicator of the economy? Basically, investors are discounting the future, because, as the valuation analysis in Chapter 10 showed, stocks are worth today the discounted value of all future cash flows. Current stock prices reflect investor expectations of the future. Stock prices adjust quickly if investor expectations of corporate profits change. Of course, the market can misjudge corporate profits, resulting in a false signal about future movements in the economy.

An alternative explanation for stock prices leading the economy involves an investor change in the required rate of return, which again would result in an immediate change in stock prices. Note that the valuation model allows for a change in confidence (psychological elements), because a change in investor confidence changes the required rate of return (in the opposite direction). Psychological elements are sometimes used in explaining market movements.

How reliable is this relationship between the stock market and the business cycle? Although it is generally considered to be reliable, it is widely known that the market has given false signals about future economic activity, particularly with regard to recessions. The old joke goes something like this—"The market has predicted nine out of the last five recessions."[7]

Recognizing that the market does not always lead the economy in the predicted manner, consider what an examination of the historical record shows:

❏ Stock prices peak roughly one year before the start of a recession.

Example 13-2 This business cycle–stock-price relationship is illustrated by what happened in 2000 to 2001. The stock markets in the United States peaked in early spring 2000, and the longest economic expansion in U.S. history–the 10-year expansion of the 1990s—is considered to have ended in March 2001.

❏ The typical contraction in stock prices is 25 percent from the peak. With recent recessions, however, it has been 40 percent or more. For example, in 2000 to 2002, the Standard & Poor's (S&P 500) Composite Index declined some 45 percent from its peak.
❏ The ability of the market to predict recoveries has been remarkably good.
❏ Stock prices almost always turn up three to five months before a recovery, with four months being very typical.

Following World War II, and preceding the recession of 2001, there were nine periods of recovery. In each of these, the market (the S&P 500) rose before the recession's trough and continued to rise as the expansion entered its early stages. Six months into recovery, stock prices were, on average, more than 25 percent higher than they had been a year earlier.

In summary, although the leading relationship between the stock market and the economy is far from perfect, investors must take it into account. Typically, by the time investors clearly recognize what the economy is doing, such as going into recession or coming out of recession, the stock market has already anticipated the event and reacted.

---

[7] The NBER defines a recession as a "significant decline in activity spread across the economy, lasting more than a few months, visibile in industrial production, real income and wholesale-retail sales."

THE RELATIONSHIP BETWEEN THE BOND MARKET, THE STOCK MARKET, AND THE ECONOMY

What is the relationship between the bond market and the stock market? Bond prices and interest rates are opposite sides of the coin—if bond prices move up (down), interest rates move down (up).

Stock investors pay attention to the bond market, because interest rates are available daily as an indicator of what is happening in the economy. The bond market can provide daily signals of what bond traders and investors think about the economy, and the stock market reacts to the state of the economy. Bond traders react to news of unemployment, or rising sales, or changes in the money supply, thereby affecting interest rates and bond prices on a daily basis. As we saw in Chapter 10, interest rates are a very important consideration in the valuation process. As we shall see later in the chapter, interest rates are one of the two key variables involved in understanding the stock market. And, as explained below, yield curves from the bond market are useful in forecasting the economy.

FORECASTS OF THE ECONOMY

Good economic forecasts are of obvious significant value to investors. Since the economy and the market are closely related, good forecasts of macroeconomic variables would be very useful. How good are such forecasts, which are widely available?

McNees concluded that forecasts made by the prominent forecasters are very similar and that differences in accuracy are very small, suggesting that investors can use any of a number of such forecasts. Obviously, not all forecasters are equally accurate, and all forecasters make errors. The only good news is that forecast accuracy apparently has increased over time.[8]

Because of its vital role in the economy, monetary policy traditionally has been assumed to have an important effect on the economy, stock prices, and interest rate. Almost all theories of the macroeconomy postulate a relationship between money and future economic activity, with the relationship depending on whether changes in money stock can be attributed to shifts in money supply or money demand. For example, increases in money supply tend to increase economic activity, whereas increases in money demand tend to reduce economic activity.

Some research indicates that an alternative measure of money called MZM has, over a period of as much as 20 years, exhibited a stable relationship with nominal GDP. MZM is defined as M2, a well-known measure of money, plus savings deposits (including money market deposit accounts, MMDAs) small time deposits, and retail money market mutual funds). This measure appears to be immune to the innovations in the mutual fund industry that caused M2, widely used to assess the relationship between money and economic activity, to lose its usefulness as an indicator.

When the Chairman Speaks Regardless of money's current role in forecasting economic activity, many investors keep an eye on the actions of the Federal Reserve because of its role in monetary policy and its impact on interest rates. When the chairman, Alan Greenspan, testifies before Congress or otherwise makes a public statement, the financial markets scrutinize every word for clues as to the future of the economy and financial markets. And when the Fed changes the key federal funds rate, which is given publicity, financial markets typically react noticeably, both positively and negatively. Historically, the Fed has reacted to a weakening economy with a lower target for the federal funds rate.

---

[8] This discussion is based on Stephen J. McNees, "How Accurate Are Macroeconomic Forecasts?" *New England Economic Review* (July–August 1988).

Robert Barro, a prominent Harvard economist, has argued that because Greenspan has carried out a relatively consistent policy of fighting inflation, investors can construct simple models to predict the Fed's behavior.[9] According to him, the actual inflation rate, as measured by the deflator for GDP (as opposed to using the Consumer Price Index, CPI), is a major determinant of Fed activity. The Fed reacts to strong employment growth, which predicts a higher rate of future inflation and thus a tendency for interest rates to rise. The Fed also tends to raise interest rates as the unemployment rate declines. In short, of all the variables that the Fed could use to influence its behavior, it is primarily the rate of inflation and the labor market that matters.

Using the Internet

Investors can go to www.bloomberg.com, click on "News," and then "Fed Watch" and review considerable information, opinions, and rumors about what the Fed is doing and is likely to do.

Not surprisingly, relationships between macrovariables are imprecise. Controversies still exist about the impact of changes in some policy variables on the economy. For example, most economists agree that monetary policy tightening can slow an overheating economy, but there is substantial disagreement about the power of monetary policy to stimulate a weak economy. Although certainly not conclusive, some estimates suggest that in the short run the response to increases in the federal funds rate (associated with monetary policy tightening) is more than twice the response to decreases in the federal funds rate (associated with monetary policy stimulus).[10]

Insights from the Yield Curve In Chapter 18, we will consider the yield curve and its role in the management of bond portfolios. The yield curve depicts the relationship between bond yields and time, holding the issuer constant, and in effect shows how interest rates vary across time on any given day. It should contain valuable information, because it reflects bond traders' views about the future of the economy. Several studies suggest that the yield curve is very useful in making economic forecasts. The professionals use the yield curve as an indicator of how the Fed is managing the economy.

It has long been recognized that the shape of the yield curve is related to the stage of the business cycle. In the early stages of an expansion, yield curves tend to be low and upward sloping, and as the peak of the cycle approaches, yield curves tend to be high and downward sloping. More specifically:

- A steepening yield curve suggests that the economy is accelerating in terms of activity as monetary policy stimulates the economy.
- When the yield curve becomes more flat, it suggests that economic activity is slowing down.
- An inverted yield curve, however, carries an ominous message—expectations of an economic slowdown. Every recession since World War II has been preceded by a downward-sloping yield curve.

Part (a) of Figure 13-2 shows Treasury yield curves for August 2001 and August 2002. They were upward sloping, which is the normal shape of the yield curve. On the other

[9] See Robert J. Barro, "How to Build Your Own Fed Crystal Ball," *Business Week*, December 4, 1999, p. 20.
[10] See Jeremy Piger, "Pushing On a String," *Monetary Trends*, The Federal Reserve Bank of St. Louis, March 2003, p. 1.

Figure 13-2

Treasury Yield Curves, Selected Periods

SOURCE: *Economic Trends*, Federal Reserve Bank of Cleveland, April 2000, p. 4 and September 2002, p. 7.

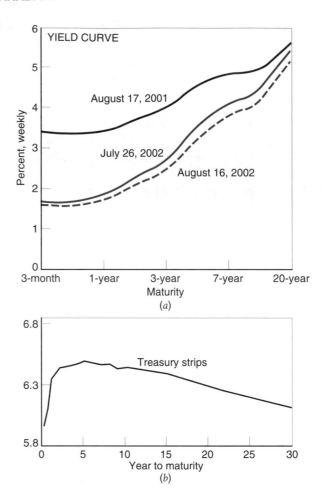

hand, part (b) of Figure 13-2 shows a Treasury yield curve in March 2000, and it is clearly downward sloping. As we now know, the latest recession officially began in March 2001.

Some researchers have developed a model to predict if the economy is going into a recession that uses as a prominent variable the yield spread between the 10-year Treasury security and the 3-month Treasury bill. According to the authors, this model was quite successful in predicting a recession four quarters in advance.[11]

Forecasts from Economic Observers Investors can find forecasts of the economy from various sources. Some of these are what are referred to as "consensus" forecasts, in the same way that we talk about consensus earnings forecasts for stocks. For example, *Blue Chip Economic Indicators* is a publication that compiles consensus forecasts from well-known economic forecasters of such important economic variables as real GDP, consumer prices, and interest rates. Thus, investors can find reputable, consistently done (but not necessarily accurate) forecasts of the economy for at least the year ahead.

---

[11] See Arturo Estrella and Frederic S. Mishkin, "The Yield Curve as a Predictor of U.S. Recessions," *Current Issues in Economics and Finance*, Vol. 2, June 1966, pp. 1–6; and Estrella and Mishkin, "Predicting U.S. Recessions: Financial Variables as Leading Indicators," *Review of Economics and Statistics*, Vol. 80, February 1998, pp. 45–61.

Understanding the Stock Market

WHAT DO WE MEAN BY THE "MARKET"?

How often have you heard someone ask, "How did the market do today?," or "How did the market react to that announcement?" Virtually everyone investing in stocks wants a general idea of how the overall market for equity securities is performing, both to guide their actions and to act as a benchmark against which to judge the performance of their securities. Furthermore, several specific uses of market measures can be identified, as discussed in the next section.

When most investors refer to the "market," they mean the stock market in general as proxied by some market index or indicator as discussed in Chapter 4. Because the "market" is simply the aggregate of all security prices, it is most conveniently measured by some index or average of stock prices.

As we know from Chapter 4, most market indexes are designed to measure a particular market segment, such as blue-chip New York Stock Exchange (NYSE) stocks (the Dow Jones Industrial Average), all stocks on the NYSE, the Nasdaq market, and foreign stocks. When discussing the market, it is possible to use a broad market index, such as the Wilshire 5000 Index. Typically, however, most investors today, when they refer to the market, use as their indicator of the market either the Dow Jones Industrial Average (reported daily in *The Wall Street Journal* and on the nightly television news) or the Standard and Poor's 500 Composite Index (favored by most institutional investors and money managers). Therefore, when we discuss the market, we are referring to the market as measured by one of these two market indexes.

Uses of Market Measures Market measures tell investors how all stocks in general are doing at any time or give them a "feel" for the market. Many investors are encouraged to invest if stocks are moving upward, whereas downward trends may encourage some to liquidate their holdings and invest in money market assets or funds.

The historical records of market measures are useful for gauging where the market is in a particular cycle and possibly for shedding light on what will happen. Assume, for example, that the market has never fallen more than X percent, as measured by some index, in a six-month period. Although this information is no guarantee that such a decline will not occur, this type of knowledge aids investors in evaluating their potential downside risk over some period of time.

Market measures are useful to investors in quickly judging their overall portfolio performance. Because stocks tend to move up or down together, the rising or falling of the market will generally indicate to the investor how he or she is likely to do. Of course, to determine the exact performance, each investor's portfolio must be measured individually, a topic to be discussed in Chapter 22.

Technical analysts need to know the historical record of the market when they are seeking out patterns from the past that may repeat in the future. Detection of such patterns is the basis for forecasting the future direction of the market using technical analysis, which is discussed in Chapter 16.

Market indexes are also used to calculate betas, an important measure of risk discussed in earlier chapters. An individual security's returns are regressed on the market's returns in order to estimate the security's beta, or relative measure of systematic risk.

WHAT DETERMINES AGGREGATE STOCK PRICES?

In Chapter 10, we examined the variables that are used to estimate the intrinsic value of stocks with the dividend discount model—dividends and the required rate of return—and with the P/E ratio model—earnings and the P/E ratio. The same models apply to the aggregate stock market as represented by a market index such as the S&P 500 Index.

To value the stock market using the fundamental analysis approach explained in Chapter 10, we use as our foundation the P/E ratio or multiplier approach, because a majority of investors focus on earnings and P/E ratios. Estimates of index earnings and the earnings multiplier are used in Equation 13-1. As explained in Chapter 10, this model uses a forward P/E ratio. We will use the S&P 500 Index as our measure of the stock market:

$$P_0 = P_0/E_1 \times E_1 \qquad\qquad (13\text{-}1)$$

where

E_1 = expected earnings on the S&P 500 Index
P_0/E_1 = the forward price-earnings ratio or multiplier

We consider each of these variables in turn.

The Earnings Stream Estimating earnings for purposes of valuing the market is not easy. The item of interest is the earnings per share for a market index or, in general, corporate profits after taxes.

Corporate profits are derived from corporate sales, which in turn are related to GDP. A detailed, top-down fundamental analysis of the economy/market would involve estimating each of these variables, starting with GDP, then corporate sales, working down to corporate earnings before taxes, and finally to corporate earnings after taxes. Each of these steps can involve various levels of difficulty.

Looking at real (inflation-adjusted) earnings growth, we would expect it to correlate closely with real GDP growth over the long run. And, in fact, for the last 30 or so years, real GDP growth has averaged about 3.1 percent annually, whereas real earnings for the S&P 500 Index has averaged about 2.7 percent annually. Therefore, when estimating real earnings growth for the future, the best guide may be expected real GDP growth.

It is reasonable to expect corporate earnings to grow, on average, at about the rate of the economy as a whole. However, for the last years of the twentieth century, operating earnings per share for the S&P 500 grew an average of 10.2 percent a year versus a rate of 5.56 percent for economic growth. This simply illustrates how difficult it is to forecast earnings accurately. Extenuating factors can cause some divergences. For example, share repurchases by firms may increase the rate of earnings growth relative to historical rates. Since earnings have to be allocated over fewer shares as firms repurchase shares, earnings per share increases. Estimates are that this could add anywhere from one-half to one and one-half percentage points to the growth rate of real earnings.

Which Earnings Should We Use? Note that an annual EPS for the S&P 500 Index, as obtained at www.spglobal.com, can be constructed in various ways. For example, as of June 2002, all four quarters for 2002 were estimates—a four-quarter total of $51.23. A one-year ahead estimate could involve the last two quarters of 2002 and the first two quarters of 2003. The past year's EPS number could be taken to be the calendar year 2001, or the last two quarters of 2001 and the first two quarters of 2002.

This is further complicated by the fact that for the S&P 500, Standard & Poor's provides both top-down and bottom-up estimates and both "as reported" estimates and operating estimates. Furthermore, S&P is now providing its "core earnings" for the S&P 500 Index, which focuses on companies' after-tax earnings generated from their principal businesses. S&P has determined that the primary reasons that core earnings and as-reported earnings differ are pension income and stock option grant expenses, with the treatment of pension gains having a very significant impact. The differences between these two earnings numbers can be substantial.

Example 13-3
In October 2002, Standard & Poor's reported that for the 12 months ended June 2002, core earnings for the S&P 500 Index were $18.48 per share versus $26.74 per share for as-reported earnings.

The Multiplier or P/E Ratio The multiplier to be applied to the earnings estimate is as important as the earnings estimate, and often more so. Investors sometimes mistakenly ignore the multiplier and concentrate only on the earnings estimate. But earnings growth is not always the leading factor in significant price changes in the market. Instead, low interest rates may lead to high P/E ratios, which in turn may account for the majority of the price changes.

Example 13-4
The S&P 500 Index increased about 150 percent between the end of 1994 and December 1998. Less than one-third of that increase was attributable to higher earnings, with the remainder being attributable to an increase in the P/E ratio. At the end of 1997, the P/E based on current earnings was 21.5. In December 1998, it was 26. Over the period 1994 to 1998, corporate earnings rose about 40 percent and the P/E ratio doubled, thereby creating the sharp rise in the S&P 500.

The multiplier is more volatile than the earnings component and, therefore, is even more difficult to predict. Consider Figure 13-3, which shows the P/E ratio for the S&P 500 Index since 1947. A trend line has been included to show the general upward swing of P/E ratios across time. Also, three different levels of P/Es are identified with the bars, showing that at different times (the 1960s and early 1970s, the late 1970s and early 1980s, and the late 1980s and early 1990s), P/Es tended to cluster together.

The P/E ratio began to rise in the early 1950s, reached a peak by 1960, and declined to the 16 to 18 area and remained around that level through 1972. As inflation heated up in 1973 and interest rates rose, the multiplier started to decline, and by 1974 it was around 7,

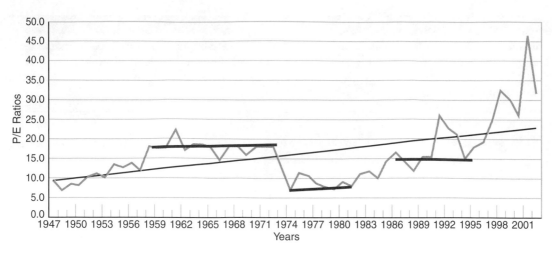

Figure 13-3

S&P 500 price/earnings ratios, 1947–2002.

less than half its previous level—a drastic cut for such a short time. Therefore, what was considered normal (about 17) in the 1960s and early 1970s was not the norm in the late 1970s and early 1980s. Most investors did not anticipate P/E ratios this low for this length of time.

The lesson from this analysis is obvious: Investors cannot simply extrapolate P/E ratios, because dramatic changes occur over time. Perhaps the most that can be said is that in the postwar period, P/E ratios of broadly based indices have ranged from an average of about 7 to an average of about 17. For the S&P 500 Composite Index, the average P/E for the period 1920 to 2001 was approximately 17, and for the period 1950 to 2001 it was 17. The variation, however, can be dramatic. The P/E ratio for the S&P 500 was 7.8 in 1978 and 32.6 in 1998. By 2000, the P/E had decreased to 26.

P/E ratios are generally depressed when interest rates and the rate of inflation are high, such as around 1980 to 1981. P/E ratios tend to be high when inflation and interest rates are low, such as the period of the mid- to late-1990s, when P/E ratios were at quite high levels by historical standards. When earnings are growing and the upward profit trend appears to be sustainable, investors are willing to pay more for today's earnings. Think of the following relationship between interest rates and P/E ratios. In 1982, yields on 10-year Treasury bonds were approximately 13 percent, and the P/E ratio on the S&P 500 Index was around 11. In the late 1990s, interest rates were around 6 percent, and the P/E ratio for 1998 was 32.6, and for 1999, 30.5. In 2001, it was 46.

Investors must be careful when using P/E ratios to place them in the proper context. P/E ratios can refer to historical data, an average for the year, or a prospective period such as the year ahead. Obviously, a significant difference can exist between P/E ratios calculated using these different definitions. Furthermore, as noted earlier, various definitions of earnings for an index such as the S&P 500 are available.

Example 13-5

As noted earlier, S&P recorded "as-reported" earnings on the S&P 500 through June 2002 as 24.74. Based on a price at the end of October 2002, the P/E ratio was 35.8. Using "core earnings" for the same period of $18.48, the P/E ratio was 47.9. Based on a bottom-up estimate of operating earnings for the same period of $41.59, the P/E ratio was 21.3. Using a bottom-up estimate of 12-month earnings ending in June 2003 of $51.12, the P/E ratio was 17.3.

Putting the Two Together Valuing the aggregate market is not easy, because the market is presumably always looking ahead, and current stock prices reflect this. Earnings estimates are typically involved, no one knows for sure how far the market is looking ahead, and no one knows for sure what the market is willing to pay for a dollar of earnings.

Example 13-6   Industry analysts are notoriously optimistic when forecasting market earnings, such as the growth for the S&P 500. In 1998, they forecast earnings growth of about 14 percent, whereas actual earnings declined about 1 percent. For 1999, they started out forecasting earnings growth of about 19 percent, on average. They then started cutting this number as more data became available.

Regardless of the difficulties, the bottom line is this—to value the level of the market, an investor must analyze both factors that determine stock prices: corporate earnings and multipliers.

Making Market Forecasts

Accurate forecasts of the stock market, particularly short-term forecasts, are impossible for anyone to do *consistently*. As discussed in Chapter 12, there is strong evidence that the market is efficient; this implies that changes in the market cannot be predicted on the basis of information about previous changes. Another implication is that even professional money managers cannot consistently forecast the market using available information, and the available evidence on the performance success of professional investors supports this proposition. Such implications are supported by a wealth of available data.

Nevertheless, most investors ultimately want to make some estimates of likely changes in the stock market. Not only do they want to try to understand what the market is doing currently and why, but they also want some reasonable estimates of the future. Part of this process, as discussed earlier, involves analyzing the overall economy. Ideally, investors need estimates of corporate earnings and estimates of the market's P/E ratio for some future period or periods. As we have seen, however, accurate estimates are difficult to obtain, given the various constructs that are available. What then can investors do to try to assess future movements in the market?

We will consider below some approaches that investors can and do use to make some types of market forecasts. Such forecasts may be implicit or explicit, crude or detailed, short-term or longer-term.

FOCUS ON THE IMPORTANT VARIABLES

It has long been known that stock prices are closely related to corporate earnings, and that interest rates play a major role in affecting both bond and stock prices. Consider an interview in late 2001 with Warren Buffett, arguably the best-known investor in the United States.[12] Buffett was asked to comment, as he did in 1999, on the likely scenario for the market. Buffett argued that long-term movements in stock prices in the past, and likely in the future, are caused by significant changes in "two critical economic variables":

1. interest rates
2. expected corporate profits

If investors wish to understand the stock market and make reasonable judgments about future movements in stock prices, they must carefully analyze interest rates and expected corporate profits.

---

[12] See "Warren Buffett on the Stock Market," *Fortune*, December 10, 2001, p. 82.

Corporate Earnings, Interest Rates, and Stock Prices As we saw in Chapter 10, interest rates and P/E ratios are inversely related. When fixed-income securities are paying less return, investors are willing to pay more for stocks; therefore, P/E ratios are higher. Stocks rise strongly as earnings climb and interest rates stay low. In other words, investors must be concerned with earnings and interest rates as they assess the outlook for stocks.

Figure 13-4 shows the three series together—interest rates, percent change in corporate profits after taxes annually, and the percent change in total returns annually for the S&P 500 Index for the period 1978 to 2002. The shaded areas indicate recessions, as

Figure 13-4

Interest rates, corporate earnings, and S&P 500 Index total returns, 1975–2002.

SOURCE: *National Economic Trends*, The Federal Reserve Bank of St. Louis, April 2003, pp. 7, 21.

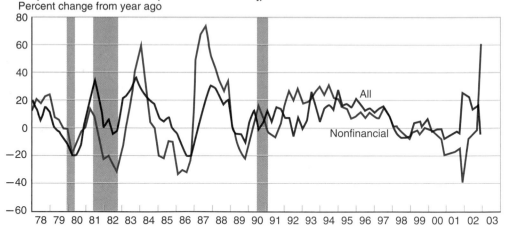

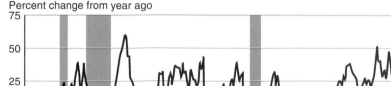

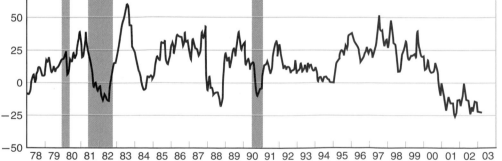

determined by the National Bureau of Economic Research. In general, in the recessionary periods, interest rates trended upward before the recession, corporate profit changes were downward, and stock return changes were downward. Also notice the similarities in profit changes and stock return changes in terms of highs and lows, and how rising (falling) interest rates are generally associated with falling (rising) stock returns.

It is logical to expect a relationship between corporate profits and stock prices. If the economy is prospering, investors will expect corporate earnings and dividends to rise and, other things being equal, stock prices to rise. To a large extent, corporate earnings growth is thought of by most market observers as the basis for share price growth. In fact, holding the P/E ratio constant, growth in price should match growth in earnings. It is worthwhile to note that S&P earnings declined almost 20 percent in 2001, which was the first decline in 10 years. The markets suffered sharp declines in 2001 and again in much of 2002, because there was no apparent recovery in earnings in sight.

Interest rates are a basic component of discount rates, with the two usually moving together. As Figure 13-4 shows, there is clearly a relationship between interest rate movements and stock prices, just as there is with corporate profits. In this case, however, the relationship is inverse; that is, as interest rates rise (fall), stock prices fall (rise), with other things being equal.

To see the interest rate relationship more clearly, Table 13-1 shows a simple analysis between the corporate Aaa bond rate and total returns for the S&P 500 Index on an annual basis. In 1989, interest rates declined and the S&P return was 31.2 percent, whereas in 1990, interest rates rose and the S&P return was −3.1 percent. The years 1991, 1992, and 1993 saw declining interest rates and S&P total returns of 30 percent, 7.4 percent, and 9.9 percent, respectively. On the other hand, interest rates rose in 1994, causing severe turmoil in both the stock market (which had a gain of 1.3 percent) and the bond market. Interest rates declined in 1995, a great year for stocks, and again in 1997 and 1998, both very good years for stocks. Rates rose in 1999, another good year for the market, and declined somewhat in 2000, when the market suffered its first decline in several years. Rates continued to decline in 2001 and 2002, but these declines could not offset the troubled economy, and the stock market suffered losses in both years.

Table 13-1 Annual Interest Rates and Total Returns on the S&P 500 Index, 1985–2002

	Interest Rates	S&P 500 Index Total Returns
1985	9.91	31
1986	8.53	18.5
1987	10.06	5.7
1988	9.61	16.3
1989	8.87	31.2
1990	9.05	−3.1
1991	8.16	30
1992	7.91	7.4
1993	7	9.9
1994	8.49	1.3
1995	6.71	37
1996	7.27	22.7
1997	6.71	33.1
1998	6.23	28.3
1999	7.64	20.9
2000	7.16	−9.1
2001	6.76	−11.9
2002	6.21	−22.1

Investments Intuition

If interest rates rise, the riskless rate of return, RF, rises, because it is tied to interest rates, and other things being equal, the required rate of return (dis- count rate) rises, because the riskless rate is one of its two components.

Note that although interest rates rose in 1996 and in 1999, the S&P had a total return of 22.7 and 20.9 percent respectively. This simply illustrates that these basic relationships do not always go in the expected direction at exactly the same time, and that two variables are involved in affecting stock returns, corporate earnings and interest rates. Reported EPS for the S&P 500 Index increased in both of those years.

Investors must take into account the role of changes in interest rates in affecting investor expectations. Investors pay close attention to announcements by the Fed that could possibly affect interest rates, as well as to any other factors that may play a role. In turn, the popular press reports possible changes in interest rates as they might affect the stock market.

Example 13-7 Consider the following headlines from *The Wall Street Journal* within a six-week period:
"Markets Fall on Absence of Rate Cut"
"Recent Rise in Long-Term Interest Rates May Mean Trouble for the Stock Market"
"As Interest Rates Rise, Will Stocks Fall?"
"Benchmark Treasury Yield Tops 8%; Stocks Fall"

Like most relationships involving investing, the relationship between interest rates and stock prices is not perfect. Nor do interest rates have a linear effect on stock prices. The best approach for investors is simply to think carefully about the likely course for corporate profits and interest rates. What we are seeking here are general clues as to the economy and the market's direction and the duration of a likely change. For example, to say that we are confident the market will go to 13,000 or 6,000 (as measured by the Dow Jones Industrial Average) one year from now is foolish. Similarly, a strong prediction that corporate earnings will rise next year by 10 percent, or that interest rates are sure to rise (or fall) X percent, is a virtually certain prescription for embarrassment.

In truth, most individual investors—indeed, most professional investors—cannot time the market consistently. What then should they do? The best approach for most investors is to recognize the futility of attempting consistently to forecast successfully the direction of the market, but also recognize that periodically situations will develop that suggest strong action. An example is 1982 when interest rates reached record peaks. Either rates were going to decline, or the U.S. economy faced a crisis situation. Interest rates did decline, and in doing so they launched one of the greatest bull markets in U.S. history.

Box 13-1 is an interesting analysis of why investors may simply choose to stand pat, and even buy, when the market appears to be ready to decline—or many people are claiming that it is. According to the evidence presented, investors lose more by missing a bull market than by dodging a bear market. This is consistent with the evidence presented in Chapter 11 on market timing—investors who miss a relatively few months in the market may lose much of the gains during that time period. The most important point, however, is the same as before—the impact of the overall market on an investor's portfolio is enormous.

BOX 13-1

Overcoming the Bear Market Blues

For more than three years, the stock market steadily marched to higher ground. Then, in February, the Federal Reserve Board, fearful of a return of inflation, began to curb monetary growth and raise interest rates. That set off the stock market's first significant downdraft since the Persian Gulf War started in 1991. Now nervous investors are wondering: Should I stay in stocks, or should I go?

During market declines, emotion tends to overtake reason and large numbers of investors make the biggest mistakes of their investment lives. The overpowering urge is to dump stocks or equity mutual funds and retreat to the safety of money market funds and bank accounts. These urges are understandable. However, investors who act on them often lock in losses and miss profit opportunities when stocks eventually rebound.

Instead of selling during market slumps, history suggests that investors should put their fears aside. If anything, it's a good time for an investor to start bargain hunting, with the intention of making an even bigger commitment to stocks. Riding out a bear market certainly can be painful. But the rewards of moving to safer ground—even when it's done with impeccable timing—are far less dramatic than is generally supposed. What's more, standing pat can be far less damaging to a portfolio than the cost of missing a major upward move in stock prices.

Want proof? Let's consider an imaginary investor with flawless timing skills, one who was able to switch his money from stocks to Treasury bills during each of the market's five worst years from 1940 through 1993. We're assuming this investor exited the market completely and then put 100 percent of his portfolio back into stocks the following year. This strategy, requiring perfect foresight, would certainly have beaten the performance of the Standard & Poor's 500 Index. But not by much. For all his brilliance, our investor would have earned a compounded annual return of 13.9 percent compared with an 11.7 percent return for the S&P 500.

Now let's look at what would have happened to an investor who missed the market's biggest upswings—switching his money out of stocks and into Treasury bills during each of the market's five best years. This unfortunate soul would have earned an average annual return of only 8.7 percent.

The lesson: There is more to lose by missing a bull market than there is to be gained by dodging a bear. And the easiest way to capture the profits provided by future bull markets is to remain fully invested in stocks over the long term. "Time cures a lot of things, including volatility," says

Investing at Market Peaks

The Results of Investing $5,000 Per Year in the S&P 500 Index at the Peak of the Market That Year

Market Top	Cumulative Investment	Account Value at Year End
1/3/74	$5,000	$3,601
7/15/75	$10,000	$9,756
9/21/76	$15,000	$17,163
1/3/77	$20,000	$20,590
9/12/78	$25,000	$26,544
10/5/19	$30,000	$36,358
11/28/80	$35,000	$53,041
1/6/81	$40,000	$55,127
11/9/82	$45,000	$71,958
10/10/83	$50,000	$92,947
11/6/84	$55,000	$103,692
12/16/85	$60,000	$141,534
12/2/86	$65,000	$172,690
8/25/87	$70,000	$185,361
10/21/88	$75,000	$220,879
10/9/89	$80,000	$295,604
7/16/90	$85,000	$290,959
12/31/91	$90,000	$384,223
12/18/92	$95,000	$418,426
12/28/93	$100,000	$465,397

SOURCE: American Funds Group.

Carl Gargula, managing director at Ibbotson Associates, a Chicago investment-consulting firm.

Still, the biggest fear investors have now is that if they were to buy stocks, they'd be plunging in at or near the top of the market. What could be worse than buying equities a day or two before the onset of a bear move?

Although it may seem counterintuitive, data show that buying at market tops is not as destructive to a portfolio's health as investors might think. Since 1940, the stock market has declined by 5 percent or more on 45 occasions. Thirteen of those declines exceeded 15 percent, and four exceeded 25 percent. In all, the stock market has spent 28 percent of that time in significant retreat. These declines have typically lasted four months, with share prices tumbling an average of 12.5 percent.

Here's where it gets interesting: The folks at the American Funds Group, a mutual fund firm in Los Angeles, recently did a study that illustrates what would have happened had an investor bought at the peak of the market not once, but every year for the last two decades. The table shows what would have happened to an investor's portfolio if $5,000 was invested in the S&P 500 Index during each of the last 20 years on the day the market peaked for that year. In other words, each investment lost money almost immediately after it was made as the market fell—the ultimate in a worried investor's nightmare.

The surprise is that after 20 years, this star-crossed investor's portfolio fared pretty darn well. Nobody's wrong all the time, but even our hopelessly unlucky investor would have earned a 13.7 percent compounded annual return. According to American Funds Group, the $100,000 this hypothetical investor would have put into the market over the 20 years would gradually have transformed itself into a portfolio valued at $465,397.

Given the astronomical odds against an investor buying at precisely the wrong moment 20 years in a row, you can bet that your own stock market performance would be even higher than his.

Of course, it's disturbing to see the value of a portfolio drop during a stock market correction. However, since stock market corrections are a fact of life, investors must learn to live with them. Avoid the urge to cut and run. It may seem like the safe thing to do at the time, but the long-term risks of missing an upturn are even more dangerous. Individuals who have the financial resources to do so should use stock market declines as opportunities to add to their portfolios, seeking out high-quality stocks for sale at discount prices. In the end, those who do will be much wealthier for their fortitude.

USING THE BUSINESS CYCLE TO MAKE MARKET FORECASTS

Earlier we established the idea that certain composite indexes can be helpful in forecasting or ascertaining the position of the business cycle. However, stock prices are one of the leading indicators, tending to lead the economy's turning points, both peaks and troughs.

What is the investor who is trying to forecast the market to do? This leading relationship between stock prices and the economy must be taken into account in forecasting likely changes in stock prices. Stock prices generally decline in recessions, and the steeper the recession, the steeper the decline. However, investors need to think about the business cycle's turning points months before they occur in order to have a handle on the turning points in the stock market. If a business cycle downturn appears to be likely in the future, the market will also be likely to turn down some months ahead of the economic downturn.

We can be somewhat more precise about the leading role of stock prices. Because of this tendency to lead the economy, the total return on stocks (on an annual basis) could be negative (positive) in years in which the business cycle peaks (bottoms). Stock prices have almost always risen as the business cycle is approaching a trough. These increases have been large, so that investors do well during these periods. Furthermore, stock prices often remain steady or even decline suddenly as the business cycle enters into the initial phase of recovery. After the previous sharp rise as the bottom is approached, a period of steady prices or even a decline typically occurs. The economy, of course, is still moving ahead.

Based on the above analysis:

1. If the investor can recognize the bottoming out of the economy before it occurs, a market rise can be predicted, at least based on past experience, before the bottom is hit. In previous recessions since World War II, the market started to rise about halfway between GDP starting to decline and starting to grow again.
2. The market's average gain over the 12 months following its bottom point is about 36 percent.
3. As the economy recovers, stock prices may level off or even decline. Therefore, a second significant movement in the market may be predictable, again based on past experience.

4. Based on the most recent 10 economic slumps in the twentieth century, the market P/E usually rises just before the end of the slump. It then remains roughly unchanged over the next year.

Some Practical Advice

Forecasting market movements is a humbling experience, and will cause everyone to look foolish sometime. The points mentioned above are based on past experience, but the past does not always repeat itself. In the spring and summer of 2002, many market observers expected a rise in the market based on an apparent ending to the economic slump. Although a profit recovery had not occurred, it appeared to many that it was time to get back in the market in anticipation of the market rising before the absolute bottom. The anticipated market rise did not occur as early as expected.

The value of being able to analyze business cycle turning points as an aid to market timing is obvious. Investors would have increased their returns, over the entire sweep of U.S. economic history, by switching into cash before the business cycle peaks and into stocks before the cycle reaches its trough. It is particularly important to switch into stocks before business cycle troughs. However, as our discussion in Chapter 11 about market timing indicated, the chances of timing the market successfully on a regular basis are small.

OTHER APPROACHES TO ASSESSING THE MARKET'S DIRECTION

A number of market indicators and macrovariables have been touted by both individuals and organizations as potential predictors of future movements in the economy and/or the market. Perhaps the best-known market indicator, and one watched by many investors, is the price/earnings ratio. Over the last 30+ years, the P/E ratio for the S&P 500 Index has typically ranged from roughly 7 to 22. Many market observers are extremely nervous when the P/E reaches levels in the high 20s and low 30s, as it did in the late 1990s. They were ultimately proven to be right, as the market declined sharply in 2000 and 2001.

Despite the market decline starting in 2000, following record highs for the market P/E, Kenneth Fisher (a money manager and columnist) argues that the level of the P/E ratio is useless for market timing. Fisher and Statman showed statistically that no link exists between market P/Es and subsequent market returns.[13] According to them, this finding holds for various definitions of the P/E ratio and various time periods up to 5 years, and is based on 125 years of data. An important reason why investors can't use the level of the market P/E ratio for timing is related to what was discussed in Chapter 11 concerning market timing. Being out of the market means that investors miss important market rallies, and missing only a few months here and there can drastically lower average returns over time.

A good example of the problems with using key variables to make market forecasts is the dividend yield. Many market participants believe that when the dividend yield on the S&P 500 Index declines below 3 percent, the market is in for a downward correction. The logic is that with stock prices high enough to make the dividend yield so low (below 3 percent), investors will abandon equities in favor of higher returns on safe fixed-income securities. The resulting sale of equities will drive down equity prices and drive up the dividend yield, restoring a balance. Dividend yield supposedly has a higher correlation with future S&P 500 changes than any other indicator over the long run.

---

[13] See Meir Statman, "Cognitive Biases in Market Forecasts," *The Journal of Portfolio Management*, 27 (Fall 2000), pp. 73–81.

The problem with key market indicators is deciding when they are signaling a change and how reliable the signal is. We can reasonably assume that the "normal" value of some of these indicators changes over time so that what is regarded as a low or high signal at one point in time does not have the same meaning at some other point in time. Dividend payouts among corporations have been in a downward trend for many years, and this trend has not been reversed. Still another problem is how quickly any change signaled by key market indicators and macrovariables might occur. In the final analysis, this is an inexact process subject to considerable interpretations as well as errors.

Example 13-8

A comparison of dividend yields shows that the dividend yield in early October 1987 was below 3 percent, and the market crashed on October 19, 1987. By early 1995, the dividend yield had been below 3 percent for well over two years, which was without precedent in market history. Some well-known forecasters expected a sharp market decline. In fall 1998, the Dow Jones Industrial Average broke the 9300 level, an all-time record, and by mid-1999 had hit new highs above 11,300. Meanwhile, the dividend yield was at its all-time low level. The market peaked in spring 2000 and declined sharply thereafter, but this was some five years after the yield declined below 3 percent. Is such a signal useful?

Investors attempting to forecast the market should pay attention to certain important variables. Interest rates are an obvious variable to watch, and a good benchmark is the Treasury's 10-year maturity bond as reported in *The Wall Street Journal*. Studies have shown that since 1970 every inverted yield curve was followed by negative earnings growth for the S&P 500 Index. Furthermore, this warning typically comes about a year in advance of the decline, providing adequate warning. The yield curve inverted in 2000 and 2000 to 2001 certainly had significant problems.

The direction of commodity prices, as opposed to levels, is also important. Finally, unit labor costs are considered by many to be an important economic indicator, with anything above 3 percent signaling a potential problem.

Does January Market Performance Forecast Annual Performance? In Chapter 12, we discussed the January effect, the observed tendency of small stocks to do particularly well in the month of January. An interesting corollary to this is to note that since 1950 there is almost a 90 percent correlation between the market's performance in January and the performance for the entire year, as measured by the S&P 500 Index. If at the end of January the market is down for the month, the market has had a gain for the year only 7 times out of 19. And if it is an odd-numbered year, such as 1999 or 2001, the correlation is perfect since 1937. Since 1950 about 60 percent of the time the S&P has performed well in January, and in all but four of those situations, the market was up for the year.

Example 13-9

For January of 2002, the S&P 500 Index declined 1.6 percent. The market performed horribly in 2002. What about 2003?

Finally, as you consider the state of the market and whether you should invest now, you might ask if any particular month is riskier than others. Some believe that October is, and the historical evidence seems to support this idea: Six of the 10 biggest down days since 1926 have occurred in October. As Mark Twain said, "October is one of the peculiarly dangerous months to speculate in stocks." However, the rest of his quote goes as follows: "The others are: July, January, September, April, November, May, March, June, December, August, and February."

USING THE FED'S MODEL TO MAKE MARKET FORECASTS

The Fed has developed a market forecasting model that has captured considerable attention both because of its relative accuracy over some time periods and because of its simplicity. This model has a simple premise—because investors can and do easily switch between stocks and bonds, based on the asset with the higher yield, stock returns will tend to restore an equilibrium relationship between the two assets.

To measure bond yields, the Fed uses the yield on 10-year Treasuries. Of course, this number can be observed on an updated basis every day. To measure stock yields, the earnings yield is used—earnings divided by stock price, using the S&P 500 Index. The earnings figure used is a forward 12-month earnings estimate based on operating earnings. Thus, on January 1, 2004, we would use an estimate of operating earnings for the S&P 500 Index for the next 12 months through the end of the year. On April 1, 2004, we would use an estimate of the next 12-month earnings through April 1, 2005.

Note the virtues of this model—it is very simple, and the variables can be obtained with relative ease. Of course, the forward 12-month earnings for the S&P 500 Index is an estimate, and is subject to error.

Using the Internet

Actual earnings, as well as earnings estimates for the S&P Index, by quarter, can be found at www. spglobal.com Click on "Special Data" on the right side and then select "Earnings" on the left side.

Earnings estimates, as well as a detailed discussion of the Fed model, are available at www.firstcall.com (click on "Market" under "Commentary" and look at "Market Analytics").

The Fed model can be used to formulate decision rules in the following ways:

- When the earnings yield on the S&P 500 is greater than the 10-year Treasury yield, stocks are relatively attractive.
- When the earnings yield is less than the 10-year Treasury yield, stocks are relatively unattractive.

An alternative way to use the Fed model is to estimate the "fair value" level of the S&P 500 Index and compare it to the actual current index value. To do this, divide the estimated earnings for the S&P Index by the current 10-year Treasury bond yield (expressed as a decimal) to obtain the estimated fair value.

- If the estimated fair value of the market is greater than the current level of the market, stocks are undervalued.
- If the estimated fair value of the market is less than the current level of the market, stocks are overvalued.

Finally, note that the Fed model implies that the reciprocal of the yield on 10-year Treasuries is an estimate of the S&P 500's equilibrium P/E ratio. That is,

Equilibrium estimate of the S&P 500 P/E ratio = 1/ yield on 10-year Treasuries

Using this formulation, we can use P/E ratios in a relative valuation format as explained in Chapter 10.

- If the S&P 500's actual P/E ratio is less than the estimated equilibrium P/E ratio, equities are relatively attractive.
- If the S&P 500's actual P/E ratio is greater than the estimated equilibrium P/E ratio, equities are relatively unattractive.

The Fed model has worked remarkably well over the last 30 years or so, but it has not always performed well. Futhermore, when interest rates are very low, it does not work as well as when rates are in a more normal range.

Potential Problems With the Fed Model The Fed model has the great virtue of simplicity, and has given some useful signals, but it is not without its problems and limitations, which are important to note.

1. As noted above, the model implies a linear relationship between the reciprocal of the Treasury bond yield and the estimated equilibrium P/E ratio. This means that with a Treasury bond yield of 4 percent, the predicted equilibrium P/E ratio is 25. However, with a Treasury bond yield of 2 percent, predicted P/E is 50, and at 1 percent it is 100. Therefore, it is highly probable that the Fed model is not as reliable when interest rates are unusually low, because the implied linear relationship overstates the estimated equilibrium P/E ratio.
2. The model relies on the estimated earnings for the S&P 500 Index for the next 12 months. There are different estimates of this number, involving top-down, bottom-up, and S&P's core earnings, and they are revised often. Therefore, it is difficult to determine exactly which number to use at any given time.
3. The model is derived by assuming that the yield on 10-year Treasuries can be substituted for the required rate of return on equities and for the return on equity (ROE, explained in Chapter 15) on the S&P 500 Index. Historically, this has often not been the case.

In conclusion, the Fed model may offer some valuable insights to investors trying to forecast the future direction of the stock market, but the model should be used with care. It is by no means a simple solution to the forecasting problem, and could easily mislead investors, particularly when interest rates are unusually low.

Using the Internet

An interesting compilation of market opinions and forecasts can be found in the "Bulls and Bears" section of www.investorhome.com. This is said to be a "random collection of statistics, articles, and predictions by individuals that have publicly declared their bullish or bearish opinions on the U.S. stock market."

Summary

▶ The recurring pattern of expansion and contraction in the economy is referred to as the business cycle. Stock prices are related to the phases of the business cycle.

▶ Leading, lagging, and coincident indicators are used to monitor the economy in terms of business cycle turning dates.

▶ It is important to remember that stock prices, one of the set of leading indicators, typically lead the economy. Therefore, although the market and the economy are clearly related, stock prices usually turn before the economy.

▶ Macroeconomic forecasts have become more accurate, but there is much room for improvement.

▶ Although money's effectiveness in forecasting the economy is controversial, investors should monitor the actions of the Federal Reserve.

▶ The "market" is the aggregate of all security prices and is conveniently measured by some average or, most commonly, by some index of stock prices.

▶ To understand the market (i.e., what determines stock prices), it is necessary to think in terms of a valuation model. The two determinants of aggregate stock prices are the expected benefits stream (earnings or dividends) and the required rate of return (alternatively, the P/E ratio).

▶ Keran's model is useful for visualizing the economic factors that combine to determine stock prices. In trying to understand the market in conceptual terms, it is appropriate to think of corporate earnings and interest rates as the determinants of stock prices.

▶ Corporate earnings are directly related to stock prices, whereas interest rates are inversely related.

▶ To value the market, investors should think in terms of corporate earnings and the P/E ratio. (Alternatively, the dividend valuation model could be used.)

▶ Forecasting market changes is difficult. The business cycle can be of help in understanding the status of the economy, and investors then need to relate the market, which typically leads, to the economy.

▶ Some intelligent estimates of possible changes in the market can be made by considering what is likely to happen to corporate profits and P/E ratios (or interest rates) over some future period, such as a year.

▶ An alternative approach to forecasting likely changes in the market is to apply a model such as the so-called Fed model, which involves a comparison of bond yields to earnings yields. Like all valuation models, the Fed model has limitations, and may result in faulty forecasts.

Key Words

Bubble	Business cycle	Composite economic indexes	Gross Domestic Product (GDP)

Questions

13-1 Why is market analysis so important?

13-2 What are the two determinants of stock prices? How are these two determinants related to a valuation model?

13-3 How can interest rates be one of the two determinants of stock prices when the interest rate does not appear in either the dividend valuation model or the earnings multiplier model?

13-4 How can the Federal Reserve affect stock prices?

13-5 What is the historical relationship between stock prices, corporate profits, and interest rates?

13-6 How can investors go about valuing the market?

13-7 What was the primary cause of the rise in stock prices in 1982?

13-8 What is the "typical" business cycle–stock price relationship?

13-9 If an investor can determine when the bottoming out of the economy will occur, when should stocks be purchased—before, during, or after such a bottom? Would stock prices be expected to continue to rise as the economy recovers (based on historical experience)?

13-10 Can money supply changes forecast stock-price changes?

13-11 What is the historical relationship between the market's P/E ratio and recessions?

13-12 Based on Table 13-1, what is the likely explanation for the stock market's lackluster performance in the last half of the 1970s?

13-13 Suppose that you know with certainty that corporate earnings next year will rise 15 percent above this year's level of corporate earnings. Based on this information, should you buy stocks?

CFA
13-14 Universal Auto is a large multinational corporation headquartered in the United States. For segment reporting purposes, the company is engaged in two businesses: production of motor vehicles and information processing services.

The motor vehicle business is by far the larger of Universal's two segments. It consists mainly of domestic U.S. passenger car production, but also includes small truck manufacturing operations in the U.S. and passenger car production in other countries. This segment of universal has had weak operating results for the past several years, including a large loss in 1992. While the company does not break out the operating results of its domestic passenger car business, that part of Universal's business is generally believed to be primarily responsible for the weak performance of its motor vehicle segment.

Idata, the information processing services segment of Universal, was started by Universal about 15 years ago. This business has shown strong, steady growth which has been entirely internal; no acquisitions have been made.

Adam's research report continued as follows:

" ... With a business recovery already underway, the expected profit surge should lead to a much higher price for Universal Auto stock. We strongly recommend purchase."
a. Discuss the business cycle approach to investment timing. (Your answer should describe actions to be taken on both stocks and bonds at different points over a typical business cycle.)
b. Assuming Adam's assertion is correct—that a business recovery is already underway— evaluate the timeliness of his recommendation to purchase Universal Auto, a cyclical stock, based on the business cycle approach to investment timing.

Problems

13-1 Given the following data for a stock index, answer the questions below:

Year	End-of-Year Price (P)	Earnings (E)	Dividends (D)	P/E	(D/E) (%)	(D/P) (%)
1998	107.21	13.12	5.35	8.17	40.78	4.99
1999	121.02	16.08	6.04	7.53	37.56	4.99
2000	154.45	16.13	6.55	9.58	40.61	4.24
2001	137.12	16.70	7.00	8.21	41.92	5.11
2002	157.62	13.21	7.18	11.93	54.35	4.56
2003	*186.24*	*15.24*	6.97			

The 2003 values in italics are estimated.
a. Calculate the 2003 values for those columns left blank.
b. Calculate the estimated total return for 2003.
c. On the assumption that $g = 0.095$, calculate k for 2003 using the formula $k = D/P + g$ and show that $k = 0.132425$.
d. Show that P/E = 12.22.
e. Assuming a projection that 2004 earnings will be 25 percent greater than the 2003 value, show that projected earnings are expected to be 19.05.
f. Assuming further that the dividend-payout ratio will be 0.40, show that projected dividends for 2004 will be 7.62.
g. Using the projected earnings and dividends for 2004, and the same k and g used in problem c, show that the expected P/E for 2004 is 10.69.
h. Using these expected values for 2004, show that the expected price is 203.61 for 2004.
i. Recalculate the values for 2004 P/E and P, using the same $g = 0.095$, but with (1) $k = 0.14$; (2) $k = 0.13$, and (3) $k = 0.12$.

Web Resources

For additional resources visit our dynamic Web site located at www.wiley.com/college/jones.

- *Two Kinds of Bears*—The case examines the current state of the business cycle and the decision-maker must form an opinion about the direction of the economy. An opinion is necessary for a top-down approach to evaluating security prices.
- Internet Exercises—This chapter analyzes the effect of market-wide and economy-wide events on stock returns. The Web exercises will take you to sites that provide information on these macroeconomic events and help you look at how the information impacts on stock returns.
  Exercise 1: Considers the idea that there are market corrections.
  Exercise 2: Asks the reader to follow particular investment strategies to outperform the S&P 500.
  Exercise 3: Asks the reader to come up with a strategy using the theory that dividend yields predict market corrections.
  Exercise 4: Asks the reader to evaluate the random walk model of stock prices and relates deviations from the model to macro economic variables.
  Exercise 5: Suggests using information on economic indicators to predict the stock market.

- Appendix 13-A—Published Information About the Economy
- Multiple Choice Self Test

Selected References

A book that captured considerable attention because of its predictions for the market is:

Shiller, Robert J. *Irrational Exuberance*. Princeton University Press, 2000.

A book about a predicted rise in the market that has generated considerable interest is:

Glassman, James K. and Hassett, Kevin A. *Dow 36,000*. Times Books, 1999.

A good overall view of the economy can be found in:

United States Government Printing Office, *Economic Report of the President*, yearly.

chapter 14

Sector/ Industry Analysis

Chapter 14 analyzes the sector/industry issue, which involves the importance of major sectors of the economy to overall investing success. Over long periods, some sectors/industries have greatly outperformed others, and over shorter periods of time, the differences in one sector's performance can be dramatic.

AFTER READING THIS CHAPTER YOU WILL BE ABLE TO:

▶ Assess the significance of sector/industry analysis in the top-down approach to security analysis.

▶ Recognize how industries are classified and the stages that industries go through over time.

▶ Understand how to go about using sector/ industry analysis as an investor.

The second step in the fundamental analysis of common stocks is industry or sector analysis. We will use these two terms throughout the discussion, since investors sometimes speak about industries and sometimes about sectors. In general, a sector is a broader definition, and can include several different industries. An industry in turn can include several different subindustries. Think of going from sectors to industries to subindustries.

An investor who is convinced that the economy and the market offer favorable conditions for investing should proceed to consider those sectors that promise the most opportunities in the coming years. In the next few years of the twenty-first century, for example, investors will not view some U.S. industries with the same enthusiasm they would have even 5 years earlier—telecommunications being a good example. On the other hand, it is obvious that some industries such as the medical equipment and biotechnology industries have, and will continue to have, an impact on many Americans with new life-saving techniques and new wonder drugs that prolong life and/or enhance the quality of life.

The actual security analysis of industries as performed by professional security analysts is typically tedious. Numerous factors are involved, including multiple demand and supply factors, a detailed analysis of price factors, labor issues, government regulation, and so forth. To do such analysis successfully requires experience, access to information, and hard work.

In this chapter, we concentrate on the *conceptual issues* involved in industry analysis. The basic concepts of such analysis are closely related to our previous discussion of valuation principles. Investors can apply these concepts in several ways, depending on the degree of rigor sought, the amount of information available, and the end objective. What we seek to accomplish here is to learn to think analytically about industries and sectors. Investors can in fact benefit from a reasonable and modest approach to sector/industry analysis without getting involved in myriad details.

What Is an Industry?

At first glance, the term *industry* may seem self-explanatory. After all, everyone is familiar with the auto industry, the drug industry, and the electric utility industry. But are these classifications as clear-cut as they seem? Apparently not, because although we have had industry classification schemes for many years, the classification system for industries continues to evolve, as shown below. Furthermore, different organizations use different classification systems.

CLASSIFYING INDUSTRIES

Standard Industrial Classification (SIC) System A classification of firms on the basis of what they produce using census data

Regardless of the problems, analysts and investors need methods with which to classify industries. One well-known and widely used system is the **Standard Industrial Classification (SIC) System** based on census data and developed to classify firms on the basis of what they produce.[1] SIC codes have 11 divisions, and within each of these divisions are several major industry groups designated by a two-digit code. The major industry groups within each division are further subdivided into three-, four-, and five-digit SIC codes to provide more detailed classifications. The larger the number of digits in the SIC system, the more specific the breakdown.

---

[1] See *Census of Manufacturers* (Washington, D.C.: U.S. Government Printing Office).

SIC codes have aided significantly in bringing order to the industry classification problem by providing a consistent basis for describing industries and companies. Analysts using SIC codes can focus on economic activity in as broad or as specific a manner as desired.

Other Industry Classifications The SIC system of industry classification is probably the most consistent system available. However, in the Investments field, various well-known organizations have developed their own industry groupings. For example, the Standard & Poor's (S&P) Corporation has provided weekly stock indexes on 11 sectors and approximately 115 industry groups for a long time. These weekly indexes have often been used to assess an industry's performance over time.

As of March 2002, S&P is using a new system known as the **Global Industry Classification Standard (GICS)** to provide "one complete, continuous set of global sector and industry definitions." This system divides everything into ten "economic sectors": Consumer Discretionary, Consumer Staples, Energy, Financials, Health Care, Industrials, Information Technology, Materials, Telecommunications Services, and Utilities. Within this framework, there are 23 industry groupings, 59 industries, and 122 subindustries. This system is intended to classify companies around the world, and already includes 25,000 companies. Peer groups are defined tightly.

This new system, developed jointly with Morgan Stanley Capital International, provides considerably more detail than S&P's previous classification system. This in turn will permit users to customize more readily portfolios and indexes.

The Value Line Investment Survey covers roughly 1700 companies, divided into approximately 90 industries, with a discussion of industry prospects preceding the company analysis. As discussed later, these industry classifications could be important, because *Value Line* ranks their expected performance (relatively) for the year ahead.

Other providers of information use different numbers of industries in presenting data. The important point to remember is that multiple industry classification systems are used.

Global Industry Classification Standard (GICS) Provides a complete continuous set of global sector and industry definitions using 10 economic sectors

The Importance of Industry/Sector Analysis

WHY INDUSTRY ANALYSIS IS IMPORTANT OVER THE LONG RUN

Sector and industry analysis is important to investor success, because over the long run, very significant differences occur in the performance of industries and major economic sectors of the economy. To see this, we will examine the performance of industry groups over long periods of time using price indexes for industries.

Standard & Poor's calculates weekly and monthly stock price indexes for a variety of industries, with data being available for approximately 60 years. Since the data are reported as index numbers, long-term comparisons of price performance can be made for any industry covered. Note that the base number for these S&P data is 1941–1943 = 10; therefore, dividing the index number for any industry for a particular year by 10 indicates the number of times the index has increased over that period.

The top part of Table 14-1 shows the long-term price performance of randomly selected industries for the years 1973, 1983, 1995, and March 2000 (using 1941 to 1943 as the base).[2] The S&P 500 Composite Index in 1973 was almost 10 times (98/10) its 1941 to 1943 level, a continuously compounded average in excess of 8 percent annually over this 31-year period. By March 2000, the index was about 150 times its base. However, this average growth rate consisted of widely varying performance over the industries covered by Standard & Poor's.

[2] All data are based on December closing index values.

Table 14-1 Standard & Poor's Weekly Stock Price Indexes for Selected Industries Using Data for Various Years, All With a Base of 1941–1943 = 10

	1941–43 = 10			
	1973	1983	1995	2000*
Automobiles	61	100	234	508
Aluminum	90	185	393	703
Beverages (Alcoholic)	133	84	463	717
Beverages (Soft Drinks)	145	157	2343	2899
Electrical Equipment	280	522	1798	6485
Entertainment	34	264	2431	7073
Foods	59	134	1037	1222
Health Care (Drugs)	218	259	2223	5263
S&P 500 Index	98	165	616	1499

	1941–43 = 10				
	1982	1986	1989	1995	2000*
Broadcast Media	889	2309	4980	9437	30946
Entertainment	307	577	1383	2431	7073
Health Care (Drugs)	248	540	949	2223	5264
Money Center Banks	65	66	111	233	419
Retail Stores Composite	104	159	375	321	901
S&P 500 Index	141	242	353	616	1499

* = end of March

SOURCE: Standard & Poor's *Statistical Service: Security Price Index Record*, various issues. Reprinted by permission of Standard & Poor's, a division of the McGraw-Hill Companies.

Over the 31-year period 1943 to 1973, the electrical equipment industry did well, rising to 28 times the base number, whereas the entertainment industry was only 3.4 times the base. By 1983, the alcoholic beverages industry was only eight times its original base, whereas electrical equipment was 52 times higher.

An examination of the entire time period, 1941 to 1943 through March 2000, shows that the entertainment industry increased more than 700-fold, whereas the electrical equipment industry did almost as well at about 650 times the base. Meanwhile, the auto industry was only about 50 times the base. Notice the dramatic difference in the alcoholic beverages industry and the soft drink beverages industry over the period ending in both 1995 and March 2000.[3]

The lower half of Table 14-1 shows selected and matched Standard & Poor's Industry Stock Price indexes for the years 1982, 1986, 1989, 1995, and March 2000 (based on 1941–1943 = 10). Therefore, Table 14-1 provides both an almost 60-year picture of industry performance (from 1941 to 1943), which approximates the maximum investing lifetime of many individuals, and a look at how much change can occur in shorter periods of time such as 3 (1986 to 1989), 4 (1982 to 1986), 7 (1982 to 1989), 13 (1982 to 1995), and roughly 18 (1982 to 2000) years.

Tremendous differences existed for industries in the 1980s, and between periods in the 1980s and 2000. Notice how money center banks did nothing between 1982 and 1986, but then almost doubled and redoubled through 1995, and almost redoubled again by March 2000. Broadcast media performed in an incredibly strong manner over the entire period from 1982 to 1995, but the change from 1995 to March 2000 is astounding. Retail stores, having declined from 1989 to 1995, almost tripled from 1995 to March 2000.

---

[3] Standard & Poor's has changed industry classifications over time because of changes in the economy.

The lesson to be learned from Table 14-1 is simple. Industry analysis pays because industries perform very differently over time and investor performance will be significantly affected by the particular industries that investors hold in their portfolios. Investors are seeking to identify the broadcast media and health care (drugs) industries of the future and to avoid the money center banks and retail stores industries of the future.

INDUSTRY PERFORMANCE OVER SHORTER PERIODS

What about shorter periods of time and recent data? Does the same principle hold true—that industries perform very differently?

Let's consider S&P's new GICS classification system, and analyze a five-year period ending in April 2002. As noted previously, there are 10 broad sectors in this new classification system, and these are shown in Table 14-2 along with two industries in the consumer discretionary and information technology sectors. The base for these new S&P industry classifications is December 30, 1994 = 100.

As we can see, these sectors performed differently over this five-year period, with the health care sector performing at more than double the annual rate of the information technology and consumer staples sector, and about 27 times the rate of the materials sector. Meanwhile, telecommunications services had a negative annual rate of price change.

Now consider the two industries shown within two of the sectors, and notice how differently they performed over this five-year period. Within the information technology sector, whereas application software was growing at almost a −27-percent annual rate, semiconductor equipment was growing at about a +27-percent annual rate.

HOW ONE INDUSTRY CAN HAVE A MAJOR IMPACT ON INVESTORS—THE TELECOM INDUSTRY

Let's consider an example of a sector moving into and out of favor with investors in a very dramatic manner. The telecommunications sector was one of the great growth stories of the late 1990s. Telecom was deregulated in 1996. Predictions of how quickly Internet traffic would grow proliferated. One of the major contributing factors to what happened

Table 14-2 Performance of Sectors and Industries Using S&P's GSIC

Sector	5 yr Performance ending 4/30/02 Annual Rate of Change	
Consumer Discretionary		11.0%
Home Improvement Retail	27.7	
Photographic Products	−18.3	
Consumer Staples		5.1
Energy		6.0
Financials		10.1
Health Care		11.6
Industrials		6.1
Information Technology		5.1
Application Software	−26.7	
Semiconductor Equipment	27.1	
Materials		0.4
Telecommunication Services		−2.6
Utilities		4.5

SOURCE: S&P Sector Scoreboard, Industry Performance, *The Outlook*, May 29, 2002, p. 12.
Reprinted by permission of Standard & Poor's, a division of The McGraw-Hill Companies.

to the telecom industry is the huge amount of money that poured into the industry after it took off. When stock prices were rising so rapidly in the late 1990s with the tech stock boom, it was easy for the industry to raise large amounts of capital by borrowing.

Figure 14-1 shows the rise of the telecom index in 1998 and 1999, which was very strong. Many of the companies in this industry were market favorites, such as Global Crossing and WorldCom, Qwest. This is a constructed index of various companies.

Amazingly, after only a couple of years ago of the telecom industry being regarded as a superstar industry, investors realized that the need for communications and bandwidth services could not grow at the rates that had been predicted. Meanwhile, the crushing debt loads these companies had assumed were catching up with them, as was the recession in the economy that started in 2001. Telecom collapsed, and in all likelihood, was the greatest bursting of a bubble in history in terms of total dollars lost. One estimate is that investors in the telecommunications industry had lost $2 trillion by mid-2002.

Figure 14-1 tells the rest of the story, and it has been ugly. The downward spiral of telecom companies seemed to be nonstop, and there were plenty of bankruptcies and accounting scandals by 2002.

CROSS-SECTIONAL VOLATILITY HAS INCREASED

Finally, consider another indication that paying attention to the relative performance of industries and sectors is important. A new study by the Frank Russell Company measures "cross-sectional volatility," or the variation in returns across various sectors of the market.[4] *Sectors* here refers to such groups of companies as utilities, retail companies, financial companies, and so forth. By examining the variations in returns among the different sectors on a month by month basis, some judgment about cross-sectional volatility can be made.

The Russell study found that cross-sectional volatility began to rise in the mid-1990s, and even after some decline in 2000 and 2001, it was twice what it was in 1995. Obviously, what happened in the technology sector contributed to this volatility. But the study found that even ignoring the tech sector, cross-sectional volatility has increased significantly.

Figure 14-1

Telecommunications Index, 1997–early 2003

SOURCE: Jack W. Wilson and Charles P. Jones, NCSU, constructed from various data.

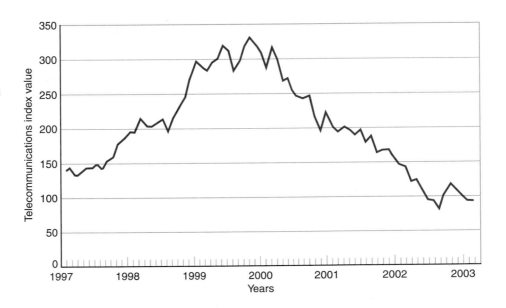

---

[4] See Walter Updegrave, "Blame the Market?" *Money*, August 2002, pp. 49–51.

An increase in cross-sectional volatility enhances the importance of industry/sector analysis. Any ability to distinguish between the top and bottom performers should pay off. (See Chapter 11, "The Importance of Stock Selection.")

Analyzing Sectors/Industries

Sectors and industries, as well as the market and companies, are analyzed through the study of a wide range of data, including sales, earnings, dividends, capital structure, product lines, regulations, innovations, and so on. Such analysis requires considerable expertise, and is usually performed by industry analysts employed by brokerage firms and other institutional investors.

A useful first step is to analyze industries in terms of their stage in the life cycle. The idea is to assess the general health and current position of the industry. A second step involves a qualitative analysis of industry characteristics designed to assist investors in assessing the future prospects for an industry. Each of these steps is examined in turn.

THE INDUSTRY LIFE CYCLE

Many observers believe that industries evolve through at least four stages: the pioneering stage, the expansion stage, the stabilization stage, and the deceleration in growth and/or decline stage. There is an obvious parallel in this idea to human development. The concept of an **industry life cycle** could apply to industries or product lines within industries. The industry life cycle concept is depicted in Figure 14-2, and each stage is discussed in the following section.

Industry Life Cycle
The stages of an industry's evolution from pioneering to stabilization and decline

Pioneering Stage In the pioneering stage, rapid growth in demand occurs. Although a number of companies within a growing industry will fail at this stage because they will not survive the competitive pressures, most experience rapid growth in sales and earnings, possibly at an increasing rate. The opportunities available may attract a number of companies, as well as venture capital. Considerable jockeying for position occurs as the companies battle each other for survival, with the weaker firms failing and dropping out.

Investor risk in an unproven company is high, but so are expected returns if the company succeeds. Profit margins and profits are often small or negative. At the pioneering stage of an industry, it can be difficult for security analysts to identify the likely survivors, just when the ability to identify the future strong performers is most valuable. By

Figure 14-2

The industry life cycle.

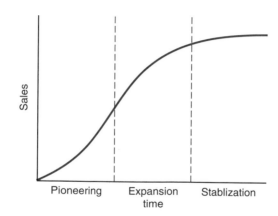

the time it becomes apparent who the real winners are, their prices may have been bid up considerably beyond what they were in the earlier stages of development.

In the early 1980s, the microcomputer business—both hardware and software— offered a good example of companies in the pioneering stage. Given the explosion in expected demand for these products, many new firms entered the business hoping to capture some share of the total market. By 1983, there were an estimated 150 manufacturers of home computers, a clearly unsustainable number over the longer run.

Expansion Stage In the second stage of an industry's life cycle, the expansion stage, the survivors from the pioneering stage are identifiable. They continue to grow and to prosper, but the rate of growth is more moderate than before.

At the expansion stage of the cycle, industries are improving their products and perhaps lowering their prices. They are more stable and solid, and at this stage they often attract considerable investment funds. Investors are more willing to invest in these industries now that their potential has been demonstrated and the risk of failure has decreased.

Financial policies become firmly established at this stage. The capital base is widened and strengthened. Profit margins are very high. Dividends often become payable, further enhancing the attractiveness of these companies to a number of investors.

Stabilization Stage Industries eventually evolve into the stabilization stage (sometimes referred to as the maturity stage), at which point the growth begins to moderate. This is probably the longest part of the industry life cycle. Products become more standardized and less innovative, the marketplace is full of competitors, and costs are stable rather than decreasing through efficiency moves, for example. Management's ability to control costs and produce operating efficiencies becomes very important in terms of affecting individual company profit margins.

Industries at this stage continue to move along, but typically the industry growth rate matches the growth rate for the economy as a whole.

Declining Stage An industry's sales growth can decline as new products are developed and shifts in demand occur. Think of the industry for home radios and black-and-white televisions. Some firms in an industry experiencing decline face significantly lower profits or even losses. Rates of return on invested capital will tend to be low.

Assessing the Industry Life Cycle The industry life cycle classification of industry evolvement helps investors to assess the growth potential of different companies in an industry. Based on the stage of the industry, they can better assess the potential of different companies within an industry. This helps in estimating the return potential, and the risk, of companies.

There are limitations to this type of analysis. First, it is only a generalization, and investors must be careful not to attempt to categorize every industry, or all companies within a particular industry, into neat categories that may not apply. Second, even the general framework may not apply to some industries that are not categorized by many small companies struggling for survival. Finally, the bottom line in security analysis is stock prices, a function of the expected stream of benefits and the risk involved.

The industry life cycle tends to focus on sales and share of the market and investment in the industry. Although all of these factors are important to investors, they are not the final items of interest. Given these qualifications to industry life cycle analysis, what are the implications for investors?

The pioneering stage may offer the highest potential returns, but it also poses the greatest risk. Several companies in a particular industry will fail or do poorly. Such risk may be appropriate for some investors, but many will wish to avoid the risk inherent in this stage.

Investors interested primarily in capital gains should avoid the maturity stage. Companies at this stage may have relatively high dividend payouts, because they have fewer growth prospects. These companies often offer continuing stability in earnings and dividend growth.

Clearly, companies in the fourth stage of the industrial life cycle, decline, are usually to be avoided. Investors should seek to spot industries in this stage and avoid them.

It is the second stage, expansion, that is probably of most interest to investors. Industries that have survived the pioneering stage often offer good opportunities, for the demand for their products and services is growing more rapidly than the economy as a whole. Growth is rapid but orderly, an appealing characteristic to investors.

QUALITATIVE ASPECTS OF INDUSTRY ANALYSIS

The analyst or investor should consider several important qualitative factors that can characterize an industry. Knowing about these factors will help investors to analyze a particular industry and will aid in assessing its future prospects.

The Historical Performance   As we have learned, some industries perform well and others poorly over long periods of time. Although performance is not always consistent and predictable on the basis of the past, an industry's track record should not be ignored. In Table 14-1, we saw that the aluminum industry performed poorly in both 1973 and 1983 (in relation to the base of 1941 to 1943). It continued to do badly in 1995 and afterward. The broadcast media industry, on the other hand, showed strength at each of the checkpoints as shown.

Investors should consider the historical record of sales and earnings growth and price performance. Although the past cannot simply be extrapolated into the future, it does provide some useful information.

Competition   The nature of the competitive conditions existing in an industry can provide useful information in assessing its future. Is the industry protected from the entrance of new competitors as a result of control of raw materials, prohibitive cost of building plants, the level of production needed to operate profitably, and so forth?

Michael Porter has written extensively on the issue of competitive strategy, which involves the search for a competitive position in an industry. The intensity of competition in an industry determines that industry's ability to sustain above-average returns.[5] This intensity is not a matter of luck, but a reflection of underlying factors that determine the strength of five basic competitive factors:

1. Threat of new entrants
2. Bargaining power of buyers
3. Rivalry between existing competitors
4. Threat of substitute products or services
5. Bargaining power of suppliers

---

[5] See Michael E. Porter, "Industry Structure and Competitive Strategy: Keys to Profitability," *Financial Analysts Journal* (July–August 1980), pp. 30–41. See also Michael Porter, *Competitive Advantage: Creating and Sustaining Superior Performance* (New York: Free Press, 1985).

Figure 14-3

The five competitive forces that determine industry profitability.

SOURCE: Reprinted with the permission of the Free Press, a division of Simon & Schuster, Inc. from COMPETITIVE ADVANTAGE: Creating and Sustaining Superior Performance by Michael E. Porter. Copyright © 1985 by Michael E. Porter.

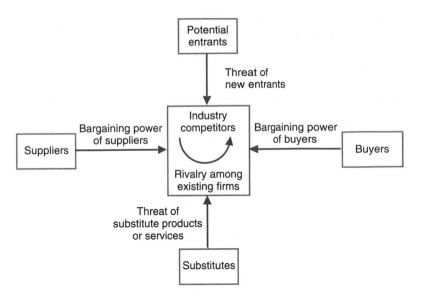

These five competitive forces are shown as a diagram in Figure 14-3. Because the strength of these five factors varies across industries (and can change over time), industries vary from the standpoint of inherent profitability.

The five competitive forces determine industry profitability because these influence the components of return on investment. The strength of each of these factors is a function of industry structure.

The important point of the Porter analysis is that industry profitability is a function of industry structure. Investors must analyze industry structure to assess the strength of the five competitive forces, which in turn determine industry profitability.

Government Effects Government regulations and actions can have significant effects on industries. The investor must attempt to assess the results of these effects or, at the very least, be well aware that they exist and may continue.

Consider the breakup of AT&T as of January 1, 1984. This one action has changed the telecommunications industry permanently, and perhaps others as well. As a second example, the deregulating of the financial services industries resulted in banks and savings and loans competing more directly with each other, offering consumers many of the same services. Such an action has to affect the relative performance of these two industries as well as some of their other competitors, such as the brokerage industry (which can now also offer similar services in many respects).

Structural Changes A fourth factor to consider is the structural changes that occur in the economy. As the United States continues to move from an industrial society to an information-communications society, major industries will be affected. New industries with tremendous potential are, and will be, emerging, whereas some traditional industries, such as steel, may never recover to their former positions.

Structural shifts can occur even within relatively new industries. For example, in the early 1980s, the personal computer industry was a young, dynamic industry with numerous competitors, some of which enjoyed phenomenal success in a short time. The introduction of personal computers by IBM in 1982, however, forever changed that industry. Other hardware manufacturers sought to be compatible with IBM's personal computer, and suppliers rushed to supply items such as software, printers, and additional memory boards. IBM's decision to enter this market significantly affected virtually every part of the industry.

Using Sector/Industry Analysis as an Investor

SECTOR ROTATION

Numerous investors use sector analysis in their investing strategy. The premise here is simple—companies within the same industry group are generally affected by the same market and economic conditions. Therefore, if an investor can spot important changes in the sector or industry quickly enough, appropriate portfolio changes can be made.

Institutional investors such as mutual funds analyze industry groupings carefully in order to determine which are losing momentum, and which are gaining. When a sector trend is spotted, these investors rotate into the favorable sector and out of a sector losing favor with investors. The strategy at the beginning of these events is to invest in the likely best-performing companies in the sector, which points out why company analysis (Chapter 15) is important. When these companies rise in price and appear to be fully valued, secondary companies are identified and invested in. Ultimately, the entire sector becomes fairly valued or overvalued, or economic conditions for the sector become less favorable, and money rotates out of this sector and into a new one.

EVALUATING FUTURE INDUSTRY PROSPECTS

Ultimately, investors are interested in expected performance in the future. They realize that such estimates are difficult and are likely to be somewhat in error, but they know that equity prices are a function of expected parameters, not past, known values. How then is an investor to proceed?

Assessing Longer-Term Prospects To forecast industry performance over the longer run, investors should ask the following questions:

1. Which industries are obvious candidates for growth and prosperity over, say, the next decade? (In the early 1980s, such industries as personal computers, the software industry, telecommunications, and cellular telephones could have been identified; in the late 1990s, technology firms could have been identified.)
2. Which industries appear to be likely to have difficulties as the United States changes from an industrial to an information-collecting and information-processing economy?

BUSINESS CYCLE ANALYSIS

A useful procedure for investors to assess industry prospects is to analyze industries by their operating ability in relation to the economy as a whole. That is, some industries perform poorly during a recession, whereas others are able to weather it reasonably well. Some industries move closely with the business cycle, outperforming the average industry in good times and underperforming it in bad times. Investors should be aware of these relationships when analyzing industries.

Most investors have heard of, and are usually seeking, growth companies. In **growth industries**, earnings are expected to be significantly above the average of all industries, and such growth may occur regardless of setbacks in the economy. Growth industries in the 1980s included genetic engineering, microcomputers, and new medical devices. Current and future growth industries include robotics and cellular telephones. Clearly, one of the primary goals of fundamental security analysis is to identify the growth industries of the near and far future.

Growth stocks suffer much less during a recession, such as 1990, than do the cyclical stocks explained below. For example, growth stocks gained 2.5 percent in 1990, whereas cyclicals lost about 20 percent.

At the opposite end of the scale are the **defensive industries**, which are least affected by recessions and economic adversity. Food has long been considered such an industry. People must eat, and they continue to drink beer, eat frozen yogurt, and so on, regardless of the economy. Public utilities might also be considered a defensive industry.

Cyclical industries are most volatile—they do unusually well when the economy prospers and are likely to be hurt more when the economy falters. Durable goods are a good example of the products involved in cyclical industries. Autos, refrigerators, and stereos, for example, may be avidly sought when times are good, but such purchases may be postponed during a recession, because consumers can often make do with the old units.

In the 1990 recession, cyclical stocks declined 20 percent, three times as much as the S&P 500. In 1994, General Motors, a prime example of a cyclical company, declined 40 percent. On the other hand, when the economy recovers, cyclicals do very well.

Cyclicals are said to be "bought to be sold." When should investors pursue cyclical industries? When the prices of companies in the industry are low, relative to the historical record, and P/Es are high. This seems counterintuitive to many investors, but the rationale is that earnings are severely depressed in a recession and therefore the P/E is high, and this may occur shortly before earnings turn around.

Countercyclical industries also exist, actually moving opposite to the prevailing economic trend. The gold mining industry is known to follow this pattern.

These three classifications of industries according to economic conditions do not constitute an exhaustive set. Additional classifications are possible and logical. For example, **interest-sensitive industries** are particularly sensitive to expectations about changes in interest rates. The financial services, banking, and real estate industries are obvious examples of interest-sensitive industries. Another is the building industry.

What are the implications of these classifications for investors? To predict the performance of an industry over shorter periods of time, investors should carefully analyze the stage of the business cycle and the likely movements in interest rates. If the economy is heading into a recession, cyclical industries are likely to be affected more than other industries, whereas defensive industries are the least likely to be affected. With such guidelines investors may make better buy or sell decisions. Similarly, an expected rise in interest rates will have negative implications for the savings and loan industry and the home building industry, whereas an expected drop in interest rates will have the opposite effect.

These statements reinforce the importance of market analysis. Not only do investors need to know the state of the economy and market before deciding to invest, but such knowledge is valuable in selecting or avoiding particular industries. Furthermore, investors need to consider the possibility of overcapacity as well as global competition.

As an example of applying business cycle considerations to industry analysis, consider the memory-chip industry. As shortages occurred in the early 1990s and prices rose,

Growth Industries Industries with expected growth in earnings significantly above the average of all industries

Defensive Industries Industries least affected by recessions and economic adversity

Cyclical Industries Industries most affected, both up and down, by the business cycle

Interest-Sensitive Industries Industries particularly sensitive to expectations about changes in the interest rate

suppliers rushed to build new plants in order to cash in on the demand for chips. By the end of 1995, memory-chip production was growing in excess of 20 percent, but sales were slipping. A glut emerged, and in 1996, prices dropped more than 80 percent. The stock prices of chip makers suffered sharp drops in mid-1996 as the results of this activity became apparent.

Investments Intuition

Clearly, business cycle analysis for industries is a logical and worthwhile part of fundamental security analysis. Industries have varying sensitivities to the business conditions and interest rate expectations at any given time, and the smart investor will think carefully about these factors.

PICKING INDUSTRIES FOR NEXT YEAR

On a shorter-run basis, investors would like to value industries along the lines discussed in Chapter 13 for the market. They would like to be able to estimate the expected earnings for an industry and the expected multiplier and combine them to produce an estimate of value. However, this is not easy to do. It requires an understanding of several relationships and estimates of several variables. Fortunately, considerable information is readily available to help investors in their analysis of industries. Investors should be aware of the primary sources of information about industries and the nature of the information available. These issues are discussed in Appendix 14-A.

To determine industry performance for shorter periods of time (e.g., one year), investors should ask themselves the following question: Given the current and prospective economic situation, which industries are likely to show improving earnings? In many respects, this is the key question for industry security analysis. Investors can turn to *IBES*, which compiles institutional brokerage earnings estimates, for analysts' estimates of earnings for various industries, which are revised during the year.

Given the importance of earnings and the availability of earnings estimates for industries and companies, are investors able to make relatively easy investment choices? The answer is no, because earnings estimates are notoriously inaccurate. In one recent year, for example, Standard & Poor's was estimating that the banking industry's profits would increase 15 percent for the year, whereas IBES estimated 29 percent—obviously a big difference.

Dreman reports on a study of 61 industries for a 17-year period. Three-fourths of all estimates within industries missed reported earnings by 30 percent or more, and 15 percent showed errors of 80 percent or more. The average forecast error grouped by industries was 50 percent (median error of 43 percent). Only 16 of the 61 industries over the 17 years showed forecast errors of 29 percent or less.[6]

Of course, investors must also consider the likely P/E ratios for industries. Which industries are likely to show improving P/E ratios? Dreman has also reported on the issue of whether, like companies, investors pay too much for favored companies in an industry. Buying the lowest 20 percent of P/Es in each of 44 industry groups over 25 years (based on the 1,500 largest companies on the Compustat database measured by market capitalization) produced an average annual return of 18 percent compared to 12.4 percent for

---

[6] David Dreman, "Cloudy Crystal Balls," *Forbes*, October 10, 1994, p. 154.

BOX 14-1

Picking Top Industries for the Year Ahead

A study by Standard & Poor's shows that investing in industries based on their prior year's performance relative to the S&P 500 is a way to beat the market.

You can outperform the general market by buying both the strongest and weakest industries of the prior year, according to a new study by S&P. But last year's leaders and laggards must be turning the corner in terms of their own performance, as measured by their nine-month moving averages (an indicator that technical analysts find useful), to qualify for purchase.

First, at the end of November of each of the past 10 years, we determined which of the industry group indexes that make up the S&P 500 Index did best over the prior 12 months relative to the S&P 500 Index itself and which did worst relative to the "500." We then eliminated any of these leaders and laggards whose relative performances for the 12-month period were below their own nine-month moving averages of relative performance.

We found that industries that ranked highest in this regard and were bought at December 31 tended to do well in the following year, as did those that ranked lowest, although, again, both the best and worst had to be showing relative strength greater than the nine-month average of their relative strength, to indicate upward momentum. Rankings at the end of November determined which industries to buy on December 31 of each year and hold until December 31 one year later.

The table at right shows the performance of the leaders and laggards based on industries in the S&P 500 from 1987 through 1996. By investing in the five strongest industries at the end of each year, an investor would have beaten the market seven out of ten years and would have achieved a compound average annual return of 13.8 percent vs. the S&P 500's annual return of 11.8 percent (before dividends).

The results would have been even better had you bought the five industries with the lowest relative strength. Although many studies have determined that investors would have done poorly buying the previous year's laggards, by including one selection criterion (relative strength for the past 12 months must be above the nine-month average of relative strength), we found the opposite to be the case. The nine-month moving average helps to identify those industry groups that are depressed but may have turned the corner.

At the end of November 1996, the five industries with the strongest 12-month relative strength that were also above their nine-month moving averages were Oil & Gas Drilling & Equipment, Semiconductors, Computer Software & Services, Money Center Banks, and Consumer Finance.

During the 10-year period, the laggards outperformed the market in 8 years, or 80 percent of the time, and posted an average compound return of 175 percent. They thus not only beat the S&P 500's return of 11.8 percent for the 10 years, but they also topped the 13.8-percent average annual gain of the top five industry groups. And they did so with lower risk. The group's relative risk rank (calculated by dividing the average return by standard deviation, a common measure of price volatility) was considerably higher than both the S&P 500 and the leaders. This means the laggards offered a higher return with lower risk.

For the year through November 1996, the five industries with the lowest 12-month relative strength, but above their nine-month moving averages of relative strength, were Paper & Forest Products, Entertainment, Paper Containers, Waste Management, and General Merchandise Retailers.

Performance of Leading and Lagging Groups in Following Years

Year	S&P 500	Laggards	Leaders
1987	2.0%	30.1%	75%
1988	12.4	17.0	193.0
1989	27.3	28.2	28.6
1990	−6.6	−3.2	−11.1
1991	26.3	35.1	35.5
1992	4.5	8.1	−0.4
1993	7.1	11.6	23.1
1994	−1.5	12.6	13.7
1995	34.1	28.3	35.3
1996	20.4	13.1	28.1
Compound Avg. Return	11.8	17.5	13.8
Times Beat Market	NA	8.0	7.0
Standard Deviation	13.0	11.4	17.4
†Relative Risk Rank	0.9	1.5	0.8

NA—Not available.

†Average return divided by standard deviation

SOURCE: Sam Stovall, "Picking Top Industries for 1997 Using 'Relative Strength'," The Outlook, January 15, 1997, pp. 8–9. Reprinted by permission of Standard & Poor's, a division of McGraw-Hill Companies, copyright 2001.

the highest 20-percent P/E group. Dreman also found that buying the lowest P/E stocks across industries produced smaller losses when the market is down relative to the market as a whole and to the highest P/E group.[7]

Other questions to consider are the likely direction of interest rates and which industries would be most affected by a significant change in interest rates. A change in interest rates, other things being equal, leads to a change in the discount rate (and a change in the multiplier). Which industries are likely to be most affected by possible future political events, such as a new administration, renewed inflation, new technology, an increase in defense spending, and so on?

Box 14-1 is an interesting discussion of a technique suggested by S&P in its publication, *The Outlook*. It indicates that picking industries on the basis of their prior year's performance relative to the S&P 500 Index can produce superior results.[8] What is interesting about this is that both last year's leaders and last year's laggards are recommended as long as they are exhibiting upward momentum.

Using the Internet

The "Research Library" portion of the www.lehman.com Web site has information organized by industries. At http://quote.yahoo.com, financial news is organized by industry. Investors can find a section on industry reports from *Individual Investor* at www.iionline.com. A large supplier of company information, Hoover's, also has industry analysis at www.hoover's.com.

As with all security analysis, we can use several procedures in analyzing industries. Much of this process is common sense. For example, if you can reasonably forecast a declining number of competitors in an industry, it stands to reason that, other things being equal, the remaining firms will be more profitable.

Summary

▶ Industry analysis is the second of three steps in a top-down framework of fundamental security analysis, following economy/market analysis but preceding individual company analysis. The objective is to identify those industries that will perform best in the future in terms of returns to stockholders.

▶ Is industry analysis valuable? Yes, because over the long term, some industries perform much better than others.

▶ Industry performance is not consistent; past price performance does not always predict future price performance. Particularly over shorter periods such as one or two years, industry performance rankings may completely reverse themselves.

▶ Although the term *industry* at first seems self-explanatory, industry definitions and classifications are not straightforward, and the trend toward diversification of activities over the years has blurred the lines even more.

---

[7] See David Dreman, "A New Approach to Low-P/E Investing," *Forbes*, September 23, 1996, p. 241.
[8] Relative strength is discussed in more detail in Chapter 16.

▶ The Standard Industrial Classification System, is a comprehensive scheme for classifying major industry groups. S&P now uses the new Global Industry Classification standard which divides everything into 10 economic sectors.

▶ A number of investment information services, such as Standard & Poor's, *Value Line*, and Media General, use their own industry classifications.

▶ To analyze industries, a useful first step is to examine their stage in the life cycle, which in its simplest form consists of the pioneering, expansion, and maturity stages. Most investors will usually be interested in the expansion stage, in which growth is rapid and risk is tolerable.

▶ A second industry analysis approach is business cycle analysis. Industries perform differently at various stages in the business cycle.

▶ A third phase involves a qualitative analysis of important factors affecting industries.

▶ Investors interested in evaluating future industry prospects have a wide range of data available for their use. These data can be used for a detailed, in-depth analysis of industries using standard security analysis techniques for examining recent ratings of industry performance (e.g., the *Forbes* data) or for ranking likely industry performance (e.g., the *Value Line* industry rankings).

Key Words

Cyclical industries

Defensive industries

Global Industry Classification Standard (GICS)

Growth industries

Industry life cycle

Interest-sensitive industries

Standard Industrial Classification (SIC) System

Questions

14-1 Why is it difficult to classify industries?

14-2 Why is industry analysis valuable?

14-3 Name some industries that you would expect to perform well in the next 5 years and in the next 10 to 15 years.

14-4 How consistent is year-to-year industry performance?

14-5 What are the stages in the life cycle for an industry? Can you think of other stages to add?

14-6 Name an industry that currently is in each of the three life cycle stages.

14-7 In which stage of the life cycle do investors face the highest risk of losing a substantial part of the investment?

14-8 Which industries are the most sensitive to the business cycle? the least sensitive?

14-9 Explain how aggregate market analysis can be important in analyzing industries in relation to the business cycle.

14-10 Explain the concept used in valuing industries.

14-11 What sources of information would be useful to an investor doing a detailed industry analysis?

14-12 Explain how Figure 14-2 might be useful to an investor doing industry analysis.

INTRODUCTION

The KCR Fund, a tax-exempt retirement plan, has owned shares of Merck & Co., Inc., a major international drug company, for many years. The investment in Merck has performed well due to rapid growth in sales and earnings.

Peter Higgens, CFA, an analyst employed by the investment manager of the DCR Fund, has been asked to recommend whether the investment in Merck should be replaced by one in Ford Motor Company.

Ford is an international manufacturer of motor vehicles, parts, and accessories, and derives 70 percent of its revenues from sales of these products in North America. Automotive and Financial Services operations have generated substantially all of Ford's earnings in the past five years. While Ford is the second largest North American auto manufacturer, it is the largest U.S. auto manufacturer overseas. The mature auto industry is sensitive to business cycles, and Japanese and European products have eroded the position of the three largest auto producers in North America.

Merck is one of the largest and "purest" of the major U.S. drug companies. It is a long-term leader in patent-protected drugs for two chronic diseases—hypertension and arthritis—and has recently captured a major position in intravenous antibiotics and anti-ulcer drugs. Merck's research and development effort is the largest in the industry. Imported drugs account for less than 5 percent of total industry sales in the United States.

The competitive environment faced by Ford is significantly different than that faced by Merck. Higgens suspects this is the major reason Merck has been more profitable than Ford, and that Merck would likely remain more profitable in the future.

CFA

14-13 Higgens is aware of three general strategies that companies may follow in seeking to create a strong competitive position:

  ❑ cost leadership
  ❑ product differentiation, and
  ❑ focus on market segments

Ford has been largely unsuccessful in exploiting these strategies. Merck, however, appears to have successfully implemented one or more of them.

Higgens is also aware of five competitive forces faced by companies. Explain how three of these competitive forces faced by Ford and Merck may have affected the relative ability of the two companies to utilize one or more of the general strategies listed above.

CFA

14-14 Universal Auto is a large multinational corporation headquartered in the United States. For segment reporting purposes, the company is engaged in two businesses: production of motor vehicles and information-processing services.

The motor vehicle business is by far the larger of Universal's two segments. It consists mainly of domestic U.S. passenger car production, but also includes small truck manufacturing operations in the U.S. and passenger car production in other countries. This segment of Universal has had weak operating results for the past several years, including a large loss in 1992. While the company does not break out the operating results of its domestic passenger car business, that part of Universal's business is generally believed to be primarily responsible for the weak performance of its motor vehicle segment.

Idata, the information-processing services segment of Universal, was started by Universal about 15 years ago. This business has shown strong, steady growth that has been entirely internal; no acquisitions have been made.

In another excerpt from the research report Adam states:

> Based on our assumption that Universal will be able to increase prices significantly on U.S. passenger cars in 1993, we project a multi-billion dollar profit improvement. . . .

A. Discuss the concept of an industrial life cycle by describing each of its four phases.
B. Identify where each of Universal's two primary businesses, passenger cars and information processing, is in such a cycle.
C. Discuss how product pricing should differ between Universal's two businesses, based on the location of each in the industrial life cycle.

Web Resources

**For additional resources visit our dynamic Web site located at
www.wiley.com/college/jones.**

- *Sector Rotation*—The case helps the reader understand and assess the prospects for different sectors of the current economy. Web site links provide summary information on sectors and industries to help in the active allocation of assets.
- Internet Exercises—This chapter looks at the importance of industry factors in the performance of individual stocks. The Web site exercises will address topics such as:
  - How to identify industry
  - Similarities and dissimilarities between firms in the same industry

  Exercise 1: Looks at how firms behave within and across industries.

  Exercise 2: Repeat the exercise for other industry definitions.

  Exercise 3: Looks at three competing theories on firm growth.

  Exercise 4: Tests the Life-cycle hypothesis of firm growth.

  Exercise 5: Tests the Core-competencies hypothesis.

  Exercise 6: Using sector SPDR funds to proxy for industries, the reader is asked to construct winning investment strategies

- Appendix 14-A—Sources of Industry Information
- Multiple Choice Self Test

Selected References

One of the most detailed and well-known analyses of industries can be found in Michael Porter's work. A well-known book of his is:

Porter, Michael E. *Competitive Advantage: Creating and Sustaining Superior Performance.* New York: Free Press, 1985.

chapter 15

Company Analysis

Chapter 15 explains fundamental security analysis for companies, showing how this is often carried out by practicing security analysts. Investors need to have a good understanding of those factors that affect security returns. For example, although earnings per share are very important in determining stock prices, the unexpected component of those earnings has been important in affecting stock price movements.

AFTER READING THIS CHAPTER YOU WILL BE ABLE TO:

► Analyze companies using the techniques of fundamental analysis.

► Understand the accounting issues and controversies that have come about recently.

► Use the concepts of return on equity (ROE) and return on assets (ROA) in security analysis.

► Recognize the importance of earnings announcements and surprises on stock prices.

► Appreciate more completely the role of the P/E (price/earnings) ratio in security analysis.

Once economy/market analysis has indicated a favorable time to invest in common stocks and industry analysis has been performed to find those industries that are expected to perform well in the future, it remains for the investor to choose promising companies within those industries. The last step in *top-down* fundamental analysis, therefore, is to analyze individual companies.

Fundamental Analysis

Fundamental analysis at the company level involves analyzing basic financial variables in order to estimate the company's intrinsic value. These variables include sales, profit margins, depreciation, the tax rate, sources of financing, asset utilization, and other factors. Additional analysis could involve the firm's competitive position in its industry, labor relations, technological changes, management, foreign competition, and so on. The end result of fundamental analysis at the company level is a good understanding of the company's financial variables and an assessment of the estimated value and potential of the company.

As discussed in Chapter 10, investors could use the dividend discount model to value common stocks. Alternatively, for a short-run estimate of intrinsic value, the earnings multiplier model could be used. Intrinsic (estimated) value is the product of the estimated earnings per share (EPS) for next year and the expected multiplier or P/E ratio, as shown in Equation 15-1.

$$\text{Stock's estimated value} = V_0 = \text{Estimated EPS} \times \text{expected P/E ratio} \qquad \textbf{(15-1)}$$

$$= E_1 \times \widehat{\text{P/E}}$$

where E_1 = earnings expected for the next year and $\widehat{\text{P/E}}$ = the price/earnings ratio expected for the next year.

As noted in Chapter 10, many investors use relative valuation techniques, comparing a company's P/E ratio, P/B ratio, and/or P/S to various benchmarks in order to assess the relative value of the company. Using these techniques, it is not necessary to make a point estimate of intrinsic value. Instead, investors are simply trying to determine if a stock is reasonably valued, overvalued, or undervalued without being too precise about the absolute amount. For many investors, this is an effective method of analysis.

For purposes of discussion, we concentrate on earnings and P/E ratios for several reasons. First, this is what investors encounter most frequently when analyzing stocks. Despite all the uproar recently about accounting scandals, EPS is still the major variable of interest to a majority of investors. Second, the close correlation between earnings changes and stock-price changes is well documented. As Siegel states in his book, *Stocks for the Long Run*, "stock values are based on corporate earnings."[1]

Figure 15-1 shows that the top 50 stocks from a sample of 650 companies studied had a five-year price appreciation of 182 percent, with a change in EPS of 199 percent; for the bottom 50 performers, with a price depreciation of -62 percent, the change in EPS was -61 percent. This figure dramatically illustrates the importance of EPS in common stock analysis. Although other comparisons of earnings and stock prices may not be as striking as those in Figure 15-1, EPS and price changes typically are very closely related both for the best-performing and worst-performing stocks and for stocks in general.

Alternatively, consider the relationship between earnings growth and price performance. A study by Elton, Gruber, and Gultekin examined the risk-adjusted excess returns

---

[1] Siegel's book is a well-known discussion of how common stocks have performed in the past. See Jeremy Siegel, *Stocks for the Long Run*, McGraw-Hill, 3rd edition, 2002.

Figure 15-1

Median change in earnings and stock price: five-year horizon.

SOURCE: V. Niederhoffer and P. J. Regan, "Earnings Changes, Analysts' Forecasts and Stock Prices," *Financial Analysis Journal* 28 (May–June 1972), p. 71. Reprinted by permission.

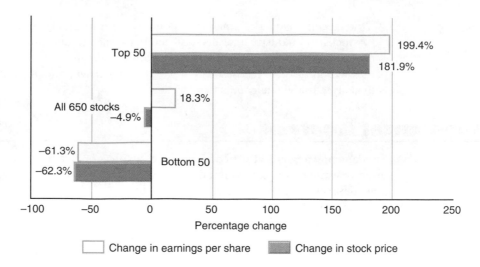

available from buying stocks on the basis of next year's growth in earnings.[2] They found that those stocks with the highest future growth in EPS showed the highest risk-adjusted returns. For the 30 percent of the companies with the highest growth in EPS, the risk-adjusted excess return was 7.48 percent; for the 30 percent with the lowest growth, the risk-adjusted excess return was −4.93 percent. Clearly, growth in reported earnings affects stock prices in a highly significant manner.

The Accounting Aspects of Earnings

If investors are to focus on a company's earnings per share (EPS), a critical variable in security analysis, they should understand the various uses of the word "earnings," how EPS is derived, and what it represents. For investors, an EPS figure is often the bottom line—the item of major interest—in a company's financial statements. Furthermore, they must understand the components of EPS before they can attempt to forecast it—and earnings forecasts remain a building block of stock valuation.

THE FINANCIAL STATEMENTS

Financial Statements
The principal published financial data about a company, primarily the balance sheet and income statement

Investors rely heavily on the **financial statements** of a corporation, which provide the major financial data about companies. To illustrate the use of financial statements in doing company analysis, we examine the 2002 financial statements for the Coca-Cola Company, a famous company with a brand name known worldwide, and a company that epitomizes the global nature of business in today's world. Coca-Cola, the soft drink, is available in more than 195 countries.

The Balance Sheet The balance sheet shows the portfolio of assets for a corporation, as well as its liabilities and owner's equity, at one point in time. The amounts at which items are carried on the balance sheet are dictated by accounting conventions. Cash is the actual dollar amount, whereas marketable securities could be at cost or market value. Stockholders' equity and the fixed assets are on a book value basis.

The balance sheet for Coca-Cola, shown in Exhibit 15-1, is for the year 2002 and also includes data for 2001. The asset side is divided into *Current Assets, Investments and*

---

[2] Edwin Elton, Martin Gruber, and Mustafa Gultekin, "Expectations and Share Prices," *Management Science,* 27 (September 1981).

Other Assets, and *Long-term Assets* (labeled by Coke as Property, Plant, and Equipment) plus, in Coca-Cola's case, *Goodwill and Other Intangible Assets*. Coca-Cola's net property, plant, and equipment is less than the current assets, whereas in the case of General Motors, for example, the fixed assets exceed the current assets. Coca-Cola is also unusual in the large amount of investments and other assets carried.

The right-hand side of the balance sheet is divided between *Current Liabilities* (payable within one year), *Long-Term Debt, Other Liabilities, Deferred Income Taxes, and Shareholders' Equity*. For 2002, Coca-Cola had $7.3 billion of current liabilities, $2.7 billion in long-term debt, and $11.8 billion in shareholders' equity plus *Other Liabilities and Deferred Income Taxes*.

The shareholders' equity includes 2.478 billion shares of stock outstanding as of 2002 (out of 5.6 billion authorized), with a par value of $0.25, $3.9 billion of capital surplus, and a substantial amount of retained earnings ($24.5 billion). The retained earnings item does not represent "spendable" funds for a company; rather it designates that part of previous earnings not paid out as dividends. Note the large amount of *treasury stock* held, representing shares of Coca-Cola being held by the company itself. This amount reduces the original stockholders' equity by more than half.

EXHIBIT 15-1

The Balance Sheet for Coca-Cola

Consolidated Balance Sheets
The Coca-Cola Company and Subsidiaries

December 31, (In millions except share data)	2002	2001
ASSETS		
CURRENT		
Cash and cash equivalents	$ 2,126	$ 1,866
Marketable securities	219	68
	2,345	1,934
Trade accounts receivable, less allowances $55 in 2002 and $59 in 2001	2,097	1,882
Inventories	1,294	1,055
Prepaid expenses and other assets	1,616	2,300
TOTAL CURRENT ASSETS	7,352	7,171
INVESTMENTS AND OTHER ASSETS		
Equity method investments		
Coca-Cola Enterprises Inc.	972	788
Coca-Cola Amatil Limited	872	791
Coca-Cola HBC S.A.	492	432
Other, principally bottling companies	2,401	3,117
Cost method investments, principally bottling companies	254	294
Other assets	2,694	2,792
	7,685	8,214
PROPERTY, PLANT, AND EQUIPMENT		
Land	385	217
Buildings and improvements	2,332	1,812
Machinery and equipment	5,888	4,881
Containers	396	195
	9,001	7,105
Less allowances for depreciation	3,090	2,652
	5,911	4,453

(continued)

TRADEMARKS WITH INDEFINITE LIVES	1,724	1,697
GOODWILL AND OTHER INTANGIBLE ASSETS	1,829	882
	$ 24,501	$ 22,417
LIABILITIES AND SHAREOWNERS' EQUITY		
Accounts payable and accrued expenses	$ 3,692	$ 3,679
Loans and notes payable	2,475	3,743
Current maturities of long-term debt	180	156
Accrued income taxes	994	851
TOTAL CURRENT LIABILITIES	7,341	8,429
LONG-TERM DEBT	2,701	1,219
OTHER LIABILITIES	2,260	961
DEFERRED INCOME TAXES	399	442
SHAREOWNERS' EQUITY		
Common stock, $.25 par value Authorized: 5,600,000,000 shares; issued: 3,490,818,627 shares in 2002 and, 3,491,465,016 shares in 2001	$ 873	$ 879
Capital surplus	3,857	3,520
Reinvested earnings	24,506	23,443
Accumulated other comprehensive (loss) and compensation on restricted stock	(3,047)	(2,788)
	26,189	25,048
Less treasury stock, at cost (1,019,839,490 shares in 2002; 1,005,237,693 shares in 2001)	14,389	13,682
	11,800	11,366
TOTAL LIABILITIES AND SHARE OWNERS' EQUITY	$ 24,501	$ 22,417

See Notes to Consolidated Financial Statements.
SOURCE: Annual Financial Statements, Coca-Cola Company.

It is important for investors to analyze a company's balance sheet carefully.[3] Investors wish to know which companies are undergoing true growth, as opposed to companies that are pumping up their performance by using a lot of debt they may be unable to service. In the latter years of the 1990s, numerous companies used large amounts of debt to improve their performance. Following the severe market downturn in 2000, 2001, and 2002, investors have become much more concerned about both the amount of debt shown on the balance sheet, as well as the amount of cash available to survive difficult periods.

The Income Statement This statement is used more frequently by investors, not only to assess current management performance but also as a guide to the company's future profitability. The income statement represents flows for a particular period, usually one year. Exhibit 15-2 shows the Consolidated Statements of Income for Coca-Cola covering the years 2002, 2001, and 2000.

The key item for investors on the income statement is the after-tax net income, which, divided by the number of common shares outstanding, produces earnings per share. Earnings from continuing operations typically are used to judge the company's success and are almost always the earnings reported in the financial press. Nonrecurring earnings, such as net extraordinary items that arise from unusual and infrequently occurring transactions, are separated from income from continuing operations.

[3] Several financial ratios that can be calculated from balance sheet data are useful in assessing the company's financial strength (e.g., the current ratio, a measure of liquidity, or the debt to total assets ratio, a measure of leverage). These ratios are part of the standard ratio analysis which is often performed by managers, creditors, stockholders, and other interested groups, and are covered in most financial management texts and courses. Some of these ratios are demonstrated later in the analysis.

EXHIBIT 15-2

Income Statement for Coca-Cola

Consolidated Statements of Income
The Coca-Cola Company and Subsidiaries

Year Ended December 31, (In millions except per share data)	2002	2001	2000
NET OPERATING REVENUES	$19,564	$17,545	$17,354
Cost of goods sold	7,105	6,044	6,204
GROSS PROFIT	12,459	11,501	11,150
Selling, administrative and general expenses	7,001	6,149	6,016
Other operating charges	—	—	1,443
OPERATING INCOME	5,458	5,352	3,691
Interest income	209	325	345
Interest expense	199	280	447
Equity income (loss)	384	152	(289)
Other income–net	(353)	39	99
Gains on issuances of stock by equity investors	—	91	—
INCOME BEFORE INCOME TAXES AND OF ACCOUNTING CHANGE	5,499	5,670	3,399
Income taxes	1,523	1,691	1,222
NET INCOME BEFORE CUMULATIVE EFFECT OF ACCOUNTING CHANGE	3,976	3,979	2,177
Cumulative effect of accounting change for SFAS No. 142, net of income taxes:			
Company operations	(367)	—	—
Equity investors	(559)	—	—
Cumulative effect of accounting change for SFAS No. 133, net of income taxes	—	(10)	—
NET INCOME	$ 3,050	$ 3,969	$ 2,177
BASIC NET INCOME PER SHARE			
Before accounting change	$ 1.60	$ 1.60	$ 0.88
Cumulative effect of accounting change	(.37)	—	—
	$ 1.23	$ 1.60	$ 0.88
DILUTED NET INCOME PER SHARE			
Before accounting change	$ 1.60	$ 1.60	$ 0.88
Cumulative effect of accounting change	(.37)	—	—
	$ 1.23	$ 1.60	$ 0.88
AVERAGE SHARES OUTSTANDING	2,478	2,487	2,477
Effect of dilutive securities	5	—	10
AVERAGE SHARES OUTSTANDING ASSUMING DILUTION	2,483	2,487	2,487

See Notes to Consolidated Financial Statements.
SOURCE: Annual Financial Statements, Coca-Cola Company.

Exhibit 15-2 clearly illustrates the "flow" in an income statement. Starting with revenues (total net sales), the cost of goods sold is deducted to obtain Gross Profit. Subtraction of selling, administrative, and general expenses results in "Operating Income," which for Coca-Cola in 2002 was $5.46 billion. Operating income is adjusted by subtracting the interest expense, which generally is an important item for large companies, because interest is tax deductible.[4]

---

[4] Note, however, that Coca-Cola had both interest income and interest expense plus other income (which was a negative) as well as equity income, and all of these items must be netted together.

These adjustments to operating income produce "Income before Income Taxes." Subtracting out income taxes results in "Net Income Before Cumulative Effect of Accounting Change." After any effects of accounting changes are deducted, "Basic Net Income Per Share" emerges. Note that for the previous two years "Basic Net Income Per Share" and "Diluted Net Income Per Share" were the same, but not in 2002 because of accounting changes.

Dividing by the *average* number of shares outstanding produces EPS for 2002 of $1.23. Although basic net income per share of $1.60 was the same in 2002 as in 2001, accounting changes reduced this number by $0.37, resulting in the final $1.23 EPS for 2002.

Any charge to earnings because of an accounting change is important to investors in trying to understand earnings. What investors seek to determine is the "true" earning power of a company, because ultimately they will be attempting to forecast future earnings. As we can see, there was a substantial accounting-change impact on Coca-Cola in 2002. The difference caused by accounting adjustments can be quite large for other companies at various times. In general, investors should rely on income before changes in accounting principles in trying to gauge true earning power.

The Cash-Flow Statement   The third financial statement of a company is the **cash-flow statement**, which incorporates elements of both the balance sheet and income statement as well as other items. It is designed to track the flow of cash through the firm. It consists of three parts:

Cash-Flow Statement Tracks the flow of cash through the firm

- ❏ cash from operating activities
- ❏ cash from investing activities
- ❏ cash from financing activities

The cash-flow statement can help investors examine the quality of the earnings. For example, if inventories are rising more quickly than sales, as happened in late 2000 and early 2001 for several companies, this can be a real sign of trouble—demand may be softening. If a company is cutting back on its capital expenditures, this could signal problems down the road. If accounts receivable are rising at a rate greater than sales are increasing, a company may be having trouble collecting money owed to it. If accounts payable are rising too quickly, a company may be conserving cash by delaying payments to suppliers, a potential sign of trouble for the company.

Example 15-1   In Motorola's financial statements, net cash used for inventories went from $678 million in 1999 to $2.3 billion in 2000, clearly a warning sign that investors should have investigated.

One item of potential importance that investors should examine in the Statement of Cash Flows is the write-off, supposedly a one-time charge. These write-offs may be labeled as such items as "charges for reorganization of businesses" or "one-time charge for strategic actions." Some firms make multiple write-offs over a period of years. Investors should determine what these write-offs are for and if they signal operating problems for the company.

Example 15-2   K-Mart wrote off about three-quarters of a billion dollars over a five-year period, mostly for store closings and inventory write-downs.

Exhibit 15-3 shows the Consolidated Statement of Cash Flows for Coca-Cola. Relative to some other companies, the changes in Coke's cash-flow statement were basically not significant. Coke generated substantial "net cash provided by operating activities" for each of the three years shown, and after investing activities and financing activities, Coke ended each of these years with a sizeable cash balance.

EXHIBIT 15-3

Consolidated Statements of Cash Flows for Coca-Cola

Consolidated Statements of Cash Flows
The Coca-Cola Company and Subsidiaries

Year Ended December 31, (In Millions)	2002	2001	2000
OPERATING ACTIVITIES			
Net Income	$3,050	$3,969	$2,177
Depreciation and amortization	806	803	773
Stock-based compensation expense	365	41	43
Deferred income taxes	40	56	3
Equity income or loss, net of dividends	(256)	(54)	380
Foreign currency adjustments	(76)	(60)	196
Gain on issuances of stock by equity investee	—	(91)	—
(Gains) losses on sales of assets, including bottling interests	3	(85)	(127)
Cumulative effect of accounting changes	926	10	—
Other operating charges	—	—	916
Other items	291	(17)	76
Net change in operating assets and liabilities	(407)	(462)	(852)
Net cash provided by operating activities	4,742	4,110	3,585
INVESTING ACTIVITIES			
Acquisitions and investments, principally trademarks and bottling companies	(544)	(651)	(397)
Purchases of investments and other assets	(156)	(456)	(508)
Proceeds from disposals of investments and other assets	243	455	290
Purchases of property, plant and equipment	(851)	(769)	(733)
Proceeds from disposals of property, plant and equipment	69	91	45
Other investing activities	52	142	138
Net cash used in investing activities	(1,187)	(1,188)	(1,165)
FINANCING ACTIVITIES			
Issuances of debt	1,622	3,011	3,671
Payments of debt	(2,378)	(3,937)	(4,256)
Issuances of stock	107	164	331
Purchases of stock for treasury	(691)	(277)	(133)
Dividends	(1,987)	(1,791)	(1,685)
Net cash used in financing activities	(3,327)	(2,830)	(2,072)
EFFECTS OF EXCHANGE RATE CHANGES ON CASH AND CASH EQUIVALENTS	32	(45)	(140)
CASH AND CASH EQUIVALENTS			
Net increase during the year	260	47	208
Balance at beginning of the year	1,866	1,819	1,611
Balance at end of year	$2,126	$1,866	$1,819

See Notes to Consolidated Financial Statements.

SOURCE: Annual Financial Statements, Coca-Cola Company.

Some Practical Advice

Given the accounting problems in today's world, many investors have concluded that cash flows are the way to go, because they cannot easily be manipulated. Although cash flows are increasingly important to investors, they need to be aware that companies can and do manipulate cash flows. WorldCom, in their summer 2002 announcement that rocked the investment community, admitted that it inflated not only earnings but cash flows as well for several quarters. Investors should pay careful attention to the first part of the Cash-Flow Statement, "Cash Flows From Operations." For example, did the company sell their accounts receivable, which will immediately pump up operating cash flows? Are some expenses being capitalized, thereby creating an asset to be written off gradually (this is what WorldCom allegedly did)? Are the proceeds from securities trading being counted as part of operating cash? Investors need to look for issues such as these if they are to avoid being fooled on the cash-flow statement.[5]

Generally Accepted Accounting Principles (GAAP) Financial reporting requirements establishing the rules for producing financial statements

Certifying the Statements The earnings shown on an income statement are derived on the basis of **generally accepted accounting principles (GAAP)**. The company adheres to a standard set of rules developed by the accounting profession on the basis of historical costs, which can be measured objectively. An auditor from an independent accounting firm certifies that the earnings have been derived according to accounting standards in a statement labeled the "auditor's report."

Example 15-3

In certifying Coca-Cola's financial statements, Ernst & Young LLP stated that, "In our opinion, the financial statements referred to above present fairly, in all material respects, the consolidated financial position of the Coca-Cola Company and subsidiaries at December 31, 2002 and 2001."

Note that the auditor's report does *not* guarantee the accuracy or the quality of the earnings in an absolute sense; rather it only attests that the statements are a *fair presentation* of the company's financial position for a particular period. Coke's auditors are certifying, in effect, that generally accepted accounting principles were applied on a consistent basis when they state: "We conducted our audits in accordance with auditing standards generally accepted in the United States." The Financial Accounting Standards Board (FASB), which succeeded the Accounting Principles Board of the American Institute of Certified Public Accountants in 1972, currently formulates accounting standards.

Reading the Footnotes Regardless of how closely a company adheres to good accounting practices, and how carefully the auditors do their job, investors still need to examine the "Notes to the Financial Statements," or footnotes, if they are really to understand the company's financial situation. The footnotes often provide important information about the accounting methods being used, any ongoing litigation, how revenue is recognized, and so forth. The footnotes can help an investor better understand the quality of the reported earnings. The footnotes are located after the consolidated financial statements, and can be found in 10-K and 10-Q Reports.

Reported Earnings GAAP earnings, the official earnings of a company as reported to stockholders and the SEC

THE PROBLEMS WITH EPS

Reported Earnings Earnings derived under GAAP and reported on the income statement are known as **reported earnings**. Although the financial statements are derived on the basis of GAAP and are certified in an auditor's report, problems exist with reported

---

[5] This discussion is based on Ann Tergesen, "Cash-Flow Hocus-Pocus," *Business Week*, July 15, 2002, pp. 130, 132.

earnings. The basic problem, simply stated, is that reported EPS for a company (i.e., accounting EPS) is the product of very complex GAAP principles, which are subject to subjective judgment. EPS is not a precise figure that is readily comparable over time, and the EPS figures for different companies often are not comparable to each other. Alternative accounting principles can be, and are, used to prepare the financial statements.

Many of the items in the balance sheet and income statement can be accounted for in more than one way. Given the number of items that constitutes the financial statements, the possible number of acceptable (i.e., that conform to GAAPs) combinations that could be used is large. A company could produce several legal and permissible EPS figures depending solely on the accounting principles used. The question that investors must try to answer is, "Which EPS best represents the 'true' position of a company?"

Because reported EPS is a function of the many alternative accounting principles in use, it is extremely difficult, if not impossible, for the "true" performance of a company to be reflected consistently in one figure. Since each company is different, is it reasonable to expect one accounting system to capture the true performance of all companies? With the business world so complex, one can make a case for the necessity of alternative treatments of the same item or process, such as inventories or depreciation.

Accountants are caught in the middle—between investors, who want a clean, clear-cut EPS figure, and company management, which wants to present the financial statements in the most favorable light. After all, management hires the accounting firm, and, subject to certain guidelines, management can change accounting firms. As long as the company follows GAAP, the accountant may find it difficult to resist management pressure to use particular principles. At some point, an accounting firm may resign as a company's auditor as a result of the problems and pressures that can arise.

The FASB faces conflicting demands when it formulates or changes accounting principles, because various interest groups want items accounted for in specific ways. The end result has been that the "standards" issued by the FASB were often compromises that did not fully resolve the particular issue; in some cases, they created additional complications.

Example 15-4

FAS 133, which is concerned with financial derivatives and hedging, was begun in 1992 and continues to evolve. The standard and its supporting documents now total more than 800 pages.

Given the accounting controversies in 2002—the collapse of Enron, the charges against Arthur Andersen, the questioning of numerous companies as to their accounting practices—the FASB, under the leadership of a new head, is planning to change directions. The new approach emphasizes broad principles rather than thousands of pages of rules designed to spell out what to do with each new variation encountered in practice.[6] In the past, some companies met the exact letter of the law, but violated the intent of the principles. The new plan is to emphasize the validity of a transaction from a business perspective, and to place the burden on corporations to demonstrate that their accounting procedures are in compliance. Given entrenched interests, the outcome is yet to be decided.

Should the FASB falter in its job, or investors actively demand more action in the way of "tighter" accounting rules, as they did in 2002 in the face of several company accounting scandals, the government can intervene and issue its own rulings. The Securities and Exchange Commission (SEC) has the authority to do so, because corporations must file detailed financial data with it. The SEC has issued some definitions of acceptable accounting practices over the years, thereby acting as a prod to the accounting groups to continue their progress.

---

[6] See Mike McNamee, "FASB: Rewriting the Book on Bookkeeping," *Business Week*, May 20, 2002, pp. 123–124.

Investments Intuition

Given the difficulties involved, and the alternative accounting treatments, investors must remember that reported EPS is not the precise figure that it first appears to be. Unless adjustments are made, the EPS of different companies may not be comparable on either a time series or a cross-sectional basis.

The Quality of Earnings Some EPS figures are better than others in the sense that they have been derived using more conservative principles. In other words, they are of higher quality. The quality of corporate earnings is currently a bigger issue than it has been at any time since the 1930s. In an article on the quality of earnings, Bernstein and Seigel stated[7]:

> A company's reported earnings figure is often taken by the unsophisticated user of financial statements as the quantitative measure of the firm's well-being. Of course, any professional knows that earnings numbers are in large part the product of conscious and often subjective choices between various accounting treatments and business options, as well as of various external economic factors. If he wants to assess the true earning power of each company, the financial statement user must make some determination of the "quality of its earnings" [emphasis added].

Quality assessments are typically difficult to make and require considerable expertise in accounting and financial analysis. However, as *Forbes* magazine recently noted, "Really smart investors must go back to the original data and reinterpret it. 'Right now,' says former SEC commissioner Steven Wallman, 'we take disaggregated data and have accountants aggregate it, only to have investors disaggregate it again.'"[8]

When it is difficult to assess the quality of a company's earnings, one alternative is to look at the first item on the Income Statement—Sales, or Revenues. Is revenue growth slowing or increasing? Unless (legitimate) revenues are growing over time, earnings will suffer, and the quality may be suspect. Because of the importance of earnings quality today, more and more information sources are focusing on it.

Example 15-5 *Forbes* magazine started an annual survey of corporate earnings quality in 2001. The primary focus is on the cash generated rather than the earnings reported. *Forbes* states that in the first list of 25 growth stocks, 17 issues with satisfactory grading declined only 2 percent, whereas the market declined 12 percent; meanwhile the seven stocks with red flags declined 28 percent on average.[9]

One of the primary reasons that earnings quality has been called into doubt in recent years is the proliferation of various EPS numbers. We examine this issue below.

What About *Pro Forma* Earnings? As if the problems with reported earnings and confusing GAAPs are not bad enough, companies recently have introduced a whole new level of confusion by reporting their own version of earnings, with varying labels

---

[7] See Leopold Bernstein and Joel Seigel, "The Concept of Earnings Quality," *Financial Analysts Journal* (July–August 1979), pp. 72–75

[8] See Bernard Condon, "Gaps in GAAP," *Forbes*, January 25, 1999, p. 76.

[9] See Nathan Vardi and Cecily J. Fluke, "Priced for Perfection," *Forbes*, June 10, 2002, pp. 206–208.

and varying procedures. Let's examine the differences in earnings numbers in today's world.[10]

- Net income is also called reported earnings. It is the "official" audited number on the income statement derived under GAAP, and filed with the SEC.
- Operating Earnings, also called "Pro Forma Earnings," takes net income and adjusts it by leaving out certain costs that are said not to be relevant to the ongoing business, such as noncash charges and one-time expenses. Operating Earnings are not audited, and there are no rules on how to calculate it, leaving companies free to do as they choose.
- EBITDA, or Earnings before interest, taxes, depreciation and amortization, is sometimes called operating profit. This number essentially is revenue minus operating expenses, and leaves out interest expense and depreciation and amortization. Telecommunications companies in particular have emphasized this number in their reporting because of their lack of real profitability.

Example 15-6 In 2001, Quest Communications reported that for the third quarter its EBITDA was $1.77 billion. However, the company actually lost $142 million because the operating profit was essentially wiped out by interest expense and depreciation. In 2002 the price of this stock declined almost 90 percent because of questions about its accounting procedures.

While the concept of pro forma earnings has been around for a number of years, its use really became muddled with the explosion of dotcoms in the late 1990s. Since many of them had no earnings in the conventional sense, they tried to report to shareholders in the most favorable light by omitting various expenses. The problem is that each company can choose its own method of calculation. Therefore, comparisons between companies are essentially meaningless. Remember, a key issue for investors is what did the company earn? If companies can decide for themselves what numbers to report, how will investors determine what the earnings really are?

Example 15-7 JDS Uniphase, a maker of fiber optics, bought a competitor for $1 billion in stock in July 2000.[11] When its assets rose sharply (at the deal's close) while the stock price declined sharply, JDS took charges of $50 billion. Although no cash was involved, under GAAP the entire amount plus other losses was deducted from net income, a total of $56 billion. For the previous five years, the total revenues for this company was only $5 billion. Now consider the alternative EPS numbers that came out of this:

Under GAAP, JDS lost $9.39.
Under Standard and Poor's (S&P) new core earnings (explained below), JDS lost $3.19.
JDS says it lost $0.36.
Wall Street numbers said JDS made $0.02.
Anyone confused?

[10] This discussion is indebted to Nanette Byrnes and David Henry, "Confused About Earnings?" *Business Week*, November 26, 2001, pp. 77–84.
[11] Ibid., pp. 79–80.

In concluding this discussion, consider a quote from an editorial in mid-2002 in *Business Week*: "There are almost as many measures of earnings today as there are companies. *Pro forma* has destroyed any serious means of measuring performance across industries and the broad economy."[12]

What Investors Can Do As the former chairman of the Federal Reserve System said in 2001, "The profession of auditing and accounting is, in fact, in crisis."[13] Investors face difficult problems with accounting issues, and as a popular press article said in 2002, "Numbers do lie."[14] In 2001 and 2002, the accounting issue really came home to investors with the Enron collapse and several other well-known companies having their accounting procedures questioned, such as Tyco, Cisco, Amazon, and on and on.

The best advice for most investors is to go ahead and use the reported EPS, because it is all that is normally available, and the majority of investors will also have to rely on this figure. Investors should, however, be aware of the potential problems involved in EPS and should constantly keep in mind its nature and derivation.

Example 15-8 As the economy approaches a recession, many analysts believe that companies use aggressive accounting techniques in order to report larger earnings. Such techniques include recognizing revenues before they are actually received or delaying the recording of expenses.

Investors can take a few precautions and additional steps to help themselves when trying to interpret financial statements and earnings reports, including[15]:

- Examine the 10-K statement for additional information. This report must be filed with the SEC and is available online.
- Read the footnotes to the financial statements. Information not disclosed in the body of the discussion of the financial statements is often contained in the footnotes, because the company must disclose the information somewhere.
- Obtain other opinions, found in sources such as *The Value Line Investment Survey*, which has its own independent analysts.
- Study the cash-flow statement. Firms need cash to operate, and it is more difficult to disguise problems where cash is concerned. Investors should calculate **free cash flow**, defined as the money left after all bills are paid and dividend payments are made. Starting with cash from operating activities on the statement of cash flows, subtract capital expenditures and cash dividends. Fast-growing companies may have negative cash flows for several years and still be okay, but mature companies with negative cash flows are often a sign of problems.

Free Cash Flow Cash flow from operations minus capital expenditures and dividends

Also note that things are changing. The SEC has implemented some new rules concerning corporate disclosures. As noted in Chapter 13, Standard & Poor's Corporation, the giant provider of financial information, has proposed a new standard to provide a better way to measure a company's performance and to provide more uniformity in earnings. S&P is

---

[12] See "A Good Idea About Earnings," *Business Week*, May 27, 2002, p. 114.
[13] Byrnes and Henry, p. 77.
[14] See Steven T. Goldberg, "Numbers Do Lie," *Kiplinger's Personal Finance*, April 2002, p. 54.
[15] Goldberg, p. 54.

calling this "core earnings." It will differ from both reported earnings (GAAP earnings) and *pro forma* earnings.[16] Specifically, core earnings will:

◨ Include many costs now excluded in *pro forma* earnings, including pension costs, expenses from stock option grants, the expenses involved in writing down certain assets, expenses involved in the restructuring of ongoing businesses, and others.
◨ Exclude certain items S&P believes do not result from a company's operating business, such as gains from a pension plan, assets sales, and income from insurance or litigation.

This move will have significant effects on the EPS of a number of companies because many companies include (exclude) the excluded (included) items above.

Example 15-9 General Electric is one of the best-performing stocks of recent years. According to an analysis of its 2001 EPS, which were reported at $1.42, S&P's new core earnings would subtract several items, including stock options expense, pension gains, and changes from asset sales. The resulting core earnings would be $1.11, which is a significant difference. Assume that the P/E ratio was 25 in each case. The stock would be valued at $35.50 under the reported EPS and $27.75 if investors used core earnings.[17]

THE GLOBAL ARENA—INTERNATIONAL ACCOUNTING

Investors who find U.S. accounting comparisons difficult have often been even more troubled by international accounting practices. Practices can vary widely among countries, and differ sharply from what U.S. investors may expect to find.

Interestingly, international accounting standards are now moving more rapidly than U.S. standards to a system based on one set of rules. The International Accounting Standards Board is formulating global rules that eliminate numerous choices, in many cases becoming stricter than U.S. standards. While U.S. accounting practices still provide more information to investors, it would appear that global accounting practices are moving toward providing more information while being based on broad principles (as noted earlier, the use of broader and easier to understand principles is apparently the way the FASB plans to move).

Current plans call for the International Accounting Standard (IAS), which resembles GAAP, to be implemented in 2005.[18] Publicly traded companies in the European Union must switch from their local accounting rules to the new IAS. Although IAS more closely resembles GAAP than the accounting standards in most countries, there will still be differences, including (among others):

◨ Whereas IAS plans to expense the cost of stock options, GAAP does not require this to date.
◨ GAAP requires research and development costs to be expensed, whereas IAS allows development costs to be capitalized.
◨ GAAP does not require consolidation of subsidiary results if the parent company owns less than 51 percent of the stock; IAS requires consolidation if the parent has "economic control."

[16] This discussion is based on Nanette Byrnes and Mara Derhovanesian, "Earnings: A Cleaner Look," *Business Week*, May 27, 2002, pp. 34–37.
[17] Ibid., p. 37.
[18] This discussion is based on Michael Maiello, "Tower of Babel," *Forbes*, July 22, 2002, p. 166.

Analyzing a Company's Profitability

On a company level, EPS is the culmination of several important factors going on within the company. Accounting variables can be used to examine these determining factors by analyzing key financial ratios. Analysts examine the components of EPS in order to try to determine whether a company's profitability is increasing or decreasing and why.

We start with the following accounting identity, which establishes the relationship between EPS and ROE:

$$\text{EPS} = \text{ROE} \times \text{Book value per share} \qquad (15\text{-}2)$$

where ROE is the return on equity and book value per share is the accounting value of the stockholders' equity on a per share basis. Book value typically changes rather slowly, making ROE the primary variable on which to concentrate. Using Coca-Cola's data from Exhibits 15-1 and 15-2, we would calculate EPS for 2002 as follows:

		For Coca-Cola	=	\$	% Return
$\text{EPS} = \dfrac{\text{Net income after taxes}}{\text{Shares outstanding}}$	=	$\dfrac{\$3,050,000,000}{2,478,000,000}$	=	\$1.23	—
$\text{ROE} = \dfrac{\text{Net income after taxes}}{\text{Stockholders' equity}}$	=	$\dfrac{\$3,050,000,000}{\$11,800,000,000}$	=	—	25.9
$\text{Book value per share} = \dfrac{\text{Stockholders' equity}}{\text{Shares outstanding}}$	=	$\dfrac{\$11,800,000,000}{2,478,000,000}$	=	\$4.76	—

ROE is the accounting rate of return that stockholders earn on their portion of the total capital used to finance the company; in other words, it is the stockholders' return on equity. Book value per share measures the accounting value of the stockholders' equity.

Example 15-10 In Coca-Cola's case in 2002 the ROE was 25.9 percent and the book value was \$4.76 per share. Therefore:

$$\text{EPS} = 0.259 \times \$4.76 = \$1.23$$

Return on Equity (ROE)
The accounting rate of return on stockholders' equity

Primary emphasis is on **return on equity (ROE)**, because it is the key component in determining earnings growth and dividend growth. The return on equity is the end result of several important variables. Analysts and investors seek to decompose the ROE into its critical components in order both to identify adverse impacts on ROE and to help predict future trends in ROE.

Different combinations of financial ratios can be used to decompose ROE—in other words, there are several ways to do this analysis. We will use a multiplicative relationship that consists of important financial ratios that easily can be calculated from a company's financial statements.

ANALYZING RETURN ON EQUITY (ROE)

$$\text{ROE} = \text{ROA} \times \text{Leverage} \qquad (15\text{-}3)$$

Return on Assets (ROA)
The accounting rate of return on a firm's assets

A major component of ROE is **return on assets (ROA)**, an important measure of a company's profitability. ROA measures the return on assets, whereas ROE measures the return to the stockholders, who finance only part of the assets (the bondholders finance the other part).

To go from ROA to ROE, the effects of leverage must be considered. The leverage ratio measures how the firm finances its assets.[19] Basically, firms can finance with either debt or equity. Debt, although a cheaper source of financing, is a riskier method, because of the fixed interest payments that must be systematically repaid on time to avoid bankruptcy. Leverage can magnify the returns to the stockholders (favorable leverage) or diminish them (unfavorable leverage). Thus, any given ROA can be magnified into a higher ROE by the judicious use of debt financing. The converse, however, applies; injudicious use of debt can lower the ROE below the ROA.

Investments Intuition

What this analysis does not show is the impact of leverage on the risk of the firm. Remember that in this analysis we are examining only the determinants of EPS. However, as we know from our discussion of valuation, two factors, EPS and a multiplier, are required to determine value. An increase in leverage may increase the riskiness of the company more than enough to offset the increased EPS, thereby lowering the company's value. *Investors must always consider both dimensions of the value of a stock, the return side and the risk side—in other words, EPS alone does not determine stock price.*

To capture more easily the effects of leverage, we use an equity multiplier rather than a debt percentage. This measure reflects the amount of assets financed per dollar of stockholders' equity. For example, a ratio of 2 would indicate that $2 in assets are being financed by $1 in stockholders' equity.

$$\text{Leverage} = \text{Total assets/Stockholders' equity}$$

Example 15-11 For Coca-Cola in 2002, dividing total assets by equity (24,501/11,800) produces an equity multiplier of 2.0764, which is used as the measure of leverage. In effect, $1 of stockholders' equity was financing $2.08 of assets.

To calculate ROE, we relate ROA and leverage as shown in Equation 15-3:

$$\text{ROE} = \text{ROA} \times \text{Leverage}$$

Example 15-12 Combining these two factors, ROA and leverage, for Coca-Cola produces the following ROE:

$$\text{ROE} = 0.1245 \times 2.0764 = 0.259 = 25.9\%$$

ANALYZING RETURN ON ASSETS (ROA)

ROA is an important measure of a firm's profitability. It is a product of two factors, as shown in Equation 15-4.

$$\text{ROA} = \text{Net income margin} \times \text{Turnover} \tag{15-4}$$

$$\text{Net income margin} = \text{Net income / Sales}$$

$$\text{Turnover} = \text{Sales / Total assets}$$

---

[19] Leverage can be measured in several ways, such as the ratio of total debt to total assets or the ratio of debt to equity.

The first ratio affecting ROA, the net income margin, measures the firm's earning power on its sales (revenues). How much net return is realized from sales given all costs? Obviously, the more the firm earns per dollar of sales, the better.

Asset turnover is a measure of efficiency. Given some amount of total assets, how much in sales can be generated? The more sales per dollar of assets, where each dollar of assets has to be financed with a source of funds bearing a cost, the better it is for a firm. The firm may have some assets that are unproductive, thereby adversely affecting its efficiency.

$$\text{ROA} = \frac{\text{Net income}}{\text{Sales}} \times \frac{\text{Sales}}{\text{Total assets}} \tag{15-5}$$

Example 15-13 Using the data for Coca-Cola for 2002 from Exhibits 15-1 and 15-2:

Net Income/Sales = $3,050,000,000/$19,564,000,000 = 0.1559

Sales/Total assets = $19,564,000/$24,501,000,000 = 0.7985

ROA = 0.1559 × 0.7985 = 0.1245 = 12.45%

ROA is a fundamental measure of firm profitability, reflecting how effectively and efficiently the firm's assets are used. Obviously, the higher the net income for a given amount of assets, the better the return. For Coca-Cola, the return on assets is 12.45 percent. The ROA can be improved by increasing the net income more than the assets (in percentage terms) or by using the existing assets even more efficiently.

One of the determinants of ROA may be able to offset poor performance in the other. The net income margin may be low, but the company may generate more sales per dollar of assets than comparable companies. Conversely, poor turnover may be partially offset by high net profitability. In either case, analysts and investors are trying to understand how these factors are impacting Coke, and how they are likely to do so in the future.

USING ROE—ESTIMATING THE INTERNAL (SUSTAINABLE) GROWTH RATE

Sustainable Growth Rate The estimated rate at which a company's earnings can grow from internal forces

An important part of company analysis is the determination of a **sustainable growth rate** in earnings and dividends. This rate represents the rate at which a company can grow from internal sources without the issuance of additional securities. It provides a benchmark for assessing a company's actual or target growth rate. A company growing faster than the sustainable growth rate will have to issue additional securities, which could dilute the existing equity (in the case of stock issues) or increase the financial risk (in the case of debt issues).

How is the sustainable growth rate calculated? The internal or sustainable growth rate, typically designated as g, is the product of the ROE and the retention rate—which is calculated as 1 minus the dividend payout ratio—as shown in Equation 15-6:

$$g = \text{ROE} \times (1 - \text{Payout ratio}) = \text{ROE} \times \text{retention rate} \tag{15-6}$$

Equation 15-6 is one of the primary calculations in fundamental security analysis and is often used by security analysts.

Example 15-14 For 2002, Coca-
The retention ra
data is, therefor
calculation for
years ago. (Co

A problem a
is that the y
can result i
Although a
tionships a

The
company'
for a com
rate will
by Equa

W
investors
growth ra
companies
company u

obtained; and (3) understand the
consider each of these topics i

A FORECAST OF E
Security Analyst
the most obvious s
casts as a part of
Line Investmen
ahead for ea
tracks ear

in th
ser

Investments in

Many investors get carried away when estimating the expected growth rate in EPS for companies they find attractive. However, when we think about it logically, there have to be limits to how fast a company can continue to grow. Clearly, some can grow extremely fast for a few years. But an analysis of companies shows that the outer limit for truly long-term growth is about 20 percent. Consider this—Cisco, one of the great growth stocks of modern times, grew almost 100% a y through March 2000.[21] This was fai... and it produced great performance for Cisco's stockholders. However, had Cisco grown at that rate for the next 10 years, it would had a total market value of $520 trillion in 2010. This would have far exceeded the combined value of every stock in the world in 2000. Simply put, very rapid growth can't last indefinitely. It is simply not possible.

Earnings Estimates

The EPS that investors use to value stocks is the future (expected) EPS. Current stock price is a function of future earnings estimates and the P/E ratio, not the past. If investors knew what the EPS for a particular company would be next year, they could achieve good results in the market.

In doing fundamental security analysis using EPS, an investor needs to (1) know how to obtain an earnings estimate; (2) consider the accuracy of any earnings estimate

---

[20] Technically, g is defined as the expected growth rate in dividends. However, the dividend growth rate is clearly influenced by the earnings growth rate. Although dividend and earnings growth rates can diverge in the short run, such differences would not be expected to continue for long periods of time. The standard assumption in security analysis is that g represents the growth rate for both dividends and earnings.

[21] This example is based on Jason Zweig, "Murphy was an Investor," *Money*, July 2002, p. 62.

role of earnings surprises in impacting stock prices. We
turn.

S

' **Estimates of Earnings** As discussed in Chapter 11, among
urces of earnings estimates are security analysts, who make such fore-
heir job. This type of earnings information is widely available. *The Value*
Survey, for example, forecasts quarterly earnings for several quarters
company covered. IBES International is a well-known New York firm that
ings estimates by analysts and makes them available.

veral studies suggest that individual analysts are by and large undistinguishable
ir ability to predict EPS. The practical implication of these findings is that the con-
sus forecast is likely to be superior to the forecasts of individual analysts.

Mechanical Estimates of Earnings An alternative method of obtaining earnings
forecasts is the use of mechanical procedures such as time series models. In deciding
what type of model to use, some of the evidence on the behavior of earnings over time
should be considered.

Time series analysis involves the use of historical data to make earnings forecasts.
The model used assumes that the future will be similar to the past. The series being forecast, EPS, is assumed to have trend elements, an average value, seasonal factors, and
error. The moving average technique is a simple example of the time series model for
forecasting EPS. Exponential smoothing, which assigns differing weights to past values, is
an example of a more sophisticated technique. A regression equation would represent another technique for making forecasts; the regression equation could handle several variables, such as trend and seasonal factors. More sophisticated models could also be used.

Studies of the behavior of the time path of earnings have produced mixed results. Most
of the early studies indicated randomness in the growth rates of annual earnings. Other studies found some evidence of nonrandomness. More recent studies, particularly those of quarterly earnings, have indicated that the time series behavior of earnings is not random.

THE ACCURACY OF EARNINGS FORECASTS

A study by Brown and Rozeff found results that "overwhelmingly" favored the analysts.[22]
Specifically, the study found that earnings forecasts made by *The Value Line Investment
Survey* (described in Appendix 15-A) were consistently superior to those produced by
well-known time series models, including the sophisticated Box-Jenkins method. Such a
finding is reassuring from an economic theory standpoint because analysts' forecasts cost
more than time series forecasts. On balance, the weight of the evidence tends to favor analysts over statistical models in predicting what the *actual* reported earnings will be.

Even if investors accept the relative superiority of analysts' estimates, the fact remains that analysts often over- or underestimate the earnings that are actually realized.
Analysts are typically far off target on their estimates. According to one study of almost
400 companies, analysts' estimates averaged 57 percent too high in the first month of a
fiscal year, and the error was still an average 12 percent by year end.

Another study by Dreman and Berry covered 66,100 analysts' consensus forecasts
for the period 1974 to 1990. Analysts were given every advantage in the study—for exam-

[22] See L. Brown and M. Rozeff, "The Superiority of Analyst Forecasts as Measures of Expectations. Evidence
from Earnings," *Journal of Finance*, 33 (March 1978): 1–16.

ple, forecasts could be made in the same quarter as earnings were reported, and the forecasts could be changed up to two weeks before the end of the quarter. Nevertheless, the average annual error was 44 percent, and only 25 percent of consensus estimates came within plus or minus 5 percent of reported earnings. Looking at the estimates on the basis of the 61 industries involved, only one industry had forecast errors averaging under 10 percent for the entire time period, and overall the average forecast error grouped by industries was 50 percent (the median error was 43 percent).[23]

Inaccurate earnings estimates can provide opportunities for investors. Analysts are frequently wrong, and if investors can make better estimates of earnings, they can expect to profit from their astuteness.

EARNINGS SURPRISES

We have established that changes in earnings and stock prices are highly correlated. We have also discussed the necessity of estimating EPS and how such estimates can be obtained. What remains is to examine the role of expectations about earnings in selecting common stocks.

The association between earnings and stock prices is more complicated than simply demonstrating a correlation (association) between earnings growth and stock-price changes. Elton, Gruber, and Gultekin found that investors could not earn excess returns by buying and selling stocks on the basis of the consensus estimate of earnings growth.[24] (The consensus estimate was defined as the average estimate of security analysts at major brokerage houses.) They also found that analysts tended to overestimate earnings for companies they expected would perform well and to underestimate for companies they expected would perform poorly.

Investors must form expectations about EPS, and these expectations will be incorporated into stock prices if markets are efficient. Although these expectations are often inaccurate, they play an important role in affecting stock prices. Malkiel and Cragg concluded that in making accurate one-year predictions, "It is far more important to know what the market will think the growth rate of earnings will be next year rather than to know the (actual) realized long-term growth rate."[25]

As Latané and Jones pointed out, new information about a stock is unexpected information.[26] The important point about EPS in terms of stock prices is the difference between what the market (i.e., investors in general) was expecting the EPS to be and what the company actually reported. Unexpected information about earnings calls for a revision in investor probability beliefs about the future and therefore an adjustment in the price of the stock.

Earnings Surprise
The difference between a firm's actual earnings and its expected earnings

To assess the impact of the surprise factor in EPS, Latané and Jones developed a model to express and use the **earnings surprise** factor in the quarterly EPS of companies. This standardized unexpected earnings (SUE) model was discussed in Chapter 12 as part of the market anomalies associated with the evidence concerning market efficiency.[27] Repeating from Chapter 12,

$$SUE = \frac{\text{Actual quarterly EPS} - \text{Forecast quarterly EPS}}{\text{Standardization variable}}$$ (15-7)

[23] See David Dreman, "Cloudy Crystal Balls," *Forbes*, October 10, 1994, p. 92.
[24] See footnote 4.
[25] Malkiel and Cragg, "Expectations and the Structure of Share Prices," p. 616.
[26] See H. Latané and C. Jones, "Standardized Unexpected Earnings—A Progress Report," *Journal of Finance*, 32 (December 1977): 1457–1465.
[27] This model is explained in Latané and Jones, "Standardized Unexpected Earnings," p. 1457 (see footnote 26). The standardization variable is the standard error of estimate for the estimating regression equation.

The SUE concept is designed to capture the surprise element in the earnings just mentioned—in other words, the difference between what the market expects the company to earn and what it actually does earn. A favorable earnings surprise, in which the actual earnings exceed the market's expectation, should bring about an adjustment to the price of the stock as investors revise their probability beliefs about the company's earnings. Conversely, an unfavorable earnings surprise should lead to a downward adjustment in price; in effect, the market has been disappointed in its expectations.[28]

In conclusion, stock prices are affected not only by the level of and growth in earnings but also by the market's expectations of earnings. Investors should be concerned with both the forecast for earnings and the difference between the actual earnings and the forecast—that is, the surprise. Therefore, fundamental analysis of earnings should include more than a forecast, which is difficult enough; it should involve the role of the market's expectations about earnings.

What happens when the quarterly earnings are reported and the figures are below analysts' estimates? Obviously, the price is likely to drop quickly, and in some cases sharply. In a number of cases, the stock market is very unforgiving about disappointments in negative earnings surprises.

Example 15-15 For its third quarter of 2000, Lucent Technologies announced on two different occasions that earnings would be less than expected. It also expressed doubt about the next fiscal year. Following the second announcement, the price declined more than 30 percent, and this was after the price had suffered earlier declines.

If the price does drop sharply following such an announcement, should an investor interested in owning the stock react quickly to take advantage of the price drop? According to one study of 2000 large companies that experienced single-day price drops of over 10 percent during the past 12 months, the average decline was 17 percent the first day the stock traded after the bad news.[29] However, on average these stocks were 25 percent cheaper 30 days after the report of bad news, with 90 percent of the stocks being lower at that time. Sixty days after the bad news, these stocks were still down an average of 23 percent, and down almost 20 percent after 90 days. Why? The initial shock is often followed by additional shocks.

THE EARNINGS GAME

Investors need to realize that the process of estimating earnings, announcing earnings and determining earnings surprises has become much more of a game, or managed process, over time. The way the "game" has been played by many companies is as follows:

1. Analysts attempt to guess what a particular company will earn each quarter.
2. The company simultaneously provides "guidance" as to what it thinks earnings will be. According to one survey, about 80 percent of companies provide guid-

---

[28] Stocks can be categorized by SUEs that are divided into increments of 1.0. Thus, SUE classifications can range from all stocks with a SUE < -4.0 (category 1), all between -4.0 and -3.0 (category 2), and so on, up to the most positive category, all stocks with SUEs >4.0 (category 10). The larger the SUE (either positive or negative), the greater the unexpected earnings, and therefore, other things being equal, the larger the adjustment in the stock's return should be. Stocks with small SUEs (between $+1.0$ and -1.0) have little or no unexpected earnings, and therefore should show little or no subsequent adjustment in stock return.

[29] See David Dreman, "Let the Dust Clear," *Forbes*, October 12, 1992, p. 166.

ance as compared to 10 percent only a few years earlier. Many companies start the new quarter by encouraging analysts to forecast strong earnings growth.

3. The "guidance number" plays a major role in the **consensus estimate** among analysts as to the expected earnings. As time passes, the company may be trying to talk the forecast down in order to increase the chances of beating the forecast. When the company feels the consensus is "right" (low enough), the company announces that it is "comfortable" with Wall Street estimates.

4. The variance of the actual reported earnings from the consensus estimate has typically constituted the earnings surprise. In the past, when the announced earnings exceeded the consensus estimate, the earnings surprise was positive and the stock price often rose.

5. Investors have had to contend with "whisper forecasts," which are unofficial earnings estimates that circulate among traders and investors before earnings are announced. A recent study suggests that these estimates are more accurate than are the consensus estimates which have been guided by the companies. If the announced earnings exceeded the consensus forecast but were below the whisper forecast, the stock price often declined.

Obviously, investors must try to understand the current earnings game and the likely impact it will have on stock prices as a result of earnings surprises. Suffice it to say that it has become more complicated as investors try to figure out which forecast the actual earnings are expected to beat. In the final analysis, however, remember—it is all a game, and almost everyone involved knows it.

Regulation FD (discussed in Chapter 1), which became effective in October 2000, changed the situation regarding how information about earnings numbers were made available. Rather than inform only a few analysts of a significant upcoming change in earnings, companies must now make public disclosure of important information to all investors at the same time. Analysts and portfolio managers claim that Regulation FD has resulted in companies disclosing less information and in stock prices being more volatile, according to a March 2001 survey released by the Association for Investment Management and Research. Of course, it is hard to document such claims, and these players obviously have a vested interest in the situation. Numerous companies are now releasing corporate information to all investors simultaneously through internet broadcasts.

Recent Changes A new trend has started among some companies that may have a major impact on how information about earnings is formulated and distributed. Warren Buffet, among others, has argued that companies should not provide guidance. In December 2002, Coca-Cola announced that it will not provide quarterly or annual EPS guidance. The company stated that, "it will continue to provide investors with perspectives on its value drivers, its strategic initiatives and those factors critical to understanding its business and operating environment." Several other companies had opted to take the same approach. Currently, therefore, many companies still provide guidance, while some no longer do.

USEFUL INFORMATION FOR INVESTORS ABOUT EARNINGS ESTIMATES

Summarizing our discussion about earnings forecasts, we can note the following useful information about the role, and use, of earnings forecasts in selecting common stocks:

1. Earnings reports are a key factor affecting stock prices. However, it is the surprise element in the reports that often moves stock prices—the difference between the actual results reported and the results expected by the market.

2. Surprises occur because analyst estimates are considerably off target. Surprises have typically involved the difference between the consensus forecast and the actual earnings, although "whisper forecasts," which are unofficial forecasts circulating among investors, may be more important in determining if there really is a surprise.

3. There appears to be a lag in the adjustment of stock prices to earnings surprises.

4. One earnings surprise tends to lead to another, with a 45-percent chance of repeating an earnings surprise.

5. The best guidelines to surprises are revisions in analyst estimates. If estimates are steadily being adjusted upward, a buy signal is indicated, and if the adjustments are downward, a sell signal is indicated.

6. Stocks with significant revisions of 5 percent or more—up or down—often show above or below average performance.

7. Investors interested in buying stocks which report bad news and suffer a sharp decline should wait awhile. Chances are the stock will be cheaper 30 and 60 days after the initial sharp decline.

8. Increasingly, earnings are being guided by companies, both as a result of significantly influencing the consensus estimate as well as by making earnings preannouncements. Some companies report earnings that are very close to the estimates time after time—General Electric and Coca-Cola (traditionally) being good examples. Some companies provide conservative guidance, which results in positive earnings surprises. Other companies are overly optimistic.

Using the Internet

A number of Web sites have information about earnings estimates and surprises. At http://quote.yahoo.com/, under "Research," is a section on earnings surprises, showing both positive and negative. Entering the symbol for a stock will allow you to access research on the company, which provides detailed information on earnings estimates—consensus estimates, number of analysts following the company, surprises, and so forth. At http://cbs.marketwatch.com, investors can reference "Earnings Headlines" as well as "Earnings Surprises." For earnings information as well as other detailed information of all types about any company, try http://justquotes.com.

SALES GROWTH—AN ALTERNATIVE TO EARNINGS

Given the accounting problems with earnings, and the difficulty in forecasting earnings, it is not surprising that investors look at other fundamental data when selecting stocks. This is particularly true with newer companies that may not have current EPS or the expectation thereof for several years. Amazon.com is a clear example of this—given its lack of profitability, investors must evaluate other dimensions.

A key variable is obviously revenues, or sales. After all, a company can't have earnings without reasonable revenues. Revenues not only lead to the accounting EPS for a company but also make possible the firm's cash which it uses to pay its bills and operate. Both of the major providers of earnings estimates, Zacks Investment Research and First Call, also plan to offer revenue estimates.

The P/E Ratio

The other half of the valuation framework in fundamental analysis is the price/earnings (P/E) ratio, or multiplier. The P/E ratio (reported in *The Wall Street Journal* and other newspapers) indicates how much per dollar of earnings investors currently are willing to pay for a stock; that is, the price for each dollar of earnings. In a sense, it represents the market's summary evaluation of a company's prospects.

Example 15-16 In March 2003, Coca-Cola was selling for about 26 times the latest 12-month earnings. Coke sold for about 49 times earnings in 1998. In mid-1993, on the other hand, Coca-Cola sold for about nine times earnings.

In effect, the P/E ratio is a measure of the relative price of a stock. In one recent year, for example, investors were willing to pay about 50 times earnings for Centel but only six times earnings for Asarco. What are the reasons for such a large difference? To answer this question, it is necessary to consider the determinants of the P/E ratio.

WHICH P/E RATIO IS BEING USED?

When discussing the P/E ratio, it is important to remember that different P/E ratios can be calculated for the same stock at one point in time, including:

- ❏ P/E based on last year's reported earnings
- ❏ P/E based on trailing 12-month earnings
- ❏ P/E based on this year's expected earnings
- ❏ P/E based on next year's expected earnings

Furthermore, the EPS could be reported EPS (based on GAAP), operating EPS, or the new core EPS being reported by Standard & Poor's Corporation. Assuming we limit ourselves to GAAP EPS, the difference can still be substantial.

Example 15-17 In mid-November 2002, Coke was trading at $44.60. P/Es were:

- ❏ Based on 2001 earnings of $1.60, the P/E was   27.9
- ❏ Based on TTM (trailing 12-month earnings) reported by
  Morningstar of $1.31, the P/E was   34
- ❏ Based on expected earnings for 2002 (mean consensus of analysts)
  of $1.77, the P/E was   25.2
- ❏ Based on expected earnings for 2003 (mean consensus of analysts)
  of $1.95, the P/E was   22.9

DETERMINANTS OF THE P/E RATIO

As we saw in Chapter 10, the expected P/E ratio is conceptually a function of three factors:

$$P/E = \frac{D_1/E_1}{k - g} \tag{15-8}$$

where

D_1/E_1 = the expected dividend payout ratio
k = the required rate of return for the stock
g = expected growth rate in dividends

Investors attempting to determine the P/E ratio that will prevail for a particular stock should think in terms of these three factors and their likely changes.

- The higher the expected payout ratio, other things being equal, the higher the P/E ratio. However, "other things" are seldom equal. If the payout rises, the expected growth rate in earnings and dividends, g, will probably decline, thereby adversely affecting the P/E ratio. This decline occurs because less funds will be available for reinvestment in the business, thereby leading to a decline in the expected growth rate, g.
- As we learned in Chapter 10, the relationship between k and the P/E ratio is inverse: Other things being equal, as k rises, the P/E ratio declines; as k declines, the P/E ratio rises. Because the required rate of return is a discount rate, P/E ratios and discount rates move inversely to each other.
- P/E and g are directly related; the higher the g, other things being equal, the higher the P/E ratio.[30]

Analyzing the P/E Ratio In analyzing a particular P/E ratio, we first ask what model describes the expected growth rate for that company. Recent rapid growth and published estimates of strong expected future growth would lead investors not to use the constant-growth version of the dividend valuation model. Instead, we should evaluate the company by using a multiple-growth model. At some point, however, this growth can be expected to slow down to a more normal rate.

$$\frac{P}{E_{n+1}} = \frac{D_{n+1}/E_{n+1}}{k - g}$$

where n is the year that the abnormal growth ends.

Relative to the discussion above on the earnings game, investors must be increasingly concerned with the impact of managing earnings expectations on the P/E ratio. If a fast-growing company is being conservative in guiding the estimates of its earnings, and it regularly reports earnings higher than the consensus, then the forward P/E ratio is actually lower than it appears to be based on the current consensus estimate of earnings. In other words, a company may appear to sell for 50 times next year's earnings, but this is based on an underestimate of next year's earnings, because the consensus estimate has been guided to be below what actually occurs. For much of the 1990s Dell Computer fit this model, regularly reporting significantly larger earnings than the consensus estimate.

WHY P/E RATIOS VARY AMONG COMPANIES

Stock prices reflect market expectations about earnings. Companies that the market believes will achieve higher earnings growth rates will tend to be priced higher than companies that are expected to show low earnings growth rates. Thus, a primary factor in explaining P/E ratio differences among companies is investor expectations about the future growth of earnings. Variations in the rate of earnings growth will also influence the P/E.

It is important to remember the role of interest rates, which are inversely related to P/E ratios (see Chapter 10). When interest rates are declining, the largest impact is on the P/E ratios of reliable growth stocks. This is because most of their earnings will occur far out in the future, and can now be discounted at lower rates.

An analysis of P/E ratios at any point in time will show the wide variation that exists in this variable as some companies have high ratios, whereas others have low ratios. For

---

[30] Harris suggests that a consensus forecast of earnings growth by analysts can be used successfully as a proxy for the dividend growth rate. See Robert S. Harris, "Using Analysts' Growth Forecasts to Estimate Shareholder Required Rates of Return," *Financial Management* (Spring 1986), pp. 58–67.

example, The *Value Line Investment Survey* presents a weekly ranking of the lowest and highest P/E stocks out of the more than 1,700 companies covered. At any point in time, the lowest P/Es will be around 1, whereas the highest may be 80 or 90. Of course, P/Es for the same company will change over time.

Fundamental Security Analysis in Practice

We have analyzed several important aspects of fundamental analysis as it is applied to individual companies. Obviously, such a process can be quite detailed, involving an analysis of a company's sales potential, competition, tax situation, cost projections, accounting practices, and so on. Nevertheless, regardless of detail and complexity, the underlying process is as described. Analysts and investors are seeking to estimate a company's earnings and P/E ratio and to determine whether the stock is undervalued (a buy) or overvalued (a sell).

In doing fundamental security analysis, investors need to use published and computerized data sources both to gather information and to provide calculations and estimates of future variables such as EPS. Appendix 15-A briefly discusses some of the major published information sources that investors have traditionally used. Exhibit 15-4 shows an excerpt from *The Value Line Investment Survey* for Coca-Cola.

The Value Line Investment Survey, as explained in Appendix 15-A, is the largest investment advisory service in the United States and is available in many libraries. As shown in Exhibit 15-4, a significant amount of information about a particular company can be reported on one page. This information can be very helpful in terms of estimates for EPS and in terms of a prediction (by *Value Line*) as to the timeliness of each stock for the coming year (see Appendix 15-A for a more detailed discussion of this coverage).

In modern investment analysis, the risk for a stock is related to its beta coefficient, as explained in Chapter 9. Beta reflects the relative systematic risk for a stock, or the risk that cannot be diversified away. The higher the beta coefficient, the higher the risk for an individual stock, and the higher the required rate of return. Beta measures the volatility of a stock's returns—its fluctuations in relation to the market.

Example 15-18 Refer to *The Value Line Investment Survey* (see Exhibit 15-4) for the beta for Coca-Cola. Assume it is around 1.10. Therefore, we know that Coca-Cola has slightly more relative systematic risk than the market as a whole. That is, on average, its price fluctuates more than the market. If, for example, the market is expected to rise 10 percent over the next year, investors could, on average, expect Coca-Cola to rise 11 percent based on its beta of 1.10. In a market decline, Coca-Cola would be expected to decline more, on average, than the market. If the market declined 10 percent, for example, Coca-Cola would be expected, on average, to decline in price by 11 percent.

Investments Intuition

It is extremely important in analyses such as these to remember that beta is a measure of volatility indicating what can be expected to happen, on average, to a stock when the overall market rises or falls. In fact, Coca-Cola, or any other stock, will not perform in the predicted way every time. If it did, the risk would disappear. Investors can always find examples of stocks that, over some specific period of time, did not move as their beta indicated they would. This is not an indictment of the usefulness of beta as a measure of volatility; rather it suggests that the beta relationship can only be expected to hold on the average.

EXHIBIT 15-4

A Page from a Weekly Issue of "Ratings and Reports," *The Value Line Investment Survey*

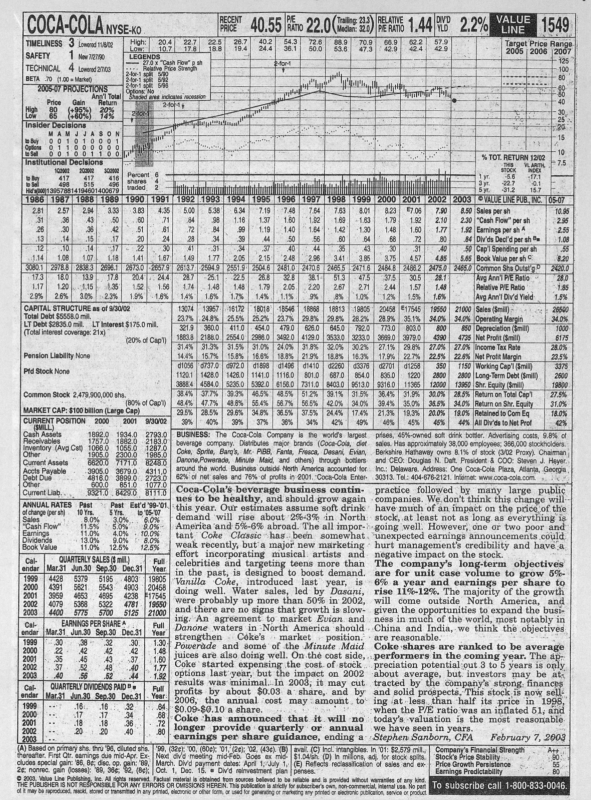

SOURCE: *The Value Line Investment Survey*, Summary of Advice and Index, February 7, 2003, p. 1549. Reproduced with the permission of Value Line Publishing, Inc.

BOX 15-1

Face-Off Coca-Cola

"It's positioned for the kind of long-term growth unique to Coca-Cola." MARC GREENBERG, DEUTSCHE BANK

YES The product line is very strong right now. Domestically, Vanilla Coke has been a huge winner, and that is only scratching the surface of what they can do outside the U.S.

YES Return on capital and free cash flow is accelerating. I don't believe the company's earnings or unit case volumes are at risk, nor do I see them lowering earnings forecasts for next year. It's entirely possible to see 5 percent volume growth.

YES The stock has sold off 15 percent since they announced the profit warning [in October]. That presents an opportunity to buy stock at an attractive valuation.

"They haven't been hitting their targets. It's one disappointment after another." JEFF KANTER, PRUDENTIAL SECURITIES

NO Talk to me a year from now, and we'll see if Vanilla Coke is still a success. Margins may not be so great. And the flagship soft drinks aren't selling as well as before.

NO I can't see the company hitting its long-term goals. Management must lower the bar on its assumptions—sustaining 5 percent volume growth is not easy for any company.

NO At 23 times current earnings, it's not cheap. This is full valuation for a company still facing headwinds. If Coke could grow earnings 12 percent largely from operations instead of a tax cut, maybe it would be attractively valued.

SOURCE: Nkiru Asika Oluwasanmi, "Face-Off," *SmartMoney*, January 2003, p. 28. Reprinted by permission of *SmartMoney*. Copyright © 2003 by *SmartMoney*. *SmartMoney* is a joint publishing venture of Dow Jones & Company, Inc. and the Hearst Corporation. All rights reserved worldwide.

In trying to understand and predict a company's return and risk, we need to remember that both are a function of two components. The systematic component is related to the return on the overall market. The other component is the unique part attributable to the company itself and not to the overall market. It is a function of the specific positive or negative factors that affect a company independent of the market.

It should come as no surprise that because security analysis always involves the uncertain future, mistakes will be made, and analysts will differ in their outlooks for a particular company. Box 15-1 illustrates two different opinions on Coca-Cola at the same point in time, with one analyst arguing that Coke is an attractive buy, whereas the other argues that the stock is fully valued.

As we might expect, security analysis in the twenty-first century is often done differently than it was in the past. The reason for this change is not so much that we have a better understanding of the basis of security analysis because the models we have discussed earlier—value as a function of expected return and risk—remain the basis of security analysis today. Rather the differences now have to do with the increasingly sophisticated use of personal computers to perform many calculations quickly and objectively.

One of the new approaches to stock picking is the use of "neural networks," whereby a computer program attempts to imitate the brain in doing security analysis and choosing stocks. One such program examines 11 different variables for 2,000 companies, searching for patterns that might be profitable to exploit and that are too subtle for humans to detect. In effect, this program searches for undervalued stocks, which is the basis of security analysis.

Summary

▶ The analysis of individual companies, the last of three steps in fundamental security analysis, encompasses all the basic financial variables of the company, such as sales, management, and competition. It involves applying the valuation procedures explained in earlier chapters.

▶ Intrinsic value (a company's justified price) can be estimated using either a dividend valuation model or an earnings multiplier model. It is then compared to the current market price in order to determine whether the stock is undervalued or overvalued.

▶ An important first step in fundamental analysis is to understand the earnings per share (EPS) of companies. The financial statements can be used to understand the accounting basis of EPS.

▶ The balance sheet shows the assets and liabilities of a specific date, whereas the income statement shows the flows during a period for the items that determine net income.

▶ Although these statements are certified by the accounting profession, alternative accounting principles result in EPS figures that are not precise, readily comparable figures. EPS is the result of the interaction of several variables.

▶ Changes in earnings are directly related to changes in stock prices. To assess expected earnings, investors often consider the earnings growth rate, which is the product of ROE and the earnings retention rate.

▶ The lack of persistence in these growth rates may lead investors to consider EPS forecasts, which are available mechanically or from analysts. Both are subject to error. The evidence is mixed on which method is better, although a recent study favors analysts' forecasts.

▶ The difference between actual and forecast EPS is important because of the role of the market's expectations about earnings. Standardized unexpected earnings (SUE) attempts to evaluate the unexpected portion of quarterly earnings.

▶ The price/earnings (P/E) ratio is the other half of the earnings multiplier model, indicating the amount per dollar of earnings investors are willing to pay for a stock. It represents the relative price of a stock, with some companies carrying high P/E ratios and others having low ones.

▶ The P/E ratio is influenced directly by investors' expectations of the future growth of earnings and the payout ratio and inversely by the required rate of return.

▶ P/E ratios vary among companies primarily because of investors' expectations about the future growth of earnings. If investors lower their expectations, the price of the stock may drop while earnings remain constant or even rise.

▶ The beta coefficient, the measure of volatility for a stock, indicates the average responsiveness of the stock's price to the overall market, with high- (low-) beta stocks exhibiting larger (smaller) changes than the overall market.

Key Words

Cash flow statement
Consensus estimate
Earnings surprise
Financial statements

Free cash flow
Generally accepted accounting
   principles (GAAP)
Reported earnings

Return on assets (ROA)
Return on equity (ROE)
Sustainable growth rate

Questions

15-1   What is the intrinsic value of a stock?

15-2   How can a stock's intrinsic value be determined?

15-3   What are the limitations of using Equation 15-1 to determine intrinsic value?

15-4   What is meant by GAAP?

15-5 What problems do estimating accounting earnings present?

15-6 What does the auditor's report signify about the financial statements?

15-7 How do auditors and management relate to each other in determining the financial statements?

15-8 What is the concept of earnings quality?

15-9 Outline, in words, the determination process for EPS.

15-10 Explain the role of financing in a company's EPS.

15-11 Assuming that a firm's return on assets exceeds its interest costs, why would it not boost ROE to the maximum through the use of debt financing since higher ROE leads to higher EPS?

15-12 How can the earnings growth rate be determined?

15-13 How well do earnings growth rates for individual companies persist across time?

15-14 How can investors obtain EPS forecasts? Which source is better?

15-15 What role do earnings expectations play in selecting stocks?

15-16 How can the unexpected component of EPS be used to select stocks?

15-17 Explain the relationship between SUE and fundamental security analysis.

15-18 Describe at least two variations in calculating a P/E ratio.

15-19 Using *The Value Line Investment Survey*, list the average annual P/E ratio for the following companies for the last five years: Apple Computer, Coca-Cola, Caterpillar, and Duke Energy. What conclusions can you draw from this analysis?

15-20 What are the variables that affect the P/E ratio? Is the effect direct or inverse for each component?

15-21 Holding everything else constant, what effect would the following have on a company's P/E ratio?
   a. An increase in the expected growth rate of earnings
   b. A decrease in the expected dividend payout
   c. An increase in the risk-free rate of return
   d. An increase in the risk premium
   e. A decrease in the required rate of return.

15-22 Why would an investor want to know the beta coefficient for a particular company? How could this information be used?

15-23 Is beta the only determinant of a company's return?

Problems

15-1 GF is a large producer of food products. In 2003, the percentage breakdown of revenues and profits was as follows:

	Revenues (%)	Profits (%)
Packaged foods	41	62
Coffee	28	19
Processed meat	19	13
Food service—other	12	6
	100	100

International operations account for about 22 percent of sales and 17 percent of operating profit.

For the 1998–2003 fiscal years, the number of shares outstanding (in millions) and selected income statement data were (in millions of dollars) as follows:

Shares Outst.	Year	Revenues	Oper Inc.	Cap. Exp.	Deprec.	Int. Exp.	Net Income Before Tax	After Tax
49.93	1999	$5472	$524	$121	$77	$31	$452	$232
49.97	2000	5960	534	262	78	39	470	256
49.43	2001	6601	565	187	89	50	473	255
49.45	2002	8351	694	283	131	152	418	221
51.92	2003	8256	721	266	133	139	535	289

a. For each year calculate operating income as a percentage of revenues.
b. Net profits after tax as a percentage of revenues.
c. After-tax profits per share outstanding (EPS). The balance sheet data for the same fiscal years (in millions of dollars) were as follows:

Year	Cash	Current Assets	Current Liabilities	Total Assets	Long-Term Debt	Common Equity
1999	$291	$1736	$ 845	$2565	$251	$1321
2000	178	1951	1047	2978	255	1480
2001	309	2019	929	3103	391	1610
2002	163	2254	1215	3861	731	1626
2003	285	2315	1342	4310	736	1872

d. Calculate the ratio of current assets to current liabilities for each year.
e. Calculate the long-term debt as a percentage of common equity.
f. For each year calculate the book value per share as the common equity divided by the number of shares outstanding.
g. Calculate ROE.
h. Calculate ROA.
i. Calculate leverage.
j. Calculate the net income margin.
k. Calculate turnover.
l. Calculate the EBIT.
m. Calculate the income ratio.
n. Calculate operating efficiency.
o. On the basis of these calculations evaluate the current status of the health of GF and the changes over the period.

15-2   Combining information from the S&P reports and some estimated data, the following calendar-year data, on a per-share basis, are provided:

Year	Price Range Low High	Earnings	Dividends	Book Value	(D/E) 100(%)	Annual Avg. P/E	ROE = E/Book TR%
1999	$26.5–$35.3	$4.56	$1.72	$25.98	37.7	7.0	17.6%
2000	28.3–37.0	5.02	1.95	29.15	38.8	6.2	17.3
2001	23.5–34.3	5.14	2.20	32.11	42.8	5.8	16.0
2002	27.8–35.0	4.47	2.20	30.86		7.7	
2003	29.0–47.8	5.73	2.30	30.30		6.8	
2004	36.6–53.5	6.75	2.40	39.85			
2005		6.75	2.60	44.00			

a. Calculate the D/E, ROE, and TR for 2002, 2003, and 2004. (Use the average of the low and high prices to calculate TRs.)
b. Show that from 2000 through 2004 the per annum growth rate in dividends was 6.9 percent and for earnings was 8.2 percent.
c. Using the current price of $47, with estimated earnings for 2005 of $6.75, show that the P/E would be evaluated as 6.96.
d. On the basis of the annual average P/E ratios shown above and your estimate in Problem c, assume an expected P/E of 7. If an investor expected the earnings of GF for 2005 to be $7.50, show that the intrinsic value would be $52.50.

e. What factors are important in explaining the difference in the P/E ratios of Coca-Cola and GF?

f. From your calculation of the growth rate of dividends in Problem b, assume that the annual rate is 7 percent. If the required rate of return for the stock is 12 percent and the expected dividend payout ratio is 0.4, show that P/E = 8.

g. If the dividend payout ratio is 0.4 and the return on equity is 15 percent, show that $g = 0.09$.

h. Using $k = 0.14$ and $g = 0.09$, with expected 2005 dividends of $2.60, show that the intrinsic value is $52.

i. Assume the "beta" for GF is 0.8 relative to Coke's beta of 1.3. Is this information of any help in explaining the different P/E ratios of these two companies?

CFA
15-3 The value of the components affecting the ROE of Merck & Co., Inc. for 1985 are indicated in Table 1. Selected 1990 income statement and balance sheet information for Merck can be found in Table 2.

A. Calculate each of the five ROE components for Merck in 1990. Using the five components, calculate ROE for Merck in 1990. Show all calculations.

B. Based on your calculations, describe how each ROE component contributed to the change in Merck's ROE between 1985 and 1990. Identify the major underlying reasons for the change in Merck's ROE.

Table 1 Merck & Co., Inc., 1985 Roe

Tax burden (net income/pretax income)	.628
Interest burden (pretax income/EBIT)	.989
Operating (or profit) margin	.245
Asset turnover	.724
Financial leverage	1.877

Table 2 Merck & Co., Inc., 1990
Selected Financial Data ($ Millions)

Income Statement Data	
Sales revenue	$7,120
Depreciation	230
Interest expense	10
Pretax income	2,550
Income taxes	900
Net income	1,650
Balance Sheet Data	
Current assets	$4,850
Net fixed assets	2,400
Total assets	7,250
Current liabilities	3,290
Long-term debt	100
Shareholders' equity	3,860
Total liabilities & shareholders' equity	7,250

CFA
15-4   In attempting to forecast the internal growth rate of BK Industries, you develop the following probability distributions:

ROE	Probability	Retention Rate	Probability
15%	0.4	40%	0.7
20%	0.6	60%	0.3

A. Assuming that ROE and retention rate are statistically independent, compute the probability distribution for the growth rate of BK.

B. Compute the expected value of the growth rate.

The following information applies to Problems 15-5 through 15-8:

INTRODUCTION

Eastover Company (EO) is a large, diversified forest products company. Approximately 75 percent of its sales are from paper and forest products, with the remainder from financial services and real estate. The company owns 5.6 million acres of timberland, which is carried at very low historical cost on the balance sheet.

Peggy Mulroney, CFA, is an analyst at the investment counseling firm of Centurion Investments. She is assigned the task of assessing the outlook for Eastover, which is being considered for purchase and comparing it to another forest products company in Centurion's portfolios, Southampton Corporation (SHC). SHC is a major producer of lumber products in the United States. Building products, primarily lumber and plywood, account for 89 percent of SHC's sales, with pulp accounting for the remainder. SHC owns 1.4 million acres of timberland, which is also carried at historical cost on the balance sheet. In SHC's case, however, that cost is not as far below current market as Eastover's.

CFA
15-5   Mulroney's supervisor asks her to first explore the relationship between industry lumber production and lumber production at EO and SHC. As part of this analysis, Mulroney runs two regressions, using industry lumber production as the independent variable and each company's lumber production as the dependent variable.

The results are indicated below:

	intercept (t-ratio)	slope coefficient (t-ratio)	R^2
Eastover	2.79 (6.08)	−0.03 (−0.25)	0.63
Southampton	1.28 (5.25)	0.10 (13.07)	0.90

The *t*-ratio critical value at the 5-percent level is 1.83.

A. The regressions produce the two intercepts and two slope coefficients shown above. Define the terms *intercept* and *slope coefficient*. State whether each of the two intercepts and each of the two slope coefficients are statistically significant.

B. Based on these regressions, identify the statistic that expresses the percentage of Eastover's and Southampton's lumber production that is explained by the independent variable (industry lumber production). State the percentage explained by the regression.

C. Based on your answer to Parts A and B above, discuss the reliability of forecasts from each of the two regressions.

CFA
15-6
Mulroney continued her examination of Eastover and Southampton by looking at the five components of return on equity (ROE) for each company. For her analysis, Mulroney elected to define equity as total shareholders' equity, including preferred stock. She also elected to use year-end data rather than averages for the balance sheet items.

A. Based on the data shown in Tables 1 and 2, calculate each of the five ROE components for Eastover and Southampton in 1990. Using the five components, calculate ROE for both companies in 1990. Show all calculations.

B. Referring to the components calculated in Part A, explain the difference in ROE for Eastover and Southampton in 1990.

C. Using 1990 data, calculate an internal (i.e., sustainable) growth rate for both Eastover and Southampton. Discuss the appropriateness of using these calculations as a basis for estimating future growth.

Table 1 Eastover Company (EO)($ Millions, Except Shares Outstanding)

	1986	1987	1988	1989	1990
Sales	$5,652	$6,990	$7,863	$8,281	$7,406
Earnings before interest & taxes (EBIT)	$ 568	$ 901	$1,037	$ 708	$ 795
Interest expense (net)	(147)	(188)	(186)	(194)	(195)
Income before taxes	$ 421	$ 713	$ 851	$ 514	$ 600
Income taxes	(144)	(266)	(286)	(173)	(206)
Tax rate	34%	37%	33%	34%	34%
Net income	$ 277	$ 447	$ 565	$ 341	$ 394
Preferred dividends	(28)	(17)	(17)	(17)	(0)
Net income to common	$ 249	$ 430	$ 548	$ 324	$ 394
Common shares outstanding (millions)	196	204	204	$ 205	$ 201

Balance Sheet Summary	1986	1987	1988	1989	1990
Current assets	$1,235	$1,419	$1,702	$1,585	$1,367
Timberland assets	649	625	621	612	615
Property, plant & equipment	4,370	4,571	5,056	5,430	5,854
Other assets	360	555	473	472	429
Total assets	$6,614	$7,242	$7,852	$8,099	$8,265
Current liabilities	$1,226	$1,186	$1,206	$1,606	$1,816
Long-term debt	1,120	1,340	1,585	1,346	1,585
Deferred taxes & other	1,000	1,000	1,016	1,000	1,000
Equity-preferred	364	350	350	400	0
Equity-common	2,904	3,366	3,695	3,747	3,864
Total liabilities & equity	$6,614	$7,242	$7,852	$8,009	$8,265

Table 2 Southampton Corporation (SCH) ($ Millions, Except Shares Outstanding

	1986	1987	1988	1989	1990
Sales	$1,306	$1,654	$1,799	$2,010	$1,793
Earnings before interest & taxes (EBIT)	$ 120	$ 230	$ 221	$ 304	$ 145
Interest expense (net)	(13)	(36)	(7)	(12)	(8)
Income before taxes	$ 107	$ 194	$ 214	$ 292	$ 137
Income taxes	(44)	(75)	(79)	(99)	(46)
Tax rate	41%	39%	37%	34%	34%
Net income	$ 63	$ 119	$ 135	$ 193	$ 91
Common shares outstanding (millions)	38	38	38	38	38

Balance Sheet Summary	1986	1987	1988	1989	1990
Current assets	$ 487	$ 504	$ 536	$ 654	$ 509
Timberland assets	512	513	508	513	518
Property, plant & equipment	648	681	718	827	1,037
Other assets	141	151	34	38	40
Total assets	$1,788	$1,849	$1,796	$2,032	$2,104
Current liabilities	$ 185	$ 176	$ 162	$ 180	$ 195
Long-term debt	536	493	370	530	589
Deferred taxes & other	123	136	127	146	153
Equity	944	1,044	1,137	1,176	1,167
Total liabilities & equity	$1,788	$1,849	$1,796	$2,032	$2,104

CFA

15-7 Mulroney recalled from her CFA studies that the constant-growth discounted dividend model (DDM) was one way to arrive at a valuation for a company's common stock. She collected current dividend and stock price data for Eastover and Southampton, shown in Table 3.

A. Using 11 percent as the required rate of return (i.e., discount rate) and a projected growth rate of 8 percent, compute a constant-growth DDM value for Eastover's stock and compare the computed value for Eastover to its stock price indicated in Table 3. Show calculations.

Table 3 Current Information

	Current Share Price	Current Dividends	1992 EPS Estimate	Current Book Value per Share
Eastover	$28	$1.20	$1.60	$17.32
Southampton	48	1.08	3.00	32.21
S&P 500	415	12.00	20.54	159.83

Mulroney's supervisor commented that a two-stage DDM may be more appropriate for companies such as Eastover and Southampton. Mulroney believes that Eastover and Southampton could grow more rapidly over the next three years and then settle in at a lower but sustainable rate of growth beyond 1994. Her estimates are indicated in Table 4.

Table 4 Projected Growth Rates

	Next 3 Years (1992, 1993, 1994)	Growth Beyond 1994
Eastover	12%	8%
Southampton	13%	7%

B. Using 11 percent as the required rate of return, compute the two-stage DDM value of Eastover's stock and compare that value to its stock price indicated in Table 3. Show calculations.

C. Discuss two advantages and three disadvantages of using a constant-growth DDM. Briefly discuss how the two-stage DDM improves upon the constant-growth DDM.

CFA 15-8 Mulroney previously calculated a valuation for Southampton for both the constant growth and two-stage DDM as shown below:

	Discounted Dividend Model Using	
	Constant Growth Approach	Two-Stage Approach
Southampton	$29	$35.50

Using only the information provided and your answers to Questions CFA 5, 6, and 7, select the stock (EO or SHC) that Mulroney should recommend as the better value, and justify your selection.

Web Resources

For additional resources visit our dynamic Web site located at www.wiley.com/college/jones.

- *I Need IBM's Beta!*—Fundamental financial data on IBM is required to forecast a change in systematic risk due to a potential shift in IBM's capital structure. The case highlights the relationship between systematic risk measures and managerial decisions.
- Internet Exercises—This chapter focuses on fundamental security analysis. Accordingly, we will look at companies' financial statements and at earnings forecasts to see how they affect stock returns.
- Exercise 1: Looks at various fundamental analytical models at *Ford Investor Services* and asks the reader to test them.

  Exercise 2: Takes the reader through Dupont Analysis.
  Exercise 3: Looks at the relationship between earnings surprises and stock returns.
  Exercise 4: Uses P/E ratios to pick stocks.
- Multiple Choice Self Test
- Appendix 15-A—Sources of Information for Common Stocks

Selected References

One of the well-known authors of books about valuation has written the following guide to valuation:

Damodaran, Aswath, *Investment Valuation: Tools and Techniques for Determining the Value of Any Asset, Second Edition*, John Wiley & Sons, New York.

chapter 16

Technical Analysis

Chapter 16 presents the other approach to security analysis, which is technical analysis. This approach is very different from fundamental analysis and is directly affected by the efficient market hypothesis discussed in Chapter 12.

AFTER READING THIS CHAPTER YOU WILL BE ABLE TO:

- ▶ Understand how technical analysis differs from fundamental analysis.
- ▶ Critically evaluate most of the techniques used in technical analysis as well as the claims made for these techniques.

- ▶ Decide what role, if any, technical analysis might play in your own investing program.

As discussed in Chapter 11, traditionally, stocks have been selected using two approaches:

❑ Fundamental analysis
❑ Technical analysis

Technical analysis is entirely different from the fundamental approach to security analysis discussed in Chapters 13, 14, and 15. How different? Consider the following quotations from popular press articles on technical analysis:

"Engage a technical analyst in a conversation about his art, and you soon feel like you're in the shadowy saloon from *Star Wars*, where freakish aliens lounge about speaking strange languages."[1]

"Spend some time with a technical analyst and you almost need a Technical-to-English translation guide. Conversations are full of references to support and resistance levels, Fibonacci retracements, double bottoms and moving averages."[2]

Although the technical approach to common stock selection is the oldest approach (dating back to the late 1800s), it remains controversial. The techniques discussed in this chapter appear at first glance to have considerable merit, because they seem intuitive and plausible, but they have been severely challenged in the last three decades by evidence supporting the Efficient Market Hypothesis discussed in Chapter 12. Despite Burton Malkiel's (a well-known proponent of efficient markets) admission that "the market is not a perfect random walk," the extensive evidence concerning the efficiency of the market has challenged the validity of technical analysis and the likelihood of its success.

Those learning about investments will in all likelihood be exposed to technical analysis, because numerous investors, investment advisory firms, and the popular press talk about it and use it. Furthermore, it may produce some insights into the psychological dimension of the market. In fact, technical analysis is becoming increasingly interrelated with behavioral finance (discussed in Chapter 11), a popular field of study today. In effect, technical indicators are being used to measure investor emotions.

Even if this approach is incorrect, many investors act as if it were correct. Therefore, the prudent course of action is to study this topic, or indeed any other recommended approach to making investing decisions, and try to make an objective evaluation of its validity and usefulness. At the very least, an informed investor will be in a better position to understand what is being said, or claimed, and better able to judge the validity of the claims.

Although technical analysis can be applied to bonds, currencies, and commodities as well as to common stocks, technical analysis typically involves the aggregate stock market, industry sectors, or individual common stocks. Therefore, we restrict our discussion in this chapter to common stocks.

What Is Technical Analysis?

Technical Analysis
The use of specific market data for the analysis of both aggregate stock prices and individual stock prices.

Technical analysis can be defined as the use of specific market-generated data for the analysis of both aggregate stock prices (market indices or industry averages) and individual stocks. Martin J. Pring, in his book *Technical Analysis*, states:

"The technical approach to investing is essentially a reflection of the idea that prices move in trends which are determined by the changing attitudes of investors toward

---

[1] See Michael Hirson, "Reading the Tea Leaves," *Individual Investor*, January 2001, p. 96.
[2] See Karen Talley, "Some Technical Analysts Fall off the Charts," *The Wall Street Journal*, February 20, 2002, p. B5B.

a variety of economic, monetary, political and psychological forces. The art of technical analysis—*for it is an art* [emphasis added]—is to identify trend changes at an early stage and to maintain an investment posture until the weight of the evidence indicates that the trend is reversed."[3]

Technical analysis is sometimes called market or internal analysis, because it utilizes the record of the market itself to attempt to assess the demand for, and supply of, shares of a stock or the entire market. Thus, technical analysts believe that the market itself is its own best source of data—as they say, "let the market tell its own story." The theory of technical analysis is that the price movement of a security captures all the information about that security.

Economics teaches us that prices are determined by the interaction of demand and supply. Technicians do not disagree, but argue that it is extremely difficult to assess all the factors that influence demand and supply. Since not all investors are in agreement on price, the determining factor at any point in time is the net demand (or lack thereof) for a stock based on how many investors are optimistic or pessimistic. Furthermore, once the balance of investors becomes optimistic (pessimistic), this mood is likely to continue for the near term and can be detected by various technical indicators. As the chief market technician of one New York firm says, "All I care about is how people feel about those particular stocks as shown by their putting money in and taking their money out."[4]

Market Data Price and volume information for stocks or indexes

Technical analysis is based on published market data as opposed to fundamental data, such as earnings, sales, growth rates, or government regulations. **Market data** primarily include the price of a stock or a market index and volume data (number of shares traded). Many technical analysts believe that only such market data, as opposed to fundamental data, are relevant. For example, they argue that accounting data are subject to all types of limitations and ambiguities, an argument that was strengthened by the Enron debacle and other accounting flaps in 2002.

Recall that in fundamental analysis, the dividend discount model and the multiplier model produce an estimate of a stock's intrinsic value, which is then compared to the market price. Fundamentalists believe that their data, properly evaluated, can be used to estimate the intrinsic value (see Chapter 10) of a stock. Technicians, on the other hand, believe that it is extremely difficult to estimate intrinsic value and virtually impossible to obtain and analyze good information consistently. In particular, they are dubious about the value to be derived from an analysis of published financial statements. Instead, they focus on market data as an indication of the forces of supply and demand for a stock or the market.

Technicians believe that the process by which prices adjust to new information is one of a gradual adjustment toward a new (equilibrium) price. As the stock adjusts from its old equilibrium level to its new level, the price tends to move in a trend. The central concern is not why the change is taking place, but rather the very fact that it is taking place at all. Technical analysts believe that stock prices show identifiable trends that can be exploited by investors. They seek to identify changes in the direction of a stock and take a position in the stock to take advantage of the trend.

The following points summarize technical analysis:

1. Technical analysis is based on published market data and focuses on internal factors by analyzing movements in the aggregate market, industry average, or stock. In contrast, fundamental analysis focuses on economic and political factors, which are external to the market itself.

[3] See Martin J. Pring, *Technical Analysis Explained* (New York: McGraw-Hill Publishers), 1991.
[4] See Jonathan Butler, "Technical Analysis: A Primer," *Worth*, October 1995, p. 128.

2. The focus of technical analysis is on identifying changes in the direction of stock prices which tend to move in trends as the stock price adjusts to a new equilibrium level. These trends can be analyzed, and changes in trends detected, by studying the action of price movements and trading volume across time. The emphasis is on likely price changes.
3. Technicians attempt to assess the overall situation concerning stocks by analyzing technical indicators, such as breadth of market data, market sentiment, momentum, and other indicators.

Perhaps the bottom line can be stated as: Stock prices (either for the market or individual stocks) tend to move in trends, and these trends take time to unfold. Such trends can be spotted by careful analysis, and acted upon by buying and selling.

A FRAMEWORK FOR TECHNICAL ANALYSIS

Technical analysis can be applied to both an aggregate of prices (the market as a whole or industry averages) and individual stocks. Technical analysis includes the use of graphs (charts) and technical indicators. Figure 16-1 depicts the technical analysis approach to investing.

Price and volume are the primary tools of the pure technical analyst, and the chart is the most important mechanism for displaying this information. Technicians believe that the forces of supply and demand result in particular patterns of price behavior, the most important of which is the trend or overall direction in price. Using a chart, the technician hopes to identify trends and patterns in stock prices that provide trading signals.

Volume data are used to gauge the general condition in the market and to help assess its trend. The evidence seems to suggest that rising (falling) stock prices are usually associated with rising (falling) volume. If stock prices rose but volume activity did not keep pace, technicians would be skeptical about the upward trend. An upward surge on contracting volume would be particularly suspect. A downside movement from some pattern or holding point accompanied by heavy volume would be taken as a bearish sign.

Figure 16-1

The technical analysis approach to common stock selection.

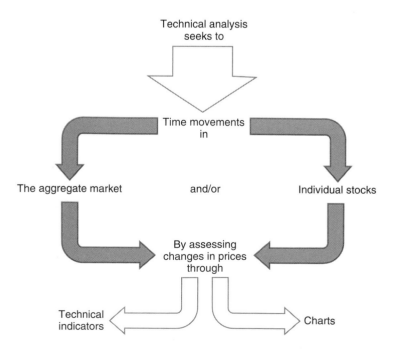

We first consider stock price and volume techniques, often referred to as charting. However, technical analysis has evolved over time, so that today it is much more than the charting of individual stocks or the market. In particular, technical indicators are used to assess market conditions (breadth) and investor sentiment. It also includes "contrary analysis," which is an intellectual process more than a technique. The idea behind contrary analysis is to go against the crowd when those in the crowd start thinking alike.

Stock Price and Volume Techniques

THE DOW THEORY

Dow Theory A technique for detecting long-term trends in the aggregate stock market

The oldest and best-known theory of technical analysis is the **Dow theory**, originally developed in the late 1800s by the editor of *The Wall Street Journal*, Charles H. Dow, who many regard as the father of technical analysis. Although Dow developed the theory to describe past price movements, William Hamilton followed up by using it to predict movements in the market. (It is not concerned with individual securities.) The Dow theory was very popular in the 1920s and 1930s, and articles offering support for it still appear periodically in the literature. Several investment advisory services are based on the Dow theory.

The theory is based on the existence of three types of price movements:

1. Primary moves, a broad market movement that lasts several years.
2. Secondary (intermediate) moves, occurring within the primary moves, which represent interruptions lasting several weeks or months.
3. Day-to-day moves, occurring randomly around the primary and secondary moves.

Bull Market An upward trend in the stock market

Bear Market A downward trend in the stock market

The Dow theory focuses on the primary trend in the market, using the daily closing price of the Dow Jones Industrial Average (DJIA). The term **bull market** refers to an upward primary move, whereas **bear market** refers to a downward primary move (in both cases, these are longer term events, occurring over months or years). A major upward move is said to occur when successive rallies penetrate previous highs, whereas declines remain above previous lows. A major downward move is expected when successive rallies fail to penetrate previous highs, while declines penetrate previous lows.

As originally conceived, the Dow Jones Industrial Average and the Dow Jones Rail Average (which was later replaced by the Transportation Average) must confirm each other for the movement to be validated. Therefore, a primary trend is bullish (bearish) when both the Industrials and the Transports are reaching significant highs (lows).

The secondary, or intermediate, moves give rise to the so-called technical corrections, which are often mentioned in the popular press. These corrections supposedly adjust for excesses that have occurred. These movements are of considerable importance in applying the Dow theory.

Finally, the day-to-day "ripples" occur often and are of minor importance. Even ardent technical analysts do not usually try to predict day-to-day movements in the market.

Figure 16-2 illustrates the basic concept of the Dow theory, although there are numerous variations. The primary trend, represented by the dotted line, is up through time period 1. Although several downward (secondary) reactions occur, these "corrections" do not reach the previous low. Each of these reactions is followed by an upward movement that exceeds the previously obtained high. Trading volume continues to build over this period. Although prices again decline after time period 1 as another correction occurs, the price recovery fails to surpass the last peak reached. (This process is referred to as an abortive recovery.) When the next downward reaction occurs, it penetrates the previous

Figure 16-2

The basic concept of the Dow theory.

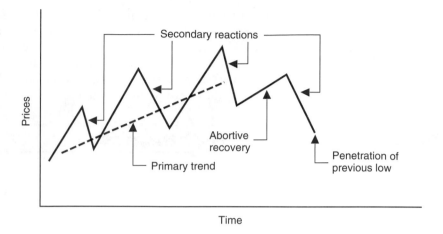

low. This movement could suggest that a primary downturn or new bear market has begun, although it is subject to confirmation.

The Dow theory is intended to forecast the start of a primary movement, but it does not tell us how long the movement will last. Another important consideration is that the confirmation referred to above is up to each user of the Dow theory. The trend will continue as long as the averages confirm each other. Only these averages matter; extensive records are not required, chart patterns are not studied, and so on.

The Dow theory is subject to a number of criticisms, and investors continue debating its merits today. Studies of its success rate have been disappointing; for example, some indicate that over periods of as much as 25 years, investors would have been more successful with a buy-and-hold policy in the same stocks. It is obvious that today's economy is vastly different from the one that existed when the theory was developed. In addition, confirmations are slow to arrive, and are often unclear when they do. The amount of price movement needed for a confirmation is ambiguous.

One problem associated with the Dow theory is that many versions are available, including several investment letters based on the Dow theory. Its users interpret the theory in various ways, and so it may predict different (and conflicting) movements at the same time.

CHARTS OF PRICE PATTERNS

To assess individual stock-price movements, technicians generally rely on charts or graphs of price movements and on relative strength analysis. The charting of price patterns is one of the classic technical analysis techniques. Technicians believe that stock prices move in trends, with price changes forming patterns that can be recognized and categorized. By visually assessing the forces of supply and demand, technicians hope to be able to predict the likely direction of future movements. The most basic measure of a stock's direction is the **trendline**, which simply shows the direction the stock is moving. If demand is increasing more rapidly than supply and the stock shows successively higher low points, it is in an uptrend. Consistently lower highs indicate that supply is increasing more rapidly, and the stock is in a downtrend. Obviously, investors seek to buy in an uptrend and sell on a downtrend.

Technicians seek to identify certain signals in a chart of stock prices, and use certain terminology to describe the events. A **support level** is the level of price (or, more correctly, a price range) at which a technician expects a significant increase in the demand for a stock—in other words, a lower bound on price where it is expected that buyers will

Trendline   The most basic measure of a stock's direction of price movement

Support Level   A price range at which a technician expects a significant increase in the demand for a stock

Resistance Level A price range at which a technician expects a significant increase in the supply of a stock

act, supporting the price and preventing additional price declines. A **resistance level**, on the other hand, is the level of price (range) at which a technician expects a significant increase in the supply of a stock—in other words, an upper bound on price where sellers are expected to act, providing a resistance to any further rise in price.

Figure 16-3 illustrates support and resistance levels. As the stock approaches $10 per share, it encounters a resistance level and drops back below this price. Conversely, as it approaches slightly less than $6 per share, it gains supports and eventually rises. If the stock breaks through the resistance level on heavy volume, this is taken as a very bullish sign and is referred to as a *breakthrough*.

Support levels tend to develop when profit taking causes a reversal in a stock's price following an increase. Investors who did not purchase earlier are now willing to buy at this price, which becomes a support level. Resistance levels tend to develop after a stock declines from a higher level. Investors are waiting to sell the stocks at a certain recovery point. At certain price levels, therefore, a significant increase in supply occurs, and the price will encounter resistance moving beyond this level.

As noted, a trendline is a line drawn on a chart to identify a trend. If a trend exhibits support and resistance levels simultaneously that appear to be well defined, the trend lines are referred to as *channel lines*, and price is said to move between the upper channel line and the lower channel line. *Momentum* is used to indicate the speed with which prices are changing, and a number of measures of momentum exist, referred to as momentum indicators. When a change in direction occurs in a short-term trend, technicians say that a *reversal* has occurred. A correction occurs when the reversal involves only a partial retracing of the prior movement. Corrections may be followed by periods of *consolidation*, with the initial trend resuming following the consolidation.

Technical analysts rely primarily on line charts, bar charts, and point-and-figure charts, although other types of charts are also used, such as candlestick charts.[5]

Bar Chart A plot of daily stock price plotted against time

Bar Charts One of the most popular charts in technical analysis, **bar charts**, are plotted with price on the vertical axis and time on the horizontal axis. Each day's price movement is represented by a vertical bar whose top (bottom) represents the high (low) price for the day.

Figure 16-3

Support and resistance levels for a stock and a breakthrough.

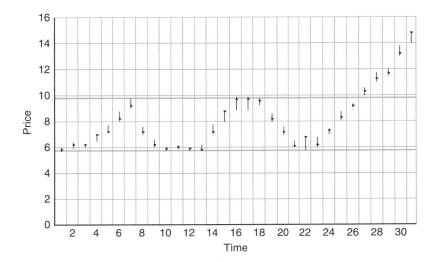

[5] Technicians also use a basic line chart, which uses only one number—usually the closing price for the day—to reflect the price movement. Another type of chart gaining some popularity in the United States is the candlestick chart. Developed in Japan, the candlestick is similar to the bar chart, although it shows the opening price as well as the high, low, and closing prices.

Figure 16-4

A bar chart for Unfloppy Disks, Inc.

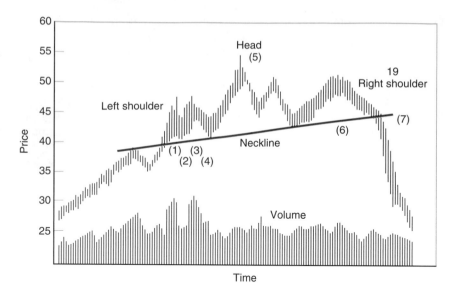

(A small, horizontal tick is often used to designate the closing price for the day.) The bottom of a bar chart usually shows the trading volume for each day, permitting the simultaneous observation of both price and volume activity. *The Wall Street Journal* carries a bar chart of the Dow Jones Averages each day on the page with New York Stock Exchange (NYSE) quotations.

Figure 16-4 shows a daily bar chart for Unfloppy Disks, Inc. The technician using charts will search for patterns in the chart that can be used to predict future price moves. Note in Figure 16-4 the strong uptrend occurring over a period of months. This trend ended with a rally on high volume (at point 1 in Figure 16-4) that forms part of the left shoulder of a famous chart pattern called a *head-and-shoulders pattern*.

The left shoulder shows initially strong demand followed by a reaction on lower volume (2), and then a second rally, with strong volume, carrying prices still higher (3). Profit taking again causes prices to fall to the so-called neckline (4), thus completing the left shoulder. (The neckline is formed by connecting previous low points.) A rally occurs, but this time on low volume, and again prices sink back to the neckline. This is the head (5). The last step is the formation of the right shoulder, which occurs with light volume (6). Growing weakness can be identified as the price approaches the neckline. As can be seen in Figure 16-4, a downside breakout occurs on heavy volume, which technicians consider to be a sell signal.

What about other patterns? Technicians have considered a very large number of such patterns. Some of the possible patterns include flags, pennants, gaps (of more than one type), triangles of various types (e.g., symmetrical, ascending, descending, and inverted), the inverted saucer or dome, the triple top, the compound fulcrum, the rising (and falling) wedge, the broadening bottom, the duplex horizontal, rectangles, and the inverted V. Figure 16-5 shows one set of price patterns said to be the most important for investors to recognize when reading charts of stock prices.

Obviously, numerous patterns are possible and can usually be found on a chart of stock prices. It is also obvious that most, if not all, of these patterns are much easier to identify in hindsight than at the time they are actually occurring.

Point-and-Figure Chart

A plot of stock prices showing only significant price changes

Point-and-Figure Charts Technicians also use **point-and-figure charts**. These types of charts are more complex in that they show only significant price changes, and volume is not shown at all. The user determines what is a significant price change

Figure 16-5

Important price patterns for investors using charts.

SOURCE: Jonathan Butler, "Technical Analysis: A Primer," *Worth*, October 1995, p. 133. Reprinted by permission of *Worth* magazine.

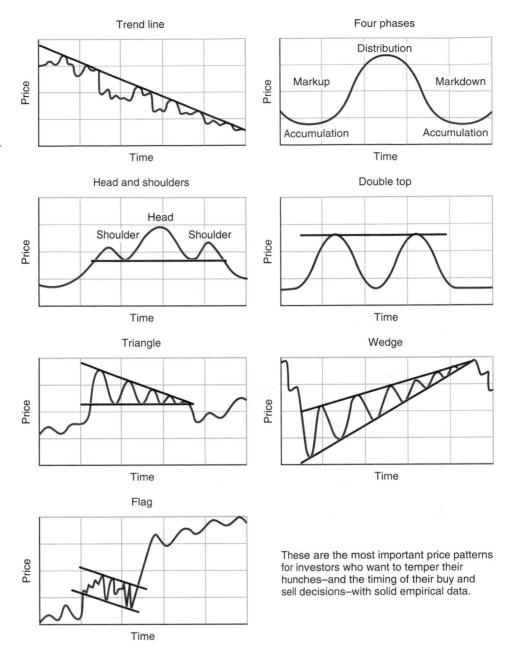

These are the most important price patterns for investors who want to temper their hunches—and the timing of their buy and sell decisions—with solid empirical data.

($1, $2, and so forth) and what constitutes a price reversal ($2, $3, $4, and so forth). Although the horizontal axis still depicts time, specific calendar time is not particularly important—the passage of time is basically ignored. (Some chartists do show the month in which changes occur.)

An X is typically used to show upward movements, whereas an O is used for downward movements. Each X or O on a particular chart may represent $1 movements, $2 movements, $5 movements, and so on, depending on how much movement is considered significant for that stock. An X or O is recorded only when the price moves by the specified amount. Figure 16-6 illustrates a point-and-figure chart.

Figure 16-6

A point-and-figure chart for Gigantic Computers.
X = $1 upward price change,
O = $1 downward price change (numbers indicate months).

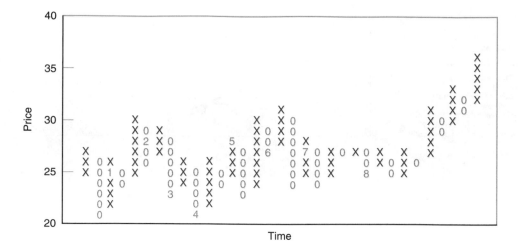

A point-and-figure chart is designed to compress many price changes into a small space. By doing so, areas of "congestion" can be identified. A congestion area is a compacted area of price fluctuations (i.e., a closely compacted horizontal band of Xs and Os). The technician studies a congestion area in search of a "breakout," which will indicate an expected upward or downward movement in stock price.

Some Evidence on Price Charts There are many chart patterns, some of which were mentioned earlier, and numerous technicians analyze and interpret these patterns. It is impossible to demonstrate conclusively the lack of predictive significance in charting. Very few scientific studies of the ability of chart patterns to predict the future direction of price movements have been conducted, although chartists are often claiming success.

Levy studied the predictive significance of "five-point" chart patterns.[6] A five-point chart pattern is one with two highs and three lows or two lows and three highs. As Levy noted,

> The avid chartist will recognize, among the 32 patterns, several variations of channels, wedges, diamonds, symmetrical triangles, head and shoulders, reverse head and shoulders, triple tops, and triple bottoms. Each of these formations allegedly reflects underlying supply/demand and support/resistance conditions that have implications as to future price behavior. A common belief among chartists is that the appearance of certain patterns followed by a "breakout" gives a profitable buy or sell signal.[7]

The results indicated that, although some patterns did produce better results than others, none performed very differently from the market. When brokerage commissions were deducted, none of the 32 patterns was found to have any "profitable forecasting ability in either [bullish or bearish] direction." The really surprising conclusion of this study, however, was that "the best performing patterns would probably be characterized as bearish by most technicians, and conversely, the worst performing patterns would, in two of the three cases, be characterized as bullish."

---

[6] See R. Levy, "The Predictive Significance of Five-Point Chart Patterns," *The Journal of Business*, 44 (July 1971): 316–323.

[7] Using daily prices for 548 NYSE stocks over a five-year period (1964 to 1969), Levy found 19,077 five-point patterns. Of these, 9,383 were followed by a breakout and were therefore studied.

Opinions about charting vary widely. Since the evidence is not conclusive—at least to everyone's satisfaction—the controversy will continue.

MOVING AVERAGES

A moving average of prices is a popular technique for analyzing both the overall market and individual stocks and is used specifically to detect both the direction and the rate of change. Some number of days of closing prices is chosen to calculate a moving average. After initially calculating the average price, the new value for the moving average is calculated by dropping the earliest observation and adding the latest one. This process is repeated daily (or weekly). The resulting moving average line supposedly represents the basic trend of stock prices. Moving averages smooth data, tending to eliminate or soften outliers in price data.

Three major decisions have to be made in constructing a moving average; furthermore, each of the three involves several alternatives.

1. *The time period over which the average is calculated.* This decision has the greatest impact on the moving average. A well-known average for identifying major trends is the 200-day moving average (alternatively, a 10-week [50 day] average is used to identify intermediate trends). Shorter trends can be captured by 10-, 20-, and 50-day averages, as well as 100-day averages. The 200-day moving average will tend to be flatter and lower on the graph than over moving averages.
2. *The price used.* Although closing prices are often used, sometimes the open, high, low, and close prices are used in different configurations.
3. *The type of moving average used.* A simple moving average is often used, but alternatives include a weighted average and an exponential average (whether simple or weighted). The latter two place greater weight on recent price activity, whereas the simple moving average places equal weight on each day's price activity.

A comparison of the current market price to the moving average produces a buy or sell signal. The general buy signal is generated when actual prices rise through the moving average on high volume, with the opposite applying to a sell signal. Specific signals of an upper turning point (a sell signal) are the following:

1. Actual price is below the moving average, advances toward it, does not penetrate the average, and starts to turn down again.
2. Following a rise, the moving average flattens out or declines, and the price of the stock or index penetrates it from the top.
3. The stock price rises above the moving average line while the line is still falling.

Buy signals would be generated if these situations were turned upside-down.

Figure 16-7 shows Coca-Cola plotted daily for a recent period, with both a 200-day moving average and a 50-day moving average included. Volume is shown at the bottom of the chart. Various publications and Web sites offer plots of a 200-day moving average, a 50-day moving average, and other moving averages for both individual stocks and market indices. Figure 16-7 illustrates the type of free information available.

Investors should remember that moving averages show what prices have already done, not what they will do. They indicate if prices, over a given time period, have gone up or gone down. Regardless of how it is constructed, the moving average is always reacting to *what has happened.*

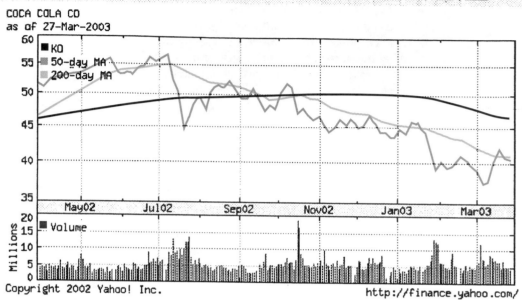

Figure 16-7

A full-screen shot from Yahoo! Finance showing a chart of Coca-Cola with two moving averages, a 50-day average and a 200-day average (the smoother line).

A variation of the moving average popular on some Web sites is the moving average convergence divergence, or MACD. This involves a longer moving average (such as the 200-day) and a shorter moving average (such as the 50-day). As a stock price rises, a bullish signal is generated if the short-term average consistently is greater than the long-term average. A warning signal is generated when the short-term average falls below the long-term average.

RELATIVE STRENGTH

Relative Strength The ratio of a stock's price to some market or industry index, usually plotted as a graph

A well-known technique used for individual stocks (or industries) is relative strength analysis. The **relative strength** for a given stock is calculated as the ratio of the stock's price to a market index, or an industry index, or the average price of the stock itself over some previous period. Relative strength could also be calculated as the ratio of an industry average relative to the market. These ratios can be plotted to form a graph of relative prices across time. In effect, the graph shows the strength of the stock relative to its industry, the market, or whatever. According to the chief market analyst at Merrill Lynch in New York, "Very often changes in trend, from good to bad or from bad to good, will be preceded by a change in the stock's relative performance."[8]

---

[8] See Butler, p. 133.

The relative strength of a stock over time may be of use in forecasting.[9] Because trends are assumed to continue for some time, a rising ratio (an upward-sloping line when relative strength is plotted) indicates relative strength. That is, it indicates a stock that is outperforming the market and that may continue to do so. A declining ratio would have the same implications for the downside. One rule of thumb is that a stock is attractive when the relative strength has improved for at least four months, but as with most technical indicators, technicians interpret some of these signals in different ways.

Figure 16-8 shows relative performance for Coca-Cola in recent years by plotting the ratio of closing monthly prices for Coke to closing monthly prices for the Standard and Poor's 500 Composite Index (S&P 500). Coca-Cola stock during this period generally declined, particularly at the end of the period shown. However, the market also declined during this time period, and both Coke and the market hit a new low in the last month shown in Figure 16-8. Therefore, except for the first few months, Coca-Cola had about the same relative strength at the end as it did much earlier in the period shown.

Relative strength is often used by technicians to identify industry sectors that look attractive prior to selecting individual stocks. This is in line with our analysis in Part IV which supports a top-down approach to security analysis, with industry analysis preceding company analysis. By focusing on the selection of promising industries, investors narrow the number of possibilities to be considered.

This group selection approach may be helpful in supporting the proposition that an individual stock showing relative strength is not an anomaly, but the technique does not protect an investor against the chance that the overall market is weak, and that one or more groups which currently appear strong are next in line to show weakness. Such a possibility once again supports the case for a top-down approach that begins with market analysis in order to assess the likelihood that now is a good time to be investing in stocks.

Figure 16-8

Coca-Cola relative strength performance, April 1999–March 2001.

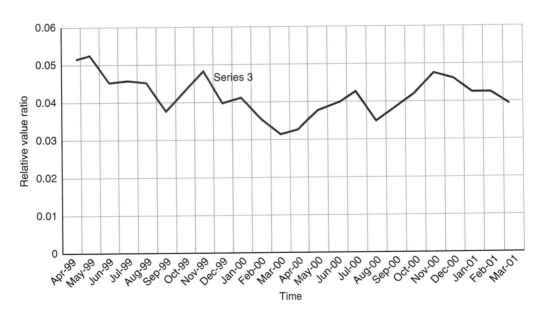

[9] Some evidence supporting relative strength can be found in Narasimhan Jegadeesh and Sheridan Titman, "Returns to Buying Winners and Selling Losers: Implications for Stock Market Efficiency," *The Journal of Finance*, 48 (March 1993): 65–91.

One of the problems with relative strength is that a stock or group could show increasing relative strength because it is declining less quickly than the market, not because it is, in fact, increasing. This suggests that relative strength is not a technique to be used in isolation.

Numerous investment information services provide information on relative strength. For example, *The Value Line Investment Survey*, discussed in Chapter 15, divides a stock's price by the Value Line Composite Average and plots this relative strength ratio for each company it covers at the top of the page. Relative strength analysis lends itself well to computerized stock analysis. This probably accounts for its popularity among institutional investors who own highly automated and sophisticated data analysis systems. The extent to which a number of institutional investors use relative strength techniques and have the means to observe changes at about the same time can affect the volatility of a stock.

USING THE COMPUTER FOR TECHNICAL ANALYSIS

Obviously, the widespread use of personal computers makes technical analysis much more accessible than previously. A few years ago, individual investors could either do the charting themselves or buy a subscription to a service that delivered hard copy of charts on a regular basis. Subsequently, one could buy software with programs and data.

The basic choice for those interested in technical analysis remains either obtaining software or using an on-line service. Software-based programs are more comprehensive, both with regard to charting and to technical indicators, which are discussed below. Software-based programs allow the user to select a trading system based on multiple technical indicators and backtest the system to determine what the profitability would have been. Few on-line services offer any type of trading system, and none allows significant historical backtesting.

Using technical analysis systems requires both a program and a data vendor, and costs can add up quickly. Data can be provided at the end-of-the-day, intraday delayed, or real-time. Most users will find Web-based services to be sufficient.

Using the Internet

Investors have many choices for obtaining charts and related information. Most well-known Web sites, such as www.quicken.com, http://yahoo.quote.com, and http://cbs.marketwatch.com provide simple charts of most stocks easily and quickly. Investors seeking more detail, such as interactive charts where comparisons can be made to indexes, and various types of indicators can be chosen, should try www.bigcharts.com. It has a database of over 50,000 securities, and includes company news and industry analysis.

A particularly comprehensive site is www.clearstation.com, which tracks all NYSE, Amex, and Nasdaq stocks and advocates fundamental analysis along with technical analysis. These charts concentrate on moving averages, which are popular with many investors, and on stochastic oscillators, which forecast change by comparing a stock's closing price to its daily price range. An interesting part of this site is the "Tag and Bag" area, which has lists of stocks, updated during the day, that are experiencing price action trends or fundamental events such as earnings surprises. At www.techrules.com, investors can obtain easy-to-use charts on thousands of stocks as well as daily commentary, support and resistance levels, volatility measures, and much more. Moneycentral.msn.com allows users to export historical price and volume data and save custom screens. Users can also quickly zoom in and out on a chart, shortening or lengthening the time period examined.

Technical Indicators

The chart remains the technician's most important tool for making buy and sell decisions. However, in addition to looking at the plot of stock prices, technicians also like to examine the overall situation by analyzing such factors as breadth and market sentiment indicators.

BREADTH INDICATORS

The Advance-Decline Line (Breadth of the Market) The advance-decline line measures, on a cumulative daily basis, the net difference between the number of stocks advancing in price and those declining in price for a group of stocks such as those on the NYSE. Subtracting the number of declines from the number of advances produces the net advance for a given day (which, of course, can be negative). This measure may include thousands of stocks.

The advance-decline line, often referred to as the breadth of the market, results from plotting a running total of these numbers across time. The line can be based on daily or weekly figures, which are readily available from daily newspapers such as *The Wall Street Journal* (typically reported on page C2, under "Stock Market Data Bank, Diaries").

The advance-decline line is compared to a stock average, in particular the DJIA, in order to analyze any divergence—that is, to determine whether movements in the market indicator have also occurred in the market as a whole. Technicians believe that divergence can signal that the trend is about to change.

The advance-decline line and the market averages normally move together. If both are rising (declining), the overall market is said to be technically strong (weak). If the advance-decline line is rising while the market average is declining, the decline in the market average should reverse itself. Particular attention is paid to a divergence between the two during a bull market. If the market rises while the line weakens or declines, this indicates a weakening in the market; the market would therefore be expected to reverse itself and start declining.

New Highs and Lows Part of the information reported for the NYSE and other stocks is the 52-week high and low prices for each stock. Technicians regard the market as bullish when a significant number of stocks each day hit 52-week highs. On the other hand, technicians see rising market indexes and few stocks hitting new highs as a troublesome sign.

Volume Volume is an accepted part of technical analysis. High trading volume, other things being equal, is generally regarded as a bullish sign. Heavy volume combined with rising prices is even more bullish.

SENTIMENT INDICATORS

Short-Interest Ratio The short interest for a security is the number of shares that have been sold short but not yet bought back. The **short-interest ratio** can be defined relative to shares outstanding or average daily volume, as in:

Short-interest ratio = Total shares sold short/Average daily trading volume   **(16-1)**

The NYSE, Amex, and Nasdaq report the short interest monthly for each stock. The NYSE and Amex indicate those securities where arbitrage or hedging may be important,

Advance-Decline Line
A technical analysis measure that relates the number of stocks rising to the number declining

Short-Interest Ratio
The ratio of total shares sold short to average daily trading volume

but the significance of these activities cannot be determined. For investors interested in the short interest, each month *The Wall Street Journal* reports NYSE and Amex issues for which a short-interest position of at least 100,000 shares existed or for which a short-position change of 50,000 shares occurred from the previous month. A list of stocks with the largest short-interest ratios broken down by exchange can be found at www.trading-ideas.com.

In effect, the ratio indicates the number of days necessary to "work off" the current short interest.[10] It is considered to be a measure of investor sentiment, and many investors continue to refer to it.

Investors sell short when they expect prices to decline; therefore, it would appear, the higher the short interest, the more investors are expecting a decline. A large short-interest position for an individual stock should indicate strong negative sentiment against a stock.

Many technical analysts interpret this ratio in the opposite manner, as a contrarian indicator (discussed below): a high short-interest ratio is taken as a bullish sign, because the large number of shares sold short represents a large number of shares that must be repurchased in order to close out the short sales. (If the ratio is low, the required purchases are not present.) In effect, the short seller must repurchase regardless of whether or not his or her expectations were correct. The larger the short-interest ratio, the larger the potential demand that is indicated. Therefore, an increase in the ratio indicates more "pent-up" demand for the shares that have been shorted.

The short-interest ratio for a given month should be interpreted in relation to historical boundaries, which historically were in the range of 1 to 2 for the NYSE. The problem is that the boundaries keep changing. In the 1960s, 1970s, and 1980s, a ratio of 2 was bullish. More recently, the ratio has been in the 3 to 6 range regardless of the market.

Short-interest figures have been distorted by hedging and arbitrage techniques that have become more popular. For example, if a fund buys Delta and shorts American Airlines, how does this affect the interpretation of the short interest? Hedged short sellers are not likely to panic if their short position moves adversely, which otherwise might lead them to buy and push the price up.

Mutual Fund Liquidity Several indicators are based on the theory of *contrary investing* discussed in Chapter 11. The idea is to trade contrary to most investors, who supposedly almost always lose—in other words, to go against the crowd. This is an old idea on Wall Street, and over the years technicians have developed several measures designed to capitalize on this concept. As mentioned above, the short interest is often used as a contrarian indicator, with high short levels in a stock viewed as being overly pessimistic.

Mutual fund liquidity can be used as a contrary opinion technique. Under this scenario, mutual funds are viewed in a manner similar to odd-lotters; that is, they are presumed to act incorrectly before a market turning point.[11] Therefore, when mutual fund liquidity is low because the funds are fully invested, contrarians believe that the market is at, or near, a peak. The funds should be building up cash (liquidity); instead, they are ex-

---

[10] For example, a ratio of 1 means that the outstanding short interest approximates a day's trading volume.

[11] According to the odd-lot theory, small investors who often buy or sell odd lots (less than 100 shares of stock) are usually wrong in their actions at market peaks and troughs. Supposedly, such investors typically buy (sell) when the market is at or close to a peak (bottom). In particular, small investors do not get involved with short sales unless they are particularly bearish.

tremely bullish and are fully invested. Conversely, when funds hold large liquid reserves, it suggests that they are bearish. Contrarians would consider this a good time to buy, because the market may be at, or near, its low point.

The Opinions of Investment Advisory Newsletters *Investors Intelligence*, an investment advisory service, samples weekly the opinions of about 150 investment advisory services and calculates an index of investment service opinions. It has found that, on average, these services are most bearish at the market bottom and least bearish at the market top. This index, published since 1963, is now available weekly and is widely quoted in the investing community.

The "bearish sentiment index" is calculated as the ratio of advisory services that are bearish to the total number with an opinion. When this index approaches 55 or 60 percent, this would indicate a bearish attitude on the part of investment advisory services. As this ratio approaches 20 percent, the opposite occurs. Thus, a contrarian should react in the opposite direction of the sentiment this ratio is exhibiting. As the ratio nears 60 percent, the contrarian becomes bullish, because a majority of the investment advisory services are bearish, and around 20 percent the contrarain becomes bearish, because most of the investment advisory services are not bearish.

The reason for this seeming contradiction to logic—that investment advisory services are wrong at the extremes—is attributed to the fact that these services tend to follow trends rather than forecast them. Thus, they are reporting and reacting to what has happened rather than concentrating on anticipating what is likely to happen.

Using the Internet

This ratio and detailed information about it, in both table and chart form, can be found at http://vtoreport.com/other/sentiment-table.htm.

CBOE Put/Call Ratio Speculators buy calls when they expect stock prices to rise, and they buy puts when they expect prices to fall. Because they are generally more optimistic than pessimistic, the put to call ratio is well below 1. The puts/calls ratio (P/C ratio) was developed as a sentiment indicator between the number of puts to calls on the Chicago Board Options Exchange. For example, a ratio of 0.60 indicates that only six puts are purchased for every 10 calls purchased.

This ratio was designed to capture the actions of unsophisticated investors trading options. A rise in this ratio indicates pessimism on the part of speculators in options. However, the P/C ratio is used as a contrarian indicator; therefore, when it reaches an excessive level, this is a buy signal to a contrarian. A low ratio would be a sell signal to a contrarian because of the rampant optimism such a ratio indicates.

Small changes are considered unimportant. Extreme readings are said to convey information. According to some sources, a ratio greater than 0.80 (based on a 10-day moving average) would be excessively bearish, and therefore a *buy* signal. A ratio less than 0.45 would be excessively bullish, and therefore a *sell* signal.[12] Like many technical indicators, the exact levels to trigger signals are open to debate. No one indicator should be used in isolation, but rather with other indicators as part of a total package.

---

[12] See Steven B. Achelis, *Technical Analysis from A to Z*, McGraw-Hill Professional Publishing, 2000.

Testing Technical Analysis Strategies

What constitutes a fair test of a technical trading rule? The adjustments that should be made include at least the following:

1. *Risk*. If the risk involved in two strategies is not comparable, a fair comparison cannot be made. As we know, other things being equal, a more risky strategy would be expected to outperform a less risky strategy.
2. *Transaction and other costs (e.g., taxes)*. Several technical trading rules appeared to produce excess returns before transaction costs were deducted. After such costs were deducted, however, the rules were inferior to a buy-and-hold strategy, which generates little costs.
3. *Consistency*. Can the rule outperform the alternative over a reasonable period of time, such as 5 or 10 years? Any rule may outperform an alternative for a short period, but it will not be too useful unless it holds up over some longer term.
4. *Out-of-sample validity*. Has the rule been tried on data other than that used to produce the rule? It is always possible to find a rule that works on a particular sample if enough rules are tried; that is, it is possible to torture the data until it confesses.

Filter Rule A rule for buying and selling stocks according to the stock's price movements

A well-known technical trading rule is the so-called **filter rule**. A filter rule specifies a breakpoint for an individual stock or a market average, and trades are made when the stock-price change is greater than this filter. For example, buy a stock if the price moves up 10 percent from some established base, such as a previous low, hold it until it declines 10 percent from its new high, and then sell it and possibly go short.

Several studies of filters have been conducted. Fama and Blume tested 24 filters (ranging from 0.50 to 50 percent) on each of the 30 Dow Jones stocks.[13] Before commissions, several of the filters were profitable, in particular, the smallest (0.5 percent). After commissions, however, average returns were typically negative or very small. Brokerage commissions more than offset any gains that could be exploited. The low correlations found in the statistical tests were insufficient to provide profitable filter trading rules.

Many different variations of the relative strength technique can be tested by varying the time period over which the average price is calculated and the percentage of the top stocks selected. If we conduct enough tests, we can find a rule that produces favorable results on a particular sample. Therefore, before we conclude that a trading rule of this type is successful, we should conduct a fair test as outlined earlier. Risks must be comparable, and appropriate costs must be deducted. Finally, the rule should be tried on a different sample of stocks.

The Challenge of the Efficient Market Hypothesis The efficient market hypothesis (EMH) discussed in Chapter 12 poses a major challenge to the usefulness of technical analysis. Virtually all statistical tests of the weak form of the EMH offer strong support for the weak form, thereby providing evidence against technical analysis which holds that stock price changes across time are dependent and that prices move in trends. Many tests of technical trading rules suggest that such rules do not generate superior risk-adjusted returns after all relevant costs have been deducted. The sum total of all of this evidence is the reason why many informed observers do not believe that technical analy-

---

[13] E. Fama and M. Blume, "Filter Rules and Stock-Market Trading," *The Journal of Business: A Supplement*, 39 (January 1969): 2–21.

sis can really work on a consistent basis. Nevertheless, proponents of technical analysis claim that it can and does work, and certainly there is some supporting evidence, which we now examine.

Some Supporting Evidence on Technical Analysis Many academic studies have been published which indicate that technical analysis does not work. That is why most academics (and textbooks) do not speak favorably about technical analysis. Nevertheless, some recent credible evidence does exist that supports technical analysis. The following articles have appeared in *The Journal of Finance*, one of the top journals in the field.

Jegadeesh found predictable patterns in stock prices based on monthly returns for the period 1934 to 1987, which is a long period of time.[14] His study showed that stocks with large losses in one month are likely to show a significant reversal in the following month, and that stocks with large gains in one month are likely to show a significant loss in the next month.

Brock, LeBaron, and Lakonishok published a paper titled "Simple Technical Trading Rules and the Stochastic Properties of Stock Returns."[15] This paper provides support for two basic technical indicators, moving averages and support and resistance. The period studied was 1897 to 1986 and used the DJIA. Subperiods were also considered.

Regarding the moving average, the results of this study suggest it does pay to be in the market when the DJIA is above its 200-day moving average and to be more cautious when it is below that average. The authors concluded that the results are "consistent with technical rules having predictive power."

Chordia and Swaminathan found that trading volume is a significant determinant of leads and lags observed in stock prices.[16] Returns on low-volume portfolios respond more slowly to information in market returns than do the returns on high volume portfolios.

Lo, Mamaysky, and Wang at Massachusetts Institute of Technology developed a systematic and automatic approach to technical pattern recognition in order to bypass the subjective nature of technical analysis.[17] Testing a large number of stocks from 1962 to 1996, they found that several technical indicators provide incremental information and may have some practical value.

The Ebb and Flow of Technical Analysis

The 1990s was the decade of common stocks, with most years showing strong performance. Accordingly, firms hired many fundamental analysts and technical analysts during that time, although most firms always have considerably more of the former than the latter. Following the market downturns in 2000 and 2001, however, several firms began to dismiss their analysts. Given that there were many more fundamental analysts than technical analysts to begin with, the result was a distinctive decrease in technical analysis at some firms. In other words, dismissing one or two technical analysts at a firm could

---

[14] See Narasimhan Jegadeesh, "Evidence of Predictable Behavior of Security Returns," *The Journal of Finance* (July 1990): 881–898.

[15] William Baron, Josef Lakonishok, and Blake LeBaron, "Simple Technical Trading Rules and the Stochastic Properties of Stock Returns," *The Journal of Finance*, 47 (December 1992): 1731–1764.

[16] Taran Chordia and Bhaskaran Swaminathan, "Trading Volume and Cross-Autocorrelation in Stock Returns," *The Journal of Finance*, 55 (April 2000): 913–935.

[17] Andrew Lo, Harry Mamaysky, and Jiang Wang, "Foundations of Technical Analysis: Computational Algorithms, Statistical Inference, and Empirical Implementation," *The Journal of Finance*, 55 (August 2000): 1705–1770.

basically eliminate this activity for that firm. This came as somewhat of a shock to the investment community in general and technical analysts in particular. Whether this trend reverses remains to be seen.

Some Conclusions About Technical Analysis

Technical analysis often appeals to those who are beginning a study of investments, because it is easy to believe that stock prices form repeatable patterns over time or that certain indicators should be related to future market (or individual stock) price movements. Most people who look at a chart of a particular stock will immediately see what they believe to be patterns in the price changes and clear evidence of trends that should have been obvious to anyone studying it. How should we view this situation?

On the one hand, academicians (and numerous practitioners) are highly skeptical of technical analysis, to say the least. Most academic discussions at the college level dismiss, or seriously disparage, this concept. A primary reason is that thorough tests of technical analysis techniques typically fail to confirm their value, given all costs and considering an alternative, such as a buy-and-hold strategy.

It is not only academics who remain skeptical of technical analysis. Box 16-1 is a critical discussion of this subject by Laszio Birinyi, Jr., president of a financial consulting firm and well-known observer of the stock market as well as a columnist for *Forbes* magazine. His conclusions are not encouraging when it comes to technical analysis.

In addition to these reasons, other troubling features of technical analysis remain. First, several interpretations of each technical tool and chart pattern are not only possible but usual. One or more of the interpreters will be correct (more or less), but it is virtually impossible to know beforehand who these will be. After the fact, we will know which indicator or chart or whose interpretation was correct, but only those investors who used that particular information will benefit. Tools such as the Dow theory are well known for their multiple interpretations by various observers who disagree over how the theory is to be interpreted.

Furthermore, consider a technical trading rule (or chart pattern) that is, in fact, successful. When it gives its signal on the basis of reaching some specified value (or forms a clear picture on a chart), it correctly predicts movements in the market or some particular stock. Such a rule or pattern, if observed by several market participants, will be self-destructive as more and more investors use it. Price will reach its equilibrium value quickly, taking away profit opportunities from all but the quickest. Some observers will start trying to act before the rest on the basis of what they expect to happen. (For example, they may act before a complete head and shoulders forms.) Price will then reach an equilibrium even more quickly, so that only those who act earliest will benefit. Eventually, the value of any such rule will be negated entirely.

Investments Intuition

No inherent reason exists for stock-price movements to repeat themselves. For example, flipping a fair coin 100 times should, on average, result in about 50 heads and 50 tails. There is some probability that the first 10 tosses could produce 10 heads. However, the chance of such a pattern repeating itself is very small.

As we saw in Chapter 12, strong evidence exists suggesting that stock-price changes over time are weak-form efficient. If this is the case, any patterns formed are accidental but not surprising.

BOX 16–1

Uncharted Territory

Technical analysis seeks to protect you with timing signals from bear markets. It doesn't work—but that doesn't mean that you should be out of the market.

Are you looking for direction as the dreary bear market drags on? One piece of advice: Don't look for it from technical analysts, who profess to find market patterns today that portend tomorrow's direction. These folks, for instance, divine that something called a "head-and-shoulders top" formation—a market high above two high points on either side—means that stocks are poised for a downward move. But such a notion is more aptly suited for a shampoo label than for market interpretation.

Chartists, as they're also known, don't regard me as a friend. A few years ago I wrote a column criticizing their approach as distinctly unhelpful. The technical analysts' reaction was harsh, to say the least—ranging from quibbling about my grammar to arguing that because technical analysis has attracted a large following, it must have merit.

Nevertheless, in a rotten investment environment in which nothing seems to work, I recently revisited the chartist approach in hopes that I was wrong. My staff and I road-tested numerous chartist tools to see if they were valid in the real world—they included trend lines, resistance, and oscillators. With the greater market information now available on the Web, I hoped that maybe the chartists' discipline had finally evolved into a useful guide. My hopes were in vain.

I have searched high and low for anyone who can persuade me that this stuff works. I turned to an academic study favorable to technical analysis, published in *Journal of Finance* in August 2000. Yet upon examination, this study proved only that certain patterns emerge, not that you can make money from them. The authors reported that their findings did "not necessarily imply that technical analysis can be used to generate excess trading profits." Providing superior returns, though, is what analysis—any analysis—should be about.

Certainly, technical analysis has grown in popularity since I wrote about it. Over the last two years, the number of those studying to be Certified Technical Analysts has doubled, to 400, from the previous two-year period. (That doesn't prove that they're on to something, however. The number of people reporting alien abductions is up, too.)

The allure of a system that promises certainty in topsy-turvy times is obvious, especially when that system is supposed to shower riches on its acolytes. In Jack D. Schwager's book, *Getting Started in Technical Analysis* (John Wiley & Sons, 1999), one chartist trader is quoted as bragging that he averaged a 25% monthly return over ten years. Sounds too good to be true. Had the trader started with $100 and achieved the results cited, after ten years he would have accumulated $43 trillion (before taxes) and created a whole new category in The Forbes 400.

Sure, the chartists have at times been right. In the summer of 1998 they made a good call in the media, suggesting that a decline in prices was imminent. Then came the Russian debt crisis and Long-Term Capital Management's demise. The Dow fell 19%, so we can grade that call as an A. Unfortunately, once the technical crowd thinks that it has spotted a trend, it can get carried away. As the fall of 1998 approached, a subsequent roundup of chartist projections in *Barron's* foresaw the Dow tumbling as low as 5000. Well, that didn't happen. By early 1999 the index was climbing nicely.

Would that I had a better market-reading system myself. My own statistical analysis, which is based on comparing trading volumes on upticks and downticks, served well in the 1990s but has faltered recently. Market strategists of whatever stripe have had a rough go. The same is true for economists. This year was going to see a deeper recession in the U.S., then a recovery; now, evidently, it is seeing a recovery in the economy but not necessarily in the market.

SOURCE: Laszio Birinyi Jr., *Forbes*, July 22, 2002, p. 206. Reprinted by permission of *Forbes* Magazine © 2002 Forbes Inc.

Yet, it is impossible to test all the techniques of technical analysis and their variations and interpretations. In fact, technical analysis has not been tested thoroughly. The techniques of this approach are simply too numerous, and technical analysis is broader than the use of only price information. Therefore, absolutely definitive statements about this subject cannot be made. A good example of the omissions in this area is the use of volume in technical strategies. Although volume is a recognized part of technical analysis, at least until recently, relatively few tests have been conducted on its use in conjunction with the rest of technical analysis.

Also, as noted above in *The Journal of Finance* articles, in recent years, some evidence has been presented that tends to support the basis of technical analysis. And, of course, other evidence has been presented. For example, Brown and Jennings have presented a different way of looking at technical analysis which provides a justification for technical analysis being useful to investors.[18] They construct a scenario that shows how each investor can learn something about what other investors know by observing the price at which a security trades. In effect, prices reveal information as well as simply convey information.

What can we conclude about technical analysis? On the basis of all available evidence, it is difficult to justify technical analysis. Until quite recently, the studies that have been done in support of this concept have produced relatively weak arguments in its favor. Studies done in support of the efficient market hypothesis, on the other hand, are much stronger in their conclusions that technical analysis does not work on a consistent, after-transactions cost basis. Regardless of the evidence, technical analysis remains popular with many investors.

Perhaps a recent quote from the popular press summarizes it best: "Whether it works or not, TA is no quick road to riches. Even die-hard technical analysts say that the method works best when accompanied by fundamental research—for example, to time entry and exit points for a stock."[19]

Summary

▶ Technical analysis, the other approach to selecting securities, is the oldest approach available to investors and in many respects the most controversial.

▶ Technical analysis relies on published market data, primarily price and volume data, to predict the short-term direction of individual stocks or the market as a whole. The emphasis is on internal factors that help to detect demand-supply conditions in the market.

▶ The rationale for technical analysis is that the net demand (or lack thereof) for stocks can be detected by various technical indicators and that trends in stock prices occur and continue for considerable periods of time. Stock prices require time to adjust to the change in supply and demand.

▶ Price and volume are primary tools of the technical analyst, as are various technical indicators.

▶ Technical analysis involves the use of charts of price patterns to detect trends that are believed to persist over time. Technical analysis can be applied to both the aggregate market and individual stocks.

▶ Aggregate market analysis originated with the Dow theory, the best-known technical theory. It is designed to detect the start of major movements.

▶ The most frequently used charts are line charts, bar charts, which show each day's price movement as well as volume, and point-and-figure charts, which show only significant price changes as they occur.

▶ Numerous chart "patterns" are recognizable to a technician. However, all patterns are subject to multiple interpretations because different technicians will read the same chart differently.

▶ A very well-known tool of technical analysis is the moving average, which is used to detect both the direction and the rate of change in prices.

▶ Another well-known technique for individual stocks is relative strength, which shows the strength of a particular stock in relation to its average price, its industry, or the market.

▶ Technical indicators of the aggregate market include, but are not limited to, the following:

1. The advance-decline line (breadth of market), which is used to assess the condition of the overall market.
2. Mutual fund liquidity, which uses the potential buying power (liquidity) of mutual funds as a bullish or bearish indicator.

---

[18] See David Brown and Robert Jennings, "On Technical Analysis," *Review of Financial Studies*, 1989, pp. 527–552.

[19] See Hirson, op. cit., p. 98.

3. Short-interest ratio, which assesses potential demand from investors who have sold short.
4. Contrary opinion, which is designed to go against the crowd. Included here are the put/call ratio and the opinions of investment advisory services. The short sale ratio can also be interpreted as a contrarian indicator, as can mutual fund liquidity.

Key Words

Advance-decline line	Filter rule	Short-interest ratio
Bar chart	Market data	Support level
Bear market	Point-and-figure chart	Technical analysis
Bull market	Relative strength	Trendline
Dow theory	Resistance level	

Questions

16-1 Describe the rationale for technical analysis.

16-2 Differentiate between fundamental analysis and technical analysis.

16-3 What do technicians assume about the adjustment of stock prices from one equilibrium position to another?

16-4 What role does volume play in technical analysis?

16-5 What is the Dow theory? What is the significance of the "confirmation" signal in this theory?

16-6 How does the Dow theory forecast how long a market movement will last?

16-7 Using a moving average, how is a sell signal generated?

16-8 Why is the advance-decline line called an indicator of breadth of the market?

16-9 Why are the opinions of investment advisory services considered a contrary opinion signal?

16-10 What is the rationale for the theory of contrary opinion?

16-11 How is the odd-lot index calculated? How is it used as a buy or sell signal?

16-12 Why is a rising short-interest ratio considered to be a bullish indicator?

16-13 Distinguish between a bar chart and a point-and-figure chart.

16-14 What is relative strength analysis?

16-15 On a rational economic basis, why is the study of chart patterns likely to be an unrewarding activity?

16-16 Is it possible to prove or disprove categorically the validity of technical analysis?

16-17 Assume that you know a technical analyst who claims success on the basis of his or her chart patterns. How might you go about scientifically testing this claim?

16-18 How do the new contrarians differ from the more traditional contrarians?

16-19 Why do stock-price movements repeat themselves?

16-20 Look at the bar chart of the Dow Jones Averages in section C1 of *The Wall Street Journal*. Does this chart cover a sufficient time period to apply the Dow theory?

16-21 With reference to Question 16-20, why would this chart, or possibly several of these charts covering a number of months, be useful in trying to apply the Dow theory?

16-22 What new financial instruments have caused the short-interest ratio to be less reliable? Why?

16-23 Describe a bullish sign when using a moving average; a bearish sign. Do the same for the advance-decline line.

16-24 Consider the plot of stock X in the following diagram. The plot shows weekly prices for one year based on a beginning price of $30.

    a. Do you see any chart patterns in this figure?

    b. Do any patterns you see in this chart help you to predict the future price of this stock?

    c. What is your forecast of this stock's price over the next three months?

    d. If this price series were to be generated using random numbers, do you think it could resemble this plot?

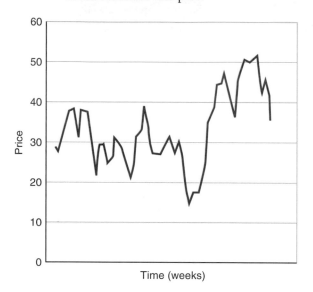

Reprinted, with permission, from the Level I 1992 *CFA Study Guide.* Copyright 1992, Association for Investment Management and Research, Charlottesville, VA. All rights reserved.

CFA

16-26 Two basic assumptions of technical analysis are that security prices adjust:

    a. rapidly to new information, and liquidity is provided by securities dealers.

    b. rapidly to new information, and market prices are determined by the interaction of supply and demand.

    c. gradually to new information, and liquidity is provided by securities dealers.

    d. gradually to new information, and market prices are determined by the interaction of supply and demand.

CFA

16-27 Which one of the following would be a bearish signal to a technical analyst?

    a. The debit balances in brokerage accounts increase.

    b. The market shows poor performance when compared to individual stocks.

    c. The yield differential between high-quality and low-quality bonds increases.

    d. The ratio of short sales by specialists to total short sales becomes abnormally low.

CFA

16-25 Under the theory of contrary opinion, the put/call ratio and the put premium are two factors in which technicians are interested. At the point where stock prices are at their lowest levels, one would expect:

    a. put trading volume to increase and put premiums to increase.

    b. put trading volume to decrease and put premiums to decrease.

    c. call trading volume to increase and put premiums to decrease.

    d. call trading volume to decrease and put premiums to remain constant.

CFA

16-28 When technical analysts say a stock has a good "relative strength," they mean the:

    a. ratio of the price of the stock to a market index has trended upward.

    b. recent trading volume in the stock has exceeded the normal trading volume.

    c. total return on the stock has exceeded the total return on other stocks in the same industry.

    d. stock has performed well compared to other stocks in the same risk category as measured by beta.

Reprinted, with permission, from the Level I 1994 *CFA Study Guide.* Copyright 1994, Association for Investment Management and Research, Charlottesville, VA. All rights reserved.

Web Resources

For additional resources visit our dynamic Web site located at www.wiley.com/college/jones.

☐ *A Free Lunch*—Technical analysis of market-level data may help in the timing of stock purchases and sales. A contrarian's measure of investor sentiment using the volume exchange-traded options is presented to help with the investment timing decision.

☐ Internet Exercises—Technical analysis tries to use trends in price movements to construct winning investment strategies. The theory of market efficiency denies the validity of technical analysis. The Web exercises for this chapter will evaluate different technical strategies for stock picking.

Exercise 1: Explores primary market moves.
Exercise 2: Explores secondary market moves.
Exercise 3: Looks at the moving average theory.
Exercise 4: Examines short interest as a means of predicting stock prices.

☐ Multiple Choice Self Test

Selected References

One of the classic commentaries on this and related subjects such as the Efficient Market Hypothesis is:

Malkiel, Burton G. *A Random Walk Down Wall Street*, 7th ed. New York: W. W. Norton, 2000.

Up-to-date coverage of technical analyis can be found in:

Achelis, Steven B. *Technical Analysis From A to Z.* New York: McGraw-Hill Professional Publishing, 2001.

And in:

Schwager, Jack D. *Getting Started in Technical Analysis*. New York: John Wiley & Sons, 1999.

chapter *17*

Bond Yields and Prices

Chapter 17 provides an analysis of bond yields and prices, including the valuation of bonds. An important part of this analysis is a consideration of how interest rates affect bond investors, which in turn helps us to understand how bond prices change over time. This chapter discusses the important concepts in bond analysis, such as yield to maturity and duration, as well as covering the mechanics of bond calculations, an important part of an investor's toolkit.

AFTER READING THIS CHAPTER YOU WILL BE ABLE TO:

▶ Understand and calculate various bond yield measures, most importantly the yield to maturity.

▶ Calculate the price of a bond as a result of understanding how to value financial assets.

▶ Determine how bond prices change as the interest rate changes.

▶ Understand, calculate, and use the concept of duration.

This chapter builds on the background developed in Part I and the return concepts discussed in Part II. The basic characteristics of bonds were discussed in Chapter 2. We now focus on the important principles governing bond yields and prices. A thorough understanding of these principles is essential to an investor's success in bond investing.

In addition to the total return concept considered in Chapter 6, which is applicable to any security, bond investors must also understand specific measures of bond yields. It is traditional in the bond markets to use various yield measures and to quote potential returns to investors on the basis of these measures. However, these measures can mislead unwary investors who fail to understand the basis on which they are constructed. Investors must understand that bond yields shown daily in sources such as *The Wall Street Journal* do not indicate the "true" yield an investor is promised when he or she buys bonds in the marketplace and holds them to maturity. On the other hand, "correct" yield quotes from your broker may lead you to expect a very different return from what you will actually earn.

How is the price of a bond determined? This question involves valuation principles similar to those learned in Chapter 10 for stocks. A bond's estimated value, exactly like a stock's estimated value, is the present value of the future cash flows to be received from owning the bond. In addition to calculating the price of a bond, we will learn why bond prices change and why some bonds are more sensitive to a change in market rates than are other bonds. As part of this analysis we will consider the important concept of duration, now widely recognized and used by bond investors.

Bond Yields

Bond yields and interest rates are the same concept. Therefore, we begin our discussion of bond yields with a brief consideration of interest rates.

Interest rates measure the price paid by a borrower to a lender for the use of resources over some time period—that is, interest rates are the price for loanable funds. The price differs from case to case, based on the demand and supply for these funds, resulting in a wide variety of interest rates. The spread between the lowest and highest rates at any point in time could be as much 10 to 15 percentage points. In bond parlance, this would be equivalent to 1,000 to 1,500 basis points, since 1 percentage point of a bond yield consists of 100 **basis points**.

Basis Points   100 basis points are equal to 1 percentage point

It is convenient to focus on the one interest rate that provides the foundation for other rates. This rate is referred to as the short-term riskless rate (designated RF in this text) and is typically proxied by the rate on Treasury bills. All other rates differ from RF because of two factors: (1) maturity differentials and (2) risk premiums.

THE BASIC COMPONENTS OF INTEREST RATES

Explaining interest rates is a complex task that involves substantial economics reasoning and study. Such a task is not feasible in this text.[1] However, we can analyze the basic determinants of nominal (current) interest rates with an eye toward recognizing the factors that affect such rates and cause them to fluctuate. The bond investor who understands the foundations of market rates can then rely on expert help for more details, and be in a better position to interpret and evaluate such help.

---

[1] Most money and banking texts, as well as texts on financial markets, contain a good, concise discussion of interest rates.

**Real Risk-Free Rate
of Interest**   The
opportunity cost of
foregoing consumption,
given no inflation

The basic foundation of market interest rates is the opportunity cost of foregoing consumption, representing the rate that must be offered to individuals to persuade them to save rather than consume. This rate is sometimes called the **real risk-free rate of interest**, because it is not affected by price changes or risk factors.[2] We will refer to it simply as the *real rate* and designate it RR in this discussion.

Nominal interest rates on Treasury bills consist of the RR plus an adjustment for *expected inflation*. A lender who lends $100 for a year at 10 percent will be repaid $110. But if inflation is 12 percent a year, the $110 that the lender receives upon repayment of the loan is worth, in terms of purchasing power, only (1/1.12) ($110), or $98.21. Lenders therefore expect to be compensated for the *expected* rate of price change in order to leave the real purchasing power of wealth unchanged. *As an approximation for discussion purposes*, this inflation adjustment can be added to the real risk-free rate of interest. Unlike RR, which is often assumed by market participants to be reasonably stable with time, adjustments for *expected* inflation vary widely over time.

Thus, for short-term risk-free securities, such as three-month Treasury bills, the nominal interest rate is a function of the real rate of interest and the *expected* inflationary premium. This is expressed as Equation 17-1, which is an approximation:[3]

$$RF \approx RR + EI \tag{17-1}$$

where

RF = short-term Treasury bill rate
RR = the real risk-free rate of interest
EI = the expected rate of inflation over the term of the instrument

Equation 17-1 is known as the *Fisher hypothesis* (named after Irving Fisher). It implies that the nominal rate on short-term risk-free securities rises point-for-point with expected inflation, with the real rate of interest remaining unaffected.[4] Turning Equation 17-1 around, estimates of the real risk-free rate of interest can be *approximated* by subtracting the *expected* inflation rate from the observed nominal interest rate.[5]

One of the best sources of expected inflation data is the survey of consumers conducted by the University of Michigan. Participants are asked to predict how much prices will change over a horizon of 5 to 10 years.

All market interest rates are affected by a *time factor* which leads to maturity differentials. That is, although long-term Treasury bonds are free from default risk in the same manner as Treasury bills, Treasury bonds typically yield more than Treasury notes, which typically yield more than Treasury bills. This typical relationship between bond maturity and yield applies to all types of bonds whether Treasuries, corporates, or municipals. The *term structure of interest rates*, discussed in Chapter 18, accounts for the relationship between time and yield—that is, the maturity differentials.

Market interest rates other than those for riskless Treasury securities are also affected by a third factor, a *risk premium*, which lenders require as compensation for the

[2] The real rate of interest cannot be measured directly. It is often estimated by dividing (1.0 + MIR) by (1.0 + EI), where MIR is the market interest rate and EI is expected inflation. This result can be approximated by subtracting estimates of inflation from nominal (market) interest rates (on either a realized or expected basis).
[3] The correct procedure is to multiply (1 + the real rate) by (1 + the expected rate of inflation) and subtract 1.0. For purposes of our discussion, the additive relationship is satisfactory.
[4] Fisher believed that inflation expectations were based on past observations as well as information about the future and that inflation expectations were slow to develop and slow to disappear.
[5] Although estimates of the real federal funds rate can be made by subtracting actual inflation for the same quarter because federal funds are of very short duration, estimates of real rates on instruments with longer maturities require measures of expected inflation over the term of the instrument.

risk involved. This risk premium is associated with the issuer's own particular situation or with a particular market factor. The risk premium is often referred to as the *yield spread* or yield differential. Yield spreads are discussed in Chapter 18.

MEASURING BOND YIELDS

Several measures of the yield on a bond are used by investors. It is very important for bond investors to understand which yield measure is being discussed, and what the underlying assumptions of any particular measure are. To illustrate these measures, we will use as an example a three-year, 10-percent coupon, AAA-rated corporate bond, with interest payments occurring exactly six months from now, one year from now, and so forth. (It is very important to note throughout this discussion that interest payments on bonds [i.e., the coupons] are paid semiannually—this is simply the actual payment mechanism that has existed for many years.) The current price of this bond is $1,052.42 because interest rates declined after the bond was issued.

Current Yield The ratio of the coupon interest to the current market price is the **current yield**, and this is the measure reported daily in *The Wall Street Journal* for those corporate bonds shown under the sections "New York Exchange Bonds" and "AMEX Bonds." The current yield is clearly superior to simply citing the coupon rate on a bond, because it uses the current market price as opposed to the face amount of a bond (almost always $1,000). However, current yield is not a true measure of the return to a bond purchaser, because it does not account for the difference between the bond's purchase price and its eventual redemption at par value.

Current Yield A bond's annual coupon divided by the current market price

Example 17-1 The current yield on this bond is $100/$1,052.10 = 9.5 percent.

Yield to Maturity The rate of return on bonds most often quoted for investors is the **yield to maturity (YTM)**, a *promised* rate of return that will occur only under certain assumptions. It is the compound rate of return an investor will receive from a bond purchased at the current market price if:

Yield to Maturity (YTM) The promised compound rate of return on a bond purchased at the current market price and held to maturity

1. the bond is held to maturity, and
2. the coupons received while the bond is held are reinvested at the calculated yield to maturity.

Barring default, an investor will actually earn this *promised* rate if, and only if, these two conditions are met. As we shall see, however, the likelihood of the second condition actually being met is extremely small.

The yield to maturity is the periodic interest rate that equates the present value of the expected future cash flows (both coupons and maturity value) to be received on the bond to the initial investment in the bond, which is its current price. This means that the yield to maturity is the internal rate of return (IRR) on the bond investment, similar to the IRR used in capital budgeting analysis (and subject to the same limitations).

To calculate the yield to maturity, we use Equation 17-2 where the market price, the coupon, the number of years to maturity, and the face value of the bond are known, and the discount rate or yield to maturity is the variable to be determined. Note in the following discussion (and in the rest of the chapter) that lower case letters, ytm, c, and *n*, are used to denote semiannual variables, whereas capital letters, YTM, C, and N are used to denote annual variables. Correct bond calculations in the United States involve the use of semiannual periods, because bond interest is typically paid twice a year.

$$P = \sum_{t=1}^{n} \frac{c_t}{(1 + ytm)^t} + \frac{FV}{(1 + ytm)^n} \qquad (17\text{-}2)$$

where

P	= the current price of the bond
n	= the number of semiannual periods to maturity
ytm	= the semiannual yield to maturity to be solved for
c	= the semiannual coupon in dollars
FV	= the face value (or maturity value or par value) which in this discussion is always $1,000

Since both the left-hand side of Equation 17-2 and the numerator values (cash flows) on the right side are known, the equation can be solved for ytm. Because of the semiannual nature of interest payments, the annual coupon on the bond is divided in half (to obtain c) and the number of periods is doubled (to obtain n). What remains (conceptually) is a trial-and-error process to find a discount rate, ytm, that equates the inflows from the bond (coupons plus maturity value) with its current price (cost).

For purposes of providing an *intuitive understanding* of yield to maturity, we illustrate the trial-and-error (iteration) process involved in this calculation by referring to the present value tables at the end of the text. The purpose is simply to demonstrate *conceptually* how to calculate the yield to maturity. Investors will normally use a calculator or computer to do computations such as these.

Example 17-2

Assume we are considering a 10-percent coupon bond with 3 years to maturity. The annual coupon is $100, or $50 every six months, and the total number of semiannual periods is six. Assume that the bond is selling at a premium with a current market price of $1,052.42. *A bond is selling at a premium if the coupon rate is greater than the current yield.* Because of the inverse relation between bond prices and market yields, it is clear that yields have declined since the bond was originally issued, because the price is greater than $1,000. Using Equation 17-2 to solve for yield to maturity, we will find that the solution is 4% on a semiannual basis[6]

$$\$1,052.42 = \sum_{t=1}^{6} + \frac{\$50}{(1 + ytm)^t} + \frac{\$1,000}{(1 + ytm)^6}$$

$1,052.42 = $50 × (present value of an annuity, 4% for six periods)
          + $1,000 × (present value factor, 4% for six periods)

$1,052.42 = $50(5.242) + $1,000(0.790)

$1,052.42 = $1,052.10 (rounding error accounts for the differential)

4% = semiannual ytm

2 × 4% = 8% = annual YTM (bond equivalent yield)

---

[6] The present value of an annuity factor for 4 percent for 6 periods, 5.242, is taken from Table A-4 in the Interest Tables at the end of the text; 0.790, the present value of $1 for 4 percent for 6 periods, is taken from Table A-2.

Bond-Equivalent Yield
Yield on an annual basis,
derived by doubling the
semiannual yield

In Example 17-2, the solution is 4 percent on a semiannual basis, which we are calling ytm, and which by convention is doubled to obtain the annual YTM of 8 percent. A YTM calculated by annualizing in this manner is referred to as the **bond-equivalent yield**.

The yield to maturity calculation for a zero-coupon bond is based on the same process expressed in Equation 17-2—equating the current price to the future cash flows to find ytm, and then doubling this result to obtain the annual YTM. Because there are no coupons, the only cash flow is the face value of the bond to be received at maturity. We will always assume a $1,000 face value for all bonds discussed. The ytm calculation for a zero-coupon bond reduces to Equation 17-3, with all terms as previously defined:

$$\text{ytm} = [\text{FV/P}]^{1/n} - 1 \qquad (17\text{-}3)$$

Multiply by 2 to obtain YTM, the bond equivalent yield on an annual basis.

Example 17-3

A zero-coupon bond has 12 years to maturity and is selling for $300. Given the 24 semi-annual periods, the power to be used in raising the ratio of $1,000/$300, or 3.3333, is 0.0417 (calculated as 1/[2 × 12]). Using a calculator with a power function produces a value of 1.0515. Subtracting the 1.0 and converting to a percent leaves a semiannual yield to maturity, ytm, of 5.15 percent. The bond equivalent yield is 10.30 percent.

An investor who purchases a bond and holds it to maturity will earn the promised yield to maturity as calculated on the purchase date (barring default or failure to receive the cash flows in a timely manner) if, and only if, the cash flows are reinvested at the calculated rate. As we will see below, reinvestment rate risk is heavily involved here, and will affect the actual outcome of virtually every bond investment. Before we consider that, however, there is one other promised yield measure investors may need to use.

Yield to Call   The
promised return on a
bond from the present to
the date that the bond is
likely to be called

Yield to Call Most corporate bonds, as well as some government bonds, are callable by the issuers, typically after some deferred call period. For bonds likely to be called, the yield to maturity calculation is unrealistic. A better calculation is the **yield to call**. The end of the deferred call period, when a bond can first be called, is often used for the yield to call calculation. This is particularly appropriate for bonds selling at a premium (i.e., high-coupon bonds with market prices above par value).[7]

To calculate the yield to first call, the YTM formula (Equation 17-2) is used, but with the number of periods until the first call date substituted for the number of periods until maturity and the call price substituted for face value. Issuers often pay a call premium for a specified period of time to call the bonds, and therefore the call price can differ from the maturity value of $1,000. These changes are shown in Equation 17-4.

$$P = \sum_{t=1}^{fc} \frac{c_t}{(1 + yc)^t} + \frac{CP}{(1 + yc)^{fc}} \qquad (17\text{-}4)$$

where

fc = the number of semiannual periods until the first call date
yc = the yield to first call on a semiannual basis
CP = the call price to be paid by the issuer if the bond is called

---

[7] That is, bonds with high coupons (and high yields) are prime candidates to be called.

Bond prices are calculated on the basis of the lowest yield measure. Therefore, for premium bonds selling above a certain level, yield to call replaces yield to maturity, because it produces the lowest measure of yield.

Realized Compound Yield After the investment period for a bond is over, an investor can calculate the **realized compound yield (RCY)**. This rate measures the compound yield on the bond investment actually earned over the investment period, taking into account all intermediate cash flows and reinvestment rates. Defined in this manner, it cannot be determined until the investment is concluded and all of the cash flows are known. Thus, if you invest $1,000 in a bond for five years, reinvesting the coupons as they are received, you will have X dollars at the conclusion of the five years, consisting of the coupons received, the amount earned from reinvesting the coupons, and the $1,000 par value of the bond payable at maturity. You can then calculate your actual realized rate of return on the investment.

Realized Compound Yield (RCY)   Yield earned based on actual reinvestment rates

■ The RCY for a bond can be calculated by dividing the total ending wealth (including the purchase price) at the bond's maturity by the amount invested, and raising the result to the *1/n* power, where *n* is the number of compounding periods. Next, subtract 1.0 from the result. Finally, because of the semiannual basis for bonds, multiply by 2 to obtain the bond equivalent rate.

The semi-annual realized compound yield can be calculated using the following formula:

$$RCY = \left[\frac{\text{Total ending wealth}}{\text{Purchase price of bond}} \right]^{1/n} - 1.0 \qquad (17\text{-}5)$$

Example 17-4

Assume an investor had $1,000 to invest three years ago. This investor purchased a 10-percent coupon bond with a three-year maturity at face value. The promised YTM for this bond was 10 percent.

Assume the investor reinvested each coupon at a semiannual rate, or ytm, of exactly 5 percent. At the end of the three years, the investor has a total ending wealth of $1,340.10 which includes the initial investment of $1,000 (in other words, the investor earned $340.10 on the $1,000, given the compounding over time).

The realized compound yield on this investment, under the circumstances described, is 5 percent on a semiannual basis or 10% on a bond-equivalent basis, calculated as:

$$[\$1,340.10 / 1,000]^{1/6} - 1.0 = 0.05 \text{ semiannually, or } 0.10 \text{ on a bond-equivalent basis.}$$

Now we are in a better position to understand the YTM calculation. The YTM on a bond assumes that all coupons are reinvested at an interest rate equal to the bond's YTM. If all coupons are reinvested at the calculated yield to maturity, the realized compound yield after the investment period ends will be equal to the rate promised to the investor at the time of purchase, the YTM. This is the case for the bond in Example 17-4. The promised YTM was 10 percent annually (bond-equivalent basis), and the actual realized compound yield was 10 percent annually (bond-equivalent basis).

If the coupons are reinvested at different rates, however, the RYC will not be equal to the promised YTM. It should be apparent that for the typical bond investment, the YTM will seldom turn out to equal the RCY. This is true because subsequent reinvestment rates will seldom equal the calculated YTM on the bond. Instead, they will vary over time, often being higher than the calculated YTM at times and lower than the calculated YTM at other times.

Remember,

❏ The YTM is a promised rate, and is totally dependent on certain conditions being met.
❏ The RCY is the actual return realized at the conclusion of the investment, and reflects exactly what was earned.

Investments Intuition

Consider what happens when investors purchase bonds at high YTMs, such as the record levels reached in the summer of 1982. Some utilities issued bonds with an 18% coupon. Those investors expecting to earn 18 percent were disappointed unless they reinvested the coupons at these record YTMs; that is, investors did not actually achieve a realized compound yield equal to the calculated YTM. For the promised YTM to become a realized yield, coupons had to be reinvested over time at the record rates existing at the purchase date of the bond, an unlikely situation for a high-YTM bond with a long maturity. The subsequent decline in interest rates during the fall of 1982 illustrates the fallacy of believing that one has "locked up" record yields during a relatively brief period of very high interest rates. Investors in this situation are sometimes said to be subject to *yield illusion*.

This analysis highlights the importance of reinvestment rates to investors and, therefore, reinvestment rate risk.

Interest on Interest
The process by which bond coupons are reinvested to earn interest

Reinvestment Risk As noted, the YTM calculation assumes that the investor reinvests all coupons received from a bond at a rate equal to the computed YTM on that bond, thereby earning **interest on interest** over the life of the bond. Interest on interest is the income earned on the reinvestment of the intermediate cash flows, which for a bond are the coupon (interest) payments made semiannually.

Example 17-5

Given the bond in Example 17-4, with a 10-percent coupon and a three-year maturity, assume that the coupons are reinvested at a rate of 5 percent semiannually. The interest on interest from this bond is as follows: The first $50, received six months after buying the bond, is reinvested and earns $50 \times (1.05)^5 = \$63.81$; the second $50 received at the end of one year is reinvested and earns $50 \times (1.05)^4 = \$60.78$; the third $50 received at the end of one and a half years is reinvested and earns $50 \times (1.05)^3 = \$57.88$; the fourth $50 received at the end of two years is reinvested and earns $50 \times (1.05)^2 = \$55.13$; the fifth $50 received is reinvested and earns $50 \times (1.05) = \$52.50$, and the last $50 is received at the end of three years and is not reinvested. Adding all six numbers together produces a total of $340.10, which added to the initial investment of $1,000 results in a total dollar return at the end of three years of $1,340.10.

Reinvestment Rate Risk
The part of interest rate risk resulting from uncertainty about the rate at which future interest coupons can be reinvested

The YTM calculation assumes that the reinvestment rate on all cash flows during the life of the bond is the calculated yield to maturity. If the investor spends the coupons, or reinvests them at a rate different from the assumed reinvestment rate, the realized compound yield that will actually be earned when the bond matures will differ from the calculated YTM which is only a promised rate. And, in fact, coupons almost always will be reinvested at rates higher or lower than the computed YTM. This gives rise to **reinvestment rate risk**. This term describes the risk that future reinvestment rates will be less than the YTM at the time the bond is purchased.

Note that a bond investor has three possible sources of dollar returns from a bond investment, which we will call the *total dollar return*:

- The coupons, which are the semiannual interest payments on a coupon-paying bond
- A capital gain or loss—the difference between the purchase price and the price received when the bond is sold, matures or is called
- Interest on interest, resulting from the reinvestment of the coupons

The interest on interest concept significantly affects the potential total dollar return from a bond investment. The exact impact is a function of coupon and time to maturity, with reinvestment becoming more important as either coupon or time to maturity, or both, rises. Specifically:

1. Holding everything else constant, the longer the maturity of a bond, the greater the reinvestment risk.
2. Holding everything else constant, the higher the coupon rate, the greater the dependence of the total dollar return from the bond on the reinvestment of the coupon payments.

Figure 17-1 illustrates the importance of the interest on interest in impacting the total dollar return from a bond. This is a 10-percent coupon, 20-year bond purchased at par ($1,000). All coupons are reinvested at 5 percent on a semiannual basis; that is, the ytm is 5 percent. At the end of 20 years (40 semiannual periods), the total dollar return on this bond will be $7,040, consisting of:

$1,000 received at maturity (no capital gain or loss)
+$2,000 in coupons received over the life of the bond
+$4,040 as a result of interest-on-interest (reinvesting each coupon at 5 percent semiannually. Note this is the largest area in Figure 17-1).

To illustrate the importance of the reinvestment rate in determining the actual yields that will be realized from a bond, Table 17-1 shows the realized compound yields actually earned under different assumed reinvestment rates for a 10-percent noncallable 20-year bond purchased at face value—which has a YTM of 10 percent. If the reinvestment rate exactly equals the YTM of 10 percent, the investor earns a 10-percent RCY when the bond is

Figure 17-1

The three components of a bond's total dollar return.

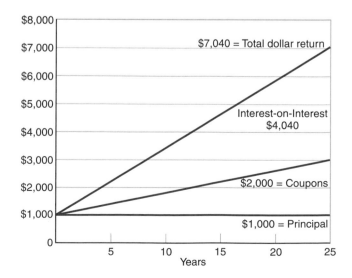

Table 17-1 Realized Compound Yields, Using Different Reinvestment Rate Assumptions, for a 10-percent 20-Year Bond Purchased at Face Value

(1) Coupon Income[a] ($)	(2) Assumed Reinvestment Rate (%)	(3) Total Return[b] ($)	(4) Amount Attributable to Reinvestment[c] ($)	(5) Realized Yields[d] (%)
2000	0	2000	0	5.57
2000	5	3370	1370	7.51
2000	8	4751	2751	8.94
2000	9	5352	3352	9.46
2000	10	6040	4040	10.00
2000	11	6830	4830	10.56
2000	12	7738	5738	11.14

[a]Coupon income = total dollars received from coupons over 20 years (40 semiannual periods) = $50-coupon received *semiannually* × 40 periods. 10-percent coupon bond generates $100 income annually.

[b]Total return = all coupons received plus all income earned from reinvesting the coupons over the life of the bond = sum of an annuity for 40 periods, $50 semiannual coupons.

Example: at 10-percent reinvestment rate, $50 × 120.80 (120.80 is the 5-percent, 40-period sum of an annuity factor) = $6,040.

[c]Amount attributable to reinvestment of coupons = total return minus coupon income. This is also known as the interest on interest. Notice that in each case it is $2,000 (the amount of the coupons) less than the Total Return.

[d]Realized yield = [Total dollar return]$^{1/n}$ − 1, where Total dollar return = (total return + cost of the bond)/cost of the bond.

Example: at 10-percent reinvestment rate, Total dollar return is $6,040 + $1,000 (the cost of the bond)/cost of the bond = $7,040/$1,000 = 7.04.

Next, raise 7.04 to the 1/40 or 0.025 power: $7.04^{.025}$ = 1.05; 1.05 − 1.0 = 0.05 on a semiannual basis: (Note: 7.04 is the same value one would obtain by raising the semiannual rate of 0.05 to the 40th power [which reflects semiannual compounding for 20 years]—that is, 1.05^{40} = 7.04).

The result of this calculation is the realized yield on a semiannual basis. To put this on an annual basis, this figure must be doubled. This has been done for the yields in Table 17-1.

held to maturity, with $4,040 of the total dollar return from the bond attributable to interest on interest (see Figure 17-1). Notice in this case that the interest on interest is the largest single component of the total dollar return of $7,040 (which includes return of principal).

If coupons are reinvested at rates above the calculated YTM, the RCY rises, and an even larger percentage of the total dollar return comes from interest on interest.

Example 17-6 To calculate the realized compound yield an investor would earn if the reinvestment rate is 12 percent, add the total return shown in Table 17-1, $7,738, to the cost of the bond, $1,000, to obtain total dollar return of $8,738. Then divide by the beginning amount and raise to the appropriate power. Therefore,

$$RCY = [\$8,738/1,000]^{1/40} - 1.0$$
$$= [8.738]^{.025} - 1.0$$
$$= 1.0557 - 1.0$$
$$= 0.0557, \text{ or } 5.57\% \text{ on a semiannual basis}$$

Once again, to place this on a bond equivalent basis, multiply by 2. The annual RCY is 5.57 percent × 2 = 11.14 percent.

Almost 75 percent of the total return comes from interest on interest ($5,738/$7,738).

On the other hand, with no reinvestment of coupons (spending them as received), the investor will achieve only a 5.57 percent RCY when the bond is held to maturity.

Clearly, the reinvestment portion of a bond's total dollar return is critical in determining the actual rate of return earned. In fact, for long-term bonds, when coupons are reinvested, the interest on interest component is typically the most important component of the bond's total dollar return.

One advantage of a zero-coupon bond is the elimination of reinvestment rate risk, because there are no coupons to be reinvested. At the time of purchase investors know the RCY that will be earned when the bond is held to maturity—it is the simply the YTM, because there are no coupons to reinvest.

Horizon Return As we have seen, each of the yield measures has problems. Current yield is clearly not a correct measure of the return that will be received on a bond. Both the yield to maturity and the yield to first call have potential problems because of the reinvestment rate assumptions made, which are basically unrealistic. What can a bond investor do in these circumstances?

Bond investors today often make specific assumptions about future reinvestment rates in order to cope with the reinvestment rate problem illustrated earlier. This is sometimes referred to as *horizon analysis*. Given their explicit assumption about the reinvestment rate, investors can calculate the **horizon (total) return** to be earned over a specified period based upon an assumed reinvestment rate.

Horizon (Total) Return
Bond returns to be earned based on assumptions about reinvestment rates

The investor makes an assumption about the reinvestment rate expected to prevail over the planned investment horizon. The investor may also make an assumption about the yield to maturity expected to prevail at the end of the planned investment horizon, which in turn is used to estimate the price of the bond at that time. Based on these assumptions, the total future dollars expected to be available at the end of the planned investment horizon can be determined. The horizon return, or expected return, is then calculated as the interest rate that equates the total future dollars to the purchase price of the bond.

Bond Prices

THE VALUATION PRINCIPLE

What determines the price of a security? The answer is *estimated* value! A security's estimated value determines the price that investors place on it in the open market.

Intrinsic Value The estimated or calculated value of a security

Recall from Chapter 10 that a security's **intrinsic value**, or estimated value, is the present value of the expected cash flows from that asset. Any security purchased is expected to provide one or more cash flows some time in the future. These cash flows could be periodic, such as interest or dividends, or simply a terminal price or redemption value, or a combination of these. Since these cash flows occur in the future, they must be discounted at an appropriate rate to determine their present value. The sum of these discounted cash flows is the estimated intrinsic value of the asset. Calculating intrinsic value, therefore, requires the use of present value techniques. Equation 17-6 expresses the concept:

$$\text{Value}_{t=0} = \sum_{t=1}^{n} \frac{\text{Cash flows}}{(1 + k)^t} \tag{17-6}$$

where

$\text{Value}_{t=0}$ = the estimated value of the asset now (time period 0)
Cash flows = the future cash flows resulting from ownership of the asset
k = the appropriate discount rate or rate of return required by an investor for an investment of this type
n = number of periods over which the cash flows are expected

To solve Equation 17-6 and derive the intrinsic value of a security, it is necessary to determine the following:

1. The expected *cash flows* from the security. This includes the size and type of cash flows, such as dividends, interest, face value *expected* to be received at maturity, or the *expected* price of the security at some point in the future.
2. The *timing* of the expected cash flows. Since the returns to be generated from a security occur at various times in the future, they must be properly documented for discounting back to time period 0 (today). Money has a time value, and the timing of future cash flows significantly affects the value of the asset today.
3. The *discount rate*, or required rate of return demanded by investors. The discount rate used will reflect the time value of the money and the risk of the security. It is an *opportunity cost*, representing the rate foregone by an investor in the next best alternative with comparable risk.

BOND VALUATION

The price of a bond should equal the present value of its expected cash flows.[8] The coupons and the principal repayment of $1,000 are known, and the present value, or price, can be determined by discounting these future payments from the issuer at an appropriate required yield, r, for the issue. Equation 17-7 is used to solve for the value of an option-free coupon bond.[9]

$$P = \sum_{t=1}^{n} \frac{c_t}{(1+r)^t} + \frac{FV}{(1+r)^n} \qquad (17\text{-}7)$$

where

P = the present value or price of the bond today (time period 0)
c = the semiannual coupons or interest payments
FV = the face value (or par value) of the bond
n = the number of semiannual periods until the bond matures
r = the appropriate semiannual discount rate or market yield

In order to conform with the existing payment practice on bonds of paying interest semiannually rather than annually, the discount rate being used (r), the coupon (c_t) on the bond, and the number of periods are all on a semiannual basis. Equation 17-7 is the equation that underlies standard bond practices.

For expositional purposes, we will illustrate the calculation of bond prices by referring to the present value tables at the end of the text; in actuality, a calculator or computer is used. The present value process for a typical coupon-bearing bond involves three steps, given the dollar coupon on the bond, the face value, and the current market yield applicable to a particular bond:

1. Using the *present value of an annuity* table (Table A-4 in the Interest Tables), determine the present value of the coupons (interest payments).
2. Using the *present value* table (Table A-2 in the Interest Tables), determine the present value of the maturity (par) value of the bond; for our purposes, the maturity value will always be $1,000.
3. Add the present values determined in steps 1 and 2 together.

[8] An investor purchasing a bond must also pay to the seller the accrued interest on that bond.
[9] This formulation is nothing new; John Burr Williams stated it in a book in 1938. See John Burr Williams, *The Theory of Investment Value* (Cambridge, Mass.: Harvard University Press, 1938).

Example 17-7 Consider newly issued bond A with a three-year maturity, sold at par with a 10-percent coupon rate. Assuming semiannual interest payments of $50 per year for each of the next six periods, the price of bond A, based on Equation 17-7, is:

$$P(A) = \sum_{t=1}^{6}\frac{\$50}{(1 + 0.05)^t} + \frac{\$1,000}{(1 + 0.05)^6} = \$50 \times (5.0757) + \$1,000 \times (0.7462)$$

$$= \$999.99, \text{ or } \$1,000$$

which, of course, agrees with our immediate recognition that the bond's price should be $1,000, since it has just been sold at par.

Now consider bond B, with characteristics identical to bond A's, issued five years ago when the interest rate demanded for such a bond was 7 percent. Assume that the current discount rate or required yield on bonds of this type is 10 percent on an annual basis, or 5 percent on a semiannual basis, and that the bond has three years left to maturity. Investors certainly will not pay $1,000 for bond B and receive the dollar coupon of $70 per year, or $35 semiannually, when they can purchase bond A and receive $100 per year. However, they should be willing to pay a price determined by the use of Equation 17-7.

$$P(B) = \sum_{t=1}^{6}\frac{\$35}{(1 + 0.05)^t} + \frac{\$1,000}{(1 + 0.05)^6} = \$35(5.0757) + \$1,000(0.7462)$$

$$= \$923.85$$

Thus, bond B is valued, as is any other asset, on the basis of its future stream of benefits (cash flows), using an appropriate market yield. Since the numerator is always specified for coupon-bearing bonds at time of issuance, the only issue in valuing a typical bond is to determine the denominator or discount rate. The appropriate discount rate is the bond's required yield.

The *required yield*, r, in Equation 17-7 is specific for each particular bond. It is the current market rate being earned by investors on comparable bonds with the same maturity and the same credit quality. (In other words, it is an opportunity cost.) Thus, market interest rates are incorporated directly into the discount rate used to solve for the fundamental value of a bond.

Since market interest rates fluctuate constantly, required yields do also. When solving for a bond price, it is customary to use the yield to maturity. If the YTM is used, we can, for convenience, restate Equation 17-7 in terms of price and YTM, as in Equation 17-8.

$$P = \sum_{t=1}^{n}\frac{c_t}{(1 + \text{ytm})^t} + \frac{FV}{(1 + \text{ytm})^n} \tag{17-8}$$

Investments Calculation

Solving for the price of a bond is an easy procedure in today's financial world using either a financial calculator or personal computer. For example, by using a basic financial calculator such as the HP-10B, price can be solved for after entering the cash flows and required yield.

Bond Price Changes

BOND PRICE CHANGES OVER TIME

We now know how to calculate the price of a bond, using the cash flows to be received and the YTM as the discount rate. Assume that we calculate the price of a 20-year bond issued five years ago and determine that it is $910. The bond still has 15 years to maturity. What can we say about its price over the next 15 years?

When everything else is held constant, including market interest rates, bond prices that differ from the bond's face value (assumed to be $1,000) must change over time. Why? On a bond's specified maturity date, it must be worth its face value or maturity value. Therefore, over time, holding all other factors constant, a bond's price must converge to $1,000 on the maturity date because that is the amount the issuer will repay on the maturity date.

After bonds are issued, they sell at discounts (prices less than $1,000) and premiums (prices greater than $1,000) during their lifetimes. Therefore, a bond selling at a discount will experience a rise in price over time, holding all other factors constant, and a bond selling at a premium will experience a decline in price over time, holding all other factors constant, as the bond's remaining life approaches the maturity date.

Figure 17-2 illustrates bond price movements over time assuming constant yields. Bond 2 in Figure 17-2 illustrates a 10-percent coupon, 30-year bond assuming that yields remain constant at 10 percent. The price of this bond does not change, beginning at $1,000 and ending at $1,000. Bond 1, on the other hand, illustrates an 8-percent coupon, 30-year bond assuming that required yields start, and remain constant, at 10 percent. The price starts below $1,000, because bond 1 is selling at a discount as a result of its coupon of 8 percent being less than the required yield of 10 percent. Bond 3 illustrates a 12-percent coupon, 30-year bond assuming that required yields start, and remain constant, at 10 percent. The price of bond 3 begins above $1,000, because it is selling at a premium (its coupon of 12 percent is greater than the required yield of 10 percent).

If all other factors are held constant, the price of all three bonds must converge to $1,000 on the maturity date. Before the maturity date, however, interest rates and bond prices are continually changing. An important issue is, how much do they change, and why.

The sensitivity of the price change is a function of certain variables, especially coupon and maturity. We now examine these variables.

BOND PRICE CHANGES AS A RESULT OF INTEREST RATE CHANGES

Bond prices change because interest rates and required yields change. Understanding how bond prices change given a change in interest rates is critical to successful bond management. The basics of bond price movements as a result of interest rate changes have been known for many years. For example, over 40 years ago, Burton Malkiel derived five theorems about the relationship between bond prices and yields.[10] Using the bond valuation

Figure 17-2

Bond price movements over time assuming constant yields for a 10-percent coupon, 15-year bond.

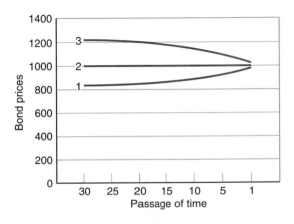

---

[10] Burton G. Malkiel, "Expectations, Bond Prices, and the Term Structure of Interest Rates," *Quarterly Journal of Economics*, May 1962, pp. 197–218.

model, he showed the changes that occur in the price of a bond (i.e., its volatility), given a change in yields, as a result of bond variables such as time to maturity and coupon. We will use Malkiel's bond theorems to illustrate how bond prices change as a result of changes in interest rates.

Bond Prices Move Inversely to Interest Rates Investors must always keep in mind *the* fundamental fact about the relationship between bond prices and bond yields: *Bond prices move inversely to market yields.* When the level of required yields demanded by investors on new issue changes, the required yields on all bonds already outstanding will also change. For these yields to change, the prices of these bonds must change. This inverse relationship is the basis for understanding, valuing, and managing bonds.

Example 17-8   Table 17-2 shows prices for a 10-percent coupon bond for market yields from 6 to 14 percent and for maturity dates from 1 to 30 years. For any given maturity, the price of the bond declines as the required yield increases and increases as the required yield declines from the 10-percent level. Figure 17-3 shows this relationship using data from Table 17-2.

An interesting corollary of the inverse relationship between bond prices and interest rates is as follows: *Holding maturity constant, a decrease in rates will raise bond prices on a percentage basis more than a corresponding increase in rates will lower bond prices.*

Example 17-9   Table 17-2 shows that for the 15-year 10-percent coupon bond, the price would be $1,172.92 if market rates were to decline from 10 to 8 percent, resulting in a price appreciation of 17.29 percent. On the other hand, a rise of 2 percentage points in market rates from 10 to 12 percent results in a change in price to $862.35, a price decline of only 13.77 percent.

Obviously, bond price volatility can work for, as well as against, investors. Money can be made, and lost, in risk-free Treasury securities as well as more risky corporate bonds.

Although the inverse relationship between bond prices and interest rates is the basis of all bond analysis, a complete understanding of bond price changes as a result of interest rate changes requires additional information. An increase in interest rates will cause bond prices to decline, but the exact amount of decline will depend on important variables unique to each bond such as time to maturity and coupon. We will examine each of these in turn.

Table 17-2 Bond Price and Market Yields for a 10-Percent Coupon Bond

Time to Maturity	Bond Prices at Different Market Yields and Maturities				
	6%	8%	10%	12%	14%
1	$1,038.27	$1,018.86	$1000	$981.67	$963.84
5	1,170.60	1,081.11	1000	926.40	859.53
10	1,297.55	1,135.90	1000	885.30	788.12
15	1,392.01	1,172.92	1000	862.35	751.82
20	1,462.30	1,197.93	1000	849.54	733.37
25	1,514.60	1,214.82	1000	842.38	723.99
30	1,553.51	1,226.23	1000	838.39	719.22

Figure 17-3

The relationship between bond prices and market yields.

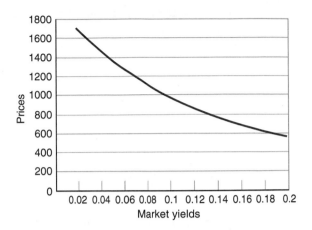

The Effects of Maturity The effect of a change in yields on bond prices depends on the maturity of the bond. An important principle is that *for a given change in market yields, changes in bond prices are directly related to time to maturity*. Therefore, as interest rates change, the prices of longer term bonds will change more than the prices of shorter term bonds, everything else being equal.

Example 17-10 Given two 10-percent coupon bonds and a drop in market yields from 10 to 8 percent, we can see from Table 17-2 that the price of the 15-year bond will be $1,172.92, whereas the price of the 30-year bond will be $1,226.23.

The principle illustrated here is simple but important. Other things being equal, bond price volatility is a function of maturity. Long-term bond prices fluctuate more than do short-term bond prices.

A related principle regarding maturity is as follows: *The percentage price change that occurs as a result of the direct relationship between a bond's maturity and its price volatility increases at a diminishing rate as the time to maturity increases.*

Example 17-11 As we saw above, a 2 percentage–point drop in market yields from 10 to 8 percent increased the price of the 15-year bond to $1,172.92, a 17.29 percent change, whereas the price of the 30-year bond changed to $1,226.23, a 26.23-percent change. Therefore, although the time doubled, the percentage change in price did not double.

This example shows that the percentage of price change resulting from an increase in time to maturity increases, but at a decreasing rate. Put simply, a doubling of the time to maturity will not result in a doubling of the percentage-price change resulting from a change in market yields.

The Effects of Coupon In addition to the maturity effect, the change in the price of a bond as a result of a change in interest rates depends on the coupon rate of the bond. We can state this principle as (other things equal): *Bond price fluctuations (volatility) and bond coupon rates are inversely related.* Note that we are talking about percentage-price fluctuations; this relationship does not necessarily hold if we measure volatility in terms of dollar price changes rather than percentage-price changes.

The Implications of Malkiel's Theorems for Investors Malkiel's derivations for bond investors lead to a practical conclusion: The two bond variables of major importance in assessing the change in the price of a bond, given a change in interest rates, are its coupon and its maturity. This conclusion can be summarized as follows: A decline (rise) in interest rates will cause a rise (decline) in bond prices, with the most volatility in bond prices occurring in longer maturity bonds and bonds with low coupons. Therefore:

1. In order to receive the maximum price impact of an expected change in interest rates, a bond buyer should purchase low-coupon, long-maturity bonds.
2. If an increase in interest rates is expected (or feared), an investor contemplating a bond purchase should consider those bonds with large coupons or short maturities, or both.

These relationships provide useful information for bond investors by demonstrating how the price of a bond changes as interest rates change. Although investors have no control over the change and direction in market rates, they can exercise control over the coupon and maturity, both of which have significant effects on bond price changes. Nevertheless, it is cumbersome to calculate various possible price changes on the basis of these theorems. Furthermore, maturity is an inadequate measure of the sensitivity of a bond's price change to changes in yields, because it ignores the coupon payments and the principal repayment.

   Investors managing bond portfolios need a measure of time designed more accurately to portray a bond's "average" life, taking into account all of the bond's cash flows, including both coupons and the return of principal at maturity. Such a measure, called duration, is available and is widely used today.

MEASURING BOND PRICE VOLATILITY: DURATION

In managing a bond portfolio, perhaps the most important consideration is the effects of yield changes on the prices and rates of return for different bonds. The problem is that a given change in interest rates can result in very different percentage-price changes for the various bonds that investors hold. We saw earlier that both maturity and coupon affect bond price changes for a given change in yields. One of the problems, however, is that we examined the effects of these two variables separately.

   Although maturity is the traditional measure of a bond's lifetime, it is inadequate, because it focuses only on the return of principal at the maturity date. Two 20-year bonds, one with an 8-percent coupon and the other with a 15-percent coupon, do not have identical *economic* lifetimes. An investor will recover the original purchase price much sooner with the 15-percent coupon bond compared to the 8-percent coupon bond. Therefore, a measure is needed that accounts for the entire pattern (both size and timing) of the cash flows over the life of the bond—the *effective maturity of the bond.* Such a concept, called duration (or Macaulay duration), was conceived over 50 years ago by Frederick Macaulay. Duration is very useful for bond management purposes, because it combines the properties of maturity and coupon.

Duration A measure of a bond's lifetime that accounts for the entire pattern of cash flows over the life of the bond

Duration Defined Duration measures the weighted average maturity of a (noncallable) bond's cash flows on a present value basis. We can also say that duration is the weighted average of the times until each payment (coupon or principal repayment) from the bond is received.[11]

---

[11] This discussion applies only to option-free bonds.

Figure 17-4

Illustration of the cash flow pattern of a 10-percent coupon, five-year maturity bond paying interest semi-annually and returning the principal of $1,000 at maturity.

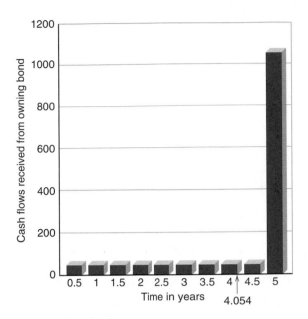

Figure 17-4 illustrates the concepts of both time to maturity and duration for a bond with five years to maturity, a 10-percent coupon, and selling for $1,000. As the figure indicates, the stream of cash flows generated by this bond over the term to maturity consists of $50 every six months, or $100 per year, plus the return of principal of $1,000 at the end of the five years. The last cash flow combines the interest payment of $50 with the principal repayment of $1,000, which occurs at the maturity date.

Although the term to maturity for the bond illustrated in Figure 17-4 is five years, its duration is only 4.054 years as indicated by the arrow. This means that the time-value-of-money–weighted average number of years needed to recover the cost of this bond is 4.054. In effect, the arrow indicates the point where the weights, which are the cash flows, are in balance.

Think of duration, as illustrated by Figure 17-4, in the following manner. Although the bond has five years to maturity, interest payments are received in each of the first four years. Therefore, describing the bond as a 5-year bond is not totally accurate, because the average time to receipt of each of the cash flows is clearly less than 5 years. Duration describes the weighted average time to each payment.

Calculating Duration To calculate duration, it is necessary to calculate a weighted time period, because duration is stated in years. The time periods at which the cash flows are received are expressed in terms of years and denoted by t in this discussion. When all of these t's have been weighted and summed, the result is the duration, stated in years.

The present values of the cash flows, as a percentage of the bond's current market price, serve as the weighting factors to apply to the time periods. Each weighting factor shows the relative importance of each cash flow to the bond's total present value, which is simply its current market price. The sum of these weighting factors will be 1.0, indicating that all cash flows have been accounted for. The sum of all the discounted cash flows from the bond will equal the bond's price.

The equation for duration is shown as Equation 17-9:

$$\text{Macaulay duration} = D = \sum_{t=1}^{n} \frac{\text{PV}(\text{CF}_t)}{\text{Market price}} \times t \tag{17-9}$$

where

t	= the time period at which the cash flow is expected to be received
n	= the number of periods to maturity
$PV(CF_t)$	= present value of the cash flow in period t, discounted at the yield to maturity
Market price	= the bond's current price or present value of all the cash flows

As Equation 17-9 shows, duration is obtained by multiplying the present value of each period's cash flow by the number of periods when each is to be received and summing. Note that *duration is expressed in years.*

Example 17-12 Table 17-3 provides an example of calculating the duration for a bond, using the same bond as shown in Figure 17-4. This is a 10-percent coupon bond with five years remaining to maturity. The bond is priced at $1,000 for ease of exposition, and the YTM is 10 percent (semiannual yield, ytm, is 5 percent).[12]

The cash flows, column 2, consist of 10 $50-coupons (the annual coupon is $100) plus the return of principal at the end of the fifth year. Notice that the final cash flow of $1,050 ($50-coupon plus $1,000 return of principal) accounts for 64.5 percent of the value of the bond. Column 4 shows the present value of the cash flows, whereas column 5 shows these present values as a percentage of the bond's price, which in this example is $1,000. Column 6 is calculated by multiplying the weights in column 5 by the time periods in column 1, and summing these products.

The duration of 4.054 years is almost one year less than the term to maturity of five years. As we will see, duration will always be less than time to maturity for bonds that pay coupons.

Table 17-3 An Example of Calculating the Duration of a Bond with a 10-Percent Coupon, Five-Year Maturity, Currently Priced at $1,000

1 Periods	2 Cash Flow	3 Pres. Val Factor—5%	4 Pres. Val of Cash Flow	5 Pres. Val /Price	6 (1) × (5)
0.5	50	0.952381	47.61905	0.047619	0.02381
1	50	0.907029	45.35147	0.045351	0.045351
1.5	50	0.863838	43.19188	0.043192	0.064788
2	50	0.822702	41.13512	0.041135	0.08227
2.5	50	0.783526	39.17631	0.039176	0.097941
3	50	0.746215	37.31077	0.037311	0.111932
3.5	50	0.710681	35.53407	0.035534	0.124369
4	50	0.676839	33.84197	0.033842	0.135368
4.5	50	0.644609	32.23045	0.03223	0.145037
5	1050	0.613913	644.6089	0.644609	3.223045
		Totals	1000	1.0	4.053911

[12] A shortcut formula can be used for coupon bonds selling at face value:

$$\text{Duration} = \frac{1 + \text{ytm}}{\text{ytm}} [1 - (1/(1 + \text{ytm})^n)]$$

Using the semiannual rate and doubling the number of periods, we must divide the answer by 2.0 to put it on an annual basis.

Understanding Duration How is duration related to the key bond variables previously analyzed? An examination of Equation 17-9 shows that the calculation of duration depends on three factors[13]:

❑ The final maturity of the bond
❑ The coupon payments
❑ The yield to maturity

1. *Duration expands with time to maturity but at a decreasing rate* (holding the size of coupon payments and the yield to maturity constant, particularly beyond 15 years time to maturity). Even between 5 and 10 years time to maturity, duration is expanding at a significantly lower rate than in the case of a time to maturity of up to 5 years, where it expands rapidly.[14] Note that for all coupon-paying bonds, duration is always less than maturity. For a zero-coupon bond, duration is equal to time to maturity.[15]
2. *Yield to maturity is inversely related to duration* (holding coupon payments and maturity constant).
3. *Coupon is inversely related to duration* (holding maturity and yield to maturity constant). This is logical, because higher coupons lead to quicker recovery of the bond's value, resulting in a shorter duration, relative to lower coupons.

Why is duration important in bond analysis and management? First, it tells us the difference between the effective lives of alternative bonds. Bonds A and B, with the same duration but different years to maturity, have more in common than bonds C and D with the same maturity but different durations. For any particular bond, as maturity increases, the duration increases at a decreasing rate.

Example 17-13 Given the 10-percent coupon bond discussed above with a yield to maturity of 10 percent and a five-year life, we saw that the duration was 4.054 years. If the maturity of this bond was 10 years, it would have an effective life (duration) of 6.76 years, and with a 20-year maturity it would have an effective life of 9.36 years—quite a different perspective. Furthermore, under these conditions, a 50-year maturity for this bond would change the effective life to only 10.91 years. The reason for the sharp differences between the term to maturity and the duration is that cash receipts received in the distant future have very small present values and therefore add little to a bond's value.

Second, the duration concept is used in certain bond-management strategies, particularly immunization, as explained in Chapter 18.

Third, and most importantly for bond investors, duration is a measure of bond-price sensitivity to interest rate movements; that is, it is a direct measure of interest rate risk. Malkiel's bond-price theorems are inadequate to examine all aspects of bond-price sensitivity. This issue is considered in some detail below because of its potential importance to bond investors.

---

[13] The duration of a bond can change significantly if there is a sinking fund or a call feature.

[14] The duration of a perpetuity is $(1 + YTM)/YTM$. This indicates that maturity and duration can differ greatly since the maturity of a perpetuity is infinite, but duration is not. That is, perpetuities have an infinite maturity but a finite duration.

[15] Deep discount bonds are an exception to the general rule. Their duration first increases with time to maturity, up to some distant point, and then decreases in duration beyond this point. This is because deep discount bonds with very long maturities behave like perpetuities.

Estimating Price Changes Using Duration The real value of the duration measure to bond investors is that it combines coupon and maturity, the two key variables that investors must consider in response to expected changes in interest rates. As noted earlier, duration is positively related to maturity and negatively related to coupon. However, bond-price changes are directly related to duration; that is, the percentage change in a bond's price, given a change in interest rates, is proportional to its duration. Therefore, duration can be used to measure interest rate exposure.

Modified Duration
Duration divided by
1 + yield to maturity

The term **modified duration** refers to Macaulay's duration in Equation 17-9 divided by (1 + ytm).

$$\text{Modified duration} = D^* = D/(1 + \text{ytm}) \tag{17-10}$$

where

D* = modified duration

ytm = the bond's semiannual yield to maturity (we divide YTM by the number of discounting periods, which for semiannual bond payments is 2)

Example 17-14 Using the duration of 4.054 years calculated earlier and the YTM of 10 percent, the modified duration based on semiannual interest would be

$$D^* = 4.054/(1 + 0.05) = 3.861$$

The modified duration can be used to calculate the percentage-price change in a bond for a given change in the yield; that is, for small changes in yield, the price movements of most bonds will vary proportionally with modified duration. This is shown by Equation 17-11, *which is an approximation.*[16]

$$\text{Percentage change in bond price} \approx -D^* \times \text{Yield change} \tag{17-11}$$

or

$$\Delta P/P \approx -D^* \Delta r \tag{17-12}$$

where

ΔP = change in price
P = the price of the bond
−D* = modified duration with a negative sign (the negative sign occurs because of the inverse relation between price changes and yield changes)
Δr = the instantaneous change in yield in decimal form

Example 17-15 Using our same bond with a modified duration of 3.861, assume an instantaneous yield change of 20 basis points (+0.0020) from 10 to 10.20 percent. The approximate change in price, based on Equation 17-12, would be (multiplying by 100 to put it on a percentage basis):

$$\Delta P/P = -3.861 \times (+0.0020) \times 100 = -0.772\%$$

---

[16] This formula can provide an exact estimate of the percentage price change if the change in yield is very small and the security does not involve options.

Given the original price of the bond of $1,000, this percentage price change would result in an estimated bond price of $992.28 (1,000 − [0.00772 × $1,000]. For very small changes in yield, Equation 17-11 or 17-12 produces a good approximation.[17]

In summary, a bond's modified duration shows the bond's percentage change in price for a 1 percentage point change (100 basis points) in its yield. It can be used to measure the price risk of a bond or a bond portfolio since the same holds true for a portfolio of bonds.

Convexity Although Equation 17-11 generally provides only an approximation, for very small changes in the required yield the approximation is quite close and at times could be exact. However, as the changes become larger the approximation becomes poorer. The problem is that modified duration produces symmetric percentage-price change estimates using Equation 17-11 (if r had decreased 0.20 percent, the price change would have been +0.772 percent) when, in actuality, the price-yield relationship is not linear. This relationship is, in fact, curvilinear, as Figure 17-4 shows.

We refer to the curved nature of the price-yield relationship as the bond's convexity (the relationship is said to be convex because it opens upward). More formally, **convexity** is a term used to refer to the degree to which duration changes as the yield to maturity changes. The degree of convexity is not the same for all bonds. Calculations of price changes should properly account for this convexity in order to improve the approximation of a bond's price change given some yield change.[18]

To understand the convexity issue, Figure 17-5 repeats the analysis from Figure 17-3 which showed a 10-percent coupon bond at different market yields and prices. We can think of modified duration graphically as the slope of a line tangent to the convex price-yield curve of Figure 17-5 at the current price and yield of the bond, which is assumed to be $1,000 and 10 percent.[19] In effect, we are using a tangent line to measure the slope of the curve that depicts bond prices as a function of market yields. For a very small change

Convexity A measure of the degree to which the relationship between a bond's price and yield departs from a straight line

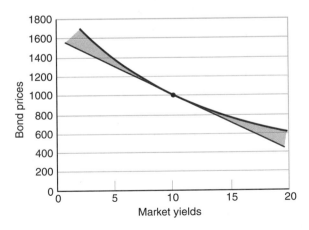

Figure 17-5

Convex relationship between yields and prices and tangent line representing modified duration for a 10-percent, 10-year bond.

---

[17] To prove this, we could solve for the price of this bond using a YTM of 10.20 percent. If we did, we would find that the price should decline to $992.32, a percentage decline of 0.768 percent as compared to our estimate of 0.772 percent. For larger changes in yield, such as 100 or 200 basis points, the approximate percentage price change is less good.
[18] An in-depth discussion of convexity is beyond the scope of this text. For a more detailed discussion, see Frank J. Fabozzi and T. Dessa Fabozzi, *The Handbook of Fixed Income Securities*. Fourth Edition. Irwin Professional Publishing, 1995.
[19] Technically, the slope of the tangent line in Figure 17-5 is equal to the negative of modified duration multiplied by the bond's current market price.

in yield, such as a few basis points, the slope of the line—the modified duration—provides a good approximation for the rate of change in price given a change in yield. As the change in yield increases, the error that results from using a straight line to estimate a bond's price behavior as given by a curve increases.[20]

As we move away from the point of tangency in Figure 17-5 in either direction, we underestimate the change in price of the bond using duration; that is, the price change is always more favorable than suggested by the duration. Notice that the shaded area in Figure 17-5 captures the convexity areas both above and below the starting point of 10 percent and $1,000. If yields decrease, prices increase, and the duration tangent line fails to indicate the true higher price, which is given by the curve. Conversely, when yields increase, prices decrease, but the duration tangent line overstates the amount of the price decrease relative to the true convex relationship. This helps to illustrate what is meant by the term *positive convexity*.

Convexity is largest for low coupon bonds, long-maturity bonds, and low yields to maturity. If convexity is large, large changes in duration are implied, with corresponding inaccuracies in forecasts of price changes. Therefore, when dealing with securities that have high convexity, the convexity effect on price change must be considered.

Convexity calculations can be made similar to those with modified duration discussed earlier. These calculations produce an approximate percentage-price change due to convexity which can be added to the approximate percentage-price change based on modified duration discussed earlier. This *total percentage price change* is still an approximation, but it is considerably improved over that using only modified duration.

Some Conclusions on Duration What does this analysis of price volatility mean to bond investors? The message is simple—to obtain the maximum (minimum) price volatility from a bond, investors should choose bonds with the longest (shortest) duration. If an investor already owns a portfolio of bonds, he or she can act to increase the average modified duration of the portfolio if a decline in interest rates is expected and the investor is attempting to achieve the largest price appreciation possible. Fortunately, duration is additive, which means that a bond portfolio's modified duration is a (market-value)—weighted average of each individual bond's modified duration.

How popular is the duration concept in today's investment world? This concept has become widely known and referred to in the popular press. Investors can find duration numbers in a variety of sources, particularly with regard to bond funds.

Although duration is an important measure of bond risk, it is not necessarily always the most appropriate one. Duration measures volatility, which is important, but is only one aspect of the risk in bonds. If an investor considers volatility to be an acceptable proxy for risk, duration is the measure of risk to use along with the correction for convexity. Duration may not be a complete measure of bond risk, but it does reflect some of the impact of changes in interest rates.

Summary

▶ The level of market interest rates for short-term, risk-free securities is a function of the real rate of interest and inflationary expectations. Inflationary expectations are the primary variable in understanding changes in market rates for short-term, default-free securities.

[20] As the yield changes, the tangency line and slope also change; that is, modified duration changes as yield changes.

▶ Other interest rates vary from the short-term risk-less rate as a result of maturity differential and risk premiums.

▶ The yield to maturity is defined as the compound rate of return an investor will receive from a bond purchased at the current market price and held to maturity.

▶ The yield to call is the expected yield to the end of the deferred call period when a bond first can be called.

▶ The horizon return is the total rate of return earned on a bond over some time period given a specified reinvestment rate of return.

▶ A security's intrinsic value is its estimated value, or the present value of the expected cash flows from that asset. To calculate intrinsic value, the expected cash flows, specified as to amounts and timing, and the discount rate or required rate of return are needed.

▶ Bonds are valued using a present value process. The cash flows for a bond—interest payments and principal repayments—are discounted at the bond's required yield.

▶ Bond prices change over time independent of other factors, because they must be worth their face value (typically, $1,000) on the maturity date.

▶ Bond prices move inversely with interest rates, with price increasing (decreasing) as the required yield decreases (increases).

▶ Changes in bond prices are directly related to time to maturity and inversely related to bond coupons.

▶ The two bond variables of major importance in assessing the change in price of a bond, given a change in interest rates, are its coupon and its maturity.

▶ Duration, stated in years, is the weighted average time to recovery of all interest payments plus principal repayment.

▶ Duration expands with time to maturity but at a decreasing rate, and it is inversely related to coupon and yield to maturity.

▶ The modified duration can be used to calculate the percentage price change in a bond for a given change in the bond's yield to maturity.

▶ The bond price-yield relationship is not linear but convex, and precise calculations of price changes should properly account for this convexity.

Key Words

Basis points	Horizon return	Real risk-free rate of interest
Bond-equivalent yield	Interest on interest	Reinvestment rate risk
Convexity	Intrinsic value	Yield to call
Current yield	Modified duration	Yield to maturity (YTM)
Duration	Realized compound yield (RCY)	

Questions

17-1 Define YTM. How is YTM determined?

17-2 Why is YTM important?

17-3 What does it mean to say that YTM is an expected yield?

17-4 If YTM is merely a promised yield, why do investors not use some other measure of yield?

17-5 What is meant by interest on interest?

17-6 Which bond is more affected by interest-on-interest considerations?
   a. Bond A—12-percent coupon, 20 years to maturity
   b. Bond B—6-percent coupon, 25 years to maturity

17-7 Distinguish between YTM and RCY. How does interest on interest affect the RCY?

17-8 How can bond investors eliminate the reinvestment rate risk inherent in bonds?

17-9 How is the intrinsic value of any asset determined? How are intrinsic value and present value related?

17-10 How is the price of a bond determined? Why is this process relatively straightforward for a bond?

17-11 What effect does the use of semiannual discounting have on the value of a bond in relation to annual discounting?

17-12 What are the implications of Malkiel's bond price theorems to bond investors? Which two bond variables are of major importance in assessing bond price changes?

17-13 How does duration differ from time to maturity? What does duration tell you?

17-14 How is duration related to time to maturity? to coupon? Do the same relationships hold for a zero-coupon bond?

17-15 Assume that a bond investor wishes to maximize the potential price volatility from a portfolio of bonds about to be constructed. What should this investor seek in the way of coupon, maturity, and duration?

17-16 Is duration a complete measure of bond risk? Is it the best measure?

17-17 When is a bond selling at a discount based on coupon rate and current yield? A premium?

17-18 What assumptions are involved in calculating the horizon return?

17-19 How is duration related to the final maturity of the bond? the coupon payments? the yield to maturity?

17-20 What is meant by convexity? Why should bond investors consider it?

Demonstration Problems

17-1 Calculate the Price of a Bond using annual coupons and semi-annual coupons: Consider a bond with the following characteristics:

C = an $80 annual coupon; c = a $40 semi-annual coupon

par = $1,000 face value

r = 0.05, the semi-annual discount rate, the going market interest rate on similar securities

n = exactly three years—the time to maturity under two different conditions:

a. Annual coupon payments, $80, are received at the end of each year Assumption A
b. Semiannual coupon payments, $40, are received every six months Assumption B

Under either condition, the price of the bond is the present value of the discounted cash flows, as follows:

Future Date	Assumption A	Assumption B
6 months		$40/(1.05)$ = $38.095
1 year	$80/(1.10)$ = $72.727	$40/(1.05)^2$ = $36.281
1.5 years		$40/(1.05)^3$ = $34.554
2 years	$80/(1.10)^2$ = $66.116	$40/(1.05)^4$ = $32.908
2.5 years		$40/(1.05)^5$ = $31.341
3 years	$80/(1.10)^3$ = $60.105	$40/(1.05)^6$ = $29.849
3 years	$1000/(1.10)^3$ = 751.315	$1000/(1.05)^6$ = 746.215
Price	$950.260	$949.243

Since the discount rate (10 percent) exceeds the coupon rate (8 percent), the bond is selling at a discount. The prices differ because of the timing of the coupon payments.

17-2   Calculate the Price of a Bond, Alternative Formula:
Here is an equivalent formula, used in bond tables, that appears to be more complex but actually is easier to calculate. For the bond described in Demonstration Problem 17-1, the value of the sum of the coupon payments can be calculated together with the discounted value of par. For the annual coupons (Assumption A):

$$P = \frac{C}{r}\left[1 - \frac{1}{(1 + r)^t}\right] + \frac{Par}{(1 + r)^t} = \frac{80}{0.10}\left[1 - \frac{1}{(1.10)^3}\right] + \frac{1,000}{(1.10)^3}$$

$$= 198.948 + 751.315 = \$950.26$$

Using semiannual coupons and discount rates (Assumption B):

$$P = \frac{C/2}{r/2}\left[1 - \frac{1}{(1 + r/2)^{2t}}\right] + \frac{Par}{(1 + r/2)^{2t}}$$

$$= \frac{40}{0.05}\left[1 - \frac{1}{(1.05)^6}\right] + \frac{1,000}{(1.05)^6}$$

$$= \$203.028 + \$746.215 = \$949.24$$

17-3   The Calculation of Duration on a Semiannual Basis:

C = an \$80 coupon = (0.08)(\$1,000); c = a \$40 semi-annual coupon

par = \$1,000 face value

r = 0.05, the semi-annual discount rate, the going market interest rate on similar securities

n = exactly three years—the time to maturity

(1) Future Date	(2) PV of Cash Flows	(3)/ 949.243	(4) Years	(3) × (4)
6 months	38.095	0.04013	0.5	0.02007
1 year	36.281	0.03822	1.0	0.03822
1.5 years	34.554	0.03640	1.5	0.05460
2 years	32.908	0.03467	2.0	0.06934
2.5 years	31.341	0.03302	2.5	0.08255
3 years	29.849	0.03145	3.0	0.09435
3 years	746.215	0.78612	3.0	2.35836
Sum	949.246	1.00120		2.71749
				Duration = 2.72 years

Problems

17-1   Using the information in Demonstration Problem 17-1, if the coupon rate for the bond is 10 percent and the discount rate is 8 percent, with the same three years to maturity, show that the price of the bond is \$1,051.54 with annual discounting and \$1,052.24 with semi-annual discounting. Use a calculator to determine the discount factors.
   What would be the price of this bond if both the coupon rate and the discount rate were 10 percent?

17-2   Using the information in Demonstration Problem 17-2, solve for the price of the bond in Problem 17-1 using both annual and semiannual discounting. Use a calculator to solve these problems.

17-3 With reference to Problem 17-2, what would be the price of the bond if the coupon were paid quarterly?

17-4 Calculate the price of a 10-percent coupon bond with eight years to maturity, given an appropriate discount rate of 12 percent, using both annual and semiannual discounting. Use the tables contained in the Interest Tables at the end of the text.

17-5 Calculate the price of the bond in Problem 17-4 if the maturity is 20 years rather than eight years. Use semiannual discounting and the tables in the appendix. Which of Malkiel's principles are illustrated when comparing the price of this bond to the price determined in Problem 17-1?

17-6 The YTM on a 10-percent, 15-year bond is 12 percent. Calculate the price of the bond.

17-7 Calculate the YTM for a 10-year zero-coupon bond sold at $400. Recalculate the YTM if the bond had been priced at $300.

17-8 Calculate the realized compound yield for a 10-percent bond with 20 years to maturity and an expected reinvestment rate of 8 percent.

17-9 Consider a 12-percent 10-year bond purchased at face value. Based on Table 17-1 and assuming a reinvestment rate of 10 percent, calculate:

a. The interest on interest
b. The total return
c. The realized return

17-10 Consider a junk bond with a 12-percent coupon and 20 years to maturity. The current required rate of return for this bond is 15 percent. What is its price? What would its price be if the required yield rose to 17 percent? 20 percent?

17-11 A 12-percent coupon bond with 10 years to maturity is currently selling for $913.50. Determine the modified duration for this bond.

17-12 Consider a 4-percent coupon bond with 15 years to maturity. Determine the YTM that would be necessary to drive the price of this bond to $300.

17-13 Determine the point at which duration decreases with maturity for a 4-percent bond with an original maturity of 15 years. Use increments in maturity of five years. The market yield on this bond is 15 percent.

17-14 Calculate the yield to first call for a 10-percent, 10-year bond that is callable five years from now. The current market price is $970 and the call price is $1,050.

17-15 Calculate the YTM for the following bonds.

a. A 12-percent, 20-year bond with a current price of $975
b. A 6-percent, 10-year bond with a current price of $836
c. A 9-percent, 8-year bond with a current price of $714

17-16 Ohio Oil's bonds, the 10s of 2018, are selling at 109 3/8. Exactly 14 years remain to maturity. Determine the

a. Current yield
b. Yield to maturity

17-17 Using Problem 17-16, assume that 28 years remain to maturity. How would the yield to maturity change? Does the current yield change?

17-18 Mittra Products' bonds, the 11s of 2019, sell to yield 12.5 percent. Exactly 15 years remain to maturity. Determine the current market price of the bonds. If the YTM had been 11.5 percent, what would the price of the bonds be? Explain why this difference occurs.

17-19 A 12-percent coupon bond has 20 years to maturity. It is currently selling for 20 percent less than face value. Determine its YTM.

17-20 Given a 10-percent, three-year bond with a price of $1,052.24, where the market yield is 8 percent, calculate its duration using the format illustrated in Table 17-3.

17-21 Using the duration from Problem 17-20, determine:
   a. The modified duration
   b. The percentage change in the price of the bond if r changes 0.50 percent.

17-22 Calculate the duration of a 12-percent coupon bond with 10 years remaining to maturity and selling at par. Use annual interest rates.

17-23 Given the duration calculated in Problem 17-22, calculate the percentage change in bond price if the market discount rate for this bond declines by 0.75 percent.

CFA
17-24 Assume a $10,000 par value zero coupon bond with a term-to-maturity at issue of 10 years and a market yield of 8 percent.

1. Determine the duration of the bond.
2. Calculate the initial issue price of the bond at a market yield of 8 percent, assuming semiannual compounding.
3. Twelve months after issue, this bond is selling to yield 12 percent.

Calculate its then-current market price. Calculate your pre-tax rate of return assuming you owned this bond during the 12-month period.

   Assume a 10-percent coupon bond with a Macaulay duration of 8 years, semiannual payments, and a market rate of 8 percent.

1. Determine the modified duration of the bond.
2. Calculate the percent change in price for the bond, assuming market rates decline by two percentage points (200 basis points).

CFA
17-25 You are asked to consider the following bond for possible inclusion in your company's fixed income portfolio:

Issuer	Coupon	Yield to Maturity	Maturity	Duration
Wiser Company	8%	8%	10 years	7.25 years

1. Explain why the Wiser bond's duration is less than its maturity.

2. Explain whether a bond's duration or its maturity is a better measure of the bond's sensitivity to changes in interest rates.

Briefly explain the impact on the duration of the Wiser Company bond under each of the following conditions:

   I. The coupon is 4 percent rather than 8 percent
   II. The yield to maturity is 4 percent rather than 8 percent
   III. The maturity is seven years rather than 10 years

Web Resources

**For additional resources visit our dynamic Web site located at
www.wiley.com/college/jones.**

☐ *No Luck At All*—The concepts of bond valuation and risk are the focus of a decision
to invest in one of three fixed-income securities. Estimating appropriate discount
rates as well as calculating and using duration is part of the case environment. The
case also presents an ethical dilemma.

☐ Internet Exercises—This chapter analyzes bond yields and prices. The Web exercises
will take you to sites that post bond prices and yields; you will get the opportunity to
see how these numbers relate to each other. You will also see the relation between
bond duration and bond price volatility.

Exercise 1: Goes over the mechanics of bond and bill pricing.

Exercise 2: Explores the notion of bond duration.

Exercise 3: Explores bond convexity.

☐ Multiple Choice Self Test

☐ Appendix 17-A—Convertible Bonds

Selected References

Basic bond information can be found in:

Faerber, Esme. *Fundamentals of the Bond Market*. McGraw Hill, 2001

Additional comprehensive information about bonds can be found in:

Thau, Annette. *The Bond Book: Everything Investors Need to Know About Treasuries, Municipals, GNMAs, Corporates, Zeros, Bond Funds, Money Market Funds, and More.* McGraw-Hill
Professional Publishing, 2000.

Detailed information on fixed-income securities, 62 chapters written by well-known authorities on
fixed-income securities, can be found in:

Fabozzi, Frank J. Editor. *The Handbook of Fixed Income Securities*. Fifth Edition. Irwin Professional Publishing, 1997.

chapter *18*

Bonds:
Analysis and
Strategy

C hapter 18 concludes Part V on fixed-income securities by discussing issues in the management of a bond portfolio. We consider why investors buy bonds as well as the issues an investor should consider in managing a bond portfolio. The basic strategies available to a bond investor are organized along the lines of passive versus active strategies, an important distinction that also applies to stock investors.

AFTER READING THIS CHAPTER YOU WILL BE ABLE TO:

▶ Analyze the reasons why investors buy bonds.
▶ Recognize important considerations in managing a bond portfolio, including the term structure of interest rates and yield spreads.

▶ Differentiate between the passive and active strategies for managing a bond portfolio.
▶ Consider how both conservative investors and aggressive investors go about building a fixed-income portfolio.

In the previous chapter, we studied the calculation of bond prices and yields as well as their relationships. From that analysis we know the importance of interest rate changes as well as the impact of coupon and time to maturity on bond prices, given a change in yields. The call feature also can affect the price and yield on a bond, as can a variety of other issuer-unique factors such as the credit rating, the collateral, sinking fund provisions, and any conversion feature that may exist.

A consideration of bond analysis and strategies is a natural capstone to our discussion of bond yields and prices. In the final analysis, bond investors construct and manage portfolios of securities, whether bonds only or combinations of bonds and other securities such as common stocks. In doing so, they may very well employ concepts we have previously studied, such as duration. They must also grapple with the overall strategy issue facing investors of whether to be active or passive in their investment approach.

Why Buy Bonds?

As noted in Chapter 6, the total return on bonds can be separated into two components, which helps to explain why bonds appeal to both conservative investors seeking steady income and aggressive investors seeking capital gains. A wide range of investors participate in the fixed-income securities marketplace, ranging from individuals who own a few government or corporate bonds to large institutional investors who own billions of dollars of bonds. Most of these investors are presumably seeking the basic *steady return–low risk* characteristics that most bonds offer; however, quite different overall objectives can be accomplished by purchasing bonds. It is worthwhile to consider these points.

As fixed-income securities, bonds are desirable to many investors, because they offer a steady stream of interest income over the life of the obligation and a return of principal at maturity. The promised yield on a bond held to maturity is known at the time of purchase. Barring default by the issuer, the buyers will have the bond principal returned to them at maturity. By holding to maturity, investors can escape the risk that interest rates will rise, thereby driving down the price of the bonds, although other risks may not be eliminated.

As an illustration of the return and risk situation for this type of investor, who is seeking steady returns, consider long-term Treasury securities for the period 1871 to 2002.[1] There is no practical risk of default. At the end of 2002, investors in these government bonds would have earned an average compound growth rate of 4.92 percent. Over the earlier subperiod from 1871 through 1935, the average annual compound return was 4.42 percent, whereas for the later subperiod from 1936 to 2002 it was 5.40 percent. The point is that government bonds, as well as corporate bonds, offer a stream of steady returns over long periods of time with small risks, as measured by the standard deviation.

Other investors are interested in bonds exactly because bond prices will change as interest rates change. If interest rates rise (fall), bond prices will fall (rise).

These investors are interested not in holding the bonds to maturity but rather in earning the capital gains that are possible if they correctly anticipate movements in interest rates. Because bonds can be purchased on margin, large potential gains are possible from speculating on interest rates over relatively short periods. (Of course, large losses are also possible.)

To obtain some idea of the changes in returns that can result from changes in interest rates, consider again Treasury bonds. Some of the total annual returns were very large, far beyond the yield component alone. In 1982, for example, the total return was approx-

---

[1] These data, and the returns below on Treasuries, are based on Jack W. Wilson and Charles P. Jones, "Long-Term Returns and Risk for Bonds," *The Journal of Portfolio Management*, Vol. 23, No. 3, Spring 1997, pp. 15–28, updated for recent years.

imately 42 percent; in 1985, 32 percent; in 1995, 31 percent; in 2000, 20 percent, and in 2002, 17 percent. Clearly, successful bond speculation in each of those years resulted in very large returns.

Of course, losses also occur as a result of interest rate changes, both for longer periods and for short periods.

Example 18-1 From November 1, 2001 to April 1, 2002, the 10-year Treasury bond rate went from 4.2 percent to 5.4 percent, and the face value of these bonds went down more than 9 percent.

Speculation has been heavy in the bond markets in recent years. In the past, bonds were viewed as very stable instruments whose prices fluctuated very little in the short run. This situation changed drastically in the 1980s, however, with the bond markets becoming quite volatile. Interest rates in the early 1980s reached record levels, causing large changes in bond prices.

Bond speculators encompass a wide range of participants from financial institutions to individual investors. All are trying to take advantage of an expected movement in interest rates. Thus, investors seeking the income component from bonds as well as investors attempting to speculate with bonds are keenly interested in the level of interest rates and any likely changes in the level. A key part of any bond analysis, therefore, must involve these interest rate considerations.

BUYING FOREIGN BONDS

Why do U.S. investors consider foreign bonds for inclusion in their portfolios? One obvious reason is that foreign bonds may offer higher returns at a given point in time than alternative domestic bonds. Investors can make a case for buying foreign bonds on the basis of potentially attractive returns.

Example 18-2 In mid-2002, European government bonds were paying more than U.S. Treasuries. British bonds, as one example, were yielding 4.7 percent when comparable Treasuries were yielding 2.8 percent. The reasons for this spread centered on differing monetary policies, and the yield differentials were expected to persist for several years.

A second important reason for buying foreign bonds is the diversification aspect. Diversification is extremely important both in a stock portfolio and a bond portfolio.

Individual investors have often found it difficult to invest directly in European bonds. Some brokerage firms do not offer foreign bonds to individual investors, whereas most that do require a minimum investment of at least $50,000. Selling foreign bonds that are directly owned also can be a problem. Secondary markets in Europe are not comparable to the huge U.S. Treasury markets. This means that individual investors selling small amounts of foreign bonds abroad will typically incur significant price concessions. Here is a case where most investors are better off to invest via bond mutual funds.

What About Currency Risk? Investors in foreign bonds (or any other security) must deal with exchange-rate risk. An adverse movement in the dollar can result in an American investor's return being lower than the return on the asset, or even negative. For example, if the euro weakens instead of strengthens, an investor's dollar-denominated return suffers. On the other hand, the euro strengthened against the dollar in 2001 to 2003, providing a currency gain.

Investors who are considering direct investment in foreign bonds face the additional issue of transaction costs. Dollars must be converted into the foreign currency to make purchases, and receipts from the foreign bonds must be converted back into dollars. On small transactions, these costs can significantly impact returns. However, this situation has improved with the introduction of the euro, which provides a common currency for multiple countries.

Important Considerations in Managing a Bond Portfolio

UNDERSTANDING THE BOND MARKET

The first consideration for any investor is to understand the basic nature of the bond market. It has been commonplace to talk about the bond market benefiting from a weak economy. If the economy is growing slowly, interest rates may decline, and bond prices rise. In effect, a decline in economic growth may lead to fewer investment opportunities, leading savers to increase their demand for bonds, which pushes bond prices up and bond yields down. Talk of a rapidly growing economy is thought to frighten bond investors.

The relationship that really matters in this view is between bond yields and inflation, not between economic growth and bond yields. As we know from Chapter 17, interest rates reflect expected inflation. If investors expect a rise in inflation, they demand more from a bond to compensate for the expected decline in the purchasing power of their cash flows from the bond investment. Therefore, an increase in expected inflation will tend to depress bond prices and increase yields.

Figure 18-1 shows a plot of the yield on 10-year Treasuries, moving averages of real Gross Domestic Product (GDP), and the growth rate of the Consumer Price Index (CPI) over the period 1962 to 1992.[2] Note that real GDP growth had no trend over the 30-year period, whereas bond yields had an upward trend for approximately the first 20 years and a downward trend thereafter. The CPI growth rate behaved in a similar manner. Inflation tended to move counter to GDP growth over business cycles, and more than offset any increased demand for bonds resulting from a weakening economy.

Figure 18-1

Real gross domestic product growth rates, consumer price index growth rates, and yields on 10-year treasuries, 1962–1992.

SOURCE: David C. Wheelock, "What Drives the Bond Market," *Monetary Trends*, The Federal Reserve Bank of St. Louis, October 1994, p. 1.

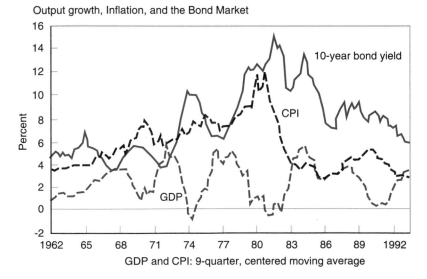

Output growth, Inflation, and the Bond Market

GDP and CPI: 9-quarter, centered moving average

---

[2] This discussion draws heavily on David C. Wheelock, "What Drives the Bond Market," *Monetary Trends*, The Federal Reserve Bank of St. Louis, October 1994, p. 1.

Consider the more recent period from 1981, which stands out in Figure 18-1. Although it appears that bond yields declined with declining GDP growth, the linkage with the growth in the CPI is clearer. Bond yields declined and bond prices rose as inflation growth declined. What makes this analysis tricky is that bond yields can continue to rise after inflation has peaked, because investors are reacting to *expectations* of future inflation rather than actual current inflation.

Therefore, although the bond market appears to like a weak economy, *the bond market clearly dislikes inflation.* Bond investors fear inflation because of its negative effect on fixed-income securities, and they favor Federal Reserve (Fed) actions that temper economic growth and reduce inflation. Investors may react quite favorably to a tightening of monetary policy, because this helps to calm inflation fears.

Leverage has become a big factor in the bond markets, and this leverage has magnified the swings in bond prices. According to some sources, leveraged speculation resulted in the bond rally of 1993 and a major debacle in 1994. *Fortune* magazine estimated that as of mid-September 1994, the rise in rates on the 30-year Treasury bond (about 1.5 percentage points) resulted in a $600 billion loss on U.S. bonds and a possible $1.5 trillion loss worldwide.[3] Is it any wonder that *Fortune* titled this article "The Great Bond Market Massacre"?

Global Factors and the Bond Markets The bond market may also respond favorably to a strengthening of the dollar. A stronger dollar increases the value of dollar-denominated assets to foreign investors.

Other events of a global nature affect the bond market. When the Brazilian crisis erupted around the end of 1998, there was a flight to safety in the form of purchases of Treasuries. As the crisis diminished, this demand for Treasuries decreased. On the other hand, with Japanese interest rates on the rise, bond investors feared that Japanese investors would liquidate their holdings of Treasuries in order to buy their own government bonds. Such a movement decreases the demand for Treasuries and hence their prices.

THE TERM STRUCTURE OF INTEREST RATES

Term Structure of Interest Rates The relationship between time to maturity and yields for a particular category of bonds

The **term structure of interest rates** refers to the relationship between time to maturity and yields for a particular category of bonds at a particular point in time. Ideally, other factors are held constant, particularly the risk of default. The easiest way to do this is to examine U.S. Treasury securities, which have no practical risk of default, have no sinking fund, and are taxable. By eliminating those that are callable and those that may have some special feature, a quite homogeneous sample of bonds is obtained for analysis.

Yield Curve A graphical depiction of the relationship between yields and time for bonds that are identical except for maturity

Yield Curves The term structure is usually plotted in the form of a **yield curve**, which is a graphical depiction of the relationship between yields and time for bonds that are identical except for maturity. The horizontal axis represents time to maturity, whereas the vertical axis represents yield to maturity.

Figure 18-2(*a*) shows yield curves for recent periods in 2002 and early 2003 for Treasury securities. These upward-sloping curves are considered to be typical; that is, interest rates that rise with maturity are considered to be the "normal" pattern. Such upward-sloping curves can have various degrees of steepness.

Figure 18-2(*b*) shows additional yield curves for Treasuries. Note the flattened yield curve in January 2002 and the downward-sloping curves for June and July, with short

---

[3] See Al Ehrbar, "The Great Bond Market Massacre," *Fortune*, October 17, 1994, pp. 77–92.

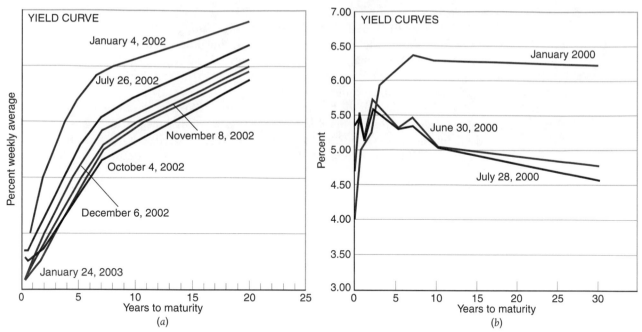

Figure 18-2

Yield curves for Treasury securities, various periods.

Source: Federal Reserve Banks of St. Louis and Cleveland.

rates above long rates. These "inverted" yield curves are unusual, and almost always precede a recession. And, in fact, as we know from Chapter 13, the latest recession is officially dated as starting in March 2001.

Most observations about yield curves involve tendencies and not exact relationships. For example, there generally is a negative relationship between short rates and the yield spread. A higher short rate typically is associated with a flatter yield curve, because long rates do not increase by quite as much. However, this relationship does not always hold.

Term Structure Theories   A theory of the term structure of interest rates is needed to explain the shape and slope of the yield curve and why it shifts over time. Theories traditionally advanced are the expectations theory, the liquidity premium theory, the preferred habitat theory, and the market segmentation theory.

Expectations Theory

States that the long-term rate of interest is equal to an average of the short-term rates that are expected to prevail over the long-term period

Forward Rates

Unobservable rates expected to prevail in the future

The *pure or "unbiased"* **expectations theory** of the term structure of interest rates asserts that financial market participants determine security yields such that the return from holding an *n*-period security equals the average return expected from holding a series of one-year securities over the same *n* periods. In other words, the long-term rate of interest is equal to an average of the present yield on short-term securities plus the expected future yields on short-term securities that are expected to prevail over the long-term period. For each period, the total rate of return is expected to be the same on all securities regardless of time to maturity.

In effect, the term structure consists of a set of forward rates and a current known rate. **Forward rates** are rates that are expected to prevail in the future; that is, they are unobservable but anticipated future rates.

Under the expectations theory, long rates must be an average of the present and future short-term rates. For example, a three-year bond would carry an interest rate that is an average of the current rate for one year and the expected forward rates for the next two years. The same principle holds for any number of periods; therefore, the market rate for any period to maturity can be expressed as an average of the current rate and the applicable forward rates. Technically, the average involved is a geometric rather than an arithmetic average.

For expositional purposes:

$_tR_n$ = the current known yield (i.e., at time t) on a security with n periods to maturity

$_{t+1}r_n$ = the yield expected to prevail one year from today (at time $t + 1$) for n periods—these are forward rates

The rate for the three-year bond referred to above must be a geometric average of the current one-year rate ($_tR_1$) and the expected forward rates for the subsequent two years.
Therefore, in equation form

$$_tR_3 = [(1 + {}_tR_1)(1 + {}_{t+1}r_1)(1 + {}_{t+2}r_1)]^{1/3} - 1.0 \qquad (18\text{-}1)$$

where

$_tR_3$ = the rate on a three-year bond
$(1 + {}_tR_1)$ = the current known rate on a one-year bond
$(1 + {}_{t+1}r_1)$ = the expected rate on a bond with one year to maturity beginning one year from now
$(1 + {}_{t+2}r_1)$ = the expected rate on a bond with one year to maturity beginning two years from now

Example 18-3

Assume the current one-year bond rate ($_tR_1$) is 0.07 and the two forward rates are 0.075 ($_{t+1}r_1$) and 0.082 ($_{t+2}r_1$). The rate for a three-year bond, $_tR_3$, would be

$$_tR_3 = [(1.07)(1.075)(1.082)]^{1/3} - 1.0$$
$$= 1.07566 - 1.0$$
$$= 0.0757 \text{ or } 7.57\%$$

The same principle applies for any number of periods. Any long-term rate is a geometric average of consecutive one-period rates.

Forward rates cannot be easily measured, but they can be inferred for any one-year future period. The expectations theory, however, does not say that these future expected rates will be correct; it simply says that there is a relationship between rates today and rates expected in the future.

Under this hypothesis, investors can expect the same return regardless of the choice of investment. Any combination of securities for a specified period will have the same expected return. For example, a five-year bond will have the same expected return as a two-year bond held to maturity plus a three-year bond bought at the beginning of the third year. The assumption under this hypothesis is that expected future rates are equal to computed forward rates. Profit-seeking individuals will exploit any differences between forward rates and expected rates, ensuring that they equilibrate.

Liquidity Preference Theory States that interest rates reflect the sum of current and expected short rates, as in the expectations theory, plus liquidity (risk) premiums

The second theory, the **liquidity preference theory**, states that interest rates reflect the sum of current and expected short rates, as in the expectations theory, plus liquidity (risk) premiums. Because uncertainty increases with time, investors prefer to lend for the short run. Borrowers, however, prefer to borrow for the long run in order to be assured of funds. Investors receive a liquidity premium to induce them to lend long term, although paying a price premium (in the form of lower yields) for investing short term. The implication of this theory is that longer term bonds should offer higher yields.

The difference between the liquidity preference theory and the expectations theory is the recognition that interest rate expectations are uncertain. Risk-averse investors seek

Market Segmentation Theory   States that investors confine their activities to specific maturity sectors and are unwilling to shift from one sector to another to take advantage of opportunities

Preferred Habitat Theory   States that investors have preferred maturity sectors in which they seek to invest but are willing to shift to other maturities if they can expect to be adequately compensated

to be compensated for this uncertainty. Forward rates and estimated future rates are not the same; they differ by the amount of the liquidity premiums.

The third hypothesis for explaining the term structure of interest rates is the **market segmentation theory**. This theory states that various institutional investors, having different maturity needs dictated by the nature of their liabilities, confine themselves to specific maturity segments. Investors are not willing to shift from one maturity sector to another to take advantage of any opportunities that may arise. Under the market segmentation theory, the shape of the yield curve is determined by the supply and demand conditions for securities within each of the multiple maturity sectors.

The **preferred habitat theory** is similar to, but not identical with, the market segmentation theory. Under this hypothesis, investors have preferred maturity sectors, or habitats. For example, a thrift institution with many five-year certificates of deposit (CDs) to pay off will not wish to take the reinvestment rate risk that would result from investing in one-year Treasury bills.

What if imbalances arise in a given maturity range between the demand and supply of funds? *The preferred habitat theory states that borrowers and lenders can be induced to shift maturities if they are adequately compensated by an appropriate risk premium*, which distinguishes this theory from the market segmentation theory. The implication of this theory for the term structure is that both expectations concerning future interest rates and risk premiums play a role, and the yield curve can take any shape.[4]

The preferred habitat theory is related to, but not identical with, the market segmentation theory. This theory states that the various institutional investors, having different maturity needs dictated by the nature of their liabilities, confine themselves to specific maturity segments. Investors are not willing to shift from one maturity sector to another to take advantage of any opportunities that may arise. Under the segmentation theory, the shape of the yield curve is determined by the supply and demand conditions for securities within each of the multiple maturity sectors.

Which of these theories is correct? The issue of the term structure has not been resolved; although many empirical studies have been done, the results are at least partially conflicting. Therefore, definitive statements cannot be made. The empirical evidence on the expectations hypothesis is equivocal at best. The evidence on the liquidity premium hypothesis is the most unequivocal. Substantial evidence suggests that risk premiums exist, but their behavior over time is subject to debate.

In actual bond practice, market observers and participants do not tend to be strict adherents to a particular theory. Rather they accept the reasonable implications of all three and try to use any available information in assessing the shape of the yield curve. For example, many market participants will focus on expectations but allow for liquidity premiums.

Since the 1930s, upward-sloping yield curves have been the norm, as would be predicted by the liquidity preference theory. This theory is more compatible than the other two with the study of investments, which emphasizes the risk-return trade-off that exists. The liquidity preference theory stresses the idea that because of larger risks, longer maturity securities require larger returns or compensation.[5]

Regardless of which of the above theories is correct, it seems to be reasonable to assert that investors demand a premium from long-term bonds because of their additional risk. After all, uncertainty increases with time, and as we shall learn, long-term bonds are more sensitive to interest rate fluctuations than are short-term bonds. Furthermore, the

[4] See Frank Fabozzi and Franco Modigliana, *Capital Markets: Institutions and Instruments*, 3rd edition, Prentice Hall, 2002. This book has good discussions of several important investment topics.
[5] The expectations theory categorizes investors as return maximizers, whereas the preferred habitat theory categorizes investors as risk minimizers.

typical shape of the yield curve is upward sloping, which indicates that investors are more averse to the risk of long bonds than to short-term securities.

Using the Yield Curve   Investors should use yield curves for the right reasons and understand their limitations. We consider both sides of the issue.

The yield curve should not be used to price a bond. Rather a bond should be viewed as a package of zero-coupon instruments, and the price of a bond should equal the value of all these zero-coupon instruments. To value each zero-coupon instrument, we need to know the spot rates, or yields, on zero-coupon Treasuries with the same maturity. It is possible to derive a **theoretical spot rate curve**, and apply these spot rates to price a bond.

Investors use yield curves as clues to the future. One study showed that the slope of the yield curve is a good predictor of changes in activity 12 to 18 months out.[6] All six recessions identified were preceded by a flattening or inverted yield curve (however, one inverted yield curve was not followed by a recession). A recent paper by a Federal Reserve bank found the slope of the yield curve to be the best predictor of economic growth. It also found a negative slope typically preceding a recession. Therefore, investors should be quite concerned when yield curves become inverted. This concern was justified once again in April 2000 when the Treasury yield curve was inverted. By year-end the economy had slowed down, layoffs occurred, and the stock market suffered one of its largest losses (which continued into 2001).

> **Theoretical Spot Rate Curve**   A graph depicting the relationship between spot rates and maturities, based on theoretical considerations

Example 18-4

Brazil, having already experienced a crisis, faced inverted yield curves in January 1999. Apparently, bond buyers felt there was more risk of being repaid in the short run than in the long run. They may have been influenced by the situation in Russia, where the yield curve inverted before Russia defaulted on its obligations.

THE RISK STRUCTURE OF INTEREST RATES—YIELD SPREADS

Assume that market interest rates on risk-free securities are determined as explained above. If the expected rate of inflation rises, the level of rates also rises. Similarly, if the real rate of interest were to decline, market interest rates would decline; that is, the level of rates would decrease. Furthermore, as seen in the term structure analysis, yields vary over time for issues that are otherwise homogeneous. The question that remains is, "Why do rates differ between different bond issues or segments of the bond market?"

The answer to this question lies in what bond analysts call the risk structure of interest rates (risk premiums), or simply yield spreads. **Yield spreads** refer to the relationships between various bond yields based on the particular issuer and issue characteristics of the bonds involved. Yield spreads are often calculated among different bonds holding maturity constant. They are a result of the following factors:

> **Yield Spreads**   The relationship between bond yield and the particular features on various bonds, such as quality, callability, and taxes

1. Differences in quality, or risk of default. Clearly, all other things being equal, a bond rated BAA will offer a higher yield than a similar bond rated AAA because of the difference in default risk.
2. Differences in call features. Bonds that are callable have higher yield to maturities (YTMs) than otherwise identical noncallable bonds. If the bond is called, bondholders must give it up, and they could replace it only with a bond carrying a lower YTM. Therefore, investors expect to be compensated for this risk.

---

[6] See Arturo Estrella and Gikas Hardouvelis, "The Term Structure as a Predictor of Real Economic Activity," *The Journal of Finance*, June 1991.

3. Differences in coupon rates. Bonds with low coupons have a larger part of their YTM in the form of capital gains.
4. Differences in marketability. Some bonds are more marketable than others, meaning that their liquidity is better. They can be sold either more quickly or with less of a price concession, or both. The less marketable a bond, the higher the YTM.
5. Differences in tax treatments.
6. Differences between countries.

Example 18-5

One yield spread of interest to some investors is the difference between the yields on investment-grade bonds, or Treasuries, and junk bonds.[7] This spread can change for a number of reasons. In February 1995, the spread between Treasuries and B-rated junk bonds was about 490 basis points (4.9 percent). By August 1995, the spread was 600 basis points, making the junk bonds relatively more attractive (the default rate for junk bonds historically is between 3 and 5 percent).[8]

Other Factors Affecting Yield Spreads Clearly, yield spreads are a function of the variables connected with a particular issue or issuer. Investors expect to be compensated for the risk of a particular issue, and this compensation is reflected in the risk premium. However, investors are not the only determining factor in yield spreads. The actions of borrowers also affect them. Heavy Treasury financing, for example, may cause the yield spreads between governments and corporates to narrow as the large increase in the supply of Treasury securities pushes up the yields on Treasuries.

The level of interest rates also plays a role in explaining yield spreads. As a general proposition, risk premiums tend to be high when the level of interest rates is high.

Yield Spreads over Time Yield spreads among alternative bonds may be positive or negative at any time. Furthermore, the size of the yield spread changes over time. Whenever the differences in yield become smaller, the yield spread is said to "narrow"; as the differences increase, it "widens."

As one example of how yield spreads change over time, consider one of the most prominent spreads—that between different categories of corporate bonds. Figure 18-3 shows the difference between Baa corporates (medium-grade bonds) and Aaa corporates (high-grade bonds). This risk premium has averaged 1.15 percentage points since 1970, 0.95 since 1984, and only 0.64 since the beginning of 1994 (perhaps because of fewer recessions and overall general prosperity relative to the longer run history). Following Russia's default on debt in August 1998, the risk premium rose by 20 basis points, as Figure 18-3 shows, as yields on Baa corporates rose. This was true despite bond yields declining since August 1998, as investors rushed to quality issues in the face of the uncertainty. Treasury yields fell even more as investors rushed to quality. Thus, the emerging markets crisis caused a change in the yield spreads, and investors trying to determine which bonds to hold have to be prepared for such shifts.[9]

[7] Bonds rated BB or below are regarded as being speculative with respect to capacity to pay interest and repay principal.
[8] The default rate on junk bonds can be found at Moody's Investor Services, which tracks the rate monthly: http://riskcalc.moodysrms.com/us/research/mdr.
[9] This discussion is based on "Risk Premiums among Corporate Bonds," *Monetary Trends*, November 1998, p. 1. This free publication of the Federal Reserve Bank of St. Louis is a good source of information on monetary matters and financial market events. See www.stls.frb.org.

Figure 18-3

An illustration of corporate yield spreads: the difference between Baa corporates and Aaa corporates.

SOURCE: Federal Reserve Bank of St. Louis, *Monetary Trends*, November 1998, p. 1.

It seems reasonable to assume that yield spreads widen during recessions, when investors become more risk averse, and narrow during times of economic prosperity. Since the probability of default is greater during a recession, investors demand more of a premium. Yield spreads were at their widest during the early 1930s when the Depression was at its worst. In contrast, yield spreads narrow during boom periods, because even financially weak companies have a good chance of surviving and paying their debt obligations. Some historical evidence supports these trends; thus, we can state that the yield spread varies inversely to the business cycle.

Understanding and Using the Yield Spread as an Investor Bond investors seeking opportunities in the bond market need to understand, and analyze, bond spreads. When bond default rates rise, yield spreads widen. This means that corporate bonds must yield more relative to Treasuries, and when their prices decline, some may represent good buys. In effect, new buyers receive higher yields, and have a chance for price appreciation if the yield spread narrows, as it eventually does in most cases.

What can cause corporate yield spreads (relative to Treasuries) to widen?

❏ Accounting debacles, such as those in 2002 involving WorldCom, Enron, and Tyco.
❏ Litigation problems, such as Halliburton and other companies involved in asbestos exposure.
❏ Excessive debt levels, which increase the risk of default and bankruptcy.
❏ Weak earnings, which increase the risk that the companies cannot service their debt

Smart bond investors understand that not all corporate yield spreads are justified. Markets sometimes overreact to particular issuers by being caught up in a current environment of despair or panic. For example, Halliburton's short-term bonds showed a yield spread in early 2002 of some 500 basis points while the company covered its interest obligations several times over. If Halliburton successfully defends itself, the yield spread will narrow. At the same time, Ford's bonds had an unusually wide yield spread for such a large and well-known company, because it has been suffering some problems, but in all likelihood, Ford is a survivor whose business will improve, the yield spread will narrow, and bond investors will profit (all the while collecting 7.35 percent on one of its bond issues).

Bond Strategies

We now consider the basic approaches that bond investors can use in managing their bond portfolios or the bond portion of their overall portfolio. An understanding of these strategies requires more than an understanding of the basic factors affecting the valuation and analysis of bonds.

Bond investing has become increasingly popular, no doubt as a result of record interest rates in recent years. Unfortunately, the theoretical framework for bond portfolio management has not developed to the same extent as that for common stocks. In some ways common stocks have been more "glamorous," and more attention has been devoted to them. Furthermore, more data exist for common stocks, undoubtedly because the most prominent stocks trade on the New York Stock Exchange where daily prices can be collected and analyzed. The same is not true for bonds. Even today investors may have difficulty obtaining instantaneous, current quotes on many bonds.

Despite the incomplete theory of bond portfolio management, investors must manage their bond portfolios and make investment decisions. Different bond investors have adopted different strategies depending on their risk preferences, knowledge of the bond market, and investment objectives.

For organizational purposes, and because this scheme corresponds to the two broad strategies that any investor can follow with any type of portfolio, we will concentrate primarily on passive and active management of bond portfolios while discussing a hybrid approach. Active and passive approaches can be distinguished by the types of inputs needed. Active management depends upon expectations data, whereas passive strategies do not.

PASSIVE MANAGEMENT STRATEGIES

As we learned in Chapter 12, which deals with efficient markets, many investors agree that securities are fairly priced in the sense that the expected return is commensurate with the risk taken. This belief can justify a **passive management strategy**, meaning that the investor does not actively seek out trading possibilities in an attempt to outperform the market. Passive bond strategies are based on the proposition that bond prices are fairly determined, leaving risk as the portfolio variable to control. In effect, passive management strategies are based on inputs that are known at the time rather than expectations. These strategies have a lower expected return and risk than do active strategies.

A *passive investment strategy does not mean that investors do nothing*. They must still monitor the status of their portfolios in order to match their holdings with their risk preferences and objectives. Conditions in the financial markets change quickly, and investors must also make fast changes when necessary. Passive management does not mean that investors accept changes in market conditions, securities, and so on if these changes cause undesirable modifications in the securities they hold.

The passive approach is supported by evidence for various periods of years showing that the performance of bond managers during the years examined failed to equal that of a market index. For example, reporting on a five-year period when the managers of fixed-income portfolios had an annualized total return of 14.4 percent compared to 14.5 percent for a bond index (and this was before fees) *Forbes* magazine noted, "The average pension fund would have done better with its bond money in a passive index fund."[10]

Passive Management Strategy A strategy whereby investors do not actively seek out trading possibilities in an attempt to outperform the market

---

[10] Taken from Steve Kichen, "The *Forbes*/TUCS Institutional Portfolio Report," *Forbes*, August 21, 1989, p. 112.

A recent comprehensive study examining the performance of bond mutual funds, using two samples of bond funds, found that such funds underperformed relevant indexes from the fixed-income area.[11] The results were robust across a wide choice of models. For the most part, this underperformance approximated the average management fees; therefore, before expenses, funds performed about as well as the indexes. There was no evidence of predictability using past performance to predict future performance.

A good case for passive bond investing was made by Mark Hulbert, a columnist for *Forbes* magazine, who publishes a report on the performance of investment advisors.[12] His analysis, based on the results achieved by investment advisors, makes a strong argument for passive bond investing, at least as regards attempts to time swings in the bond market. As Hulbert concludes, "Timing the bond market is just about impossible. My advice is: Resist the temptation to try."[13]

Strategies for investors following a passive bond management approach include buy-and-hold and indexing.

Buy and Hold An obvious strategy for any investor interested in nonactive trading policies is simply to buy and hold. This investor carefully chooses a portfolio of bonds and does not attempt to trade them in a search for higher returns. An important part of this strategy is to choose the most promising bonds that meet the investor's requirements. Making this selection requires some knowledge of bonds and markets. Simply because an investor is following a basic buy-and-hold strategy does not mean that the initial selection is unimportant.

The buy-and-hold investor must have knowledge of the yield advantages of various bonds (e.g., agency securities over U.S. Treasuries), the default risk, call risk, the marketability of a bond, any current income requirements, and taxes.

One alternative for the buy-and-hold investor is to try to duplicate the overall bond market by purchasing a broad cross section of bonds. Another is selectively to build a portfolio of bonds based on characteristics that match those that the investor is seeking whether a high level of safety, an intermediate maturity, large coupons, and so forth. Regardless of the bonds sought, individual investors have traditionally faced a very difficult job, because the bond market caters to institutional investors, using real-time databases not available to individuals. Therefore, individual investors could not determine current prices. As of the beginning of 1999, however, this situation was changing dramatically.

Using the Internet

An important development occurred in early 1999 when a new firm, Bond Exchange, created a platform that securities firms can use to sell bonds to investors. Investors can see a demo at www.bond-exchange.com. Investors can search by type, rating, coupon, industry, and more. Prices (and markups) are generally very favorable compared to the past. E*Trade and Vanguard Brokerage Services now use this platform. This is the first real breakthrough for individual investors interested in bonds, allowing them to build a bond portfolio by buying and selling at fair prices.

Investors interested in municipal bonds should check www.investinginbonds.com. This site contains the previous day's prices for approximately 1,000 actively traded municipals, and it allows you to search a database of bonds by state. Note that this is a reference site, and prices do not represent actual trading prices.

---

[11] See Christopher Blake, Edwin Elton, and Martin Gruber, "The Performance of Bond Mutual Funds," *The Journal of Business*, July 1993, pp. 371–403.

[12] Hulbert publishes the *Hulbert Financial Digest*, which has become a well-known source of information on the performance of financial newsletters that are sold to investors.

[13] See Mark Hulbert, "A Fool's Game," *Forbes*, August 8, 1991, p. 119.

Still another variation for bond investors who do not wish to be active in the market but instead protect themselves from some risk is the *ladder approach*. Under a laddering approach, investors protect themselves to some degree against rises in interest rates by purchasing bonds with different maturity dates. The investor chooses dates that mesh with his or her own situation. For example, with $100,000 to invest, an investor could put approximately $20,000 in each of five bonds, with the first bond maturing two years from now, the second one maturing three years from now, and so forth. Thus, if interest rates rise, the investor will have some principal returned periodically which can be reinvested in new bonds with a higher yield. If interest rates decline, some of the previous higher yields are locked up until those bonds mature. Any type of bond can be used in a laddering strategy.

Indexing If investors decide that they are unlikely to outperform a market index, they may opt to buy a portfolio that will match the performance of a well-known bond index such as the Shearson Lehman Index or Salomon Brothers Index.[14] Mutual funds designed to match the performance of some index are known as **bond index funds**. Index funds are available for both bonds and stocks (stock index funds are discussed in Chapter 11). Whereas the typical actively managed bond fund has an expense ratio of almost 1 percent, the average expense ratio of bond index funds is half that, and some are less.

Bond Index Funds Mutual funds holding a bond portfolio designed to match a particular market index

Example 18-6

The *Vanguard Total Bond Market Index* is one of the largest bond index funds. Its expense ratio is a mere 0.2 percent. This fund outperformed 89 percent of actively managed bond funds over the period 1996 to 1998.

How important are expense ratios for bond funds? Very important! With high-grade corporates yielding 5 or 6 percent and Treasuries even less in recent years (sometimes 4 percent or less), the impact of a 0.2-percent expense ratio subtracted from these returns versus about one percent subtracted from these returns is obvious.

How popular has bond indexing become? Not very, despite outperforming active funds. At the beginning of 1999, about 30 bond index funds were in operation, accounting for only 2 percent of overall assets in bond funds.

IMMUNIZATION—A STRUCTURED PORTFOLIO STRATEGY

Because interest rates change over time, investors face uncertainty about the realized returns from bonds. This, of course, is the nature of interest rate risk. The strategy of immunizing (protecting) a portfolio against interest rate risk (i.e., changes in the general level of interest rates) is called **immunization**. This is one form of a structured portfolio strategy, which aims to have a portfolio achieve the performance of a benchmark that has been specified beforehand.

Immunization The strategy of immunizing (protecting) a portfolio against interest rate risk by canceling out its two components, price risk and reinvestment rate risk

To see how such a strategy works, think of interest rate risk as being composed of two parts:

1. The *price risk*, resulting from the inverse relationship between bond prices and required rates of return.
2. The *reinvestment rate risk*, resulting from the uncertainty about the rate at which future coupon income can be reinvested. As discussed in Chapter 17, the YTM calculation assumes that future coupons from a given bond investment will be reinvested at the calculated yield to maturity. If interest rates change so that this assumption is no longer operable, the bond's realized YTM will differ from the calculated (expected) YTM.

[14] In practice, it is not feasible to exactly replicate a broad bond index. For example, the Lehman Brothers Aggregate Bond Index covers more than 6,000 securities. Most bond-index funds use a sampling approach to replicate the index as much as possible.

Notice that these two components of interest rate risk move in opposite directions:

- ▣ If interest rates rise, reinvestment rates (and therefore income) rise, whereas the price of the bond declines.
- ▣ If interest rates decline, reinvestment rates (and therefore income) decline, whereas the price of the bond rises.

In effect, the favorable results on one side can be used to offset the unfavorable results on the other. This is what immunization is all about—protecting a bond portfolio against interest rate risk by canceling out the two components of interest rate risk, reinvestment rate risk and price risk.

The duration concept discussed earlier is the basis for immunization theory. Specifically, a portfolio is said to be immunized (the effects of interest rate risk are neutralized) if the duration of the portfolio is made equal to a preselected investment horizon for the portfolio. Note carefully what this statement says. An investor with, as an example, a 10-year horizon does not choose bonds with 10 years to maturity but bonds with a duration of 10 years—quite a different statement. The duration strategy will usually require holding bonds with maturities in excess of the investment horizon.[15]

Exhibit 18-1 outlines the concept of immunization, showing the essential points. Think of it simply as a strategy to protect against the adverse consequences of interest rate risk, thereby allowing the portfolio holder to achieve a prespecified rate of return over a selected period of time.

EXHIBIT 18–1

Understanding the Concept of Immunization

Immunization

Seeks to
Protect a Portfolio Against Interest Rate Risk
By
Playing the Two Components of Interest Rate Risk
Against Each Other

The Objective Is to Have the Portfolio Earn a Prespecified
Rate of Return

With an Immunized Portfolio:

IF Interest Rates Go UP ⇑
Reinvestment Rates ↑
While
The Prices of the Bonds ↓

IF Interest Rates Go Down ⇓
Reinvestment Rates ↓
While
The Prices of the Bonds ↑

The Key to Immunization Is Duration

---

[15] For additional information on reinvestment rate risk, see R. W. McEnally, "How to Neutralize Reinvestment Rate Risk," *The Journal of Portfolio Management*, Spring 1980. Also, see William L. Nemerever, "Managing Bond Portfolios Through Immunization Strategies," reprinted in *The Revolution in Techniques for Managing Bond Portfolios* (Charlottesville, Va.: Institute of Chartered Financial Analysts, 1983).

For an example of the immunization concept, consider Table 18-1 which illustrates for a portfolio consisting of one bond what ideally could happen with a portfolio of several bonds. Assume an investor has a five-year investment horizon after which she wishes to liquidate her bond portfolio and spend the proceeds. The current yield to maturity for AAA-rated bonds, the only investment grade our investor is willing to consider, is 7.9 percent for both five-year and six-year bonds because of the flatness of the yield curve. In order to simplify the calculations, we will assume that interest is paid annually so that we can concentrate on the immunization principle.

Because the YTM is 7.9 percent, our investor, understanding the reinvestment rate implications of bonds, expects that after five years her investment should yield an ending wealth ratio of $(1.079)^5$, or 1.46254, or $1.46254 per dollar invested today. That is, if she invests $1,000 in a bond today and the intermediate coupons are reinvested at 7.9 percent each, as the YTM calculation assumes, the ending wealth for this investment in a bond that can be purchased for face value should be $1,000 $(1.079)^5$, or $1,462.54.

Table 18-1   Ending Wealth for a Bond Following a Change in Market Yields With and Without Immunization

Bond A: Purchased for $1,000, five-year maturity, 7.9% coupon, 7.9% yield to maturity
Bond B: Purchased for $1,000, six-year maturity, 7.9% coupon, 7.9% yield to maturity,
**   duration = 5.00 years**

Part A: Ending Wealth for Bond A if Market Yields Remain Constant at 7.9%

Years	Cash Flow	Reinvestment Rate (%)	Ending Wealth
1	$ 79	—[a]	$ 79.00
2	79	7.9	164.24
3	79	7.9	256.22
4	79	7.9	355.46
5	79	7.9	462.54
5	1,000	—	1,462.54

Part B: Ending Wealth for Bond A if Market Yields Decline to 6% in Year 3

Years	Cash Flow	Reinvestment Rate (%)	Ending Wealth
1	$ 79	—	$ 79.00
2	79	7.9	164.24
3	79	6.0	253.10
4	79	6.0	347.29
5	79	6.0	477.13
5	1,000	—	1,447.13

Part C: Ending Wealth for Bond B if Market Yields Decline to 6% in Year 3
**   (Bond B has a duration of five years.)**

Years	Cash Flow	Reinvestment Rate (%)	Ending Wealth
1	$ 79	—	$ 79.00
2	79	7.9	164.24
3	79	6.0	253.10
4	79	6.0	347.29
5	79	6.0	477.13
5	1,017.92[b]	—	1,465.05

[a]Cash flows are received at the end of the year.

[b]The price of bond B with one year left to maturity and a market yield of 6% is $1,017.92.

Our investor can purchase bond A, with a 7.9-percent coupon and a five-year maturity, or bond B, with a 7.9-percent coupon, a six-year maturity, and a duration of five years. The top panel of Table 18-1 illustrates what happens if bond A is purchased and market yields remain constant for our investor's five-year investment horizon. Because the intermediate cash flows are reinvested at exactly 7.9 percent each year, the ending amounts cumulate toward the final ending wealth of $1,462.54, or a wealth ratio of 1.46254. Notice in these examples that we separate year five from the other four because of the return of principal ($1,000) at the end of year five; obviously, no compound interest is earned on the return of this $1,000 at the end of the year. In a similar manner, no interest is earned on the first year's cash flow of $79, which is assumed to occur at the end of the year.

Now consider what would happen if our investor bought bond A and in the third year of its five-year life, market yields for this and comparable bonds declined to 6.0 percent and remained at that level for the remainder of the five-year period. As a result, the intermediate cash flows in the last three years of the bond's life would be reinvested at 6 percent rather than at 7.9 percent. Therefore, the reinvestment rate risk present in bond investments has a negative impact on this particular bond investment.

The results of a drop in the reinvestment rate are shown in the middle panel of Table 18-1, using the same format as previously. As this panel shows, at the end of year five, the ending amount of wealth for bond A now is only $1,447.13, representing a shortfall for the investor's ending-wealth objective. This result occurred because she did not immunize her bond portfolio against interest rate risk, but instead purchased a bond based on matching the maturity of the bond with her investment horizon. As explained above, to protect against this interest rate risk, it is necessary to purchase a bond whose duration is equal to the investor's investment horizon.

Assume that a $1,000 bond with a coupon rate of 7.9 percent and a six-year maturity could have been purchased at the same time. The duration of this bond, which we call bond B, is exactly five years, matching the investor's investment horizon. In this case, the bond would be immunized against interest rate risk, because any shortfall arising from a declining reinvestment rate would be offset by a higher price for the bond at the end of the investment horizon, because the drop in interest rates produces an increase in the price of the bond. Note that at the end of five years, which is our investor's investment horizon, bond B has one year left to maturity and could be sold in the market.

The bottom panel of Table 18-1 illustrates the same process as before for bond B. Notice that the ending cash flows are the same for the first four years as they were for the previous situation with the five-year bond. At the end of year five, the bond still has one year to go to maturity. Its price has risen because of the drop in interest rates. As the analysis in Table 18-1 demonstrates, the ending wealth is more than enough to meet the investor's objective of $1,462.54 per $1,000 invested.

Thus, the example in Table 18-1 illustrates the basic concept of immunization. By choosing a bond or a portfolio of bonds with a duration equal to a predetermined investment horizon, it is possible, in principle, to immunize the portfolio against interest rate risk.

Immunization is only one of the structured portfolio strategies. These strategies occupy a position between passive strategies and active strategies. Although the classic immunization discussed here could possibly be thought of as a passive strategy, we must be aware of the real-world problems involved in implementing such a strategy. In truth, this strategy is not easy to implement, and it is not a passive strategy in application. To achieve immunization as discussed here requires frequent rebalancing, because duration should always be equal to the investment horizon. An investor simply cannot set duration equal to investment horizon at the beginning of the process and ignore the bond, or portfolio, thereafter.[16]

ACTIVE MANAGEMENT STRATEGIES

Active Management Strategies Strategies designed to provide additional returns by trading activities

Although bonds are often purchased to be held to maturity, frequently they are not. Many bond investors use **active management strategies**. Such strategies have traditionally sought to profit from active management of bonds by either:

1. Forecasting changes in interest rates, because we know that bond prices will change as well or
2. Identifying relative mispricing between various fixed-income securities.

Notice that, unlike the passive strategy, the key inputs are not known at the time of the analysis. Instead, investors have expectations about interest rate changes and mispricings among securities.

We will consider each of these alternatives in turn. We will also examine briefly some of the newer techniques for actively managing a bond portfolio.

Forecasting Changes in Interest Rates Changes in interest rates are the chief factor affecting bond prices because of the inverse relationship between changes in bond prices and changes in interest rates. When investors project interest rate declines, they should take action to invest in bonds, and the right bonds, for price appreciation opportunities. When interest rates are expected to rise, the objective is to minimize losses by not holding bonds or holding bonds with short maturities.

Example 18-7 The Federal Reserve reversed its course in both 1994 and 1999 and significantly tightened its interest rate policy. The result was the two worse years for bonds since 1980, which each showing negative returns for the year.

How does an investor forecast interest rates? Not very well on a consistent and accurate basis, because interest rate forecasting is a notoriously difficult proposition. Nevertheless, reasonable forecasts can be made about the likely growth rate of the economy and the prospects for inflation, both of which affect interest rates and, therefore, bond investors. Assuming that an investor has a forecast of interest rates, what strategy can be used? The basic strategy is to change the maturity of the portfolio. Specifically, an investor should lengthen (shorten) the maturity of a bond portfolio when interest rates are expected to decline (rise).

Duration plays an important role in active strategies involving interest rate forecasting. If interest rates are expected to fall, the duration of the portfolio would be increased; duration would be reduced if interest rates are expected to rise. A portfolio's duration may be changed by swapping bonds to achieve a new target duration or using interest-rate futures contracts.

---

[16] There are several variations of the basic immunization strategy. The most popular variation is called *horizon-matching*, or combination matching. This involves a portfolio that is duration-matched and also cash-matched in the first few years.

An alternative variation is *contingent* immunization, which involves active management plus a lower floor return that is ensured for the horizon period. The portfolio manager must act to earn the floor return by immunizing the portfolio if necessary. Otherwise, the manager can actively manage the portfolio or some portion thereof.

It is important to be aware of the trade-offs in strategies involving maturity.

1. Short maturities sacrifice price appreciation opportunities and usually offer lower coupons (income), but serve to protect the investor when rates are expected to rise.
2. Longer maturities have greater price fluctuations; therefore, the chance for bigger gains (and bigger losses) is magnified. However, longer maturities may be less liquid than Treasury bills.

An important component in forecasting interest rates is the yield curve, discussed earlier in connection with the term structure of interest rates. The shape of the yield curve at any point in time contains potentially valuable information about the future course of interest rates. Bond market participants in particular, and investors in general, pay close attention to yield curves as an aid in forecasting interest rates and as part of deciding what segments of the bond market to invest in.

Example 18-8   Consider the situation in mid-1992. The yield curve for Treasury securities had a range of rates that represented a historic high. The difference between 3-month bills and 30-year bonds was approximately 4.5 percent (450 basis points), an incredible difference by historic standards. The normal difference between longs and shorts is less than 2 percent (200 basis points). Many observers at the time predicted that long rates would decrease, thereby making the yield curve more "normal."

One form of interest rate forecasting, *horizon analysis*, involves the projection of bond performance over a planned investment horizon. The investor evaluates bonds that are being considered for purchase over a selected holding period in order to determine which will perform the best. To do this, the investor must make assumptions about reinvestment rates and future market rates and calculate the *horizon returns* for the bonds being considered based on that set of assumptions. Note that this concept is different from the yield to maturity concept, which does not require expectations to be integrated into the analysis. Horizon analysis requires users to make assumptions about reinvestment rates and future yields but allows them to consider how different scenarios will affect the performance of the bonds being considered. Horizon analysis was discussed in Chapter 17.

Bond Swaps An active bond management strategy involving the purchase and sale of bonds in an attempt to improve the rate of return on the bond portfolio

Identifying Mispricings Among Securities Managers of bond portfolios attempt to adjust to the constantly changing environment for bonds (and all securities) by engaging in what are called **bond swaps**. The term usually refers to the purchase and sale of bonds in an attempt to improve the rate of return on the bond portfolio by identifying temporary mispricings in the bond market. These are relative mispricings among different types of bonds.

Example 18-9   In late 1998, the convertibles of HealthSouth were yielding the same as its straight debt, possibly because hedge funds sold unusual amounts of convertibles to raise cash, thereby depressing prices.

Using the Internet

Investors can obtain information on global events, including U.S. interest rates and bond markets, from Morgan Stanley Dean Witter's Web site at www.ms.com. Access the "Global Strategy Bulletin" for a list of headline stories.

Use of Newer Techniques The bond markets have changed rapidly in recent years because numerous structural changes and record interest rates have occurred. These changes have been accompanied by new techniques for the active management of fixed-income portfolios.

The distinction between the bond market and the mortgage market is now blurred, with mortgage instruments competing in the capital markets in the same manner as bonds. The mortgage has been transformed into a security, and the mortgage market has become more uniform and standardized. These securities are alternatives to bonds, especially corporate bonds, and can be used in the portfolio as substitutes.

Financial futures are now a well-known part of the investor's alternatives. Their use has grown tremendously, in particular to hedge positions and to speculate on the future course of interest rates. Futures will be discussed in more detail in Chapter 20.

Building a Fixed-Income Portfolio

Having reviewed some active and passive strategies for managing a bond portfolio, we will now consider how to build a fixed-income portfolio. The first consideration, which is true throughout the range of investment decisions, is to decide on the risk-return trade-off that all investors face. If investors seek higher expected returns, they must be prepared to accept greater risk. In building a fixed-income portfolio, it is useful to think of the two broad approaches an investor can take, a conservative or an aggressive approach. We will use these two broad strategies below to organize the discussion.

CONSERVATIVE INVESTORS

Conservative investors view bonds as fixed-income securities that will pay them a steady stream of income. In most cases, the risk is small, and Treasury issues have practically no risk of default. These investors tend to use a buy-and-hold approach.

Investors following this strategy seek to maximize their current income subject to the risk (quality of issue) they are willing to assume: corporates should return more than Treasury issues, BAA should return more than A or AA or AAA, longer maturities should return more than short maturities, and so on.

Even conservative investors in bonds must consider a number of factors. Assume that an investor wishes to purchase only Treasury issues, thereby avoiding the possible risk of default. Careful consideration should be given to the maturity of the issue, since the range is from Treasury bills of a few months' duration to bonds maturing in the twenty-first century. Reinvestment rate risk must be considered, as must call risk for a few Treasury issues. For investors who may need their funds back before the bonds mature, interest rate risk is relevant.

The investor's choice will depend to a large extent on interest rate forecasts. Even conservative buy-and-hold investors should probably avoid long-term issues if interest rates are expected to rise over an extended period of time. Finally, these investors may wish to consider the differences in coupons between issues. Previous discussion has shown that the lower the coupon on a bond, the higher the price volatility. Although many investors in this group may plan to hold to maturity, conditions can change, and they may need to sell some of these bonds before maturity.

Box 18-1 contains a consideration of some issues that investors would face, and should think about carefully, if interest rates are expected to rise.

BOX 18-1

Prepare for Rising Rates

The Federal Reserve's refusal to ease credit further at its late September Federal Open Market Committee meeting is just one more sign that yields have bottomed. Interest rates may not rise much, if at all, for the rest of 2002. But at some point the return of federal deficits, the likelihood of some pick-up in the economy, and the pressure on the dollar's value in world markets all point to higher rates, especially at the longer end of the interest-rate spectrum.

Still, financial planners believe most investors should still have at least a quarter, if not more, of their portfolios in interest-paying assets. Keeping your money there will become a challenge as rates rise and, as a result, prices fall—meaning lower principal values. Our suggestion is to look at all your bonds and bond funds one by one, think about what would happen if rates were to rise, and decide whether you would still buy that asset today.

EASY DECISIONS

The easiest decision comes with bonds that are a year or less from maturity or to the date when they may be called (redeemed by the issuer for the face amount). There's no reason to sell, because you're due to get your principal back. A year from now, when rates are higher than they are now, you'll be able to reinvest on better terms.

Certificates of deposit and savings bonds do not expose you to any risk of principal loss. If you can roll a CD into one that pays better, do it. But don't pay a stiff penalty and don't bite on really long-term CDs unless you're absolutely okay with earning 4% for the next five years.

WHEN THE PRINCIPAL IS AT RISK

What about assets whose principal value is at risk should the rate picture deteriorate?

Treasuries, in particular, are risky. When the 10-year T-bond's yield fell below 3.7% last week, the statisticians announced that this was a 40-year low. Another way to express this is that the price of a 10-year Treasury bond is at a 40-year high. Would you buy gold, or real estate, or stocks under those conditions? Or keep it?

If you have some long-term Treasuries issued at dramatically higher yields, such as in the early 1990s, take the profits and put the money in short CDs. The same is true with high-grade corporate bonds and funds, those rated A or better. Unless you need the cash flow and can hold to maturity, why leave the gains on the table?

OTHER KEEPERS

If you're holding high-yield, or junk, bond funds, note that their performance depends more on the health of the companies than on rate trends. And, in a rare piece of good news, Moody's Investors Service just issued some positive comments on junk. Junk bond funds are okay to keep unless the economy really deteriorates and defaults mount.

A couple of columns ago I discussed *stable-value funds*, an insurance company invention that own fixed-rate "guaranteed investment contracts." Keep them—they have good yields with little risk. Same with real estate investment trusts, unless you happen to own one that has its own specific troubles. For example, New York City and San Francisco office leasing is proving to be slow. REITs that specialize in one location, as opposed to those spread out nationally, are riskier.

Finally, what about money funds? They are the ultimate defense against rising rates. The term is so short that if something starts moving rates higher, those 1.7% yields could go up in a hurry. The Federal Reserve isn't ready to tighten, but if they do, you'll be happy to be sitting it out in a money fund. Come to think of it, hasn't that been true for about three years now?

SOURCE: Jeffrey R. Kosnett, "Prepare for Rising Rates," Kiplinger.com, October 2, 2002. Used by permission.

Example 18-10 As an example of what can happen to conservative investors when they are buying and holding a bond portfolio, consider the situation facing municipal bond investors in mid-1992. Most municipal bonds can be called after 10 years. Many investors bought municipals in 1982 when interest rates were at record highs. On July 1, 1992, several billion dollars of municipals were redeemed, and more calls were expected in the future on the typical call dates, January 1 and July 1. Investors were forced to give up high-yielding municipals at a time when interest rates were quite low. Moreover, in trying to replace the income stream, they had to consider alternatives with lower quality (and therefore greater risk) and/or longer maturity (and therefore subject to interest rate risk as rates rose), or simply resign themselves to a bond portfolio with a new, lower return.

Indirect investing is another possibility. In addition to the bond funds holding Treasuries, municipals, and corporates, or mixtures of any of these, with a wide range of maturities, investors can consider *flexible-income funds*. These funds invest in bonds of all types, convertible securities, and stocks. The emphasis on these funds tends to be on income, but their investment strategies vary greatly. The annual yields on these funds may be only a percentage point or so below long-term Treasury yields, and their total returns tend to be much higher. Examples include Vanguard Wellsley Income, USAA Income, and Berwyn Income.

AGGRESSIVE INVESTORS

Aggressive investors are interested in capital gains that arise from a change in interest rates. There is a substantial range of aggressiveness, from the really short-term speculator to the somewhat less aggressive investor who is willing to realize capital gains over a longer period while possibly earning high yields.

The short-term speculator studies interest rates carefully and moves into and out of securities on the basis of interest rate expectations. If rates are expected to fall, this investor can buy long-term, low-coupon issues and achieve maximum capital gains if the interest rate forecast is correct. Treasury bonds can be bought on margin, further magnifying gains (or losses). Treasury securities, for example, can be purchased on 10-percent margin. The speculator often uses Treasury issues (the highest quality bond available) or high-grade corporates in doing this kind of bond trading. It is not necessary to resort to low-quality bonds.

Another form of aggressive behavior involves seeking the highest total return whether from interest income or capital gains. Investors who follow this strategy plan on a long horizon in terms of holding a portfolio of bonds, but engage in active trading during certain periods when such actions seem particularly appropriate. One such period was 1982, when bonds were offering record yields to maturity and interest rates were widely expected to decline. Even mildly aggressive investors could purchase Treasury bonds yielding high-coupon income and have a reasonable expectation of capital gains. The downside risk in this strategy at that time was small. These investors still needed to consider maturity and coupon questions, however, because no interest rate decline can be assumed with certainty.

Using Duration As noted in Chapter 17, duration can be used as a measure of a bond, or bond fund's, volatility. Investors can determine how much the price will move up or down as interest rates change. By comparing different durations, an investor can find a level of volatility that is suitable for his or her risk tolerance.

Example 18-11 As the stock market declined more and more during 2000 to 2002, many investors shifted into bonds. Suppose an investor thought at some point that interest rates would decline and wanted to invest aggressively in bonds in order to take advantage of the expected decline. Zero-coupon bonds have maximum price volatility. Buying a bond mutual fund that holds zero-coupon Treasuries eliminates credit (default) risk while providing maximum volatility, and the longer the duration, the greater the volatility. Consider the American Century Target Maturity 2030 fund, which holds long-term government securities. This fund, in 2002, had a very high duration of about 28. For the first nine months of the year, this fund had a return of 26 percent. Of course, if interest rates rise only 1 percent, and the duration of this fund remains 28, shareholders will suffer a loss of approximately 28 percent.

THE INTERNATIONAL PERSPECTIVE

When investors build bond portfolios, they should consider the opportunities available in the international bond markets. Investors can invest directly or indirectly in foreign bonds by making their own decisions and using their broker or by purchasing shares in an investment company holding foreign bonds.

Example 18-12 Assume that you were a bond speculator in the spring of 1992. Large amounts of money had already been made in U.S. bonds by speculators borrowing at rates lower than the rates being paid on the short-term Treasuries they bought. When interest rates declined, they made large capital gains. Assuming U.S. opportunities had been mostly exploited, what about foreign opportunities?

Investors looking at foreign bonds observed that a five-year French government bond could be bought with a yield more than 2 percentage points greater than a five-year U.S. Treasury bond.[17] Thus, investors willing to switch to a bond denominated in French francs could pick up a substantial increase in yield. Furthermore, since the French yield curve was inverted (sloped downward), there was a good chance of earning a capital gain on the French bond as rates returned to more normal relationships.

As we know by now, larger returns are associated with larger risks. In the case of foreign bonds such as the French example, investors were implicitly betting on the future direction of interest rates in these foreign countries, which in turn reflected bets on their economies. A slowdown would favor the odds of lower interest rates and higher bond prices. Furthermore, investors in foreign bonds face exchange rate or currency risk. Adverse currency fluctuations could significantly reduce the returns to a cash bond investor and wipe out an investor on margin. Therefore, the investors had to decide whether to hedge the position against adverse currency movements. Investors who were bullish on the foreign currency, such as the French franc, could take unhedged positions, whereas investors who were bearish would probably choose to hedge their positions.

In Chapter 2, we noted that investors always have an alternative to direct investing. They can invest indirectly by purchasing shares of investment companies that, in turn, invest in the securities in which they are interested. In the case of European bonds, the practical way for investors to invest is through mutual funds. Among the foreign bond funds, short-term world multimarket income funds have been popular. Such funds were recently emphasizing short-term European securities because of their relatively high returns. They differ from money market mutual funds in that their prices can fluctuate, whereas money market fund prices typically are maintained at a constant value of $1 per share.

Investors interested in foreign bonds can also purchase world bond funds which invest in long-term bonds. Such funds invariably are betting on the future course of interest rates because of the inverse relation between bond prices and interest rates. Investors can

---

[17] This information, as well as the analysis below, is based on Robert Lenzner, "How to Play Foreign Yields," *Forbes*, March 16, 1992, p. 71.

also invest in a few funds that buy the short-term debt securities of only one country. For example, Fidelity, the largest mutual fund company, has separate funds that specialize in German securities and British securities.

Investment companies with funds specializing in foreign government bonds include Fidelity, T. Rowe Price, Putnam, Scudder, and Templeton. Some of these funds hedge European currencies. Alliance Capital, for example, with both a money market and a short-term bond fund, hedges the European currencies, thereby minimizing currency risk.

How does the U.S. dollar affect the foreign bond investor? If the U.S. economy improves, the dollar will probably rise. If the dollar rises against the currencies involved in the foreign bonds, their returns to U.S. investors are impacted.

Summary

▶ A wide range of investors are interested in bonds, ranging from those who seek a steady stream of interest income and return of principal to those seeking capital gains by speculating on future interest rate movements.

▶ In understanding what drives the bond market, fears of inflation play a key role.

▶ The term structure of interest rates denotes the relationship between market yields and time to maturity. A yield curve graphically depicts this relationship with upward-sloping curves being the norm.

▶ None of the prevalent theories proposed to explain term structure—the expectations theory, the liquidity preference theory, the preferred habitat theory, and the market segmentation theory—is dominant.

▶ Yield spreads are the relationship between bond yields and particular bond features such as quality and callability. Differences in type, quality, and coupon account for most of the yield spreads.

▶ Bond investment strategies can be divided into passive and active strategies.

▶ Passive bond strategies, whereby the investor does not actively seek out trading possibilities in an attempt to outperform the market, include buy and hold and indexing.

▶ Immunization is the strategy of protecting (immunizing) a portfolio against interest rate risk by attempting to have the two components of interest rate risk, reinvestment rate risk and price risk, cancel each other out.

▶ Active management strategies can be broadly divided into forecasting changes in interest rates and identifying relative mispricing between various fixed-income securities. New techniques include the use of mortgage instruments and strategies with financial futures.

▶ Interest rate swaps are now a significant item in the management of bond portfolios by institutions.

▶ In building a bond portfolio, investors must make a decision on the risk-return trade-off faced by all investors. Conservative investors will probably consider some issues that are different from those considered by aggressive investors.

Key Words

Active management strategy
Bond index funds
Bond swaps
Expectations theory
Forward rates

Immunization
Liquidity preference theory
Market segmentation theory
Passive management strategy
Preferred habitat theory

Term structure of interest rates
Theoretical spot rate curve
Yield curve
Yield spreads

Questions

18-1 Describe two different types of investors interested in bonds as an investment.

18-2 List some of the problems involved for U.S. investors in purchasing and selling foreign bonds.

18-3 What is the key factor in analyzing bonds? Why?

18-4 Identify and explain at least two passive bond management strategies.

18-5 Explain the concept of immunization. What role, if any, does duration play in this concept?

18-6 Identify and explain two specific active bond management strategies. Are the two related?

18-7 Assume you have correctly forecast that interest rates will soon decline sharply. Also assume that you will invest only in fixed-income securities and that your time horizon is one year; how would you construct a portfolio?

18-8 When would investors find bonds with long maturities, selling at large discounts, particularly unattractive as investment opportunities?

18-9 What is meant by the term "bond swaps"?

18-10 How can horizon analysis be used to manage a bond portfolio?

18-11 Assume that you are interested in some British government bonds that are currently yielding three percentage points more than comparable Treasury securities. If you think the British economy will slow down, is this favorable or unfavorable for your decision to purchase British bonds? If you are also bullish on the British pound, does this suggest a hedged or unhedged position when you buy the bonds?

CFA
18-12 The concepts of spot and forward rates are most closely associated with which one of the following explanations of the term structure of interest rates?

a. Expectations hypothesis
b. Liquidity premium theory
c. Preferred habitat hypothesis
d. Segmented market theory

CFA
18-13 The interest rate risk of a bond normally is:

a. greater for shorter maturities
b. lower for longer duration
c. lower for higher coupons
d. none of the above

CFA
18-14 Robert Devlin and Neil Parish are portfolio managers at the Broward Investment Group. At their regular Monday strategy meeting, the topic of adding international bonds to one of their portfolios came up. The portfolio, an ERISA-qualified pension account for a U.S. client, was currently 90 percent invested in U.S. Treasury bonds, and 10 percent invested in 10-year Canadian government bonds.

Devlin suggested buying a position in 10-year West German government bonds, while Parish argued for a position in 10-year Australian government bonds.

a. Briefly discuss the three major issues that Devlin and Parish should address in their analysis of the return prospects for German and Australian bonds relative to those of U.S. bonds.

Having made no changes to the original portfolio, Devlin and Parish hold a subsequent strategy meeting and decide to add positions in the government bonds of Japan, United Kingdom, France, West Germany, and Australia.

b. Identify and discuss two reasons for adding a broader mix of international bonds to the pension portfolio.

Problems

CFA
18-1 The table below shows selected data on a German government bond (payable in deutsche marks) and a U.S. government bond. Identify the components of return and calculate the

total return in U.S. dollars for *both* of these bonds for the year 1991. Show the calculations for *each* component. (Ignore interest on interest in view of the short time period.)

		Market Yield		Modified Duration	Exchange Rate (DM/$U.S.)	
	Coupon	1/1/91	1/1/92		1/1/91	1/1/92
German government bond	8.50%	8.50%	8.00%	7.0	1.55	1.50
U.S. government bond	8.00%	8.00%	6.75%	6.5	—	—

CFA
18-2   Bill Peters is the investment officer of a $60 million pension fund. He has become concerned about the big price swings that have occurred lately in the fund's fixed-income securities. Peters has been told that such price behavior is only natural given the recent behavior of market yields. To deal with the problem, the pension fund's fixed-income money manager keeps track of exposure to price volatility by closely monitoring bond duration. The money manager believes that price volatility can be kept to a reasonable level as long as portfolio duration is maintained at approximately seven to eight years.

a. Discuss the concepts of duration and convexity and explain how each fits into the price/yield relationship. In the situation described above, explain why the money manager should have used both duration and convexity to monitor the bond portfolio's exposure to price volatility.

b. One of the bonds held in the portfolio is a 15-year, 8-percent U.S. Treasury bond with a modified duration of 8.0 years and a convexity of 94.36. It has been suggested that the fund swap out of the 15-year bond and into a barbell position made up of the following two U.S. Treasury issues:

Bond	Coupon	Maturity	Modified Duration	Convexity
1	8%	5 years	3.97 years	19.58
2	8%	30 years	9.73 years	167.56

Construct a barbell position from these two bonds that results in a modified duration of 8.0 years. Compare the price volatility of the barbell position to the bond currently held under each of the following interest rate environments:

i.   market rates drop by 50 basis points (e.g., from 9 percent to 8.50 percent), and
ii. market rates drop by 250 basis points (e.g., from 9 percent to 6.50 percent).

CFA
18-3   On June 1, 1989, a bond portfolio manager is evaluating the following data concerning three bonds held in his portfolio.

Bond	Bond Rating	Coupon	Maturity	Call Price (Date)	Market Price	Yield to Maturity	Modified Duration	Change in Market Price*
X	AA	0%	8/14/94	Noncallable	59.44	10.25%	5.2 years	+5.1%
Y	AA	14.00	3/30/98	Noncallable	116.60	11.00	5.2	+5.5
Z	AA	10.25	7/15/97	100 (6/1/90)	98.63	10.50	5.2	+2.4

*Following a 100 basis–point decline in rates

It is noted that all three bonds have the same modified duration and thus are expected to rise in price by 5.20 percent for a 100 basis–point decline in interest rates. However, the data show that a different change in price occurs for each bond.

Discuss three reasons for the discrepancy between the expectations and the actual change in market price for the bonds.

Web Resources

For additional resources visit our dynamic Web site located at www.wiley.com/college/jones.

- *Bond Market Tricks*—The decision-maker must estimate future interest rates and calculate expected returns to recommend a bond for purchase by her company. The case presents an exercise in realized compound yield calculation and horizon return analysis.
- Internet Exercises—This chapter discusses passive and active bond portfolio management strategies. The Web exercises will enable you to understand the term structure of interest rates and their role in the forecasting of interest rates. You will also work on exercises that examine the relative superiority of passive versus active strategies.
  Exercise 1: Looks at international comparisons of bond yields.
  Exercise 2: Looks at the yield curve.
  Exercise 3: Looks at forward rates and spot rates.
- Multiple Choice Self Test

Selected References

Bond return strategies for investors are discussed in:

Crescenzi, Anthony. *The Strategic Bond Investor: Strategies and Tools to Unlock the Power of the Bond Market*. McGraw-Hill Trade, 2002.

A good discussion of how to use bonds as investing alternatives can be found in:

Richelson, Hildy and Stan Richelson. *The Money-Making Guide to Bonds: Straightforward Strategies for Picking the Right Bonds and Bond Funds*. Bloomberg Press, 2002.

A complete discussion for maximizing returns in bond portfolios can be found in:

Fabozzi, Frank J. *Bond Portfolio Management*. McGraw-Hill, 2001.

chapter *19*

Options

C hapter 19 analyzes options, a derivative security used by many investors. The importance of derivative securities lies in the flexibility they provide investors in managing investment risk. Derivative instruments can also be used to speculate in various markets.

AFTER READING THIS CHAPTER YOU WILL BE ABLE TO:

▶ Understand why investors use options in their investment strategies.

▶ Describe the option alternatives available to investors, and how the options markets operate.

▶ Analyze basic option strategies.

▶ Understand the valuation of options.

Equity-Derivative Securities Securities that derive their value in whole or in part by having a claim on the underlying common stock

Rather than trade directly in common stocks, investors can purchase **equity-derivative securities** representing a claim—an option—on a particular stock and index options representing a claim on some index. Equity options give the holder the right to receive or deliver shares of stock under specified conditions. The option need not be exercised (and often will not be worth exercising). Instead, an investor can simply buy and sell these, which are securities that derive all or part of their value from the equity of the same corporation. Gains or losses will depend on the difference between the purchase price and the sales price.

This chapter primarily discusses put and call equity options. Other equity-derivative securities are covered elsewhere—Appendix 17-A covers convertible securities and Appendix 19-B covers warrants. All are equity-derivative securities.[1] We concentrate mostly on options on individual stocks, but also consider index options, or options on stock indexes (both domestic and foreign, sectors such as gold/silver and utilities, and themes such as volatility). In Chapter 20, we consider futures contracts, which together with options constitute the most commonplace derivative instruments. Since we are focusing on investing instruments, we concentrate our discussion on *financial derivatives* as opposed to derivatives involving commodities such as gold, oil, and corn.

The emphasis here is on how puts and calls work, and on their importance to portfolio managers. As derivative securities, options are innovations in *risk management*, not in risk itself, and as such should be both welcomed and used by investors and portfolio managers. Again, our emphasis is on equity securities, and our examples revolve around common stocks.

Why Have Derivative Securities?

Over the years some people have asked why do we have derivative instruments such as options and futures, which allow investors to speculate on securities and indexes. Investors can easily lose their entire investment in the derivative security, and they have as the alternative buying either the underlying security or some index (typically, via an exchange-traded fund [ETF] or index mutual fund).

One important reason for the existence of derivatives is that they contribute to market completeness. A complete market is one where all identifiable payoffs can be obtained by trading the securities that are in that market. Although a truly complete market is not likely to exist, incomplete markets occur as a result of investors not being able to exploit all opportunities that may exist. Derivatives are one more means of achieving a more complete market, allowing investors to construct payoff patterns that would otherwise not be available.

Financial derivatives have several important applications, including risk management, trading efficiency, and speculation. Derivatives offer an opportunity to limit the risk faced by both individual investors and firms. They can also be used as a substitute for the underlying positions, and may offer lower transaction costs as well as more liquidity. Finally, derivatives do permit speculation, which involves taking a market position when a change in prices or interest rates is expected.

Introduction

Options Contracts giving the owner the right to buy or sell the underlying asset

Options, which represent claims on an underlying common stock, are created by investors and sold to other investors. The corporation whose common stock underlies these claims has no direct interest in the transaction, being in no way responsible for the creating, terminating, or executing put and call contracts.

[1] Rights are another equity-derivative security. They are not discussed further because of their minor importance to most investors.

Call An option to buy a stock at a stated price within a specified period of months

A **call** option gives the holder the right to buy (or "call away") 100 shares of a particular common stock at a specified price any time prior to a specified expiration date.[2] Investors purchase calls if they expect the stock price to rise, because the price of the call and the common stock will move together. Therefore, calls permit investors to speculate on a rise in the price of the underlying common stock without buying the stock itself.

Example 19-1

A Coca-Cola six-month call option at $50 per share gives the buyer the right (an option) to purchase 100 shares of Coke at $50 per share from a writer (seller) of the option anytime during the six months before the specified expiration date. The buyer pays a premium (the price of the call) to the writer for this option.

Put An option to sell a stock at a stated price within a specified period of months

A **put** option gives the buyer the right to sell (or "put away") 100 shares of a particular common stock at a specified price prior to a specified expiration date. If exercised, the shares are sold by the owner (buyer) of the put contract to a writer (seller) of this contract who has been designated to take delivery of the shares and pay the specified price. Investors purchase puts if they expect the stock price to fall, because the value of the put will rise as the stock price declines. Therefore, puts allow investors to speculate on a decline in the stock price without selling the common stock short.

Example 19-2

A writer (seller) of a Coca-Cola six-month put at $50 per share is obligated, under certain circumstances, to receive from the holder of this put 100 shares of Coke for which the writer will pay $50 per share. The writer received a premium (the price of the put) for selling this option.

WHY OPTIONS MARKETS?

An investor can always purchase shares of common stock if he or she is bullish about the company's prospects or sell short if bearish. Why then should we create these indirect claims on a stock as an alternative way to invest? Several reasons have been advanced, including the following:

1. Puts and calls expand the opportunity set available to investors, making available risk-return combinations that would otherwise be impossible or that improve the risk-return characteristics of a portfolio. For example, an investor can sell the stock short and buy a call, thereby decreasing the risk on the short sale for the life of the call.[3]
2. In the case of calls, an investor can control (for a short period) a claim on the underlying common stock for a much smaller investment than required to buy the stock itself. In the case of puts, an investor can duplicate a short sale without a margin account and at a modest cost in relation to the value of the stock. The

---

[2] It is important to remember throughout this discussion that the standard option contract on the organized exchanges is for 100 shares of the underlying common stock; therefore, when we speak of buying or selling *a* call or *a* put, we mean one contract representing an option on 100 shares of stock.

[3] Most stocks do not have puts and calls available in the organized options markets. Several hundred stocks constitute the active options market.

buyer's maximum loss is known in advance. If an option expires worthless, the most the buyer can lose is the cost (price) of the option.

3. Options provide leverage—magnified percentage gains in relation to buying the stock; furthermore, options can provide greater leverage than fully margined stock transactions.

4. Using options on a market index such as the Standard & Poor's 500 Composite Index (S&P 500), an investor can participate in market movements with a single trading decision.

Understanding Options

OPTIONS TERMINOLOGY

To understand puts and calls, one must understand the terminology used in connection with them. Our discussion here applies specifically to options on the organized exchanges as reported daily in such sources as *The Wall Street Journal*.[4] Important options terms include the following:

Exercise (Strike) Price
The per-share price at which the common stock may be purchased from (in the case of a call) or sold to a writer (in the case of a put)

1. *Exercise (strike) price.* The **exercise (strike) price** is the per-share price at which the common stock may be purchased (in the case of a call) or sold to a writer (in the case of a put). Most stocks in the options market have options available at several different exercise prices, thereby providing investors with a choice. For stocks with prices greater than $25, the strike price changes in increments of $5, whereas for those under $25, the increment is $2.50. As the stock price changes, options with new exercise prices are added.[5]

Expiration Price The date an option expires

2. *Expiration date.* The **expiration date** is the last date at which an option can be exercised.[6] All puts and calls are designated by the month of expiration. The options exchanges currently offer sequential options and other shorter term patterns. The expiration dates for options contracts vary from stock to stock but do not exceed nine months.

Option Premium The price paid by the option buyer to the seller of the option

3. *Option premium.* The **option premium** is the price paid by the option buyer to the writer (seller) of the option whether put or call. The premium is stated on a per-share basis for options on organized exchanges, and since the standard contract is for 100 shares, a $3 premium represents $300, a $15 premium represents $1500, and so forth. Information on options premiums can be found on *The Wall Street Journal*'s "Listed Options Quotation" page.[7] The most active contracts for the day are reported along with some individual equity options. Information about index options is also available on this page.

---

[4] Puts and calls existed for many years before these organized exchanges. They could be bought or sold in the over-the-counter market through brokers who were part of the Put and Call Dealers and Brokers Association. Members of this association endeavored to satisfy investor demands for particular options on a case-by-case basis. The terms of each individual contract (price, exercise date, and so on) had to be negotiated between buyer and seller. This was clearly a cumbersome, inefficient process.

[5] Options sold on these exchanges are protected against stock dividends and stock splits; therefore, if either is paid during the life of an option, both the exercise price and the number of shares in the contract are adjusted as necessary.

[6] American-style options can be exercised any time prior to expiration; European-style options can be exercised only at expiration.

[7] The WSJ page shows only a few of the options traded. More complete information is available in other sources, such as Barron's, and from various brokers via the Internet or directly by contacting the brokers..

Long-Term Equity
Anticipation Securities
(LEAPS) Options on
individual securities
with maturities up to
two years

The options page of *The Wall Street Journal*, as well as other sources, also carries the information for long-term options known as **long-term equity anticipation securities (LEAPS)**, which were introduced in 1990. These long-term options, available on roughly 450 stocks and several indexes, trade on four U.S. exchanges. All LEAPS options for stocks expire in January, and for indexes, December. Maturities extend out to about two and one-half years.

LEAPS are typically more expensive than short-term options, but with a longer maturity, they may cost less per share when calculated on a daily basis. Like short-term options, they can be used to hedge or speculate.

Example 19-3

S&P Index LEAPS are available on the S&P 100 and S&P 500. If the S&P 500 Index LEAP is currently valued at 100, this implies a value for the S&P 500 of 1000 (based on a value of one-tenth of the index). The multiplier is $100. In late July 2003, a December 05 call with a strike price of 100 was $10.90/share.

HOW OPTIONS WORK

As noted, a standard call (put) contract gives the buyer the right to purchase (sell) 100 shares of a particular stock at a specified exercise price any time before the expiration date. Both puts and calls are created by sellers who write a particular contract. Sellers (writers) are investors, either individuals or institutions, who seek to profit from their beliefs about the underlying stock's likely price performance, just as the buyer does.

The buyer and the seller have opposite expectations about the likely performance of the underlying stock, and therefore the performance of the option.

- ❏ The call writer expects the price of the stock to remain roughly steady or perhaps move down.
- ❏ The call buyer expects the price of the stock to move upward relatively soon.
- ❏ The put writer expects the price of the stock to remain roughly steady or perhaps move up.
- ❏ The put buyer expects the price of the stock to move down relatively soon.

Example 19-4

Consider an individual named Carl who is optimistic about Coca-Cola's prospects. Carl instructs his broker to buy a May call option on Coca-Cola at a strike price of $65. Assume the stock price is $64½ and the premium is $6⅜ (i.e., about $637.50, since 100 shares are involved). Carl pays this premium plus brokerage commissions.

Three courses of action are possible with any option:

1. *The option may expire worthless.* Assume the price of Coke fluctuates up and down but is at $50 on the expiration date. The call gives the buyer (owner) the right to purchase Coke at $65, but this would make no sense when Coke can be purchased on the open market at $50. Therefore, the option will expire worthless.
2. *The option may be exercised.* If Coke appreciates, Carl could exercise the option by paying $6,500 (the $65 exercise price multiplied by 100 shares) and receiving 100 shares of Coke.[8]

---

[8] Assume the price has appreciated to $80 before expiration. Carl now owns 100 shares of Coca-Cola worth $80 per share, for which he paid $65 per share (plus the $6⅜ per share for the call option itself). An immediate sale of the stock in the market would result in a $862 *gross profit* (brokerage costs are not included here), or [$8000 − ($6500 + $638)].

3. *The option can be sold in the secondary market.* If Coke appreciates, the value (price) of the call will also appreciate. Carl can easily *sell the call in the secondary market* to another investor who wishes to speculate on Coke, because listed options are traded continuously. Most investors trading puts and calls do not exercise those that are valuable; instead, they simply sell them on the open market, exactly as they would the common stock if they owned it.[9]

Puts work the same way as calls except in reverse. A writer creates a particular put contract and sells it for the premium that the buyer pays. The writer believes that the underlying common stock is likely to remain flat or appreciate, whereas the buyer believes that the stock price is likely to decline. Unlike a buyer, a writer may have to take action in the form of taking delivery of the stock.

Example 19-5   Assume a writer sells an August Coca-Cola put at an exercise price of $70 when the stock price is 69\frac{7}{16}$. The premium is 5$\frac{3}{4}$, or $575, which the buyer of the put pays and the writer receives (brokerage costs would be involved in both cases). Suppose the price of Coke declines to $60 near the expiration date.

The put owner (buyer), who did not own Coke previously, could instruct the broker to purchase 100 shares of Coke in the open market for $6,000. The buyer could then exercise the put, which means that a chosen writer must accept the 100 shares of Coke and pay the put owner $70 per share, or $7,000 total (although the current market price is only $60). The put buyer grosses $425 ($7,000 received less $6,000 cost of 100 shares less the $575 paid for the put). The put writer suffers an immediate *paper* loss, because the 100 shares of Coke are worth $60 per share but have a cost of $70 per share, although the premium received by the writer reduces this loss. (Brokerage costs have once again been omitted in the example.)

As in the case of a call, two other courses of action are possible in addition to the exercise of the put. The put may expire worthless because the price of the common did not decline or did not decline enough to justify exercising the put. Far more likely, however, the put owner can sell the put in the secondary market for a profit (or a loss). As in the case of calls, most put investors simply buy and sell their options in the open market.

THE MECHANICS OF TRADING

The Options Exchanges Five option exchanges constitute the secondary market: the Chicago Board Options Exchange (CBOE), the American, the Philadelphia, the Pacific, and the newer International Securities Exchange (ISE) in New York. Traditionally, the first four exchanges controlled the trading of U.S. options, each handling different options and competing very little. The ISE began trading in May 2000, and now has a substantial share of U.S. trading volume in options. This all-electronic market is extremely efficient, and has forced the other four exchanges to handle all options. This competition has led to lower costs and narrower spreads for customers, and quicker access to the market.

---

[9] One of the implications of the option pricing model to be considered later is that American calls on stocks that do not pay a cash dividend should never be exercised before the expiration date. Calls on stocks paying a cash dividend might be exercised before the expiration date.

The options markets provide liquidity to investors, which is a very important requirement for successful trading. Investors know that they can instruct their broker to buy or sell whenever they desire at a price set by the forces of supply and demand. These exchanges have made puts and calls a success by standardizing the exercise date and exercise price of contracts. One Coca-Cola May 50 call option is identical to every other Coca-Cola May 50 call option.

The same types of orders discussed in Chapter 5, in particular, market, limit, and stop orders, are used in trading puts and calls.[10] Certificates representing ownership are not used for puts and calls; instead, transactions are handled as bookkeeping entries. Option trades settle on the next business day after the trade.

The secondary markets for puts and calls have worked well in the years since the CBOE started operations in 1973. Trading volume has been large, and the number of puts and calls available has expanded.

Options Clearing Corporation (OCC) Stands between buyers and sellers of options to ensure fulfillment of obligations

The Clearing Corporation The options clearing corporation (OCC) performs a number of important functions that contribute to the success of the secondary market for options. It functions as an intermediary between the brokers representing the buyers and the writers. That is, once the brokers representing the buyer and the seller negotiate the price on the floor of the exchange, they no longer deal with each other but with the OCC.

Through their brokers, call writers contract with the OCC itself to deliver shares of the particular stock, and buyers of calls actually receive the right to purchase the shares from the OCC. Thus, the OCC becomes the buyer for every seller and the seller for every buyer, guaranteeing that all contract obligations will be met. This prevents the problems that could occur as buyers attempted to force writers to honor their obligations. The net position of the OCC is zero, because the number of contracts purchased must equal the number sold.

Investors wishing to exercise their options inform their brokers, who in turn inform the OCC of the exercise. The OCC randomly selects a broker on whom it holds the same written contract, and the broker randomly selects a customer who has written these options to honor the contract. Writers chosen in this manner are said to be assigned an obligation or to have received an assignment notice. Once assigned, the writer cannot execute an offsetting transaction to eliminate the obligation; that is, a call writer who receives an assignment must sell the underlying securities, and a put writer must purchase them.

One of the great advantages of a clearinghouse is that transactors in this market can easily cancel their positions prior to assignment. Since the OCC maintains all the positions for both buyers and sellers, it can cancel out the obligations of both call and put writers wishing to terminate their position.[11] With regard to puts and calls, margin refers to the collateral that option *writers* provide their brokers to ensure fulfillment of the contract in case of exercise. Options cannot be purchased on margin. Buyers must pay 100 percent of the purchase price.[12]

---

[10] Although available, the manner in which some types of orders are executed on some of the options exchanges varies from that used on the stock exchanges.

[11] For example, a call writer can terminate the obligation to deliver the stock any time before the expiration date (or assignment) by making a "closing purchase transaction" at the current market-determined price of the option. The OCC offsets the outstanding call written with the call purchased in the closing transaction. A put writer can also close out a position at any time by making an offsetting transaction.

[12] To protect itself, the OCC requires that its member firms whose customers have written options provide collateral to it in order to protect the OCC against defaults by writers. The member firms, in turn, require its customers who have *written* options to provide collateral for their written positions.

Payoffs and Profits from Basic Option Positions

We can better understand the characteristics of options by examining their potential payoffs and profits. The simplest way to do this is to examine their value at expiration. At the expiration date, an option has an *investment value*, or *payoff*, that can be easily determined. At the expiration date, the investment value is equal to the price of the option as determined in the marketplace. In addition, we can also examine the net *profit*, which takes into account the price of the stock, the exercise price of the option, and the cost of the option. We consider both variables because option traders are interested in their net profits, but option valuation is perhaps better understood by focusing on payoffs.

As part of this analysis, we use letters to designate the key variables:

S_T = the value of the stock at expiration

E = the exercise price of the option

CALLS

Buying a Call Consider first the buyer of a call option. At expiration, the investment value or *payoff* to the call holder is:

Payoff to call buyer at expiration:

$$= S_T - E \text{ if } S_T > E$$
$$= 0 \qquad \text{if } S_T \leq E$$

This payoff to a call buyer is illustrated in Figure 19-1(a). The payoff is $0 until the exercise price is reached, at which point the payoff rises as the stock price rises.

Figure 19-1

Payoff profiles for call and put options at expiration.

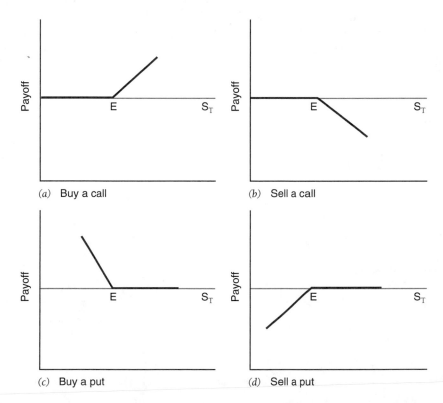

(a) Buy a call

(b) Sell a call

(c) Buy a put

(d) Sell a put

Example 19-6

Assume an investor buys a Coca-Cola three-month call with an exercise price of $50. The payoff for the call at expiration is a function of the stock price at that time. For example, at expiration the value of the call relative to various possible stock prices would be calculated as in the following partial set of prices:

Coca-Cola stock price at expiration	$40	45	50	55	60
Coca-Cola call price at expiration	$0	0	0	5	10

Notice that the payoff is not the same as the net profit to the option holder or writer. For example, if Coca-Cola is at $60 per share, the payoff to the option buyer is $10, but the net profit must reflect the cost of the call. In general, the profit to an option holder is the value of the option less the price paid for it.

Example 19-7

Figure 19-2 illustrates the *profit* situation for a call buyer. The price of the stock is assumed to be $48, and a six-month call is available with an exercise price of $50 for a premium of $4 (i.e., $400). If this call expires worthless, the maximum loss is the $400 premium. Up to the exercise price of $50, the loss is $4. The breakeven point for the investor is the sum of the exercise price and the premium, or $50 + $4 = $54. Therefore, the profit-loss line for the call buyer crosses the breakeven line at $54. If the price of the stock rises above $54, the value of the call will increase with it, at least point for point, as shown by the two parallel lines above the $0 profit-loss line.

Selling (Writing) a Call A call writer of an uncovered (naked) call incurs losses if the stock's price increases, as shown by the payoff profile in Figure 19-1(*b*) (note carefully that we are not talking here about covered call writing—writing a covered call is a different situation, as explained below). The payoff is flat at the amount of the premium until the exercise price is reached, at which point it declines as the stock price rises. The uncovered call writer loses if the stock price rises, exactly as the call buyer gains if the stock price rises.[13]

Figure 19-2

Profit and loss to the buyer of a call option.

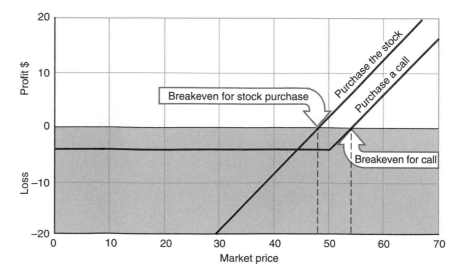

---
[13] The author is indebted to William Dukes for helpful comments in this discussion.

Figure 19-3

Profit and loss to
the writer of a call
option.

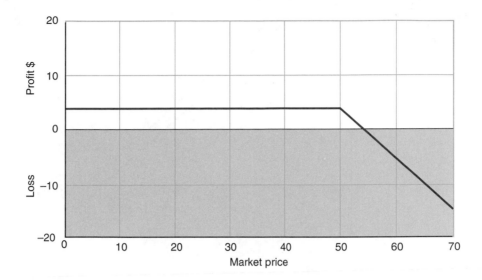

Payoff to call writer at expiration:

$$= -(S_T - E) \text{ if } S_T > E$$

$$= 0 \qquad \text{if } S_T \le E$$

The net *profit* line in Figure 19-3 shows a similar pattern to that of the call buyer except now the profit is positive up to the exercise price, because the call writer is receiving the premium. The horizontal axis intercept in Figure 19-3 occurs at the breakeven point for the option writer—the sum of the exercise price and the option premium received (note that the breakeven point is identical to that of the call buyer). As the stock price exceeds the breakeven point, the uncovered call writer loses.

The mirror images of the payoff and net profit profiles for the call buyer (Figure 19-2) and the call writer (Figure 19-3) illustrate an important point. Options trading is *a zero-sum game*. What the option buyer (writer) gains, the option writer (buyer) loses. With commissions, options trading could be unprofitable for both buyers and sellers and must be unprofitable for both taken together, since it is a zero-sum game.

PUTS

Buying a Put A put buyer makes money if the price of the stock declines. Therefore, as Figure 19-1(*c*) illustrates, the payoff pattern is flat at the $0 axis to the right of the exercise price; that is, stock prices greater than the exercise price result in a $0 payoff for the put buyer. As the stock declines below the exercise price, the payoff for the put option increases. The larger the decline in the stock price, the larger the payoff.

Payoff to put buyer at expiration:

$$= 0 \qquad \text{if } S_T \ge E$$

$$= E - S_T \text{ if } S_T < E$$

Once again, the profit line parallels the payoff pattern for the put option at expiration. As Figure 19-4 illustrates, the investor breaks even (no net profit) at the point where the stock price is equal to the exercise price minus the premium paid for the put. Beyond that point, the net profit line parallels the payoff line representing the investment value of the put.

Figure 19-4

Profit and loss to the buyer of a put option.

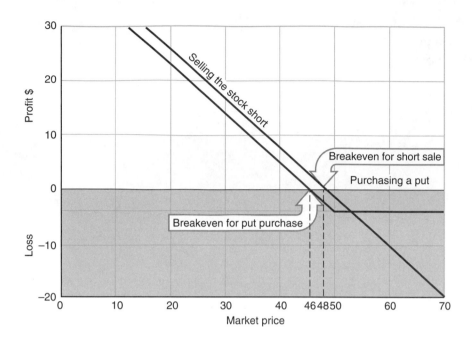

Selling (Writing) a Put The payoff pattern for the put writer is the mirror image of that for the put buyer as shown in Figure 19-1(d). The put writer retains the premium if the stock price rises and loses if the stock price declines. The put writer exchanges a fixed payoff for unknown losses.

Payoff to put writer at expiration:

$$= 0 \qquad \text{if } S_T \geq E$$
$$= -(E - S_T) \text{ if } S_T < E$$

Writers (sellers) of puts are seeking the premium income exactly as call writers are. The writer obligates himself or herself to purchase a stock at the specified exercise price during the life of the put contract. If stock prices decline, the put buyer may purchase the stock and exercise the put by delivering the stock to the writer, who must pay the specified price.

Note that the put writer may be obligated to purchase a stock for, say, $50 a share when it is selling in the market for $40 a share. This represents an immediate paper loss (less the premium received for selling the put). Also note that the put writer can cancel the obligation by purchasing an identical contract in the market.

Example 19-8 Figure 19-5 illustrates the profit-loss position for the seller of a put. Using the previous figures, we see that a six-month put is sold at an exercise price of $50 for a premium of $4. The seller of a naked put receives the premium and hopes that the stock price remains at or above the exercise price. As the price of the stock falls, the seller's position declines. The seller begins to lose money below the breakeven point, which in this case is $50 − $4 = $46. Losses could be substantial if the price of the stock declined sharply. The price of the put will increase point for point as the stock price declines.

Figure 19-5

Profit and loss to the writer of a put option.

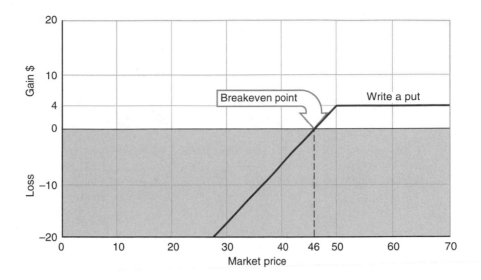

Some Observations on Buying and Selling Options Options are attractive because of the small investment required and the potentially large payoff. According to the studies that have been done, the odds favor the sellers. Writing calls produces steady, although not extraordinary, returns. Call writing is often profitable, and call buying is often unprofitable. When buying options investors should generally avoid options that expire in a few weeks—about 75 percent of the option premium disappears in the last three weeks of the option's life. Selling uncovered options can be very risky. In effect, the reward (premium) does not justify the risk for most investors.

Some Basic Options Strategies

In the previous section, we examined the payoffs and profit/losses for basic "uncovered" positions involving options (and their underlying stocks). The six uncovered positions are: long stock, short stock, buy call, write call, buy put, and write put. In this section, we analyze "covered" positions involving hedges. Spreads and combinations, which are also covered positions, are discussed in Appendix 19-A.

Hedge A strategy using derivatives to offset or reduce the risk resulting from exposure to an underlying asset

A **hedge** is a combination of an option and its underlying stock designed such that the option protects the stock against loss or the stock protects the option against loss. We consider below the more popular hedges.

COVERED CALLS

Covered Call A strategy involving the sale of a call option as a supplement to a long position in an underlying asset

A **covered call** involves the purchase of stock and the sale of a call on that stock; that is, it is a long position in the stock and a short position in a call. The position is "covered," because the writer owns the stock and could deliver it if called to do so as a result of the exercise of the call option by the holder. In effect, the investor is willing to sell the stock at a fixed price, limiting the gains if the stock rises in exchange for cushioning the loss, by the amount of the call premium, if the stock declines.

BOX 19-1

The Options Game

Why buying and selling calls has a place in even a conservative investor's playbook.

I am not much of a gambler. Years ago I was at the Desert Inn in Las Vegas and tried using a "system" for winning big at roulette. I don't recall the fine points, but it involved doubling my bet every time I lost. I was down so far, so fast, it left my head spinning. I spent the rest of the night playing blackjack, determinedly eking out small gains until, many tedious hours later, I was even.

For a long time I shunned options in the stock market as just another form of gambling. But a few years back, I bought some long-term call options, or "Leaps" (for Long-term Equity Anticipation Securities), which worked out quite nicely. Then a broker suggested I sell some calls on stocks I already own. In the process, I learned that selling these "covered calls" is deemed sufficiently conservative to be permitted in tax-advantaged retirement accounts. Though I consider myself a cautious investor, I now believe options have a place in every investor's arsenal.

Let's start with the basics, since most people I know, including myself, find options terminology confusing. A call option is the right to buy a share of stock at a fixed price at a fixed date in the future. A put is the opposite, the right to sell a share. Generally speaking, you buy a call when you think the stock price is going to rise, and a put when you think it will fall. So why are options considered riskier than stocks? After all, in buying or selling shares, you're also predicting whether the price will rise or fall. The difference is that because calls and puts often expire worthless, you can easily lose *all* of your investment.

Since options trades are actually contracts, they always have two sides: For every call or put that's bought, there's someone selling it. This is where things get trickier. Selling a call is a bet that the price will drop below the strike price and that you won't have to deliver the shares you promised when you sold someone the right to buy them. Selling a put is a bet the price will rise above the strike price, and therefore the buyer will not exercise the right to sell you the shares.

If you sell calls or puts and bet right, you simply keep the sale proceeds. If you bet wrong, you can get into trouble quickly. Say you sold calls on shares you don't own and the price skyrockets. You have to go into the market—and into your pocket—to buy them for delivery, and since there's no limit to how high the price might go (think Qual-comm during the late '90s), there's no limit to your potential loss.

To make this simpler, let's forget about puts entirely. Sure, buying a put can be an insurance policy against a declining market, but it's an expensive one, and *selling* a put is simply too risky for me.

Calls are another matter. First of all, consider the actual risk. Yes, you can lose 100 percent of your investment. But stocks, too, can go to zero or close to it, as we've learned the hard way the past few years. And because an option price is always a fraction of the share price, you may be putting very little money at risk. If you sell covered calls, your potential losses are also capped by the fact that you already own the shares. Sure, you may have to deliver them at a price far below what they would then fetch in the market, but you're not out any additional money.

I first bought some calls several years ago on shares of Tyco International. The stock had been hammered by short sellers, and then had been really clobbered when the Securities and Exchange Commission announced an investigation. Tyco denied any wrongdoing, and if the company was exonerated, there was potential for big gains. But if it wasn't, the share could go even lower.

I had no idea what the SEC would conclude, but this is a situation where I like to buy calls. The negative sentiment meant that sellers were plentiful, driving down prices on the call options. But I needed an option lasting long enough for the SEC to reach a decision, which is when I discovered Leaps. I was able to buy options expiring more than a year in the future at a strike price barely above where the battered stock was already trading, for about $1 a share. (Finding real-time option prices isn't easy. Unless you have something like a Bloomberg terminal, you have to ask a broker, which is a good way to make him actually earn his commission.) I bought 10 contracts, covering 100 shares each, for a total of $1,000. When the SEC exonerated Tyco eight months later, the stock—and option—prices soared, and I scored a big gain—all with just $1,000 at risk.

I had a similar experience buying calls on beleaguered Monsanto after it was attacked by antibioengineering activists. I figured the depressed stock would rebound once the benefits of such products as vitamin-enhanced "golden rice" became manifest. Little did I anticipate that Monsanto would be acquired by Pharmacia, which in turn was bought by Pfizer. My stake soared at each juncture. I exercised the optons, and when the Pfizer deal closes, I'll own a nice position in the company for an extremely modest investment.

Yes, I've had losses, especially over the past three years in a steeply declining market. My $45 strike price Nortel Networks call options, needless to say, expired worthless this January. Still, with Nortel having plunged to less than $2, my loss was far smaller than if I had bought the shares outright. And as readers of my weekly online column already know, I recently hit a home run with AOL options at a strike price of $7.50. It doesn't take many of these to offset the losses.

So my rules of thumb are quite simple: I reserve buying call options for special situations that have driven a stock price down and soured investor opinion. And I buy only options with a long enough term—so far, at least a year—for the special situation to work itself out.

When I *sell* calls, I put the strategy into reverse. I have found this an excellent way to respond when the market hits one of my selling thresholds, as it did in November's rally. With the market feeling pretty euphoric, I sold covered calls on AIG and Microsoft for a lofty price of about $3.50 per share. Selling options on 500 shares of each stock generated $3,500 in cash right away.

At the time, AIG was trading at about $63, and the strike price was $70, with the contract expiring in January. That meant if AIG shares managed to reach that threshold—and that would require a 10 percent rise in just three months—I would have to deliver the 500 shares. Even if that happened and I wound up having to sell them for less than they were trading for, I figured I would still be happy to realize the $35,000 in proceeds.

After selling call options, you don't have to sit by passively and wait for the contracts to expire. By early December, with the market slumping again, those AIG options I sold for $3.50 were fetching just 20 cents, and the Microsoft options were at 90 cents. I could have stepped in and bought them back, keeping most of my profit and avoiding having to worry about what happened over the next month. But I decided to stand pat and let the hand play out. Odds are these options will expire worthless, and if not—if a sudden rally drives the stocks above the strike prices—I will still benefit from the discipline of selling into a rally, which is in line with my overall investing strategy. As this column went to press, I was still waiting to see whether my bet would pay off.

So here are my rules for selling calls: Sell only covered calls, look for big premiums suggesting a euphoric market sentiment about a stock's prospects, and sell short-term contracts. I have now sold calls on more than a dozen occasions, and every one of them has resulted in a net profit.

In other words, I take a cautious, common-sense approach to options trading. Long-term, patient stock ownership remains the backbone of my investment approach, and options are a very small percentage of my portfolio. So far, my options trading has been very profitable. Yet curiously, my approach seems to be very unusual. Most options traders are technophiles and big institutions with sophisticated computerized strategies that seize on minor arbitrage possibilities and volatility aberrations. While I may just be experiencing beginner's luck, I'm beginning to suspect that the professionals have left some big opportunities for the rest of us.

SOURCE: James B. Stewart, "The Options Game," *SmartMoney*, February 2003, pp. 46, 48. Reprinted by permission of SmartMoney. Copyright ©2003 by *SmartMoney*. *SmartMoney* is a joint publishing venture of Dow Jones & Company, Inc. and Hearst Communications, Inc. All rights reserved worldwide.

Using our previous notation, the payoff profile at expiration is:

$$
\begin{array}{c|c|c}
 & S_T < E & S_T > E \\
\hline
\text{Payoff of stock} & S_T & S_T \\
\hline
-\text{ Payoff of call} & -0 & -(S_T - E) \\
\hline
\text{Total payoff} & S_T & E
\end{array}
$$

Figure 19-6 illustrates the *payoffs* on the covered call hedge by showing all three situations: purchase of the stock, writing a call, and the combined position. The sale of the call truncates the combined position if the stock price rises above the exercise price. In effect, the writer has sold the claim to this gain for the call premium. At expiration, the position is worth, at most, the exercise price and the profit is the call premium received by selling the call.

As Figure 19-6 shows, if the stock price declines, the position is protected by the amount of the call premium received. Therefore, the breakeven point is lower compared to simply owning the stock, and the loss incurred as the stock price drops will be less with the covered call position by the amount of the call premium.

Figure 19-6

Payoff profiles for a covered call.

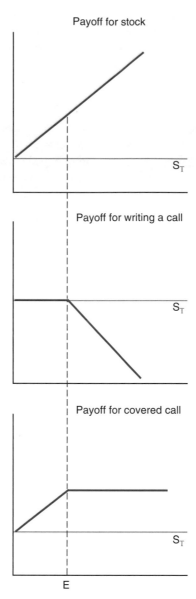

Payoff for stock

S_T

Payoff for writing a call

S_T

Payoff for covered call

S_T

E

Example 19-9   Assume that an investor purchased 100 shares of Coca-Cola last year for $40 per share and this year, with the stock price at $48, writes a (covered) six-month call with an exercise price of $50. The writer receives a premium of $4. This situation is illustrated in Figure 19-7.

   If called on to deliver his or her 100 shares, the investor will receive $50 per share, plus the $4 premium, for a gross profit of $14 per share (since the stock was purchased at $40 per share). However, the investor gives up the additional potential gain if the price of this stock rises above $50—shown by the flat line to the right of $50 for the covered call position in Figure 19-7. If the price rises to $60 after the call is sold, for example, the investor will gross $14 per share but could have grossed $20 per share if no call had been written.

Figure 19-7

Profit and loss for a covered call position.

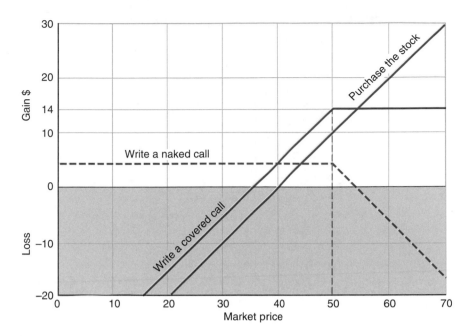

Writing a naked call is also illustrated (by the broken line) in Figure 19-7. If the call is not exercised, the writer profits by the amount of the premium, $4. The naked writer's breakeven point is $54. This position will be profitable if the price of the stock does not rise above the breakeven point. Notice that the potential gain for the naked writer is limited to $4. The potential loss, however, is large. If the price of the stock were to rise sharply, the writer could easily lose an amount in excess of what was received in premium income.

PROTECTIVE PUTS

Protective Put A strategy involving the purchase of a put option as a supplement to a long position in an underlying asset

A **protective put** involves buying a stock (or owning it already) and a put for the same stock; that is, it is a long position in both the stock and a put. The put acts as insurance against a decline in the underlying stock, guaranteeing an investor a minimum price at which the stock can be sold. In effect, the insurance acts to limit losses or unfavorable outcomes. The largest profit possible is infinite.

The payoff profile is:

	$S_T < E$	$S_T > E$
Payoff of stock	S_T	S_T
+ Payoff of put	$E - S_T$	0
Total payoff	E	S_T

Above the exercise price, the payoff reflects the increase in the stock price. Below the exercise price, the payoff is worth the exercise price at expiration.

Figure 19-8 shows the protective put versus an investment in the underlying stock. As always, the payoff for the stock is a straight line, and the payoff for the option strategy is an asymmetrical line consisting of two segments. The payoff for the protective put clearly illustrates what is meant by the term *truncating* the distribution of returns. Below a certain stock price (the exercise price), the payoff line is flat or horizontal. Therefore, the loss is limited to the cost of the put. Above the breakeven point, the protective put strategy

Figure 19-8

Payoff profile and profit/losses for a protected put position.

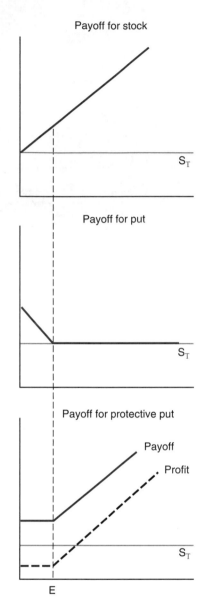

shares in the gains as the stock price rises. This is the true benefit of derivative securities and the reason for their phenomenal growth—derivatives provide a quick and inexpensive way to alter the risk of a portfolio.

Figure 19-8 illustrates how a protective put offers some insurance against a decline in the stock price. This insurance feature limits losses, but at a cost if the insurance turns out not to be needed—the cost of the put. Above the exercise price, the profit is less than the payoff profile for the investment because of the cost of the put. Below the exercise price, losses in the stock price are partially offset by gains from the put, resulting in a constant loss equal to the cost of the put.

This position is identical to purchasing a call except for a different intercept on the vertical axis.

The protective put illustrates a well-known concept called portfolio insurance, which is explained below.

PORTFOLIO INSURANCE

Portfolio Insurance
An asset management
technique designed to
provide a portfolio with
a lower limit on value
while permitting it to
benefit from rising
security prices

The potential return-risk modification properties of options, and particularly the insurance aspects discussed above, are well illustrated by the technique known as **portfolio insurance**. This term refers to investment strategies designed to hedge portfolio positions by providing a minimum return on the portfolio while simultaneously providing an opportunity for the portfolio to participate in rising security prices. This asset management technique became very popular in the 1980s, with many billions of dollars of assets being insured.

There are several methods of insuring a portfolio, including options, futures, and the creation of *synthetic options*. In practice, it is common to use futures contracts on market indexes (as discussed in Chapter 20). However, in principle, options can be used in portfolio insurance strategies, and their use illustrates the basic nature of a hedge.

The idea behind portfolio insurance as regards options is simple. A protective put can be purchased that allows the portfolio to be sold for an amount sufficient to provide the minimum return. The remaining portfolio funds are invested in the usual manner. The protective put provides insurance for the portfolio by limiting losses in the event stock prices decline. The portfolio's value at the end of the period must equal or exceed the exercise price of the put.

Example 19-10 An investor wishes to ensure a minimum return of 5 percent. For simplicity, we assume the investor starts with $1.[14]

- One unit of a stock market index sells for $0.9097.
- A European put on this index can be bought for $0.0903.
- The put has a strike price of $1.05.

The investor has used portfolio insurance to ensure a 5-percent minimum return. If the value of the stock index exceeds $1.05 by the end of the investing period, the investor is ahead that much and allows the put to expire worthless. If the value of the index is less then $1.05 by the end of the period, the investor can exercise the option and sell the stock index for $1.05, thereby earning the required 5-percent minimum return on the initial investment of $1.00. Portfolio insurance has provided protection against the downside while allowing the investor to participate in stock price advances.

This example illustrates the conceptual use of puts in portfolio insurance strategies. In practice, however, puts and calls are not used to insure portfolios, because those typically available to investors are American and not European. The exercise-at-any-time feature of American options makes them not only more valuable than corresponding European options but also much more costly for portfolio insurance purposes. Furthermore, it generally is not possible to find puts and calls with the exact time to expiration, exercise price, and so on that matches a particular portfolio.

It should also be noted that portfolio insurance is not costless. The costs include:

- The *cost of the option* itself. In our example, the put cost $0.0903. Obviously, if stocks advance and the put expires worthless, the cost of the put has been lost relative to an uninsured strategy. This can be thought of as the insurance premium.
- An *opportunity cost*. An investor who places 100 percent of investment funds in the stock index would participate fully in any market rise. In our example, the insured investor would participate in only 90.97 percent of any market rise.

---

[14] This example is based on Richard J. Rendleman and Richard W. McEnally, "Assessing the Costs of Portfolio Insurance," *Financial Analysts Journal* (May–June 1987): 27–37.

Option Valuation

A GENERAL FRAMEWORK

In this section, we examine the determinants of the value of a put or call. Special terminology is used to describe the relationship between the exercise price of the option and the current stock price. If the price of the common stock, S, exceeds the exercise price of a call, E, the call is said to be *in the money* and has an immediate exercisable value. On the other hand, if the price of the common is less than the exercise price of a call, it is said to be *out of the money*. Finally, calls that are *near the money* are those with exercise prices slightly greater than current market price, whereas calls that are *at the money* are those with exercise prices equal to the stock price.

These same definitions also apply to puts but in reverse. In summary,

If $S > E$, a call is in the money and a put is out of the money.

If $S < E$, a call is out of the money and a put is in the money.

If $S = E$, an option is at the money.

INTRINSIC VALUES AND TIME VALUES

The price of a call option can be dichotomized in the following manner. If a call is in the money (the market price of the stock exceeds the exercise price for the call option), it has an *immediate* value equal to the difference in the two prices. This value will be designated as the *intrinsic value* of the call; it could also be referred to as the option's minimum value, which in this case is positive. If the call is out of the money (the stock price is less than the exercise price), the intrinsic value is zero; in this case, the price of the option is based on its speculative appeal. Summarizing, where $S_0 =$ current stock price:

$$\text{Intrinsic value of a call} = \text{Maximum } (S_0 - E), 0 \qquad \textbf{(19-1)}$$

Example 19-11   Assume that on October 1 Compaq Computer closes at $27\frac{5}{8}$ and that a December call option with a strike price of 25 is available. This option is in the money, because the stock price is greater than the exercise price.

Intrinsic value of December 25 call $= \$27\frac{5}{8} - \$25 = \$2\frac{5}{8}$

Puts work in reverse. If the market price of the stock is less than the exercise price of the put, the put is in the money and has an intrinsic value. Otherwise, it is out of the money and has a zero intrinsic value. Thus:

$$\text{Intrinsic value of a put} = \text{Maximum } (E - S_0), 0 \qquad (19\text{-}2)$$

Example 19-12 Assume there is a Compaq Computer December put available on October 1 with a strike price of $30. The current market price is $27\frac{5}{8}$.

$$\text{Intrinsic value of Compaq Computer December 30 put} = \$30 - \$27\tfrac{5}{8}$$
$$= \$2\tfrac{3}{8}$$

An option's premium almost never declines below its intrinsic value. The reason is that market arbitrageurs, who constantly monitor option prices for discrepancies, would purchase the options and exercise them, thus earning riskless returns. **Arbitrageurs** are speculators who seek to earn a return without assuming risk by constructing riskless hedges. Short-lived deviations are possible, but they will quickly be exploited.

Arbitraguers Investors who seek discrepancies in security prices in an attempt to earn riskless returns

Option prices almost always exceed intrinsic values, with the difference reflecting the option's potential appreciation typically referred to as the *time value*. This is somewhat of a misnomer, because the actual source of value is volatility in price. However, price volatility decreases with a shortening of the time to expiration—hence the term *time value*.

Because buyers are willing to pay a price for potential future stock-price movements, time has a positive value—the longer the time to expiration for the option, the more chance it has to appreciate in value. However, when the stock price is held constant, options are seen as a *wasting asset* whose value approaches intrinsic value as expiration approaches. In other words, as expiration approaches, the time value of the option declines to zero.[15]

The time value can be calculated as the difference between the option price and the intrinsic value:

$$\text{Time value} = \text{Option price} - \text{Intrinsic value} \qquad (19\text{-}3)$$

Example 19-13 For the Compaq Computer options referred to earlier:

$$\text{Time value of December 25 call} = \$3\tfrac{1}{2} - \$2\tfrac{5}{8} = \$\tfrac{7}{8}$$
$$\text{Time value of December 30 put} = \$3 - \$2\tfrac{3}{8} = \$\tfrac{5}{8}$$

We can now understand the premium for an option as the sum of its intrinsic value and its time value, or

$$\text{Premium or Option price} = \text{Intrinsic value} + \text{Time value} \qquad (19\text{-}4)$$

Example 19-14 For the Compaq Computer options:

$$\text{Premium for December 25 call} = \$2\tfrac{5}{8} + \$\tfrac{7}{8} = \$3\tfrac{1}{2}$$
$$\text{Premium for December 30 put} = \$2\tfrac{3}{8} + \$\tfrac{5}{8} = \$3$$

[15] For an American option, time value cannot be zero because the option can be exercised at any time.

Notice an important point about options based on the preceding discussion. An investor who owns a call option and wishes to acquire the underlying common stock will always find it preferable to sell the option and purchase the stock in the open market rather than exercise the option (at least if the stock pays no dividends). Why? Because otherwise, he or she will lose the speculative premium on the option.

Example 19-15 Consider the Compaq December 25 call option, with the market price of the common at $27\frac{5}{8}$. An investor who owned the call and wanted to own the common would be better off to sell the option at $3\frac{1}{2}$ and purchase the common for $27\frac{5}{8}$, for a net investment of $24\frac{1}{8}$. Exercising the call option, the investor would have to pay $25 per share for shares of stock worth $27\frac{5}{8}$ in the market, but at a cost of $3\frac{1}{2}$ per share. (Brokerage commissions are ignored in this example.)

On the other hand, it can be optimal to exercise an American put early (on a nondividend paying stock). A put sufficiently deep in the money should be exercised early, because the payment received at exercise can be invested to earn a return.

The time to maturity is clearly a major determinant of the value of an option. Most investors should generally avoid deep in the money options, because they are expensive and their profit potential is limited. Similarly, most investors generally should avoid deep out-of-the-money options. Although the premium is low, the chances of a large return are also low. Most investors will generally be better served with slightly in the money or out of the money options, or options that are at the money.

BOUNDARIES ON OPTION PRICES

In the previous section, we learned what the premium, or price, of a put or call consists of, but we do not know why options trade at the prices they do and the range of values they can assume. In this section, we learn about the boundaries for option prices, and in the next section, we discuss the exact determinants of options prices.

The value of an option must be related to the value of the underlying security. The basic relationship is most easy to understand by considering an option immediately prior to expiration when there is no time premium. If the option is not exercised, it will expire immediately, leaving the option with no value. Obviously, investors will exercise it only if it is worth exercising (if it is in the money).

Figure 19-9(a) shows the values of call options at expiration, assuming a strike price of $50. At expiration, a call must have a value that is the maximum of 0 or its intrinsic value. Therefore, the line representing the value of a call option must be horizontal at $0 up to the exercise price and then rise as the stock price exceeds the exercise price. Above $50 the call price must equal the difference between the stock price and the exercise price, or its intrinsic value.

For puts the situation is reversed. At expiration, a put must have a value that is the maximum of 0 or its intrinsic value. Therefore, the line in Figure 19-9(b) representing the value of a put option must be horizontal beyond the exercise price. Below $50 the put price must equal the difference between the exercise price and the stock price. Note that a put option has a strict upper limit on intrinsic value, whereas the call has no upper limit. A put's strike price is its maximum intrinsic value.

What is the maximum price an option can assume? To see this think of a call. Since the call's value is derived from its ability to be converted into the underlying stock, it can never sell for more than the stock itself. It would not make sense to pay more for a call on

Figure 19-9

Determining the boundaries on option prices.

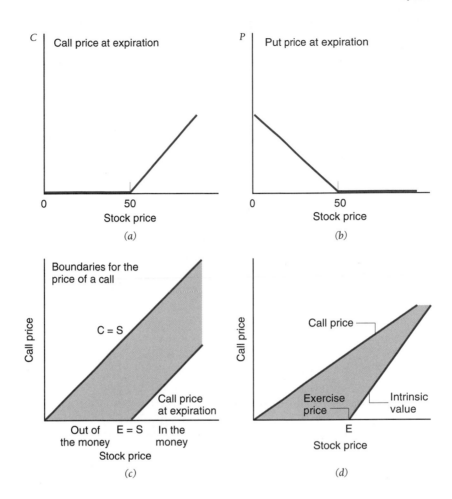

one share of stock than the price of the stock itself. Therefore, the maximum price for a call is the price of the underlying stock.

Based on the preceding, we can establish the absolute upper and lower boundaries for the price of a call option as shown in Figure 19-9(c). The upper boundary is a 45-degree line from the origin representing a call price equal to the stock price.[16] The lower boundary is the price of the option at expiration, which must be either zero or its in-the-money value. This is represented by the 45-degree line starting at the exercise price. Once again, the lower boundary can be interpreted as the value of the call at the moment the call is exercised, or its intrinsic value.

Finally, Figure 19-9(d) illustrates more precisely and realistically the variation in price for a call option by illustrating how the price of a call varies with the stock price and the exercise price. The call price is always above intrinsic value and rises as the stock price increases beyond the exercise price. The time value, represented by the shaded area in Figure 19-9(d), decreases beyond the exercise price.

To understand fully the price of a call option, we must use a formal model of call prices, the Black-Scholes model. The price of a put can also be found from this model because of a parity relationship between puts and calls.

---

[16] Think of this as a call with a zero exercise price and an infinite maturity.

THE BLACK-SCHOLES MODEL

Black-Scholes Model

A widely used model
for the valuation of
call options

Fischer Black and Myron Scholes have developed a model for the valuation of call options that is widely accepted and used in the investments community.[17] The formula itself is mathematical and appears to be very complex; however, it is widely available on calculators and computers. Numerous investors estimate the value of calls using the **Black-Scholes model**.

The Black-Scholes model uses five variables to value the call option of a *nondividend-paying stock*.[18] These five variables, all but the last of which are directly observable in the market, are as follows:

1. The price of the underlying stock
2. The exercise price of the option
3. The time remaining to the expiration of the option
4. The interest rate
5. The volatility of the underlying stock

The first two variables are of obvious importance in valuing an option, because, as noted before, they determine the option's intrinsic value—whether it is in the money or not. If it is out of the money, it has only a time value based on the speculative interest in the stock.

Time to expiration (measured as a fraction of a year) is also an important factor in the value of an option, because value generally increases with maturity. The relationship between time and value is not proportional, however. The time value of an option is greatest when the market price and the exercise price are equal.[19]

The interest rate affects option values because of the opportunity cost involved. Buying an option is a substitute to some degree for buying on margin on which interest must be paid. The higher interest rates are, therefore, the more interest cost is saved by the use of options. This adds to the value of the option and results in a direct relationship between the value of a call option and interest rates in the market.

The last factor, and the only one not directly observable in the marketplace, is the stock's volatility. The greater the volatility, the *higher* the price of a call option because of the increased potential for the stock to move up. Therefore, a positive relation exists between the volatility of the stock and the value of the call option.[20]

The Black-Scholes option pricing formula can be expressed as[21]:

$$CP = CMP[N(d_1)] - \frac{EP}{e^{rt}}[N(d_2)]$$ **(19-5)**

---

[17] F. Black and M. Scholes, "The Pricing of Options and Corporate Liabilities," *The Journal of Political Economy*, 81 (May–June 1973): 637–654.

[18] Options traded on organized exchanges are not protected against cash dividends, and this can have significant effects on option values. When a cash dividend is paid, the stock price should decline to reflect this payment. Any event that reduces the stock price reduces the value of a call and increases the value of a put.

[19] If the option is already in the money, a rise in the stock price will not result in the same percentage gain in the option price that would occur in the previous situation. For out of the money options, part of the time remaining will be used for the price of the stock to reach the exercise price.

[20] "Volatility" as used in the options model is not the same concept as a stock's beta as used in Chapter 7. Volatility is used here as a measure of the variability in the stock price as opposed to sensitivity to market movements.

[21] This version of the model applies to nondividend-paying stocks. Adjustments can be made for stocks that pay dividends.

where

    CP   = the price of the call option
    CMP = current market price of the underlying common stock
    $N(d_1)$ = the cumulative density function of d_1
    EP   = the exercise price of the option
    e = the base of natural logarithms = approximately 2.71828
    r = the continuously compounded riskless rate of interest on an annual basis
    t = the time remaining before the expiration date of the option, expressed as a fraction of a year
    $N(d_2)$ = the cumulative density function of d_2

To find d_1 and d_2, it is necessary to solve these equations:

$$d_1 = \frac{\ln(CMP/EP) + (r + 0.5\sigma^2)t}{(\sigma[(t)^{1/2}])} \quad \text{(19-6)}$$

$$d_2 = d_1 - (\sigma[(t)^{1/2}]) \quad \text{(19-7)}$$

where

    $\ln(CMP/EP)$ = the natural log of (CMP/EP)
    σ = the standard deviation of the annual rate of return on the underlying common stock

The five variables previously listed are needed as inputs. Variables 1–4 are immediately available. Variable 5 is not, however, because what is needed is the variability expected to occur in the stock's rate of return. Although historical data on stock returns are typically used to estimate this standard deviation, variability does change over time. A formula user should try to incorporate expected changes in the variability when using historical data. To do so, the user should examine any likely changes in either the market's or the individual stock's variability.

Variables 1–3 should be identical for a given stock for everyone using the Black-Scholes model. Variable 4 should be identical or very close among formula users depending on the exact proxy used for the riskless rate of interest. Variable 5 will vary among users, providing different option values. Empirical studies have shown that estimates of the variance obtained from other than historical data are more valuable than the estimates based on historical data. Since the price of an option can be observed at any time, it is possible to solve the Black-Scholes formula for the implied standard deviation of the stock's return. Henry Latané and Richard Rendleman found that better forecasts of the actual standard deviation could be obtained by preparing forecasts from the model itself.[22]

Example 19-16 The following is an example of the use of the Black-Scholes option pricing formula:

Assume

    CMP = $40

    EP   = $45

    r = 0.10

[22] H. Latané and R. Rendleman, Jr., "Standard Deviations of Stock Price Ratios Implied in Option Prices," *The Journal of Finance* (May 1976): 369–382.

$$t = 0.5 \text{ (6 months)}$$

$$\sigma = 0.45$$

Step 1: Solve for d_1.

$$d_1 = \frac{\ln(40/45) + [(0.10 + 0.5(0.45)^2]0.5}{0.45[(0.5)^{1/2}]}$$

$$= \frac{-0.1178 + 0.1006}{0.3182}$$

$$= -0.054$$

Step 2: Use a cumulative probability distribution table to find the value of $N(d_1)$.

$$N(d_1) = 0.4801$$

where $d_1 = -0.054$

Step 3: Find d_2.

$$d_2 = -0.054 - [0.45((0.5)^{1/2})]$$

$$= -0.372$$

Step 4: Find $N(d_2)$.

$$N(d_2) \approx 0.3557$$

Step 5: Solve for CP, the price of the call.

$$CP = CMP[0.4801] - EP[\text{antilog} - (0.1)(0.5)][0.3557]$$

$$= 19.20 - 45(0.9512)(0.3557)$$

$$= 19.20 - 15.23$$

$$= \$3.97$$

The theoretical (fair) value of the option, according to the Black-Scholes formula, is $3.97. If the current market price of the option is greater than the theoretical value, it is overpriced; if less, it is underpriced.

Investors can use knowledge gained from understanding the Black-Scholes valuation model in their trading activities.

PUT OPTION VALUATION

To establish put prices, we can take advantage of the principle of put-call parity.

Put-Call Parity The formal relationship between a call and a put on the same item that must hold if no arbitrage is to occur

The **put-call parity** principle expresses the relationship between the prices of puts and calls on the same stock that must hold if arbitrage is to be ruled out. In other words, unless the price of the put and the call bear a certain relationship to each other, there will be opportunities for earning riskless profits (arbitrage). The put-call parity can be expressed as

$$\text{Price of put} = EP/(e^{rt}) - CMP + CP \tag{19-8}$$

where all terms are as defined before.

Example 19-17 Use the information for the call given earlier. Since the Black-Scholes model uses continuous interest, the discount factor is expressed in continuous form.[23] It is equal to e^{rt}, or $e^{10(0.5)}$. Using a calculator, this value is 1.051. Therefore,

$$\text{Price of put} = 45/1.051 - 40 + 3.96 = \$6.78$$

SUMMARIZING THE FACTORS AFFECTING OPTIONS PRICES

If we allow for stocks that pay dividends, we can summarize the factors affecting options prices into a table with six elements, as shown in Table 19-1. The + sign indicates a direct relation, and a negative sign a negative relation. The assumption behind Table 19-1 is that all other variables remain fixed as we consider any of the six variables individually.

Table 19-1 Effects of Various Variables on Options Prices

Variable	Calls	Puts
Stock price	+	−
Exercise price	−	+
Time to expiration	+	+
Stock volatility	+	+
Interest rates	+	−
Cash dividends	−	+

HEDGE RATIOS

A key concept with options is their use as a hedging device. Although risky assets themselves, options can be used to control risk. In particular, options can be used to control the riskiness inherent in common stocks.

To hedge a long stock position with options, an investor would write one call option while simultaneously buying a certain number of shares of common. This number is given by the **hedge ratio**, which is $N(d_1)$ from the Black-Scholes model.[24] The hedge ratio for an option, commonly referred to as the option's *delta*, indicates the change in the price of the option for a $1 change in the price of the common. Since the hedge ratio with a call option is $N(d_1)$, for a put option it is $N(d_1) - 1$.

Hedge Ratio The ratio of options written to shares of stock held long in a riskless portfolio

Example 19-18 In the preceding example, $N(d_1)$ was 0.48; therefore, for every call option written, 0.48 shares of the common would be required to hedge the position. For a standard 100-share option contract, 48 shares of stock would be required. A $1 increase in the price of the stock should produce a $0.48 change in the price of the option. The loss on the call options written is $100 \times \$0.48$, or $48, which is offset by the gain on the 48 shares of stock of $48. A perfectly hedged position leaves total wealth unchanged.

[23] The value e^k is the equivalent of $(1 + r)$ in continuous compounding. If r is 5 percent, the value of e^k is $e^{0.05}$, or 1.051.
[24] Technically, the hedge ratio is the slope of the functional relationship between the value of the option (vertical axis) and the value of the stock (horizontal axis), evaluated at the current stock price.

The fact that hedge ratios are less than 1.0 indicates that option values change with stock prices on less than a one-for-one basis. That is, dollar movements in options prices are smaller than dollar movements in the underlying stock. However, *percentage* price changes on the option generally will be greater than percentage price changes on the stock.

USING THE BLACK-SCHOLES MODEL

What does it mean if we calculate an intrinsic value for an option that is significantly different from the market price? Although this may represent an investment opportunity, we must remember that the original Black-Scholes model is based on some simplifying assumptions, such as the payment of no dividends, a constant variance, and continuous stock prices. The standard deviation cannot be observed and must be estimated. Therefore, any observed discrepancies could reflect errors in the estimation of the stock's volatility.

Development of the Black-Scholes model was a significant event and has had a major impact on all options investors both directly and indirectly. This model has been the basis of extensive empirical investigations into how options are priced. How well does this model work?

The numerous studies that have been conducted offer general support for the Black-Scholes model and the proposition that options are efficiently priced by the market. Some deficiencies have been noted.[25] The deviations and biases that appear to remain in option pricing models may derive from several sources. For example, the true stock-price volatility is unobservable. Despite any statistically significant biases that may exist in the prices generated by the option pricing models, however, the validity of these models remains intact. What are the implications of this for market efficiency?

Using the Internet

Sophisticated investors often analyze options by comparing a stock's volatility and its implied volatility. Options are overpriced if implied volatility is greater than historical volatility. Ivolatility.com allows users to see a stock's implied volatility, historical volatility and current volatility. Investors can focus on trading strategies at www.optioninvestor.com. Trading ideas are arranged by strategy type, such as play of the day, calls, puts, and so forth. Data and commentary are available at www.schaeffersresearch.com, as is a Black-Scholes pricing calculator.

One interesting use of volatility is the VIX, an index of options volatility provided by the CBOE. Many observers believe that when this index hits 50, it is time to buy. In fact, this indicator has proven reliable several times in recent years. Current and historical data for this measure can be found at www.cboe.com.

An Investor's Perspective on Puts and Calls

WHAT PUTS AND CALLS MEAN TO INVESTORS

Earlier we examined some simple strategies using puts and calls and briefly considered some more sophisticated strategies. It is important for investors to have an overall perspective on puts and calls and consider what they really add to the investment process.

---

[25] See Dan Galai, "A Survey of Empirical Tests of Option-Pricing Models," in Menachem Brenner, ed., *Option Pricing: Theory and Applications* (Lexington, Mass.: Lexington Books, 1983), pp. 45–80.

Options contracts are important to investors in terms of the two dimensions of every investment decision that we have emphasized throughout this book—the return and risk from an asset or portfolio. Options can be used for various types of hedging, which is concerned with the management of risk. Options also offer speculators a way to leverage their investment with a strict limit on downside risk.

The return-risk modification properties of puts and calls vary significantly from other derivative instruments such as futures contracts, which we consider in Chapter 20. The important point about options and portfolio return and risk is that the impact of options is not symmetrical. As discussed earlier, the distribution of payoffs is *truncated*, because in the case of buying a call, the most the investor can lose is the premium regardless of what happens to the stock price. The same is true when purchasing a put—relative to the profit-loss line when selling short—the distribution of possible profits and losses from purchasing a put is truncated. If the stock price continues to rise, adversely affecting the investor, the most that can be lost from the put purchase is the premium.

Some Practical Advice

Investors who consider buying options as a way to trade in securities should remember a couple of key points:

❏ With options, you have approximately a 50-percent chance of losing your entire investment. Thus, this is a high-risk investment.

❏ With options, there is a small chance of making a large profit, often 5 to 10 times the original investment, and sometimes more.

Given these two points, options may be attractive to some investors and very unattractive to others.

THE EVOLUTIONARY USE OF OPTIONS

Puts and calls on organized options exchanges have been available to investors since 1973, although financial derivatives were being used long before then. Puts and calls have been popular with individual investors since the beginning of CBOE trading, although the manner in which they are viewed has changed somewhat. At first, options were viewed more or less as speculative instruments and were often purchased for their leverage possibilities. Covered option writing was used to enhance portfolio yields. During the 1980s many investors were selling puts in order to capitalize on the rising trend in stock prices. This strategy worked well until the famous market crash in October 1987. As a result of the losses, many investors once again viewed options as speculative instruments, and options volume did not return to the level reached in 1987 for several years. From the standpoint of the late 1990s, the average daily volume of contracts has more than doubled, and estimates of the future growth rate reflect a strong interest in options.

The current emphasis by the brokerage industry is on educating investors as to how options can be used efficiently as part of their portfolio. Investor desire to hedge their portfolios against a market decline (often predicted in the late 1990s by market observers because of the strong upward movement in the market) as well as the introduction of new products—for example, options on new indexes, country funds, American Depository Receipts (ADRs), and the new LEAPS—seems to be drawing the public back into the market.

By the 1980s, options had proved to be a respectable investment alternative and had begun to attract institutional attention.[26] Changes in regulations occurred that, in effect, encouraged institutional interest in options. Pension funds, insurance companies, and

---

[26] This discussion is based on "Money Management Begins to Accept Options As a Prudent Investment," *The Wall Street Journal*, September 22, 1980, p. 27.

banks began to receive clearance for the trading of options, provided that such trading met the guidelines under which they normally operate.

Options today are increasingly valued in strategic portfolio management, because they allow investors to create strategies that expand the set of outcomes beyond what could be achieved in the absence of options. In other words, investors and investment managers sometimes need the nonsymmetrical distributions of returns that options can provide. Options strategies increase the set of contingencies that can be provided for.[27]

At some brokerage firms, such as E Trade, options volume has increased significantly and now accounts for a sizeable percentage of the firm's revenues. The on-line brokerage firms have made options trading much easier, and options information, recommendations, and strategies much more accessible. Nevertheless, many investors with a strong interest in options are turning to so-called "options boutiques" that cater to options traders. These specialized brokers, such as OptionsXpress, Wall Street Access, and Wallstreet*E Online Trading, offer complex trades at lower prices than regular brokerage firms, specialized risk-assessment tools, and a staff specifically trained in options.

Stock-Index Options

Stock-Index Options
Option contracts on a stock market index such as the S&P 500

An important part of the options market for many investors is **stock-index options**. Rather than concentrate on options for individual securities, investors can buy puts and calls on various market indexes, thereby taking a position on broad market movements.

THE BASICS OF STOCK-INDEX OPTIONS

As of the beginning of 2001, stock-index options were available on a variety of market indexes, including (but not limited to) the S&P 100 Index, the S&P 500 Index, the Dow Jones Industrial Average (DJIA) Index, the Russell 2000 Index, the Major Market Index, the Value Line Index, the S&P Midcap Index, the Japan Index, and the Nasdaq-100 Index. Index options were also available on some industry subindexes, including Pharmaceuticals, Gold/Silver, Oil Services and Semiconductors. In addition, long-term index options (LEAPS) were available for the S&P 100 and 500 indexes and for the DJIA Index.[28]

Stock-index options enable investors to trade on general stock market movements or industries in the same way that they can trade on individual stocks. Thus, an investor who is bullish on the market can buy a call on a market index, and an investor who is bearish on the overall market can buy a put. The investor need only make a market decision, not an industry or an individual stock decision.

Overall, stock-index options are similar to the options listed on the options exchanges. As usual, the exercise price and the expiration date are uniformly established. Investors buy and sell them through their broker in the normal manner. Index option information is read in the same manner as that for stock options.

Unlike stock options which require the actual delivery of the stock upon exercise, buyers of index options receive cash from the seller upon exercise of the contract. The amount of cash settlement is equal to the difference between the closing price of the index and the strike price of the option multiplied by a specified dollar amount.

---

[27] This discussion is based on Richard Bookstaber, "The Use of Options in Performance Structuring," *Journal of Portfolio Management* (Summer 1985): 36–37.

[28] In 1986, the S&P 500 Index option was converted to a European-style contract; meaning it cannot be exercised until the contract expires. The predictable exercise date appeals to institutional investors when they attempt to hedge their portfolios against losses in volatile markets. Hedgers using standard index options may find their hedges exercised before the contracts expire, thereby giving an edge to the European-style contracts. The Institutional Index is also European-style.

Example 19-19 Assume an investor holds an S&P 100 Index option (OEX)—the S&P 100 Index consists of 100 blue-chip stocks on which the CBOE has listed options. The strike price is 580, and the investor decides to exercise the option on a day that the S&P 100 Index closes at 588.5. The investor will receive a cash payment from the assigned writer equal to $100 multiplied by the difference between the option's strike price and the closing value of the index, or

$$
\begin{array}{ll}
\text{S\&P 100 Index close} & = 588.5 \\
\text{S\&P 100 Index option strike price} & = \underline{580.0} \\
& 8.5
\end{array}
$$

$$
8.5 \times \$100 = \$850
$$

Note the use of the $100 multiplier for this index option. The multiplier performs a function similar to the unit of trading (100 shares) for a stock option in that it determines the total dollar value of the cash settlement. Since options on different indexes may have different multipliers, it is important to know the multiplier for the stock index being used.

STRATEGIES WITH STOCK-INDEX OPTIONS

The strategies with index options are similar to those for individual stock options. Investors expecting a market rise buy calls, and investors expecting a market decline buy puts. The maximum losses from these two strategies—the premiums—are known at the outset of the transaction. The potential gains can be large because of the leverage involved with options.

Example 19-20 In early April, an investor expects the stock market to rise strongly over the next two to three months. This investor decides to purchase an S&P 100 Index May 590 call, currently selling for 24, on a day when the S&P 100 Index closed at 588.5.

Assume that the market rises, as the investor expected, to a mid-May level of 623.81 (a 6-percent increase). The investor could exercise the option and receive a cash settlement equal to the difference between the index close (623.81) and the exercise price of 590, multiplied by $100, or[29]

$$
\begin{array}{l}
623.81 \text{ S\&P 100 Index close} \\
\underline{-590.00 \text{ S\&P 100 Call exercise price}} \\
33.81 \times \$100 = \$3381
\end{array}
$$

The leverage offered by index options is illustrated in this example by the fact that a 6-percent rise in the index leads to a 40.9-percent profit on the option position [($3381 − $2400)/$2400 = 40.88%]. Obviously, leverage can, and often does, work against an investor. If the market declined or remained flat, the entire option premium of $2400 could be lost unless the buyer of this option sold at some point before expiration. As with any option, however, the investor has a limited loss of known amount—the premium paid.

Investors can use stock-index options to hedge their positions. For example, an investor who owns a diversified portfolio of stocks may be unwilling to liquidate his or her portfolio but is concerned about a near-term market decline. Buying a put on a market

---

[29] Before exercising, the investor should determine if a better price could be obtained by selling the option.

index will provide some protection to the investor in the event of a market decline. In effect, the investor is purchasing a form of market insurance. The losses on the portfolio holdings will be partially offset by the gains on the put. If the market rises, the investor loses the premium paid but gains with the portfolio holdings. A problem arises, however, in that the portfolio holdings and the market index are unlikely to be a perfect match. The effectiveness of this hedge will depend on the similarity between the two.

Example 19-21   Assume an investor has a portfolio of New York Stock Exchange (NYSE) blue-chip common stocks currently worth $59,000. It is early April and this investor is concerned about a market decline over the next couple of months. The S&P 100 Index (OEX) is currently at 588.5, and an S&P 100 Index May 590 put is available for 10. In an attempt to protect the portfolio's profits against a market decline, the investor purchases one of these puts, which represent an aggregate exercise price of $59,000, calculated as (590 × 100 = $59,000).[30]

Assume that the market declines about 10 percent by the May expiration. If the OEX Index is 530 at that point, the investor collects from the put as follows:

Put exercise price = 590

OEX Index price = 530

60 × $100 = $6,000

If the value of the investor's portfolio declines approximately 10 percent, the loss on the portfolio of $5,900 will be somewhat offset by the net gain on the put contract of $6,000 − $1,000 premium paid for the put. It is important to note, however, that a particular portfolio's value may decline more or less than the overall market as represented by one of the market indexes such as the S&P 100 or 500 Index. For example, poorly diversified portfolio may decline less or more than the change in the index.

As before, if the option is held to expiration and a market decline (of a significant amount) does not occur, the investor could lose the entire premium paid for the put(s). In our example, the investor could lose the entire $1,000 paid for the put. This could be viewed as the cost of obtaining "market insurance."

Stock-index options can be useful to institutional investors (or individuals) who do not have funds available immediately for investment but anticipate a market rise. Buying calls will allow such investors to take advantage of the rise in prices if it does occur. Of course, the premium could be lost if the anticipations are incorrect.

Investors can sell (write) index options either to speculate or to hedge their positions. As we saw in the case of individual options, however, the risk can be large. If the seller is correct in his or her beliefs, the profit is limited to the amount of the premium; if incorrect, the seller faces potential losses far in excess of the premiums received from selling the options. It is impractical (or impossible) to write a completely covered stock-index option because of the difficulty of owning a portfolio that exactly matches the index at all points in time. Although the writer of an individual stock call option can deliver the stock if the option is exercised, the writer of a stock-index call option that is exercised must settle in cash and cannot be certain that gains in the stock portfolio will *fully* offset losses on the index option.[31]

---

[30] The exercise value of an index option, like any stock option, is equal to 100 (shares) multiplied by the exercise price. Divide portfolio value by exercise value to calculate number of puts needed, and round off.

[31] Writers of index options are notified of their obligation to make a cash settlement on the business day following the day of exercise.

THE POPULARITY OF STOCK-INDEX OPTIONS

Stock-index options appeal to speculators because of the leverage they offer. A change in the underlying index of less than 1 percent can result in a change in the value of the contract of 15 percent or more. Given the increased volatility in the financial markets in recent years, investors can experience rapid changes in the value of their positions.

Introduced in 1983, stock-index options quickly became a popular investment in the United States. Much of the initial volume was accounted for by professional speculators and trading firms. As familiarity with index options increased, individual investors assumed a larger role in this market.

Summary

▶ Equity-derivative securities consist of puts and calls, created by investors, and warrants and convertible securities, created by corporations.

▶ A call (put) is an option to buy (sell) 100 shares of a particular stock at a stated price any time before a specified expiration date. The seller receives a premium for selling either of these options, and the buyer pays the premium.

▶ Advantages of options include a smaller investment than transacting in the stock itself, knowing the maximum loss in advance, leverage, and an expansion of the opportunity set available to investors.

▶ Buyers of calls expect the underlying stock to perform in the opposite direction from the expectations of put buyers. Writers of each instrument have opposite expectations from the buyers.

▶ The basic strategies for options involve a call writer and a put buyer expecting the underlying stock price to decline, whereas the call buyer and the put writer expect it to rise. Options may also be used to hedge against a portfolio position by establishing an opposite position in options on that stock.

▶ More sophisticated options strategies include combinations of options, such as strips, straps, straddles, and spreads, which include money spreads and time spreads.

▶ Options have an intrinsic value ranging from $0 to the "in the money" value. Most sell for more than this, representing a speculative premium.

▶ According to the Black-Scholes option valuation model, value is a function of the price of the stock, the exercise price of the option, time to maturity, the interest rate, and the volatility of the underlying stock.

▶ The available empirical evidence seems to suggest that the options market is efficient, with trading rules being unable to exploit any biases that exist in the Black-Scholes or other options pricing models.

▶ Interest rate options and stock-index options are also available to investors.

▶ Stock-index options are a popular innovation in the options area that allows investors to buy puts and calls on broad stock market indexes and industry subindexes.

▶ The major distinction with these option contracts is that settlement is in cash.

▶ In effect, stock-index options allow investors to make only a market decision and to purchase a form of market insurance.

▶ The strategies with index options are similar to those for individual stock options. Investors can both hedge and speculate.

Key Words

Arbitrageurs
Black-Scholes model
Call
Covered call

Equity-derivative securities
Expiration date
Exercise (strike) price
Hedge

Hedge ratio
Long-term Equity Anticipation
  Securities (LEAPS)
Option premium

Options
Options clearing corporation
   (OCC)

Portfolio insurance
Protective put
Put

Put-call parity
Stock-index options

Questions

19-1 Distinguish between a put and a call and a warrant.

19-2 What are the potential advantages of puts and calls?

19-3 Explain the following terms used with puts and calls:
  a. Strike price
  b. Naked option
  c. Premium
  d. Out-of-the-money option

19-4 Who writes puts and calls? Why?

19-5 What role does the options clearing corporation play in the options market?

19-6 What is the relationship between option prices and their intrinsic values? Why?

19-7 What is meant by the time premium of an option?

19-8 Explain the factors used in the Black-Scholes option valuation model. What is the relationship between each factor and the value of the option?

19-9 Give three reasons why an investor might purchase a call.

19-10 Why do investors write calls? What are their obligations?

19-11 What is a straddle? When would an investor buy one?

19-12 What is a spread? What is its purpose?

19-13 Explain two types of spreads.

19-14 Why is the call or put writer's position considerably different from the buyer's position?

19-15 What is an index option? What index options are available?

19-16 What are the major differences between a stock option and an index option?

19-17 How can a put be used to protect a particular position? a call?

19-18 How does writing a covered call differ from writing a naked call?

19-19 Which is greater for an option relative to the underlying common, dollar movements or return volatility? Why?

19-20 What is the significance of the industry subindex stock index options?

19-21 Assume that you own a diversified portfolio of 50 stocks and fear a market decline over the next six months.
  a. How could you protect your portfolio during this period using stock-index options?
  b. How effective would this hedge be?
  c. Other things being equal, if your portfolio consisted of 150 stocks, would the protection be more effective?

19-22 Assume that you expect interest rates to rise and that you wish to speculate on this expectation. How could interest rate options be used to do this?

19-23 What does it mean to say that an option is worth more alive than dead?

CFA
19-24 Which is the *most risky* transaction to undertake in the stock-index option markets if the stock market is expected to increase substantially after the transaction is completed?

  a. Write an uncovered call option
  b. Write an uncovered put option
  c. Buy a call option
  d. Buy a put option

CFA
19-25 Which *one* of the following comparative statements about common stock call options and warrants is *correct*?

	Call option	Warrant
a. Issued by the company	No	Yes
b. Sometimes attached to bonds	Yes	Yes
c. Maturity greater than one year	Yes	No
d. Convertible into the stock	Yes	No

19-26 All of the following factors influence the market price of options on a common stock *except* the:

a. expected return on the underlying stock.
b. volatility of the underlying stock.
c. relationship between the strike price of the options and the market price of the underlying stock.
d. option's expiration date.

19-27 Investor A uses options for defensive and income reasons. Investor B uses options as an aggressive investment strategy. An appropriate use of options for Investors A and B respectively would be:

a. writing covered calls/buying puts on stock not owned.
b. buying out of the money calls/buying puts on stock owned.
c. writing naked calls/buying in the money calls.
d. selling puts on stock owned/buying puts on stock not owned.

Problems

19-1 The common stock of Teledyne trades on the NYSE. Teledyne has never paid a cash dividend. The stock is relatively risky. Assume that the beta for Teledyne is 1.3 and that Teledyne closed at a price of $162. Hypothetical option quotes on Teledyne are as follows:

Strike	Call			Put		
Price	Apr	Jul	Oct	Apr	Jul	Oct
140	$23\frac{1}{2}$	s	s	$\frac{3}{8}$	s	s
150	16	21	25	1	$3\frac{3}{4}$	r
160	$8\frac{7}{8}$	14	20	3	7	9
170	3	9	$13\frac{1}{4}$	9	10	11
180	$1\frac{1}{4}$	$5\frac{1}{4}$	9	r	20	r

r = not traded; s = no option offered.

Based on the Teledyne data, answer the following questions:

a. Which calls are in the money?
b. Which puts are in the money?
c. Why are investors willing to pay $1\frac{1}{4}$ for the 180 call but only 1 for the 150 put, which is closer to the current market price?

19-2 Based on the Teledyne data answer the following:

a. Calculate the intrinsic value of the April 140 and the October 170 calls.
b. Calculate the intrinsic value of the April 140 and the October 170 puts.
c. Explain the reasons for the differences in intrinsic values between a and b.

19-3 Using the Teledyne data, answer the following:

a. What is the cost of 10 October 150 call contracts in total dollars? From the text, what is the commission? Total cost?
b. What is the cost of 20 October 160 put contracts in total dollars? What is the commission? Total cost?
c. On the following day, Teledyne closed at $164. Which of the options would you have expected to increase? Decrease?
d. The new quote on the October 150 call was 26. What would have been your one-day profit on the 10 contracts?

e. The new quote on the October 160 put was $7\frac{1}{2}$. What would have been your one-day profit on the 20 contracts?

f. What is the most you could lose on these 20 contracts?

19-4 You are considering some put and call options and have available the following data:

	Call ABC	Call DEF	Put ABC
Time to expiration (months)	3	6	3
Annual risk-free rate	8%	8%	8%
Exercise price	$50	$50	$50
Option price	$ 3		$ 4
Stock price	$45	$45	$45

a. Comparing the two calls, should DEF sell for more or less than ABC? Why?

b. What is the time value for ABC?

c. Based on the information for the call and the put for ABC, determine if put-call parity is working.

19-5 Assume that the value of a call option using the Black-Scholes model is $8.94. The interest rate is 8 percent and the time to maturity is 90 days. The price of the underlying stock is $47.375, and the exercise price is $45. Calculate the price of a put using the put-call parity relationship.

19-6 Calculate, using the Black-Scholes formula, the value of a call option given the following information:

> Interest rate = 7%
> Time to expiration = 90 days
> Stock price = $50
> Exercise price = $45
> Standard deviation = 0.4

What is the price of the put using the same information?

19-7 Using the information in Problem 19-6, determine the sensitivity of the call value to a change in inputs by recalculating the call value if

a. the interest rate doubles to 14 percent but all other values remain the same.

b. the standard deviation doubles to 0.8 but all other values remain the same.

Which change causes the greatest change in the value of the call? What can you infer from this?

19-8 Given the following information, determine the number of shares of stock that must be purchased to form a hedged position if one option contract (covering 100 shares of stock) is to be written.

> Stock price = $100
> Exercise price = $95
> Interest rate = 8%
> Time to expiration = 180 days
> Standard deviation = 0.6

19-9 Given the information in Problem 19-8, determine how the value of the call would change if

a. the exercise price is $100

b. the time to expiration is 80 days (use the original exercise price of $95)

c. the time to expiration is 8 days

19-10 Determine the value of Ribex call options if the exercise price is $40, the stock is currently selling for $2 out of the money, the time to expiration is 90 days, the interest rate is 0.10, and the variance of return on the stock for the past few months has been 0.81.

19-11 Using the information in Problem 19-10, decide intuitively whether the put or the call will sell at a higher price and verify your answer.

Web Resources

For additional resources visit our dynamic Web site located at www.wiley.com/college/jones.

- *Exercise May Be Unhealthy*—Decisions concerning employee stock options as compensation relate to the principles of option valuation. The Black-Scholes Option Pricing Formula proves useful in evaluating the value of employee stock options as well a methods used to offset the risk of options.
- Alternate Case:
- *Career Options*—A career choice is a major investment decision with considerable uncertainty about the future. In the case, a finance major investigates his employment alternatives in the investments field and learns about the requirements for the Chartered Financial Analyst and Certified Financial Planner designations.
- Internet Exercises—This chapter discusses the pricing and use of options. The Web exercises will aid in the understanding of the different factors that affect option pricing. We will also look at how their use can transform portfolio return distributions.
  Exercise 1: Computing option returns.
  Exercise 2: Looking at simple option strategies.
  Exercise 3: Looks at the relation between call and put options.
  Exercise 4: Relating volatility to option prices.
  Exercise 5: Explores the maturity structure of option prices.
  Exercise 6: Computing implied volatilities.
  Exercise 7: Using implied volatilities to price options.
- Multiple Choice Self Test
- Appendix 19-A—Spreads and Combinations: Combinations of Options and Spreads
- Appendix 19-B—Warrants: Characteristics of Warrants

Selected References

A good overall discussion of options and associated strategies is available in:

> Schaeffer, Bernard G. *The Option Advisor: Wealth-Building Techniques Using Equity & Index Options.* John Wiley & Sons, 1997.

A book by a leading expert in options is:

> McMillan, Lawrence G. *Options as a Strategic Investment*, 4th edition. Prentice Hall Press.

chapter *20*

Futures

Chapter 20 covers futures, the other derivative security of importance to many investors. Although our discussion pertains in general to all markets, we concentrate specifically on financial futures as opposed to commodity futures. As with options, futures allow investors to manage investment risk and to speculate in the equity, fixed-income, and currency markets.

AFTER READING THIS CHAPTER YOU WILL BE ABLE TO:

▶ Understand why financial futures have been developed for use by investors.

▶ Describe the alternatives available to investors in the futures markets as well as how futures markets operate.

▶ Analyze basic strategies involving futures contracts.

utures markets play an important role in today's Investments world. New instruments in this area have proliferated, and techniques involving the use of futures, such as program trading, have captured wide media attention. Of particular importance to many investors is the array of financial futures now available. Anyone studying Investments should understand what futures contracts are, the wide variety of choices now available, and how financial futures can be used both to hedge portfolio positions and to speculate in fixed-income and equity areas. Futures contracts are an important component of derivative securities and, like options, are a major innovation in risk management.

Understanding Futures Markets

WHY FUTURES MARKETS?

Physical commodities and financial instruments typically are traded in *cash markets*. A cash contract calls for immediate delivery and is used by those who need a commodity now (e.g., food processors). Cash contracts cannot be canceled unless both parties agree. The current cash prices of commodities and financial instruments can be found daily in such sources as *The Wall Street Journal*.

There are two types of cash markets, spot markets and forward markets. Spot markets are markets for immediate delivery.[1] The spot price refers to the current market price of an item available for immediate delivery.

Forward markets are markets for deferred delivery. The forward price is the price of an item for deferred delivery.

Example 20-1

Suppose that a manufacturer of high school and college class rings is gathering orders to fill for this school year and wishes to ensure an established price today for gold to be delivered six months from now, when the rings will actually be manufactured. The spot (current) price of gold is not the manufacturer's primary concern, because the gold will not be purchased until it is needed for the manufacturing process. However, to reduce the risk involved with the future price of gold, the manufacturer wished to contract now for gold to be delivered in six months at a price established today. This will allow the manufacturer to price its rings more accurately, having locked in the price of gold.

Our manufacturer could find a gold supplier who was willing to enter into a forward commitment or contract, which is simply a commitment today to transact in the future. The other party to the contract, such as a mining company, agrees to deliver the gold six months from now at a price negotiated today. Both parties have agreed to a deferred delivery at a sales price that is currently determined. No funds have been exchanged. Both parties have reduced their risk in the sense that the mining company knows what it will receive for the gold when it is sold six months from now, and the ring manufacturer knows what it will pay for the gold when it actually needs to take delivery six months from now.

Investments Intuition

Obviously, one of the parties may be disappointed six months later when the price of gold has changed, but that is the advantage of hindsight. If investors could foresee the future, they would know what to do to start with and would not have to worry about risk. The forward and futures markets were developed to allow individuals to deal with the risks they face, because the future is uncertain.

[1] "Immediate" means in the normal course of business. For example, it may normally take two days for an item to be delivered after being ordered.

Forward contracts are centuries old, traceable to at least the ancient Romans and Greeks. Organized futures markets, on the other hand, effectively go back to the mid-nineteenth century in Chicago. Futures markets are, in effect, organized and standardized forward markets. An organized futures exchange standardizes the nonstandard forward contracts, establishing such features as contract size, delivery dates, and condition of the items that can be delivered. Only the price and number of contracts are left for futures traders to negotiate. Individuals can trade without personal contact with each other because of the centralized marketplace. Performance is guaranteed by a clearinghouse, relieving one party to the transaction from worry that the other party will fail to honor its commitment.

An important economic function performed by futures markets is price discovery. Because the price of a futures contract reflects current expectations about values at some future date, transactors can establish current prices against later transactions. The futures markets also serve a valuable economic purpose by allowing hedgers to shift price risk to speculators. The risk of price fluctuations is shifted from participants unwilling to assume such risk to those who are.

◼ Price discovery and price risk management are the primary functions of futures markets.

CURRENT U.S. FUTURES MARKETS

To most people, futures trading traditionally has meant trading in commodities such as gold, wheat, and oil. However, money can be thought of simply as another commodity, and financial futures have become a particularly viable investment alternative for numerous investors. Therefore, futures contracts currently traded on U.S. futures exchanges can be divided into two broad categories:

1. Commodities—agricultural, metals, and energy-related
2. Financials—foreign currencies and debt and equity instruments

Although financial futures are relatively new (compared to commodity futures), they now account for about two-thirds of all futures traded in the United States. Thus, the futures market to a large extent is a financial futures market.

Each category can be further subdivided as shown in Exhibit 20-1. As we can see, the futures markets involve trading in a variety of both commodities and financials.

For each type of contract, such as corn or silver, different delivery dates are available. Each contract will specify the trading unit involved and, where applicable, the deliverable grade necessary to satisfy the contract. Investors can also purchase options on futures contracts. Appendix 20-A explains futures options.

One of the striking features of Exhibit 20-1 is the proliferation of foreign-based futures contracts on U.S. futures exchanges. This is true for interest rate futures and stock-index futures, and is good evidence of the move toward globalization that is occurring throughout the investing world.

FOREIGN FUTURES MARKETS

European futures exchanges are quite competitive. Most of these systems are now fully automated order-matching systems.

Japan, which banned financial futures until 1985, is now very active in developing futures exchanges. With regard to stock-index futures, the Nikkei 225 contract, the most active Japanese index futures contract, trades on the Osaka Securities Exchange.

Exhibit 20-1 Futures Contracts Traded in the United States, by Category

The major commodities traded in the United States can be classified into the following categories (as shown in *The Wall Street Journal*):

I. Commodities

Grains and oilseeds	Wheat, corn, oats, soybean oils, soybean meal, flaxseed, rye, and canola
Livestock and meats	Cattle (both live and feeders), pork bellies, and hogs
Foods	Cocoa, coffee, orange juice, and sugar
Fibers	Cotton
Metals	Copper, gold, platinum, silver, and palladium
Oil	Gasoline, heating oil, crude oil, gas oil, propane
Wood	Lumber

II. Financials

Interest rates	Treasury bills, Treasury notes, Treasury bonds, municipal bond index, 30-day federal funds, Eurodollar, 1-month Libor, Sterling, Long Gilt, Euromark, EuroSwiss, EuroLira, German Government Bond, Italian Government Bond, French Government Bond, Canadian Government Bond
Stock Indexes	S&P 500 Index, S&P MidCap 400, NYSE Composite Index, Major Market Index, KR-CRB Index, KC Value Line Index, Russell 2000, CAC 40, Nikkei 225 Index, GSCL FT-SE 100 Index, Toronto 35 Index
Foreign currencies	Japanese yen, German mark, Canadian dollar, British pound, Swiss franc, Australian dollar, and U.S. Dollar Index

FUTURES CONTRACTS

Forward Contract A commitment today to transact in the future. Both parties have agreed to a deferred delivery at a sales price that is currently determined, with no funds having been exchanged

A **forward contract** is an agreement between two parties that calls for delivery of a commodity (tangible or financial) as a specified future time at a price agreed upon today. Each contract has a buyer and a seller. Forward markets have grown primarily because of the growth in swaps, which in general are similar to forward contracts.

◾ Forward contracts involve credit risk—either party can default on their obligation. These contracts also involve liquidity risk because of the difficulties involved in getting out of the contract. On the other hand, forward contracts can be customized to the specific needs of the parties involved.

Futures Contract A commitment to buy or sell at a specified future settlement date a designated amount of a specific commodity or asset

A **futures contract** is a standardized, transferable agreement providing for the deferred delivery of either a specified grade and quantity of a designated commodity within a specified geographical area or of a financial instrument (or its cash value). In simple language, a futures contract locks in a price for delivery on a future date.

The futures price at which this exchange will occur at contract maturity is determined today. The trading of futures contracts means only that commitments have been made by buyers and sellers; therefore, "buying" and "selling" do not have the same meaning in futures transactions as they do in stock and bond transactions. Although these commitments are binding because futures contracts are legal contracts, a buyer or seller can eliminate the commitment simply by taking an opposite position in the same commodity or financial instrument for the same futures month.

◾ Futures contracts are standardized and easily traded. Credit risk is removed by the clearinghouse (explained below) which ensures performance on the contract. On the other hand, they cannot readily be customized to fit particular needs.

Futures contracts are not securities and are not regulated by the Securities and Exchange Commission (SEC). The Commodity Futures Trading Commission (CFTC), a federal regulatory agency, is responsible for regulating trading in all domestic futures markets. In practice, the National Futures Association, a self-regulating body, has assumed some of the duties previously performed by the CFTC. In addition, each futures exchange has a supervisory body to oversee its members.

The Structure Of Futures Markets

FUTURES EXCHANGES

As noted, futures contracts are traded on designated futures exchanges, which are voluntary, nonprofit associations composed of members. There are several major U.S. exchanges.[2] The exchange provides an organized marketplace where established rules govern the conduct of the members. The exchange is financed by both membership dues and fees charged for services rendered.

All memberships must be owned by individuals, although they may be controlled by firms. The limited number of memberships, like stock exchange seats, can be traded at market-determined prices. Members can trade for their own accounts or as agents for others. For example, floor traders trade for their own accounts, whereas floor brokers (or commission brokers) often act as agents for others. Futures commission merchants (FCMs) act as agents for the general public, for which they receive commissions. Thus, a customer can establish an account with an FCM, who in turn may work through a floor broker at the exchange.

THE CLEARINGHOUSE

The clearinghouse, a corporation separate from, but associated with, each exchange plays an important role in every futures transaction. Since all futures trades are cleared through the clearinghouse each business day, exchange members must either be members of the clearinghouse or pay a member for this service. From a financial requirement basis, being a member of the clearinghouse is more demanding than being a member of the associated exchange.

Essentially, the clearinghouse for futures markets operates in the same way as the clearinghouse for options, which was discussed in some detail in Chapter 19. Buyers and sellers settle with the clearinghouse, not each other. Thus, the clearinghouse, and not another investor, is actually on the other side of every transaction and ensures that all payments are made as specified. It stands ready to fulfill a contract if either buyer or seller defaults, thereby helping to facilitate an orderly market in futures. The clearinghouse makes the futures market impersonal, which is the key to its success, because any buyer or seller can always close out a position and be assured of payment. The first failure of a clearinghouse member in modern times occurred in the 1980s, and the system worked perfectly in preventing any customer from losing money. Finally, as explained below, the clearinghouse allows participants easily to reverse a position before maturity, because the clearinghouse keeps track of each participant's obligations.

---

[2] Major U.S. futures exchanges include the following: Chicago Board of Trade (CBT), Chicago Mercantile Exchange (CME), Commodity Exchange, New York (COMEX), Kansas City Board of Trade (KCBT), Mid-America Commodity Exchange (MCE), Coffee Sugar & Cocoa Exchange (CSCE), New York Cotton Exchange (CTN), New York Futures Exchange (NYFE), New York Mercantile Exchange (NYM), the International Petroleum Exchange (PE), the Philadelphia Board of Trade (PBT), and the Twin Cities Board of Trade (TCBT).

The Mechanics of Trading

BASIC PROCEDURES

Because the futures contract is a commitment to buy or sell at a specified future settlement date, a contract is not really being sold or bought, as in the case of Treasury bills, stocks, or Certificates of Deposit (CDs), because no money is exchanged at the time the contract is negotiated. Instead, the seller and the buyer simply are agreeing to make and take delivery, respectively, at some future time for a price agreed upon today. As noted above, the terms *buy* and *sell* do not have the same meanings here. It is more accurate to think in terms of

Short Position An agreement to sell an asset at a specified future date at a specified price

Long Position An agreement to purchase an asset at a specified future date at a specified price

❑ A **short position** (seller), which commits a trader to deliver an item at contract maturity.
❑ A **long position** (buyer), which commits a trader to purchase an item at contract maturity.

Selling short in futures trading means only that a contract not previously purchased is sold. For every futures contract, someone sold it short and someone else holds it long. Like options, futures trading is a zero-sum game.

Whereas an options contract involves the *right* to make or take delivery, a futures contract involves an *obligation* to take or make delivery. However, futures contracts can be settled by delivery or by offset. Delivery, or settlement of the contract, occurs in months that are designated by the various exchanges for each of the items traded. Delivery occurs in less than 2 percent of all transactions.

Offset Liquidation of a futures position by an offsetting transaction

Offset is the typical method of settling a contract. Indeed, about 95 percent of futures contracts are closed before the contract expires by offset. Holders liquidate a position by arranging an offsetting transaction. This means that buyers sell their positions, and sellers buy in their positions sometime prior to delivery. When an investor offsets his or her position, it means that their trading account is adjusted to reflect the final gains (or losses) and their position is closed.

Thus, to eliminate a futures market position, the investor simply does the reverse of what was done originally. As explained above, the clearinghouse makes this easy to accomplish. It is essential to remember that if a futures contract is not offset, it must be closed out by delivery.

❑ An option involves the right, but not the obligation to take action, but
❑ A futures contract involves an obligation—either offset occurs or delivery occurs.

Each exchange establishes price fluctuation limits on the various types of contracts. Typically, a minimum price change is specified. In the case of corn, for example, it is 0.25¢ per bushel, or $12.50 per contract. A daily price limit is in effect for all futures contracts except stock-index futures. For corn it is 10¢ per bushel ($500 per contract) above and below the previous day's settlement price.

With stocks, shortselling can be done only on an uptick, but futures have no such restriction. Stock positions, short or long, can literally be held forever. However, futures positions must be closed out within a specified time either by offsetting the position or by making or taking delivery.

Unlike stocks, there are no specialists on futures exchanges. Each futures contract is traded in a specific "pit" in an auction market process in which every bid and offer competes without priority as to time or size. A system of "open outcry" is used, whereby any offer to buy or sell must be made to all traders in the pit.

Brokerage commissions on commodities contracts are paid on the basis of a completed contract (purchase and sale) rather than each purchase and sale, as in the case of stocks. As with options, no certificates exist for futures contracts.

The *open interest* indicates contracts that are not offset by opposite transactions or delivery. That is, it measures the number of unliquidated contracts at any point in time on a cumulative basis.[3] The open interest increases when an investor goes long on a contract and is reduced when the contract is liquidated.

MARGIN

Futures Margin The earnest money deposit made by a transactor to ensure the completion of a contract

Recall that in the case of stock transactions, the term *margin* refers to the down payment in a transaction in which money is borrowed from the broker to finance the total cost. **Futures margin**, on the other hand, is not a down payment, because ownership of the underlying item is not being transferred at the time of the transaction.[4] Instead, it refers to the "good faith" (or earnest money) deposit made by both buyer and seller to ensure the completion of the contract. In futures trading, unlike stock trading, margin is the norm. All futures markets participants, whether buyers or sellers, must deposit minimum specified amounts in their futures margin accounts to guarantee contract obligations.

❑ In effect, futures margin is a performance bond.

Initial Margin That part of a transaction's value a customer must pay to initiate the transaction, with the other part being borrowed from the broker

Each clearinghouse sets its own minimum **initial margin** requirements (in dollars). Furthermore, brokerage houses can require a higher margin and typically do so. The margin required for futures contracts, which is small in relation to the value of the contract itself, represents the equity of the transactor (either buyer or seller). It is not unusual for the initial margin to be only a few thousand dollars although the value of the contract is much larger. As a generalized approximation, the margin requirement for futures contracts is about 6 percent of the value of the contract. Since the equity is small, the risk is magnified.

Example 20-2

Assume the initial margin is equal to 5 percent of the total value and an investor holds one contract in an account. If the price of the contract changes by 5 percent because the price of the underlying commodity changes by 5 percent, this is equivalent to a 100-percent change in the investor's equity. This example shows why futures trading can be so risky!

Maintenance Margin The percentage of a security's value that must be on hand at all times as equity

Margin Call A demand from the broker for additional cash or securities as the result of the actual margin declining below the maintenance margin

In addition to the initial margin requirement each contract requires a **maintenance margin** (or variation margin), below which the investor's equity cannot drop. If the market price of a futures contract moves adversely to the owner's position, the equity declines. A **margin call** occurs when the price goes against the investor, requiring the transactor to deposit additional cash or to close out the account. If the account balance is below the initial margin but above the maintenance margin, no action is required. When the account balance goes below the maintenance margin level, a margin call is issued that requires the account holder to restore the account back to the initial margin level (not the maintenance margin level).

---

[3] The open interest can be measured using either the open long positions or the open short positions, but not both.

[4] Because no credit is being extended, no interest expense is incurred on that part of the contract not covered by the margin as is the case when stocks are purchased on margin. With futures, customers often receive interest on margin money deposited. A customer with a large enough requirement (roughly, $15,000 and over) can use Treasury bills as part of the margin.

To understand how the margin process for futures contracts works, we must first understand how profits and losses from futures contracts are debited and credited daily to an investor's account. All futures contracts are **marked to the market** daily, which means that all profits and losses on a contract are credited and debited to each investor's account every trading day.[5] Those contract holders with a profit can withdraw the gains, whereas those with a loss will receive a margin call when the equity falls below the specified variation margin. This process is referred to as daily resettlement, and the price used is the contract's settlement price.[6]

Marked to the Market
The daily posting of all profits and losses on a contract to each account

Example 20-3

Table 20-1 illustrates how accounts are marked to the market daily. Consider an investor who buys a stock-index futures contract on the Dow Jones Industrial Average (DJIA) using the Chicago Board of Trade's CBOT® DJIA^SM futures contract.[7] Assume that the investor's brokerage firm requires an initial margin of $7,000. The maintenance margin is $4,000 per contract.

This contract has a multiplier of $10. Price quotes are in points ($10), and the tick size is $10. The value of a CBOT DJIA Index futures contract is equal to $10 times the current index level. For example, if the index is trading at 10,000, one of these futures contracts is equivalent to investing $100,000 in the DJIA portfolio. The seller of such a contract (the short position) is agreeing to sell $10 times the index and the buyer (the long position) is agreeing to buy $10 times the index on the expiration date of the contract. On the settlement day of this futures contract, the final settlement price is $10 times the Special Opening Quotation of the index.

Assume investor A buys a contract with the DJIA at 10,000, whereas investor B, believing the DJIA will decline, sells (goes short) one contract at the same time. After day 1, the settlement price is 9,925. The buyer will have a debit in his or her account of $75 \times$10 = $750, because the price declined and the buyer was long. Conversely, the seller will have a credit of the same amount in his or her account because the seller was short and the price declined. At the end of day 1, the value of the buyer's account is $7,000 − $750 = $6,250, whereas the value of the seller's account is $7,000 + $750 = $7,750. In effect, both accounts have been marked to the market.

Table 20-1 An Example of Investor Accounts, Using Stock-Index Futures, Marked to the Market

	Buyer (Long)	Seller (Short)
Account after one day		
Original equity (initial margin)	$ 7,000	$7,000
Day 1 mark to the market	(750)	750
Current equity	$ 6,250	7,750
Account after two weeks		
Original equity	$ 7,000	$7,000
Cumulative mark to the market	4,000	(4,000)
Current equity	$11,000	$3,000
Withdrawable excess equity	$ 4,000	
Margin call		$4,000

[5] This is not true of forward contracts, where no funds are transferred until the maturity date.
[6] The settlement price does not always reflect the final trade of the day. The clearinghouse establishes the settlement price at the close of trading.
[7] Information about futures contracts on the Dow Jones Industrial Average can be found at the Chicago Board of Trade's Web site, www.cbot.com.

Now assume that two weeks have passed, during which time each account has been marked to the market daily (we also assume no margin calls have been necessary).[8] The settlement price on this contract has reached 10,400, with a move on the last day of this two-week period of 150 points. The aggregate change in market value for each investor is the difference between the current price and the initial price multiplied by $10, the value of one point in price. This will be

$$10,400 - 10,000 = 400 \times \$10 = \$4,000$$

As shown in Table 20-1, this amount is currently credited to the buyer because the price moved up as the buyer expected. Conversely, this same amount is currently debited to the seller, who is now on the wrong side of the price movement. Therefore, starting with an initial equity or margin of $7,000, after two weeks the cumulative mark to the market is $4,000. This results in a current equity of $11,000 for the buyer and $3,000 for the seller. The buyer has a withdrawable excess equity of $4,000 because of the favorable price movement, whereas the seller now faces a margin call, because the maintenance margin for this contract is $4,000.[9] In this example, the market declined sharply on the last day of the two-week period, bringing the seller's equity below the required maintenance level. The seller would now have to put up funds to return the account to the initial margin requirement level of $7,000.

Investments Intuition

This example illustrates what is meant by the expression that futures trading, like options trading, is a zero-sum game. The aggregate gains and losses net to zero. The aggregate profits enjoyed by the winners must be equal to the aggregate losses suffered by the losers. This also means that the net exposure to changes in the commodity's price must be zero.

Using Futures Contracts

Who uses futures, and for what purpose? Traditionally, participants in the futures market have been classified as either *hedgers* or *speculators*. Because both groups are important in understanding the role and functioning of futures markets, we will consider each in turn. The distinctions between these two groups apply to financial futures as well as to the more traditional commodity futures.

HEDGERS

Hedgers are parties at risk with a commodity or an asset, which means they are exposed to price changes. They buy or sell futures contracts in order to offset their risk. In other words, hedgers actually deal in the commodity or financial instrument specified in the futures contract.[10] By taking a position opposite to that of one already held, at a price set today, hedgers plan to reduce the risk of adverse price fluctuations—that is, to hedge the risk of unexpected price changes. In effect, this is a form of insurance.

---

[8] We are condensing the time element here for the sake of simplicity. The account would be marked to the market each day of this two-week period, and therefore each investor's equity would change every single day.

[9] If the investor's current equity drops below the maintenance level required (which in this case is $4,000), he or she receives a margin call and must add enough money to restore the account to the initial margin level.

[10] The cash position may currently exist (a cash hedge) or may be expected to exist in the future (an anticipatory hedge).

In a sense, the real motivation for all futures trading is to reduce price risk. With futures, risk is reduced by having the gain (loss) in the futures position offset the loss (gain) on the cash position. A hedger is willing to forego some profit potential in exchange for having someone else assume part of the risk. Figure 20-1 illustrates the hedging process as it affects the return-risk distribution. Notice that the unhedged position not only has a greater chance of a larger loss but also a greater chance of a larger gain. The hedged position has a smaller chance of a low return but also a smaller chance of a high return.

Investments Intuition

The use of hedging techniques illustrates the trade-off that underlies all investing decisions: Hedging reduces the risk of loss, but it also reduces the return possibilities relative to the unhedged position. Thus, hedging is used by people who are uncertain of future price movements and who are willing to protect themselves against adverse price movements at the expense of possible gains. There is no free lunch!

HOW TO HEDGE WITH FUTURES

The key to any hedge is that a futures position is taken opposite to the position in the cash market. That is, the nature of the cash market position determines the hedge in the futures market. A commodity or financial instrument held (in effect in inventory) represents a long position, because these items could be sold in the cash market. On the other hand, an investor who sells a futures position not owned has created a short position. Since investors can assume two basic positions with futures contracts, long and short, there are two basic hedge positions.

Short Hedge A transaction involving the sale of futures (a short position) while holding the asset (a long position)

1. The short (sell) hedge. A cash market inventory holder must sell (short) the futures. Investors should think of short hedges as a means of protecting the value of their portfolios. Since they are holding securities, they are long on the cash position and need to protect themselves against a decline in prices. A **short hedge** reduces, or possibly eliminates, the risk taken in a long position.

Long Hedge A transaction where the asset is currently not held but futures are purchased to lock in current prices

2. The long (buy) hedge. An investor who currently holds no cash inventory (holds no commodities or financial instruments) is, in effect, short on the cash market; therefore, to hedge with futures requires a long position. Someone who is not currently in the cash market but who expects to be in the future and who wants to lock in current prices and yields until cash is available to make the investment can use a **long hedge** which reduces the risk of a short position.

Hedging is not an automatic process. It requires more than simply taking a position. Hedgers must make timing decisions as to when to initiate and end the process. As conditions change, hedgers must adjust their hedge strategy.

Figure 20-1

Return distribution for hedged and unhedged positions.

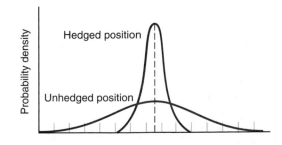

Basis The difference between the cash price of an item and the futures price of the item

One aspect of hedging that must be considered is "basis" risk. The **basis** for financial futures often is defined as the difference between the cash price and the futures price of the item being hedged:[11]

Basis = Cash price − Futures price

The basis must be zero on the maturity date of the contract. In the interim, the basis fluctuates in an unpredictable manner and is not constant during a hedge period. Basis risk, therefore, is the risk hedgers face as a result of unexpected changes in the basis. Although changes in the basis will affect the hedge position during its life, a hedge will reduce risk as long as the variability in the basis is less than the variability in the price of the asset being hedged. At maturity, the futures price and the cash price must be equal, resulting in a zero basis. (Transaction costs can cause discrepancies.)

The significance of basis risk to investors is that risk cannot be entirely eliminated. Hedging a cash position will involve basis risk.

SPECULATORS

In contrast to hedgers, speculators buy or sell futures contracts in an attempt to earn a return. They are willing to assume the risk of price fluctuations, hoping to profit from them. Unlike hedgers, speculators typically do not transact in the physical commodity or financial instrument underlying the futures contract. In other words, they have no prior market position. Some speculators are professionals who do this for a living; others are amateurs, ranging from the very sophisticated to the novice. Although most speculators are not actually present at the futures markets, floor traders (or locals) trade for their own accounts as well as others and often take very short-term (minutes or hours) positions in an attempt to exploit any short-lived market anomalies.

Speculators are essential to the proper functioning of the futures market, absorbing the excess demand or supply generated by hedgers and assuming the risk of price fluctuations that hedgers wish to avoid. Speculators contribute to the liquidity of the market and reduce the variability in prices over time.

Why speculate in futures markets? After all, one could speculate in the underlying instruments. For example, an investor who believed interest rates were going to decline could buy Treasury bonds directly and avoid the Treasury bond futures market. The potential advantages of speculating in futures markets include:

1. Leverage. The magnification of gains (and losses) can easily be 10 to 1.
2. Ease of transacting. An investor who thinks interest rates will rise will have difficulty selling bonds short, but it is very easy to take a short position in a Treasury bond futures contract.
3. Transaction costs. These are often significantly smaller in futures markets.

By all accounts, an investor's likelihood of success when speculating in futures is not very good. The small investor is up against stiff odds when it comes to *speculating* with futures contracts. Futures should be used for hedging purposes.

Financial Futures

Financial Futures Futures contracts on financial assets

Financial futures are futures contracts on equity indexes, fixed-income securities, and currencies. They give investors greater opportunity to fine tune the risk-return characteristics of their portfolios. In recent years, this flexibility has become increasingly important

---

[11] The typical definition for basis is the cash price minus the futures price. For financial futures, the definition is often reversed.

as interest rates have become much more volatile and as investors have sought new techniques to reduce the risk of equity positions. The drastic changes that have occurred in the financial markets in the last 15 to 20 years could be said to have generated a genuine need for new financial instruments that allow market participants to deal with these changes.

The procedures for trading financial futures are the same as those for any other commodity with few exceptions. At maturity, stock-index futures settle in cash, because it would be impossible or impractical to deliver all the stocks in a particular index.[12] Unlike traditional futures contracts, stock-index futures typically have no daily price limits (although they can be imposed).

We will divide the subsequent discussion of financial futures into the two major categories of contracts, interest rate futures and stock-index futures. Hedging and speculative activities within each category are discussed separately.

Using the Internet

Specifications for the various financial futures contracts, including initial and maintenance margins, can be found at http://www.ccstrade.com/ccs/services/ref/specs/margins/. The Chicago Mercantile Exchange has an extensive Web site at www.cme.com. Included are price quotes, on-line courses, on-line simulated trading, and other educational resources. The CBOT has similar information at www.cbot.com. At www.futuresmag.com, investors can find daily technical information on the markets as well as links to a large number of sites involving futures. A series of papers covering various topics about futures can be found at http://www.e-analytics.com/fudir.htm.

INTEREST RATE FUTURES

Bond prices are highly volatile, and investors are exposed to adverse price movements. Financial futures, in effect, allow bondholders and others who are affected by volatile interest rates to transfer the risk. One of the primary reasons for the growth in financial futures is that portfolio managers and investors are trying to protect themselves against adverse movements in interest rates. An investor concerned with protecting the value of fixed-income securities must consider the possible impact of interest rates on the value of these securities.

Today's investors have the opportunity to consider several different interest rate futures contracts that are traded on various exchanges.[13] The Chicago Mercantile Exchange trades contracts on Treasury bills and the one-month LIBOR rate as well as eurodollars. The Chicago Board of Trade (CBT) specializes in longer-maturity instruments, including Treasury notes (of various maturities, such as two-year and five-year) and Treasury bonds (of different contract sizes).

Exhibit 20-2 describes some futures contracts (not an exhaustive list) on fixed-income securities. Contracts are available on various maturities of U.S. Treasury notes in trading units of $100,000 and $200,000, on Treasury bonds in units of both $50,000 and $100,000, and on Treasury bills in trading units of $1 million. The contracts for U.S. Treasury bonds are by far the most important.

---

[12] Gains and losses on the last day of trading are credited and debited to the long and short positions in the same way—marked to the market—as was done for every other trading day of the contract. Therefore, not only is there no physical delivery of securities, but also the buyer does not pay the full value of the contract at settlement.

[13] The Chicago Board of Trade launched financial futures trading in 1975 by opening trading in Government National Mortgage Association (GNMA or Ginnie Mae) bonds. The concept accelerated in 1976, when the International Monetary Market started trading in Treasury bills. Treasury bond futures appeared in 1977.

Exhibit 20-2 **Characteristics of Interest Rate Futures Contracts**

Contract	Where Traded[a]	Contract Size or Trading Unit	Minimum Fluctuations
Treasury bonds	CBT	$100,000 per value 8% coupon[b]	$1/32$ or $31.25
10-Year Treasury notes	CBT	$100,000 par value	$1/32$ or $31.25
Treasury bills	CME	$1 million face value	1 basis point or $25
5-Year & 2-Year Treasury notes	CBT	$100,000 & $200,000 par value	$1/32$ or $31.25

[a]CBT = Chicago Board of Trade; CME = Chicago Mercantile Exchange.
[b]Bonds with other coupons are usable with price adjustments.

Reading Quotes As an illustration of the quotation (reporting) system for interest rate futures, Exhibit 20-3 shows some hypothetical quotations for the Treasury bond contract on the CBT. These hypothetical quotations are intended only to illustrate relationships that typically exist. The value of the contract is $100,000, and the price quotations are percentages of par, with 32nds shown. Since one point is $1,000, $1/32$ is worth $31.25. Thus, a price of $75^{16}/_{32}$ is equal to $75,500. Exhibit 20-3 indicates that there were eight different contract months for the Treasury bond contract, covering a period of approximately two years—since the first contract, December, could have been purchased prior to that month.

In this illustration, the December futures contract opened at $74^{20}/_{32}$ of par, traded in a range of $74^{30}/_{32}$ to $74^{20}/_{32}$, and settled at $74^{25}/_{32}$, which translates into a yield of 11.816.[14] Notice that the change in price, $+^{8}/_{32}$, is opposite the change in yields, −0.042. In both cases, changes are measured from the previous day's respective variables.

Hedging with Interest Rate Futures We now consider an example of using interest rate futures to hedge an investment position. Obviously, other examples could be constructed involving various transactors, such as a corporation or financial institution; various financial instruments, such as a portfolio of Ginnie Maes (GNMAs) or Treasury bills; and various scenarios under which the particular hedger is operating. Our objective is simply to illustrate the basic concepts. Here we concentrate on the short hedge, since it is by far the more common. We discuss the concept of the long hedge below.

Short Hedge Suppose an investor has a bond portfolio and wishes to protect the value of his or her position.[15] This type of hedge is sometimes referred to as *inventory hedge*.

Exhibit 20-3 **Hypothetical Quotes for One Day for the Various Maturities of the Treasury Bond Futures Contracts**

	Open	High	Low	Settle	Change	Yield Settle Change	Open Interest
December 19X0	74–20	74–30	74–20	74–25	+8	11.816–0.042	100,845
March 19X1	74–06	74–13	74–03	74–07	+8	11.911–0.041	24.566
June	73–28	73–31	73–21	73–25	+8	11.985–0.042	16,548
September	73–13	73–16	73–09	73–13	+8	12.049–0.042	12,563
December	72–32	73–06	72–30	73–03	+8	12.103–0.043	8,576
March 19X2	72–22	72–30	72–23	72–27	+8	12.146–0.042	7,283
June	72–15	72–23	72–16	72–20	+8	12.184–0.042	4,801
September	72–12	72–17	72–10	72–14	+8	12.217–0.042	702

[14] Futures prices on Treasury bonds are quoted with reference to an 8-percent, 20-year bond. Settlement prices are translated into a settlement yield to provide a reference point for interest rates.
[15] This example is taken from *U.S. Treasury Bond Futures* (Chicago: Chicago Board of Trade), p. 10.

Example 20-4   A pension fund manager holds $1 million of 11.75-percent Treasury bonds due 2005. The manager plans to sell the bonds three months from now (June 1) but wishes to protect the value of the bonds against a rise in interest rates. Since assets are owned (a long position), a short hedge is used.

To protect the position, the manager hedges by going short (selling) in the futures market. As illustrated in Exhibit 20-4, the manager sells 10 September contracts (since each contract is worth $100,000) at a current price of 83–06. In this example, interest rates rise, producing a loss on the cash side (i.e., in the prices of the bonds held in the cash market) and a gain on the futures side (i.e., the manager can cover the short position at a lower price, which produces a profit). The futures position thus offsets 67 percent of the cash market loss.[16]

The manager in this example could offset only 67 percent of the cash market loss, because the T-bond contract is based on 8-percent coupon bonds, whereas the manager was holding 11.75-percent bonds. The dollar value of higher coupon bonds changes by a larger dollar amount than the dollar value of lower coupon bonds for any change in yields. One way to overcome this difference is to execute a "weighted" short hedge, adjusting the number of futures contracts used to hedge the cash position. With the example data in Exhibit 20-4, selling 14 September contracts would offset 93.4 percent of the cash market loss.[17]

Other Hedges   An alternative hedge is the *anticipatory hedge*, whereby an investor purchases a futures contract as an alternative to buying the underlying security. At some designated time in the future, the investor will purchase the security and sell the futures contract. This results in a net price for the security position at the future point in time which is equal to the price paid for the security minus the gain or loss on the futures position.

Consider an investor who would like to purchase an interest rate asset now but will not have the cash for three months. If rates drop, the asset will cost more at that point in time. By purchasing a futures contract on the asset now, as a hedge, the investor can lock in the interest rate implied by the interest rate futures contract. This may be a good sub-

Exhibit 20-4   Illustration of Hedges Using Interest Rate Futures: A Short Hedge

Cash Market	Futures Market
Short Hedge	

June 1
  Holds $1 million 11¾% Treasury bonds due 2005.
	June 1
	  Sells 10 T-bond futures contracts at a price
	    of 83–06

Current market price: 117–23 (yields 9.89%)	

September 1
  Sells $1million of 11¾% bonds at 104–12 (yields 11.25%)
	September 1
	  Buys 10 T-bond futures contracts at 74–09

Loss: $133,437.50	Gain: $89,062.50

[16] The $89,062.50 gain is calculated as follows: The gain per contract is $83\frac{6}{32} - 74\frac{9}{32} = 8\frac{29}{32}$, or 8.90625 percent of par value. Multiplying the gain of 8.90625 percent by par value = $8906.25 per contract, and for 10 contracts, the total gain is $89,062.50.

[17] The market value of the 14 futures contracts changes from $1,164,625 to $1,039,937.50. The cash market values change from $1,177,187.50 to $1,043,750. Different Treasury bonds are related to the nominal 8-percent coupon, 20-year maturity bond used in the contract by means of a set of conversion factors that represent the relative values of the various deliverable bonds. The conversion factor for the 11.75-percent coupon bond used in this example, rounded off, is 1.40.

stitute for not being able to lock in the current interest rate because of the lack of funds now to do so. At the conclusion of this transaction, the investor will pay a *net* price that reflects the ending cash price minus the gain on the futures contract. In effect, the gain on the futures increases the rate of return earned on the interest rate asset.

Speculating with Interest Rate Futures Investors may wish to speculate with interest rate futures as well as to hedge with them. To do so, investors make assessments of likely movements in interest rates and assume a futures position that corresponds with this assessment. If the investor anticipates a rise in interest rates, he or she will sell one (or more) interest rate futures, because a rise in interest rates will drive down the prices of bonds and therefore the price of the futures contract. The investor sells a contract with the expectation of buying it back later at a lower price. Of course, a decline in interest rates will result in a loss for this investor, since the price will rise.

Example 20-5

Assume that in November a speculator thinks interest rates will rise over the next two weeks and wishes to profit from this expectation. The investor can sell one December Treasury bond futures contract at a price of, say, 90–20. Two weeks later, the price of this contract has declined to 88–24 because of rising interest rates. This investor would have a gain of $1^{28}/_{32}$, or $1875 (each $^1/_{32}$ is worth $31.25), and could close out this position by buying an identical contract.

The usefulness of interest rate futures for pursuing such a strategy is significant. A speculator who wishes to assume a short position in bonds cannot do so readily in the cash market (either financially or mechanically). Interest rate futures provide the means to short bonds easily.

In a similar manner, investors can speculate on a decline in interest rates by purchasing interest rate futures. If the decline materializes, bond prices and the value of the futures contract will rise. Because of the leverage involved, the gains can be large; however, the losses can also be large if interest rates move in the wrong direction.

STOCK-INDEX FUTURES

Stock-index futures trading was initiated in 1982 with several contracts quickly being created. Although stock-index futures are unavailable on individual stocks as in the case of options, investors can trade futures contracts on major market indexes such as the DJIA and the Standard & Poor's 500 Composite Index (S&P 500). Contracts are also available on a "mini" S&P Index, the Nasdaq 100, the Russell 2000, and the Nikkei 225 Stock Average (Japanese market). Other indexes also are available.[18]

The S&P 500 contract is the most popular stock-index futures contract, accounting by far for the bulk of trading in stock-index futures. The value of an S&P 500 contract is determined by using a multiplier of $250. The minimum tick is 0.10, or $25.

Delivery is not permitted in stock-index futures because of its impracticality. Instead, each remaining contract is settled by cash on the settlement day by taking an offsetting position using the price of the underlying index.[19]

Stock-index futures offer investors the opportunity to act on their investment opinions concerning the future direction of the market. They need not select individual

---

[18] There is also a futures contract on the S&P Midcap 400 Index. It has a value of $500 times the index.
[19] The final settlement price is set equal to the closing index on the maturity date.

stocks, and it is easy to short the market. Furthermore, investors who are concerned about unfavorable short-term market prospects but remain bullish for the longer run can protect themselves in the interim by selling stock-index futures.

Hedging With Stock-Index Futures Common stock investors hedge with financial futures for the same reasons that fixed-income investors use them. Investors, whether individuals or institutions, may hold a substantial stock portfolio that is subject to the risk of the overall market; that is, systematic risk. A futures contract enables the investor to transfer part or all of the risk to those willing to assume it. Stock-index futures have opened up new, and relatively inexpensive, opportunities for investors to manage market risk through hedging.

Chapter 8 pointed out the two types of risk inherent in common stocks: systematic risk and nonsystematic risk. Diversification will eliminate most or all of the nonsystematic risk in a portfolio, but not the systematic risk. Although an investor could adjust the beta of the portfolio in anticipation of a market rise or fall, this is not an ideal solution because of the changes in portfolio composition that might be required.

Investors can use financial futures on stock market indexes to hedge against an overall market decline. That is, investors can hedge against systematic or market risk by selling the appropriate number of contracts against a stock portfolio. In effect, stock-index futures contracts give an investor the opportunity to protect his or her portfolio against market fluctuations.

To hedge market risk, investors must be able to take a position in the hedging asset (in this case, stock-index futures) such that profits or losses on the hedging asset offset changes in the value of the stock portfolio. Stock-index futures permit this action, because changes in the futures prices themselves generally are highly correlated with changes in the value of the stock portfolios that are caused by marketwide events. The more diversified the portfolio, and therefore the lower the nonsystematic risk, the greater the correlation between the futures contract and the stock positions.

Figure 20-2 shows the price of the S&P 500 Index futures plotted against the value of a portfolio that is 99 percent diversified. That is, market risk accounts for 99 percent of its total risk.[20] The two track each other very closely, which demonstrates that stock-index futures can be very effective in hedging the market risk of a portfolio.

Figure 20-2

The value of a well-diversified stock portfolio versus the price of the S&P 500 Index futures.

SOURCE: Charles S. Morris, "Managing Stock Market Risk with Stock Index Futures," *Economic Review* (June 1989): 9.

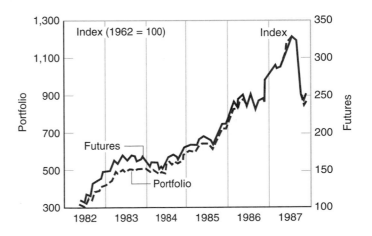

[20] This example is taken from Charles S. Morris, "Managing Stock Market Risk with Stock Index Futures," *Economic Review* (June 1989): 3–16.

Short Hedges Since so much common stock is held by investors, the short hedge is the natural type of contract for most investors. Investors who hold stock portfolios hedge market risk by selling stock-index futures, which means they assume a short position.

A short hedge can be implemented by selling a forward maturity of the contract. The purpose of this hedge is to offset (in total or in part) any losses on the stock portfolio with gains on the futures position. To implement this defensive strategy, an investor would sell one or more index futures contracts. Ideally, the value of these contracts would equal the value of the stock portfolio. If the market falls, leading to a loss on the cash (the stock portfolio) position, stock-index futures prices will also fall, leading to a profit for sellers of futures.

The reduction in price volatility that can be accomplished by hedging is shown in Figure 20-3, which compares the performance of a well-diversified portfolio (the unhedged portfolio) with the same portfolio hedged by sales of the S&P 500 Index futures. Clearly, there is much less variability in the value of the hedged portfolio as compared to the value of the unhedged portfolio. In fact, the volatility of the returns is 91 percent lower.[21] Notice in particular what happened in the great market crash of October 1987. The value of the unhedged portfolio fell some 19 percent, whereas the value of the hedged portfolio fell only 6 percent.

Table 20-2 (top) illustrates the concept of a short hedge using the Standard & Poor's Index when it is at 1140. Assume that an investor has a portfolio of stocks valued at $290,000 that he or she would like to protect against an anticipated market decline. By selling one S&P stock index future also priced at 1140, the investor has a short position of $285,000, because the value of the contract is $250 times the index quote. As Table 20-2 illustrates, a decline in the stock market of 10 percent results in a loss on the stock portfolio of $29,000 and a gain on the futures position of $28,500 (ignoring commissions). Thus, the investor almost makes up on the short side what is lost on the long side.

Long Hedges The long hedger, while awaiting funds to invest, generally wishes to reduce the risk of having to pay more for an equity position when prices rise. Potential users of a long hedge include the following:

1. Institutions with a regular cash flow who use long hedges to improve the timing of their positions.
2. Institutions switching large positions who wish to hedge during the time it takes to complete the process. (This could also be a short hedge.)

Figure 20-3

The value of a well-diversified portfolio versus the value of the same portfolio hedged by sales of S&P 500 Index futures.

SOURCE: Charles S. Morris, "Managing Stock Market Risk with Stock Index Futures," *Economic Review* (June 1989): 10.

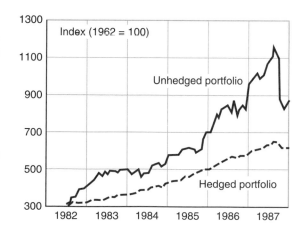

[21] See ibid.

Table 20-2 Examples of Short and Long Hedges Using Stock-Index Futures

	Short Hedge		
	Current Position	Position after a 10% Market Drop	Change in Position
(Long Position) $ value of portfolio	$290,000	$261,000	$(29,000)
(Short position) sell one S&P 500 futures contract at 1140	285,000	256,500	28,500
Gain or loss from hedging			(500)

	Long Hedge		
	Current Position	Position or Cost Following a 10% Market Rise	Change in Position or Cost of Position
Buy three S&P 500 futures contracts at 1140 each	$855,000	$940,500	$85,500
Cost of stock position	850,000	935,000	(85,000)
Gain or loss from hedging			500

Assume an investor with $850,000 to invest believes that the stock market will advance but has been unable to select the stocks he or she wishes to hold. The S&P stock index future is at 1140. By purchasing three S&P 500 Index futures, each representing an aggregate dollar value of 1140 × $250 = $285,000, the investor will gain if the market advances. As shown in Table 20-2, a 10-percent market advance will increase the value of the futures contract $28,500 (1140 × 1.10 = 1254; 1254 × $250 = $313,500; $313,500 − $285,000 = $28,500). With three contracts, the total gain is three times larger, or $85,500. Even if the investor has to pay 10 percent more (on average) for stocks purchased after the advance, he or she still gains, because the net hedge result is positive.

Limitations of Hedging with Stock-Index Futures Although hedging with stock-index futures can reduce an investor's risk, typically risk cannot be eliminated completely. As with interest rate futures, basis risk is present with stock-index futures. It represents the difference between the price of the stock-index futures contract and the value of the underlying stock index. A daily examination of the "Futures Prices" page of *The Wall Street Journal* will show that each of the indexes quoted under the respective futures contracts differs from the closing price of the contracts.[22]

Basis risk as it applies to common stock portfolios can be defined as the risk that remains after a stock portfolio has been hedged.[23] Note here that stock-index futures hedge only systematic (market) risk. That is, when we consider a stock portfolio hedged with stock-index futures, the basis risk is attributable to nonsystematic (nonmarket or firm-specific) risk.

Figure 20-4(a) illustrates the effects of basis risk by comparing the value of a relatively undiversified portfolio with the price of the S&P 500 futures contract. In contrast to Figure 20-2, where the portfolio was 99 percent diversified, this portfolio is only 66 percent diversified. Although the two series are related, the relationship is in no way as close as that illustrated in Figure 20-2. Therefore, stock-index futures will be less effective

---

[22] Futures prices are generally more volatile than the underlying indexes and therefore diverge from them. The index futures tend to lead the actual market indexes. If investors are bullish, the futures are priced at a premium, with greater maturities usually associated with greater premiums. If investors are bearish, the futures are normally priced at a discount, which may widen as maturity increases.

[23] This discussion is based heavily on Morris, "Managing Stock Market Risk with Stock Index Futures," pp. 11–13.

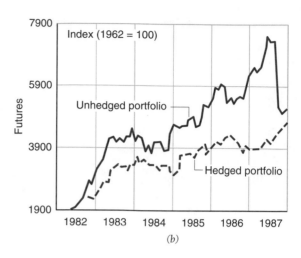

Figure 20-4

(*a*) The value of a relatively undiversified stock portfolio and the price of the S&P index futures contract. (*b*) The value of the unhedged portfolio and the same portfolio hedged by sales of S&P 500 futures contracts.

SOURCE: Charles S. Morris, "Managing Stock Market Risk with Stock Index Futures," *Economic Review* (June 1989): 12, 13.

Program Trading   The use of computer-generated buy and sell orders for entire portfolios based on arbitrage opportunities

Index Arbitrage   Exploitation of price differences between stock-index futures and the index of stocks underlying the futures contract

at hedging the total risk of the portfolio, as shown in Figure 20-4(*b*). In this situation, the variance of returns on the hedged portfolio is only 27 percent lower than the unhedged position. Note that in the crash of October 1987 both portfolios fell sharply, demonstrating that the hedge was relatively ineffective. (It did better than the unhedged position, but not by much.)

From this analysis, we can conclude that stock-index futures generally do not provide a good hedge for relatively undiversified portfolios.

Index Arbitrage and Program Trading A force of considerable magnitude hit Wall Street in the 1980s. It is called **program trading**, and it has captured much attention and generated considerable controversy. It leads to headlines attributing market plunges at least in part to program trading, as happened on October 19, 1987, when the DJIA fell over 500 points. Because program trading typically involves positions in both stocks and stock-index futures contracts, we consider the topic within the general discussion of hedging.

The terms *program trading* and **index arbitrage** often are used together. In general terms, index arbitrage refers to attempts to exploit the differences between the prices of the stock-index futures and the prices of the index of stocks underlying the futures contract. For example, if the S&P 500 futures price is too high relative to the S&P 500 Index, investors could short the futures contract and buy the stocks in the index. In theory, arbitrageurs should be able to build a hedged portfolio that earns arbitrage profits equaling the difference between the two positions. If the price of the S&P 500 futures is deemed too low, investors could purchase the futures and short the stocks, again exploiting the differences between the two prices.

If investors are to be able to take advantage of discrepancies between the futures price and the underlying stock-index price, they must be able to act quickly. Program trading involves the use of computer-generated orders to coordinate buy and sell orders for entire portfolios based on arbitrage opportunities. The arbitrage occurs between portfolios of common stocks, on the one hand, and index futures and options on the other. Large institutional investors seek to exploit differences between the two sides. Specifically, when stock-index futures prices rise substantially above the current value of the stock-index itself (e.g., the S&P 500), they sell the futures and buy the underlying stocks, typically in "baskets" of several million dollars. Because the futures price and the stock-index value must be equal when the futures contract expires, these investors are seeking to "capture the premium" between the two, thereby earning an arbitrage profit. That is, they seek high risk-free returns by arbitraging the difference between the cash value of the underlying securities and the prices of the futures contracts on these securities. In effect, they have a hedged position and should profit regardless of what happens to stock prices.

Normally, program traders and other speculators "unwind" their positions during the last trading hour of the day the futures expire. At this time, the futures premium goes to zero, because, as noted, the futures price at expiration must equal the stock-index value.

The headlines about program trading often reflect the results of rapid selling by the program traders. For whatever reason, traders decide to sell the futures. As the price falls, stock prices also fall. When the futures price drops below the price of the stock index, tremendous selling orders can be unleashed. These volume sell orders in stocks drive the futures prices even lower.

Speculating with Stock-Index Futures In addition to the previous hedging strategies (and others not described), investors can speculate with stock-index futures if they wish to profit from stock market volatility by judging and acting on the likely market trends. Stock-index futures are effective instruments for speculating on movements in the stock market because

1. Minimal costs are involved in establishing a futures position.
2. Stock-index futures mirror the market, offering just as much risk.

We can refer to one group of speculators as "active traders." These individuals are willing to risk their capital on price changes they expect to occur in the futures contracts. Such individuals are often sophisticated investors who are seeking the opportunity for large gains and who understand the risk they are assuming.

The strategies of active traders basically include long and short positions. Traders who expect the market to rise buy index futures. Because of the high leverage, the profit opportunities are great; however, the loss opportunities are equally great. The same is true for traders expecting a market decline who assume a short position by selling a stock-index futures contract. Selling a contract is a convenient way to go short the entire market. It can be done at any time. (No wait for an uptick is required, as with stock short sales.)

Another form of speculation involves spreaders, who establish both long and short positions at the same time. Their objective is to profit from changes in price relationships between two futures contracts. Spreads include the following:

1. The intramarket spread, also known as a calendar or time spread. This spread involves contracts for two different settlement months, such as buying a March contract and selling a June contract.
2. The intermarket spread, also known as a quality spread. This spread involves two different markets, such as buying a New York Stock Exchange (NYSE) contract and selling an S&P contract (both for the same month).

Spreaders are interested in relative price as opposed to absolute price changes. If two different contracts appear to be out of line, the spreader hopes to profit by buying one contract and selling the other and waiting for the price difference to adjust. This adjustment may require the spread between the two contracts to widen in some cases and narrow in others.

SINGLE STOCK FUTURES

A very recent innovation in financial futures is the single stock futures, SSFs. These are futures contracts on individual stocks such as IBM, GE, Dell, and Microsoft as well as on the exchange-traded fund for the DJIA, called DIAMONDS. These futures are traded on new exchanges such as OneChicago, a joint venture of the Chicago Board Options Exchange, the

Chicago Mercantile Exchange, and the CBT, and on the Nasdaq Liffe Market (NQLX), a joint venture of the Nasdaq Stock Market and the London International Financial Futures and Options Exchange. Both exchanges are wholly electronic futures exchanges. SSFs are regulated by both the SEC and the Commodity Futures Trading Commission.

Like other futures contracts, SSFs are standardized agreements between two parties to buy or sell 100 shares of a specified stock in the future at a price determined today. On the NQLX, contracts are available covering seven different months over the current year and the next year. The minimum price fluctuation ("tick") is 1¢ per share, or $1 per contract (contracts are for 100 shares). The initial margin requirement is 20 percent, providing substantial leverage for these contracts.

Using SSFs As we would expect from what we have learned, an investor buys or "goes long" a SSF contract if he or she believes that the price of a particular stock will rise, and sells or "goes short" a SSF contract if the price is expected to decline. Shorting is easily accomplished, relative to stock trading, because no uptick in price is required. As always with a futures contract, both a buy and sell are involved, and which is done first really does not matter in terms of the process working smoothly.

Example 20-6 Assume an investor buys 10 contracts on Microsoft at $50 and sells them two months later at $60. The profit on this position would be:

$$[\$60 - \$50] \times 100 \text{ shares} \times 10 \text{ contracts} = \$10,000$$

The primary advantages of SSFs may be the low cost and ease with which short selling can be accomplished. Some investors will view the 20-percent margin requirement as an advantage, but it can also be a significant disadvantage if the price moves against the investor, particularly when multiple contracts are involved.

Example 20-7 Assume an investor shorts 10 contracts on Microsoft at $50 and buys them back at $57. The loss on this position would be:

$$[\$50 - \$57] \times 100 \text{ shares} \times 10 = -\$7,000.$$

How SSFs Differ From Stocks and Options SSFs have price and risk profiles that are similar to stocks. For example, if the stock price goes up, the futures price will also go up in all but the most unusual circumstances. On the other hand, the payoff profile for options is often nonlinear, consisting of two or more different segments. Options truncate the returns distribution, whereas futures do not. There are several variables that affect the prices of options, whereas futures prices are more straightforward.

On the other hand, SSFs are like any other futures in some respects, and therefore differ from stocks. Margin for futures represents funds to ensure that obligations are met, not funds to finance part of the purchase or short sell of the stock. There is no interest to pay on the loan as in the case of margin with stocks. Profits and losses are credited to an investor's account daily.

The Future of SSFs Because SSFs are a very recent innovation, it is difficult to say how successful they will be and the total impact they will have on investors. They clearly offer investors one more tool in hedging risk and constructing specific return-risk profiles. At their introduction, some critics immediately questioned their necessity, or even desirability. However, it is worthwhile to remember that foreign-currency futures, exchange-traded funds, and stock-index futures were also attacked by some critics at their introduction. Each has gone on to be quite successful. Exchange-traded futures (ETFs), for example, started slowly, but total volume today is very respectable.

Summary

▶ Futures markets play an important role in risk management.

▶ Spot markets are markets for immediate delivery. Forward markets are markets for deferred delivery.

▶ An organized futures exchange standardizes the nonstandard forward contracts, with only the price and number of contracts left for futures traders to negotiate.

▶ A futures contract designates a specific amount of a particular item to be delivered at a specified date in the future at a currently determined market price.

▶ Buyers assume long positions and sellers assume short positions. A short position indicates only that a contract not previously purchased is sold.

▶ Most contracts are settled by offset, whereby a position is liquidated by an offsetting transaction. The clearinghouse is on the other side of every transaction and ensures that all payments are made as specified.

▶ Contracts are traded on designated futures exchanges, which set minimum price changes and may establish daily price limits.

▶ Futures positions must be closed out within a specified time. There are no certificates and no specialists to handle the trading. Each futures contract is traded in an auction market process by a system of "open outcry."

▶ Margin, the norm in futures trading, is the "good faith" deposit made to ensure completion of the contract.

▶ All futures contracts are marked to the market daily; that is, all profits and losses are credited and debited to each investor's account daily.

▶ Hedgers buy or sell futures contracts to offset the risk in some other position.

▶ Speculators buy or sell futures contracts in an attempt to earn a return, and are valuable to the proper functioning of the market.

▶ Interest rate futures, one of the two principal types of financial futures, allow investors to hedge against, and speculate on, interest rate movements. Numerous contracts are available on both domestic instruments and foreign instruments.

▶ Investors can, among other transactions, execute short hedges to protect their long positions in bonds.

▶ Stock-index futures are available on the NYSE Composite Index, the S&P 500 Index, and numerous other indexes, both domestic and foreign.

▶ Investors can use stock-index futures to hedge the systematic risk of common stocks, that is, broad market movements.

▶ Short hedges protect a stock position against a market decline, and long hedges protect against having to pay more for an equity position because prices rise before the investment can be made.

▶ Index arbitrage refers to attempts to exploit the differences between the prices of the stock-index futures and the prices of the index of stocks underlying the futures contract.

Key Words

Basis
Financial futures
Forward contract
Futures contract
Futures margin
Index arbitrage

Initial margin
Long hedge
Long position
Maintenance margin
Margin call

Marked to the market
Offset
Program trading
Short hedge
Short position

Questions

20-1 Carefully describe a futures contract.

20-2 Explain how futures contracts are valued daily and how most contracts are settled.

20-3 Describe the role of the clearinghouses in futures trading.

20-4 What determines if an investor receives a margin call?

20-5 Describe the differences between trading in stocks and trading in futures contracts.

20-6 How do financial futures differ from other futures contracts?

20-7 Explain the differences between a hedger and a speculator.

20-8 What is meant by basis? When is the basis positive?

20-9 Given a futures contract on Treasury bonds, determine the dollar price of a contract quoted at 80–5, 90–24, and 69–2.

20-10 When might a portfolio manager with a bond position use a short hedge involving interest rate futures?

20-11 Is it possible to construct a perfect hedge? Why or why not?

20-12 What is the difference between a short hedge and a weighted short hedge using interest rate futures?

20-13 Why would an investor have preferences among the different stock-index futures?

20-14 Which type of risk does stock-index futures allow investors to hedge? Why would this be desirable?

20-15 Explain how a pension fund might use a long hedge with stock-index futures.

20-16 When would an investor likely do the following?
   a. Buy a call on a stock index.
   b. Buy a put on interest rate futures.

20-17 What is program trading? How does it work?

CFA
20-18 Michelle Industries issued a Swiss Franc-denominated five-year discount note for SFr 200 million. The proceeds were converted to U.S. dollars to purchase capital equipment in the U.S. The company wants to hedge this currency exposure and is considering the following alternatives:

   (i) At-the-money Swiss Franc call options
   (ii) Swiss Franc forwards
   (iii) Swiss Franc futures

Contrast the essential characteristics of *each* of these *three* derivative instruments. **Evaluate** the suitability of *each* in relation to Michelle's hedging objective, including *both* advantages and disadvantages.

CFA
20-19 Futures contracts *differ* from forward contracts in the following ways:

   I. Futures contracts are standardized.
   II. For Futures, performance of each party is guaranteed by a clearinghouse.
   III. Futures contracts require a daily settling of any gains or losses.
      a. I and II only
      b. I and III only
      c. II and III only
      d. I, II, and III

Copyright, 1994, Association for Investment Management and Research.

CFA
20-20 To preserve capital in a declining stock market, a portfolio manager should:

   a. buy stock index futures.
   b. sell stock index futures.
   c. buy call options.
   d. sell put options.

Copyright, 1992, Association for Investment Management and Research. Reproduced and republished from *CFA® Program Materials* with permission from the Association for Investment Management and Research. All Rights Reserved.

CFA
20-21 An investor in the common stock of companies in a foreign country may wish to hedge against the _____ in the investor's home currency and can do so by _____ the foreign currency in the forward market.

   a. depreciation; selling
   b. appreciation; purchasing
   c. appreciation; selling
   d. depreciation; purchasing

CFA
20-22 Which of the following best describes a stock-index arbitrage strategy?

a. taking a long or short position in the cash (spot) market represented by a market basket of stocks
b. trading in stock-index futures contracts and in individual stocks when a divergence occurs between the cash (stock) price of the market and the futures price

c. trading call and put stock options in each stock represented in a market index
d. selling stock-index futures contracts when the stock market falls

Problems

20-1 Assume that an investor buys one March NYSE Composite Index futures contract on February 1 at 67.5. The position is closed out after five days. The prices on the four days after purchase were 67.8, 68.1, 68, and 68.5. The initial margin is $3500.

a. Calculate the current equity on each of the next four days.
b. Calculate the excess equity for these four days.
c. Calculate the final gain or loss for the week.
d. Recalculate (a), (b), and (c) assuming that the investor had been short over this same period.

20-2 Given the information in Problem 20-1, assume that the investor holds until the contract expires. Ignore the four days after purchase and assume that on the next to last day of trading in March the investor was long and the final settlement price on that date was 70.5. Calculate the cumulative profit.

20-3 Calculate the dollar gain or loss on Treasury bond futures contracts ($100,000) per contract for the following transactions. In each case the position is held six months before closing it out.

a. Sell 10 T-bond contracts at a price of 82–80 and buy 10 at 76–12.
b. Sell 10 T-bond contracts at a price of 80–14 and buy 10 at 77.
c. Buy 15 T-bond contracts at 62–10 and sell 15 at 64–24.
d. Sell one T-bond contract at 70–14 and buy one at 78–08.

20-4 Assume a portfolio manager holds $1 million of 8.5 percent Treasury bonds due 2004 to 2009. The current market price is 76–2, for a yield of 11.95 percent. The manager fears a rise in interest rates in the next three months and wishes to protect this position against such a rise by hedging in futures.

a. Ignoring weighted hedges, what should the manager do?
b. Assume T-bond futures contracts are available at 68, and the price three months later is 59–12. If the manager constructs the correct hedge, what is the gain or loss on this position?
c. The price of the Treasury bonds three months later is 67–8. What is the gain or loss on this cash position?
d. What is the net effect of this hedge?

CFA
20-5 Chris Smith of XYZ Pension Plan has historically invested in the stocks of only U.S. domiciled companies. Recently, he has decided to add international exposure to the plan portfolio.

A. **Identify** and **briefly discuss** *three* potential problems that Smith may confront in selecting international stocks that he did not face in choosing U.S. stocks. Rather than select individual stocks, Smith decides to use Nikkei futures to obtain his Japanese portfolio exposure. The Nikkei Index is now at 15,000 with a 2 percent dividend yield and the Japanese risk-free interest rate is 5 percent.

B. Calculate the price at which Smith can expect a six-month Nikkei futures contract to trade. **Show** all work.

Web Resources

For additional resources visit our dynamic Web site located at www.wiley.com/college/jones.

- ☐ *Trading Negative Beta Portfolios*—The case describes the institutional characteristics of futures contracting. The decision-maker creates a financial futures hedge for price risk management.
- ☐ Alternate Case:
- ☐ *A Financial Market Where?*—The focus is on the operations of a low-cost, yet real financial market in Iowa—the Iowa Electronic Markets. Those with limited cash can take advantage of their beliefs in a variety of different delayed delivery contracts.
- ☐ Internet Exercises—The Web exercises for this chapter parallel the treatment in the text; in particular, we will address the use of futures for hedging.
  Exercise 1: Looks at the distribution characteristics of futures returns.
  Exercise 2: Discusses hedging using futures positions.
  Exercise 3: Looks at the return characteristics of hedged positions.
  Exercise 4: Discusses the use of bankruptcy index futures contracts.
  Exercise 5: Looks the relative volatility of spot prices and futures prices.

- ☐ Multiple Choice Self Test
- ☐ Appendix 20-A—Futures Options

Selected References

A good primer on the futures market for anyone interested in futures is:

> Lofton, Todd. *Getting Started in Futures*, 4th ed., John Wiley & Sons, 2001.

A guide to single stock futures is:

> Mitchell, Kennedy. *Single Stock Futures: An Investor's Guide*, John Wiley & Sons, 2002.

Investors may wish to consider on-line trading of futures in depth:

> Silverman, David. *Direct Access Trading: A Complete Guide to Trading Electronically*, John Wiley & Sons, 2001.

chapter 21

Portfolio Management

Chapter 21 considers the practice of portfolio management—how investors should go about actually managing their money, or having it managed for them. In particular, we consider why and how portfolio management should be thought of as an ongoing, systematic, and dynamic process. An understanding of portfolio management as a process allows any portfolio manager to apply a consistent framework to managing the portfolio of any investor whether an individual or institution. It also allows us to consider some topics of importance to all investors, such as taxes, protection against inflation, probabilities of potential market returns, the life cycle of investors, and other related issues.

AFTER READING THIS CHAPTER YOU WILL BE ABLE TO:

▶ Discuss why portfolio management should be considered, and implemented as, a process.

▶ Describe the steps involved in the portfolio management process.

▶ Apply the process to any type of investment situation.

▶ Assess related issues of importance, such as asset allocation.

Portfolio management involves a series of decisions and actions that must be made by every investor whether an individual or institution. Portfolios must be managed whether investors follow a passive approach or an active approach to selecting and holding their financial assets. As we saw when we examined portfolio theory, the relationships among the various investment alternatives that are held as a portfolio must be considered if an investor is to hold an optimal portfolio and achieve his or her investment objectives.

Portfolio management can be thought of as a process. Having the process clearly in mind is very important, allowing investors to proceed in an orderly manner.

In this chapter, we outline the portfolio management process, making it clear that a logical and orderly flow does exist. This process can be applied to each investor and by any investment manager. Details may vary from client to client, but the process remains the same.

Portfolio Management as a Process

Portfolio Management Process A sequence of steps to be followed when investing

The **portfolio management process** has been described by Maginn and Tuttle in a book that forms the basis for portfolio management as envisioned by the Association for Investment Management and Research (AIMR), and advocated in its curriculum for the Chartered Financial Analyst (CFA) designation.[1] This is an important development because of its contrast with the past, where portfolio management was treated on an ad hoc basis, matching investors with portfolios on an individual basis. Portfolio management should be structured so that any investment organization can carry it out in an effective and timely manner without serious omissions.

Maginn and Tuttle emphasize that portfolio management is a *process*, integrating a set of activities in a logical and orderly manner. Given the feedback loops and monitoring that is included, the process is both continuous and systematic. It is a dynamic and flexible concept, and extends to all portfolio investments, including real estate, gold, and other real assets.

The portfolio management process extends to all types of investment organizations and investment styles. In fact, Maginn and Tuttle specifically avoid advocating how the process should be organized by money management companies or others, who should make the decisions, and so forth. Each investment management organization should decide for itself how best to carry out its activities consistent with viewing portfolio management as a process.

Having structured portfolio management as a process, any portfolio manager can execute the necessary decisions for an investor. The process provides a framework and a control over the diverse activities involved, and allows every investor, an individual or institution, to be accommodated in a systematic, orderly manner.

As outlined by Maginn and Tuttle, portfolio management is an ongoing process by which:

1. Objectives, constraints, and preferences are identified for each investor. This leads to the development of an explicit investment policy statement which is used to guide the money management process.
2. Capital market expectations for the economy, industries and sectors, and individual securities are considered and quantified.

---

[1] See John L. Maginn, CFA, and Donald L. Tuttle, CFA, eds., *Managing Investment Portfolios*, 2nd ed. (Charlottesville, Va: Association for Investment Management and Research, 1990). This chapter follows the format advocated in this book and is indebted to it for much of the discussion.

3. Strategies are developed and implemented. This involves asset allocation, portfolio optimization, and selection of securities.
4. Portfolio factors are monitored and responses are made as investor objectives and constraints and/or market expectations change.
5. The portfolio is rebalanced as necessary by repeating the asset allocation, portfolio strategy, and security selection steps.
6. Portfolio performance is measured and evaluated to ensure attainment of the investor objectives.

Figure 21-1 explains the portfolio construction, monitoring, and revision process. Notice that we begin with the specification of investor objectives, constraints, and preferences. This specification leads to a statement of portfolio policies and strategies. Next, capital market expectations for the economy as well as individual assets must be determined and quantified.

The combination of portfolio policies/strategies and capital market expectations provides the investment manager with the basis for portfolio construction and revision. This includes the asset allocation decision, a very important determinant of the success of the investment program. Also included here are the portfolio optimization and security selection stages of portfolio management; that is, we must determine appropriate portfolio strategies and techniques for each asset class and the selection of individual securities.

Monitoring is an important part of the process. As indicated in Figure 21-1, the portfolio manager should monitor both investor-related input factors as well as economic and market input factors and rebalance as necessary. For example, the manager may need to respond to any changes in investor objectives and constraints and/or capital market expectations. Portfolio rebalancing is an important part of any ongoing portfolio management process.

The process is ultimately focused on the attainment of investor objectives. In order to determine how well investor objectives are being met, we must measure and evaluate portfolio performance. This topic is discussed in Chapter 22.

Figure 21-1

The portfolio construction, monitoring, and revision process.

SOURCE: John L. Maginn and Donald L. Tuttle, "The Portfolio Management Process and Its Dynamics." Copyright 1990 Association for Investment Management and Research. Reproduced and republished from John L. Maginn, CFA, and Donald L. Tuttle, CFA, eds., *Managing Investment Portfolios*, 2nd ed., with permission from the Association for Investment Management and Research. All rights reserved.

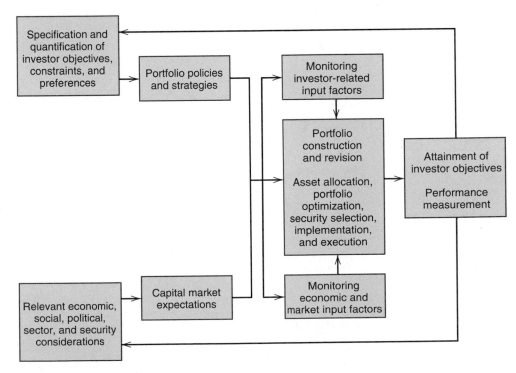

We will discuss these steps in more detail below, but first we consider the differences between individual investors and institutional investors. As we noted in Chapter 2, investors can invest directly and indirectly through institutional investors, and an understanding of both types of investment decision making is important.

INDIVIDUAL INVESTORS vs INSTITUTIONAL INVESTORS

Significant differences exist among investors as to objectives, constraints, and preferences. We are primarily interested here in the viewpoint of the individual investor, but the basic investment management process applies to all investors, individuals, and institutions. Furthermore, individuals are often the beneficiaries of the activities of institutional investors, and an understanding of how institutional investors fit into the investment management process is desirable.

A major difference between the two occurs with regard to time horizon, because institutional investors are often thought of on a perpetual basis, but this concept has no meaning when applied to individual investors. As explained below, for individual investors, it is often useful to think of a life-cycle approach, as people go from the beginning of their careers to retirement. This approach is less useful for institutional investors, because they typically maintain a relatively constant profile across time.

Kaiser has summarized the differences between individual investors and institutional investors as follows[2]:

1. Individuals define risk as "losing money," whereas institutions use a quantitative approach, typically defining risk in terms of standard deviation (as in the case of the returns data presented in Chapter 6).
2. Individuals can be characterized by their personalities, whereas for institutions, we consider the investment characteristics of those with a beneficial interest in the portfolios managed by the institutions.
3. Goals are a key part of what individual investing is all about, along with their assets, whereas for institutions, we can be more precise as to their total package of assets and liabilities.
4. Individuals have great freedom in what they can do with regard to investing, whereas institutions are subject to numerous legal and regulatory constraints.
5. Taxes often are a very important consideration for individual investors, whereas many institutions, such as pension funds, are free of such considerations.

The implications of all of this for the investment management process are as follows:

- **For individual investors**: Because each individual's financial profile is different, an investment policy for an individual investor must incorporate that investor's unique factors. In effect, preferences are self-imposed constraints.
- **For institutional investors**: Given the increased complexity in managing institutional portfolios, it is critical to establish a well-defined and effective policy. Such a policy must clearly delineate the objectives being sought, the institutional investor's risk tolerance, and the investment constraints and preferences under which it must operate.

---

[2] See Ronald W. Kaiser, "Individual Investors," in *Managing Investment Portfolios*, 2nd ed., John L. Maginn, CFA and Donald L. Tuttle, CFA, eds. (Charlottesville, Va.: Association for Investment Management and Research, 1990), p. 3–2.

The primary reason for establishing a long-term investment policy for institutional investors is twofold:

1. It prevents arbitrary revisions of a soundly designed investment policy.
2. It helps the portfolio manager to plan and execute on a long-term basis and resist short-term pressures that could derail the plan.[3]

Formulate an Appropriate Investment Policy

Investment Policy The overall investing guidelines to be followed for a client

The determination of portfolio policies—referred to as the **investment policy statement**—is the first step in the investment process. It summarizes the objectives, constraints, and preferences for the investor. A recommended approach in formulating an investment policy statement is simply to provide information, in the following order, for any investor—individual or institutional:

- *Objectives*:
  - Return requirements
  - Risk tolerance

followed by:

- *Constraints and Preferences*:
  - Liquidity
  - Time horizon
  - Laws and regulations
  - Taxes
  - Unique preferences and circumstances

We discuss each of these in turn below.

OBJECTIVES

Portfolio objectives are always going to center on return and risk, because these are the two aspects of most interest to investors. Indeed, return and risk are the basis of all financial decisions in general and investing decisions in particular. Investors seek returns, but must assume risk in order to have an opportunity to earn the returns. A good starting point here is to think in terms of the return-risk trade-off developed in Chapter 1 and emphasized throughout the text. Expected return and risk are related by an upward sloping tradeoff, as shown in Figure 21-2(*a*).

Alternatively, the life-cycle approach can be depicted as shown in Figure 21-2(*b*). Here we see four different phases in which individual investors view their wealth, although it is important to note that the boundaries between the stages are not necessarily clear-cut and can require years to complete. Furthermore, an individual can be a composite of these stages at the same time. The four stages are:

1. *Accumulation Phase*: In the early stage of the life cycle, net worth is typically small, but the time horizon is long. Investors can afford to assume large risks.

---

[3] See "Portfolio Management: The Portfolio Construction Process," in *1997 CFA Level I Candidate Readings*, AIMR, Charlottesville, VA, 1997, p. 177.

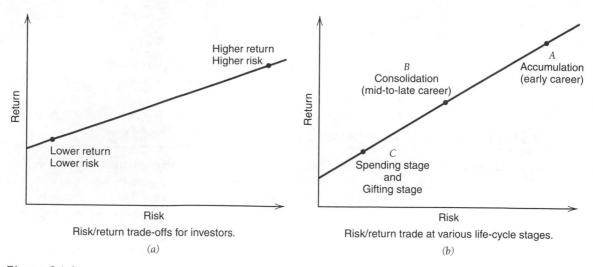

Risk/return trade-offs for investors.

(a)

Risk/return trade at various life-cycle stages.

(b)

Figure 21-2

Risk/return position at various life-cycle stages.

2. *Consolidation Phase*: In this phase, involving the mid-to-late career stage of the life cycle when income exceeds expenses, an investment portfolio can be accumulated. A portfolio balance is sought to provide a moderate trade-off between risk and return.

3. *Spending Phase*: In this phase, living expenses are covered from accumulated assets rather than earned income. Although some risk taking is still preferable, the emphasis is on safety, resulting in a relatively low position on the risk-return trade-off.

4. *Gifting Phase*: In this phase, the attitudes about the purpose of investments changes. The basic position on the trade-off remains about the same as in phase 3.

We know from Chapter 7 that investors must think in terms of expected returns, which implicitly or explicitly involves probability distributions. The future is uncertain, and the best that investors can do is to make probabilistic estimates of likely returns over some holding period, such as one year. Because the future is uncertain, mistakes are inevitable, but this is simply the nature of investing decisions. Estimates of expected returns must be made regardless of the uncertainties, using the best information and investment processes available.

In the final analysis, perhaps the best way to think about investor objectives is to think about an investor's risk tolerance. Investors must decide how much risk they are willing to take, and then attempt to maximize expected returns given this level of risk. If an investor is uncomfortable taking the risk of placing 100 percent of investable funds in stocks, that suggests some strategies and some likely outcomes for expected return.

Establishing a Portfolio Risk Level Investors should establish a portfolio risk level that is suitable for them, and then seek the highest returns consistent with that level of risk. We will assume here that investors have a long-run horizon. If not, they probably should avoid stocks, or at least minimize any equity position.

Assuming you are a long-term investor, and that you own an S&P 500–type portfolio, ask yourself what is the worst that is likely to happen to you as an investor in stocks. Ignoring the Great Depression, which hopefully will not occur again, consider the worst events that have occurred. During the bear market of 1973 to 1974, investors could have lost about 37 percent of their investment in S&P 500 stocks. During the bear market of 2000 to 2002, investors could have lost over 40 percent. Therefore, it is reasonable to assume that with a long-time horizon, investors will face one or more bear markets with approximately 40 percent declines. This is in line with the long-term standard deviation of S&P 500 returns of about 20 percent—with two standard deviations on either side of the mean return encompassing 95 percent of all returns.

If an investor can accept a loss (at least on paper) of approximately 40 percent once or twice in an investing lifetime, and is otherwise optimistic about the economy and about stocks, the investor can assume the risk of U.S. stocks. On the other hand, if such a potential decline is unacceptable, an investor will have to construct a portfolio with a lower risk profile. For example, a portfolio of 50 percent stocks and 50 percent Treasury bills would cut the risk in half. Other alternatives consisting of stocks and bonds would also decrease the risk.

Using the Internet

Investors can measure the overall risk of their portfolio at www.riskgrades.com. After registering, users can enter their portfolio and have the risk analyzed, along with its diversification efficiency. The average of all the world's equities (measured by standard deviation) is assigned a value of 100, and risk for any portfolio is stated as a percentage of that number.

Investment Policy Statement A statement of a few sentences describing policies to be followed for the client

Inflation Considerations An **investment policy statement** often will contain some statement about inflation-adjusted returns because of the impact of inflation on investor results over long periods of time. For example, a wealthy individual's policy statement may be stated in terms of maximum after-tax, *inflation-adjusted* total return consistent with the investor's risk profile, whereas another investor's primary return objective may be stated as *inflation-adjusted capital preservation*, perhaps with a growth-oriented mix to reflect the need for capital growth over time.

Inflation is clearly a problem for investors. The inflation rate of 13 percent in 1979 to 1980 speaks for itself in terms of the awful impact it had on investors' real wealth. But even with a much lower inflation—say, 3 percent—the damage is substantial. It can persist steadily, eroding values. At a 3 percent inflation rate, for example, the purchasing power of a dollar is cut in half in less than 25 years. Therefore, someone retiring at age 60 who lives to approximately age 85 and does not protect him or herself from inflation will suffer a drastic decline in purchasing power over the years.

The very low inflation rates of the late 1990s and early 2000s probably lulled many investors into thinking that inflation is no longer a serious problem, and that they did not need to consider this issue as being very important. However, for the last 80 or so years, the compound annual rate of inflation has been approximately 3 percent. It is reasonable to assume that in the future inflation will be higher than it has been recently, and therefore this is an issue that investors need to consider.

Contrary to some people's beliefs, common stocks are not always an inflationary hedge. In the 1970s, for example, inflation more than doubled to an average annual rate of about 7.5 percent, and the average stock showed a return of slightly less than 6 percent. On the other hand, one of the primary reasons for the strong stock market in the late 1990s was the low (by historical standards) and steady rate of inflation.

CONSTRAINTS AND PREFERENCES

To complete the investment policy statement, these items are described for a particular investor as the circumstances warrant. Since investors vary widely in their constraints and preferences, these details may also vary widely.

Time Horizon Investors need to think about the time period involved in their investment plans. The objectives being pursued may require a policy statement that speaks to specific planning horizons. In the case of an individual investor, for example, this could well be the investor's expected lifetime. In the case of an institutional investor, the time horizon can be quite long. For example, for a company with a defined-benefit retirement plan whose employees are young, and which has no short-term liquidity needs, the time horizon can be quite long.

Liquidity Needs As noted in Chapter 2, liquidity is the ease with which an asset can be sold without a sharp change in price as the result of selling. Obviously, cash equivalents (money market securities) have high liquidity, and are easily sold at close to face value. Many stocks also have great liquidity, but the price at which they are sold will reflect their current market valuations.

Investors must decide how likely they are to sell some part of their portfolio in the short run. As part of the asset allocation decision, they must decide how much of their funds to keep in cash equivalents.

Tax Considerations Individual investors, unlike some institutional investors, must consider the impact of taxes on their investment programs. The treatment of ordinary income as opposed to capital gains is an important issue, because typically there is a differential tax rate. Furthermore, the tax laws in the United States have been changed several times, making it difficult for investors to forecast the tax rate that will apply in the future.

In addition to the differential tax rates and their changes over time, the capital gains component of security returns benefits from the fact that the tax is not payable until the gain is realized. This tax deferral is, in effect, a tax-free loan that remains invested for the benefit of the taxpayer. As explained below, some securities become "locked up" by the reluctance of investors to pay the capital gains that will result from selling the securities. For example, think about a stock bought for, say, $2 per share 40 years ago that today, after stock splits and growth, is worth $150 per share. Almost the entire proceeds from the sale of such a stock will be taxable if the security is sold—even with a favorable capital gains rate, the tax bill will be sizable.

Retirement programs offer tax sheltering whereby any income and/or capital gains taxes are avoided until such time as the funds are withdrawn. Investors with various retirement and taxable accounts must grapple with the issue of which type of account should hold stocks as opposed to bonds (given that bonds generate higher current income).

Legal and Regulatory Requirements Investors must obviously deal with regulatory requirements growing out of both common law and the rulings and regulations of state and federal agencies. Individuals are subject to relatively few such requirements, whereas a particular institutional portfolio, such as an endowment fund or a pension fund, is subject to several legal and regulatory requirements.

With regard to fiduciary responsibilities, one of the most famous concepts is the Prudent Man Rule.[4] This rule, which concerns fiduciaries, goes back to 1830, although it was not formally stated until more than 100 years later. Basically, the rule states that a fiduciary, in managing assets for another party, shall act like people of "prudence, discretion and intelligence" act in governing their own affairs.

---

[4] This discussion is indebted to "Portfolio Management: The Portfolio Construction Process," in John L. Maginn, CFA, and Donald L. Tuttle, CFA, eds., *Managing Investment Portfolios*, 2nd ed. (Charlottesville, Va: Association for Investment Management and Research, 1990).

The important aspect of the Prudent Man Rule is its flexibility, because interpretations of the rule can change with time and circumstances. Unfortunately, some judicial rulings have specified a very strict interpretation, negating the value of flexibility for the time period and circumstances involved. Also unfortunately, in the case of state laws governing private trusts, the standard continues to be applied to individual investments rather than the portfolio as a whole, which violates all of the portfolio-building principles we learned earlier.

One of the important pieces of federal legislation governing institutional investors is the Employment Retirement Income Security Act, referred to as ERISA. This act, administered by the Department of Labor, regulates employer-sponsored retirement plans. It requires that plan assets be diversified and that the standards being applied under the act be applied to *management of the portfolio as a whole.*

The investment policy thus formulated is an operational statement. It clearly specifies the actions to be taken to try to achieve the investor's goals, or objectives, given the preferences of the investor and any constraints imposed. Although portfolio investment considerations are often of a qualitative nature, they help to determine a quantitative statement of return and risk requirements that are specific to the needs of any particular investor.

Unique Needs and Circumstances Investors often face a variety of unique circumstances. For example, a trust established on their behalf may specify that investment activities be limited to particular asset classes, or even specified assets. Or an individual may feel that their life span is threatened by illness and wish to benefit within a certain period of time.

Example 21-1

To illustrate the application of the investment management process, consider a question from the Level I CFA Examination.[5] The answer is contained in a succinct but sufficient form.

A. **Outline** a generalized framework that could be used to establish investment policies applicable to all investors.
B. **List** and **briefly discuss** *five* differences in investment policy that might result from the application of your Part A framework to:

(1) the pension plan of a young, fast-growing consumer products company; and
(2) the modest life insurance proceeds received by a 60-year-old widow with two grown children.

ANSWERS:
A. FRAMEWORK

Objectives	*Constraints*
Return	Time Horizon
Risk	Liquidity Needs
	Tax Considerations
	Legal/Regulatory Issues
	Unique Needs and Circumstances

---

[5] This question and answer are taken from Question 8 of the 1989 Level I Examination. Reprinted in I: *The CFA Study Guide,* 1991, The Institute of Chartered Financial Analysts, Charlottesville, Va., pp. 165 and 173. Copyright, 1991, Association for Investment Management and Research. Reproduced and republished from *CFA® Program Materials* with permission from the Association for Investment Management Research. All rights reserved.

B. APPLICATION DIFFERENCES

	Pension Fund	*Widow's Portfolio*
Return	Total Return Objective	Income-Oriented Objective with Some Inflation Protection
Risk	Above-Average Capacity; Company Bears Risk	Somewhat Below-Average Capacity Indicated; Widow Bears Risk; Safety Important
Time Horizon	Long Term; Infinite	Medium Term; Finite Life
Liquidity	Low; Cash Flow Accrues	Probably Medium to High; No Reinvestment Likely
Tax	U.S. Tax-Exempt	Federal (and Probably State) Income Taxes Paid On Most Investment Receipts
Legal/Regulatory	Governed by ERISA	"Prudent Man" Rule Applies (State)
Unique Needs and Circumstances	Cash Flow Reinvested; Opportunity for Compounding	Widow's Needs Are Immediate and Govern Now; Children's Needs Should Be Considered in Planning for the Future

Determine and Quantify Capital Market Expectations

Having considered their objectives and constraints, the next step is to determine a set of investment strategies based on the policy statement. Included here are such issues as asset allocation, portfolio diversification, and the impact of taxes. Once the portfolio strategies are developed, they are used along with the investment manager's expectations for the capital market and for individual assets to choose a portfolio of assets. Most importantly, the asset allocation decision must be made.

FORMING EXPECTATIONS

The forming of expectations involves two steps:

1. *Macroexpectational factors*: These factors influence the market for bonds, stocks, and other assets on both a domestic and international basis. These are expectations about the capital markets.
2. *Microexpectational influences*: These factors involve the cause agents that underlie the desired return and risk estimates and influence the selection of a particular asset for a particular portfolio.

RATE OF RETURN ASSUMPTIONS

Most investors base their actions on some assumptions about the rate of return expected from various assets. Obviously, it is important for investors to plan their investing activities on realistic rate of return assumptions.

As a starting point, investors should study carefully the historical rates of return available in such sources as the data provided by Ibbotson Associates or the comparable data discussed in Chapter 6. We know the historical mean returns, both arithmetic and geometric, and the standard deviation of the returns for major asset classes such as stocks, bonds, and bills.

Having analyzed the historical series of returns, there are several difficulties in forming expectations about future returns. For example, how much should investors be influenced by recent stock market returns, particularly when they are unusually good returns?

Example 21-2

The cumulative gain on the S&P 500 Index for 1995 and 1996 was 69.2 percent, the best two-year period in a generation and one of the best in the history of stock market returns for this index (only four other consecutive two-year periods were better as measured by the S&P 500). The average gain of more than 30 percent a year for the years 1995 and 1996 was three times the annual average gain for common stocks over many years.

Do investors form unrealistic expectations about future returns as a result of such activity? Over the past four decades, bear markets have occurred on average about once every four years. In the four previous cases of two-year cumulative returns averaging 30 percent per year or more (comparable to 1995 to 1996), the average annual return for the next five years was negative in two cases (−7.5 and −11.2 percent), and less than 9 percent in two cases of positive returns. Moreover, most observers believe that stock returns tend to "revert toward the mean" over time—that is, periods of unusually high returns tend to be followed by periods of lower returns (although not necessarily losses), and the opposite is also true.

Following the bottom that was reached in the stock market in August 1982, the S&P 500 Composite Index has shown a compound annual average return of approximately 17.5 percent a year. This is 60 percent larger than the long-run average return of about 10.7 percent a year. And the return was negative in only one year, 1990, until the period 2000–2002. Therefore, it is valid to ask how investor expectations about stock returns are influenced by this now substantial, but unusual by historical standards, time period. How are investors, particularly relatively new investors, affected by this history as they form expectations about future returns?

Investors should recognize some key points about future rates of return. In estimating the expected return on stocks (as proxied by the S&P 500), Ibbotson Associates combines the riskless rate and expected risk premium of large company stocks over riskless bonds. The expected equity risk premium to be used in this calculation is based on the *arithmetic mean* of equity risk premiums and not the geometric mean, because this is an additive relationship. As stated in the Ibbotson Associates *Yearbook*, ". . . the arithmetic mean is correct because an investment with uncertain returns will have a higher expected ending wealth value than an investment that earns, with certainty, its compound or geometric rate of return each year."[6]

A second key point that investors should recognize in thinking about expected rates of return, and the returns they can realistically expect to achieve, is that common stock returns involve considerable risk. Although we know that the annual average compound rate of return on common stocks for the period 1920 to 2001 was 10.5 percent, that does not mean that all investors can realistically expect to achieve this historical rate of return. To see this, we can analyze the probabilities of actually realizing various compound rate of returns over time.

Jones and Wilson have analyzed data for the S&P 500 Index for the period 1920 to 2001 using "corrected" S&P observations.[7] The annual geometric mean of these data for

---

[6] See Roger G. Ibbotson and Rex A. Sinquefield, *Stocks, Bonds, Bills, and Inflation (SBBI)*, updated in *Stocks, Bonds, Bills, and Inflation 1996 Yearbook*, p. 155. Chicago: Ibbotson Associates. All rights reserved.

[7] See Charles P. Jones and Jack W. Wilson, "Probabilities Associated with Common Stock Returns," *The Journal of Portfolio Management* (Fall 1995): 21–32.

Table 21-1 Estimated probabilities for Receiving a Specified Return, or Greater, for Various Holding Periods, for the Period 1920–2001 Based on a Geometric Mean of 10.5037% and a Standard Deviation of 20.7430%

Per annum return %	Years											
	1	2	3	4	5	10	15	20	25	30	35	40
75	0.007	0.000	0.000	0.000	0.000	0.000	0.000	0.000	0.000	0.000	0.000	0.000
70	0.011	0.001	0.000	0.000	0.000	0.000	0.000	0.000	0.000	0.000	0.000	0.000
65	0.017	0.001	0.000	0.000	0.000	0.000	0.000	0.000	0.000	0.000	0.000	0.000
60	0.025	0.003	0.000	0.000	0.000	0.000	0.000	0.000	0.000	0.000	0.000	0.000
55	0.036	0.006	0.001	0.000	0.000	0.000	0.000	0.000	0.000	0.000	0.000	0.000
50	0.052	0.011	0.002	0.001	0.000	0.000	0.000	0.000	0.000	0.000	0.000	0.000
45	0.075	0.021	0.006	0.002	0.001	0.000	0.000	0.000	0.000	0.000	0.000	0.000
40	0.105	0.038	0.015	0.006	0.003	0.000	0.000	0.000	0.000	0.000	0.000	0.000
35	0.144	0.067	0.033	0.017	0.009	0.000	0.000	0.000	0.000	0.000	0.000	0.000
30	0.194	0.111	0.068	0.042	0.027	0.003	0.000	0.000	0.000	0.000	0.000	0.000
29	0.206	0.123	0.077	0.050	0.033	0.005	0.001	0.000	0.000	0.000	0.000	0.000
28	0.218	0.135	0.088	0.059	0.041	0.007	0.001	0.000	0.000	0.000	0.000	0.000
27	0.230	0.148	0.101	0.070	0.049	0.010	0.002	0.000	0.000	0.000	0.000	0.000
26	0.243	0.162	0.114	0.082	0.060	0.014	0.004	0.001	0.000	0.000	0.000	0.000
25	0.257	0.178	0.129	0.095	0.072	0.019	0.006	0.002	0.001	0.000	0.000	0.000
24	0.270	0.194	0.145	0.111	0.086	0.027	0.009	0.003	0.001	0.000	0.000	0.000
23	0.285	0.211	0.162	0.128	0.102	0.036	0.014	0.006	0.002	0.001	0.000	0.000
22	0.300	0.229	0.182	0.147	0.120	0.048	0.021	0.009	0.004	0.002	0.001	0.000
21	0.315	0.248	0.202	0.168	0.141	0.064	0.031	0.016	0.008	0.004	0.002	0.001
20	0.331	0.268	0.224	0.191	0.164	0.083	0.045	0.025	0.014	0.008	0.005	0.003
19	0.347	0.289	0.248	0.216	0.190	0.107	0.064	0.039	0.025	0.016	0.010	0.006
18	0.364	0.311	0.273	0.243	0.218	0.135	0.089	0.060	0.041	0.028	0.020	0.014
17	0.381	0.334	0.300	0.272	0.249	0.169	0.120	0.088	0.065	0.048	0.036	0.028
16	0.398	0.358	0.328	0.303	0.282	0.208	0.159	0.125	0.099	0.079	0.064	0.052
15	0.416	0.382	0.357	0.336	0.318	0.252	0.206	0.172	0.145	0.123	0.105	0.090
14	0.434	0.408	0.387	0.371	0.356	0.301	0.261	0.230	0.204	0.183	0.164	0.148
13	0.453	0.433	0.419	0.406	0.396	0.354	0.323	0.298	0.277	0.258	0.242	0.227
12	0.472	0.460	0.451	0.443	0.437	0.411	0.391	0.375	0.361	0.348	0.336	0.326
11	0.491	0.487	0.484	0.481	0.479	0.470	0.463	0.458	0.453	0.448	0.444	0.440
10	0.510	0.514	0.517	0.519	.0522	0.531	0.537	0.543	0.548	0.553	0.557	0.561
9	0.529	0.541	0.550	0.558	0.565	0.591	0.611	0.627	0.642	0.655	0.666	0.677
8	0.548	0.568	0.583	0.596	0.607	0.650	0.681	0.707	0.728	0.747	0.764	0.779
7	0.568	0.596	0.616	0.634	0.649	0.706	0.746	0.778	0.804	0.825	0.844	0.860
6	0.587	0.623	0.649	0.671	0.689	0.757	0.804	0.838	0.865	0.887	0.904	0.919
5	0.607	0.649	0.681	0.706	0.728	0.804	0.853	0.887	0.912	0.931	0.946	0.957
4	0.626	0.675	0.711	0.740	0.764	0.846	0.894	0.925	0.946	0.961	0.972	0.979
3	0.645	0.701	0.741	0.772	0.798	0.881	0.926	0.952	0.969	0.979	0.986	0.991
2	0.665	0.726	0.769	0.802	0.829	0.910	0.950	0.971	0.983	0.990	0.994	0.996
1	0.683	0.750	0.796	0.830	0.857	0.934	0.968	0.984	0.991	0.996	0.998	0.999
0	0.702	0.773	0.821	0.855	0.882	0.953	0.980	0.991	0.996	0.998	0.999	1.000
−1	0.720	0.795	0.844	0.878	0.904	0.967	0.988	0.995	0.998	0.999	1.000	1.000
−2	0.738	0.816	0.865	0.899	0.923	0.978	0.993	0.998	0.999	1.000	1.000	1.000
−3	0.755	0.836	0.884	0.917	0.939	0.986	0.996	0.999	1.000	1.000	1.000	1.000
−4	0.772	0.854	0.902	0.932	0.952	0.991	0.998	1.000	1.000	1.000	1.000	1.000
−5	0.789	0.872	0.918	0.946	0.964	0.994	0.999	1.000	1.000	1.000	1.000	1.000
−6	0.805	0.888	0.931	0.957	0.972	0.997	1.000	1.000	1.000	1.000	1.000	1.000
−7	0.820	0.902	0.943	0.966	0.980	0.998	1.000	1.000	1.000	1.000	1.000	1.000
−8	0.835	0.915	0.954	0.974	0.985	0.999	1.000	1.000	1.000	1.000	1.000	1.000
−9	0.849	0.927	0.963	0.980	0.989	0.999	1.000	1.000	1.000	1.000	1.000	1.000
−10	0.862	0.938	0.970	0.985	0.993	1.000	1.000	1.000	1.000	1.000	1.000	1.000

Table 21-1 (continued)

Per annum return %	Years											
	1	2	3	4	5	10	15	20	25	30	35	40
−15	0.918	0.976	0.992	0.997	0.999	1.000	1.000	1.000	1.000	1.000	1.000	1.000
−20	0.957	0.992	0.999	1.000	1.000	1.000	1.000	1.000	1.000	1.000	1.000	1.000
−25	0.980	0.998	1.000	1.000	1.000	1.000	1.000	1.000	1.000	1.000	1.000	1.000
−30	0.992	1.000	1.000	1.000	1.000	1.000	1.000	1.000	1.000	1.000	1.000	1.000
−35	0.998	1.000	1.000	1.000	1.000	1.000	1.000	1.000	1.000	1.000	1.000	1.000
−40	0.999	1.000	1.000	1.000	1.000	1.000	1.000	1.000	1.000	1.000	1.000	1.000
−45	1.000	1.000	1.000	1.000	1.000	1.000	1.000	1.000	1.000	1.000	1.000	1.000

that time period was 10.5037 percent and the standard deviation was 20.743 percent. The differences in this mean and that provided by Ibbotson Associates and others stems from a difference in the data used for the earlier years of the S&P 500 and a slightly longer period.

Jones and Wilson determined from a statistical analysis of the data that the historical returns on the S&P 500 Index are lognormally distributed, which means that we can use compound rates of return to estimate probabilities based on the mean and standard deviation of the logs of annual total returns. These probabilities are calculated and reported as the probabilities of achieving any specified *compound* annual average rate of return over any specified holding period. It is important to note that these are probabilities of achieving *at least* the stated compound rate of return or more.

Table 21-1 shows the probabilities of achieving at least a specified compound rate of return, or *more*, based on the history of the S&P 500 Index over the period 1920 to 2001. In analyzing Table 21-1, remember that the approximate geometric mean for the revised S&P 500 for this period was approximately 10.5 percent. These probabilities should be interpreted in the following manner: "Based *solely* on the entire history of annual returns on the S&P Index for the period 1920 to 2001, where the geometric mean was approximately 10.5 percent, what are the probabilities of achieving *at least* a specified *compound* rate of return over various holding periods?"

As Table 21-1 shows, the probability of achieving approximately 10.5 percent or more on a compound basis is (essentially) 50 percent regardless of the holding period. Note that for rates of return of 10.5037 percent or more, the probabilities of achieving that rate of return *decrease* over time, contrary to assertions of many market observers that the risk of owning common stocks decreases over time. On the other hand, the probabilities of achieving at least a 9-percent rate of return, or an 8-percent rate of return, or any lower return, increase over time, because these rates of return are below the geometric mean return for the period. Nevertheless, after 40 years, the probability of earning a compound rate of return of 9 percent or more on the S&P 500, based on this long history, is only 0.677—thus, investors have a one in three chance of earning 9 percent or less if the future is like the past. Even for a compound rate of return of 8 percent or more, the probability after 40 years is only 78 percent, which means there is a substantial risk of earning 8 percent or less.

The message from Table 21-1 is important. Based on the known history of stock returns, the chance that an investor will actually achieve some compound rate of return over time from owning common stocks may not be as high as he or she believes. Common stocks are risky, and expected returns are not guaranteed.

Developing and Implementing Investing Strategies

Having considered the objectives and constraints and formed capital market expectations, the next step is portfolio construction and revision based on the policy statement and capital market expectations. Included here are such issues as asset allocation, portfolio optimization, and security selection. In summary, once the portfolio strategies are developed, they are used along with the investment manager's expectations for the capital market and for individual assets to choose a portfolio of assets.

The portfolio construction process can be viewed from a broad perspective as consisting of the following steps (again, given the development of the investment policy statement and the formulation of capital market expectations):

1. Define the universe of securities eligible for inclusion in a particular portfolio. For institutional investors, this traditionally meant asset classes, in particular stocks, bonds, and cash equivalents. More recently, institutional investors have broadened their investment alternatives to include foreign securities, small stocks, real estate, venture capital, and so forth. This step is really the asset allocation decision, probably the key decision made by investment managers.
2. Utilize an optimization procedure to select securities and determine the proper portfolio weights for these securities.

Both of these steps are discussed in more detail as follows.

ASSET ALLOCATION

The asset allocation decision involves deciding the percentage of investable funds to be placed in stocks, bonds, and cash equivalents. It is the most important investment decision made by investors, because it is the basic determinant of the return and risk taken. This is a result of holding a well-diversified portfolio, which we know from Part II is the primary lesson of portfolio management.

The returns of a well-diversified portfolio within a given asset class are highly correlated with the returns of the asset class itself. Within an asset class, diversified portfolios will tend to produce similar returns over time. However, different asset classes are likely to produce results that are quite dissimilar. Therefore, differences in asset allocation will be the key factor over time causing differences in portfolio performance.

To appreciate the importance of the asset allocation decision, think of an investor with a five-year investment horizon making this decision at the beginning of 1995. If this investor had placed all of his or her portfolio funds in stocks, the investor would have enjoyed great success as the market compounded at 20+ percent for the next five years. On the other hand, think of this investor making the decision at the beginning of 2000, with a three-year horizon. A 100-percent commitment to stocks would have resulted in large losses as the market declined sharply. In contrast, the investor who placed all of his or her funds in bonds at the beginning of 2000 would have been spared this debacle and enjoyed nice returns.

The Asset Allocation Decision Factors to consider in making the asset allocation decision include the investor's return requirements (current income versus future income), the investor's risk tolerance, and the time horizon. This is done in conjunction with the investment manager's expectations about the capital markets and about individual assets, as described above.

How asset allocation decisions are made by investors remains a subject that is not fully understood. It is known that actual allocation decisions often differ widely from how investors say they will allocate assets.

According to some analyses, asset allocation is closely related to the age of an investor. This involves the so-called life-cycle theory of asset allocation. This makes intuitive sense, because the needs and financial positions of workers in their 50s will differ on average from those who are starting out in their 20s. According to the life-cycle theory, for example, as individuals approach retirement, they become more risk averse.

Table 21-2 illustrates the asset allocation decision by presenting two examples to show how major changes during life can affect asset allocation. One investor is "conservative" and one "aggressive." They begin their investment programs with different allocations and end with different allocations, but their responses to major changes over the life cycle are similar. Both investors have a minimum of 50 percent allocated to stocks at all stages of the life cycle because of the need for growth.

Table 21-2, published in *AAII Journal*, a magazine for individual investors, is illustrative only. Different investors will choose different allocations. Life-style changes could cause investors to move from one stage to the other, or changes in life may not cause a change in the allocation percentages. Moreover, even among similar age groups, goals can vary substantially. Overall, asset allocation decisions may depend more upon goals than age. The important point is that all investors must make the asset allocation decision, and this decision will have a major impact on the investment results achieved.

It seems reasonable to assert that the level of risk tolerance affects the asset allocation decision. One study examined the risk preferences of households using financial data for a large random sample of U.S. households. The definition of risk used was *relative risk aversion*, defined as investors' tolerance for risk as measured relative to his or her wealth level. This study found differences in relative risk aversion across three distinct categories of individuals—those aged 65 and older, those with very high levels of wealth, and those with incomes below the poverty level. The study also found clear patterns for asset allocation over wealth and income levels, with the proportion allocated to risky assets rising consistently with both income and wealth.

Using the Internet

There are many Internet sources of information available concerning asset allocation. For example, for an explanation of how to determine the current asset allocation in a portfolio, see http://www.aaii.com/promo/20021111/pswkshp.shtml. For a discussion of how to make asset allocation work for you, see http://moneycentral.msn.com/articles/invest/prepare/1259.asp. At www.vanguard.com, under "Research Funds and Stocks," investors can fill out a questionnaire which will lead to a recommended asset allocation for their situation. Morningstar has a wide range of tools available to analyze a portfolio at www.morningstar.com. Some of these are free and some involve a premium package for a fee. Many of these tools can be accessed free at www.troweprice.com, a mutual fund company, even if the investor does not have an account with this company (registration is free).

Table 21-2 How Major Changes Can Affect Your Asset Allocation

Asset Category	Conservative			Aggressive		
	Early Career (%)	Late Career (%)	Retirement (%)	Early Career (%)	Late Career (%)	Retirement (%)
Cash	10	10	10	10	10	10
Bonds	20	30	40	0	10	10
Large-Cap Stocks	40	40	40	30	40	50
Small-Cap Stocks	15	10	5	30	20	15
International Stocks	15	10	5	30	20	15

SOURCE: Maria Crawford Scott, "How Major Changes in Your Life Can Affect Your Asset Allocation," *AAII Journal*, October 1995, p. 17

Types of Asset Allocation William Sharpe has outlined several types of asset allocation.[8] If all major aspects of the process have been considered, the process is referred to as *integrated asset allocation*. These include issues specific to an investor, particularly the investor's risk tolerance, and issues pertaining to the capital markets, such as predictions concerning expected returns, risks, and correlations. If some of these steps are omitted, the asset allocation approaches are more specialized. Such approaches include:

1. *Strategic asset allocation* This type of allocation is usually done once every few years, using simulation procedures to determine the likely range of outcomes associated with each mix. The investor considers the range of outcomes for each mix, and chooses the preferred one, thereby establishing a long-run, or strategic asset mix.
2. *Tactical asset allocation* This type of allocation is performed routinely, as part of the ongoing process of asset management. Changes in asset mixes are driven by changes in predictions concerning asset returns. As predictions of the expected returns on stocks, bonds, and other assets change, the percentages of these assets held in the portfolio changes. In effect, tactical asset allocation is a market-timing approach to portfolio management intended to increase exposure to a particular market when its performance is expected to be good and decrease exposure when performance is expected to be poor.

PORTFOLIO OPTIMIZATION

Stated at its simplest, portfolio construction involves the selection of securities to be included in the portfolio and the determination of portfolio funds (the weights) to be placed in each security. As we know from Chapter 7, the Markowitz model provides the basis for a scientific portfolio construction resulting in efficient portfolios. An efficient portfolio, as discussed in Chapter 8, is one with the highest level of expected return for a given level of risk or the lowest risk for a given level of expected return.

On a formal basis, the Markowitz model provides a formal model of optimization, which allows investors to construct portfolios that are efficient.

Monitor Market Conditions and Investor Circumstances

It is important to monitor market conditions, the relative asset mix, and the investor's circumstances. Investing is an ongoing and dynamic process, and changes occur rapidly and frequently.

MONITORING MARKET CONDITIONS

The need to monitor market conditions is obvious. Investment decisions are made in a dynamic marketplace where change occurs on a continuing basis. Key macrovariables, such as inflation and interest rates, should be tracked on a regular basis. Information about the prospects for corporate earnings is obviously important because of the impact of earnings on stock prices.

---

[8] See William F. Sharpe, "Asset Allocation," in *Managing Investment Portfolios*, 2nd ed., John L. Maginn, CFA and Donald L. Tuttle, CFA, eds. (Charlottesville, Va.: Association for Investment Management and Research, 1990), p. 7-21–7-27.

CHANGES IN INVESTOR'S CIRCUMSTANCES

An investor's circumstances can change for several reasons. These can be easily organized on the basis of the framework for determining portfolio policies outlined above.

- ❏ *Change in Wealth*: A change in wealth may cause an investor to behave differently, possibly accepting more risk in the case of an increase in wealth, or becoming more risk averse in the case of a decline in wealth.
- ❏ *Change in Time Horizon*: Traditionally, we think of investors aging and becoming more conservative in their investment approach.
- ❏ *Change in Liquidity Requirements*: A need for more current income could increase the emphasis on dividend-paying stocks, whereas a decrease in current income requirements could lead to greater investment in small stocks whose potential payoff may be years in the future.
- ❏ *Change in Tax Circumstances*: An investor who moves to a higher tax bracket may find municipal bonds more attractive. Also, the timing of the realization of capital gains can become more important.
- ❏ *Change in Legal/Regulatory Considerations*: Laws affecting investors change regularly, whether tax laws or laws governing retirement accounts, annuities, and so forth.
- ❏ *Change in Unique Needs and Circumstances*: Investors face a number of possible changes during their life depending on many economic, social, political, health, and work-related factors.

Rebalancing the Portfolio

Portfolio Rebalancing
Periodically rebalancing a portfolio to maintain some specified or desired asset allocation decision

Even the most carefully constructed portfolio is not intended to remain intact without change. Portfolio managers spend much of their time monitoring their portfolios and doing **portfolio rebalancing**. The key is to know when and how to do such rebalancing, because a trade-off is involved: the cost of trading versus the cost of not trading.[9]

The cost of trading involves commissions, possible impact on market price, and the time involved in deciding to trade. The cost of not trading involves holding positions that are not best suited for the portfolio's owner, holding positions that violate the asset allocation plan, holding a portfolio that is no longer adequately diversified, and so forth.

One of the problems involved in rebalancing is the "lock-up" problem. This situation arises in taxable accounts subject to capital gains taxes. Even at low levels of turnover, the tax liabilities generated can be larger than the gains achieved by the active management driving the turnover. In the absence of taxes, such as with tax-deferred IRA and 401(k) plans, investors would simply seek to hold those securities with the highest risk-adjusted expected rates of return. With a lock-up problem, however, investors may be reluctant to rebalance the portfolio because of the capital gains taxes that will result on the accrued appreciation which, until realized, remains untaxed.

Individual investors, having taken the time to make the asset allocation decision, often forget to rebalance their portfolios. This means that they may lose the benefits of having an asset allocation plan. Rebalancing reduces the risks of sharp losses—in general, a rebalanced portfolio is less volatile than one that is not rebalanced.

---

[9] This discussion is indebted to Robert D. Arnott and Robert M. Lovell, Jr., "Monitoring and Rebalancing the Portfolio," in *Managing Investment Portfolios*, 2nd ed., edited by John L. Maginn and Donald L. Tuttle. New York: Warren, Gorham and Lamont, 1990.

BOX 21-1

Rebalancing Is Worth the Effort

A periodic review and revision of your asset allocation can become a disciplined way to sell high and buy low, allowing you to lock in gains and reduce risk. To rebalance or not to rebalance, that is the question.

Rebalancing simply means periodically reviewing your portfolio to ensure that it is still fulfilling your investment goals. If, for example, an investor set up a portfolio that was 60% stocks and 40% bonds three years ago, the outperformance of bonds in recent years could mean that the portfolio no longer reflects the desired allocation strategy. In fact, it would have flip-flopped to 40% stocks and 60% bonds. In that case, you might want to rebalance—meaning sell some bonds and buy more stocks—to get the portfolio back to the asset allocation you want.

Many investors dislike rebalancing, however, because it means selling winners in favor of losers. Rebalancing can also generate trading fees, as well as taxes on any gains booked by selling securities.

But most financial professionals believe the benefits outweigh these disadvantages.

"You want to rebalance to avoid owning a portfolio dominated by overvalued securities," says David Braverman, senior director of portfolio services at Standard & Poor's. "Rebalancing can reduce the risk of your portfolio and, often, boost returns as well."

That's because rebalancing forces you to sell high and buy low.

"Think of it as an exercise to remind yourself that you do have to sell," says David Blitzer, S&P's managing director for investment analysis. "Rebalancing gives you a discipline for determining what to sell and when to sell it. The idea is that no one is going to be the perfect market timer. Rebalancing is a guaranteed way to buy low, though perhaps not at the low, and sell high, though perhaps not at the high."

How often should you rebalance? Most experts suggest you do it once a year, though some say you might want to consider rebalancing even more frequently if the markets are especially volatile.

"I use the 5% rule with my clients," says Larry Swedroe, a financial planner with Buckingham Asset Management in St. Louis. "If a portfolio shifts more than 5% away from a desired asset allocation, that's when you want to think about rebalancing."

If you haven't rebalanced in the past year, you should think about it. Take a look at all your investments, whether they are in a taxable brokerage or mutual fund account, or a tax-deferred account like a 401(k) plan or an individual retirement account (IRA). Calculate how much is in stocks and how much is in bonds. Then determine whether you are comfortable with your allocations. S&P is currently recommending an asset allocation of 65% stocks, 15% bonds, and 20% cash.

It is also important to drill down deeper than that. Within your stock portfolio, for example, you probably want a split between U.S. stocks and foreign issues. Many financial planners advocate keeping at least 10% of your equity portfolio in foreign stocks.

Similarly, many investors prefer to keep their bond portfolios invested in a mix of U.S. Treasuries, municipals, and corporate bonds.

Once you determine how to bring your asset allocation back to where you want it, there are several ways to get it done.

Some advisers suggest making as many changes as possible in a tax-deferred account like a 401(k) or an IRA because that will reduce your immediate tax liability. Also, since few 401(k) accounts charge trading fees, it is a way to cut down on transaction costs.

You can also rebalance without incurring a tax liability by using new money instead of moving around existing money in your portfolio.

"Try to rebalance using new cash, rather than selling current investments," says Swedroe. "If you have too much in bonds right now, invest some new money in stocks, instead of having to sell the bond position to raise money to put more in stocks."

If rebalancing is going to cause a tax liability, you might want to consider waiting until the end of the year. Then you can determine whether to pay the tax in the current year, or defer it to the following year.

"I meet with each of my clients in November, and we map out a strategy for rebalancing," says Alan Kahn, president of AJK Financial in Syosset, New York. "If we see the portfolio is going to incur net gains because of the rebalancing, we calculate the tax implications and decide whether the trades should be made in December, which puts the tax into the current year, or in January, which defers the tax to the following year. The important thing to remember is that you are in control of the portfolio; it isn't taking control of itself."

SOURCE: Portfolio Strategies, "Rebalancing Is Worth the Effort," *The Outlook*, March 26, 2003, p. 12. Reprinted by permission of Standard & Poor's, a division of McGraw-Hill Companies, copyright 2003.

Rebalancing is difficult for many investors, because it represents a contrarian strategy. To rebalance, investors are selling those asset classes that have appreciated and reinvesting the funds in those that have not. This is very difficult to do psychologically. During the stock market bubble in the late 1990s, it was almost impossible to do as the market continued to rise and rise. Ultimately, of course, the benefits of rebalancing emerged as stocks plummeted and bonds appreciated.

Box 21-1 is a good discussion of the rebalancing issue from a practical standpoint, as presented in S&P's *Outlook*. Note that the tax liability issue is discussed in this article.

Performance Measurement

The portfolio management process is designed to facilitate making investment decisions in an organized, systematic manner. Clearly, it is important to evaluate the effectiveness of the overall decision-making process. The measurement of portfolio performance allows investors to determine the success of the portfolio management process and of the portfolio manager. It is a key part of monitoring the investment strategy that was based on investor objectives, constraints, and preferences.

Performance measurement is important to both those who employ a professional portfolio manager on their behalf as well as to those who invest personal funds. It allows investors to evaluate the risks that are being taken, the reasons for the success or failure of the investing program, and the costs of any restrictions that may have been placed on the investment manager. This, in turn, could lead to revisions in the process.

Unresolved issues remain in performance measurement despite the development of an entire industry to provide data and analyses of *expost* performance. Nevertheless, it is a critical part of the investment management process, and the logical capstone in its own right of the entire study of investments. We therefore consider this issue next as a separate and concluding chapter of the text.

Summary

▶ Portfolio management should be thought of as a process that can be applied to each investor. It is continuous, systematic, dynamic, and flexible.

▶ The portfolio management process can be applied to each investor to produce a set of strategy recommendations for accomplishing a given end result.

▶ The entire process consists of: developing explicit investment policies, consisting of objectives, constraints, and preferences; determining and quantifying capital market expectations; constructing the portfolio; monitoring portfolio factors and responding to changes; rebalancing the portfolio when necessary; and measuring and evaluating portfolio performance

▶ The first step is to develop an investment policy for the investor consisting of carefully stated objectives, constraints, and preferences.

▶ The portfolio construction process can be thought of in terms of the asset allocation decision and the portfolio optimization decision.

▶ Asset allocation is the most important investment decision made by investors. Types of asset allocation include strategic and tactical.

Key Word

Questions

21-1 What is meant by the portfolio management process?

21-2 Must each investment management firm be organized the same way in order to carry out the investment process?

21-3 What are some of the differences between individual investors and institutional investors?

21-4 What is meant by the *investment policy*?

21-5 How can the investment policy be thought of as an operational statement for investment managers to follow?

21-6 Why is the asset allocation decision the most important decision made by investors?

21-7 Explain the difference between tactical asset allocation and strategic asset allocation.

21-8 How does a well-specified investment policy help institutional investors?

21-9 In forming expectations about future returns from stocks, to what extent should investors be influenced by the more recent past (e.g., the previous 15 years) versus the history of stock market returns starting used here in 1920?

CFA
21-10 a. **Outline** a generalized framework that could be used to establish investment policies applicable to all investors.
   b. **List** and **briefly discuss** *five* differences in investment policy that might result from the application of your Part A framework to:
   1. the pension plan of a young, fast-growing consumer products company, and
   2. the modest life insurance proceeds received by a 60-year-old widow with two grown children. (Note: you may find a matrix format helpful in organizing your answers to Part B.)

CFA
21-11 a. **List** the objectives and constraints that must be considered in developing an investment policy statement.

b. **Explain** why the asset allocation decision is the primary determinant of total portfolio performance over time.

c. **Describe** *three* reasons why successful implementation of asset allocation decisions is even more difficult in practice than in theory.

CFA
21-12 You are being interviewed for a junior portfolio manager's job at Progressive Counselors, Inc., and are eager to demonstrate your grasp of portfolio management basics.

a. Portfolio management is a process whose *four* key steps are applicable in all investment management situations. **List** these *four* key steps.

    An endowment fund has a conservative Board of Trustees. The Board establishes an annual budget that relies on gifts as well as investment income. Gift income is unpredictable, having represented from 10 to 50 percent (averaging 30 percent) of annual spending over the past 10 years. If the gift component of any year's total income falls short of this average level, the shortfall is met from liquidity reserves.

b. **List** and **briefly discuss** the objectives and constraints that must be considered in developing an Investment Policy Statement for this endowment fund.

CFA
21-13

INTRODUCTION

The following information is available on two U.S.-based accounts managed by Omega Trust Company.

ACCOUNT 1: THE FOOTE FAMILY

Dr. and Mrs. Sheraton Foote are both 35 years old and have a combined annual income of $250,000. They are both professionals and intend to remain childless. They pay a marginal income tax rate of 40 percent on dividends, interest, and realized capital gains, and dislike paying taxes. Their managed account, which Mrs. Foote inherited, is just over $1,000,000 in value. The Footes do not expect to use the principal in or the income from their managed account until their planned retirement at age 65. Any funds remaining at their death will be left to Hope Ministries.

ACCOUNT 2: HOPE MINISTRIES

Hope Ministries is a tax exempt charitable organization which was established to provide financial assistance to homeless people. The Foundation's charter requires that all income earned from its endowment fund must be used in operations; any increase in the value of the principal of the endowment fund, whether realized or not, must be retained in the endowment fund. Hope currently requires $90,000 annual income from its $1,500,000 endowment fund.

The Omega Trust Company uses the CAPM in managing investment portfolios, combining U.S. Treasury bills (as a proxy for the risk-free rate) and co-mingled funds having differing characteristics. A summary of prevailing expectations for selected capital markets and for each of Omega's co-mingled funds are outlined in Table VIII:

Use the Introduction and Table VIII to answer the following questions about the Foote Family.

a. **Create** and **justify** an investment policy statement for *the Foote Family* based solely on the information provided. Be specific and complete as to the objectives and constraints.

b. **Create** and **justify** an asset allocation for *the Foote Family* portfolio, considering both the requirements of the policy statement created in Part A and the returns that are required by the prevailing security market line. Use only the co-mingled funds (A, B, C) shown in Table VIII.

Assume the Footes have received an additional $350,000 from a new inheritance and invested in a broadly-diversified portfolio and small-capitalization stocks having a 12 percent expected return and a beta of 1.4. They are considering borrowing an additional $150,000 at an interest rate of 8 percent to increase this investment to $500,000.

c. **Explain** the effect of the borrowing on the expected return on the $350,000 inheritance. **Show** any calculations.

d. **State** whether the borrowing is appropriate for the Footes. **Justify** your statement with reference to the investment policy statement you created in Part A.

CFA
21-14 Use the Introduction from above and Table VIII to answer the following questions about Hope Ministries.

a. **Create** and **justify** an investment policy statement for *Hope Ministries* based solely on the information provided. Be specific

Table VIII Omega Trust Company Investment Choices

Investment	Expected Return	Beta
U.S. Treasury Bills (risk-free rate)	4.0%	0.0
S&P 500 (the equity market portfolio)	12.0%	1.0
Fund A (aggressive equity)	16.5% (including 1.0% from dividends)	1.7
Fund B (diversified equity)	13.0% (including 3.0% from dividends)	1.1
Fund C (global bond)	8.0% (including 8.0% from interest)	0.5

and complete as to the objectives and constraints.

b. **Create** and **justify** an asset allocation for the *Hope Ministries* portfolio, considering both the requirements of the policy statement created in Part A and the returns which are required by the prevailing security market line. Use only the three co-mingled funds (A,B,C) shown in Table VIII.

Web Resources

For additional resources visit our dynamic Web site located at www.wiley.com/college/jones.

- *Lost Coast Investment Club*—The case examines the differences between on-line brokerage accounts and highlights the importance of transaction costs in achieving investment objectives. Web site links also help the reader understand brokerage issues and characteristics.

- Internet Exercises—The Web exercises for this chapter explore asset allocation from the viewpoint of the goals of individual investors. A good Web site of information on portfolio construction from the point of view of the individual is the Vanguard's Personal Financial Portfolio Planning site maintained by Vanguard.
  Exercise 1: Relates Stock returns and Inflation.
  Exercise 2: Relates the length of the holding period to the characteristics of return distributions.

- Multiple Choice Self Test

chapter 22

Evaluation of Investment Performance

Chapter 22 explains what is involved in the evaluation of investment performance. Although it might seem like a straightforward process to determine how well an investor's portfolio has performed, such is not the case. Chapter 22 emphasizes the so-called composite measures of portfolio performance and includes a discussion of The Association for Investment and Management Research (AIMR) Performance Presentation Standards as well as a brief consideration of some other issues such as performance attribution.

AFTER READING THIS CHAPTER YOU WILL BE ABLE TO:

▶ Understand the issues involved in evaluating portfolio performance.

▶ Evaluate critically popular press claims about the performance of various portfolios, such as mutual funds, available to investors.

▶ Analyze the performance of portfolios using the well-known measures of Sharpe, Treynor, and Jensen.

We have now discussed in an organized and systematic manner the major components of the investing process. One important issue that remains is the "bottom line" of the investing process: evaluating the performance of a portfolio. The question to be answered is: Is the return on a portfolio, less all expenses, adequate to compensate for the risk that was taken? Every investor should be concerned with this issue because after all, the objective of investing is to increase, or at least protect, financial wealth. Unsatisfactory results must be detected so that changes can be made.

Evaluating portfolio performance is important regardless of whether an individual investor manages his or her own funds or invests indirectly through investment companies. Direct investing can be time consuming and has high opportunity costs. If the results are inadequate, why do it (unless the investor simply enjoys it)? On the other hand, if professional portfolio managers (such as mutual fund managers) are employed, it is necessary to know how well they perform. If manager A consistently outperforms manager B, other things being equal, investors will prefer manager A. Alternatively, if neither A nor B outperforms an index fund, other things being equal, investors may prefer neither. The obvious point is that performance has to be evaluated before intelligent decisions can be made about existing portfolios.

Portfolio evaluation has changed significantly over time. Prior to the mid-1960s, evaluation was not a major issue, even for investment firms, but it is in today's highly competitive money-management environment. Currently, thousands of mutual funds are operating, with several trillion dollars under management. The pension fund universe is even larger, with many employing multiple managers. The majority of all U.S. pension plans with assets greater than $2 billion employ multiple managers. In addition to these money managers, trusts, discretionary accounts, and endowment funds have portfolios that must be evaluated.

Evaluation techniques have become more sophisticated, and the demands by portfolio clients more intense. The broad acceptance of modern portfolio theory has changed the evaluation process and how it is viewed.

In this chapter, we discuss the evaluation of portfolio performance, with an eye to understanding the critical issues involved and the overall framework within which evaluation should be conducted. We also review the well-known measures of composite portfolio performance and the problems associated with them.

Framework for Evaluating Portfolio Performance

When evaluating a portfolio's performance, certain factors must be considered. We discuss below some of the obvious factors that investors should consider and outline the performance presentation standards recently recommended by AIMR, which now plays a prominent role in performance evaluation.

To illustrate our discussion about comparisons, assume that in early 2004 you are evaluating the GoGrowth mutual fund, a domestic equity fund in the category of large growth (it emphasizes large-capitalization growth stocks). This fund earned a total return of 20 percent for its shareholders for 2003. It claims in an advertisement that it is the #1 performing mutual fund in its category. As a shareholder, you are trying to assess GoGrowth's performance. What can you conclude about the performance of this fund?

SOME OBVIOUS FACTORS TO CONSIDER IN MEASURING PORTFOLIO PERFORMANCE

Differential Risk Levels Based on our discussion throughout this text of the risk-return trade-off that underlies all investment actions, we can legitimately say relatively little about GoGrowth's performance. The primary reason is that investing is always a two-dimensional process based on both return and risk. These two factors are opposite sides of the same coin, and both must be evaluated if intelligent decisions are to be made. Therefore, if we know nothing about the risk of this fund, little can be said about its performance. After all, GoGrowth's managers may have taken twice the risk of comparable portfolios to achieve this 20-percent return.

Given the risk that all investors face, it is totally inadequate to consider only the returns from various investment alternatives. Although all investors prefer higher returns, they are also risk averse. To evaluate portfolio performance properly, we must determine whether the returns are large enough given the risk involved. If we are to assess portfolio performance correctly, we must evaluate performance on a risk-adjusted basis.

Differential Time Periods It is not unusual to pick up a publication from the popular press and see two different mutual funds of the same type—for example, small-capitalization growth funds or balanced funds—advertise themselves as the #1 performer. How can this occur?

The answer is simple. Each of these funds is using a different time period over which to measure performance. For example, one fund could use the 10 years ending December 31, 2003, whereas another fund uses the five years ending June 30, 2003. GoGrowth could be using a one-year period ending on the same date or some other combination of years. Mutual fund sponsors may emphasize different time periods in promoting their performance. Funds can also define the group or index to which comparisons are made.

Although it seems obvious when one thinks about it, investors tend not to be careful when making comparisons of portfolios over various time periods. As with the case of differential risk, the time element must be adjusted for if valid performance of portfolio results is to be obtained.

Appropriate Benchmarks A third reason why we can say little about the performance of GoGrowth is that its 20-percent return, given its risk, is meaningful only when compared to a legitimate alternative. Obviously, if the average-risk fund or the market returned 25 percent in 2003, and GoGrowth is an average-risk fund, we would find its performance unfavorable. Therefore, we must make *relative* comparisons in performance measurement, and an important related issue is the benchmark to be used in evaluating the performance of a portfolio.

Benchmark Portfolio
An alternative portfolio against which to measure a portfolio's performance

It is critical in evaluating portfolio performance to compare the returns obtained on the portfolio being evaluated with the returns that could have been obtained from a comparable alternative. The measurement process must involve relevant and obtainable alternatives; that is, the **benchmark portfolio** must be a legitimate alternative that accurately reflects the objectives of the portfolio being evaluated.[1]

An equity portfolio consisting of Standard & Poor's Composite 500 Index (S&P 500) stocks should be evaluated relative to the S&P 500 Index or other equity portfolios that could be constructed from the Index, after adjusting for the risk involved. On the other hand, a portfolio of small-capitalization stocks should not be judged against the benchmark of the S&P 500. Or, if a bond portfolio manager's objective is to invest in bonds rated A or higher, it would be inappropriate to compare his or her performance with that of a junk bond manager.

---

[1] For a discussion of benchmarks, see Jeffrey V. Bailey, "Evaluating Benchmark Quality," *Financial Analysts Journal* (May–June 1992): 33–39.

It may be more difficult to evaluate equity funds that hold some mid-cap and small stocks while holding many S&P 500 stocks. Comparisons for this group can be quite difficult.

Example 22-1

Most of the largest equity funds underperformed the S&P 500 Composite Index for the years 1994, 1995, and 1996. Why? These funds held more small and mid-cap stocks than are in the S&P 500 Index, and such stocks underperformed the large capitalization stocks in those years.

The S&P 500 has been the most frequently used benchmark for evaluating the performance of institutional portfolios such as those of pension funds and mutual funds. However, many observers now agree that multiple benchmarks are more appropriate to use when evaluating portfolio returns for reasons such as those described in Example 22-1. Customized benchmarks also can be constructed to evaluate a manager's style that is unusual.

Constraints on Portfolio Managers In evaluating the portfolio manager rather than the portfolio itself, an investor should consider the objectives set by (or for) the manager and any constraints under which he or she must operate. For example, if a mutual fund's objective is to invest in small, speculative stocks, investors must expect the risk to be larger than that of a fund invested in S&P 500 stocks, with substantial swings in the annual realized returns.

It is imperative to recognize the importance of the *investment policy statement* (discussed in Chapter 21) pursued by a portfolio manager in determining the portfolio's results. In many cases, the investment policy determines the return and/or the risk of the portfolio. For example, Brinson, Hood, and Beebower found that for a sample of pension plans the asset allocation decision accounted for approximately 94 percent of the total variation in the returns to these funds.[2] In other words, more than 90 percent of the movement in a fund's returns, relative to the market's returns, is attributable to a fund's asset allocation policy.

If a portfolio manager is obligated to operate under certain constraints, these must be taken into account. For example, if a portfolio manager of an equity fund is prohibited from selling short, it is unreasonable to expect the manager to protect the portfolio in this manner in a bear market. If the manager is further prohibited from trading in options and futures, the only protection left in a bear market may be to reduce the equity exposure.

Other Considerations Of course, other important issues are involved in measuring the portfolio's performance, including evaluating the manager as opposed to the portfolio itself if the manager does not have full control over the portfolio's cash flows. It is essential to determine how well diversified the portfolio was during the evaluation period, because, as we know, diversification can reduce portfolio risk.

All investors should understand that even in today's investment world of computers and databases, exact, precise universally agreed-upon methods of portfolio evaluation remain an elusive goal. One popular press article summarized the extent of the problem by noting that, "most investors . . . don't have the slightest idea how well their portfolios are

---

[2] See Gary P. Brinson, Randolph Hood, and Gilbert L. Beebower, "Determinants of Portfolio Performance," *Financial Analysts Journal* (July/August 1986): 39–44.

actually performing." This article suggests some do-it-yourself techniques as well as some "store-bought solutions" and discusses some new trends in the money management industry to provide investors with better information.

As we will see below, investors can use several well-known techniques to assess the actual performance of a portfolio relative to one or more alternatives. In the final analysis, when investors are selecting money managers to turn their money over to, they evaluate these managers only on the basis of their published performance statistics. If the published "track record" looks good, that is typically enough to convince many investors to invest in a particular mutual fund. However, the past is no guarantee of an investment manager's future. Short-term results may be particularly misleading.

USING TODAY'S INFORMATION SOURCES AND TOOLS TO EVALUATE PORTFOLIO PERFORMANCE

Like most areas of investing, the Internet has dramatically changed the situation for investors when it comes to evaluating portfolio performance, particularly for mutual funds. Numerous sources of information are available, and convenient tools and techniques can be quickly accessed.

When it comes to mutual funds, *Morningstar* (discussed in Chapter 3) is considered one of the primary sources of information. One of its best-known features is the one to five star ratings that it assigns mutual funds, with five stars being the highest rating. This rating system measures a fund's risk-adjusted performance by analyzing the degree to which fund returns underperform Treasury bills. *Morningstar* recently revised this ranking system to be less sensitive to market movements and to rate funds within 48 different categories rather than using only four broad peer groups.

At the *Morningstar* site (www.morningstar.com), annual fund returns are available for several years, as is a comparison of these returns to both the category the fund is in (e.g., large growth) and a proper benchmark index. These comparisons are available for 1, 3, 5, and 10 years. The returns and risk for a fund are categorized for various periods as to low, average, above average, and so forth. Finally, both the standard deviation and the beta for a fund are available under the "rankings" section of this Web site.

AIMR'S PRESENTATION STANDARDS

Performance Presentation Standards (PPS) Minimum standards for presenting investment performance as presented by the AIMR

The AIMR (see Appendix 1-A), based on years of discussion, has issued *minimum* standards for presenting investment performance.[3] These **Performance Presentation Standards (PPS)** are a set of guiding ethical principles with two objectives:

1. To promote full disclosure and fair representation by investment managers in reporting their investment results.
2. To ensure uniformity in reporting in order to enhance comparability among investment managers.

Some aspects of the standards are mandatory and others are recommended. Table 22-1 summarizes many of the key points of most relevance to this discussion. We will encounter some of these points as we consider how to go about evaluating portfolios.

---

[3] Association for Investment Management and Research, *Performance Presentation Standards 1993*, Charlottesville, Va. 1993.

Table 22-1 AIMR'S Performance Presentations Standards

1. **Total Return**—must be used to calculate performance
2. **Accrual accounting**—use accrual, not cash, accounting except for dividends and for periods before 1993
3. **Time-weighted rates of return**—to be used on at least a quarterly basis and geometric linking of period returns
4. **Cash and cash equivalents**—to be included in composite returns
5. **All portfolios included**—all actual discretionary portfolios are to be included in at least one composite
6. **No linkage of simulated portfolios with actual performance**
7. **Asset-weighting of composites**—beginning-of-period values to be used
8. **Addition of new portfolios**—to be added to a composite after the start of the next measurement period
9. **Exclusion of terminated portfolios**—excluded from all periods after the period in place
10. **No restatement of composite results**—after a firm's reorganization
11. **No portability of portfolio results**
12. **All cost deducted**—subtracted from gross performance
13. **10-year performance record**—minimum period to be presented
14. **Present annual returns for all years**

There are additional requirements for international portfolios and for real estate. In addition, performance presentations must disclose several items of information, such as a complete list of a firm's composites, whether performance results are gross or net of investment management fees, and so on.

Source: *Performance Presentation Standards 1993*, Association for Investment Management and Research, Charlottesville, Va. 1993.

Return and Risk Considerations

Performance measurement begins with portfolio valuations and transactions translated into rate of return. Prior to 1965, returns were seldom related to measures of risk. In evaluating portfolio performance, however, investors must consider both the realized return and the risk that was assumed. Therefore, whatever measures or techniques are used, these parameters must be incorporated into the analysis.

MEASURES OF RETURN

When portfolio performance is evaluated, the investor should be concerned with the total change in wealth. As discussed throughout this text, a proper measure of this return is the total return (TR), which captures both the income component and the capital gains (or losses) component of return. Note that the Performance Presentation Standards require the use of total return to calculate performance.

In the simplest case, the market value of a portfolio can be measured at the beginning and ending of a period, and the rate of return can be calculated as

$$R_p = \frac{V_E - V_B}{V_B} \tag{22-1}$$

where V_E is the ending value of the portfolio and V_B is its beginning value.

This calculation assumes that no funds were added to or withdrawn from the portfolio by the client during the measurement period. If such transactions occur, the portfolio return as calculated, R_p, may not be an accurate measure of the portfolio's performance. For example, if the client adds funds close to the end of the measurement period, use of Equation 22-1 would produce inaccurate results, because the ending value was not determined by the actions of the portfolio manager. Although a close approximation of portfolio performance might be obtained by simply adding any withdrawals or subtracting any contributions that are made very close to the end of the measurement period, timing issues are a problem.

Dollar-Weighted Rate of
Return (DWR)
Equates all cash flows,
including ending market
value, with beginning
market value of the
portfolio

Dollar-Weighted Returns Traditionally, portfolio measurement consisted of calculating the **dollar-weighted rate of return (DWR)**, which is equivalent to the internal rate of return (IRR) used in several financial calculations. The IRR measures the actual return earned on a beginning portfolio value and on any net contributions made during the period.

The DWR equates all cash flows, including ending market value, with the beginning market value of the portfolio. Because the DWR is affected by cash flows to the portfolio, it measures the rate of return to the portfolio owner. Thus, it accurately measures the investor's return. However, because the DRW is heavily affected by cash flows, it is inappropriate to use when making comparisons to other portfolios or to market indexes, a key factor in performance measurement. In other words, it is a misleading measure of the manager's ability, because the manager does not have control over the timing of the cash inflows and outflows. Clearly, if an investor with $1,000,000 allocates these funds to a portfolio manager by providing half at the beginning of the year and half at mid-year, the portfolio value at the end of the year will differ from another manager who received the entire $1,000,000 at the beginning of the year. This is true even if both managers had the same two 6-month returns during that year.

Time-Weighted Rate of
Return (TWR)
Measures the actual rate
of return earned by the
portfolio manager

Time-Weighted Returns In order to evaluate a manager's performance properly, we should use the **time-weighted rate of return (TWR)**. TWRs are unaffected by any cash flows to the portfolio; therefore, they measure the actual rate of return earned by the portfolio manager.

We wish to determine how well the portfolio manager performed regardless of the size or timing of the cash flows. Therefore, the time-weighted rate of return measures the compound rate of growth of the portfolio during the evaluation period. It is calculated by computing the geometric average of the portfolio subperiod returns. That is, we calculate the geometric mean of a set of return relatives (and subtract out the 1.0).

Which Measure to Use? The dollar-weighted return and the time-weighted return can produce different results, and at times these differences are substantial. In fact, the two will produce identical results only in the case of no withdrawals or contributions during the evaluation period and with all investment income being reinvested. The time-weighted return captures the rate of return actually earned by the portfolio *manager*, whereas the dollar-weighted return captures the rate of return earned by the portfolio *owner*.

For evaluating the performance of the portfolio manager, the time-weighted return should be used, because he or she generally has no control over the deposits and withdrawals made by the clients. The objective is to measure the performance of the portfolio manager independent of the actions of the client, and this is better accomplished by using the time-weighted return. As we can see in Table 22-1, the Performance Presentation Standards require that returns be computed using the TWR approach.

RISK MEASURES

Why can we not measure investment performance on the basis of a properly calculated rate of return measure? After all, rankings of mutual funds are often done this way in the popular press, with one-year, three-year, and sometimes five-year returns shown. Are rates of return, or averages, good indicators of performance?

As stated in Chapter 1 and restated above, we must consider risk when making judgments about performance. Differences in risk will cause portfolios to respond differently to changes in the overall market and should be accounted for in evaluating performance.

We now know that the two prevalent measures of risk used in investment analysis are total risk and nondiversifiable, or systematic, risk. The standard deviation for a portfolio's set of returns can be calculated easily with a calculator or computer and is a measure of total risk. As we know from portfolio theory, part of the total risk can be diversified away.

Beta, a relative measure of systematic risk, can be calculated with any number of software programs. However, we must remember that betas are only estimates of systematic risk. Betas can be calculated using weekly, monthly, quarterly, or annual data, and each will produce a different estimate. Such variations in this calculation could produce differences in rankings which use beta as a measure of risk. Furthermore, betas can be unstable, and they change over time.

Risk-Adjusted Measures of Performance

Based on the concepts of capital market theory, and recognizing the necessity to incorporate both return and risk into the analysis, three researchers—William Sharpe, Jack Treynor, and Michael Jensen—developed measures of portfolio performance in the 1960s. These measures are often referred to as the **composite (risk-adjusted) measures** of portfolio performance, meaning that they incorporate both realized return and risk into the evaluation. These measures are often still used, as evidenced by *Morningstar*, perhaps the best-known source of mutual fund information, reporting the Sharpe ratio explained below.

Composite (Risk-Adjusted) Measures of Portfolio Performance Portfolio performance measures combining return and risk into one calculation

Reward-to-Variability Ratio (RVAR) Sharpe's measure of portfolio performance calculated as the ratio of excess portfolio return to the standard deviation

THE SHARPE PERFORMANCE MEASURE

William Sharpe, whose contributions to portfolio theory have been previously discussed, introduced a risk-adjusted measure of portfolio performance called the **reward-to-variability ratio (RVAR)** based on his work in capital market theory.[4] This measure uses a benchmark based on the *ex post* capital market line.[5] This measure can be defined as

$$RVAR = [\overline{TR}_p - \overline{RF}]/SD_p \qquad (22\text{-}2)$$

$$= \text{Excess return/Risk}$$

$\overline{TR}_p$ = The average TR for portfolio p during some period of time (we will use annual data)

$\overline{RF}$ = the average risk-free rate of return during the period

SD_p = the standard deviation of return for portfolio p during the period

$\overline{TR}_p - \overline{RF}$ = the excess return (risk premium) on portfolio p

Table 22-2 Return and Risk Data for Five Equity Mutual Funds, 15-year Period

Mutual Fund	Average Return	Standard Deviation	Beta	R^2
Dreyfus Growth	15.86	22.85	1.46	.64
Ivy Growth	18.10	13.44	.96	.79
Kemper Growth	18.59	21.68	1.45	.69
Magellan (Fidelity)	22.09	17.27	1.24	.79
Windsor (Vanguard)	18.39	11.82	.60	.39
S&P 500	16.35	12.44		
RF	7.96			

[4] W. Sharpe, "Mutual Fund Performance," *Journal of Business* (January 1966): 119–138.
[5] Sharpe used it to rank the performance of 34 mutual funds over the period 1954–1963.

Table 22-3 Risk-Adjusted Measures for Five Equity Mutual Funds, 15-year Period

Mutual Fund	RVAR	RVOL	Jensen's Alpha
Dreyfus	.35	5.40	−3.95
Ivy	.75	10.54	2.67
Kemper	.49	7.33	−1.04
Magellan	.82	11.42	4.21
Windsor	.88	17.38	5.35
S&P 500	.67		

The numerator of Equation 22-2 measures the portfolio's excess return, or the return above the risk-free rate. (RF could have been earned without assuming risk.) This is also referred to as the risk premium. The denominator uses the standard deviation, which is a measure of the total risk or variability in the return of the portfolio. Note the following about RVAR:

1. It measures the excess return per unit of total risk (standard deviation).
2. The higher the RVAR, the better the portfolio performance.
3. Portfolios can be ranked by RVAR.

As an example of calculating the Sharpe ratio, consider the data for five equity mutual funds for a recent 15-year period chosen randomly for illustrative purposes only: Dreyfus (D), Ivy (I), Kemper (K), Magellan (M), and Windsor (W). Table 22-2 shows annual shareholder returns, the standard deviation of these returns, the beta for the fund, the average return for the S&P 500 Index for those years, and the average yield on Treasury bills as a proxy for RF. On the basis of these data, Sharpe's RVAR can be calculated using Equation 22-2, with results as reported in Table 22-3.

Based on these calculations, we see that three of these five funds—I, W, and M—outperformed the S&P 500 Index on an excess return-risk basis during this period, although the average return exceeded that for the S&P 500 for four of the funds. Since this is an ordinal (relative) measure of portfolio performance, different portfolios can easily be ranked on this variable. Using only the Sharpe measure of portfolio performance, we would judge the portfolio with the highest RVAR best in terms of *ex post* performance. A RVAR value for the appropriate market index can also be calculated and used for comparison purposes.

As we can see, W, I, and M have RVAR ratios that exceed the RVAR of 0.67 for the S&P 500 for the period. The average return for three of these funds—I, K, and W—were very close together—18.10, 18.59, and 18.39 percent, respectively. However, their standard deviations were very different—13.44, 21.68, and 11.82 percent, respectively. Therefore, their RVAR ratios differed significantly. In effect, Kemper's risk was very high in relation to its average return as compared in particular to Windsor, which showed slightly less average return but with a much lower standard deviation.

Sharpe's measure for these funds is illustrated graphically in Figure 22-1. The vertical axis is rate of return, and the horizontal axis is standard deviation of returns. The vertical intercept is RF.

Figure 22-1

Sharpe's measure
of performance
(RVAR) for five
mutual funds,
Fifteen-year period
(D = Dreyfus;
I = Ivy;
K = Kemper;
M = Magellan;
W = Windsor).

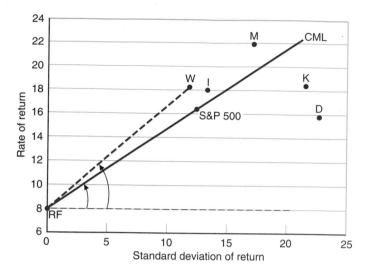

As Figure 22-1 shows, RVAR measures the slope of the line from RF to the portfolio being evaluated. The steeper the line, the higher the slope (RVAR) and the better the performance. The arrow indicates the slope for the S&P 500 and for Windsor, the fund with the greatest slope.

Because of their better performance, Windsor, Magellan, and Ivy have the higher slopes, whereas Kemper's and Dreyfus's slopes are lower than that of the S&P 500. Because the RVAR for these three portfolios is greater than the RVAR for the market measure (in this case the S&P 500), these portfolios lie above the CML, indicating superior risk-adjusted performance. The other two lie below the CML, indicating inferior risk-adjusted performance.

Using the Internet

Sharpe ratios for a number of mutual funds can be found at **fidelity.com/goto/screens**. Choose a category of mutual funds such as "Large Value." In the "View" screen, click on "Risk."

THE TREYNOR PERFORMANCE MEASURE

Reward-to-Volatility Ratio (RVOL)

Treynor's measure of portfolio performance calculated as the ratio of excess portfolio return to beta

At approximately the same time as Sharpe's measure was developed (the mid-1960s), Jack Treynor presented a similar measure called the **reward-to-volatility ratio (RVOL)**.[6] Like Sharpe, Treynor sought to relate the return on a portfolio to its risk. Treynor, however, distinguished between total risk and systematic risk, implicitly assuming that portfolios are well diversified; that is, he ignored any diversifiable risk. He used as a benchmark the *ex post* security market line.

In measuring portfolio performance, Treynor introduced the concept of the characteristic line, which was used in earlier chapters to partition a security's return into its systematic and nonsystematic components. It is used in a similar manner with portfolios, depicting the relationship between the returns on a portfolio and those of the market. The slope of the characteristic line measures the relative volatility of the fund's returns. As we know, the slope of this line is the beta coefficient, which is a measure of the volatility (or responsiveness) of the portfolio's returns in relation to those of the market index.

---

[6] J. Treynor, "How to Rate Management of Investment Funds," *Harvard Business Review* (January–February 1965), pp. 63–75.

Characteristic lines can be estimated by regressing each portfolio's returns on the market proxy returns using either raw returns for the portfolios and raw proxy returns or excess portfolio returns and excess market proxy returns where the risk-free rate has been subtracted out. The latter method is theoretically better and is used here.

Treynor's measure relates the average excess return on the portfolio during some period (exactly the same variable as in the Sharpe measure) to its systematic risk as measured by the portfolio's beta. The reward-to-volatility ratio is

$$RVOL = [\overline{TR}_p - \overline{RF}]\beta_p$$

$\overline{TR}_p - \overline{RF}$ = Average excess return on portfolio p

β_p = The beta for portfolio p

(22-3)

In this case, we are calculating the excess return per unit of systematic risk. As with RVAR, higher values of RVOL indicate better portfolio performance. Portfolios can be ranked on their RVOL, and assuming that the Treynor measure is a correct measure of portfolio performance, the best-performing portfolio can be determined.

Using the data in Table 22-1, we can calculate RVOL for the same five portfolios illustrated and for the S&P 500, which has a beta of 1.0. These calculations indicate that three funds outperformed the market on the basis of their excess return/systematic risk ratio—I, M, and W. The two funds with the highest betas, D and K, had RVOL ratios lower than the beta for the S&P 500. Although the beta for Magellan was higher than those for the other two top performers, I and W, its higher return was sufficient to compensate for this larger risk (at least in these comparisons).

Figure 22-2 illustrates the graph of the Treynor measure in a manner similar to Figure 22-1 for the Sharpe measure. In this graph, we are viewing the *ex post* SML. Again, three funds plot above the line—I, M, and W—and two funds plot below—D and K. Once again, if we were to draw lines to each fund's return—risk point, the steepest line would have the largest slope and represent the best performance.

The use of RVOL, of course, implies that systematic risk is the proper measure of risk to use when evaluating portfolio performance; therefore, it implicitly assumes a completely diversified portfolio. (Similarly, the use of RVAR implies that total risk is the proper measure to use when evaluating portfolios.) As we now know, systematic risk is a proper measure of risk to use when portfolios are perfectly diversified so that no

Figure 22-2

Treynor's measure of performance (RVOL) for five mutual funds, Fifteen-year period (D = Dreyfus; I = Ivy; K = Kemper; M = Magellan; W = Windsor).

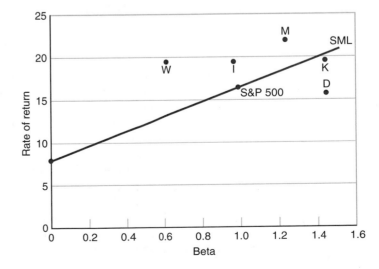

nonsystematic risk remains. (A procedure for measuring the degree of diversification is discussed below.)

Comparing the Sharpe and Treynor Measures Given their similarity, when should RVAR or RVOL be used, and why? Actually, given the assumptions underlying each measure, both can be said to be correct. Therefore, it is usually desirable to calculate both measures for the set of portfolios being evaluated.

The choice of which to use could depend on the definition of risk. If an investor thinks it correct to use total risk, RVAR is appropriate; however, if the investor thinks that it is correct to use systematic risk, RVOL is appropriate.

What about the rankings of a set of portfolios using the two measures? If the portfolios are perfectly diversified—that is, the correlation coefficient between the portfolio return and the market return is 1.0—the rankings will be identical. For typical large, professionally managed portfolios, such as broad-based equity mutual funds, the two measures often provide identical, or almost identical, rankings.

As the portfolios become less well diversified, the possibility of differences in rankings increases. This leads to the following conclusion about these two measures: RVAR takes into account how well diversified a portfolio was during the measurement period. Differences in rankings between the two measures can result from substantial differences in diversification in the portfolio. If a portfolio is inadequately diversified, its RVOL ranking can be higher than its RVAR ranking. The nonsystematic risk would not affect the RVOL calculation. Therefore, a portfolio with a low amount of systematic risk and a large amount of total risk could show a high RVOL value and a low RVAR value. Such a difference in ranking results from the substantial difference in the amount of diversification of the portfolio.

This analysis leads to an important observation about the Sharpe and Treynor measures. Investors who have all (or substantially all) of their assets in a portfolio of securities should rely more on the Sharpe measure, because it assesses the portfolio's total return in relation to total risk, which includes any unsystematic risk assumed by the investor. However, for those investors whose portfolio constitutes only one (relatively) small part of their total assets—that is, they have numerous other assets—systematic risk may well be the relevant risk. In these circumstances, RVOL is appropriate, because it considers only systematic or nondiversifiable risk.

Measuring Diversification Portfolio diversification is typically measured by correlating the returns on the portfolio with the returns on the market index. This is accomplished as part of the process of fitting a characteristic line whereby the portfolio's returns are regressed against the market's returns. The square of the correlation coefficient produced as a part of the analysis, called the **coefficient of determination**, or R^2, is used to denote the degree of diversification. The coefficient of determination indicates the percentage of the variance in the portfolio's returns that is explained by the market's returns. If the fund is totally diversified, the R^2 will approach 1.0, indicating that the fund's returns are completely explained by the market's returns. The lower the coefficient of determination, the less the portfolio's returns are attributable to the market's returns. This indicates that other factors, which could have been diversified away, are being allowed to influence the portfolio's returns.

The R^2 figures in Table 22-2 indicate that four of the funds had R^2 in the range of 0.64 to 0.79. The R^2 for Windsor was only 0.39, indicating that it was exposed to more nonsystematic risk than the other funds, presumably because the portfolio managers expected to earn adequate returns to compensate for this risk.

Coefficient of Determination The square of the correlation coefficient, measuring the percentage of the variance in the dependent variable that is explained by the independent variable

JENSEN'S DIFFERENTIAL RETURN MEASURE

Differential Return Measure (Alpha) Jensen's measure of portfolio performance calculated as the difference between what the portfolio actually earned and what it was expected to earn given its level of systematic risk

A measure related to Treynor's RVOL is Jensen's **differential return measure** (or **alpha**). Jensen's measure of performance, like Treynor's measure, is based on the capital asset pricing model (CAPM). The expected return for any security (i) or, in this case, portfolio (p) is given as

$$E(R_{pt}) = RF_t + \beta_p(E(R_{Mt}) - RF_t) \tag{22-4}$$

with all terms as previously defined.

Notice that Equation 22-4, which covers any *ex ante* period t, can be applied to *ex post* periods if the investor's expectations are, on the average, fulfilled. Empirically, Equation 22-4 can be approximated as Equation 22-5.

$$R_{pt} = RF_t + \beta_p[R_{Mt} - RF_t] + E_{pt} \tag{22-5}$$

where

R_{pt}	= the return on portfolio p in period t
RF_t	= the risk-free rate in period t
R_{Mt}	= the return on the market in period t
E_{pt}	= a random error term for portfolio p in period t
$[R_{Mt} - RF_t]$	= the market risk premium during period t

Equation 22-5 relates the realized return on portfolio p during any period t to the sum of the risk-free rate and the portfolio's risk premium plus an error term. Given the market risk premium, the risk premium on portfolio p is a function of portfolio p's systematic risk—the larger its systematic risk, the larger the risk premium.

Equation 22-5 can be written in what is called the risk premium (or, alternatively, the excess return) form by moving RF to the left side and subtracting it from R_{pt}, as in Equation 22-6:

$$R_{pt} - RF_t = \beta_p[R_{Mt} - RF_t] + E_{pt} \tag{22-6}$$

where

$R_{pt} - RF_t$ = the risk premium on portfolio p

Equation 22-6 indicates that the risk premium on portfolio p is equal to the product of its beta and the market risk premium plus an error term. In other words, the risk premium on portfolio p should be proportional to the risk premium on the market portfolio if the CAPM model is correct and investor expectations were generally realized (in effect, if all assets and portfolios were in equilibrium).

A return proportional to the risk assumed is illustrated by Fund Y in Figure 22-3. This diagram shows the characteristic line in excess return form, where the risk-free rate each period, RF_t, is subtracted from both the portfolio's return and the market's return.[7]

Equation 22-6 can be empirically tested by fitting a regression for some number of periods. Portfolio excess returns (risk premiums) are regressed against the excess returns (risk premiums) for the market. If managers earn a return proportional to the risk assumed, this relationship should hold. That is, there should be no intercept term (alpha) in the regression, which should go through the origin, as in the case of Fund Y in Figure 22-3.

---

[7] This version is usually referred to as a characteristic line in risk premium or excess return form.

Figure 22-3

Jensen's measure of performance for three hypothetical funds.

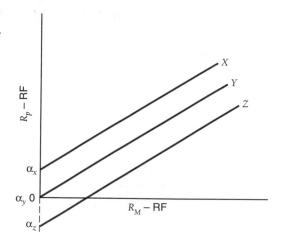

Given these expected findings, Jensen argued that an intercept term, alpha, could be added to Equation 22-6 as a means of identifying superior or inferior portfolio performance. Therefore, Equation 22-6 becomes Equation 22-7 where α_p is the alpha or intercept term:

$$R_{pt} - RF_t = \alpha_p + \beta_p[R_{Mt} - RF_t] + E_{pt} \tag{22-7}$$

The CAPM asserts that equilibrium conditions should result in a zero intercept term. Therefore, the alpha should measure the contribution of the portfolio manager, since it represents the average incremental rate of return per period beyond the return attributable to the level of risk assumed. Specifically,

1. If alpha is significantly positive, this is evidence of superior performance (illustrated in Figure 22-3 with portfolio X, which has a positive intercept).
2. If alpha is significantly negative, this is evidence of inferior performance (illustrated in Figure 22-3 with portfolio Z, which has a negative intercept).
3. If alpha is insignificantly different from zero, this is evidence that the portfolio manager matched the market on a risk-adjusted basis (as in the case of portfolio Y).

Note that Equation 22-7 can be rearranged to demonstrate better what α_p really is. Rearranging terms, Equation 22-7 becomes

$$\alpha_p = (\overline{R}_p - \overline{RF}) - [\beta_p(\overline{R}_M - \overline{RF})] \tag{22-8}$$

where the bars above the variables indicate averages for the period measured.

Equation 22-8 states that α_p is the difference between the actual excess return on portfolio p during some period and the risk premium on that portfolio that should have been earned given its level of systematic risk and the use of the CAPM. It measures the constant return that the portfolio manager earned above, or below, the return of an unmanaged portfolio with the same (market) risk.

As noted, this difference can be positive, negative, or zero. It is important to recognize the role of statistical significance in the interpretation of Jensen's measure. Although the estimated alpha may be positive or negative, it may not be significantly different (statistically) from zero. If it is not, we would conclude that the manager of the portfolio being evaluated performed as expected. That is, the manager earned an average risk-adjusted return neither more nor less than would be expected given the risk assumed.

Jensen's performance measure can be estimated by regressing excess returns for the portfolio being evaluated against excess returns for the market (in effect, producing a characteristic line in excess return form). When this was done for the five mutual funds evaluated earlier, the results are as shown in Table 22-2.

Three of the funds showed positive alphas, and reasonably high ones given the alphas typically observed for mutual funds. If significant, the 5.35 for Windsor would indicate that this fund, on the average, earned an annual risk-adjusted rate of return that was more than 5 percent above the market average. In other words, Windsor earned a positive return attributable to factors other than the market, presumably because of the ability of its managers. However, the standard errors for each fund indicate that the alphas are not significantly different from zero.[8] Therefore, we cannot conclude that these funds exhibited superior performance. As in any regression equation, the coefficients must be statistically significant for any conclusions to be drawn.

Portfolios often fail to meet this statistical significance test because of the variability in security returns. This means that although the manager may actually add value, it cannot be detected statistically. The larger the number of observations, the more likely we are to find statistical significance.

Superior and inferior portfolio performance can result from at least two sources. First, the portfolio manager may be able to select undervalued securities consistently enough to affect portfolio performance. Second, the manager may be able to time market turns, varying the portfolio's composition in accordance with the rise and fall of the market. Obviously, a manager with enough ability may be able to do both.

A computational advantage of the Jensen measure is that it permits the performance measure to be estimated simultaneously with the beta for a portfolio. That is, by estimating a characteristic line in risk premium form, estimates of both alpha and beta are obtained at the same time. However, unlike the Sharpe and Treynor measures, each period's returns must be used in the estimating process rather than an average return for the entire period. Thus, if performance is being measured on an annual basis, the annual returns on RF, RM, and R_p must be obtained.

A Comparison of the Three Composite Measures The Sharpe measure, which uses the standard deviation, evaluates portfolio performance on the basis of both the portfolio's return and its diversification. Treynor's measure considers only the systematic risk of the portfolio and, like the Sharpe measure, can be used to rank portfolios on the basis of realized performance. Although the Sharpe and Treynor measures rank portfolios, they do not tell us in percentage terms how much a fund outperformed (or underperformed) some benchmark.

Like the Treynor measure, Jensen's alpha uses beta as the measure of risk. Jensen's measure is not suitable for ranking portfolio performance, but it can be modified to do so. With proper adjustments the Jensen and Treynor measures can produce, identical relative rankings of portfolio performance.[9]

If a portfolio is completely diversified, all three measures will agree on a ranking of portfolios. The reason for this is that with complete diversification, total variance is equal to systematic variance. When portfolios are not completely diversified, the Treynor and Jensen measures can rank relatively undiversified portfolios much higher than the Sharpe measure does. Since the Sharpe measure uses total risk, both systematic and nonsystematic components are included.

---

[8] A general rule of thumb is that a coefficient should be twice its standard error in order to be significant at the 5-percent level. Alternatively, *t* values can be examined in order to test the significance of the coefficients. For a reasonably large number of observations, and therefore degrees of freedom, *t* values of approximately 2.0 would indicate significance at the 5-percent level.

[9] Jensen's alpha divided by beta is equivalent to Treynor's measure minus the average risk premium for the market portfolio for the period.

Another difference in the measures is that the Sharpe and Treynor measures use average returns over the measurement period, including the average risk-free rate. The Jensen measure uses the period-by-period returns and risk-free rate.

Problems with Portfolio Measurement

Using the three risk-adjusted performance measures just discussed to evaluate portfolios is not without problems. Investors should understand their limitations and be guided accordingly.

First, these measures are derived from capital market theory and the CAPM and are therefore dependent on the assumptions involved with this theory, as discussed in Chapter 9. For example, if the Treasury bill rate is not a satisfactory proxy for the risk-free rate, or if investors cannot borrow and lend at the risk-free rate, this will have an impact on these measures of performance.

An important assumption of capital market theory that directly affects the use of these performance measures is the assumption of a market portfolio that can be proxied by a market index. We have used the S&P 500 Index as a market proxy, as is often done. However, there are potential problems.

Richard Roll has argued that beta is not a clear-cut measure of risk.[10] If the definition of the market portfolio is changed, for example, by using the New York Stock Exchange Index instead of the S&P 500, the beta can change. This could, in turn, change the rankings of portfolios. In addition, if the proxy for the market portfolio is not efficient, the SML used may not be the true SML. Errors can occur when portfolios are plotted against an incorrect SML. This is referred to as *benchmark error*.

Although a high correlation exists among most of the commonly used market proxies, this does not eliminate the problem—that some may be efficient but others are not. This relates to Roll's major point, mentioned in Chapter 9, that using a market portfolio other than the "true" market portfolio does not constitute a test of the CAPM. Rather it is a test only of whether or not the chosen market proxy is efficient. According to Roll, no unambiguous test of the CAPM has yet been conducted. This point should be kept in mind when we consider performance measures based on the CAPM, such as the Treynor and Jensen measures.

The movement to global investing increases the problem of benchmark error. The efficient frontier changes when foreign securities are added to the portfolio. The measurement of beta will be affected by adding foreign securities. Given that a world portfolio is likely to have a smaller variance than the S&P 500 Index, any measure of systematic risk is likely to be smaller.

A long evaluation period is needed to determine successfully performance that is truly superior. Over short periods, luck can overshadow all else, but luck cannot be expected to continue. According to some estimates, the number of years needed to make such an accurate determination is quite large. As we saw in Table 22-1, the Performance Presentation Standards stipulate the presentation of at least a 10-year performance record.

Theoretically, each of the three performance measures discussed should be independent of its respective risk measure. However, over the years some researchers have found a relationship between them. In some cases, the relationship was negative, and in others, it was positive. It can be shown that a fundamental relationship does exist between the composite performance measures and their associated risk measure.[11] Given an

---

[10] See R. Roll, "Ambiguity When Performance Is Measured by the Securities Market Line," *The Journal of Finance*, 33 (September 1978): 1051–1069; "Performance Evaluation and Benchmark Error, Part I," *The Journal of Portfolio Management*, 6 (Summer 1980): 5–12, and Part II (Winter 1981): 17–22.

[11] See J. Wilson and C. Jones, "The Relationship Between Performance and Risk: Whence the Bias?" *The Journal of Financial Research*, 4 (Summer 1981): 109–117.

empirical CML, the relation between Sharpe's measure and the standard deviation can be instantly derived. Similarly, given an empirical SML, the relationship between Jensen's and Treynor's performance measures and beta can be derived instantly. The only other variable needed to do these calculations is the mean market return for the period.

Other Issues in Performance Evaluation

MONITORING PERFORMANCE

Portfolio evaluation of managed portfolios should be a continuing process. The results of the portfolio must be calculated using some of the techniques discussed above. In addition, a monitoring process should evaluate the success of the portfolio relative to the objectives and constraints of the portfolio's owners.

PERFORMANCE ATTRIBUTION

Performance Attribution
A part of portfolio evaluation that seeks to determine why success or failure occurred

Most of this chapter has considered how to measure a portfolio manager's performance. However, portfolio evaluation also is concerned with the reasons why a manager did better or worse than a properly constructed benchmark with complete risk adjustment. This part of portfolio evaluation is called **performance attribution**, which seeks to determine, after the fact, why a particular portfolio had a given return over some specified time period and, therefore, why success or failure occurred.

Typically, performance attribution is a top-down approach; it looks first at the broad issues and progresses by narrowing the investigation. Its purpose is to decompose the total performance of a portfolio into specific components that can be associated with specific decisions made by the portfolio manager.

Performance attribution often begins with the policy statement that guides the management of the portfolio. The portfolio normally would have a set of portfolio weights to be used. If the manager uses a different set, this will account for some of the results. In effect, we are looking at the asset allocation decision referred to in Chapter 21. If the manager chooses to allocate portfolio funds differently than the weights that occur in the benchmark portfolio, what are the results?

After this analysis, performance attribution might analyze sector (industry) selection and security selection. Did the manager concentrate on or avoid certain sectors, and if so what were the results? Security selection speaks for itself.

Part of this process involves identifying a benchmark of performance to use in comparing the portfolio's results. This bogey is designed to measure passive results, ruling out both asset allocation and security selection decisions. Any differences between the portfolio's results and the bogey must be attributable to one or more of these decisions made by the portfolio manager.

Another way to think about performance attribution is to recognize that performance different from a properly constructed benchmark comes from one of two sources, or both:

1. Market timing
2. Security selection

Techniques are available to decompose the performance of a portfolio into these two components.[12]

---

[12] See R. Henriksson, "Market Timing and Mutual Fund Performance: An Empirical Investigation," *Journal of Business* (1984): 73–96.

CAN PERFORMANCE BE PREDICTED?

The objective of performance evaluation is to measure the performance of a portfolio and its manager over the same time period. Having assessed how well a portfolio manager has performed over the past, is such information valuable in predicting future portfolio performance? After all, in choosing a mutual fund or closed-end fund, won't investors rely heavily on both the absolute and relative results reported by the fund?

Most studies suggest the correlation between past relative performance and future performance is weak. For example, if average returns for a 5- or 10-year period are correlated with average returns for the subsequent 5- or 10-year period, the correlations are quite low, typically less than 0.20. Therefore, past relative returns do not successfully predict future relative returns, but may provide some help.

Summary

▶ Evaluation of portfolio performance, the bottom line of the investing process, is an important aspect of interest to all investors and money managers.

▶ The framework for evaluating portfolio performance consists of measuring both the realized return and the differential risk of the portfolio being evaluated, determining an appropriate benchmark portfolio to use to compare a portfolio's performance, and recognizing any constraints that the portfolio manager may face.

▶ AIMR has issued a set of Performance Presentation Standards designed to promote full disclosure by investment managers in reporting their investment results and help ensure uniformity in reporting.

▶ The time-weighted, as opposed to the dollar-weighted, return captures the rate of return actually earned by the portfolio manager. Total returns are used in the calculations.

▶ The two prevalent measures of risk are total risk (standard deviation) and systematic risk (beta).

▶ The most often used measures of portfolio performance are the composite measures of Sharpe, Treynor, and Jensen, which bring return and risk together in one calculation.

▶ The Sharpe and Treynor measures can be used to rank portfolio performance and indicate the relative positions of the portfolios being evaluated. Jensen's measure is an absolute measure of performance.

▶ Both the Sharpe and Treynor measures relate the excess return on a portfolio to a measure of its risk. Sharpe's RVAR uses standard deviation, whereas Treynor's RVOL uses beta.

▶ Since RVAR implicitly measures the lack of complete diversification in a portfolio and RVOL assumes complete diversification, portfolio rankings from the two measures can differ if portfolios are not well diversified.

▶ The coefficient of determination can be used to measure the degree of diversification in a portfolio.

▶ The Sharpe measure is more appropriate when the portfolio constitutes a significant portion of an investor's wealth, whereas the Treynor measure is more appropriate when the portfolio constitutes only a small part of that wealth.

▶ Jensen's differential return measures the difference between what the portfolio was expected to earn, given its systematic risk, and what it actually did earn. By regressing the portfolio's excess return against that of the market index, alpha can be used to capture the superior or inferior performance of the portfolio manager.

▶ Based on capital market theory, alphas are expected to be zero. Significantly positive or negative alphas are used to indicate corresponding performance.

▶ The composite measures are not without their limitations and problems. If there are problems with capital market theory and the CAPM, such problems carry over to performance measurement.

▶ One problem in particular is the market portfolio, which can be measured only imprecisely. Failure to use the true *ex ante* market portfolio may result in different betas and different rankings for portfolios because of benchmark error.

▶ Performance attribution is concerned with why a portfolio manager did better or worse than an expected benchmark. It involves decomposing performance to determine why the particular results occurred.

Key Words

Benchmark portfolio

Coefficient of determination

Composite (risk-adjusted) measures of portfolio performance

Differential return measure (Alpha)

Dollar-weighted rate of return (DWR)

Performance attribution

Performance Presentation Standards (PPS)

Reward-to-variability ratio (RVAR)

Reward-to-volatility ratio (RVOL)

Time-weighted rate of return (TWR)

Questions

22-1 Outline the framework for evaluating portfolio performance.

22-2 Why can the evaluation of a portfolio be different from the evaluation of a portfolio manager?

22-3 Explain how the three composite measures of performance are related to capital market theory and the CAPM.

22-4 What role does diversification play in the Sharpe and Treynor measures?

22-5 How can one construct a characteristic line for a portfolio? What does it show?

22-6 How can portfolio diversification be measured? On the average, what degree of diversification would you expect to find for a typical mutual fund?

22-7 For what type of mutual fund discussed in Chapter 3 could you expect to find complete diversification?

22-8 In general, when may an investor prefer to rely on the Sharpe measure? the Treynor measure?

22-9 Explain how Jensen's differential return measure is derived from the CAPM.

22-10 Why is the Jensen measure computationally efficient?

22-11 What role does statistical significance play in the Jensen measure?

22-12 How does Roll's questioning of the testing of the CAPM relate to the issue of performance measurement?

22-13 Illustrate how the choice of the wrong market index could affect the rankings of portfolios.

22-14 In theory, what would be the proper market index to use?

22-15 Explain why the steeper the angle, the better the performance in Figures 22-1 and 22-2.

22-16 Do the Sharpe and Jensen measures produce the same rankings of portfolio performance?

CFA

22-17 A plan sponsor with a portfolio manager who invests in small capitalization, high-growth stocks should have the plan sponsor's performance measured against which *one* of the following?

a. S&P 500 Index
b. Wilshire 5000 Index
c. Dow Jones Industrial Average
d. S&P 400 Index

CFA

22-18 Which *one* of the following is a valid benchmark against which a portfolio's performance can be measured over a given time period?

a. The portfolio's dollar-weighted rate of return
b. The portfolio's time-weighted rate of return
c. The portfolio manager's "normal" portfolio
d. The average beta of the portfolio

Problems

22-1 The following data are available for five portfolios and the market for a recent 10-year period:

	Annual Return (%)	Standard Deviation (%)	Average β_p	R^2
1	14	21	1.15	0.70
2	16	24	1.1	0.98
3	26	30	1.3	0.96
4	17	25	0.9	0.92
5	10	18	0.45	0.60
S&P 500	12	20		
RF	6			

a. Rank these portfolios using the Sharpe measure.
b. Rank these portfolios using the Treynor measure.
c. Compare the rankings of portfolios 1 and 2. Are there any differences? How can you explain these differences?
d. Which of these portfolios outperformed the market?

22-2 Consider the five funds shown below:

	α	β	R^2
1	2.0	1.0	0.98
2	1.6[a]	1.1	0.95
3	3.5	0.9	0.90
4	1.2	0.8	0.80
5	0.9[a]	1.20	0.60

[a]Significant at 5-percent level.

a. Which fund's returns are best explained by the market's returns?
b. Which fund had the largest total risk?
c. Which fund had the lowest market risk? The highest?
d. Which fund(s), according to Jensen's alpha, outperformed the market?

22-3 Draw a diagram showing characteristic lines in risk premium form for two portfolios. Assume that the alphas for each portfolio are statistically significant.

a. Label each axis.
b. How could you determine which fund has the larger beta?
c. Which fund has the larger alpha?
d. Which fund outperformed the market?

22-4 Annual total returns for nine years are shown below for eight mutual funds. Characteristic lines are calculated using annual market returns. The *ex post* values are as follows:

Fund	−(1) R_p(%)	(2) σ_p(%)	(3) α_p	(4) β_p	(5) R^2
A	17.0	20.0	7.53	0.88	0.82
B	19.0	17.8	11.70	0.65	0.57
C	12.3	25.0	3.12	0.83	0.47
D	20.0	24.5	9.00	1.00	0.72
E	15.0	17.4	6.15	0.79	0.88
F	19.0	18.0	10.11	0.83	0.89
G	8.6	19.0	−1.37	0.91	0.95
H	20.0	21.5	9.52	0.93	0.78

where

$\overline{R_p}$ = mean annual total return for each fund
σ_P = standard deviation of the annual yields
α_P = the constant of the characteristic line
β_P = the slope

Using an 8.6-percent risk-free return:

a. Calculate Sharpe's RVAR for each of these eight funds and rank the eight funds from high to low performance.
b. Calculate Treynor's RVOL for each fund and perform the same ranking as in part a.
c. Use the R^2 in column 5 to comment on the degree of diversification of the eight mutual funds. Which fund appears to be the most highly diversified? Which fund appears to be the least diversified?
d. The returns, standard deviations, and characteristic lines were recalculated using the annual Treasury bill rate. The results are shown in the following table in excess yield form:

Fund	$\overline{R}$	σ_P	α_P	SE(α)	β_P	t values
A	8.60	20.00	6.57	(3.53)	0.87	2.15
B	10.30	16.90	8.81	(4.78)	0.61	2.23
C	3.70	25.50	1.58	(7.37)	0.86	0.24
D	11.50	25.00	8.98	(5.23)	1.03	1.96
E	6.30	18.09	4.34	(2.51)	0.81	1.91
F	10.80	18.20	8.69	(2.40)	0.83	4.21
G	-0.02	19.80	-2.22	(1.65)	0.92	-1.49
H	11.30	23.40	8.88	(4.20)	0.95	2.40

In the column to the right of the α_P is the calculated standard error of alpha [SE(α)]. The critical value of t for 7 degrees of freedom (number of observations minus 2) for a two-tailed test at the 5-percent level is 2.365. With a large number of degrees of freedom (more observations), the critical value of t is close to 2.00. The calculated t values are shown in the last column of the table (t for α_P). If the absolute value in that column exceeds 2.365, that fund's alpha is significantly different from zero. On the basis of this test, which funds exhibit above, or below, average performance?
e. Compare the values of α and β calculated in excess yield form with those calculated initially. Can you suggest any generalizations about the relative magnitudes of these values?

22-5 Given the following information:

Period	Market Return	RF	Portfolio 1	Portfolio 2
1	0.12	.07	0.14	0.16
2	0.10	.07	0.18	0.20
3	0.02	.08	0.06	0.04
4	0.20	.08	0.30	0.26
5	0.16	.07	0.21	0.21
6	-0.03	.08	-0.04	-0.06
7	-0.05	.07	-0.04	-0.01
8	0.13	.07	0.14	0.12
9	0.30	.08	0.28	0.32
10	-0.15	.09	-0.20	-0.25

a. Rank the portfolios on RVAR
b. Rank the portfolios on RVOL
c. Rank the portfolios on alpha

d. Which portfolio had the smaller nonsystematic risk?

e. Which portfolio had the larger beta?

f. Which portfolio had the larger standard deviation?

g. Which portfolio had the larger average return?

h. How are the answers to (f) and (g) related to the results for the composite performance measures?

22-6 Given the following information for three portfolios for a six-year period:

Period	Market Return	RF	Portfolio 1	Portfolio 2	Portfolio 3
1	0.10	.05	0.15	0.16	0.17
2	0.02	.06	0.09	0.11	0.13
3	0.20	.08	0.26	0.28	0.18
4	0.30	.09	0.34	0.36	0.42
5	−0.04	.08	−0.02	−0.03	−0.16
6	0.16	.07	0.16	0.17	0.17

Answer (a) through (d) without doing the calculations.

a. Which portfolio would you expect to have the largest beta?

b. Which portfolio would you expect to have the largest standard deviation?

c. Which portfolio would you expect to have the largest R^2?

d. Which portfolio would you expect to rank first on the basis of RVAR?

e. Determine the rankings of the three portfolios on RVAR and RVOL.

f. How did the portfolios rank in terms of R^2?

g. Which portfolio had the largest alpha?

h. Which portfolio exhibited the best performance based on the composite measures of performance?

22-7 The following information is available for two portfolios, a market index, and the risk-free rate:

Period	Market Return	RF	Portfolio 1	Portfolio 2
1	0.10	.06	0.10	0.20
2	0.12	.08	0.12	0.24
3	0.20	.08	0.20	0.40
4	0.04	.08	0.04	0.08
5	0.12	.08	0.12	0.24

a. Without doing calculations, determine the portfolio with a beta of 1.0.

b. Without doing calculations, determine the beta of portfolio 2.

c. Without doing calculations, determine the R^2 for each portfolio.

e. Without doing calculations, what would you expect the alpha of portfolio 1 to be?

f. What would you expect the RVAR and RVOL to be for portfolio 1 relative to the market?

The administrator of a large pension fund wants to evaluate the performance of four portfolio managers. Each portfolio manager invests only in U.S. common stocks. Assume that during the most recent 5-year period, the average annual total rate of return including dividends on the S&P 500 was 14 percent, and the average nominal rate of return on government Treasury bills was 8 percent. The following table shows risk and return measures for each portfolio.

Portfolio	Average Annual Rate of Return	Standard Deviation	Beta
P	0.17	0.20	1.1
Q	0.24	0.18	2.1
R	0.11	0.10	0.5
S	0.16	0.14	1.5
S&P 500	0.14	0.12	1.0

CFA
22-8   The Treynor portfolio performance measure for Portfolio P is:

a. 0.082
b. 0.099
c. 0.155
d. 0.450

CFA
22-9   The Sharpe portfolio performance measure for Portfolio Q is:

a. 0.076
b. 0.126
c. 0.336
d. 0.880

CFA
22-10   When plotting Portfolio R relative to the Security Market Line (SML), Portfolio R lies:

a. on the SML.
b. below the SML.
c. above the SML.
d. insufficient data given.

CFA
22-11   When plotting Portfolio S relative to the Capital Market Line (CML), Portfolio S lies:

a. on the CML.
b. below the CML.
c. above the CML.
d. insufficient data given.

CFA
22-12   An analyst wants to evaluate Portfolio X, consisting entirely of U.S. common stocks, using both the Treynor and Sharpe measures of portfolio performance. The table shows the average annual rate of return for Portfolio X, the market portfolio (as measured by the Standard & Poor's 500 Index), and U.S. Treasury bills (T-bills) during the past 8 years.

	Average Annual Rate of Return	Standard Deviation of Return	Beta
Portfolio X	10%	18%	0.60
S&P 500	12%	13%	1.00
T-bills	6%	n/a	n/a

n/a = not applicable

A. **Calculate** *both* the Treynor measure and the Sharpe measure for *both* Portfolio X *and* the S&P 500. **Briefly explain** whether Portfolio X underperformed, equaled, or outperformed the S&P 500 on a risk-adjusted basis using *both* the Treynor measure and the Sharpe measure.

B. Based on the performance of Portfolio X relative to the S&P 500 calculated in Part A, **briefly explain** the reason for the conflicting results when using the Treynor measure versus the Sharpe measure.

Web Resources

For additional resources visit our dynamic Web site located at www.wiley.com/college/jones.

▣ *Joy's Contribution*—The case describes a relatively new method of measuring risk-adjusted performance—M^2. Risk-adjusted returns help settle an argument about whose clients are treated best by brokers offering wrap accounts.

▣ Internet Exercises—In this chapter, the exercises will ask you to compute measures of portfolio performance. We will also explore performance attribution.
Exercise 1: Asks the reader to compute different performance measures.
Exercise 2: Leads the reader to try and explain portfolio performance expost.

▣ Multiple Choice Self Test

Selected References

Some of the problems in performance measurement are discussed in:

Ferguson, Robert. "The Trouble with Performance Measurement" *The Journal of Portfolio Management* (Spring 1986): 4–9.

A short discussion of performance measurement can be found in:

Good, Walter. "Measuring Performance" *The Financial Analysts Journal* (May–June 1983), 19–23.

The relationships among the composite measures are explained in:

Wilson, Jack, and Jones, Charles. "The Relationship Between Performance and Risk: Whence the Bias?" *Journal of Financial Research* (Summer 1981): 109–117.

Glossary

A

Abnormal Return Return on a security beyond that expected on the basis of its risk

Active Investment Strategies Strategies designed to provide additional returns by trading activities

Advance-Decline Line A technical analysis measure that relates the number of stocks rising to the number declining

American Depository Receipts (ADRs) Securities representing an ownership interest in the equities of foreign companies

Arbitrageurs Investors who seek discrepancies in security prices in an attempt to earn riskless returns

Arbitrage Pricing Theory (APT) An equilibrium theory of expected returns for securities involving few assumptions about investor preferences

Ask Quote The price at which the specialist or dealer offers to sell shares

Asset Allocation Decision The allocation of a portfolio's funds to classes of assets, such as cash equivalents, bonds, and equities

Asset-Backed Securities (ABS) Securities issued against some type of asset-linked debts bundled together, such as credit card receivables or mortgages

Asset Management Account Brokerage accounts involving various services for investors, such as investment of cash balances and check-writing privileges

Auction Market A securities market with a physical location, such as the New York Stock Exchange, where the prices of securities are determined by the actions of buyers and sellers

Average Annual Return A hypothetical rate of return used by mutual funds that, if achieved annually, would have produced the same cumulative total return if performance had been constant over the entire period

B

Bar Chart A plot of daily stock price plotted against time

Basis The difference between the futures price of an item and the spot price of the item

Basis Points 100 basis points are equal to 1 percentage point

Bear Market A downward trend in the stock market

Behavioral Finance The study of investment behavior based on the belief that investors do not always act rationally

Benchmark Portfolio An alternative portfolio against which to measure a portfolio's performance

Beta A measure of volatility, or relative systematic risk, for a stock or a portfolio

Bid Quote The price at which the specialist or dealer offers to buy shares

Black-Scholes Model A widely used model for the valuation of call options

Blocks Transactions involving at least 10,000 shares

Blue Chip Stocks Stocks with long records of earnings and dividends—well-known, stable, mature companies

Bonds Long-term debt instruments representing the issuer's contractual obligation

Bond-Equivalent Yield Yield on an annual basis, derived by doubling the semiannual yield

Bond Ratings Letters assigned to bonds by rating agencies to express the relative probability of default

Bond Swaps An active bond management strategy involving the purchase and sale of bonds in an attempt to improve the rate of return on the bond portfolio

Book Value The accounting value of the equity as shown on the balance sheet

Bottom-Up Approach Approach to fundamental analysis that focuses directly on a company's fundamentals

Broker An intermediary who represents buyers and sellers in securities transactions and receives a commission

Bubble When speculation pushes asset prices to unsustainable highs

Bull Market An upward trend in the stock market

Business Cycle The recurring patterns of expansion, boom, contraction, and recession in the economy

Buy-Side Analysts Analysts employed by money management firms to search for equities for their firms to buy as investing opportunities

C

Call An option to buy a specified number of shares of stock at a stated price within a specified period

Call Provision Gives the issuer the right to call in a security and retire it by paying off the obligation

Capital Asset Pricing Model (CAPM) Relates the required rate of return for any security with the risk for that security as measured by beta

Capital Gain (Loss) The change in price of a security over some period of time

Capital Market The market for long-term securities such as bonds and stocks

Capital Market Line (CML) The trade-off between expected return and risk for efficient portfolios

Capital Market Theory Describes the pricing of capital assets in financial markets

Cash Account The most common type of brokerage account in which a customer may make only cash transactions

Cash Flow Statement The third financial statement of a company, designed to track the flow of cash through the firm

Characteristic Line A regression equation used to estimate beta by regressing stock returns on market returns

Chartered Financial Analyst (CFA) A professional designation for people in the investments field

Closed-End Investment Company An investment company with a fixed capitalization whose shares trade on exchanges and OTC

Coefficient of Determination The square of the correlation coefficient, measuring the percentage of the variance in the dependent variable that is explained by the independent variable

Common Stock An equity security representing the ownership interest in a corporation

Composite Economic Indexes Leading, coincident, and lagging indicators of economic activity

Composite (Risk-Adjusted) Measures of Portfolio Performance Portfolio performance measures combining return and risk into one calculation

Consensus Estimate Most likely EPS value expected by analysts

Contrary Opinion (Contrarian Investing) The theory that it pays to trade contrary to most investors

Conversion Premium With convertible securities, the dollar difference between the market price of the security and its conversion value

Conversion Price Par value divided by the conversion ratio

Conversion Ratio The number of shares of common stock that the owner of a convertible security receives upon conversion

Conversion Value A convertible security's value based on the current price of the common stock

Convertible Bonds Bonds that are convertible, at the holder's option, into shares of common stock of the same corporation

Convertible Securities Bonds or preferred stock convertible into common stock

Convexity A measure of the degree to which the relationship between a bond's price and yield departs from a straight line

Corporate Bonds Long-term debt securities of various types sold by corporations

Correlation Coefficient A statistical measure of the extent to which two variables are associated

Covariance An absolute measure of the extent to which two variables tend to covary, or move together

Covered Call A strategy involving the sale of a call option to supplement a long position in an underlying asset

Cumulative Abnormal Return (CAR) The sum of the individual abnormal returns over the time period under examination

Cumulative Wealth Index Cumulative wealth over time, given an initial wealth and a series of returns on some asset

Currency Risk The risk that the changes in the value of the dollar and the foreign currency involved will be unfavorable

Current Yield A bond's annual coupon divided by the current market price

Cyclical Industries Industries most affected, both up and down, by the business cycle

D

Data Mining The search for apparent patterns in stock returns by intensively analyzing data

Dealers (Market Makers) An individual (firm) who makes a market in a stock by buying from and selling to investors

Debenture An unsecured bond backed by the general worthiness of the firm

Defensive Industries Industries least affected by recessions and economic adversity

Derivative Securities Securities that derive their value in whole or in part by having a claim on some underlying security

Differential Return Measure (Alpha) Jensen's measure of portfolio performance calculated as the difference between what the portfolio actually earned and what it was expected to earn given its level of systematic risk

Direct Access Notes (DANs) Issued at par ($1,000) with fixed coupon rates, and maturities ranging from nine months to 30 years. The company issuing the bonds typically "posts" the maturities and rates it is offering for one week, allowing investors to shop around

Direct Investing Investors buy and sell securities themselves, typically through brokerage accounts

Discount Broker Brokerage firms offering execution services at prices typically significantly less than full-line brokerage firms

Diversifiable Risk Unique risk related to a particular security that can be diversified away; nonsystematic risk

Dividend Discount Model (DDM) A model for determining the estimated price of a stock by discounting all future dividends

Dividend Reinvestment Plan (DRIP) A plan offered by a company whereby stockholders can reinvest dividends in additional shares of stock at no cost

Dividends Cash payments declared and paid quarterly by corporations to stockholders

Dividend Yield Dividend divided by current stock price

Dollar-Weighted Rate of Return (DWR) Equates all cash flows, including ending market value, with the beginning market value of the portfolio

Dow Jones Industrial Average (DJIA) A price-weighted series of 30 leading industrial stocks, used as a measure of stock market activity

Dow Jones World Stock Index A capitalization-weighted index designed to be a comprehensive measure of worldwide stock performance

Dow Theory A technique for detecting long-term trends in the aggregate stock market

Duration A measure of a bond's lifetime that accounts for the entire pattern of cash flows over the life of the bond

E

EAFE Index The Europe, Australia, and Far East Index, a value-weighted index of the equity performance of major foreign markets

Earnings Multiplier The P/E ratio for a stock

Earnings Surprises The difference between a firm's actual earnings and its expected earnings

Economic Value Added (EVA) A technique for focusing on a firm's return on capital in order to determine if stockholders are being rewarded

Efficient Frontier (set) The Markowitz trade-off between expected portfolio return and portfolio risk (standard deviation) showing all efficient portfolios given some set of securities

Efficient Market (EM) A market in which prices of securities quickly and fully reflect all available information

Efficient Market Hypothesis (EMH) The proposition that securities markets are efficient, with the prices of securities reflecting their economic value

Efficient Portfolio A portfolio with the highest level of expected return for a given level of risk or a portfolio with the lowest risk for a given level of expected return

Efficient Set (Frontier) The set of portfolios generated by the Markowitz portfolio model

Electronic Communications Networks (ECNs) A computerized trading network for buying and selling securities electronically

Emerging Markets Markets of less developed countries, characterized by high risks and potentially large returns

Equity-Derivative Securities Securities that derive their value in whole or in part by having a claim on the underlying common stock

Equity Risk Premium The difference between the return on stocks and the risk-free rate

E/P Ratio The reciprocal of the P/E ratio

Event Study An empirical analysis of stock price behavior surrounding a particular event

Exchange Rate Risk The variability in returns on securities caused by currency fluctuations

Exchange-Traded Funds (ETFs) An index fund priced and traded on exchanges like any share of stock

Expectations Theory States that the long-term rate of interest is equal to an average of the short-term rates that are expected to prevail over the long-term period

Expected Return The *ex ante* return expected by investors over some future holding period

Exercise (Strike) Price The per-share price at which the common stock may be purchased from (in the case of a call) or sold to a writer (in the case of a put)

Expiration Date The date an option expires

F

Factor Model Used to depict the behavior of security prices by identifying major factors in the economy that affect large numbers of securities

Filter Rule A rule for buying and selling stocks according to a stock's price movements

Financial Assets Pieces of paper evidencing a claim on some issuer

Financial Futures Futures contracts on financial assets

Financial Statements The principal published financial data about a company, primarily the balance sheet and income statement

Fixed-Income Securities Securities with specified payment dates and amounts, primarily bonds

Forward Contract A commitment today to transact in the future at a price that is currently determined, with no funds having been exchanged

Forward Rates Unobservable rates expected to prevail in the future

Fourth Market A communications network linking large institutional investors

Free Cash Flow The money left after all of a firm's bills are paid and dividend payments are made

Full-Service Broker A brokerage firm offering a full range of services, including information and advice

Fundamental Analysis The analysis of a stock's value using basic data such as its earnings, sales, risk, and so forth

Futures Contract Agreement providing for the future exchange of a particular asset at a currently determined market price

Futures Margin The earnest money deposit made by a transactor to ensure the completion of a contract

G

Generally Accepted Accounting Principles (GAAP) Financial reporting requirements establishing the rules for producing financial statements

Geometric Mean The compound rate of return over time

Global Funds Mutual funds that keep a minimum of 25 percent of their assets in U.S. securities

Global Industry Classification Standard (GICS) Provides a complete, continuous set of global sector and industry definitions using 10 economic sectors

Government Agency Securities Securities issued by federal credit agencies (fully guaranteed) or by government-sponsored agencies (not guaranteed)

Gross Domestic Product (GDP) The basic measure of a country's output used in National Income accounts

Growth Industries Industries with expected earnings growth significantly above the average of all industries

H

Hedge A strategy using derivatives to offset or reduce the risk resulting from exposure to an underlying asset

Hedge Ratio The ratio of options written to shares of stock held long in a riskless portfolio

Homogeneous Expectations Investors have common expectations as to securities' returns and risks

Horizon (Total) Return Bond returns to be earned based on assumptions about reinvestment rates

I

Immunization The strategy of immunizing (protecting) a portfolio against interest rate risk by canceling out its two components, price risk and reinvestment rate risk

Index Arbitrage Exploitation of price differences between stock-index futures and the index of stocks underlying the futures contract

Index Funds Mutual funds holding a bond or stock portfolio designed to match a particular market index

Index Options Puts and calls on various market indexes

Indifference Curves Curves describing investor preferences for risk and return

Indirect Investing The buying and selling of the shares of investment companies which, in turn, hold portfolios of securities

Industry Life Cycle The stages of an industry's evolution from pioneering to stabilization and decline

Initial Margin That part of a transaction's value a customer must pay to initiate the transaction, with the other part being borrowed from the broker

Initial Public Offering (IPO) Common stock shares of a company being sold for the first time

Instinet (Institutional Network) An electronic trading network, part of the fourth market

Institutional Investors Pension funds, investment companies, bank trust departments, life insurance companies, and so forth, all of whom manage large portfolios of securities

Interest on Interest The process by which bond coupons are reinvested to earn interest

Interest Rate Options Option contracts on fixed-income securities such as Treasury bonds

Interest Rate Risk The variability in a security's returns resulting from changes in interest rates

Interest Rate Swaps A contract between two parties to exchange a series of cash flows based on fixed-income securities

Interest-Sensitive Industries Industries particularly sensitive to expectations about changes in interest rates

Intermarket Trading System (ITS) A form of a central routing system, consisting of a network of terminals linking together several stock exchanges

Internal (Sustainable) Growth Rate (g) The estimated earnings growth rate, calculated as the product of ROE and the retention rate

International Funds Mutual funds that concentrate primarily on international stocks

Intrinsic Value The estimated value of a security

Investment The commitment of funds to one or more assets that will be held over some future time period

Investment Banker Firm specializing in the sale of new securities to the public, typically by underwriting the issue

Investment Company A financial company that sells shares in itself to the public and uses these funds to invest in a portfolio of securities

Investment Policy A statement of a few sentences describing policies to be followed for a client

Investment Policy Statement The first step in the portfolio management process, involving investor objectives, constraints and preferences

Investments The study of the investment process

J

January Effect The observed tendency for stocks to be higher in January than in other months

Junk Bonds Bonds that carry ratings of BB or lower, with correspondingly higher yields

L

LEAPS Puts and calls with longer maturity dates, up to two years

Limit Order An order to buy or sell at a specified (or better) price

Liquidity The ease with which an asset can be bought or sold quickly with relatively small price changes

Liquidity Preference Theory States that interest rates reflect the sum of current and expected short rates, as in the expectations theory, plus liquidity (risk) premiums

Long Hedge A transaction where the asset is currently not held but futures are purchased to lock in current prices

Long Position When an investor owns an asset, he/she is said to be in the long position.

Long-Term Equity Anticipation Securities (LEAPS) Options on individual stocks with maturities up to two years

M

Maintenance Margin The percentage of a security's value that must be on hand at all times as equity

Margin The investor's equity in a transaction, with the remainder borrowed from a brokerage firm

Margin Account An account that permits margin trading, requiring $2000 to open

Margin Call A demand from the broker for additional cash or securities as a result of the actual margin declining below the maintenance margin

Marked to the Market The daily posting of all profits and losses on a contract to each account

Marketable Securities Financial assets that are easily and cheaply traded in organized markets

Market Anomalies Techniques or strategies that appear to be contrary to an efficient market

Market Data Price and volume information for stocks or indexes

Market Maker A broker/dealer who is registered to trade in a particular security in the OTC market

Market Model Relates the return on each stock to the return on the market, using a linear relationship with intercept and slope

Market Order An order to buy or sell at the best price when the order reaches the trading floor

Market Portfolio The portfolio of all risky assets, with each asset weighted by the ratio of its market value to the market value of all risky assets

Market Risk The variability in a security's returns resulting from fluctuations in the aggregate market

Market Risk Premium The difference between the expected return for the equities market and the risk-free rate of return

Market Segmentation Theory States that investors confine their activities to specific maturity sectors and are unwilling to shift from one sector to another to take advantage of opportunities

Modified Duration Duration divided by 1 + yield to maturity

Momentum Investing Investing on the basis of recent movements in the price of a stock

Money Market The market for short-term, highly liquid, low-risk assets such as Treasury bills and negotiable CDs

Money Market Funds (MMFs) A mutual fund that invests in money market instruments

Mortgage-Backed Securities Securities whose value depends upon some set of mortgages

Municipal Bonds Securities issued by political entities other than the federal government and its agencies, such as states and cities

Mutual Funds The popular name for open-end-investment companies

N

Nasdaq National Market System (Nasdaq/NMS) A combination of the competing market markers in OTC stocks and the up-to-the-minute reporting of trades using data almost identical to that shown for the NYSE and Amex

Nasdaq Stock Market (Nasdaq) The automated quotation system for the OTC market, showing current bid-ask prices for thousands of stocks

National Association of Securities Dealers (NASD) A self-regulating body of brokers and dealers overseeing OTC practices

National Market System (NMS) The market system for U.S. securities called for, but left undefined, by the Securities Acts Amendments of 1975

Negotiated Market A market involving dealers, such as Nasdaq

Net Asset Value (NAV) The total market value of the securities in an investment company's portfolio divided by the number of investment company fund shares currently outstanding

New York Stock Exchange (NYSE) The major secondary market for the trading of equity securities

Nondiversifiable Risk Variability in a security's return directly associated with overall movements in the general market; systematic risk

Nonsystematic (Nonmarket) Risk Risk attributable to factors unique to a security

O

Offset Liquidation of a futures position by an offsetting transaction

Open-End Investment Company An investment company whose capitalization constantly changes as new shares are sold and outstanding shares are redeemed

Option Premium The price paid by the option buyer to the seller of the option

Options Rights to buy or sell a stated number of shares of a security within a specified period at a specified price

Options Clearing Corporation (OCC) Stands between buyers and sellers of options to ensure fulfillment of obligations

Over-the-Counter (OTC) Market A network of securities dealers linked together to make markets in securities

P

Par Value (Face Value) The redemption value of a bond paid at maturity, typically $1,000

Passive Investment Strategy A strategy whereby investors do not actively seek out trading possibilities in an attempt to outperform the market

Payout Ratio Dividends divided by earnings

Performance Attribution A part of portfolio evaluation that seeks to determine why success or failure occurred

Performance Presentation Standards (PPS) Minimum standards for presenting investment performance as formulated by the AIMR

Perpetuity A security without a maturity date

P/E Ratio (Earnings Multiplier) The ratio of stock price to earnings, using historical, current, or estimated data

Point-and-Figure Chart A plot of stock prices showing only significant price changes

Portfolio The securities held by an investor taken as a unit

Portfolio Insurance An asset management technique designed to provide a portfolio with a lower limit on value while permitting it to benefit from rising security prices

Portfolio Management The second step in the investment decision process, involving the management of a group of assets (i.e., a portfolio) as a unit

Portfolio Management Process Viewing the management of a client's portfolio as an integrated series of steps to follow

Portfolio Rebalancing Periodically rebalancing a portfolio to maintain some specified or desired asset allocation decision

Portfolio Weights Percentages of portfolio funds invested in each security, summing to 1.0

Preferred Habitat Theory States that investors have preferred maturity sectors in which they seek to invest but are willing to shift to other maturities if they can expect to be adequately compensated

Preferred Stock An equity security with an intermediate claim (between the bondholders and the stockholders) on a firm's assets and earnings

Price to Book Value The ratio of stock price to per share stockholders' equity

Price/Sales Ratio (PSR) A company's total market value divided by its sales

Primary Market The market for new issues of securities, typically involving investment bankers

Program Trading Involves the use of computer-generated orders to buy and sell securities based on arbitrage opportunities between common stocks and index futures and options

Prospectus Provides information about an initial public offering of securities to potential buyers

Protective Put A strategy involving the purchase of a put option as a supplement to a long position in an underlying asset

Put An option to sell a specified number of shares of stock at a stated price within a specified period

Put-Call Parity The formal relationship between a call and a put on the same item which must hold if no arbitrage is to occur

R

Real Assets Physical assets, such as gold or real estate

Real Risk-Free Rate of Interest The opportunity cost of foregoing consumption, given no inflation

Realized Compound Yield (RCY) Yield earned based on actual reinvestment rates

Realized Return Actual return on an investment for some previous period of time

Reinvestment Rate Risk That part of interest rate risk resulting from uncertainty about the rate at which future interest coupons can be reinvested

Relative Strength The ratio of a stock's price to some market or industry index, usually plotted as a graph

Reported Earnings GAAP earnings, the "official" earnings of a company, as reported to stockholders and the SEC

Required Rate of Return The minimum expected rate of return necessary to induce an investor to purchase a security

Resistance Level A price range at which a technician expects a significant increase in the supply of a stock

Return on Assets (ROA) The accounting rate of return on a firm's assets

Return on Equity (ROE) The accounting rate of return on stockholders' equity

Return Relative The total return for an investment for a given time period stated on the basis of 1.0

Reward-to-Variability Ratio (RVAR) Sharpe's measure of portfolio performance calculated as the ratio of excess portfolio return to the standard deviation

Reward-to-Volatility Ratio (RVOL) Treynor's measure of portfolio performance calculated as the ratio of excess portfolio return to beta

Risk The chance that the actual return on an investment will be different from the expected return

Risk-Averse Investor An investor who will not assume a given level of risk unless there is an expectation of adequate compensation for having done so

Risk-Free Rate of Return The return on a riskless asset, often proxied by the rate of return on Treasury securities

Risk Premium That part of a security's return above the risk-free rate of return

S

Secondary Markets Markets where existing securities are traded among investors

Securities and Exchange Commission (SEC) A federal government agency established by the Securities Exchange Act of 1934 to protect investors

Security Analysis The first part of the investment decision process, involving the valuation and analysis of individual securities

Security Market Line (SML) The graphical depiction of the CAPM

Sell-Side Analysts "Wall Street" analysts who cover stocks and make recommendation on them to investors

Semistrong Form That part of the efficient market hypothesis stating that prices reflect all publicly available information

Senior Securities Securities, typically debt securities, ahead of common stock in terms of payment or in case of liquidation

Separation Theorem The idea that the decision of which portfolio of risky assets to hold is separate from the decision of how to allocate investable funds between the risk-free asset and the risky asset

Shelf Rule Permits qualified companies to file a short form registration and "place on the shelf" securities to be sold over time under favorable conditions

Short Hedge A transaction involving the sale of futures (a short position) while holding the asset (a long position)

Short-Interest Ratio The ratio of total shares sold short to average daily trading volume

Short Position An agreement to sell an asset at a specified future date at a specified price

Short Sale The sale of a stock not owned but borrowed in order to take advantage of an expected decline in the price of the stock

Single-Country Fund Investment companies, primarily closed-end funds, concentrating on the securities of a single country

Single Index Model A model that relates returns on each security to the returns on a market index

Size Effect The observed tendency for smaller firms to have higher stock returns than large firms

Specialist A member of an organized exchange who is charged with maintaining an orderly market in one or more stocks by buying or selling for his or her own account

Spread The purchase and sale of an equivalent option varying in only one respect to reduce risk in an option position

Standard Deviation A measure of the dispersion in outcomes around the expected value

Standard & Poor's Depository Receipts (SPDRs) Tradable securities representing a claim on the S&P 500 Index. Commonly referred to as "spiders"

Standard & Poor's 500 Composite Index (S&P 500) Market value index of stock market activity covering 500 stocks

Standard Industrial Classification (SIC) System A classification of firms on the basis of what they produce using census data

Standardized Unexpected Earnings (SUE) A variable used in the selection of common stocks, calculated as the ratio of unexpected earnings to a standardization factor

Stock Dividend A payment by the corporation in shares of stock rather than cash

Stock Index Options Option contracts on a stock market index such as the S&P 500

Stock Split The issuance by a corporation of shares of common stock in proportion to the existing shares outstanding

Stop Order An order specifying a certain price at which a market order takes effect

Straddle A combination of a put and a call on the same stock with the same exercise date and exercise price

Strategic Asset Allocation Asset allocation typically done once every few years, establishing a long-run or strategic asset mix

Street Name When customers' securities are held by a brokerage firm in its name

Strong Form That part of the efficient market hypothesis stating that prices reflect all information, public and private

SuperDOT An electronic order-routing system for NYSE-listed securities

SuperMontage A new Nasdaq system displaying its order book in more detail, showing multiple orders to buy and sell; in effect, it has features similar to the ECNs

Support Level A price range at which a technician expects a significant increase in the demand for a stock

Sustainable Growth Rate A firm's expected growth rate in earnings and dividends, often calculated as the product of ROE and the retention rate of earnings

Systematic (Market) Risk Risk attributable to broad macro-factors affecting all securities

T

Tactical Asset Allocation A type of allocation performed routinely as part of the ongoing process of asset management

Technical Analysis The use of specific market data for the analysis of both aggregate stock prices and individual stock prices

Term Structure of Interest Rates The relationship between time to maturity and yields for a particular category of bonds

Theoretical (Calculated) Value of a Warrant What a warrant should be worth if markets are functioning exactly correct

Theoretical Spot Rate Curve A graph depicting the relationship between spot rates and maturities, based on theoretical considerations

Third Market An OTC market for exchange-listed securities

Time-Weighted Rate of Return (TWR) Measures the actual rate of return earned by the portfolio manager

Top-Down Approach Approach to fundamental analysis that proceeds from market/economy to industries to companies

Total Return (TR) Percentage measure relating all cash flows on a security for a given time period to its purchase price

Treasury Bill A short-term money market instrument sold at discount by the U.S. government

Treasury Bond Long-term bonds sold by the U.S. government

Treasury Inflation-Indexed Securities (TIPS) Treasury securities fully indexed for inflation

Trendline The most basic measure of a stock's direction of stock movement

U

Underwrite The process by which investment bankers purchase an issue of securities from a firm and resell it to the public

Unit Investment Trust An unmanaged form of investment company, typically holding fixed-income securities, offering investors diversification and minimum operating costs

W

Warrant A corporate-created option to purchase a stated number of common shares at a specified price within a specified time (typically several years)

Weak Form That part of the efficient market hypothesis stating that prices reflect all price and volume data

Wrap Account A new type of brokerage account where all costs are wrapped in one fee

Y

Yield The income component of a security's return

Yield Curve A graphical depiction of the relationship between yields and time for bonds that are identical except for maturity

Yield Spreads The relationship between bond yields and the particular features on various bonds such as quality, callability, and taxes

Yield to Call The promised return on a bond from the present to the date that the bond is likely to be called

Yield to Maturity (YTM) The promised compounded rate of return on a bond purchased at the current market price and held to maturity

Z

Zero-Coupon Bond A bond sold with no coupons at a discount and redeemed for face value at maturity

Interest Tables

Table A-1 Compound (Future) Value Factors for $1 Compounded at R Percent for N Periods

N	1%	2%	3%	4%	5%	6%	7%	8%	9%	10%	11%	12%	13%
1	1.01	1.02	1.03	1.04	1.05	1.06	1.07	1.08	1.09	1.1	1.11	1.12	1.13
2	1.02	1.04	1.061	1.082	1.103	1.124	1.145	1.166	1.188	1.21	1.232	1.254	1.277
3	1.03	1.061	1.093	1.125	1.158	1.191	1.225	1.26	1.295	1.331	1.368	1.405	1.443
4	1.041	1.082	1.126	1.17	1.216	1.262	1.311	1.36	1.412	1.464	1.518	1.574	1.53
5	1.051	1.104	1.159	1.217	1.276	1.338	1.403	1.469	1.539	1.611	1.685	1.762	1.842
6	1.062	1.126	1.194	1.265	1.34	1.419	1.501	1.587	1.677	1.772	1.87	1.974	2.082
7	1.072	1.149	1.23	1.316	1.407	1.504	1.606	1.714	1.828	1.949	2.076	2.211	2.353
8	1.083	1.172	1.267	1.369	1.477	1.594	1.718	1.851	1.993	2.144	2.305	2.476	2.658
9	1.094	1.195	1.305	1.423	1.551	1.689	1.838	1.999	2.172	2.358	2.558	2.773	3.004
10	1.105	1.219	1.344	1.48	1.629	1.791	1.967	2.159	2.367	2.594	2.839	3.106	3.395
11	1.116	1.243	1.384	1.539	1.71	1.898	2.105	2.332	2.58	2.853	3.152	3.479	3.836
12	1.127	1.268	1.426	1.601	1.796	2.012	2.252	2.518	2.813	3.138	3.498	3.896	4.335
13	1.138	1.294	1.469	1.665	1.886	2.133	2.41	2.72	3.066	3.452	3.883	4.363	4.898
14	1.149	1.319	1.513	1.732	1.98	2.261	2.579	2.937	3.342	3.797	4.31	4.887	5.535
15	1.161	1.346	1.558	1.801	2.079	2.397	2.759	3.172	3.642	4.177	4.785	5.474	6.254
16	1.173	1.373	1.605	1.873	2.183	2.54	2.952	3.426	3.97	4.595	5.311	6.13	7.067
17	1.184	1.4	1.653	1.948	2.292	2.693	3.159	3.7	4.328	5.054	5.895	6.866	7.986
18	1.196	1.428	1.702	2.026	2.407	2.854	3.38	3.996	4.717	5.56	6.544	7.69	9.024
19	1.208	1.457	1.754	2.107	2.527	3.026	3.617	4.316	5.142	6.116	7.263	8.613	10.197
20	1.22	1.486	1.806	2.191	2.653	3.207	3.87	4.661	5.604	6.727	8.062	9.646	11.523
21	1.232	1.516	1.86	2.279	2.786	3.4	4.141	5.034	6.109	7.4	8.949	10.804	13.021
22	1.245	1.546	1.916	2.37	2.925	3.604	4.43	5.437	6.659	8.14	9.934	12.1	14.714
23	1.257	1.577	1.974	2.465	3.072	3.82	4.741	5.871	7.258	8.954	10.026	13.552	16.627
24	1.27	1.608	2.033	2.563	3.225	4.049	5.072	6.341	7.911	9.85	12.239	15.179	18.788
25	1.282	1.641	2.094	2.666	3.386	4.292	5.427	6.848	8.623	10.835	13.585	17	21.231
30	1.348	1.811	2.427	3.243	4.322	5.743	7.612	10.063	13.268	17.449	22.892	29.96	39.116
35	1.417	2	2.814	3.946	5.516	7.686	10.677	14.785	20.414	28.102	38.575	52.8	72.069
40	1.489	2.208	3.262	4.801	7.04	10.286	14.974	21.725	31.409	45.259	65.001	93.051	132.782
45	1.565	2.438	3.782	5.841	8.985	13.765	21.002	31.92	48.327	72.89	109.53	163.98	244.641
50	1.645	2.692	4.384	7.107	11.467	18.42	29.457	46.902	74.358	117.39	184.56	289.00	450.735

Table A-1 Compound (Future) Value Factors for $1 Compounded at R Percent for N Periods (Continued)

N	14%	15%	16%	18%	20%	22%	24%	25%	30%	35%	40%	45%	50%
1	1.14	1.15	1.16	1.18	1.2	1.22	1.25	1.25	1.3	1.35	1.4	1.45	1.5
2	1.3	1.323	1.346	1.392	1.44	1.488	1.538	1.563	1.69	1.823	1.96	2.103	2.25
3	1.482	1.521	1.561	1.643	1.728	1.816	1.907	1.953	2.197	2.46	2.744	3.049	3.375
4	1.689	1.749	1.811	1.939	2.074	2.215	2.364	2.441	2.856	3.322	3.842	4.421	5.063
5	1.925	2.011	2.1	2.288	2.488	2.703	2.932	3.052	3.713	4.484	5.378	6.41	7.594
6	2.195	2.313	2.436	2.7	2.986	3.297	3.635	3.815	4.827	6.053	7.53	9.294	11.391
7	2.502	2.66	2.826	3.185	3.583	4.023	4.508	4.768	6.275	8.172	10.541	13.476	17.086
8	2.853	3.059	3.278	3.759	4.3	4.908	5.59	5.96	8.157	11.032	14.758	19.541	25.629
9	3.252	3.518	3.803	4.435	5.16	5.987	6.931	7.451	10.604	14.894	20.661	28.334	38.443
10	3.707	4.046	4.411	5.234	6.192	7.305	8.594	9.313	13.786	20.107	28.925	41.085	57.665
11	4.226	4.652	5.117	6.176	7.43	8.912	10.657	11.642	17.922	27.144	40.496	59.573	86.498
12	4.818	5.35	5.936	7.288	8.916	10.872	13.215	14.552	23.298	36.644	56.694	86.381	129.746
13	5.492	6.153	6.886	8.599	10.699	13.264	16.386	18.19	30.288	49.47	79.371	125.25	194.62
14	6.261	7.076	7.988	10.147	12.839	16.182	20.319	22.737	39.374	66.784	111.12	181.61	291.929
15	7.138	8.137	9.266	11.974	15.407	19.742	25.196	28.422	51.186	90.158	155.56	263.34	437.894
16	8.137	9.358	10.748	14.129	18.488	24.086	31.243	35.527	66.542	121.71	217.79	381.84	656.841
17	9.276	10.761	12.468	16.672	22.186	29.384	38.741	44.409	86.504	164.31	304.91	553.67	985.261
18	10.575	12.375	14.463	19.673	26.623	35.849	48.039	55.511	112.45	221.82	426.87	802.83	1477.892
19	12.056	14.232	16.777	23.214	31.948	43.736	59.568	69.389	146.19	299.46	597.63	1164.1	2216.838
20	13.743	16.367	19.461	27.393	38.338	53.358	73.864	86.736	190.05	404.27	836.68	1687.9	3325.257
21	15.668	18.822	22.574	32.324	46.005	65.096	91.592	108.42	247.06	545.76	1171.3	2447.5	4987.885
22	17.861	21.645	26.186	38.142	55.206	79.418	113.57	135.52	321.18	716.78	1639.8	3548.9	7481.828
23	20.362	24.891	30.376	45.008	66.247	96.889	140.83	169.40	417.53	994.66	2297.8	5145.9	11222.74
24	23.212	28.625	35.236	53.109	79.497	118.20	174.63	211.75	542.80	1342.7	3214.2	7461.6	16834.11
25	26.462	32.919	40.874	62.669	95.396	144.21	216.54	264.69	705.64	1812.7	4499.8	10819.	25251.17
30	50.95	66.212	85.85	143.37	237.37	389.75	634.82	807.79	2619.9	8128.5	24201.	69348.	191751.1
35	98.1	133.17	180.31	327.99	590.66	1053.4	1861.0	2465.1	9727.8	36448.	130161.	444508.	
40	188.88	267.86	378.72	750.37	1469.7	2847.0	5455.9	7523.1	36118.	163437.	700037.		
45	363.67	538.76	795.44	1716.6	3657.2	7694.7	15994.	22958.	134106.	732857.			
50	700.23	1083.6	1670.7	3927.3	9100.4	20796.	46890.	70064.	497929.				

Table A-2 Present Value Factors (at R Percent) for $1 Received at the End of N Periods

N	1%	2%	3%	4%	5%	6%	7%	8%	9%	10%	11%	12%	13%
1	.990	.980	.971	.962	.952	.943	.935	.926	.917	.909	.901	.893	.885
2	.980	.961	.943	.925	.907	.890	.873	.857	.842	.826	.812	.797	.783
3	.971	.942	.915	.889	.864	.840	.816	.794	.772	.751	.731	.712	.693
4	.961	.924	.888	.855	.823	.792	.763	.735	.708	.683	.659	.636	.613
5	.951	.906	.863	.822	.784	.747	.713	.681	.650	.621	.593	.567	.543
6	.942	.888	.837	.790	.746	.705	.666	.630	.596	.564	.535	.507	.480
7	.932	.871	.813	.760	.711	.665	.623	.583	.547	.513	.482	.452	.425
8	.923	.853	.789	.731	.677	.627	.582	.540	.502	.467	.434	.404	.376
9	.914	.837	.766	.703	.645	.592	.544	.500	.460	.424	.391	.361	.333
10	.905	.820	.744	.676	.614	.558	.508	.463	.422	.386	.352	.322	.295
11	.896	.804	.722	.650	.585	.527	.475	.429	.388	.350	.317	.287	.261
12	.887	.788	.701	.625	.557	.497	.444	.397	.356	.319	.286	.257	.231
13	.879	.773	.681	.601	.530	.469	.415	.368	.326	.290	.258	.229	.204
14	.870	.758	.661	.577	.505	.442	.388	.340	.299	.263	.232	.205	.181
15	.861	.743	.642	.555	.481	.417	.362	.315	.275	.239	.209	.183	.160
16	.853	.728	.623	.534	.458	.394	.339	.292	.252	.218	.188	.163	.141
17	.844	.714	.605	.513	.436	.371	.317	.270	.231	.198	.170	.146	.125
18	.836	.700	.587	.494	.416	.350	.296	.250	.212	.180	.153	.130	.111
19	.828	.686	.570	.475	.396	.331	.277	.232	.194	.164	.138	.116	.098
20	.820	.673	.554	.456	.377	.312	.258	.215	.178	.149	.124	.104	.087
21	.811	.660	.538	.439	.359	.294	.242	.199	.164	.135	.112	.093	.077
22	.803	.647	.522	.422	.342	.278	.226	.184	.150	.123	.101	.083	.068
23	.795	.634	.507	.406	.326	.262	.211	.170	.133	.112	.091	.074	.060
24	.788	.622	.492	.390	.310	.247	.197	.158	.126	.102	.082	.066	.053
25	.780	.610	.478	.375	.295	.233	.184	.146	.116	.092	.074	.059	.047
30	.742	.552	.412	.308	.231	.174	.131	.099	.075	.057	.044	.033	.026
35	.706	.500	.355	.253	.181	.130	.094	.068	.049	.036	.026	.019	.014
40	.672	.453	.307	.208	.142	.097	.067	.046	.032	.022	.015	.011	.008
45	.639	.410	.264	.171	.111	.073	.048	.031	.021	.014	.009	.006	.004
50	.608	.372	.228	.141	.087	.054	.034	.021	.013	.009	.005	.003	.002

Table A-2 Present Value Factors (at R Percent) for $1 Received at the End of N Periods (Continued)

							R =						
N	14%	15%	16%	18%	20%	22%	24%	25%	30%	35%	40%	45%	50%
1	.877	.870	.862	.847	.833	.820	.806	.800	.769	.741	.714	.690	.667
2	.769	.756	.743	.718	.694	.672	.650	.640	.592	.449	.510	.476	.444
3	.675	.658	.641	.609	.579	.551	.524	.512	.455	.406	.364	.328	.296
4	.592	.572	.552	.516	.482	.451	.423	.410	.350	.301	.260	.226	.198
5	.519	.497	.476	.437	.402	.370	.341	.328	.269	.223	.186	.156	.132
6	.456	.432	.410	.370	.335	.303	.275	.262	.207	.165	.133	.108	.088
7	.400	.376	.354	.314	.279	.249	.222	.210	.159	.122	.095	.074	.059
8	.351	.327	.305	.266	.233	.204	.179	.168	.123	.091	.068	.051	.039
9	.308	.284	.263	.225	.194	.167	.144	.134	.094	.067	.048	.035	.026
10	.270	.247	.227	.191	.162	.137	.116	.107	.073	.050	.035	.024	.017
11	.237	.215	.195	.162	.135	.112	.094	.086	.056	.037	.025	.017	.012
12	.208	.187	.168	.137	.112	.092	.076	.069	.043	.027	.018	.012	.008
13	.182	.163	.145	.116	.093	.075	.061	.055	.033	.020	.013	.008	.005
14	.160	.141	.125	.099	.078	.062	.049	.044	.025	.015	.009	.006	.003
15	.140	.123	.108	.084	.065	.051	.040	.035	.020	.011	.006	.004	.002
16	.123	.107	.093	.071	.054	.042	.032	.028	.015	.008	.005	.003	.002
17	.108	.093	.080	.060	.045	.034	.026	.023	.012	.006	.003	.002	.001
18	.095	.081	.069	.051	.038	.028	.021	.018	.009	.005	.002	.001	.001
19	.083	.070	.060	.043	.031	.023	.017	.014	.007	.003	.002	.001	
20	.073	.061	.051	.037	.026	.019	.014	.012	.005	.002	.001	.001	
21	.064	.053	.044	.031	.022	.015	.011	.009	.004	.002	.001		
22	.056	.046	.038	.026	.018	.013	.009	.007	.003	.001	.001		
23	.049	.040	.033	.022	.015	.010	.007	.006	.002	.001			
24	.043	.035	.028	.019	.013	.008	.006	.005	.002	.001			
25	.038	.030	.024	.016	.010	.007	.005	.004	.001	.001			
30	.020	.015	.012	.007	.004	.003	.002	.001					
35	.010	.008	.006	.003	.002	.001	.001						
40	.005	.004	.003	.001	.001								
45	.003	.002	.011	.001									
50	.001	.001	.001										

Table A-3 Compound Sum Annuity Factors for $1 Compounded at R Percent for N Periods

N	1%	2%	3%	4%	5%	6%	7%	8%	9%	10%	11%	12%	13%
1	1	1	1	1	1	1	1	1	1	1	1	1	1
2	2.01	2.02	2.03	2.04	2.05	2.06	2.07	2.08	2.09	2.1	2.11	2.12	2.13
3	3.03	3.06	3.091	3.122	3.152	3.184	3.215	3.246	3.278	3.31	3.342	3.374	3.407
4	4.06	4.122	4.184	4.246	4.31	4.375	4.44	4.506	4.573	4.641	4.71	4.779	4.85
5	5.101	5.204	5.309	5.416	5.526	5.637	5.751	5.867	5.985	6.105	6.228	6.353	6.48
6	6.152	6.308	6.468	6.633	6.802	6.975	7.153	7.336	7.523	7.716	7.913	8.115	8.232
7	7.214	7.434	7.662	7.898	8.142	8.394	8.654	8.923	9.2	9.487	9.783	10.089	10.405
8	8.286	8.583	8.892	9.214	9.549	10.897	10.26	10.637	11.028	11.436	11.859	12.3	12.757
9	9.369	9.755	10.159	10.583	11.027	11.491	11.978	12.488	13.021	13.579	14.164	14.776	15.416
10	10.462	10.95	11.464	12.006	12.578	13.181	13.816	14.487	15.193	15.937	16.722	17.549	18.42
11	11.567	12.169	12.808	13.486	14.207	14.972	15.784	16.645	17.56	18.531	19.561	20.655	21.814
12	12.683	13.412	14.192	15.026	15.917	16.87	17.888	18.977	20.141	21.384	22.713	24.133	25.65
13	13.809	14.68	15.618	16.627	17.713	18.882	20.141	21.495	22.953	24.523	26.212	28.029	29.985
14	14.947	15.971	17.086	18.292	19.599	21.015	22.55	24.215	26.019	27.975	30.095	32.393	34.883
15	16.097	17.291	18.599	20.024	21.579	23.276	25.129	27.152	29.361	31.722	34.405	37.28	40.417
16	17.258	18.639	20.157	21.825	23.657	25.673	27.888	30.324	33.003	35.95	39.19	42.753	46.672
17	18.43	20.012	21.762	23.698	25.84	28.213	30.84	33.75	36.974	40.545	44.501	48.884	53.739
18	19.615	21.412	23.414	25.645	28.132	30.906	33.999	37.45	41.301	45.599	50.396	55.75	61.725
19	20.811	22.841	25.117	27.671	30.539	33.76	37.379	41.446	46.018	51.159	56.939	63.44	70.749
20	22.019	24.297	26.87	29.778	33.066	36.786	40.995	45.762	51.16	57.275	64.203	72.052	80.947
21	23.239	25.783	28.676	31.969	35.719	39.993	44.865	50.423	56.765	64.002	72.265	81.699	92.47
22	24.472	27.299	30.537	34.248	38.505	43.392	49.006	55.457	62.873	71.403	81.214	92.503	105.491
23	25.716	28.845	32.453	36.618	41.43	46.996	53.436	60.893	69.532	79.543	91.148	104.60	120.205
24	26.973	30.422	34.426	39.083	44.502	50.816	58.177	66.765	76.79	88.497	102.17	118.15	136.831
25	28.243	32.03	36.459	41.646	47.727	54.865	63.249	73.106	84.701	98.347	114.41	133.33	155.62
30	34.785	40.568	47.575	56.085	66.439	79.058	94.461	113.28	136.30	164.49	199.02	241.33	293.199
35	41.66	49.994	60.462	73.652	90.32	111.43	138.23	172.31	215.71	271.02	341.59	431.66	546.681
40	48.886	60.402	75.401	95.026	120.8	154.76	199.63	259.05	337.88	442.59	581.82	767.09	1013.704
45	56.481	71.893	92.72	121.02	159.7	212.74	285.74	386.50	525.85	718.90	986.63	1358.2	1874.165
50	64.463	84.579	112.79	152.66	209.34	290.33	406.52	573.77	815.08	1163.9	1668.7	2400.0	3459.507

Table A-3 Compound Sum Annuity Factors for $1 Compounded at R Percent for N Periods (Continued)

N	14%	15%	16%	18%	20%	22%	24%	25%	30%	35%	40%	45%	50%
1	1	1	1	1	1	1	1	1	1	1	1	1	1
2	2.14	2.15	2.16	2.18	2.2	2.22	2.24	2.25	2.3	2.35	2.4	2.45	2.5
3	3.44	3.472	3.506	3.572	3.64	3.708	3.778	3.813	3.99	4.172	4.36	4.552	4.75
4	4.921	4.993	5.066	5.215	5.368	5.524	5.684	5.766	6.187	6.633	7.104	7.601	8.125
5	6.61	6.742	6.877	7.154	7.442	7.74	8.048	8.207	9.043	9.954	10.196	12.022	13.188
6	8.536	8.754	8.977	9.442	9.93	10.442	10.98	11.259	12.756	14.438	16.324	18.431	20.781
7	10.73	11.067	11.414	12.142	12.916	13.74	14.615	15.073	17.583	20.492	23.853	27.726	32.172
8	13.233	13.727	14.24	15.327	16.499	17.762	19.123	19.842	23.858	28.664	34.395	11.202	49.258
9	16.085	16.786	17.519	19.086	20.799	22.67	24.712	25.802	32.015	39.696	49.153	60.743	74.887
10	19.337	20.304	21.321	23.521	25.959	28.657	31.643	33.253	42.619	54.59	69.814	89.077	113.33
11	23.045	24.349	25.733	28.755	32.15	35.962	40.238	42.566	56.405	74.697	98.739	130.16	170.995
12	27.271	29.002	30.85	34.931	39.581	44.874	50.895	54.208	74.327	101.84	139.23	189.73	257.493
13	32.089	34.352	36.786	42.219	48.497	55.746	64.11	68.76	97.625	138.48	195.92	276.11	387.239
14	37.581	40.505	43.672	50.818	59.196	69.01	80.496	86.949	127.91	187.95	275.3	401.36	581.859
15	43.842	47.58	51.66	60.965	72.035	85.192	100.81	109.68	167.28	254.73	386.42	582.98	873.788
16	50.98	55.717	60.925	72.939	87.442	104.93	126.01	138.10	218.47	344.89	541.98	846.32	1311.682
17	59.118	65.075	71.673	87.068	105.93	129.02	157.25	173.63	285.01	466.61	759.78	1228.1	1968.523
18	68.394	75.836	84.141	103.74	128.11	158.40	195.99	218.04	371.51	630.92	1064.6	1781.3	2953.784
19	78.969	88.212	98.603	123.41	154.74	194.25	244.03	273.55	483.97	852.74	1491.5	2584.6	4431.676
20	91.025	102.44	115.38	146.62	186.68	237.98	303.60	342.94	630.16	1152.2	2089.2	3748.7	6648.513
21	104.76	118.81	134.84	174.02	225.02	291.34	377.46	429.68	820.21	1556.4	2925.8	5436.7	9973.77
22	120.43	137.63	157.41	206.34	271.03	356.44	469.05	538.10	1067.2	2102.2	4097.2	7884.2	14961.65
23	138.29	159.27	183.60	244.48	326.23	435.86	582.63	673.62	1388.4	2839.0	5737.1	11433.	22443.48
24	158.65	184.16	213.97	289.49	392.48	532.75	723.46	843.03	1806.0	3833.7	8032.9	16579.	33666.22
25	181.87	212.79	249.21	342.60	471.98	650.95	898.09	1054.7	2348.8	5176.5	11247.	24040.	50500.34
30	356.78	434.74	530.31	790.94	1181.8	1767.0	2640.9	3227.1	8729.9	23221.	60501.	154106.	383500.1
35	693.57	881.17	1120.7	1816.6	2948.3	4783.6	7750.2	9856.7	32422.	104136.	325400.	987794.	
40	1342.0	1779.0	2360.7	4163.2	7343.8	12936.	22728.	30088.	120392.	466960.			
45	2490.5	3585.1	4965.2	9531.5	18281.	34971.	66640.	91831.	447019.				
50	4994.5	7217.7	10435.	21813.	45497.	94525.	195372.	280255.					

Table A-4 Present Value Annuity Factors (at R Percent Per Period) for $1 Received Per Period for Each of N Periods

N	1%	2%	3%	4%	5%	6%	7%	8%	9%	10%	11%	12%	13%
1	0.990	0.980	0.971	0.962	0.952	0.943	0.935	0.926	0.917	0.909	0.901	0.893	0.885
2	1.970	1.942	1.913	1.886	1.859	1.833	1.808	1.783	1.759	1.736	1.713	1.690	1.668
3	2.941	2.884	2.829	2.775	2.723	2.673	2.624	2.577	2.531	2.487	2.444	2.402	2.361
4	3.902	3.808	3.717	3.630	3.546	3.465	3.387	3.312	3.240	3.170	3.102	3.037	2.974
5	4.853	4.713	4.580	4.452	4.329	4.212	4.100	3.993	3.890	3.791	3.696	3.605	3.517
6	5.795	5.601	5.417	5.242	5.076	4.917	4.767	4.623	4.486	4.355	4.231	4.111	3.998
7	6.728	6.472	6.230	6.002	5.786	5.582	5.389	5.206	5.033	4.868	4.712	4.564	4.423
8	7.652	7.325	7.020	6.733	6.463	6.210	5.971	5.747	5.535	5.335	5.146	4.968	4.799
9	8.566	8.162	7.786	7.435	7.108	6.802	6.515	6.247	5.995	5.759	5.537	5.328	5.132
10	9.471	8.983	8.530	8.111	7.722	7.360	7.024	6.710	6.418	6.145	5.889	5.650	5.426
11	10.368	9.787	9.253	8.760	8.306	7.887	7.499	7.139	6.805	6.495	6.207	5.938	5.687
12	11.255	10.575	9.954	9.385	8.863	8.384	7.943	7.536	7.161	6.814	6.492	6.194	5.918
13	12.134	11.348	10.635	9.986	9.394	8.853	8.358	7.904	7.487	7.103	6.750	6.424	6.122
14	13.004	12.106	11.296	10.563	9.899	9.295	8.745	8.244	7.786	7.367	6.982	6.628	6.302
15	13.865	12.849	11.938	11.118	10.380	9.712	9.108	8.559	8.061	7.606	7.191	6.811	6.462
16	14.718	13.578	12.561	11.652	10.838	10.106	9.447	8.851	8.313	7.824	7.379	6.974	6.604
17	15.562	14.292	13.166	12.166	11.274	10.477	9.763	9.122	8.544	8.022	7.549	7.120	6.729
18	16.398	14.992	13.754	12.659	11.690	10.828	10.059	9.372	8.756	8.201	7.702	7.250	6.840
19	17.226	15.678	14.324	13.134	12.085	11.158	10.336	9.604	8.950	8.365	7.839	7.366	6.938
20	18.046	16.351	14.877	13.590	12.462	11.470	10.594	9.818	9.129	8.514	7.963	7.469	7.025
21	18.857	17.011	15.415	14.029	12.821	11.764	10.836	10.017	9.292	8.649	8.075	7.562	7.102
22	19.660	17.658	15.937	14.451	13.163	12.042	11.061	10.201	9.442	8.772	8.176	7.654	7.170
23	20.456	18.292	16.444	14.857	13.489	12.303	11.272	10.371	9.580	8.883	8.266	7.718	7.230
24	21.243	18.914	16.936	15.247	13.799	12.550	11.469	10.529	9.707	8.985	8.348	7.784	7.283
25	22.023	19.523	17.413	15.622	14.094	12.783	11.654	10.675	9.823	9.077	8.422	7.843	7.330
30	25.808	22.396	19.600	17.292	15.372	13.765	12.409	11.258	10.274	9.427	8.694	8.055	7.496
35	29.409	24.999	21.487	18.665	16.374	14.498	12.948	11.655	10.567	9.644	8.855	8.176	7.586
40	32.835	27.355	23.115	19.793	17.159	15.046	13.332	11.925	10.757	9.779	8.951	8.244	7.634
45	36.095	29.490	24.519	20.720	17.774	15.456	13.606	12.108	10.881	9.863	9.008	8.283	7.661
50	39.196	31.424	25.730	21.482	18.256	15.762	13.801	12.233	10.962	9.915	9.042	8.304	7.675

Table A-4 Present Value Annuity Factors (at R Percent Per Period) for $1 Received Per Period for Each of N Periods (Continued)

R =

N	14%	15%	16%	18%	20%	22%	24%	25%	30%	35%	40%	45%	50%
1	0.877	0.870	0.862	0.847	0.833	0.820	0.806	0.800	0.769	0.741	0.714	0.690	0.667
2	1.647	1.626	1.605	1.566	1.528	1.492	1.457	1.440	1.361	1.289	1.224	1.165	1.111
3	2.322	2.283	2.246	2.174	2.106	2.042	1.981	1.952	1.816	1.696	1.589	1.493	1.407
4	2.914	2.855	2.798	2.690	2.589	2.494	2.404	2.362	2.166	1.997	1.849	1.720	1.605
5	3.433	3.352	3.274	3.127	2.991	2.864	2.745	2.689	2.436	2.220	2.035	1.876	1.737
6	3.889	3.784	3.685	3.498	3.326	3.167	3.020	2.951	2.643	2.385	2.168	1.983	1.824
7	4.288	4.160	4.039	3.812	3.605	3.416	3.242	3.161	2.802	2.508	2.263	2.057	1.883
8	4.639	4.487	4.344	4.078	3.837	3.619	3.421	3.329	2.925	2.598	2.331	2.109	1.922
9	4.946	4.772	4.607	4.303	4.031	3.786	3.566	3.463	3.019	2.665	2.379	2.144	1.948
10	5.216	5.019	4.833	4.494	4.192	3.923	3.682	3.571	3.092	2.715	2.414	2.168	1.965
11	5.453	5.234	5.029	4.656	4.327	4.035	3.776	3.656	3.147	2.752	2.438	2.185	1.977
12	5.660	5.421	5.197	4.793	4.439	4.127	3.851	3.725	3.190	2.779	2.456	2.196	1.985
13	5.842	5.583	5.342	4.910	4.533	4.203	3.912	3.780	3.223	2.799	2.469	2.204	1.990
14	6.002	5.724	5.468	5.008	4.611	4.265	3.962	3.824	3.249	2.814	2.478	2.210	1.993
15	6.142	5.847	5.575	5.092	4.675	4.315	4.001	3.859	3.268	2.825	2.484	2.214	1.995
16	6.265	5.954	5.668	5.162	4.730	4.357	4.033	3.887	3.283	2.834	2.489	2.216	1.997
17	6.373	6.047	5.749	5.222	4.775	4.391	4.059	3.910	3.295	2.840	2.492	2.218	1.998
18	6.467	6.128	5.818	5.273	4.812	4.419	4.080	3.928	3.304	2.844	2.494	2.219	1.999
19	6.550	6.198	5.877	5.316	4.843	4.442	4.097	3.942	3.311	2.848	2.496	2.220	1.999
20	6.623	6.259	5.929	5.353	4.870	4.460	4.110	3.954	3.316	2.850	2.497	2.221	1.999
21	6.687	6.312	5.973	5.384	4.891	4.476	4.121	3.963	3.320	2.852	2.498	2.221	2.000
22	6.743	6.359	6.011	5.410	4.909	4.488	4.130	3.970	3.323	2.853	2.498	2.222	2.000
23	6.792	6.399	6.044	5.432	4.925	4.499	4.137	3.976	3.325	2.854	2.499	2.222	2.000
24	6.835	6.434	6.073	5.451	4.937	4.507	4.143	3.981	3.327	2.855	2.499	2.222	2.000
25	6.873	6.464	6.097	5.467	4.948	4.514	4.147	3.985	3.329	2.856	2.499	2.222	2.000
30	7.003	6.566	6.177	5.517	4.979	4.534	4.160	3.995	3.332	2.857	2.500	2.222	2.000
35	7.070	6.617	6.215	5.539	4.992	4.541	4.164	3.998	3.333	2.857	2.500	2.222	2.000
40	7.105	6.642	6.233	5.548	4.997	4.544	4.166	3.999	3.333	2.857	2.500	2.222	2.000
45	7.123	6.654	6.242	5.552	4.999	4.545	4.166	4.000	3.333	2.857	2.500	2.222	2.000
50	7.133	6.661	6.246	5.554	4.999	4.545	4.167	4.000	3.333	2.857	2.500	2.222	2.000

Index